The Asheville Reader

# THE ANCIENT WORLD

EDITED BY
## Brian S. Hook
## Merritt W. Moseley Jr.
## Kathleen W. Peters

*Copley Custom Publishing Group*
Acton, Massachusetts 01720

ISBN 1-58152-328-9

## Acknowledgments:

**pp. 6–10, 13–16:** From *The Ancient Near East, Volume II* by James Pritchard. Copyright © 1975 by Princeton University Press, 2003 renewed PUP. Reprinted by permission of Princeton University Press.

**pp. 19–25:** Excerpts from Robert Francis Harper, trans., *The Code of Hammurabi King of Babylon about 2250 B.C.* (Chicago: The University of Chicago Press, 1904). Adapted by Kathleen Peters.

**pp. 27–33:** From *The Hymns of Zarathustra: Being a Translation of the Gathas Together with Introduction and Commentary* edited by Jacques Duchesne-Guillemin, translated by Mrs. M. Henning. Copyright © 1952 by John Murray, Ltd. Reprinted by permission of the publisher.

**pp. 84–87:** From *The Complete Dead Sea Scrolls in English* by Geza Vermes (Allen Lane, The Penguin Press, 1997). Copyright © 1962, 1965, 1968, 1975, 1995, 1997 by Geza Vermes. Reprinted by permission of the publisher.

**pp. 90–91:** From *The Eclogues* by Vergil, translated by Guy Lee. Copyright © 1980 by Francis Cairns Publications Ltd. Reprinted by permission of the publisher.

**pp. 149–158, 160–163:** From *Ancient Egyptian Literature A Book of Readings, Volume I: The Old and Middle Kingdoms* edited by Miriam Lichtheim. Copyright © 1973 by University of California Press. Reprinted by permission.

**pp. 166–169, 173–187:** From *Ancient Egyptian Literature A Book of Readings, Volume II: The New Kingdom* edited by Miriam Lichtheim. Copyright © 1976 by University of California Press. Reprinted by permission.

# Contents

# Introduction

*The Asheville Reader: The Ancient World* was created to be used in the first course in the Humanities sequence at the University of North Carolina at Asheville. Humanities is a multi-course, interdisciplinary program in culture, ideas, sensations, and social movements. At the center of Humanities is the student's encounter with primary works. This reader contains a selection of such primary works designed to illustrate the breadth and richness of ancient texts from diverse cultures.

It is designed to be employed in combination with complete texts, including, for instance, ancient epics, dramas, or entire works of religion or philosophy as well as a secondary textbook.

Within the sections, which are divided according to cultural origins, we have arranged the selections in chronological order, but the book is also designed to support other ways of organizing learning, including thematic approaches.

The editors wish to thank all those who have contributed suggestions that have helped in the construction of the reader, and especially those who have made selections and written introductions: Peter Burian, Keith Green, Grant Hardy, Lora Holland, John McClain, Keya Maitra and Sophie Mills; the teaching staff, administration, and support staff of the Humanities program at the University of North Carolina at Asheville; our students; Nanette Johnson, graphic designer; and Lucy Miskin, our always patient editor at Copley Publishing Group.

Brian S. Hook
Merritt W. Moseley, Jr.
Kathleen W. Peters

# Contributors

Keith Green, East Tennessee State University (KG)
Grant Hardy, UNC Asheville History Department (GH)
Lora Holland, UNC Asheville Classics Department(LH)
Brian S. Hook, UNC Asheville Classics Department (BSH)
Keya Maitra, UNC Asheville Philosophy Department (KM)
John McClain, UNC Asheville Humanities Program (JM)
Sophie Mills, UNC Asheville Classics Department (SJVM)
Merritt W. Moseley, Jr., UNC Asheville Literature Department (MM)
Kathleen W. Peters, UNC Asheville Classics Department (KP)

# 1. Ancient Southwest Asia:
## Mesopotamia, Israel, and Second Temple Judaism and Early Christianity

## INTRODUCTION

Written language first developed in the region of Mesopotamia, circa 3300 B.C.E. The writing system is called cuneiform, and our oldest cuneiform documents are written in the Sumerian language. The Sumerians employed cuneiform as a record-keeping device for economic and administrative concerns and shortly thereafter came the development of cuneiform literature. By the mid-third millennium, Sumerian became extinct as a spoken language as Semitic languages rose to prominence. Akkadian, the new *lingua franca* of Mesopotamia, adopted the cuneiform writing system and it spread from Mesopotamia west to Syria-Palestine, where the Ugaritians not only adopted cuneiform, but also developed the alphabet. Neighboring cultures further modified the writing system, abandoning cuneiform while keeping the alphabet, and so developed the alphabetic scripts of Hebrew, Moabite, Phoenician and Aramaic, etc.

Despite the proliferation of writing systems, the literacy rate in ancient Southwest Asia was very low; reading and writing were the prerogative of a select few. A professional scribal class was charged with recording, transcribing, or copying both traditional and original works. Yet in the earliest periods of written language, rarely did an author record his or her name; texts were anonymous. It is only with the increasing importance of literature that we find the signatures of authors and scribes.

Typically, economic and administrative records were stored in archives. Literature, on the other hand, was housed in private libraries, those belonging to kings and priests, the nobility, and of course, the scribes. Comparatively speaking, many Mesopotamian libraries have survived from this ancient time, thanks in part to the durability of clay tablets. But though much literature has survived, much has also been lost. Despite the popularity of clay as a writing medium in Mesopotamia, we know that scribes also wrote on more perishable materials such as leather and wood. In Syria-Palestine, papyrus rolls were the most popular medium for record keeping, though clay, wood and leather were also used. Thus, the literary compendia of those Southwest Asian cultures that wrote on papyrus, leather and wood fell victim to the damp climate and the conflagrations of cultures. Consequently, the literature available for our study is limited to that which survived on clay tablets, in the texts of monumental inscriptions, and in references on potsherds and graffiti. The exception is the sacred literature of the Hebrew Bible, which seems to have survived by the attentions of scribes and editors, who collected, copied, and collated many textual traditions and, as evidenced by the Dead Sea Scrolls, preserved them in remote areas and dry climates.

What scholars have found in the ruins of ancient libraries is a body of literature in both poetry and prose, in an impressive array of genres: stories, poems, hymns, law codes, laments, prophecies, scientific treatises and historiographic works. Much of the literature, indeed those works deemed of the highest literary merit, has a timeless quality; works such as Qoheleth, the Hymns of Zarathustra, and the *Adoration of Inanna* address universal concerns. There are compositions constrained by time; *The Banquet of Ashurnasirpal*, the biblical chronology in Second Kings, and the *Code of Hammurabi* were particularly meaningful to a specific place and time. There was little of what we would describe as secular literature or history. In the ancient world, there was sacred history—history told through the filtering lens of theology; from Hammurabi's *Code* to Second Kings and the Gospel of Matthew, the divine was ever-present. Their epic literature describes a world imbued with magic; their mythic literature is essentially didactic and etiological. Scientific treatises document astronomical events and physical ailments. Wisdom texts are contemplative and aim to pass on knowledge gained through experience. They are characterized by the use of metaphors, symbols, examples and language from everyday life and thus attracted a broad audience. Poetic texts contain elements common today, such as parallelism, meter, and the use of formulaic expressions, though the process of translation into English inhibits us from recognizing many poetic elements of ancient literature. Prophetic literature prognosticated events of national import. As one scholar notes, the prophets themselves "could play either a supportive or destabilizing role" within an administration or in society at large.[1] Generally speaking, Mesopotamian prophetic literature tended to support the king and his initiatives. Israelite prophetic literature is distinctive for its criticism leveled not only at kings, priests and governmental institutions, but also at the wealthy elite guilty of perpetuating social ills.

Despite the variety and vitality of literature, oral tradition must have remained strong; it provided the illiterate majority their main access to cultural traditions. We know that much of the literature functioned as performance pieces. Hebrew Psalms contain directions for a choirmaster and chorus. Even epic literature could be used for public recitation; the Babylonian myth of

*Marduk vs. Tiamat* was recited every New Year, using statues of the gods to reenact a dramatic battle. Nevertheless, it was in writing that the traditions survived. Eventually, papyrus scrolls, clay tablets, and wooden boards were replaced with books, or more properly codices.[2] With the dawn of the Common Era, we see the importance of literature increase within the general population of the provinces of the Roman Empire. Indeed, selections of sacred Hebrew literature were compiled into one canon at this time.[3] The twenty-four books of the Hebrew Bible, portions of which were written as early as 1200 B.C.E. and others as late as 165 B.C.E., reflect a variety of literary genres: wisdom, epic, mythic and prophetic literature, as well as sacred history, legal codes, songs, poems, and laments. Outside of the Hebrew Bible, there is an additional body of literature called the Apocrypha. These are fifteen traditional, cherished and important Jewish works of the last few centuries B.C.E. that did not make it into the official canon, but were still considered foundational texts for the community.[4] First Maccabees is an apocryphal book that recounts recapture of the Jerusalem Temple from the Romans, and the subsequent purification and rededication of the temple; Jews commemorate this event each year with the celebration of Hanukkah.

Other Jewish works survived antiquity, including four books by the historian Josephus, who is notable for his chronicling of events we otherwise have little literary evidence for. The Dead Sea Scrolls, the library of the Essene community of Qumran, give us some perspective on Jewish sectarian movements outside of the mainstream establishment. The community's War Scroll allows us to understand more fully the apocalyptic theology of some Jewish, and then later Christian, believers.

In literature, the new traditions of Christianity survived and spread throughout the Mediterranean world. The twenty-seven books of the New Testament, the scriptures which, together with the Hebrew Bible (the Christian Old Testament), make up the Christian Bible. Just as with the books of the Hebrew Bible, there are no original texts of any New Testament document, only copies. The literature of the New Testament was written between about 50 and 125 C.E.; the earliest writings in the Christian scriptures are the letters of Paul, and the earliest of those is probably the letter to the church at Thessalonica, about 50 C.E. These letters, The Acts of the Apostles and the Gospel of Matthew evidence a distinct literary genre: conversion literature. Other elements of the biblical books, such as the parables and sermons of Jesus, follow in the tradition of wisdom literature. Though we speak of a New Testament in the context of the ancient world, there were many other Christian writings in the first centuries of the Common Era and it was not until the fourth century (ca. 367 C.E.) that Christians (after a gradual process, and not without lingering disagreements) came to agree on which books constituted the divinely inspired books of the New Testament, in other words which were the canonical texts. This decision helped to establish orthodoxy: that is, the official determination of what Christians believed. Another step in the establishment of orthodoxy was the adumbration of creeds, including the Nicene Creed (product of the Council of Nicaea convened by the Emperor Constantine in 325 C.E.) and the Apostles' Creed, included here.

In the early centuries of the Common Era, we come across evidence of an intellectual and literary conundrum within the Christian world: what were the early Christians to do with the vast amount of "pagan" literature that they inherited? Christians had two options with respect to this literature, 1) like Jerome, they could regard it with caution or reject it, or 2) like Augustine, they could assimilate it. Tertullian (160–225 C.E.) was an early Church theologian who exemplifies an approach that considered Vergil in particular a proto-Christian, a "natural Christian," and so justified his appreciation of both Christian and non-Christian literature. Vergil's *Fourth Eclogue* is an example of a literary classic re-read and re-interpreted for a new or different society. In the contemporary world, we can appreciate the *Fourth Eclogue* for what it was, but we can recognize also that it represents a bridge between the ancient world and the early medieval world, and illustrates one way by which literature belonging to one time and place was preserved (though transformed) by the readers of another place and time.

KP

## Notes

[1] J. Blenkinsopp, *A History of Prophecy in Israel*, 2nd Edition (Louisville: Westminster John Knox Press, 1996), 3.

[2] Codices are parchment bound together on one side rather than stitched end to end and rolled in the manner of scrolls.

[3] Note, however, that there are differences between the version of the Bible (the Masoretic text) considered authoritative for medieval and modern Judaism, and the third century B.C.E. translation of Hebrew scriptures into Greek, known as the Septuagint (abbv. LXX). Jerome used Hebrew and Greek manuscripts, as well as the Greek Septuagint, for his translation of the Latin Vulgate, which in turn served the medieval Christian world (and much of the modern Christian world) as the Old and New Testaments.

Note also that the books of the Hebrew Bible contain references to other ancient Hebrew works, such as the Annals of the Kings of Israel, athe Annals of the Kings of Judah, and the Book of Jashar, that do not appear to have survived antiquity.

[3] Because the books of the Apocrypha were included in the Septuagint, Eastern Orthodox and Roman Catholic churches consider the Apocrypha "second canon." Jewish and Protestant traditions do not include the apocryphal books in the canon.

# Enheduanna

## Twenty-Fourth Century B.C.E.

Under the leadership of Sargon of Akkad (2371–2316 B.C.E.), a usurper of obscure origins, local principalities and independent Sumerian city-states disappeared as the various cultures of Mesopotamia became politically united. With the formation of this Akkadian Empire (2350–2160 B.C.E.), Mesopotamia witnessed what scholars believe to be the world's first true empire. Sargon ruled for 55 years.

In order to ensure the stability of his reign, Sargon appointed family and friends to positions of authority. One such appointee was his daughter Enheduanna to the position of high priestess of Inanna (a.k.a. Ishtar) at the traditional sanctuary of Ur. This set in motion a policy for subsequent rulers to place their daughters and sisters in such positions, a politically astute move that tied religion to politics, the temple to the king.

Scholars regard Enheduanna as the world's first identifiable author and the first historically verified woman of literature. From her life, we have artifacts including a portrait, several inscriptions, cylinder seals and religious hymns. Her most famous work is the following hymnal prayer, *The Adoration of Inanna of Ur*. Inanna was the Sumerian goddess who was the patron deity of the Sargonid line. In the hymn, Enheduanna credits the earthly successes of Sargon to Inanna's divine guidance.

In addition to the political history contained within references of the hymn, Enheduanna lays the complex composite nature of the great goddess before the reader. Inanna is both the goddess of love and war; she is simultaneously cruel and caring. Historians typically consider such dualities reflective of the unpredictable and erratic nature of life in the land of the two rivers.

The hymn is a prayer of both praise and supplication, for Enheduanna seems to have encountered some difficulties from which she begs reprieve from the goddess. Although *The Adoration of Inanna of Ur* reads as a private prayer between petitioner and deity, its hymnal character and written form indicate that the text may well have been used for more public liturgy.

KP

# The Adoration of Inanna[1] of Ur

Queen of all the *me*,[2] radiant light,
Life-giving woman, beloved of An (and) Urash,
Hierodule[3] of An, much bejewelled,
Who loves the life-giving tiara, fit for *en*-ship,[4]
Who grasps in (her) hand, the seven *me*,
My queen, you who are the guardian of all the great *me*,
You have lifted the *me*, have tied the *me* to your hands,
Have gathered the *me*, pressed the *me* to your breast.

You have filled the land with venom, like a dragon.
Vegetation ceases, when you thunder like Ishkur,
You who bring down the Flood from the mountain,
Supreme one, who are the Inanna of heaven (and) earth,
Who rain flaming fire over the land,
Who have been given the *me* by An, queen who rides the beasts,
Who at the holy command of An, utters the (divine) words,
Who can fathom your great rites!

Destroyer of the foreign lands, you have given wings to the storm,
Beloved of Enlil you made it (the storm) blow over the land,
You carried out the instructions of An.
My queen, the foreign lands cower at your cry,
In dread (and) fear of the South Wind, mankind
Brought you their anguished clamor,
Took before you their anguished *outcry*
Opened before you wailing and weeping,
Brought before you the "great" lamentations in the city streets.

In the van of battle, everything was struck down before you,
My queen, you are all devouring in your power,
You kept on attacking like an attacking storm,
Kept on blowing (louder) than the howling storm,
Kept on thundering (louder) than Ishkur,
Kept on moaning (louder) than the evil winds,
Your feet grew not weary,
You caused wailing to be uttered on the "lyre of lament."
My queen, the Anunna, the great gods,
Fled before you like fluttering bats,

Could not stand before your awesome face,
Could not approach your awesome forehead.
Who can soothe your angry heart!
Your baleful heart is beyond soothing!
Queen, happy of "liver," joyful of heart,                          40
(But) whose anger cannot be soothed, daughter of Sin,[5]
Queen, paramount in the land, who has (ever) paid you (enough) homage!

The mountain who kept from paying homage to you—vegetation became
    "tabu" for it,
You burnt down its great gates,
Its rivers ran with blood because of you, its people had nothing to drink,
Its troops were led off willingly (into captivity) before you,
Its forces disbanded themselves willingly before you,
Its strong men paraded willingly before you,
The amusement places of its cities were filled with turbulence,
Its adult males were driven off as captives before you.                50

Against the city that said not "yours is the land,"
That said not "It belongs to the father who begot you,"
You promised your holy word, turned away from it,
Kept your distance from its womb,
Its woman spoke not of love with her husband,
In the deep night she whispered not (tenderly) with him,
Revealed not to him the "holiness" of her heart.

Rampant wild cow, elder daughter of Sin,
Queen, greater than An, who has (ever) paid you (enough) homage!
You who in accordance with the life giving *me*, great queen of queens,   60
Have become greater than your mother who gave birth to you, (as soon as)
    you came forth from the holy womb,
Knowing, wise, queen of all the lands,
Who multiplies (all) living creatures (and) peoples—I have uttered your
    holy song.
Life-giving goddess, fit for the *me*, whose acclamation is exalted,
Merciful, life-giving woman, radiant of heart, I have uttered it before you in
    accordance with the *me*.

I have entered before you in my holy *gipar*,
I the *en*, Enheduanna,
Carrying the *masab*-basket, I uttered a joyous chant,
(But now) I no longer dwell in the goodly place you established.
Came the day, the sun scorched me                                        70

Came the shade (of night), the South Wind overwhelmed me,
My honey-sweet voice has become *strident*,
Whatever gave me pleasure has turned into dust.

Oh Sin, king of heaven, my (bitter) fate,
To An declare, An will deliver me,
Pray declare it to An, he will deliver me.

The kingship of heaven has been seized by the woman (Inanna),
At whose feet lies the flood-land.
That woman (Inanna) so exalted, who has made me tremble together the
    city (Ur),
Stay *her*, let her heart be soothed by me.                              80
I, Enheduanna will offer supplications to her,
My tears, like sweet drinks.
Will I proffer to the holy Inanna, I will greet her in peace,
Let not Ashimbabbar (Sin) be troubled.

She (Inanna) has changed altogether the rites of holy An,
Has seized the Eanna[6] from An,
Feared not the great An,
That house (the Eanna) whose charm was irresistible, whose allure was
    unending,
That house she has turned over to destruction,
Her . . . that she brought there has . . .                                90
My wild cow (Inanna) assaults there its men, makes them captive.

I, what am I among the living creatures!
May An give over (to punishment) the rebellious lands that hate your
    (Inanna's) Nanna,
May An split its cities asunder,
May Enlil curse it,
May not its tear-destined child be soothed by her mother,

Oh queen who established lamentations,
Your "boat of lamentations," has *landed* in an inimical land,
There will I die, while singing the holy song.
As for me, my Nanna watched not over me,                            100
I have been attacked most cruelly.
Ashimbabbar has not spoken my verdict.
But what matter, whether he spoke it or not!
I, accustomed to triumph, have been driven forth from (my) house,
Was forced to flee the cote like a swallow, my life is devoured,

Was made to walk among the mountain thorns,
The life-giving tiara of *en*-ship was taken from me,
*Eunuchs* were assigned to me—"These are becoming to you," it was told me.

Dearest queen, beloved of An,
Let your holy heart, the noble, return to me,                                    110
Beloved wife of Ushumgalanna (Dumuzi[7]),
Great queen of the horizon and the zenith,
The Anunna have prostrated themselves before you.
Although at birth you were the younger *sister*,
How much greater you have become than the Anunna, the great gods!
The Anunna kiss the ground before you.

It is not my verdict that has been completed, it is a strange verdict that has
        been *turned* into my verdict,
The fruitful bed has been abolished,
(So that) I have not interpreted to man the commands of Ningal.[8]
For me, the radiant *en* of Nanna,                                              120
May your heart be soothed, you who are the queen beloved of An.

"You are known, you are known"—it is not of Nanna that I have recited it,
        it is of you that I have recited it.
You are known by your heaven-like height,
You are known by your earth-like breadth,
You are known by your destruction of rebel-lands,
You are known by your massacring (their people),
You are known by your devouring (their) dead like a dog,
You are known by your fierce countenance.
You are known by the raising of your fierce countenance,
You are known by your flashing eyes.                                            130
You are known by your *contentiousness* (and) disobedience,
You are known by your many triumphs"—
It is not of Nanna that I have recited it, it is of you that I have recited it.
My queen, I have extolled you, who alone are exalted,
Queen beloved of An, I have *erected* your daises,
Have heaped up the coals, have conducted the rites,
Have set up the nuptial chamber for you, may your heart be soothed for me,
Enough, more than enough innovations, great queen, have I made for you.
What I have recited to you in the deep night,
The *gala*-singer will repeat for you in midday.                               140
It is because of your captive spouse, your captive son,
That your wrath is so great, your heart so unappeased.

The foremost queen, the prop of the *assembly*,
Accepted her prayer.
The heart of Inanna was restored,
The day was favorable for her, she was clothed with beauty, was filled with
    joyous allure,
How she carried (her) beauty—like the rising moonlight!
Nanna who came forth in wonder true,
(and) her mother Ningal, proffered prayers to her,
Greeted her at the doorsill (of the temple).                 150
To the hierodule whose command is noble,
The destroyer of foreign lands, presented by An with the *me*,
My queen garbed in allure, O Inanna, praise!

## Notes

Oftentimes, editors/translators will leave untranslated those terms whose definitions are uncertain. These terms will appear transliterated in italics or all caps. When an English word appears in italics, it signifies a dubious translation. An interpolation provided by the editor/translator for clarity will be in parentheses. Words or phrases in brackets indicate a hypothetical reconstruction of a missing portion of the text.

[1] Inanna was the Mespotamian goddess of love, sexuality, and a myriad of other attributes. She was both the Morning and Evening Star.

[2] The *me* are the divine powers assigned to all universal entities that keep those entities functioning and in harmony.

[3] Hierodule is a person, frequently a slave, who lives in service to a temple. In this instance, Enheduanna refers to Inanna's subordinate position in service to An, the god of Heaven.

[4] *En* means high priestess or high priest.

[5] Sin is the moon god and patron deity of the city of Haran (also Harran) in northern Mesopotamia.

[6] Eanna is the temple of An (the god of Heaven) and Inanna, his daughter. Eanna was located in the city of Uruk in Southern Mesopotamia.

[7] Dumuzi was a shepherd-god and consort of Inanna.

[8] Ningal is a deity frequently paired with Sin and was a patron deity of Haran in Northern Mesopotamia.

# Ashurnasirpal

## Ninth Century B.C.E.

*The Banquet of Ashurnasirpal II* is the product of the ninth century
Assyrian king by that name. Ashurnasirpal commissioned the work to cele-
brate the achievements of his reign and to mark the awesome strength of the
Assyrian Empire.

The conquests of Assyria created a sphere of influence stretching at times
from Egypt to Anatolia, and regions east of Mesopotamia. This political and
military supremacy of Assyria is typically recognized as a series of two empires
(ca. 1350–1150 B.C.E. and ca. 860–612 B.C.E.), separated by a period of
decline. The second of these empires (known to historians as the Neo-Assyrian
Empire) is characterized by the gross brutality of their military machine (for
example, a favorite form of Assyrian execution was impalement on stakes).
Conquered peoples spared slaughter were deported to Assyria for forced labor.
Politically, such population displacement served to break resistance and
encourage assimilation. Historians believe that Ashurnasirpal II inaugurated
this practice of population deportation; they certainly consider him one of the
most brutal of all Assyrian kings.

Ironically, the brutality of Neo-Assyrian might is coupled with tremendous cultural creativity and achievement. This "Assyrian Paradox" produced
our oldest known biological garden (i.e., zoo) and library. *The Banquet of
Ashurnasirpal II* celebrates both aspects of this paradox. The cuneiform inscription, with accompanying depiction of the king, is from a stone slab excavated
in the mid-twentieth century. Crafted as a monumental inscription to deco-
rate the Calah palace of the king, it was intended to inform and impress visitors with the achievements of Ashurnasirpal's reign.

Assyriologists value the text for the terrific amount of information
gleaned from the descriptive elements which praise the Assyrian pantheon,
geographically trace military campaigns (and in so doing, locate various population groups), and denote valuable resources as well as sources of pride, such
as engineering technology. Historians are not the only scholars interested in
this inscription; paleobotonists study the list of plants, both extant and now
extinct, for information on the ecological history of the region, while paleozo-
ologists are interested in the catalogue of animal species. There are hyperbolic
elements within the text, the traditional propaganda expected in a piece of

political braggadocio; still in all, *The Banquet of Ashurnasirpal II* contributes significantly to our general knowledge of Mesopotamian civilization.

KP

# The Banquet of Ashurnasirpal II

## (i)

(This is) the palace of Ashurnasirpal, the high priest of Ashur, chosen by Enlil and Ninurta, the favorite of Anu and of Dagan (who is) destruction (personified) among all the great gods—the legitimate king, the king of the world, the king of Assyria, son of Tukulti-Ninurta, great king, legitimate king, king of the world, king of Assyria (who was) the son of Adad-nirari, likewise great king, legitimate king, king of the world and king of Assyria—the heroic warrior who always acts upon trust-inspiring signs given by his lord Ashur and (therefore) has no rival among the rulers of the four quarters (of the world); the shepherd of all mortals, not afraid of battle (but) an onrushing flood which brooks no resistance; the king who subdues the unsubmissive (and) rules over all mankind; the king who always acts upon trust-inspiring signs given by his lords, the great gods, and therefore has personally conquered all countries; who has acquired dominion over the mountain regions and received their tribute; he takes hostages, triumphs over all the countries from beyond the Tigris to the Lebanon and the Great Sea, he has brought into submission the entire country of Laqe and the region of Suhu as far as the town of Rapiqu; personally he conquered (the region) from the source of the Subnat River to Urartu.

I returned to the territory of my own country (the regions) from the pass (which leads to) the country Kirrure as far as Gilzani, from beyond the Lower Zab River to the town of Til-bari which is upstream of the land of Zamua—from Til-sha-abtani to Til-sha-sabtani—(also) Hirimu and Harrutu (in) the fortified border region of Babylonia (Karduniash). I listed as inhabitants of my own country (the people living) from the pass of Mt. Babite to the land of Hashmar.

Ashur, the Great Lord, has chosen me and made a pronouncement concerning my world rule with his own holy mouth (as follows): Ashurnasirpal is the king whose fame is power!

I took over again the city of Calah in that wisdom of mine, the knowledge which Ea, the king of the subterranean waters, has bestowed upon me, I removed the old hill of rubble; I dug down to the water level; I heaped up a (new) terrace (measuring) from the water level to the upper edge 120 layers of bricks; upon that I erected as my royal seat and for my personal enjoyment 7 (text: 8) beautiful halls (roofed with) boxwood, *Magan-ash*, cedar, cypress, terebinth, *tarpi'u* and *mehru* (beams); I sheathed doors made of cedar, cypress,

13

juniper, boxwood and *Magan-ash* with bands of bronze; I hung them in their doorways; I surrounded them (the doors) with decorative bronze bolts; to proclaim my heroic deeds I painted on their (the palaces') walls with vivid blue paint how I have marched across the mountain ranges, the foreign countries and the seas, my conquests in all countries; I had lapis lazuli colored glazed bricks made and set (them in the wall) above their gates. I brought in people from the countries over which I rule, those who were conquered by me personally, (that is) from the country Suhi (those of) the town Great [. . .], from the entire land of Zamua, the countries BitZamani and [Kir]rure, the town of Sirqu which is across the Euphrates, and many inhabitants of Laqe, of Syria and (who are subjects) of Lubarna, the ruler of Hattina; I settled them therein (the city of Calah).

I dug a canal from the Upper Zab River; I cut (for this purpose) straight through the mountain(s); I called it Patti-hegalli ("Channel-of-Abundance"); I provided the lowlands along the Tigris with irrigation; I planted orchards at its (the city's) outskirts, with all sorts of fruit trees.

I pressed the grapes and offered (them) as first fruits in a libation to my lord Ashur and to all the sanctuaries of my country. I (then) dedicated that city to my lord Ashur.

[I collected and planted in my garden] from the countries through which I marched and the mountains which I crossed, the trees (and plants raised from) seeds from wherever I discovered (them, such as): cedars, cypress, *šimmešallu*-perfume trees, *burāšu*-junipers, myrrh-producing trees, *daprānu*-junipers, nut-bearing trees, date palms, ebony, *Magan-ash*, olive trees, *tamarind*, oaks, *tarpi'u*-terebinth trees, *luddu*-nut-bearing trees, pistachio and *cornel*-trees, *meḫru*-trees, ŠE.MUR-trees, *tijatu*-trees, Kanish oaks, willows, *ṣadānu*-trees, pomegranates, plum trees, fir trees, *ingirašu*-trees, *kamēššeru*-pear trees, *supurgillu*-bearing trees, fig trees, grape vines, *angašu*-pear trees, aromatic *ṣumlalu*-trees, *titip*-trees, *ḫip/būtu*-trees, *zanzaliqqu*-trees, "swamp-apple" trees, *ḫambuqūqu*-trees, *nuḫurtu*-trees, *urzīnu*-trees, resinous *kanaktu*-trees [. . .]. In the gardens in [Calah] they vied with each other in fragrance; the paths i[n the gardens were well *kept*], the irrigation weirs [distributed the water *evenly*]; its pomegranates glow in the pleasure garden like the stars in the sky, they are interwoven like grapes on the vine; . . . in the pleasure garden [. . .] in the garden of happiness flourished like ce[dar trees] (break).

## (ii)

I erected in Calah, the center of my overlordship, temples such as those of Enlil and Ninurta which did not exist there before; I rebuilt in it the (following) temples of the great gods: the temples of Ea-sharru (and) Damkina, of

Adad (and) Shala, of Gula, Sin, Nabu, Beletnathi, Sibittu (and of) Ishtar-kid-muri. In them I established the (sacred) pedestals of the(se), my divine lords. I decorated them splendidly; I roofed them with cedar beams, made large cedar doors, sheathed them with bands of bronze, placed them in their doorways. I placed figural representations made of shining bronze in their doorways. I made (the images of) their great godheads sumptuous with red gold and shining stones. I presented them with golden jewelry and many other precious objects which I had won as booty.

I lined the inner shrine of my lord Ninurta with gold and lapis lazuli, I placed right and left of IM[1] objects made of bronze, I placed at his pedestal fierce *ušumgallu*-dragons of gold. I performed his festival in the months Shabatu and Ululu. I arranged for them (the materials needed for) scatter and incense offerings so that his festival in Shabatu should be one of great display. I fashioned a statue of myself as king in the likeness of my own features out of red gold and polished stones and placed it before my lord Ninurta.

I organized the abandoned towns which during the rule of my fathers had become hills of rubble, and had many people settle therein; I rebuilt the old palaces across my entire country in due splendor; I stored in them barley and straw.

Ninurta and Palil, who love me as (their) high priest, handed over to me all the wild animals and ordered me to hunt (them). I killed 450 big lions; I killed 390 wild bulls from my open chariots in direct assault as befits a ruler; I cut off the heads of 200 ostriches as if they were caged birds; I caught 30 elephants in pitfalls. I caught alive 50 wild bulls, 140 ostriches (and) 20 big lions with my own [. . .] and *stave*.

## (iii)

I received five live elephants as tribute from the governor of Suhu (the Middle Euphrates region) and the governor of Lubda (S.E. Assyria toward Babylonia); they used to travel with me on my campaigns.

I organized herds of wild bulls, lions, ostriches and male and female monkeys and had them breed like flocks (of domestic animals).

I added land to the land of Assyria, *many* people to its people.

When Ashurnasirpal, king of Assyria, inaugurated the palace in Calah, a palace of joy and (erected with) great ingenuity, he invited into it Ashur, the great lord and the gods of his entire country, (he prepared a banquet of) 1,000 fattened head of cattle, 1,000 calves, *10,000* stable sheep, 15,000 lambs—for my lady Ishtar (alone) 200 head of cattle (and) 1,000 *siḫḫu*-sheep—1,000 spring lambs, 500 stags, 500 gazelles, 1,000 *ducks*, 500 *geese*, 500 *kurkû*-geese,

1,000 *mesuku*-birds, 1,000 *qāribu*-birds, 10,000 doves, 10,000 *sukanūnu*-doves, 10,000 other (assorted) small birds, 10,000 (assorted) fish, 10,000 jer-boa, 10,000 (assorted) eggs; 10,000 loaves of bread, 10,000 (jars of) beer, 10,000 skins with wine, 10,000 pointed bottom vessels with *šu'u*-seeds in sesame oil, 10,000 small pots with *ṣarhu*-condiment, 1,000 wooden crates with vegetables, 300 (containers with) oil, 300 (containers with) salted *seeds*, 300 (containers with) mixed *raqqūte*-plants 100 with *kudimmu*-spice, 100 (containers with) . . . , 100 (containers with) parched barley, 100 (containers with) green *abaḫšinnu*-stalks, 100 (containers with) fine mixed beer, 100 pomegranates, 100 bunches of grapes, 100 mixed *zamru*-fruits, 100 pistachio cones, 100 with the fruits of the *šūši*-tree, 100 with garlic, 100 with onions, 100 with *kunipḫu* (seeds), 100 with the . . . of turnips, 100 with *ḫinḫinnu*-spice, 100 with *budû*-spice, 100 with honey, 100 with rendered butter, 100 with roasted . . . barley, 100 with roasted *šu'u*-seeds, 100 with *karkartu*-plants, 100 with fruits of the *ti'atu*-tree, 100 with *kasû*-plants, 100 with milk, 100 with cheese, 100 jars with "mixture," 100 with pickled *arsuppu*-grain, ten homer of shelled *luddu*-nuts, ten homer of shelled pistachio nuts, ten homer of fruits of the *šūšu*-tree, ten homer of fruits of the *ḫabbaqūqu*-tree, ten homer of dates, ten homer of the fruits of the *titip*-tree, ten homer of *cumin*, ten homer of *saḫḫunu*, ten homer of *uriānu*, ten homer of *andaḫšu*-bulbs, ten homer of *šišanibbe*-plants, (iv) ten homer of the fruits of the *simbūru*-tree, ten homer of thyme, ten homer of perfumed oil, ten homer of sweet smelling mat-ters, ten homer of . . . , ten homer of the fruits of the *naṣubu*-tree, ten homer of *zimzimmu*-onions, ten homer of olives.

When I inaugurated the palace at Calah I treated for ten days with food and drink 47,074 persons, men and women, who were bid to come from across my entire country, (also) 5,000 important persons, delegates from the country Suhu, from Hindana, Hattina, Hatti, Tyre, Sidon, Gurguma, Malida, Hubushka, Gilzana, Kuma (and) Musasir, (also) 16,000 inhabitants of Calah from all ways of life, 1,500 officials of all my palaces, altogether 69,574 invited guests from all the (mentioned) countries including the people of Calah; I (furthermore) provided them with the means to clean and anoint themselves. I did them due honors and sent them back, healthy and happy, to their own countries.

## Note

[1] Meaning unclear.

# Hammurabi

## Eighteenth Century B.C.E.

Hammurabi reigned as King of Babylon for roughly 40 years (ca. 1792–1750 B.C.E.). He was a great warrior and diplomat, who succeeded in uniting city-states in both Northern and Southern Mesopotamia into an empire. During the second year of his reign, Hammurabi published a collection of legal decisions, some new, some inherited, which he intended to be used as a manual of jurisprudence throughout his empire. This collection was distributed on clay tablets and on inscribed stelae (a stela is an upright stone marker); the stelae were erected in temple courtyards, where the public could have access to them. The *Code* must have been updated over the course of his reign, for the most famous and best-preserved copy (the 7.5ft diorite stela now housed in the Louvre Museum in Paris) makes historical allusions to events in the latter years of his reign.

Hammurabi's *Code* is not the oldest Mesopotamian legal code (those of Urukagina [2351 B.C.E.], Gudea [2144–2124], and Ur-Nammu [2110–2100] predate that of Hammurabi), but it is by far the most complete, with almost three hundred cases to provide precedent and guide judicial proceedings. Gloria Fiero asserts: "written law represented a significant advance in the development of human rights in that it protected the individual from the capricious decisions of monarchs." Though such optimism may be a bit overstated, written law codes did serve to remove legal proceedings from the domain of the family and establish justice as the prerogative of the state. In the course of asserting this prerogative, the *Code*'s Prologue tells us that Hammurabi commissioned it under the divine auspices of Shamash, the solar deity who was the god of justice, and with the blessings of the entire Mesopotamian pantheon. Violations of Hammurabi's *Code* were thus a violation of divine law. As for adjudication of the law, scholars believe that most cases were heard before a panel of local judges; oaths were sworn and witnesses were called. However, for the most complex of cases, guilt was determined by the river ordeal, wherein the accused was thrown into a river for the River god to proclaim guilt (by drowning the accused) or innocence (by allowing the accused to survive).

In the following selections of the *Code*, you can discern three classes of society: the nobility, a so-called middle class (farmers, merchants, artisans) and slaves. Punishment for particular crimes depended upon the social class of the accused and the victim; if a noble injured a noble, the system of *lex talionis* (law of retaliation, i.e., "eye for an eye") prevailed. Injury done to a slave by a noble was as if done to a piece of property, not a human being, and thus the punishment was far less severe. You will see that corporal and capital punishment are quite common; imprisonment is nowhere mentioned. Monetary fines were also common, but reserved for those who could afford to pay them. Hammurabi, the self-titled King of Justice, loftily claims to "prevent the strong from oppressing the weak, giving justice to the orphan and the widow." Interestingly though, the *Code* devotes little, if any, time to such moral concerns. Rather, economic concerns dominate the case law.

Given that in its original form, the *Code* does not systematically group the cases by subject matter, we have arranged the selections so as to address Domestic Life, Professional Life and Religious Life. Though we do not know the extent to which the *Code* was used over subsequent centuries, we can appreciate the glimpse into the moral values and economic concerns of ancient Mesopotamia that Hammurabi's *Code* affords.

KP

# from *The Code of Hammurabi*

## Prologue

When the lofty Anu, king of the Annunaki, and Bel, lord of heaven and earth, he who determines the destiny of the land, committed the rule of all mankind to Marduk, the chief son of Ea; when they made him great among the Igigi;[1] when they pronounced the lofty name of Babylon; when they made it famous among the quarters of the world and in its midst established an everlasting kingdom whose foundations were firm as heaven and earth—at that time, Ann and Bel called me, Hammurabi, the exalted prince, the worshiper of the gods, to cause justice to prevail in the land, to destroy the wicked and the evil, to prevent the strong from oppressing the weak, to go forth like the Sun over the Black Head Race, to enlighten the land and to further the welfare of the people. Hammurabi, the governor named by Bel, am I, who brought about plenty and abundance . . . the exalted one, who makes supplication to the great gods; the descendant of Sumulailu, the powerful son of Sinmuballit, the ancient seed of royalty, the powerful king, the Sun of Babylon, who caused light to go forth over the lands of Sumer and Akkad; the king, who caused the four quarters of the world to render obedience; the favorite of Nana, am I. When Marduk sent me to rule the people and to bring help to the country, I established law and justice in the land and promoted the welfare of the people.

## Domestic Life

### Engagement

159: If a man, who has brought a present to the house of his father-in-law and has given the marriage settlement, look with longing upon another woman and say to his father-in-law, "I will not take thy daughter;" the father of the daughter shall take to himself whatever was brought to him.

160: If a man bring a present to the house of his father-in-law and give a marriage settlement and the father of the daughter say, "I will not give thee my daughter;" he (i.e., the father-in-law) shall double the amount which was brought to him and return it.

180: If a father do not give a dowry to his daughter, a bride or devotee, after her father dies she shall receive as her share in the goods of her father's house the portion of a son, and she shall enjoy it as long as she lives. After her (death) it belongs to her brothers.

## Marriage

128: If a man take a wife and do not arrange with her the (proper) contracts, that woman is not a (legal) wife.

145: If a man take a wife and she do not present him with children and he set his face to take a concubine, that man may take a concubine and bring her into his house. That concubine shall not rank with his wife.

148: If a man take a wife and she become afflicted with disease, and if he set his face to take another, he may. His wife, who is afflicted with disease, he shall not put away. She shall remain in the house which he has built and he shall maintain her as long as she lives.

## Children

138: If a man would put away his wife who has not borne him children, he shall give her money to the amount of her marriage settlement and he shall make good to her the dowry which she brought from her father's house and then he may put her away.

194: If a man give his son to a nurse (i.e., a wet-nurse who will breastfeed the child) and that son die in the hands of the nurse, and the nurse substitute another son without the consent of his father or mother, they shall call her to account, and because she has substituted another son without the consent of his father or mother, they shall cut off her breast.

195: If a son strike his father, they shall cut off his fingers.

185: If a man take in his name a young child as a son and rear him, one may not bring claim for that adopted son.

186: If a man take a young child as a son and, when he takes him, he is rebellious toward his father and mother (who have adopted him), that adopted son shall return to the house of his father.

188: If an artisan take a son for adoption and teach him his handicraft, one may not bring claim for him.

189: If he do not teach him his handicraft, that adopted son may return to his father's house.

## Adultery

129: If the wife of a man be taken in lying with another man, they shall bind them and throw them into the water. If the husband of the woman would save his wife, or if the king would save his male servant (he may).

130: If a man force the (betrothed) wife of another who has not known a male and is living in her father's house, and he lie in her bosom and they take him, that man shall be put to death and that woman shall go free.

131: If a man accuse his wife and she has not been taken in lying with another man, she shall take an oath in the name of god and she shall return to her house.

132: If the finger have been pointed at the wife of a man because of another man, and she have not been taken in lying with another man, for her husband's sake she shall throw herself into the river.

153: If a woman bring about the death of her husband for the sake of another man, they shall impale her.

## Divorce

137: If a man set his face to put away a concubine who has borne him children or a wife who has presented him with children, he shall return to that woman her dowry and shall give to her the income of field, garden, and goods and she shall bring up her children; from the time that her children are grown up, from whatever is given to her children they shall give to her a portion corresponding to that of a son and the man of her choice may marry her.

138: If a man would put away his wife who has not borne him children, he shall give her money to the amount of her marriage settlement and he shall make good to her the dowry which she brought from her father's house and then he may put her away.

139: If there was no marriage settlement, he shall give to her one mina of silver[2] for a divorce.

141: If the wife of a man who is living in his house, set her face to go out and play the part of a fool, neglect her house, belittle her husband, they shall call her to account; if her husband say "I have put her away," he shall let her go. On her departure nothing shall be given to her for her divorce. If her husband say: "I have not put her away," her husband may take another woman. The first woman shall dwell in the house of her husband as a maid servant.

142: If a woman hate her husband, and say: "Thou shalt not have me," they shall inquire into her antecedents for her defects; and if she [has] been a careful mistress and be without reproach and her husband [has] been going about and greatly belittling her, that woman has no blame. She shall receive her dowry and shall go to her father's house.

143: If she [has] not been a careful mistress, have gadded about, have neglected her house and have belittled her husband, they shall throw that woman into the water.

## Widowhood

172: If her husband have not given her a gift, they shall make good her dowry and she shall receive from the goods of her husband's house a portion corresponding to that of a son. If her children scheme to drive her out of the house, the judges shall inquire into her antecedents and if the children be in the wrong, she shall not go out from her husband's house. If the woman set her face to go out, she shall leave to her children the gift which her husband gave her; she shall receive the dowry of her father's house, and the husband of her choice may take her.

173: If that woman bear children to her later husband into whose house she has entered and later on that woman die, the former and the later children shall divide her dowry.

177: If a widow, whose children are minors, set her face to enter another house, she cannot do so without the consent of the judges. When she enters another house, the judges shall inquire into the estate of her former husband and they shall intrust the estate of her former husband to the later husband and that woman, and they shall deliver to them a tablet (to sign). They shall administer the estate and rear the minors. They may not sell the household goods. He who purchases household goods belonging to the sons of a widow shall forfeit his money. The goods shall revert to their owner.

## Inheritance

162: If a man take a wife and she bear him children and that woman die, her father may not lay claim to her dowry. Her dowry belongs to her children.

166: If a man take wives for his sons and do not take a wife for his youngest son, after the father dies, when the brothers divide, they shall give from the goods of the father's house to their youngest brother, who has not taken a wife, money for a marriage settlement in addition to his portion and they shall enable him to take a wife.

167: If a man take a wife and she bear him children and that woman die, and after her (death) he take another wife and she bear him children and later the father die, the children of the mothers shall not divide (the estate). They shall receive the dowries of their respective mothers and they shall divide equally the goods of the house of the father.

168: If a man set his face to disinherit his son and say to the judges: "I will disinherit my son," the judges shall inquire into his antecedents, and if the son have not committed a crime sufficiently grave to cut him off from sonship, the father may not cut off his son from sonship.

169: If he have committed a crime against his father sufficiently grave to cut him off from sonship, they shall condone his first (offense). If he commit a grave crime a second time, the father may cut his son off from sonship.

## Professional Life

215: If a physician operate on a man for a severe wound (or make a severe wound upon a man) with a bronze lancet and save the man's life; or if he open an abscess (in the eye) of a man with a bronze lancet and save that man's eye, he shall receive ten shekels of silver (as his fee).

218: If a physician operate on a man for a severe wound with a bronze lancet and cause the man's death; or open an abscess (in the eye) of a man with a bronze lancet and destroy the man's eye, they shall cut off his fingers.

221: If a physician set a broken bone for a man or cure his diseased bowels, the patient shall give five shekels of silver to the physician.

224: If a veterinary physician operate on an ox or an ass for a severe wound and save its life, the owner of the ox or ass shall give to the physician, as his fee, one-sixth of a shekel of silver.

228: If a builder build a house for a man and complete it, (that man) shall give him two shekels of silver per SAR of house as his wage.

234: If a boatman build a boat of 60 GUR for a man, he shall give to him two shekels of silver as his wage.

257: If a man hire a field-laborer, he shall pay him 8 GUR of grain per year.

258: If a man hire a herdsman, he shall pay him 6 GUR of grain per year.

271: If a man hire oxen, a wagon and a driver, he shall pay 180 KA of grain per day.

273: If a man hire a laborer, from the beginning of the year until the fifth month, he shall pay 6 SE of silver per day; from the sixth month till the end of the year he shall pay 5 SE of silver per day.

## Religious Life

6: If a man steal the property of a god (temple) or palace, that man shall be put to death; and he who receives from his hand the stolen (property) shall also be put to death.

45: If a man rent his field to a tenant for crop-rent and receive the crop-rent of his field and later Adad (i.e., the Storm God) inundate the field and carry away the produce, the loss (falls on) the tenant.

110: If a priestess who is not living in a MAL.GE.A, open a wine-shop or enter a wine-shop for a drink, they shall burn that woman.

127: If a man point the finger at a priestess or the wife of another and cannot justify it, they shall drag that man before the judges and they shall brand his forehead.

249: If a man hire an ox and a god strike it and it die, the man who hired the ox shall take an oath before god and go free.

266: If a visitation of god happen to a fold, or a lion kill, the shepherd shall declare himself innocent before god, and the owner of the fold shall suffer the damage.

## Property

199: If one destroy the eye of a man's slave or break a bone of a man's slave he shall pay one-half his price.

213: If he strike the female slave of a man and bring about a miscarriage, he shall pay two shekels of silver.

219: If a physician operate on the slave of a freeman for a severe wound with a bronze lancet and cause his death, he shall restore a slave of equal value.

229: If a builder build a house for a man and do not make its construction firm, and the house which he has built collapse and cause the death of the owner of the house, that builder shall be put to death.

233: If a builder build a house for a man and do not make its construction meet the requirements and a wall fall in, that builder shall strengthen that wall at his own expense.

235: If a boatman build a boat for a man and he (does) not make its construction seaworthy and that boat meet with a disaster in the same year in which it was put into commission, the boatman shall reconstruct that boat and he shall strengthen it at his own expense and he shall give the boat when strengthened to the owner of the boat.

237: If a man hire a boatman and a boat and freight it with grain, wool, oil, dates or any other kind of freight, and that boatman be careless and he sink the boat or wreck its cargo, the boatman shall replace the boat which he sank and whatever portion of the cargo he wrecked.

244: If a man hire an ox or an ass and a lion kill it in the field, it is the owner's affair.

245: If a man hire an ox and cause its death through neglect or abuse, he shall restore an ox of equal value to the owner of the ox.

## Life at Court

1: If a man bring an accusation against a man, and charge him with a (capital) crime, but cannot prove it, he, the accuser, shall be put to death.

2: If a man charge a man with sorcery, and cannot prove it, he who is charged with sorcery shall go to the river, into the river he shall throw himself and if the river overcome him, his accuser shall take to himself his house (estate). If the river show that man to be innocent and he come forth unharmed, he who charged him with sorcery shall be put to death. He who threw himself into the river shall take to himself the house of his accuser.[3]

3: If a man, in a case (pending judgment), bear false (threatening) witness, or do not establish the testimony that he has given, if that case be a case involving life, that man shall be put to death.

4: If a man (in a case) bear witness for grain or money (as a bribe), he shall himself bear the penalty imposed in that case.

5: If a judge pronounce a judgment, render a decision, deliver a verdict duly signed and sealed and afterward alter his judgment, they shall call that judge to account for the alteration of the judgment which he had pronounced, and he shall pay twelve-fold the penalty which was in said judgment; and, in the assembly, they shall expel him from his seat of judgment, and he shall not return, and with the judges in a case he shall not take his seat.

## Notes

[1] Igigi is a collective name for the Babylonian gods, typically those that were chief among the pantheon.

[2] In Mesopotamia, silver was the most common metal used in currency. One mina equaled approximately five hundred grams of silver.

[3] This is an example of trial by ordeal and here the River god judged the accused. Unlike the ordeal associated with medieval Europe, wherein the accused was proven innocent if they drowned, in Mesopotamia the accused was proven innocent if they survived.

# Zarathustra

## Sixth Century B.C.E.?

Zarathustra, also called by the westernized name Zoroaster, was a shadowy figure. It is unclear when he lived—scholars have tended to place him around the 6th century B.C.E., though others claim a date as much as a millenium earlier. The sacred text of Zoroastrianism, the *Zend Avesta*, includes seventeen hymns or Gathas, comprising the Yasna, thought to be the work of Zarathustra. In these hymns he represents himself as a prophet, living in a pastoral society in which cattle-herding is a key concern. He seeks an earthly protector-monarch, much like Confucius.

Zarathustra claimed inspiration from the god Ahura Mazda (or Wise Lord). His metaphysics features a cosmic dualism in which the forces of good or light struggle against those of evil, headed by Ahriman. Some scholars view Zarathustra as a monotheist, while others detect a sort of trinity comprising the Holy Spirit; Order or Right; and Good Mind. Right and Good Mind are the sons of the Wise Lord; in turn, Good Mind is the father of Devotion.

Zoroastrianism has strongly influenced western thought; both Judaism and Christianity include such ideas as a dualistic struggle between the forces of light and darkness, angels and demons, and a final apocalyptic battle, Persian ideas which filtered into Jewish thought during the Babylonian captivity. Zarathustra's ideas were also known in ancient Greece, where Cnidus compared his master, Plato, to Zoroaster.

The main modern followers of Zoroastrianism are the Parsees of India.

MM

# Three Hymns from the *Zend Avesta*

## Yasna 50

*1*

> What help shall my soul expect from anyone,
> In whom am I to put my trust as a protector for my cattle,
> In whom for myself, in the invocation,
> But in the Right, in thee, Wise Lord, and the Best Mind[1]?

*2*

> How is he to obtain the cattle which brings prosperity, O Wise One,
> He who desires it, together with its pastures?
> —Those who, among the many that behold the sun,
> Live uprightly, according to Righteousness . . .

*3*

> He also, O Wise One, shall receive from Righteousness the cattle
> —Promised with the Dominion and the Good Mind—
> Who, by the power of his (?) fortune (?),
> Shall make the neighbouring lands prosper for himself
> Which are still in a wicked one's possession.

*4*

> I will worship you with praise, O Wise Lord,
> Together with Righteousness, Best Mind, and the Dominion,
> Who, desired by the zealous . . .

*5*

> The signs of the hand which shall bring us to bliss
> Are assured to us indeed by you, Wise Lord as Righteousness,
> Together with a visible, manifest help,
> Because you look with favour upon your prophet.

*6*

> To me, Zarathustra, the prophet and sworn friend of Righteousness,
> Lifting my voice with veneration, O Wise One,
> May the creator of the mind's force show, as Good Mind,
> His precepts, that they may be the path of my tongue.

*7*

> I will harness for you, O Wise One with Righteousness,
> By the spur of your praise the swiftest steeds,
> (?) Broad (?) and strong through the Good Mind,
> Upon which you shall draw near. May you be ready to aid me!

*8*

> With hands outstretched I will approach you, O Wise One,
> With verses which are the song of zeal,
> You, as Righteousness, with the veneration of the zealous one,
> You, with all the strength of the Good Mind.

*9*

> With these hymns I would come before you, O Wise One,
> Praising you as Righteousness, with the deeds of the Good Mind.
> When I shall deal as I will with my portion of bliss,
> May I set into motion the hymns of the man of insight.

*10*

> The deeds which I shall do and those which I have done ere now,
> And the things which are precious to the eye, through Good Mind,
> The light of the sun, the sparkling dawn of the days,
> All this is for your praise, O Wise Lord, as Righteousness!

*11*

> I will call myself and be your praiser, O Wise One,
> While I can and may, through Righteousness.
> May the creator of existence further through Good Mind
> Its fulfilment of that which is most renewing
> In accord with the will (of the creator).

## Yasna 45

*1*

I will speak: hear now and attend,
You who from nearby or from afar come for instruction.
Do you all make your wisdom of him, for he is manifest.
May the false teacher not destroy the second existence,
Who for his evil choice has been reckoned wicked, through the tongue.

•   •   •

*2*

I will speak of the two spirits
Of whom the holier said unto the destroyer at the beginning of existence:
"Neither our thoughts nor our doctrines nor our minds' forces,
Neither our choices nor our words nor our deeds,
Neither our consciences nor our souls agree."

*3*

I will speak of the beginning of this existence,
Of the things which the Wise Lord has told me, he who knows.
Those of you who do not carry out the word
As I shall think and speak it,
For them the end of existence shall be "Woe!"

*4*

I will speak of the things which are best in this existence.
He who created it according to Righteousness,
I know, O Wise One, he is the father of the active Good Mind,
Whose daughter is beneficent Devotion.
Not to be deceived is the all-divining Lord.

*5*

I will speak of the word which the Most Holy Wise Lord
Has told me as the best for mankind to hear:
"Those who for me shall give heed and obedience to him,
Shall attain Integrity and Immortality through the deeds of Good Mind."

*6*

I will speak of the greatest of all,[2]
Praising him as Righteousness, who is benevolent towards the living.
Let the Wise Lord hear, as the Holy Spirit,
Whom I have praised when I took counsel with the Good Mind!
By his mind's force may he teach me the supreme good,

*7*

He who gives salvation or perdition
To those who are living or have been or shall be:
The soul of the righteous rewarded with Immortality,
Everlasting torments for the wicked.
(Of these torments also is the Wise Lord the creator, through his
    Dominion.)

*8*

(Listeners:)[3]
"Seek to win him for us by praises of veneration
—For I have now beheld this with mine eye,
Knowing the Wise Lord by the Righteousness of his Good Spirit,
Of his good deed and his good word—
And may we offer him hymns of praise in the house of song!

*9*

"Seek to propitiate him for us with the Good Mind,
Him who gives us fortune and misfortune at will.
May the Wise Lord through his Dominion over the village,
Through the intimacy of the Good Mind with Righteousness,
Prosper our cattle and our men!

*10*

Seek to glorify him for us with hymns of Devotion,
Him who is beheld in the soul as the Wise Lord,
Because he has promised with his Righteousness and his Good Mind
That Integrity and Immortality shall be ours in his Dominion,
Strength and endurance in his house!"

● ● ●

## 11

(Zarathustra:)
Whoever (? therefore ?) shall henceforth bear ill-will to the false gods
And to those who bear ill-will to the saviour
(That is, to those who shall not submit themselves to him),
To him shall the holy conscience of the coming saviour, the master of his
    house,
Stand in stead of sworn friend, of brother or father, O Wise Lord!

## Yasna 30

### 1

Now will I speak to those who will hear
Of the things which the initiate should remember:
The praises and prayer of the Good Mind to the Lord
And the joy which he shall see in the light who has remembered them
    well.

### 2

Hear with your ears that which is the sovereign good;
With a clear mind look upon the two sides
Between which each man must choose for himself,
Watchful beforehand that the great test may be accomplished in our
    favour.

•    •    •

### 3

Now at the beginning the twin spirits have declared their nature,
The better and the evil,
In thought and word and deed. And between the two
The wise ones choose well, not so the foolish.

### 4

And when these two spirits came together,
In the beginning they established life and non-life,
And that at the last the worst existence should be for the wicked,
But for the righteous one the Best Mind.

5

Of these two spirits, the evil one chose to do the worst things;
But the Most Holy Spirit, clothed in the most steadfast heavens,
Joined himself unto Righteousness;
And thus did all those who delight to please the Wise Lord by honest
    deeds.

6

Between the two, the false gods also did not choose rightly,
For while they pondered they were beset by error,
So that they chose the Worst Mind.
Then did they hasten to join themselves unto Fury,
That they might by it deprave the existence of man.

7

And to him[4] came Devotion, together with Dominion, Good Mind and
    Righteousness:
She gave endurance of body and the breath of life,
That he may be thine apart from them,
As the first by the retributions through the metal.

8

And when their punishment shall come to these sinners,[5]
Then, O Wise One, shall thy Dominion, with the Good Mind,
Be granted to those who have delivered Evil into the hands of
    Righteousness, O Lord!

9

And may we be those that renew this existence!
O Wise One, and you other Lords, and Righteousness, bring your
    alliance,
That thoughts may gather where wisdom is faint.

10

Then shall Evil cease to flourish,
While those who have acquired good fame
Shall reap the promised reward
In the blessed dwelling of the Good Mind, of the Wise One,
    and of Righteousness.

*11*

> If you, O men, understand the commandments which the Wise One has
> given,
> Well-being and suffering—long torment for the wicked and salvation for
> the righteous—
> All shall hereafter be for the best.

## Notes

[1] A Trinity, of sorts, comprising three aspects of the Divine.

[2] The Wise Lord (Mazda).

[3] In this and the next two stanzas, listeners who have been convinced by the Prophet
are speaking.

[4] I.e., Man. These are his helpers.

[5] This refers to an eschatology or vision of the end of time.

# The Hebrew Bible: Book of Judges

Judges belongs to a larger literary unit known as the Deuteronomistic History, that includes the books of Joshua, Judges, 1 and 2 Samuel, 1 and 2 Kings. This history is bound by a common interpretive theme: an evaluation of Israel's adherence to the Covenant tradition. Judges should also be read in conjunction with and following Exodus and Joshua, for the three books provide a sequential history of the initial promise, conquest and settlement of the Promised Land. There are four important features that distinguish the selection of Judges 4–5; the chapters reflect (1) the socio-historical background of Early Israel, (2) the governmental structure of tribal society, (3) the distinctive role of women in the narrative, and (4)preserve an example of archaic Hebrew poetry.

Archaeologically speaking, the setting suggested in Judges is that of the Early Iron Age (1200–1000 B.C.E.), a time when tribal units migrated into the hills of Judea. These settlers became agriculturists, living in small village complexes. Natural resources in this region of the Fertile Crescent were scarce so, not surprisingly, the account reflects the difficulties the new settlers faced. Paramount among the difficulties were issues of intertribal and international cooperation and competition; stories of war, conflict, and intrigue dominate the book. Therefore, scholars discern a second interpretive theme running through Judges. The folktales highlight a time when there was no king; chaos and social upheaval reigned instead as "every man did what was right in his own eyes" (17:6; 21:25). Scholars contend that the theme reflects the views of a pro-monarchic political faction.[1] This group recognized that long-term success necessitated the reconfiguration of their political structure as a monarchy like that of the Canaanites.[2] In this way, Judges functions not only as a sacred history, but as a work of political propaganda, and stands as testimony to a critical period in Israelite history. In the meantime, administration of Israelite society fell to tribal leaders, or judges (*shofet*), from whom the book of Judges takes its name. These judges functioned in various capacities that ranged from adjudicator to general to religious leader. According to the written tradition, both men and women could hold this leadership position.

Judges 4–5 tells the story of Deborah, judge, prophetess and military advisor. During her extraordinary tenure, the Israelites wage war against the Canaanites. Deborah (with Yahweh by her side) guides the Israelite general to success despite inferior numbers and weapons. A second extraordinary woman, Jael, aids the war effort by assassinating the Canaanite military commander. In the midst of this external struggle, Deborah must also face factional infighting among the Israelite tribes (5:15–17). The story is unusual, to say the least, in its portrayal of women intimately involved in a war effort. Sociologists reason that the rise to power of marginalized groups such as women indeed necessitated a background of social unrest. Only amidst social instability could Deborah have played such a public—and powerful—role in a traditionally male-dominated society.

Pay special attention to the so-called Song of Deborah (5:1–31). Scholars assign the Song a compositional date of 1200–1000 B.C.E., making it one of the oldest pieces of Hebrew poetry in existence. The Song is a victory hymn, celebrating Yahweh's participation in the war (v. 4–5; cf. 4:14–15, 23); it acclaims the Divine Warrior, who mired the Canaanites' chariots in floodwaters. Yahweh's presence on the battlefield is an example of Theophany, a revelatory experience in which a deity becomes visibly manifest. Yahweh's theophanic intercession in Israelite history is a persistent motif throughout the Hebrew Bible. The Song of Deborah also attests to the ritual functions afforded women, including leadership roles in chant, dance, and song. Though the archaic grammatical constructions of the ancient hymn are lost in translation, we are able to observe antithetic parallelism of thematic units. There are cooperative (v. 13–15) and uncooperative tribes (v. 15–17), the cursed (v. 23) and the blessed (v. 24), enemies who perish (v. 31a) and friends who are eternal (31b).

KP

## Notes

[1] Based on passages in 1 Samuel (cf. 8:1–22), it appears that an anti-kingship faction believed an earthly king ruling a Kingdom of Israel would threaten the hegemony of Yahweh and the Kingdom of God. Additionally, the installation of a monarch would only serve to lessen the distinctiveness of Israel; Israel would become "like the nations" (8:20) that surrounded it.

[2] "Canaanite" is the general designation used throughout the Hebrew Bible for the non-Israelite inhabitants, cities and/or kingdoms of Syria-Palestine.

# The Hebrew Bible: Judges 4–5

**4** And the people of Israel again did what was evil in the sight of the LORD, after Ehud died. [2] And the LORD sold them into the hand of Jabin king of Canaan, who reigned in Hazor; the commander of his army was Sis′era, who dwelt in Haro′sheth-ha-goiim. [3] Then the people of Israel cried to the LORD for help; for he had nine hundred chariots of iron, and oppressed the people of Israel cruelly for twenty years.

4 Now Deb′orah, a prophetess, the wife of Lapp′idoth, was judging Israel at that time. [5] She used to sit under the palm of Deb′orah between Ramah and Bethel in the hill country of E′phraim; and the people of Israel came up to her for judgment. [6] She sent and summoned Barak the son of Abin′o-am from Kedesh in Naph′tali, and said to him, "The LORD, the God of Israel, commands you, 'Go, gather your men at Mount Tabor, taking ten thousand from the tribe of Naph′tali and the tribe of Zeb′ulun.[a] [7] And I will draw out Sis′era, the general of Jabin's army, to meet you by the river Kishon with his chariots and his troops; and I will give him into your hand.'" [8] Barak said to her, "If you will go with me, I will go; but if you will not go with me, I will not go." [9] And she said, "I will surely go with you; nevertheless, the road on which you are going will not lead to your glory, for the LORD will sell Sis′era into the hand of a woman." Then Deb′orah arose, and went with Barak to Kedesh. [10] And Barak summoned Zeb′ulun and Naph′tali to Kedesh; and ten thousand men went up at his heels; and Deb′orah went up with him.

11 Now Heber the Ken′ite had separated from the Ken′ites, the descendants of Hobab the father-in-law of Moses, and had pitched his tent as far away as the oak in Za-anan′nim, which is near Kedesh.

12 When Sis′era was told that Barak the son of Abin′o-am had gone up to Mount Tabor, [13] Sis′era called out all his chariots, nine hundred chariots of iron, and all the men who were with him, from Haro′sheth-ha-goiim to the river Kishon. [14] And Deb′orah said to Barak, "Up! For this is the day in which the LORD has given Sis′era into your hand. Does not the LORD go out before you?" So Barak went down from Mount Tabor with ten thousand men following him. [15] And the LORD routed Sis′era and all his chariots and all his army before Barak at the edge of the sword; and Sis′era alighted from his chariot and fled away on foot. [16] And Barak pursued the chariots and the army to Haro′sheth-ha-goiim, and all the army of Sis′era fell by the edge of the sword; not a man was left.

17 But Sis′era fled away on foot to the tent of Ja′el, the wife of Heber the Ken′ite; for there was peace between Jabin the king of Hazor and the house of Heber the Ken′ite. ¹⁸And Ja′el came out to meet Sis′era, and said to him, "Turn aside, my lord, turn aside to me; have no fear." So he turned aside to her into the tent, and she covered him with a rug. ¹⁹And he said to her, "Pray, give me a little water to drink; for I am thirsty." So she opened a skin of milk and gave him a drink and covered him. ²⁰And he said to her, "Stand at the door of the tent, and if any man comes and asks you, 'Is any one here?' say, No." ²¹But Ja′el the wife of Heber took a tent peg, and took a hammer in her hand, and went softly to him and drove the peg into his temple, till it went down into the ground, as he was lying fast asleep from weariness. So he died. ²²And behold, as Barak pursued Sis′era, Ja′el went out to meet him, and said to him, "Come, and I will show you the man whom you are seeking." So he went in to her tent; and .there lay Sis′era dead, with the tent peg in his temple.

23 So on that day God subdued Jabin the king of Canaan before the people of Israel. ²⁴And the hand of the people of Israel bore harder and harder on Jabin the king of Canaan, until they destroyed Jabin king of Canaan.

5 Then sang Deb′orah and Barak the son of Abin′o-am on that day:
² "That the leaders took the lead in Israel,
    that the people offered themselves willingly,
    bless the LORD!

³ "Hear, O kings; give ear, O princes;
    to the Lord I Will sing,
    I will make melody to the Lord, the God of Israel.

⁴ "Lord, when thou didst go forth from Se′ir,
    when thou didst march from the region of Edom,
the earth trembled,
    and the heavens dropped,
    yea, the clouds dropped water.
⁵ The mountains quaked before the LORD,
    yon Sinai before the LORD, the God of Israel.

⁶ "In the days of Shamgar, son of Anath,
    in the days of Ja′el, caravans ceased
    and travelers kept to the byways.
⁷ The peasantry ceased in Israel, they ceased
    until you arose, Deb′orah,
    arose as a mother in Israel.
⁸ When new gods were chosen,
    then war was in the gates.
Was shield or spear to be seen

among forty thousand in Israel?

9 My heart goes out to the commanders of Israel
   who offered themselves willingly among the people.
   Bless the LORD.

10 "Tell of it, you who ride on tawny asses,
   you who sit on rich carpets
   and you who walk by the way.
11 To the sound of musicians at the watering places,
   there they repeat the triumphs of the LORD,
   the triumphs of his peasantry in Israel.

"Then down to the gates marched the people of the LORD.

12 "Awake, awake, Deb'orah!
   Awake, awake, utter a song!
   Arise, Barak, lead away your captives,
   O son of Abin'o-am.
13 Then down marched the remnant of the noble;
   the people of the LORD marched down for him against the mighty.
14 From E'phraim they set out thither into the valley,
   following you, Benjamin, with your kinsmen;
 from Machir marched down the commanders,
   and from Zeb'ulun those who bear the marshal's staff;
15 the princes of Is'sachar came with Deb'orah,
   and Is'sachar faithful to Barak;
   into the valley they rushed forth at his heels.
 Among the clans of Reuben
   there were great searchings of heart.b
16 Why did you tarry among the sheepfolds,
   to hear the piping for the flocks?
 Among the clans of Reuben
   there were great searchings of heart.
17 Gilead stayed beyond the Jordan;
   and Dan, why did he abide with the ships?
 Asher sat still at the coast of the sea, settling down by his landings.
18 Zeb'ulun is a people that jeoparded their lives to the death;
   Naph'tali too, on the heights of the field.

19 "The kings came, they fought;
   then fought the kings of Canaan,
   at Ta'anach, by the waters of Megid'do;
     they got no spoils of silver.

20 From heaven fought the stars,
    from their courses they fought against Sis′era.
21 The torrent Kishon swept them away,
    the onrushing torrent, the torrent Kishon.
    March on, my soul, with might!

22 "Then loud beat the horses' hoofs
    with the galloping, galloping of his steeds.

23 "Curse Meroz, says the angel of the LORD,
    curse bitterly its inhabitants,
  because they came not to the help of the LORD,
    to the help of the LORD against the mighty.

24 "Most blessed of women be Ja′el,
    the wife of Heber the Ken′ite,
    of tent-dwelling women most blessed.
25 He asked water and she gave him milk,
    she brought him curds in a lordly bowl.
26 She put her hand to the tent peg
    and her right hand to the workmen's mallet;
  she struck Sis′era a blow,
    she crushed his head,
    she shattered and pierced his temple.
27 He sank, he fell,
    he lay still at her feet;
  at her feet he sank, he fell;
    where he sank, there he fell dead.

28 "Out of the window she peered,
    the mother of Sis′era gazed through the lattice:
  'Why is his chariot so long in coming?
    Why tarry the hoofbeats of his chariots?'
29 Her wisest ladies make answer,
    nay, she gives answer to herself,
30 'Are they not finding and dividing the spoil?—
    A maiden or two for every man;
  spoil of dyed stuffs for Sis′era,
    spoil of dyed stuffs embroidered,
    two pieces of dyed work embroidered for my neck as spoil?'

31 "So perish an thine enemies, O LORD!
    But thy friends be like the sun as he rises in his might."

## Notes

[a] According to literary tradition, the Israelite population of the pre-monarchic period (ca. 1200–1000 B.C.E.) was organized in a system of 12 clan-based tribes. Each tribe was assigned land for settlement and each was expected to support the larger Israelite community in times of war and religious celebration.

[b] Reuben, along with Gilead, Dan and Asher (v. 17) are the Israelite tribes that did not participate in the battle, much to the consternation of the narrator. The tribes of Zebulun and Naphtali (v. 18) are praised for their bravery in face of battle, while the town of Meroz and its inhabitants (v. 23) are cursed for their lack of engagement.

# The Hebrew Bible: Book of 2 Kings

    2 Kings is the last book of the Deuteronomistic History. In both 1 and 2 Kings, the editor (the Deuteronomist) provides a royal history of the Israelite and Judean monarchies. He gives a brief summary of events, an evaluation of each king's fidelity to the Covenant, and a final judgment. Remember, the Deuteronomist is interested in telling the sacred history of Israel, and to that end, a king's success or failure is gauged by the pious standard of King David.[1] As compilations of prose and verse, prophecy and court history, 1 and 2 Kings are essentially based on contemporary sources (ca. 10th–6th centuries B.C.E.), with the editorial framework and commentary furnished by an editor. The books of 1 and 2 Kings, along with the rest of the Deuteronomistic History, took their final form by the fifth century B.C.E.

    2 Kings 18–20 is one of the longest accounts devoted to the reign of a single king. The chapters detail the reign of Hezekiah of Judah (727–698 B.C.E.) and tell of his rebellion against the mighty Assyrians, his provisions for the inevitable siege of Jerusalem, his consultation with the prophet Isaiah, and his illness and recovery. Interspersed are references to the fall of the Northern Kingdom to the Assyrians (ca. 722/721 B.C.E.), various regional skirmishes, and the assassination of the Assyrian king Sennacherib (ca. 681 B.C.E.).

    Though some events in these chapters are historically verifiable (the rebellion of Hezekiah, the fall of the Northern Kingdom, the death of Sennacherib, Judean vassalage to Assyria), the Deuteronomist takes great liberty with the chronological arrangement of events. Dramatic embellishment heightens the confrontation between Yahweh and His enemies, contrasts the fate of the Northern Kingdom with that of the South, and contrasts Hezekiah with the kings who preceded him. The narrative is didactic; the editor's goal is to illustrate that the Northern Kingdom was conquered because its kings violated Covenant stipulations (18:12). By contrast, Hezekiah purified the cult of the Southern Kingdom, destroying all altars and images of other deities. As a result, "Yahweh was with him; wherever he went, he prospered" (18:7).

    2 Kings 18–20 is a fine example of Israelite literary accomplishment, both in narrative and verse. Through character speeches of the charismatic *dramatis personae*, the reader is drawn in to the confrontation between three Assyrian officials (the Tartan, the Rabsaris, and the Rabshakeh) and three Judean officials, where the power of Yahweh is pitted against the power of

Sennacherib. Though Yahweh is the hero, you'll notice that the prophet Isaiah plays a central role in the narrative; Isaiah is a more significant figure than even King Hezekiah. Isaiah is an intimate within the king's court, and Hezekiah seeks guidance from the prophet on issues ranging from military strategy to medical advice. Isaiah is a spokesman of God, and his presence by the king's side illustrates the close relationship between religion and politics in the ancient world.

2 Kings 18–20 gives us insight into the way particular editors of the Hebrew Bible interpreted secular history in writing a sacred history, as the Deuteronomist took historical events and adapted them to fit a theological agenda. Through these chapters, we see the editor demonstrate the salvific power of Yahweh for those who obey His Covenant and the horrific consequences for those who do not.

KP

## Note

[1] For the secular history of Israel and Judah, the editor refers to "The Chronicles of the Kings of Israel" and "The Annals of the Kings of Judah," two works which unfortunately are lost to us.

# The Hebrew Bible: 2 Kings 18–20

**18** In the third year of Hoshe´a son of Elah, king of Israel, Hezeki´ah the son of Ahaz, king of Judah, began to reign.[a] [2]He was twenty-five years old when he began to reign, and he reigned twenty-nine years in Jerusalem. His mother's name was Abi the daughter of Zechari´ah. [3]And he did what was right in the eyes of the LORD, according to all that David his father had done. [4]He removed the high places, and broke the pillars, and cut down the Ashe´rah. And he broke in pieces the bronze serpent that Moses had made, for until those days the people of Israel had burned incense to it; it was called Nehush´tan.[b] [5]He trusted in the LORD the God of Israel; so that there was none like him among all the kings of Judah after him, nor among those who were before him. [6]For he held fast to the LORD; he did not depart from following him, but kept the commandments which the LORD commanded Moses. [7]And the LORD was with him; wherever he went forth, he prospered. He rebelled against the king of Assyria, and would not serve him. [8]He smote the Philistines as far as Gaza and its territory, from watchtower to fortified city.

9 In the fourth year of King Hezeki´ah, which was the seventh year of Hoshe´a son of Elah, king of Israel, Shalmane´ser king of Assyria came up against Sama´ria and besieged it [10]and at the end of three years he took it. In the sixth year of Hezeki´ah, which was the ninth year of Hoshe´a king of Israel, Sama´ria was taken. [11]The king of Assyria carried the Israelites away to Assyria, and put them in Halah, and on the Habor, the river of Gozan, and in the cities of the Medes, [12]because they did not obey the voice of the LORD their God but transgressed his covenant, even all that Moses the servant of the LORD commanded; they neither listened nor obeyed.

13 In the fourteenth year of King Hezeki´ah Sennach´erib king of Assyria came up against all the fortified cities of Judah and took them. [14]And Hezeki´ah king of Judah sent to the king of Assyria at Lachish, saying, "I have done wrong; withdraw from me; whatever you impose on me I will bear." And the king of Assyria required of Hezeki´ah king of Judah three hundred talents of silver and thirty talents of gold. [15]And Hezeki´ah gave him all the silver that was found in the house of the LORD, and in the treasuries of the king's house. [16]At that time Hezeki´ah stripped the gold from the doors of the temple of the LORD, and from the doorposts which Hezeki´ah king of Judah had overlaid and gave it to the king of Assyria. [17]And the king of Assyria sent the Tartan, the Rab´saris, and the Rab´shakeh with a great army from Lachish to King Hezeki´ah at Jerusalem. And they went up and came to Jerusalem. When they

arrived, they came and stood by the conduit of the upper pool, which is on the highway to the Fuller's Field. [18] And when they called for the king, there came out to them Eli'akim the son of Hilki'ah, who was over the household, and Shebnah the secretary, and Jo'ah the son of Asaph, the recorder.

19 And the Rab'shakeh said to them, "Say to Hezeki'ah, 'Thus says the great king, the king of Assyria: On what do you rest this confidence of yours? [20] Do you think that mere words are strategy and power for war? On whom do you now rely, that you have rebelled against me? [21] Behold, you are relying now on Egypt, that broken reed of a staff, which will pierce the hand of any man who leans on it. Such is Pharaoh king of Egypt to all who rely on him. [22] But if you say to me, "We rely on the LORD our God," is it not he whose high places and altars Hezeki'ah has removed, saying to Judah and to Jerusalem, "You shall worship before this altar in Jerusalem"? [23] Come now, make a wager with my master the king of Assyria: I will give you two thousand horses, if you are able on your part to set riders upon them. [24] How then can you repulse a single captain among the least of my master's servants, when you rely on Egypt for chariots and for horsemen? [25] Moreover, is it without the LORD that I have come up against this place to destroy it? The LORD said to me, Go up against this land, and destroy it.'"

26 Then Eli'akim the son of Hilki'ah, and Shebnah, and Jo'ah, said to the Rab'shakeh, "Pray, speak to your servants in the Aramaic language, for we understand it; do not speak to us in the language of Judah within the hearing of the people who are on the wall."[c] [27] But the Rab'shakeh said to them, "Has my master sent me to speak these words to your master and to you, and not to the men sitting on the wall, who are doomed with you to eat their own dung and to drink their own urine?"

28 Then the Rab'shakeh stood and called out in a loud voice in the language of Judah: "Hear the word of the great king, the king of Assyria! [29] Thus says the king: 'Do not let Hezeki'ah deceive you, for he will not be able to deliver you out of my hand. [30] Do not let Hezeki'ah make you to rely on the LORD by saying, The LORD will surely deliver us, and this city will not be given into the hand of the king of Assyria.' [31] Do not listen to Hezeki'ah; for thus says the king of Assyria: 'Make your peace with me and come out to me; then every one of you will eat of his own vine, and every one of his own fig tree, and every one of you will drink the water of his own cistern; [32] until I come and take you away to a land like your own land, a land of grain and wine, a land of bread and vineyards, a land of olive trees and honey, that you may live, and not die. And do not listen to Hezeki'ah when he misleads you by saying, The LORD will deliver us. [33] Has any of the gods of the nations ever delivered his land out of the hand of the king of Assyria? [34] Where are the gods of

Hamath and Arpad? Where are the gods of Sepharva′im, Hena, and Ivvah? Have they delivered Sama′ria out of my hand?ᵈ ³⁵ Who among all the gods of the countries have delivered their countries out of my hand, that the LORD should deliver Jerusalem out of my hand?'"

36 But the people were silent and answered him not a word, for the king's command was, "Do not answer him." ³⁷ Then Eli′akim the son of Hilki′ah, who was over the household, and Shebna the secretary, and Jo′ah the son of Asaph, the recorder, came to Hezeki′ah with their clothes rent, and told him the words of the Rab′shakeh.

**19** When King Hezeki′ah heard it, he rent his clothes, and covered himself with sackcloth, and went into the house of the LORD. ²And he sent Eli′akim, who was over the household, and Shebna the secretary, and the senior priests, covered with sackcloth, to the prophet Isaiah the son of Amoz. ³They said to him, "Thus says Hezeki′ah, This day is a day of distress, of rebuke, and of disgrace; children have come to the birth, and there is no strength to bring them forth. ⁴It may be that the LORD your God heard all the words of the Rab′shakeh, whom his master the king of Assyria has sent to mock the living God, and will rebuke the words which the LORD your God has heard; therefore lift up your prayer for the remnant that is left." ⁵When the servants of King Hezeki′ah came to Isaiah, ⁶Isaiah said to them, "Say to your master, 'Thus says the LORD: Do not be afraid because of the words that you have heard, with which the servants of the king of Assyria have reviled me. ⁷Behold, I will put a spirit in him, so that he shall hear a rumor and return to his own land; and I will cause him to fall by the sword in his own land.'"

8 The Rab′shakeh returned, and found the king of Assyria fighting against Libnah; for he heard that the king had left Lachish. ⁹And when the king heard concerning Tirha′kah king of Ethiopia, "Behold, he has set out to fight against you," he sent messengers again to Hezeki′ah, saying,ᵉ ¹⁰"Thus shall you speak to Hezeki′ah king of Judah: 'Do not let your God on whom you rely deceive you by promising that Jerusalem will not be given into the hand of the king of Assyria. ¹¹Behold, you have heard what the kings of Assyria have done to all lands, destroying them utterly. And shall you be delivered? ¹²Have the gods of the nations delivered them, the nations which my fathers destroyed, Gozan, Haran, Rezeph, and the people of Eden who were in Telassar? ¹³Where is the king of Hamath, the king of Arpad, the king of the city of Sepharva′im, the king of Hena, or the king of Ivvah?'"

14 Hezeki′ah received the letter from the hand of the messengers. and read it; and Hezeki′ah went up to the house of the LORD, and spread it before the LORD. ¹⁵And Hezeki′ah prayed before the Lord, and said: "O LORD the God of Israel, who art enthroned above the cherubim, thou art the God, thou

alone, of all the kingdoms of the earth; thou hast made heaven and earth. [16] Incline thy ear, O LORD, and hear; open thy eyes, O LORD, and see; and hear the words of Sennach´erib, which he has sent to mock the living God. [17] Of a truth, O LORD, the kings of Assyria have laid waste the nations and their lands, [18] and have cast their gods into the fire; for they were no gods, but the work of men's hands, wood and stone; therefore they were destroyed. [19] So now, O LORD our God, save us, I beseech thee, from his hand, that all the kingdoms of the earth may know that thou, O LORD, art God alone."

20 Then Isaiah the son of Amoz sent to Hezeki´ah, saying, "Thus says the LORD, the God of Israel: Your prayer to me about Sennach´erib king of Assyria I have heard. [21] This is the word that the LORD has spoken concerning him:

> "She despises you, she scorns you—
>     the virgin daughter of Zion;
> she wags her head behind you—
>     the daughter of Jerusalem.

[22] "Whom have you mocked and reviled?
>     Against whom have you raised your voice
> and haughtily lifted your eyes?
>     Against the Holy One of Israel!
[23] By your messengers you have mocked the Lord,
>     and you have said, 'With my many chariots
> I have gone up the heights of the mountains,
>     to the far recesses of Lebanon;
> I felled its tallest cedars,
>     its choicest cypresses;
> I entered its farthest retreat,
>     its densest forest.
[24] I dug wells
>     and drank foreign waters,
> and I dried up with the sole of my foot
>     all the streams of Egypt.'

[25] "Have you not heard
>     that I determined it long ago?
> I planned from days of old
>     what now I bring to pass,
> that you should turn fortified cities
>     into heaps of ruins,
[26] while their inhabitants, shorn of strength,

are dismayed and confounded,
and have become like plants of the field,
and like tender grass,
like grass on the housetops;
blighted before it is grown?
27 "But I know your sitting down
and your going out and coming in,
and your raging against me.
28 Because you have raged against me
and your arrogance has come into my ears,
I will put my hook in your nose
and my bit in your mouth,
and I will turn you back on the way
by which you came.

29 "And this shall be the sign for you: this year you shall eat what grows of itself, and in the second year what springs of the same; then in the third year sow, and reap, and plant vineyards, and eat their fruit. 30 And the surviving remnant of the house of Judah shall again take root downward, and bear fruit upward; 31 for out of Jerusalem shall go forth a remnant, and out of Mount Zion a band of survivors. The zeal of the LORD will do this.

32 "Therefore thus says the Lord concerning the king of Assyria, He shall not come into this city or shoot an arrow there, or come before it with a shield or cast up a siege mound against it. 33 By the way that he came, by the same he shall return, and he shall not come into this city, says the LORD. 34 For I will defend this city to save it, for my own sake and for the sake of my servant David."

35 And that night the angel of the LORD went forth, and slew a hundred and eighty-five thousand in the camp of the Assyrians; and when men arose early in the morning, behold, these were all dead bodies. 36 Then Sennach′erib king of Assyria departed, and went home, and dwelt at Nin′eveh. 37 And as he was worshiping in the house of Nisroch his god, Adram′melech and Share′zer, his sons, slew him with the sword, and escaped into the land of Ar′arat. And Esarhad′don his son reigned in his stead.

**20** In those days Hezeki′ah became sick and was at the point of death. And Isaiah the prophet the son of Amoz came to him, and said to him, "Thus says the LORD, 'Set your house in order; for you shall die, you shall not recover.'" 2 Then Hezeki′ah turned his face to the wall, and prayed to the LORD, saying, 3 "Remember now, O LORD, I beseech thee, how I have walked before thee in faithfulness and with a whole heart, and have done what is good in thy sight." And Hezeki′ah wept bitterly. 4 And before Isaiah had gone out of the middle court, the word of the LORD came to him: [5]"Turn back, and say to Hezeki'ah the prince of my people, Thus says the Lord, the God of David your father: I have heard your prayer, I have seen your tears; behold, I will heal you; on the third day you shall go up to the house of the LORD. [6]And I will add fifteen years to your life. I will deliver you and this city out of the hand of the king of Assyria, and I will defend this city for my own sake and for my servant David's sake." [7]And Isaiah said, "Bring a cake of figs. And let them take and lay it on the boil, that he may recover."

8 And Hezeki'ah said to Isaiah, 'What shall be the sign that the LORD will heal me, and that I shall go up to the house of the LORD on the third day?" [9]And Isaiah said, "This is the sign to you from the LORD, that the LORD will do the thing that he has promised: shall the shadow go forward ten steps, or go back ten steps?" [10]And Hezeki'ah answered, "It is an easy thing for the shadow to lengthen ten steps; rather let the shadow go back ten steps." [11]And Isaiah the prophet cried to the LORD; and he brought the shadow back ten steps, by which the sun had declined on the dial of Ahaz.

12 At that time Mero'dach-bal'adan the son of Bal'adan, king of Babylon, sent envoys with letters and a present to Hezeki'ah; for he heard that Hezeki'ah had been sick. [13]And Hezeki'ah welcomed them, and he showed them all his treasure house, the silver, the gold, the spices, the precious oil, his armory, all that was found in his storehouses; there was nothing in his house or in all his realm that Hezeki'ah did not show them. [14]Then Isaiah the prophet came to King Hezeki'ah, and said to him, "What did these men say? And whence did they come to you?" And Hezeki'ah said, "They have come from a far country, from Babylon." [15]He said, "What have they seen in your house?" And Hezeki'ah answered, "They have seen all that is in my house; there is nothing in my storehouses that I did not show them."

16 Then Isaiah said to Hezeki'ah, "Hear the word of the LORD: [17]Behold, the days are coming, when all that is in your house, and that which your fathers have stored up till this day, shall be carried to Babylon; nothing shall be left, says the LORD. [18]And some of your own sons, who are born to you, shall be taken away; and they shall be eunuchs in the palace of the king of Babylon." [19]Then said Hezeki'ah to Isaiah, "The word of the LORD which you have spoken is good." For he thought, "Why not, if there will be peace and security in my days?"

20 The rest of the deeds of Hezeki'ah, and all his might, and how he made the pool and the conduit and brought water into the city, are they not written in the Book of the Chronicles of the Kings of Judah? [21]And Hezeki'ah slept with his fathers; and Manas'seh his son reigned in his stead.

## Notes

<sup>a</sup> The third year of King Hoshea's reign was 730/729 B.C.E., though the date of King Hezekiah's accession is considered to have actually been ca. 715 B.C.E.

<sup>b</sup> In Numbers 21:6–9, we read of a people wandering in the wilderness, complaining of hunger and thirst. Provoked, God sent venomous serpents to attack them; many died. The people repented, asking Moses to intercede with God on their behalf. God relents and orders Moses to construct a bronze serpent and place it upon a pole. Any bite victim could approach the image, gaze upon it and be healed. It seems that by the time of King Hezekiah, the bronze serpent had become a cult statue revered for its apotropaic (healing) powers.

<sup>c</sup> The officials of Judah spoke Hebrew, but they also understood Aramaic, which by that time had become the *lingua franca* for governmental business in Southwest Asia. The Judean officials ask that the Babylonian officials please refrain from speaking Hebrew, so that their diplomatic exchange might remain confidential and away from the interested on-lookers.

<sup>d</sup> The king of Assyria is here issuing a challenge to the people of Judah. He notes that the gods of neighboring city-states and nations in Syria-Palestine (Hamath, Arpad, etc.) were useless in preventing Assyrian conquest. Even the Israelite capital of Samaria is noted for its collapse at the hands of the mighty king.

<sup>e</sup> "King Tirhakah of Ethiopia" is a reference to Taharqo, the King of Kush (ancient Nubia), who reigned from 695–669 B.C.E. The chronology presented in this verse places Taharqo on the throne in 701 B.C.E. and appears to be a mistake on the part of the biblical author, though Taharqo could have been active at this time as a general commanding the Kushite army. Regardless, the reference to the movement of Taharqo and his army is an allusion to a Judean-Kushite alliance. The Kushite empire would benefit from a weakened Assyrian empire, and so the Kushites were eager to come to the assistance of Judah.

# The Hebrew Bible: Book of Qoheleth/Ecclesiastes

Qoheleth, the Hebrew name of the book known in the Christian canon as Ecclesiastes, is attributed to King David's son and successor (1:1). Though he is unnamed in the superscription, the regnal history of Israel identifies this son as Solomon. Contemporary scholars dispute this attribution, noting that the superscription is a later editorial gloss and that the grammatical complexity of the term qoheleth as it is used in the body of the book as well as its associated definition "assembly" render the name ambiguous at best.[1] What we can say is that the author seems to have been a teacher (perhaps a leader of the assembly), who incorporated proverbs and sayings into an essay on life. Our oldest manuscript is from the 2nd century B.C.E., though the book was probably composed in the mid 3rd century B.C.E. Qoheleth belongs to the literary genre known as wisdom literature and is didactic in intent. Unlike prophets who receive revelation from Yahweh in the form of oracles or visions, and priests who communicate with the deity through sacrifices, chanting and divination, wisdom teachers speak from life experience. Wisdom literature is "curiously ahistorical"[2] and, in contrast to much of the Hebrew Bible, is unconcerned with contemporary politics. Rather, the main theme of Qoheleth is the utter futility of life.[3]

Qoheleth (the author) engages in debate and disputation with traditional understandings of the Universe and God, and humankind's relationship to each. In chapters one and two, Qoheleth examines the purpose of work and deeds. Keep in mind that in the ancient world, one's name, passed on through progeny and great deeds (cf. *The Epic of Gilgamesh*) is one's enduring legacy. By contrast, Qoheleth concludes that deeds and reputation are not remembered, all earthly toil is in vain. Qoheleth also explores the purpose of acquired knowledge and wisdom. Though wisdom is held in esteem by both ancient and modern societies, Qoheleth scorns it. Wisdom yields no advantage (2:14), only frustration (1:18; cf. 9:13–18). Perhaps 3:1–8 is the most well known of section of the book, due in part to the popularity of the song written by Pete Seeger inspired by these verses:

3:1 For everything there is a season, and a time for every matter under heaven:

50

a time to be born, and a time
to die;
a time to plant, and a time to
pluck up what is planted;
a time to kill, and a time to heal;
a time to break down, and a time
to build up; . . . . (3:1–3)

. . . and so on. But despite the orderliness of the universe, as ordained by God, the *raison d'être* is beyond humankind's understanding. There may well be a time for everything under heaven but humankind can only passively watch as events unfold (3:9–11). As for the end of time, and the notion of reward for the just and punishment for the wicked, Qoheleth concludes "all are from the dust, and all turn to dust again" (3:20). We will never know what the afterlife truly holds. Interestingly, Qoheleth addresses the relationship between animals and humans, asking whether humans are superior to animals. He determines that the issue of superiority is moot for our fate is one and the same: both animals and humans, we all die (3:18–21). Qoheleth's recommendation in light of his fatalism is indulgent: "Go, eat your bread with enjoyment, and drink your wine with a merry heart" (9:7; cf. 2:24, 3:12–13, 5:18, 8:15).

The pessimism endemic to the book of Qoheleth makes it one of the most controversial books in the canon. Indeed, it almost did not make canon; early rabbinic and Christian theologians hotly debated the book's sacred authority. The redemptive epilogue and the book's attribution to Solomon probably influenced its inclusion in the Hebrew Bible.

KP

## Notes

[1] Qoheleth appears with and without the definite article, as a masculine noun with a feminine construction, as a personal name and as a title.

[2] Stephen Harris and Robert Platzner, *The Old Testament, An Introduction to the Hebrew Bible* (Boston: McGraw Hill, 2003), p. 296.

[3] An epilogue was later added that provides the work with a more positive spin on the responsibilities and purposes of a life with God (cf. 12:9–14).

# The Hebrew Bible: Qoheleth/Ecclesiastes 1–4

**1** The words of the preacher, the son of David, king in Jerusalem.
² Vanity of vanities, says the Preacher,
  vanity of vanities! All is vanity.
³ What does man gain by all the toil
  at which he toils under the sun?
⁴ A generation goes, and a generation comes,
  but the earth remains for ever.
⁵ The sun rises and the sun goes down,
  and hastens to the place where it rises.
⁶ The wind blows to the south,
  and goes round to the north;
round and round goes the wind,
  and on its circuits the wind returns.
⁷ All streams run to the sea,
  but the sea is not full;
to the place where the streams flow,
  there they flow again.
⁸ All things are full of weariness;
  a man cannot utter it;
the eye is not satisfied with seeing,
  nor the ear filled with hearing.
⁹ What has been is what will be,
  and what has been done is what will be done;
  and there is nothing new under the sun.
¹⁰ Is there a thing of which it is said,
  "See, this is new"?
It has been already,
  in the ages before us.
¹¹ There is no remembrance of former things,
  nor will there be any remembrance
of later things yet to happen
  among those who come after.

12 I the Preacher have been king over Israel in Jerusalem. ¹³ And I applied my mind to seek and to search out by wisdom all that is done under heaven; it is an unhappy business that God has given to the sons of men to be busy

with. <sup>14</sup> 1 have seen everything that is done under the sun; and behold, all is vanity and a striving after wind.
<sup>15</sup> What is crooked cannot be made straight,
and what is lacking cannot be numbered.
16 I said to myself, "I have acquired great wisdom, surpassing all who were over Jerusalem before me; and my mind has had great experience of wisdom and knowledge." <sup>17</sup>And I applied my mind to know wisdom and to know madness and folly. I perceived that this also is but a striving after wind.
<sup>18</sup> For in much wisdom is much vexation,
and he who increases knowledge increases sorrow.

2 I said to myself, "Come now, I will make a test of pleasure; enjoy yourself." But behold, this also was vanity. <sup>2</sup>I said of laughter, "It is mad," and of pleasure, "What use is it?" <sup>3</sup>I searched with my mind how to cheer my body with wine—my mind still guiding me with wisdom—and how to lay hold on folly, till I might see what was good for the sons of men to do under heaven during the few days of their life. <sup>4</sup>I made great works; I built houses and planted vineyards for myself; <sup>5</sup>I made myself gardens and parks, and planted in them all kinds of fruit trees. <sup>6</sup>I made myself pools from which to water the forest of growing trees. <sup>7</sup>I bought male and female slaves, and had slaves who were born in my house; I had also great possessions of herds and flocks, more than any who had been before me in Jerusalem. <sup>8</sup>I also gathered for myself silver and gold and the treasure of kings and provinces; I got singers, both men and women, and many concubines, man's delight.

9 So I became great and surpassed all who were before me in Jerusalem; also my wisdom remained with me. <sup>10</sup>And whatever my eyes desired I did not keep from them; I kept my heart from no pleasure, for my heart found pleasure in all my toil, and this was my reward for all my toil. <sup>11</sup>Then I considered all that my hands had done and the toil I had spent in doing it, and behold, all was vanity and a striving after wind, and there was nothing to be gained under the sun.

12 So I turned to consider wisdom and madness and folly; for what can the man do who comes after the king? Only what he has already done. <sup>13</sup>Then I saw that wisdom excels folly as light excels darkness. <sup>14</sup>The wise man has his eyes in his head, but the fool walks in darkness; and yet I perceived that one fate comes to all of them. <sup>15</sup>Then I said to myself, "What befalls the fool will befall me also; why then have I been so very wise?" And I said to myself that this also is vanity. <sup>16</sup>For of the wise man as of the fool there is no enduring remembrance, seeing that in the days to come all will have been long forgotten. How the wise man dies just like the fool! <sup>17</sup>So I hated life, because what

is done under the sun was grievous to me; for all is vanity and a striving after wind.

18 I hated all my toil in which I had toiled under the sun, seeing that I must leave it to the man who will come after me; [19] and who knows whether he will be a wise man or a fool? Yet he will be master of all for which I toiled and used my wisdom under the sun. This also is vanity. [20] So I turned about and gave my heart up to despair over all the toil, of my labors under the sun [21] because sometimes a man who has toiled with wisdom and knowledge and skill must leave all to be enjoyed by a man who did not toil for it. This also is vanity and a great evil. [22] What has a man from all the toil and strain with which he toils beneath the sun? [23] For all his days are full of pain, and his work is a vexation; even in the night his mind does not rest. This also is vanity.

24 There is nothing better for a man than that he should eat and drink, and find enjoyment in his toil. This also, I saw, is from the hand of God; [25] for apart from him who can eat or who can have enjoyment? [26] For to the man who pleases him God gives wisdom and knowledge and joy; but to the sinner he gives the work of gathering and heaping, only to give to one who pleases God. This also is vanity and a striving after wind.

**3** For everything there is a season, and a time, for every matter under heaven:
> [2] a time to be born, and a time to die;
> a time to plant, and a time to pluck up what is planted;
> [3] a time to kill, and a time to heal;
> a time to break down, and a time to build up;
> [4] a time to weep, and a time to laugh;
> a time to mourn, and a time to dance;
> [5] a time to cast away stones, and a time to gather stones together;
> a time to embrace, and a time to refrain from embracing;
> [6] a time to seek, and a time to lose;
> a time to keep, and a time to cast away;
> [7] a time to rend, and a time to sew;
> a time to keep silence, and a time to speak;
> [8] a time to love, and a time to hate;
> a time for war, and a time for peace.

[9] What gain has the worker from his toil?

10 I have seen the business that God has given to the sons of men to be busy with. [11] He has made everything beautiful in its time; also he has put eternity into man's mind, yet so that he cannot find out what God has done from the beginning to the end. [12] I know that there is nothing better for them than to be happy and enjoy themselves as long as they live; [13] also that it is God's gift

to man that every one should eat and drink and take pleasure in all his toil. [14] I know that whatever God does endures for ever; nothing can be added to it, nor anything taken from it; God has made it so, in order that men should fear before him. [15] That which is, already has been; that which is to be, already has been; and God seeks what has been driven away.

16 Moreover I saw under the sun that in the place of justice, even there was wickedness, and in the place of righteousness, even there was wickedness. [17] I said in my heart, God will judge the righteous and the wicked, for he has appointed a time for every matter, and for every work. [18] I said in my heart with regard to the sons of men that God is testing them to show them that they are but beasts. [19] For the fate of the sons of men and the fate of beasts is the same; as one dies, so dies the other. They all have the same breath, and man has no advantage over the beasts; for all is vanity. [20] All go to one place; all are from the dust, and all turn to dust again. [21] Who knows whether the spirit of man goes upward and the spirit of the beast goes down to the earth? [22] So I saw that there is nothing better than that a man should enjoy his work, for that is his lot; who can bring him to see what will be after him?

4 Again I saw all the oppressions that are practiced under the sun. And behold, the tears of the oppressed, and they had no one to comfort them! On the side of their oppressors there was power, and there was no one to comfort them. [2] And I thought the dead who are already dead more fortunate than the living who are still alive; [3] but better than both is he who has not yet been, and has not seen the evil deeds that are done under the sun.

4 Then I saw that all toil and all skill in work come from a man's envy of his neighbor. This also is vanity and a striving after wind.

5 The fool folds his hands, and eats his own flesh.

6 Better is a handful of quietness than two hands full of toil and a striving after wind.

7 Again, I saw vanity under the sun: [8] a person who has no one, either son or brother, yet there is no end to all his toil, and his eyes are never satisfied with riches, so that he never asks, "For whom am I toiling and depriving myself of pleasure?" This also is vanity and an unhappy business.

9 Two are better than one, because they have a good reward for their toil. [10] For if they fall, one will lift up his fellow; but woe to him who is alone when he falls and has not another to lift him up. [11] Again, if two lie together, they are warm; but how can one be warm alone? [12] And though a man might prevail against one who is alone, two will withstand him. A threefold cord is not quickly broken.

13 Better is a poor and wise youth than an old and foolish king, who will no longer take advice, [14] even though he had gone from prison to the throne

or in his own kingdom had been born poor. [15] I saw all the living who move about under the sun, as well as that youth, who was to stand in his place; [16] there was no end of all the people; he was over all of them. Yet those who come later will not rejoice in him. Surely this also is vanity and a striving after wind. . . .

# The Hebrew Bible: Book of Amos

The superscription to the book of Amos introduces the prophet as a shepherd (1:1), while chapter 7:14 describes his vocation as that of an orchard worker. In either case, the biographical information tells us that Amos does not belong to the guild of professional prophets who operated for hire within cultic and administrative centers. Rather, the spirit of Yahweh called him to leave his home in the Southern Kingdom of Judah and travel to the Northern Kingdom of Israel, where he delivered oracles from God to the general population. Amos' prophecy is not comforting and sanguine, like that of prophets paid for their oracles, but rather it contains a harsh message, one that his audience does not want to hear. The message of Amos finds its place within the genre of oracular literature that began circulating in Israel during the eighth century B.C.E., and historical references within the book support an eighth century date for Amos' activity.

The years from 800–725 B.C.E. witnessed a period of relative affluence for the Northern Kingdom of Israel. Their perennial enemy and neighbor to the north, the Aramaens, no longer posed a threat. Commerce and trade flourished. Archaeological excavations testify to a period of intense construction and revitalization of the kingdom's infrastructure. Accordingly, the people of Israel interpreted their successes as reward, the promised blessings of the Covenant with Yahweh.[1] It must have appeared unusual for a prophet to preach doom amidst prosperity, but Amos' oracles highlighted a decadent core of social ills. His criticism was leveled at the political, social, economic and religious elite of Israel.

The selection that follows (chapters 1–6) begins with the prophet evoking a traditional oracular formula, the war oracle. Amos relates Yahweh's indictment against the neighboring enemy kingdoms of Phoenicia, Philistia, Ammon, Moab, Aram-Damascus, and Edom. Each oracle asserts Yahweh's universal dominion over all peoples, not just Israel. Departing from the condemnation leveled at foreign nations, Amos shifts attention to the Israelites and Judeans themselves (2:4–8). Here the traditional oracles of victory and praise are missing; instead, Amos (speaking for Yahweh) charges the Israelites with ethical and moral turpitude. They stand accused of mistreating the needy and oppressing the poor (cf. 2:6–7; 4:1; 8:4). They emphasize cultic ritual to the detriment of true religiosity (cf. 5:21–25). For these crimes, Yahweh cries:

Let justice roll down like
waters,
and righteousness like an
ever-flowing stream (5:24)

The tone of the book is overwhelmingly pessimistic and foreshadows the destruction of the Northern Kingdom in 722/721 B.C.E. at the hand of the Assyrians; however, the timeless relevance of these words on behalf of the poor and oppressed makes Amos the most oft-quoted biblical prophet by contemporary rights activists, most famously Dr. Martin Luther King, Jr.

Interspersed with the war oracles are literary devices such as the biographical notes mentioned above, lamentations (5:1–2), and wisdom sayings (3:3–6; 5:13). Though he was an agricultural worker by trade, Amos demonstrates sophisticated skill as a rhetorician with his use of numerical sequencing (cf 1:3, 6, 9: "For three transgressions . . . and for four . . ."). Scholars attribute the core of the book, the oracles and visions, to the prophet himself, making Amos the first of the so-called "Writing Prophets." This core, along with miscellaneous additions, was edited by his disciples and completed in the main by the mid-sixth century B.C.E. Eventually, what we now know as the book of Amos took its place alongside other prophetic works in the Septuagint (ca. the third century B.C.E.).

KP

## Note

1 According to the book of Exodus (cf. Exodus 24), Yahweh made a pact or covenant (Hebrew *berith*) with Israel wherein they would be His chosen people, and be rewarded with the proverbial "land of milk and honey," in return for their unwavering worship of Him alone. However, the covenant was conditional: blessings or curses would befall the people of Israel depending upon their adherence to the covenant. According to prophets such as Amos, the people were both knowingly and unwittingly in violation of the covenant. The violations prompted the prophets to deliver harsh judgments and dire warnings of doom.

# The Hebrew Bible: Amos 1–5

**1** The words of Amos, who was among the shepherds of Teko′a, which he saw concerning Israel in the days of Uzzi′ah king of Judah and in the days of Jerobo′am the son of Jo′ash, king of Israel, two years before the earthquake. ² And he said:

"The LORD roars from Zion,
and utters his voice from Jerusalem;
the pastures of the shepherds mourn,
and the top of Carmel withers."

³ Thus says the LORD:
"For three transgressions of Damascus,
and for four, I will not revoke the punishment;
because they have threshed Gilead
with threshing sledges of iron.
⁴ So I will send a fire upon the house of Haz′ael,
and it shall devour the strongholds of Ben-ha′dad.
⁵ I will break the bar of Damascus,
and cut off the inhabitants from the Valley of Aven,
and him that holds the scepter from Beth-eden;
and the people of Syria shall go into exile to Kir,"
says the LORD.

⁶ Thus says the LORD:
"For three transgressions of Gaza,
and for four, I will not revoke the punishment;
because they carried into exile a whole people
to deliver them up to Edom.
⁷ So I will send a fire upon the wall of Gaza,
and it shall devour her strongholds.
⁸ I will cut off the inhabitants from Ashdod,
and him that holds the scepter from Ash′kelon;
I will turn my hand against Ekron;
and the remnant of the Philistines shall perish,"
says the Lord GOD.

⁹ Thus says the LORD:
"For three transgressions of Tyre,
and for four, I will not revoke the punishment;

because they delivered up a whole people to Edom,
   and did not remember the covenant of brotherhood.
[10] So I will send a fire upon the wall of Tyre,
   and it shall devour her strongholds."

[11] Thus says the LORD:
"For three transgressions of Edom,
   and for four, I will not revoke the punishment;
because he pursued his brother with the sword,
   and cast off all pity,
and his anger tore perpetually,
   and he kept his wrath for ever.
[12] So I will send a fire upon Teman,
   and it shall devour the strongholds of Bozrah."

[13] Thus says the LORD:
"For three transgressions of the Ammonites,
   and for four, I will not revoke the punishment;
because they have ripped up women with child in Gilead,
   that they might enlarge their border.
[14] So I will kindle a fire in the wall of Rabbab,
   and it shall devour her strongholds,
with shouting in the day of battle,
   with a tempest in the day of the whirlwind;
[15] and their king shall go into exile,
   he and his princes together,"
                                         says the LORD.

2 Thus says the LORD:
"For three transgressions of Moab,
   and for four, I will not revoke the punishment;
because he burned to lime
   the bones of the king of Edom.
[2] So I will send a fire upon Moab,
   and it shall devour the strongholds of Ker'ioth,
and Moab shall die amid uproar,
   amid shouting and the sound of the trumpet;
[3] I will cut off the ruler from its midst,
   and will slay all its princes with him,"
                                         says the LORD.

[4] Thus says the LORD:
"For three transgressions of Judah,

and for four, I will not revoke the punishment;
because they have rejected the law of the LORD,
   and have not kept his statutes,
but their lies have led them astray,
   after which their fathers walked.
[5] So I will send a fire upon Judah,
   and it shall devour the strongholds of Jerusalem."

[6] Thus says the LORD:
"For three transgressions of Israel,
   and for four, I will not revoke the punishment;
because they sell the righteous for silver,
   and the needy for a pair of shoes—
[7] they that trample the head of the poor into the dust of the earth,
   and turn aside the way of the afflicted;
a man and his father go in to the same maiden,
   so that my holy name is profaned;
[8] they lay themselves down beside every altar
   upon garments taken in pledge;
and in the house of their God they drink
   the wine of those who have been fined.

[9] "Yet I destroyed the Amorite before them,
   whose height was like the height of the cedars,
and who was as strong as the oaks;
   I destroyed his fruit above, and his roots beneath.
[10] Also I brought you up out of the land of Egypt,
   and led you forty years in the wilderness,
   to possess the land of the Amorite.
[11] And I raised up some of your sons for prophets,
   and some of your young men for Nazirites.[a]
   Is it not indeed so, O people of Israel?"
                                        says the LORD.

[12] "But you made the Nazirites drink wine,
   and commanded the prophets,
   saying, 'You shall not prophesy.'

[13] "Behold, I will press you down in your place,
   as a cart full of sheaves presses down.
[14] Flight shall perish from the swift,
   and the strong shall not retain his strength,
nor shall the mighty save his life;

<sup>15</sup> he who handles the bow shall not stand,
   and he who is swift of foot shall not save himself,
   nor shall he who rides the horse save his life;
<sup>16</sup> and he who is stout of heart among the mighty
   shall flee away naked in that day,"

                         says the LORD.

**3** Hear this word that the LORD has spoken against you, O people of Israel, against the whole family which I brought up out of the land of Egypt:
<sup>2</sup> "You only have I known of
   all the families of the earth;
therefore I will punish you
   for all your iniquities.

<sup>3</sup> "Do two walk together,
   unless they have made an appointment?
<sup>4</sup> Does a lion roar in the forest,
   when he has no prey?
Does a young lion cry out from his den,
   if he has taken nothing?
<sup>5</sup> Does a bird fall in a snare on the earth,
   when there is no trap for it?
Does a snare spring up from the ground,
   when it has taken nothing?
<sup>6</sup> Is a trumpet blown in a city,
   and the people are not afraid?
Does evil befall a city,
   unless the LORD has done it?
<sup>7</sup> Surely the Lord GOD does nothing,
   without revealing his secret
   to his servants the prophets.
<sup>8</sup> The lion has roared;
   who will not fear?
The Lord GOD has spoken;
   who can but prophesy?"

<sup>9</sup> Proclaim to the strongholds in Assyria,
   and to the strongholds in the land of Egypt,
and say, "Assemble yourselves upon the mountains of Sama´ria,
   and see the great tumults within her,
   and the oppressions in her midst."
<sup>10</sup> "They do not know how to do right," says the LORD,

"those who store up violence and robbery in their strongholds."
[11] Therefore thus says the Lord GOD:
"An adversary shall surround the land,
and bring down your defenses from you,
and your strongholds shall be plundered."

12 Thus says the LORD: "As the shepherd rescues from the mouth of the lion two legs, or a piece of an ear, so shall the people of Israel who dwell in Sama'ria be rescued, with the corner of a couch and part of a bed."

[13] "Hear, and testify against the house of Jacob,"
says the Lord GOD, the God of hosts,
[14] "that on the day I punish Israel for his transgressions,
I will punish the altars of Bethel,
and the horns of the altar shall be cut off
and fall to the ground.
[15] I will smite the winter house with the summer house;
and the houses of ivory shall perish,
and the great houses shall come to an end,"
says the LORD.

4 "Hear this word, you cows of Bashan,
who are in the mountain of Sama'ria,
who oppress the poor, who crush the needy,
who say to their husbands, 'Bring, that we may drink!'
[2] The Lord GOD has sworn by his holiness
that, behold, the days are coming upon you,
when they shall take you away with hooks,
even the last of you with fishhooks.
[3] And you shall go out through the breaches,
every one straight before her;
and you shall be cast forth into Harmon,"
says the LORD.

[4] "Come to Bethel, and transgress;
to Gilgal, and multiply transgression;
bring your sacrifices every morning,
your tithes every three days;
[5] offer a sacrifice of thanksgiving of that which is leavened,
and proclaim freewill offerings, publish them;
for so you love to do, O people of Israel!"
says the Lord GOD.

<sup>6</sup> "I gave you cleanness of teeth in all your cities,
    and lack of bread in all your places,
yet you did not return to me,"

says the LORD.

<sup>7</sup> "And I also withheld the rain from you
    when there were yet three months to the harvest;
I would send rain upon one city,
    and send no rain upon another city;
one field would be rained upon,
    and the field on which it did not rain withered;
<sup>8</sup> so two or three cities wandered to one city
    to drink water, and were not satisfied;
yet you did not return to me,"

says the LORD.

<sup>9</sup> "I smote you with blight and mildew;
    I laid waste your gardens and your vineyards;
your fig trees and your olive trees
    the locust devoured;
yet you did not return to me,"

says the LORD.

<sup>10</sup> "I sent among you a pestilence after the manner of Egypt;
    I slew your young men with the sword;
I carried away your horses;
    and I made the stench of your camp go up into your nostrils;
yet you did not return to me,"

says the LORD.

<sup>11</sup> "I overthrew some of you,
    as when God overthrew Sodom and Gomor'rah,
and you were as a brand plucked out of the burning;
    yet you did not return to me,"

says the LORD.

<sup>12</sup> "Therefore thus I will do to you, O Israel,
    because I will do this to you,
    prepare to meet your God, O Israel!"

<sup>13</sup> For lo, he who forms the mountains, and creates the wind,
    and declares to man what is his thought;
who makes the morning darkness,

and treads on the heights of the earth—
the. LORD, the God of hosts, is his name!

**5** Hear this word which I take up over you in lamentation, O house of
Israel:
² "Fallen, no more to rise,
  is the virgin Israel;
forsaken on her land,
  with none to raise her up."
³ For thus says the Lord GOD:
  "The city that went forth a thousand
  shall have a hundred left,
and that which went forth a hundred
  shall have ten left
  to the house of Israel."

⁴ For thus says the LORD to the house of Israel:
  "Seek me and live;
⁵  but do not seek Bethel,
and do not enter into Gilgal
  or cross over to Beer-sheba;
for Gilgal shall surely go into exile,
  and Bethel shall come to nought."

⁶ Seek the LORD and live,
  lest he break out like fire in the house of Joseph,
and it devour, with none to quench it for Bethel,
⁷ O you who turn justice to wormwood,
  and cast down righteousness to the earth!

⁸ He who made the Plei´ades and Orion,
  and turns deep darkness into the morning,
  and darkens the day into night,
who calls for the waters of the sea,
  and pours them out upon the surface of the earth,
  the LORD is his name,
⁹ who makes destruction flash forth against the strong,
  so that destruction comes upon the fortress.

¹⁰ They hate him who reproves in the gate,
  and they abhor him who speaks the truth.
¹¹ Therefore because you trample upon the poor
  and take from him exactions of wheat,

you have built houses of hewn stone,
    but you shall not dwell in them;
you have planted pleasant vineyards,
    but you shall not drink their wine.
12 For I know how many are your transgressions,
    and how great are your sins—
you who afflict the righteous, who take a bribe,
    and turn aside the needy in the gate.
13 Therefore he who is prudent will keep silent in such a time;
    for it is an evil time.

14 Seek good, and not evil,
    that you may live;
and so the LORD, the God of hosts, will be with you,
    as you have said.
15 Hate evil, and love good,
    and establish justice in the gate;
it may be that the LORD, the God of hosts,
    will be gracious to the remnant of Joseph.

16 Therefore thus says the LORD, the God of hosts, the Lord:
"In all the squares there shall be wailing;
    and in all the streets they shall say, 'Alas! alas!'
They shall call the farmers to mourning
    and to wailing those who are skilled in lamentation,
    17 and in all vineyards there shall be wailing,
    for I will pass through the midst of you,"
                         says the LORD.

18 Woe to you who desire the day of the LORD!
    Why would you have the day of the LORD?
It is darkness, and not light;
    19 as if a man fled from a lion,
    and a bear met him;
or went into the house and leaned with his hand against the wall,
    and a serpent bit him.
20 Is not the day of the LORD darkness, and not light,
    and gloom with no brightness in it?

21 "I hate, I despise your feasts,
    and I take no delight in your solemn assemblies.
22 Even though you offer me your burnt offerings and cereal offerings,
    I will not accept them,

and the peace offerings of your fatted beasts
   I will not look upon.
23 Take away from me the noise of your songs;
   to the melody of your harps I will not listen.
24 But let justice roll down like waters,
   and righteousness like an ever-flowing stream.

25 "Did you bring to me sacrifices and offerings the forty years in the wilderness, O house of Israel? 26 You shall take up Sakkuth your king, and Kaiwan your star-god, your images, which you made for yourselves; 27 therefore I will take you into exile beyond Damascus," says the LORD, whose name is the God of hosts.

## Note

ª Nazirite means literally "those consecrated" and denotes those men (and later women) who have taken a religious vow to avoid drinking alcohol, touching the body of a deceased person, and cutting their hair. The duration of the vow was up to each individual. Notable Nazirites in the biblical tradition are Samson and Samuel.

# Apocrypha: Book of 1 Maccabees

1 Maccabees belongs to a diverse collection of fifteen religious works known as the Apocrypha. These works circulated among the Jewish communities of the Greco-Roman world, but were not accorded canonical stature. In short, they were important texts, but not of sacred authority. 1 Maccabees is essentially a prose account of early Jewish history, from the death of Alexander the Great (323 B.C.E.) to the foundational decades of the Hasmonean dynasty (135 B.C.E.). A postscript (16:23–24) dates editorial activity as late as ca. 100 B.C.E. The chronological history, told in the fashion of 1 and 2 Kings, recounts an ancient "Clash of Civilizations," as Jews attempted to maintain their distinctive identity amidst the cultural and political imperialism of the Greco-Roman world. 1 Maccabees focuses our attention on the perspective of the conquered, on the consequences of Hellenistic universalism, and brings to mind the contemporary "Clash of Civilizations" in the age of globalization.

1 Maccabees 1–4 covers the period of the Hasmonean (a.k.a. Maccabean) Revolt. In the wake of Alexander the Great's death, the Seleucids (in Syria) and the Ptolemies (in Egypt) vied for control of Syria-Palestine (300–175 B.C.E.). By 175 B.C.E., the Seleucids controlled Judea, and the Seleucid king Antiochus Epiphanes (175–164 B.C.E.) outlawed ethnic customs in an effort to bring cultural homogeny to his empire. For Jews this meant the prohibition of the Torah. The persecution of practicing Jews took many forms, among them: (1) Antiochus imposed the death sentence for any who practiced circumcision or observed the Sabbath; (2) he forced Jews to violate dietary laws and participate in pagan rituals; (3) he desecrated the temple in Jerusalem by rededicating it to Zeus (1 Maccabees 1:41–60). Occasional references in the selection convey the tensions this clash of cultures wrought within the Jewish community, as some Jews assimilated to Hellenistic practices (1:34, 43; 2:23; cf. 4:2), others tried to delicately balance the decrees of the state with their beliefs, and still others stood defiantly against the king (2:19–22). Amidst this turmoil, a powerful movement of resistance developed, led by a priestly family called the Hasmoneans and their leader, the priest Mattathias (2:1–26). They revolted against the Seleucids in 167 B.C.E. and by 164 B.C.E. the Hasmonean forces under Judas Maccabeus took Jerusalem. They purified

and rededicated the temple to Yahweh, and they inaugurated the yearly festival of Hanukkah to commemorate the occasion (4:36–59). Eleven years after the Seleucids took control, the Jews secured their own independent state.

Like the editor of the Deuteronomistic History, the author of 1 Maccabees worked with an agenda. Compare the role of Yahweh in 1 Maccabees 1–4 to that of His role in Judges 4–5 and 2 Kings 18–20, where the God of the Hebrew Bible actively intervened in the narrative action, particularly in battle. In 1 Maccabees there is no Theophany; the only war hero is Judas Maccabeus. The poetic stanzas (particularly 3:3–9) celebrate (or mourn) human activity, not Yahweh's power. Note the language of the chronicler, who uses allusions to Biblical ancestors and to the law in order to emphasize the legitimacy of the rebellion and, concomitantly, the legitimacy of the Hasmonean family. Examples such as this highlight a pragmatic and secular purpose to the text. Because the Hasmoneans were not descendants of King David, nor were they of the highest priestly order, their revolt against the Seleucids was also a *coup d'etat* over against the Jewish hereditary aristocracy. 1 Maccabees functioned as political propaganda, demonstrating that the Hasmonean rule was divinely ordained. Despite a tenuous claim to dynastic legitimacy, the Hasmonean monarchs stayed in power one hundred and thirty-three years, until they were deposed by the Romans in 37 B.C.E.

KP

# Apocrypha: 1 Maccabees 1–4

**1** After Alexander son of Philip, the Macedonian, who came from the land of Kittim, had defeated Darius, king of the Persians and the Medes, he succeeded him as king. (He had previously become king of Greece.) ² He fought many battles, conquered strongholds, and put to death the kings of the earth. ³ He advanced to the ends of the earth, and plundered many nations. When the earth became quiet before him, he was exalted, and his heart was lifted up. ⁴ He gathered a very strong army and ruled over countries, nations, and princes, and they became tributary to him.

5 After this he fell sick and perceived that he was dying. ⁶ So he summoned his most honored officers, who had been brought up with him from youth, and divided his kingdom among them while he was still alive. ⁷ And after Alexander had reigned twelve years, he died.

8 Then his officers began to rule, each in his own place. ⁹ They all put on crowns after his death, and so did their sons after them for many years; and they caused many evils on the earth.

10 From them came forth a sinful root, Antiochus Epiphanes, son of Antiochus the king; he had been a hostage in Rome. He began to reign in the one hundred and thirty-seventh year of the kingdom of the Greeks.

11 In those days lawless men came forth from Israel, and misled many, saying, "Let us go and make a covenant with the Gentiles round about us, for since we separated from them many evils have come upon us." ¹² This proposal pleased them, ¹³ and some of the people eagerly went to the king. He authorized them to observe the ordinances of the Gentiles. ¹⁴ So they built a gymnasium in Jerusalem, according to Gentile custom, ¹⁵ and removed the marks of circumcision, and abandoned the holy covenant. They joined with the Gentiles and sold themselves to do evil.

16 When Antiochus saw that his kingdom was established, he determined to become king of the land of Egypt, that he might reign over both kingdoms. ¹⁷ So he invaded Egypt with a strong force, with chariots and elephants and cavalry and with a large fleet. ¹⁸ He engaged Ptolemy king of Egypt in battle, and Ptolemy turned and fled before him, and many were wounded and fell. ¹⁹ And they captured the fortified cities in the land of Egypt, and he plundered the land of Egypt.

20 After subduing Egypt, Antiochus returned in the one hundred and forty-third year. He went up against Israel and came to Jerusalem with a strong force. ²¹ He arrogantly entered the sanctuary and took the golden altar, the

lampstand for the light, and all its utensils. <sup>22</sup> He took also the table for the bread of the Presence,<sup>a</sup> the cups for drink offerings, the bowls, the golden censers, the curtain, the crowns, and the gold decoration on the front of the temple; he stripped it all off. <sup>23</sup> He took the silver and the gold, and the costly vessels; he took also the hidden treasures which he found. <sup>24</sup> Taking them all, he departed to his own land.

He committed deeds of murder,
    and spoke with great arrogance.
<sup>25</sup> Israel mourned deeply in every community,
<sup>26</sup>     rulers and elders groaned,
    maidens and young men became faint,
        the beauty of the women faded.
<sup>27</sup> Every bridegroom took up the lament;
    she who sat in the bridal chamber was mourning.
<sup>28</sup> Even the land shook for its inhabitants,
    and all the house of Jacob was clothed with shame.

29 Two years later the king sent to the cities of Judah a chief collector of tribute, and he came to Jerusalem with a large force. <sup>30</sup> Deceitfully he spoke peaceable words to them, and they believed him; but he suddenly fell upon the city, dealt it a severe blow, and destroyed many people of Israel. <sup>31</sup> He plundered the city, burned it with fire, and tore down its houses and its surrounding walls. <sup>32</sup> And they took captive the women and children, and seized the cattle. <sup>33</sup> Then they fortified the city of David with a great strong wall and strong towers, and it became their citadel. <sup>34</sup> And they stationed there a sinful people, lawless men. These strengthened their position; <sup>35</sup> they stored up arms and food, and collecting the spoils of Jerusalem they stored them there, and became a great snare.

<sup>36</sup> It became an ambush against the sanctuary,
    an evil adversary of Israel continually.
<sup>37</sup> On every side of the sanctuary they shed innocent blood;
    they even defiled the sanctuary.
<sup>38</sup> Because of them the residents of Jerusalem fled;
    she became a dwelling of strangers;
    she became strange to her offspring,
        and her children forsook her.
<sup>39</sup> Her sanctuary became desolate as a desert;
    her feasts were turned into mourning,
    her sabbaths into a reproach,
        her honor into contempt.
<sup>40</sup> Her dishonor now grew as great as her glory;
    her exaltation was turned into mourning.

41 Then the king wrote to his whole kingdom that all should be one people, [42] and that each should give up his customs, [43] All the Gentiles accepted the command of the king. Many even from Israel gladly adopted his religion; they sacrificed to idols and profaned the sabbath. [44] And the king sent letters by messengers to Jerusalem and the cities of Judah; he directed them to follow customs strange to the land, [45] to forbid burnt offerings and sacrifices and drink offerings in the sanctuary, to profane sabbaths and feasts, [46] to defile the sanctuary and the priests, [47] to build altars and sacred precincts and shrines for idols, to sacrifice swine and unclean animals, [48] and to leave their sons uncircumcised. They were to make themselves abominable by everything unclean and profane, [49] so that they should forget the law and change all the ordinances. [50] "And whoever does not obey the command of the king shall die."

51 In such words he wrote to his whole kingdom. And he appointed inspectors over all the people and commanded the cities of Judah to offer sacrifice, city by city. [52] Many of the people, every one who forsook the law, joined them, and they did evil in the land; [53] they drove Israel into hiding in every place of refuge they had.

54 Now on the fifteenth day of Chislev, in the one hundred and forty-fifth year, they erected a desolating sacrilege upon the altar of burnt offering. They also built altars in the surrounding cities of Judah, [55] and burned incense at the doors of the houses and in the streets. [56] The books of the law which they found they tore to pieces and burned with fire. [57] Where the book of the covenant was found in the possession of any one, or if any one adhered to the law, the decree of the king condemned him to death. [58] They kept using violence against Israel, against those found month after month in the cities. [59] And on the twenty-fifth day of the month they offered sacrifice on the altar which was upon the altar of burnt offering. [60] According to the decree, they put to death the women who had their children circumcised, [61] and their families and those who circumcised them; and they hung the infants from their mothers' necks.

62 But many in Israel stood firm and were resolved in their hearts not to eat unclean food. [63] They chose to die rather than to be defiled by food or to profane the holy covenant; and they did die. [64] And very great wrath came upon Israel.

**2** In those days Mattathias the son of John, son of Simeon, a priest of the sons of Joarib, moved from Jerusalem and settled in Modein. [2] He had five sons, John surnamed Gaddi, [3] Simon called Thassi, [4] Judas called Maccabeus, [5] Eleazar called Avaran, and Jonathan called Apphus. [6] He saw the blasphemies being committed in Judah and Jerusalem, [7] and said,

"Alas! Why was I born to see this,

the ruin of my people, the ruin of the holy city,
and to dwell there when it was given over to the enemy,
the sanctuary given over to aliens?
[8] Her temple has become like a man without honor;
[9]     her glorious vessels have been carried into captivity.
Her babes have been killed in her streets,
    her youths by the sword of the foe.
[10] What nation has not inherited her palaces
    and has not seized her spoils?
[11] All her adornment has been taken away;
    no longer free, she has become a slave.
[12] And behold, our holy place, our beauty,
    and our glory have been laid waste;
the Gentiles have profaned it.
[13]     Why should we live any longer?"

14 And Mattathias and his sons rent their clothes, put on sackcloth, and mourned greatly.

15 Then the king's officers who were enforcing the apostasy came to the city of Modein to make them offer sacrifice. [16] Many from Israel came to them; an Mattathias and his sons were assembled. [17] Then the king's officers spoke to Mattathias as follows: "You are a leader, honored and great in this city, and supported by sons and brothers. [18] Now be the first to come and do what the king commands, as all the Gentiles and the men of Judah and those that are left in Jerusalem have done. Then you and your sons will be numbered among the friends of the king, and you and your sons will be honored with silver and gold and many gifts."

19 But Mattathias answered and said in a loud voice: "Even if all the nations that live under the rule of the king obey him, and have chosen to do his commandments, departing each one from the religion of his fathers, [20] yet I and my sons and my brothers will live by the covenant of our fathers. [21] Far be it from us to desert the law and the ordinances. [22] We will not obey the king's words by turning aside from our religion to the right hand or to the left."

23 When he had finished speaking these words, a Jew came forward in the sight of all to offer sacrifice upon the altar in Modein, according to the king's command. [24] When Mattathias saw it, he burned with zeal and his heart was stirred. He gave vent to righteous anger; he ran and killed him upon the altar. [25] At the same time he killed the king's officer who was forcing them to sacrifice, and he tore down the altar. [26] Thus he burned with zeal for the law, as Phinehas did against Zimri the son of Salu.[b]

27 Then Mattathias cried out in the city with a loud voice, saying: "Let every one who is zealous for the law and supports the covenant come out with me!" [28] And he and his sons fled to the hills and left all that they had in the city.

29 Then many who were seeking righteousness and justice went down to the wilderness to dwell there, [30] they, their sons, their wives, and their cattle, because evils pressed heavily upon them. [31] And it was reported to the king's officers, and to the troops in Jerusalem the city of David, that men who had rejected the king's command had gone down to the hiding places in the wilderness. [32] Many pursued them, and overtook them; they encamped opposite them and prepared for battle against them on the sabbath day. [33] And they said to them, "Enough of this! Come out and do what the king commands, and you will live." [34] But they said, "We will not come out, nor will we do what the king commands and so profane the sabbath day." [35] Then the enemy hastened to attack them. [36] But they did not answer them or hurl a stone at them or block up their hiding places, [37] for they said, "Let us all die in our innocence; heaven and earth testify for us that you are killing us unjustly." [38] So they attacked them on the sabbath, and they died, with their wives and children and cattle, to the number of a thousand persons.

39 When Mattathias and his friends learned of it, they mourned for them deeply. [40] And each said to his neighbor: "If we all do as our brethren have done and refuse to fight with the Gentiles for our lives and our ordinances, they will quickly destroy us from the earth." [41] So they made this decision that day: "Let us fight against every man who comes to attack us on the sabbath day; let us not all die as our brethren died in their hiding places."

42 Then there united with them a company of Hasideans, mighty warriors of Israel, every one who offered himself willingly for the law. [43] And all who became fugitives to escape their troubles joined them and reinforced them. [44] They organized an army, and struck down sinners in their anger and lawless men in their wrath; the survivors fled to the Gentiles for safety. [45] And Mattathias and his friends went about and tore down the altars; [46] they forcibly circumcised all the uncircumcised boys that they found within the borders of Israel. [47] They hunted down the arrogant men, and the work prospered in their hands. [48] They rescued the law out of the hands of the Gentiles and kings, and they never let the sinner gain the upper hand.

49 Now the days drew near for Mattathias to die, and he said to his sons: "Arrogance and reproach have now become strong; it is a time of ruin and furious anger. [50] Now, my children, show zeal for the law, and give your lives for the covenant of our fathers.

51 "Remember the deeds of the fathers, which they did in their generations; and receive great honor and an everlasting name. [52] Was not Abraham found faithful when tested, and it was reckoned to him as righteousness? [53] Joseph in the time of his distress kept the commandment, and became lord of Egypt. [54] Phinehas our father, because he was deeply zealous, received the covenant of everlasting priesthood. [55] Joshua, because he fulfilled the command, became a judge in Israel. [56] Caleb, because he testified in the assembly, received an inheritance in the land. [57] David, because he was merciful, inherited the throne of the kingdom for ever. [58] Elijah because of great zeal for the law was taken up into heaven. [59] Hananiah, Azariah, and Mishael believed and were saved from the flame. [60] Daniel because of his innocence was delivered from the mouth of the lions.

61 "And so observe, from generation to generation, that none who put their trust in him will lack strength. [62] Do not fear the words of a sinner, for his splendor will turn into dung and worms. [63] Today he will be exalted, but tomorrow he will not be found, because he has returned to the dust, and his plans will perish. [64] My children, be courageous and grow strong in the law, for by it you will gain honor.

65 "Now behold, I know that Simeon your brother is wise in counsel; always listen to him; he shall be your father. [66] Judas Maccabeus has been a mighty warrior from his youth; he shall command the army for you and fight the battle against the peoples. [67] You shall rally about you all who observe the law, and avenge the wrong done to your people. [68] Pay back the Gentiles in full, and heed what the law commands."

69 Then he blessed them, and was gathered to his fathers. [70] He died in the one hundred and forty-sixth year and was buried in the tomb of his fathers at Modein. And all Israel mourned for him with great lamentation.

**3** Then Judas his son, who was called Maccabeus, took command in his place. [2] All his brothers and all who had joined his father helped him; they gladly fought for Israel.
[3] He extended the glory of his people.
>    Like a giant he put on his breastplate;
> he girded on his armor of war and waged battles,
>    protecting the host by his sword.
[4] He was like a lion in his deeds,
>    like a lion's cub roaring for prey.
[5] He searched out and pursued the lawless;
>    he burned those who troubled his people.
[6] Lawless men shrank back for fear of him;
>    all the evildoers were confounded;

and deliverance prospered by his hand.
[7] He embittered many kings,
but he made Jacob glad by his deeds,
and his memory is blessed for ever.
[8] He went through the cities of Judah;
he destroyed the ungodly out of the land;
thus he turned away wrath from Israel.
[9] He was renowned to the ends of the earth;
he gathered in those who were perishing.

10 But Apollonius gathered together Gentiles and a large force from Samaria to fight against Israel. [11] When Judas learned of it, he went out to meet him, and he defeated and killed him. Many were wounded and fell, and the rest fled. [12] Then they seized their spoils; and Judas took the sword of Apollonius, and used it in battle the rest of his life.

13 Now when Seron, the commander of the Syrian army, heard that Judas had gathered a large company, including a body of faithful men who stayed with him and went out to battle, [14] he said, "I will make a name for myself and win honor in the kingdom. I will make war on Judas and his companions, who scorn the king's command." [15] And again a strong army of ungodly men went up with him to help him, to take vengeance on the sons of Israel.

16 When he approached the ascent of Beth-horon, Judas went out to meet him with a small company. [17] But when they saw the army coming to meet them, they said to Judas, "How can we, few as we are, fight against so great and strong a multitude? And we are faint, for we have eaten nothing today." [18] Judas replied, "It is easy for many to be hemmed in by few, for in the sight of Heaven there is no difference between saving by many or by few. [19] It is not on the size of the army that victory in battle depends, but strength comes from Heaven. [20] They come against us in great pride and lawlessness to destroy us and our wives and our children, and to despoil us; [21] but we fight for our lives and our laws. [22] He himself will crush them before us; as for you, do not be afraid of them."

23 When he finished speaking, he rushed suddenly against Seron and his army, and they were crushed before him. [24] They pursued them down the descent of Beth-horon to the plain; eight hundred of them fell, and the rest fled into the land of the Philistines. [25] Then Judas and his brothers began to be feared, and terror fell upon the Gentiles round about them. [26] His fame reached the king, and the Gentiles talked of the battles of Judas.

27 When King Antiochus heard these reports, he was greatly angered; and he sent and gathered all the forces of his kingdom, a very strong army.

<sup>28</sup> And he opened his coffers and gave a year's pay to his forces, and ordered them to be ready for any need. <sup>29</sup> Then he saw that the money in the treasury was exhausted, and that the revenues from the country were small because of the dissension and disaster which he had caused in the land by abolishing the laws that had existed from the earliest days. <sup>30</sup> He feared that he might not have such funds as he had before for his expenses and for the gifts which he used to give more lavishly than preceding kings. <sup>31</sup> He was greatly perplexed in mind, and determined to go to Persia and collect the revenues from those regions and raise a large fund.

32 He left Lysias, a distinguished man of royal lineage, in charge of the king's affairs from the river Euphrates to the borders of Egypt. <sup>33</sup> Lysias was also to take care of Antiochus his son until he returned. <sup>34</sup> And he turned over to Lysias half of his troops and the elephants, and gave him orders about all that he wanted done. As for the residents of Judea and Jerusalem, <sup>35</sup> Lysias was to send a force against them to wipe out and destroy the strength of Israel and the remnant of Jerusalem; he was to banish the memory of them from the place, <sup>36</sup> settle aliens in all their territory, and distribute their land. <sup>37</sup> Then the king took the remaining half of his troops and departed from Antioch his capital in the one hundred and forty-seventh year. He crossed the Euphrates River and went through the upper provinces.

38 Lysias chose Ptolemy the son of Dorymenes, and Nicanor and Gorgias, mighty men among the friends of the king, <sup>39</sup> and sent with them forty thousand infantry and seven thousand cavalry to go into the land of Judah and destroy it, as the king had commanded. <sup>40</sup> So they departed with their entire force, and when they arrived they encamped near Emmaus in the plain. <sup>41</sup> When the traders of the region heard what was said of them, they took silver and gold in immense amounts, and fetters, and went to the camp to get the sons of Israel for slaves. And forces from Syria and the land of the Philistines joined with them.

42 Now Judas and his brothers saw that misfortunes had increased and that the forces were encamped in their territory. They also learned what the king had commanded to do to the people to cause their final destruction. <sup>43</sup> But they said to one another, "Let us repair the destruction of our people, and fight for our people and the sanctuary." <sup>44</sup> And the congregation assembled to be ready for battle, and to pray and ask for mercy and compassion.

<sup>45</sup> Jerusalem was uninhabited like a wilderness;
    not one of her children went in or out.
The sanctuary was trampled down,
    and the sons of aliens held the citadel;
    it was a lodging place for the Gentiles.

Joy was taken from Jacob;[c]
    the flute and the harp ceased to play.

46 So they assembled and went to Mizpah, opposite Jerusalem, because Israel formerly had a place of prayer in Mizpah. [47] They fasted that day, put on sackcloth and sprinkled ashes on their heads, and rent their clothes. [48] And they opened the book of the law to inquire into those matters about which the Gentiles were consulting the images of their idols. [49] They also brought the garments of the priesthood and the first fruits and the tithes, and they stirred up the Nazirites[d] who had completed their days; [50] and they cried aloud to Heaven, saying,

    "What shall we do with these?
    Where shall we take them?
[51] Thy sanctuary is trampled down and profaned,
    and thy priests mourn in humiliation.
[52] And behold, the Gentiles are assembled against us to destroy us;
    thou knowest what they plot against us.
[53] How will we be able to withstand them,
    if thou dost not help us?"

54 Then they sounded the trumpets and gave a loud shout. [55] After this Judas appointed leaders of the people, in charge of thousands and hundreds and fifties and tens. [56] And he said to those who were building houses, or were betrothed, or were planting vineyards, or were fainthearted, that each should return to his home, according to the law. [57] Then the army marched out and encamped to the south of Emmaus.

58 And Judas said, "Gird yourselves and be valiant. Be ready early in the morning to fight with these Gentiles who have assembled against us to destroy us and our sanctuary. [59] It is better for us to die in battle than to see the misfortunes of our nation and of the sanctuary. [60] But as his will in heaven may be, so he will do."

**4** Now Gorgias took five thousand infantry and a thousand picked cavalry, and this division moved out there by night [2] to fall upon the camp of the Jews and attack them suddenly. Men from the citadel were his guides. [3] But Judas heard of it, and he and his mighty men moved out to attack the king's force in Emmaus [4] while the division was still absent from the camp. [5] When Gorgias entered the camp of Judas by night, he found no one there, so he looked for them in the hills, because he said, "These men are fleeing from us."

6 At daybreak Judas appeared in the plain with three thousand men, but they did not have armor and swords such as they desired. [7] And they saw the camp of the Gentiles, strong and fortified, with cavalry round about it; and these men were trained in war. [8] But Judas said to the men who were with him,

"Do not fear their numbers or be afraid when they charge. [9] Remember how our fathers were saved at the Red Sea, when Pharaoh with his forces pursued them. [10] And now let us cry to Heaven, to see whether he will favor us and remember his covenant with our fathers and crush this army before us today. [11] Then all the Gentiles will know that there is one who redeems and saves Israel."

12 When the foreigners looked up and saw them coming against them, [13] they went forth from their camp to battle. Then the men with Judas blew their trumpets [14] and engaged in battle. The Gentiles were crushed and fled into the plain, [15] and all those in the rear fell by the sword. They pursued them to Gazara, and to the plains of Idumea, and to Azotus and Jamnia; and three thousand of them fell. [16] Then Judas and his force turned back from pursuing them, [17] and he said to the people, "Do not be greedy for plunder, for there is a battle before us; [18] Gorgias and his force are near us in the hills. But stand now against our enemies and fight them, and afterward seize the plunder boldly."

19 Just as Judas was finishing this speech, a detachment appeared, coming out of the hills. [20] They saw that their army had been put to flight, and that the Jews were burning the camp, for the smoke that was seen showed what had happened. [21] When they perceived this they were greatly frightened, and when they also saw the army of Judas drawn up in the plain for battle, [22] they all fled into the land of the Philistines. [23] Then Judas returned to plunder the camp, and they seized much gold and silver, and cloth dyed blue and sea purple, and great riches. [24] On their return they sang hymns and praises to Heaven, for he is good, for his mercy endures for ever. [25] Thus Israel had a great deliverance that day.

26 Those of the foreigners who escaped went and reported to Lysias all that had happened. [27] When he heard it, he was perplexed and discouraged, for things had not happened to Israel as he had intended, nor had they turned out as the king had commanded him. [28] But the next year he mustered sixty thousand picked infantrymen and five thousand cavalry to subdue them. [29] They came into Idumea and encamped at Beth-zur, and Judas met them with ten thousand men.

30 When he saw that the army was strong, he prayed, saying, "Blessed art thou, O Savior of Israel, who didst crush the attack of the mighty warrior by the hand of thy servant David, and didst give the camp of the Philistines into the hands of Jonathan, the son of Saul, and of the man who carried his armor. [31] So do thou hem in this army by the hand of thy people Israel, and let them be ashamed of their troops and their cavalry. [32] Fill them with cowardice; melt the boldness of their strength; let them tremble in their destruction. [33] Strike

them down with the sword of those who love thee, and let all who know thy name praise thee with hymns."

34 Then both sides attacked, and there fell of the army of Lysias five thousand men; they fell in action. [35] And when Lysias saw the rout of his troops and observed the boldness which inspired those of Judas, and how ready they were either to live or to die nobly, he departed to Antioch and enlisted mercenaries, to invade Judea again with an even larger army.

36 Then said Judas and his brothers, "Behold, our enemies are crushed; let us go up to cleanse the sanctuary and dedicate it." [37] So all the army assembled and they went up to Mount Zion. [38] And they saw the sanctuary desolate, the altar profaned, and the gates burned. In the courts they saw bushes sprung up as in a thicket, or as on one of the mountains. They saw also the chambers of the priests in ruins. [39] Then they rent their clothes, and mourned with great lamentation, and sprinkled themselves with ashes. [40] They fell face down on the ground, and sounded the signal on the trumpets, and cried out to Heaven. [41] Then Judas detailed men to fight against those in the citadel until he had cleansed the sanctuary.

42 He chose blameless priests devoted to the law, [43] and they cleansed the sanctuary and removed the defiled stones to an unclean place. [44] They deliberated what to do about the altar of burnt offering, which had been profaned. [45] And they thought it best to tear it down, lest it bring reproach upon them, for the Gentiles had defiled it. So they tore down the altar, [46] and stored the stones in a convenient place on the temple hill until there should come a prophet to tell what to do with them. [47] Then they took unhewn stones, as the law directs, and built a new altar like the former one. [48] They also rebuilt the sanctuary and the interior of the temple, and consecrated the courts. [49] They made new holy vessels, and brought the lampstand, the altar of incense, and the table into the temple. [50] Then they burned incense on the altar and lighted the lamps on the lampstand, and these gave light in the temple. [51] They placed the bread on the table and hung up the curtains. Thus they finished all the work they had undertaken.

52 Early in the morning on the twenty-fifth day of the ninth month, which is the month of Chislev, in the one hundred and forty-eighth year, [53] they rose and offered sacrifice, as the law directs, on the new altar of burnt offering which they had built. [54] At the very season and on the very day that the Gentiles had profaned it, it was dedicated with songs and harps and lutes and cymbals. [55] All the people fell on their faces and worshiped and blessed Heaven, who had prospered them. [56] So they celebrated the dedication of the altar for eight days, and offered burnt offerings with gladness; they offered a sacrifice of deliverance and praise. [57] They decorated the front of the temple

with golden crowns and small shields; they restored the gates and the chambers for the priests, and furnished them with doors. [58] There was very great gladness among the people, and the reproach of the Gentiles was removed.

59 Then Judas and his brothers and all the assembly of Israel determined that every year at that season the days of the dedication of the altar should be observed with gladness and joy for eight days, beginning with the twenty-fifth day of the month of Chislev.

60 At that time they fortified Mount Zion with high walls and strong towers round about, to keep the Gentiles from coming and trampling them down as they had done before. [61] And he stationed a garrison there to hold it. He also fortified Beth-zur, so that the people might have a stronghold that faced Idumea.

## Notes

[a] We first encounter the "bread of the Presence" in Lev 24:5–9. These verses contain instructions for the baking of twelve loaves of bread made from the choicest flour. The loaves are to be placed on a table of gold before the altar of Yahweh. There they serve as a bread offering to God and a symbol of the Israelites' commitment to the covenant. This ritual food sacrifice was to be carried out every Sabbath by Aaron and upon his death, by the descendants of his priestly line. Such food sacrifices are vestiges of ritual practice conducted before cult statues, which the ancients considered the embodiment of their gods; the gods needed the food for sustenance.

[b] The reference to Phinehas is an allusion to Numbers 25:6–15. According to that tradition, God brought a plague upon Israel in response to their intermarriage with the Midianites, a neighboring enemy population. Phinehas, son of Aaron the priest, kills an Israelite man and his Midianite wife by spearing them through the stomach. The plague is thus lifted and Yahweh blesses Phinehas and his descendants with perpetual priesthood. Throughout the biblical text, we perceive growing concern over intermarriage, for such intermingling of cultures invites the temptation to worship foreign gods.

[c] Jacob is one of the patriarchs, son of Isaac and grandson of Abraham. In Genesis 32:28, Jacob's name is changed to Israel. From this point on, Jacob/Israel becomes the embodiment of the nation of Israel. His faith and adherence to the covenant symbolize that of the nation. In this verse in First Maccabees, Jacob is used as a synonym for the state of Israel.

[d] Nazirite means literally "those consecrated" and denotes those men (and later women) who have taken a religious vow to avoid drinking alcohol, touching the body of a deceased person, and cutting their hair. The duration of the vow was up to each individual. Notable Nazirites in the biblical tradition are Samson and Samuel.

# The Dead Sea Scrolls:
# The War Scroll

Judaism of the Hellenistic period was not monolithic; there were numerous sectarian groups, the most famous of which are the Pharisees, Sadducees
and Essenes. Though many factors contributed to the diversity of early
Judaism, among the most important was that until the late first century C.E.,
there was no scriptural canon, no Hebrew Bible. Different communities could
embrace a variety of sacred literature and traditions. There were also varying
degrees to which Jews accepted or rejected foreign rule and culture. So-called
Hellenistic Jews, such as the Pharisees, wore the toga, went to the gymnasium,
spoke Greek and incorporated Hellenistic notions into Jewish religious traditions. Other sects rejected any Hellenistic cultural influence. The Essenes were
just such a group.

Comparatively little is known about the Essenes; for millennia, the writings of the New Testament, the Jewish historian Josephus and the Alexandrian
philosopher Philo provided our only information. Based on these sources, we
learned that the group advocated an ascetic lifestyle and shunned urban life.
They believed only in fate (not in free will), in resurrection, in the immortality of the soul, and in angels. The Essenes denied the sanctity of the Jerusalem
temple, arguing that the Hellenistic Jews had defiled its holy precinct.
Notably, the Essenes were an apocalyptic group. The theology of apocalypti-
cism, borrowed from the Persians, is defined by the expectation of a battle
between the dual forces of the universe (good vs. evil, light vs. darkness,
Yahweh vs. Satan) and the victory of divine justice at the end of time. Many
Jews, such as the Essenes, believed that it was only in the aftermath of this cosmic battle that the nation of Israel would finally and forever make manifest the
promise to Abraham.

The Essenes have received a great deal of attention since the dramatic discovery of the Dead Sea Scrolls in 1947, for the Essenes are identified with the
religious community that produced the scrolls. The Essene community of
Qumran, on the western shore of the Dead Sea (an area that now belongs to
the modern state of Israel), assembled the literature of their faith, stored those
manuscripts in sealed jars and then hid the jars within a series of caves.

Though the Dead Sea Scrolls are perhaps most well known to the general public for their biblical witness, the collection contains a diverse array of literature—biblical and extrabiblical. The literature remains sacred in nature, but reflects the particular religious tenets of the Essenes at Qumran, such as initiation rules, the Rule of the Community (which sets forth guidelines for organization, discipline, and daily life) and various hymns and prayers. The account of their apocalyptic vision is contained in the War Scroll, a portion of which follows. According this document, at the end of time (or *eschaton*, which according to their faith was well under way), the Sons of Light (the Essenes of Qumran) follow their divinely chosen Teacher of Righteousness[1] into a pitched battle against the Sons of Darkness (other Jews and all foreigners). To the Sons of Light belongs the ultimate victory, when Yahweh ushers in the Kingdom of Heaven.

KP

## Note

[1] There has been much speculation about the identity of this teacher. Based on the evidence within the scrolls themselves, as well as archaeological data, mainstream scholarship agrees that the teacher was one of the original founders of the Qumran community and lived in the second century B.C.E. Though some conspiracy theorists and religious ideologues want to identify Jesus, James and John the Baptist in the texts, historical criticism, paleographic analysis and Carbon 14 dating of the scrolls eliminate this possibility.

# from The Dead Sea Scrolls: The War Scroll

I *For the M[aster. The Rule of] War on the unleashing of the attack of the sons of light against the company of the sons of darkness, the army of Belial:[1] against the band of Edom, Moab, and the sons of Ammon, and [against the army of the sons of the East and] the Philistines, and against the bands of the Kittim of Assyria and their allies the ungodly of the Covenant.*

The sons of Levi, Judah, and Benjamin, the exiles in the desert, shall battle against them in . . . all their bands when the exiled sons of light return from the Desert of the Peoples to camp in the Desert of Jerusalem; and after the battle they shall go up from there (to Jerusalem?).

[The king] of the Kittim [shall enter] into Egypt, and in his time he shall set out in great wrath to wage war against the kings of the north, that his fury may destroy and cut the horn of [Israel]. This shall be a time of salvation for the people of God, an age of dominion for all the members of His company, and of everlasting destruction for all the company of Belial. The confusion of the sons of Japheth[2] shall be [great] and Assyria shall fall unsuccoured. The dominion of the Kittim shall come to an end and iniquity shall be vanquished, leaving no remnant; [for the sons] of darkness there shall be no escape. [The sons of righteous]ness shall shine over all the ends of the earth; they shall go on shining until all the seasons of darkness are consumed and, at the season appointed by God, His exalted greatness shall shine eternally to the peace, blessing, glory, joy, and long life of all the sons of light.

On the day when the Kittim fall, there shall be battle and terrible carnage before the God of Israel, for that shall be the day appointed from ancient times for the battle of destruction of the sons of darkness. At that time, the assembly of gods and the hosts of men shall battle, causing great carnage; on the day of calamity, the sons of light shall battle with the company of darkness amid the shouts of a mighty multitude and the clamour of gods and men to (make manifest) the might of God. And it shall be a time of [great] tribulation for the people which God shall redeem; of all its afflictions none shall be as this, from its sudden beginning until its end in eternal redemption.

On the day of their battle against the Kittim [they shall set out for] carnage. In three lots shall the sons of light brace themselves in battle to strike down iniquity, and in three lots shall Belial's host gird itself to thrust back the company [of God. And when the hearts of the detach]ments of foot-soldiers faint, then shall the might of God fortify [the hearts of the sons of light]. And with the seventh lot, the mighty hand of God shall bring down [the army of

Belial, and all] the angels of his kingdom, and all the members [of his company in everlasting destruction] . . .

XI Truly, the battle is Thine! Their bodies are crushed by the might of Thy hand and there is no man to bury them.

Thou didst deliver Goliath of Gath, the mighty warrior, into the hands of David Thy servant, because in place of the sword and in place of the spear he put his trust in Thy great Name; for Thine is the battle. Many times, by Thy great Name, did he triumph over the Philistines. Many times hast Thou also delivered us by the hand of our kings through Thy loving-kindness, and not in accordance with our works by which we have done evil, nor according to our rebellious deeds.

Truly the battle is Thine and the power from Thee! It is not ours. Our strength and the power of our hands accomplish no mighty deeds except by Thy power and by the might of Thy great valour. This Thou hast taught us from ancient times, saying, *A star shall come out of Jacob, and a sceptre shall rise out of Israel. He shall smite the temples of Moab and destroy all the children of Sheth. He shall rule out of Jacob and shall cause the survivors of the city to perish. The enemy shall be his possession and Israel shall accomplish mighty deeds* (Num. xxiv, 17–19).

By the hand of Thine anointed, who discerned Thy testimonies, Thou hast revealed to us the [times] of the battles of Thy hands that Thou mayest glorify Thyself in our enemies by levelling the hordes of Belial, the seven nations of vanity, by the hand of Thy poor whom Thou hast redeemed [by Thy might] and by the fullness of Thy marvellous power. (Thou hast opened) the door of hope to the melting heart: Thou wilt do to them as Thou didst to Pharaoh, and to the captains of his chariots in the Red Sea. Thou wilt kindle the downcast of spirit and they shall be a flaming torch in the straw to consume ungodliness and never to cease till iniquity is destroyed.

From ancient times Thou hast fore[told the hour] when the might of Thy hand (would be raised) against the Kittim, saying, *Assyria shall fall by the sword of no man, the sword of no mere man shall devour him* (Isa. xxxi, 8). For Thou wilt deliver into the hands of the poor the enemies from all the lands, to humble the mighty of the peoples by the hand of those bent to the dust, to bring upon the [head of Thine enemies] the reward of the wicked, and to justify Thy true judgement in the midst of all the sons of men, and to make for Thyself an everlasting Name among the people [whom Thou hast redeemed] . . . of battles to be magnified and sanctified in the eyes of the remnant of the peoples, that they may know . . . when Thou chastisest Gog[3] and all his assembly gathered about him . . .

For Thou wilt fight with them from heaven . . . **XII** For the multitude of the Holy Ones [is with Thee] in heaven, and the host of the Angels is in Thy holy abode, praising Thy Name. And Thou hast established in [a community] for Thyself the elect of Thy holy people. [The list] of the names of all their host is with Thee in the abode of Thy holiness; [the reckoning of the saints] is in Thy glorious dwelling-place. Thou hast recorded for them, with the graving-tool of life, the favours of [Thy] blessings and the Covenant of Thy peace, that Thou mayest reign [over them] for ever and ever and throughout all the eternal ages. Thou wilt muster the [hosts of] Thine [el]ect, in their Thousands and Myriads, with Thy Holy Ones [and with all] Thine Angels, that they may be mighty in battle, [and may smite] the rebels of the earth by Thy great judgements, and that [they may triumph] together with the elect of heaven.

For Thou art [terrible], O God, in the glory of Thy kingdom, and the congregation of Thy Holy Ones is among us for everlasting succour. We will despise kings, we will mock and scorn the mighty; for our Lord is holy, and the King of Glory is with us together with the Holy Ones. Valiant [warriors] of the angelic host are among our numbered men, and the Hero of war is with our congregation; the host of His spirits is with our foot-soldiers and horsemen. [They are as] clouds, as clouds of dew (covering) the earth, as a shower of rain shedding judgement on all that grows on the earth.

> Rise up, O Hero!
> Lead off Thy captives, O Glorious One!
> Gather up Thy spoils, O Author of mighty deeds!
> Lay Thy hand on the neck of Thine enemies
>     and Thy feet on the pile of the slain!
> Smite the nations, Thine adversaries,
>     and devour the flesh of the sinner with Thy sword!
> Fill Thy land with glory
>     and Thine inheritance with blessing!
> Let there be a multitude of cattle in Thy fields,
>     and in Thy palaces silver and gold and precious stones!

> O Zion, rejoice greatly!
> O Jerusalem, show thyself amidst jubilation!
> Rejoice, all you cities of Judah;
> keep your gates ever open
>     that the hosts of the nations
>     may be brought in!

Their kings shall serve you
    and all your oppressors shall bow down before you;
    [they shall lick] the dust [of your feet].
Shout for joy, [O daughters of] my people!
Deck yourselves with glorious jewels
    and rule over [the kingdoms of the nations!
Sovereignty shall be to the Lord]
    and everlasting dominion to Israel.
. . .

## Notes

[1] Belial is the Angel of Darkness created by God. He is the embodiment of evil and commands an army of his minions, the Sons of Darkness. The Sons comprise both human and divine agents. The community of Qumran believed that Belial controlled the political, social and religious life of Israel at that time. The community waited in anticipation for the coming apocalypse, when the Angel of Light (God) would lead them in battle against Belial and his forces.

[2] Japheth was the third son of Noah. In the ancient literary traditions, the sons of Noah were each credited with the founding of the various human races. Japheth was considered the progenitor of the Europeans. The inhabitants of Syria-Palestine were acquainted with Europeans, such as the Celts and Germans, in their capacity as Roman mercenaries.

[3] Gog first appears in Ezekial 38:2, where he is described as the king of the land of Magog. Gog is mentioned here in the apocalyptic literature of Dead Sea Scrolls and again in the apocalyptic book of Revelation, chapter 20. Though both the Gog and Magog remain unidentified, Ezekial locates them in a region north of Judah. Both Jeremiah (6:22) and Ezekiel write of a northern enemy, and given their historical context, that enemy is understood to be Babylon. Overtime, Gog comes to symbolize one of the commanders of the forces of evil during the apocalyptic battle at the end of times.

# Vergil

## 70–19 B.C.E.

Publius Vergilius Maro stands as one of the greatest authors of any age, not only of the so-called Golden Age of Roman literature. As one scholar states, without exaggeration, the record of Vergil's influence "is Western literature." Vergil's reputation from antiquity until the twentieth century stands at the opposite extreme to the relative neglect that he suffers in general today. If any of his works is known today, it is his masterpiece, the *Aeneid*. But Vergil's first work was a book of pastoral poetry, the *Eclogues*, modeled on Theocritus' pastoral idylls. Unlike epic poetry, which finds modern analogues in certain movies and novels, pastoral poetry, offering the lives and loves of shepherds, is something of an antique. Vergil's Fourth Eclogue, however, may sound familiar to modern ears. In it, he celebrates the imminent birth of a boy, who will cause wars to end, the earth to bring forth its fruits spontaneously, and all life to live together in harmony. In short, this child will introduce a new Golden Age. Many Christians believed that Vergil was prophesying the birth of Christ, and to them this "Messianic" eclogue proved that Vergil, though pagan, was gifted with divine insight. Tertullian, writing about 200 C.E., called Vergil a "naturally Christian soul" (*anima naturaliter Christiana*), and in Dante's *Divine Comedy*, Vergil represents the height of human reason, who leads Dante wisely through the errors of sin to the very rim of Paradise.

Vergil addresses the eclogue to Asinius Pollio, who was consul in the year 40 B.C.E. In that same year, a meeting was brokered between two members of the Second Triumvirate, Octavian, who controlled the West, and Mark Antony, who held the East. The tense alliance between these two men was renewed and secured by an arranged marriage between Octavian's sister and Mark Antony. Scholars today generally suggest that Vergil is celebrating this union and its future offspring, that the "Virgin" referred to is the goddess of Justice, who fled the earth after the Golden Age, and that the "traces of sin" refer to civil wars. Nevertheless, the general echoes from the Messianic passages of Isaiah 9 and 11 are striking. The Old Testament had been translated into Greek before Vergil's day, but there is no evidence that he was familiar with Isaiah's prophecy, and the parallels are not exact: Vergil, after all, suggests a more progressive return to the Golden Age as the boy ages and becomes a man. In the end, Vergil's choice to express his political hope in language like Isaiah's was a coincidence, but it communicates a powerful vision. For

Christian readers as different and impressive as St. Augustine, Dante, and Alexander Pope, that vision could have been inspired by none other than God.

BSH

# Fourth Eclogue

Sicilian Muses, grant me a slightly grander song.
Not all delight in trees and lowly tamarisks;
Let woods, if woods we sing, be worthy of a consul.
        Now the last age of Cumae's prophecy[1] has come;
The great succession of centuries is born afresh.
Now too returns the Virgin; Saturn's rule returns;
A new begetting now descends from heaven's height.
O chaste Lucina,[2] look with blessing on the boy
Whose birth will end the iron race at last and raise
A golden through the world: now your Apollo rules.
And, Pollio, this glory enters time with you;
Your consulship begins the march of the great months;
With you to guide, if traces of our sin remain,
They, nullified, will free the lands from lasting fear.
He will receive the life divine, and see the gods
Mingling with heroes, and himself be seen of them,
And rule a world made peaceful by his father's virtues.
        But first, as little gifts for you, child, Earth untilled
Will pour the straying ivy rife, and baccaris,
And colocasia mixing with acanthus' smile.
She-goats unshepherded will bring home udders plumped
With milk, and cattle will not fear the lion's might.
Your very cradle will pour forth caressing flowers.
The snake will perish, and the treacherous poison-herb
Perish; Assyrian spikenard commonly will grow.
And then, so soon as you can read of heroes' praise
And of your father's deeds, and know what manhood means,
Soft spikes of grain will gradually gild the fields,
And reddening grapes will hang in clusters on wild brier,
And dewy honey sweat from tough Italian oaks.
Traces, though few, will linger yet of the old deceit,
Commanding men to tempt Thetis[3] with ships, to encircle
Towns with walls, to inflict deep furrows on the Earth.
There'll be a second Tiphys[4] then, a second Argo
To carry chosen heroes; there'll even be second wars,
And once more great Achilles will be sent to Troy.

Later, when strength of years has made a man of you,
The carrier too will quit the sea, no naval pines
Barter their goods, but every land bear everything.
The soil will suffer hoes no more, nor vines the hook.
The sturdy ploughman too will now unyoke his team,
And wool unlearn the lies of variable dye,
But in the fields the ram himself will change his fleece,
Now to sweet-blushing murex, now to saffron yellow,
And natural vermilion clothe the grazing lambs.
   'Speed on those centuries', said the Parcae[5] to their spindles,
Concordant with the steadfast nod of Destiny.
O enter (for the time approaches) your great glory,
Dear scion of gods, great aftergrowth of Jupiter!
Look at the cosmos trembling in its massive round,
Lands and the expanse of ocean and the sky profound;
Look how they all are full of joy at the age to come!
O then for me may long life's latest part remain
And spirit great enough to celebrate your deeds!
Linus will not defeat me in song, nor Thracian Orpheûs,[6]
Though one should have his father's aid and one his mother's,
Orpheus Callíopë and Linus fair Apollo.
If Pan too challenged me, with Arcady as judge,
Pan too, with Arcady as judge, would own defeat.
   Begin, small boy, to know your mother with a smile
(Ten lunar months have brought your mother long discomfort)
Begin, small boy: him who for parent have not smiled
No god invites to table nor goddess to bed.

## Notes

[1] A grand but obscure line, combining the prophecies of the Sibyl at Cumae on the Bay of Naples with an apparent reference to the Etruscan belief of a fixed cycle of ages.

[2] Roman goddess of childbirth.

[3] Thetis, a sea-nymph and Achilles' mother, is here used as a metonymy for the sea itself, and as a foreshadowing of the mention of Achilles and war.

[4] The helmsman of the Argonauts; their ship was the Argo.

[5] The Fates, who spin the threads of life and destiny.

[6] Famous mythical poets.

# The New Testament:
# The Gospel of Matthew

There were many Christian writings in the early centuries of the faith, including "gospels" attributed to Thomas, to Mary Magdalene, to Jesus's twin brother; apocalyptic writings; letters attributed to apostles and other figures mentioned in what is now the Bible as well as early bishops and theologians. Not until the fourth century C.E. was the New Testament firmly identified with the contents it has continued to show up to the present. A letter from Athanasius, the bishop of Alexandria, written in 367 C.E. was the first document to list as the official, orthodox books to be accepted as scripture by Christians the twenty-seven books now commonly called the New Testament.

Bart Ehrman explains that canonization relied on four criteria for inclusion: the books included must be

*Ancient.* Books written closer to the time of Jesus were more authoritative.

*Apostolic.* Books should be written by an apostle or someone close to the apostles.

*Catholic.* i.e., widely acceptable or in wide use at the time.

*Orthodox.* Books had to be theologically consistent with what was becoming the orthodox position in the Christian church.[1]

Athanasius identified four gospels, the four which have remained at the beginning of the Christian bible: the books of Matthew, Mark, Luke and John. (Gospel is an English word meaning "good news" or "good tale.") The Gospels are not really biographies of Jesus, which explains their omission of most of his life: instead, they are accounts of his rather short career as a teacher, reformer, and Messiah. They are written by Christians for other Christians.

From the second century on, Matthew's was the most widely cited Gospel. Scholars disagree on its dating but a likely date for its composition is 80–85 C.E. The author was a Jewish Christian probably writing from Antioch. He seems to be writing primarily for a Jewish Christian audience, as evidenced by his many references to the Jewish scriptures. It is in the Gospel of Matthew that Jesus declares that he has not come to change the Jewish Law. Matthew is also frequently concerned to relate the life and mission of Jesus to prophecies in the Hebrew bible.

92

His chapters 24–28 include "the little Apocalypse" (24: 1–36)—an apocalypse is a vision of the end time—several parables about the end of time and a discussion of the Last Judgment. Jesus often taught in parables, stories illustrating religious lessons, often by analogy or metaphor. Chapters 26–28 tell the story of the last days of Jesus's life before his crucifixion and his appearance to his followers after his resurrection.

MM

## Note

1 *Lost Christianities: The Battles for Scripture and the Faiths We Never Knew* (Oxford University press, 2003): 242–243.

# from The New Testament:
# The Gospel of Matthew

**24** Jesus left the temple and was going away, when his disciples came to point out to him the buildings of the temple. [2] But he answered them, "You see all these, do you not? Truly, I say to you, there will not be left here one stone upon another, that will not be thrown down."

3 As he sat on the Mount of Olives, the disciples came to him privately, saying, "Tell us, when will this be, and what will be the sign of your coming and of the close of the age?" [4] And Jesus answered them, "Take heed that no one leads you astray. [5] For many will come in my name, saying, 'I am the Christ,' and they will lead many astray. [6] And you will hear of wars and rumors of wars; see that you are not alarmed; for this must take place, but the end is not yet. [7] For nation will rise against nation, and kingdom against kingdom, and there will be famines and earthquakes in various places: [8] all this is but the beginning of the sufferings.

9 "Then they will deliver you up to tribulation, and put you to death; and you will be hated by all nations for my name's sake. [10] And then many will fall away, and betray one another, and hate one another. [11] And many false prophets will arise and lead many astray. [12] And because wickedness is multiplied, most men's love will grow cold. [13] But he who endures to the end will be saved. [14] And this gospel of the kingdom will be preached throughout the whole world, as a testimony to all nations; and then the end will come.

15 "So when you see the desolating sacrilege spoken of by the prophet Daniel, standing in the holy place (let the reader understand), [16] then let those who are in Judea flee to the mountains; [17] let him who is on the housetop not go down to take what is in his house; [18] and let him who is in the field not turn back to take his mantle. [19] And alas for those who are with child and for those who give suck in those days! [20] Pray that your flight may not be in winter or on a sabbath. [21] For then there will be great tribulation, such as has not been from the beginning of the world until now, no, and never will be. [22] And if those days had not been shortened, no human being would be saved; but for the sake of the elect those days will be shortened. [23] Then if any one says to you, 'Lo, here is the Christ!' or 'There he is!' do not believe it. [24] For false Christs and false prophets will arise and show great signs and wonders, so as to lead astray, if possible, even the elect. [25] Lo, I have told you beforehand. [26] So, if they say to you, 'Lo, he is in the wilderness,' do no go out; if they say,

'Lo, he is in the inner rooms,' do not believe it. [27] For as the lightning comes from the east and shines as far as the west, so will be the coming of the Son of man. [28] Wherever the body is, there the eagles will be gathered together.

29 "Immediately after the tribulation of those days the sun will be darkened, and the moon will not give its light, and the stars will fall from heaven, and the powers of the heavens will be shaken; [30] then will appear the sign of the Son of man in heaven, and then all the tribes of the earth will mourn, and they will see the Son of man coming on the clouds of heaven with power and great glory; [31] and he will send out his angels with a loud trumpet call, and they will gather his elect from the four winds, from one end of heaven to the other.

32 "From the fig tree learn its lesson: as soon as its branch becomes tender and puts forth its leaves, you know that summer is near. [33] So also, when you see all these things, you know that he is near, at the very gates. [34] Truly, I say to you, this generation will not pass away till all these things take place. [35] Heaven and earth will pass away, but my words will not pass away.

36 "But of that day and hour no one knows, not even the angels of heaven, nor the Son, but the Father only. [37] As were the days of Noah, so will be the coming of the Son of man. [38] For as in those days before the flood they were eating and drinking, marrying and giving in marriage, until the day when Noah entered the ark, [39] and they did not know until the flood came and swept them all away, so will be the coming of the Son of man. [40] Then two men will be in the field; one is taken and one is left. [41] Two women will be grinding at the mill; one is taken and one is left. [42] Watch therefore, for you do not know on what day your Lord is coming. [43] But know this, that if the householder had known in what part of the night the thief was coming, he would have watched and would not have let his house be broken into. [44] Therefore you also must be ready; for the Son of man is coming at an hour you do not expect.

45 "Who then is the faithful and wise servant, whom his master has set over his household, to give them their food at the proper time? [46] Blessed is that servant whom his master when he comes will find so doing. [47] Truly, I say to you, he will set him over all his possessions. [48] But if that wicked servant says to himself, 'My master is delayed' [49] and begins to beat his fellow servants, and eats and drinks with the drunken, [50] the master of that servant will come on a day when he does not expect him and at an hour he does not know, [51] and will punish him, and put him with the hypocrites; there men will weep and gnash their teeth.

25 . . . 14 "For it will be as when a man going on a journey called his servants and entrusted to them his property; [15] to one he gave five talents,[a] to another two, to another one, to each according to his ability. Then he went away. [16] He who had received the five talents went at once and traded with

them; and he made five talents more. [17] So also, he who had the two talents made two talents more. [18] But he who had received the one talent went and dug in the ground and hid his master's money. [19] Now after a long time the master of those servants came and settled accounts with them. [20] And he who had received the five talents came forward, bringing five talents more, saying, 'Master, you delivered to me five talents; here I have made five talents more.' [21] His master said to him, 'Well done, good and faithful servant; you have been faithful over a little, I will set you over much; enter into the joy of your master.' [22] And he also who had the two talents came forward, saying, 'Master, you delivered to me two talents; here I have made two talents more.' [23] His master said to him, 'Well done, good and faithful servant; you have been faithful over a little, I will set you over much; enter into the joy of your master.' [24] He also who had received the one talent came forward, saying, 'Master, I knew you to be a hard man, reaping where you did not sow, and gathering where you did not winnow; [25] so I was afraid, and I went and hid your talent in the ground. Here you have what is yours.' [26] But his master answered him, 'You wicked and slothful servant! You knew that I reap where I have not sowed, and gather where I have not winnowed? [27] Then you ought to have invested my money with the bankers, and at my coming I should have received what was my own with interest. [28] So take the talent from him, and give it to him who has the ten talents. [29] For to every one who has will more be given, and he will have abundance; but from him who has not, even what he has will be taken away. [30] And cast the worthless servant into the outer darkness; there men will weep and gnash their teeth.'

31 "When the Son of man comes in his glory, and all the angels with him, then he will sit on his glorious throne. [32] Before him will be gathered all the nations, and he will separate them one from another as a shepherd separates the sheep from the goats, [33] and he will place the sheep at his right hand, but the goats at the left. [34] Then the King will say to those at his right hand, 'Come, O blessed of my Father, inherit the kingdom prepared for you from the foundation of the world; [35] for I was hungry and you gave me food, I was thirsty and you gave me drink, I was a stranger and you welcomed me, [36] I was naked and you clothed me, I was sick and you visited me, I was in prison and you came to me.' [37] Then the righteous will answer him, 'Lord, when did we see thee hungry and feed thee, or thirsty and give thee drink? [38] And when did we see thee a stranger and welcome thee, or naked and clothe thee? [39] And when did we see thee sick or in prison and visit thee?' [40] And the King will answer them, 'Truly, I say to you, as you did it to one of the least of these my brethren, you did it to me.' [41] Then he will say to those at his left hand, 'Depart from me, you cursed, into the eternal fire prepared for the devil and his angels;

⁴²for I was hungry and you gave me no food, I was thirsty and you gave me no drink, ⁴³I was a stranger and you did not welcome me, naked and you did not clothe me, sick and in prison and you did not visit me.' ⁴⁴Then they also will answer, 'Lord, when did we see thee hungry or thirsty or a stranger or naked or sick or in prison, and did not minister to thee?' ⁴⁵Then he will answer them, 'Truly, I say to you, as you did it not to one of the least of these, you did it not to me.' ⁴⁶And they will go away into eternal punishment, but the righteous into eternal life."

**26** When Jesus had finished all these sayings, he said to his disciples, ²"You know that after two days the Passover^b is coming, and the Son of man will be delivered up to be crucified."

3 Then the chief priests and the elders of the people gathered in the palace of the high priest, who was called Ca′iaphas, ⁴and took counsel together in order to arrest Jesus by stealth and kill him. ⁵But they said, "Not during the feast, lest there be a tumult among the people."

6 Now when Jesus was at Bethany in the house of Simon the leper, ⁷a woman came up to him with an alabaster jar of very expensive ointment, and she poured it on his head, as he sat at table. ⁸But when the disciples saw it, they were indignant, saying, "Why this waste? ⁹For this ointment might have been sold for a large sum, and given to the poor." ¹⁰But Jesus, aware of this, said to them, "Why do you trouble the woman? For she has done a beautiful thing to me. ¹¹For you always have the poor with you, but you will not always have me. ¹²In pouring this ointment on my body she has done it to prepare me for burial. ¹³Truly, I say to you, wherever this gospel is preached in the whole world, what she has done will be told in memory of her."

14 Then one of the twelve, who was called Judas Iscariot, went to the chief priests ¹⁵and said, "What will you give me if I deliver him to you?" And they paid him thirty pieces of silver. ¹⁶And from that moment he sought an opportunity to betray him.

17. Now on the first day of Unleavened Bread the disciples came to Jesus, saying, "Where will you have us prepare for you to eat the passover?" ¹⁸He said, "Go into the city to such a one, and say to him, 'The Teacher says, My time is at hand; I will keep the passover at your house with my disciples.'" ¹⁹And the disciples did as Jesus had directed them, and they prepared the passover.

20 When it was evening, he sat at table with the twelve disciples; ²¹and as they were eating, he said, "Truly, I say to you, one of you will betray me." ²²And they were very sorrowful, and began to say to him one after another, "Is it I, Lord?" ²³He answered, "He who has dipped his hand in the dish with me, will betray me. ²⁴The Son of man goes as it is written of him, but woe to that

man by whom the Son of man is betrayed! It would have been better for that man if he had not been born." [25] Judas, who betrayed him, said, "Is it I, Master?" He said to him, "You have said so."

26 Now as they were eating, Jesus took bread, and blessed, and broke it, and gave it to the disciples and said, "Take, eat; this is my body." [27] And he took a cup, and when he had given thanks he gave it to them, saying, "Drink of it, all of you; [28] for this is my blood of the covenant, which is poured out for many for the forgiveness of sins. [29] I tell you I shall not drink again of this fruit of the vine until that day when I drink it new with you in my Father's kingdom."

30 And when they had sung a hymn, they went out to the Mount of Olives. [31] Then Jesus said to them, "You will all fall away because of me this night; for it is written, 'I will strike the shepherd, and the sheep of the flock will be scattered.' [32] But after I am raised up, I will go before you to Galilee." [33] Peter declared to him, "Though they all fall away because of you, I will never fall away." [34] Jesus said to him, "Truly, I say to you, this very night, before the cock crows, you will deny me three times." [35] Peter said to him, "Even if I must die with you, I will not deny you." And so said all the disciples.

36 Then Jesus went with them to a place called Gethsem´ane, and he said to his disciples, "Sit here, while I go yonder and pray." [37] And taking with him Peter and the two sons of Zeb´edee, he began to be sorrowful and troubled. [38] Then he said to them, "My soul is very sorrowful, even to death; remain here, and watch with me." [39] And going a little farther he fell on his face and prayed, "My Father, if it be possible, let this cup pass from me; nevertheless, not as I will, but as thou wilt." [40] And he came to the disciples and found them sleeping; and he said to Peter, "So, could you not watch with me one hour? [41] Watch and pray that you may not enter into temptation; the spirit indeed is willing, but the flesh is weak." [42] Again, for the second time, he went away and prayed, "My Father, if this cannot pass unless I drink it, thy will be done." [43] And again he came and found them sleeping, for their eyes were heavy. [44] So, leaving them again, he went away and prayed for the third time, saying the same words. [45] Then he came to the disciples and said to them, "Are you still sleeping and taking your rest? Behold, the hour is at hand, and the Son of man is betrayed into the hands of sinners. [46] Rise, let us be going; see, my betrayer is at hand."

47 While he was still speaking, Judas came, one of the twelve, and with him a great crowd with swords and clubs, from the chief priests and the elders of the people. [48] Now the betrayer had given them a sign, saying, "The one I shall kiss is the man; seize him." [49] And he came up to Jesus at once and said, "Hail, Master!" And he kissed him. [50] Jesus said to him, "Friend, why are you

here?" Then they came up and laid hands on Jesus and seized him. [51]And behold, one of those who were with Jesus stretched out his hand and drew his sword, and struck the slave of the high priest, and cut off his ear. [52]Then Jesus said to him, "Put your sword back into its place; for all who take the sword will perish by the sword. [53]Do you think that I cannot appeal to my Father, and he will at once send me more than twelve legions of angels? [54]But how then should the scriptures be fulfilled, that it must be so?" [55]At that hour Jesus said to the crowds, "Have you come out as against a robber, with swords and clubs to capture me? Day after day I sat in the temple teaching, and you did not seize me. [56]But all this has taken place, that the scriptures of the prophets might be fulfilled." Then all the disciples forsook him and fled.

57 Then those who had seized Jesus led him to Ca´iaphas the high priest, where the scribes and the elders had gathered. [58]But Peter followed him at a distance, as far as the courtyard of the high priest, and going inside he sat with the guards to see the end. [59]Now the chief priests and the whole council sought false testimony against Jesus that they might put him to death, [60]but they found none, though many false witnesses came forward. At last two came forward [61]and said, "This fellow said, 'I am able to destroy the temple of God, and to build it in three days.'" [62]And the high priest stood up and said, "Have you no answer to make? What is it that these men testify against you?" [63]But Jesus was silent. And the high priest said to him, "I adjure you by the living God, tell us if you are the Christ, the Son of God." [64]Jesus said to him, "You have said so. But I tell you, hereafter you will see the Son of man seated at the right hand of Power, and coming on the clouds of heaven." [65]Then the high priest tore his robes, and said, "He has uttered blasphemy. Why do we still need witnesses? You have now heard his blasphemy. [66]What is your judgment?" They answered, "He deserves death." [67]Then they spat in his face, and struck him; and some slapped him, [68]saying, "Prophesy to us, you Christ! Who is it that struck you?"

69 Now Peter was sitting outside in the courtyard. And a maid came up to him, and said, "You also were with Jesus the Galilean." [70]But he denied it before them all, saying, "I do not know what you mean." [71]And when he went out to the porch, another maid saw him, and she said to the bystanders, "This man was with Jesus of Nazareth." [72]And again he denied it with an oath, "I do not know the man." [73]After a little while the bystanders came up and said to Peter, "Certainly you are also one of them, for your accent betrays you." [74]Then he began to invoke a curse on himself and to swear, "I do not know the man." And immediately the cock crowed. [75]And Peter remembered the saying of Jesus, "Before the cock crows, you will deny me three times." And he went out and wept bitterly.

**27** When morning came, all the chief priests and the elders of the people took counsel against Jesus to put him to death; [2] and they bound him and led him away and delivered him to Pilate the governor.

3 When Judas, his betrayer, saw that he was condemned, he repented and brought back the thirty pieces of silver to the chief priests and the elders, [4] saying, "I have sinned in betraying innocent blood." They said, "What is that to us? See to it yourself." [5] And throwing down the pieces of silver in the temple, he departed; and he went and hanged himself. [6] But the chief priests, taking the pieces of silver, said, "It is not lawful to put them into the treasury, since they are blood money." [7] So they took counsel, and bought with them the potter's field, to bury strangers in. [8] Therefore that field has been called the Field of Blood to this day. [9] Then was fulfilled what had been spoken by the prophet Jeremiah, saying, "And they took the thirty pieces of silver, the price of him on whom a price had been set by some of the sons of Israel, [10] and they gave them for the potter's field, as the Lord directed me."

11 Now Jesus stood before the governor; and the governor asked him, "Are you the King of the Jews?" Jesus said to him, "You have said so." [12] But when he was accused by the chief priests and elders, he made no answer. [13] Then Pilate said to him, "Do you not hear how many things they testify against you?" [14] But he gave him no answer, not even to a single charge; so that the governor wondered greatly.

15 Now at the feast the governor was accustomed to release for the crowd any one prisoner whom they wanted. [16] And they had then a notorious prisoner, called Barab'bas [17] So when they had gathered, Pilate said to them, "Whom do you want me to release for you, Barab'bas or Jesus who is called Christ?" [18] For he knew that it was out of envy that they had delivered him up. [19] Besides, while he was sitting on the judgment seat, his wife sent word to him, "Have nothing to do with that righteous man, for I have suffered much over him today in a dream." [20] Now the chief priests and the elders persuaded the people to ask for Barab'bas and destroy Jesus. [21] The governor again said to them, "Which of the two do you want me to release for you?" And they said, "Barab'bas." [22] Pilate said to them, "Then what shall I do with Jesus who is called Christ?" They all said, "Let him be crucified." [23] And he said, "Why, what evil has he done?" But they shouted all the more, "Let him be crucified."

24 So when Pilate saw that be was gaining nothing, but rather that a riot was beginning, he took water and washed his hands before the crowd, saying, "I am innocent of this man's blood; see to it yourselves." [25] And all the people answered, "His blood be on us and on our children!" [26] Then he released for them Barab'bas, and having scourged Jesus, delivered him to be crucified.

27 Then the soldiers of the governor took Jesus into the praetorium,[c] and they gathered the whole battalion before him. [28] And they stripped him and put a scarlet robe upon him, [29] and plaiting a crown of thorns they put it on his head, and put a reed in his right hand. And kneeling before him they mocked him, saying, "Hail, King of the Jews!" [30] And they spat upon him, and took the reed and struck him on the head. [31] And when they had mocked him, they stripped him of the robe, and put his own clothes on him, and led him away to crucify him.

32 As they were marching out, they came upon a man of Cyre′ne, Simon by name; this man they compelled to carry his cross. [33] And when they came to a place called Gol′gotha (which means the place of a skull), [34] they offered him wine to drink, mingled with gall;[d] but when he tasted it, he would not drink it. [35] And when they had crucified him, they divided his garments among them by casting lots; [36] then they sat down and kept watch over him there. [37] And over his head they put the charge against him, which read, "This is Jesus the King of the Jews." [38] Then two robbers were crucified with him, one on the right and one on the left. [39] And those who passed by derided him, wagging their heads [40] and saying, "You who would destroy the temple and build it in three days, save yourself! If you are the Son of God, come down from the cross." [41] So also the chief priests, with the scribes and elders, mocked him, saying, [42] "He saved others; he cannot save himself. He is the King of Israel; let him come down now from the cross, and we will believe in him. [43] He trusts in God; let God deliver him now, if he desires him; for he said, 'I am the Son of God.'" [44] And the robbers who were crucified with him also reviled him in the same way.

45 Now from the sixth hour there was darkness over all the land until the ninth hour. [46] And about the ninth hour Jesus cried with a loud voice, "Eli, Eli, la′ma sabach-tha′ni?" that is, "My God, my God, why hast thou forsaken me?" [47] And some of the bystanders hearing it said, "This man is calling Eli′jah." [48] And one of them at once ran and took a sponge, filled it with vinegar, and put it on a reed, and gave it to him to drink. [49] But the others said, "Wait, let us see whether Eli′jah will come to save him." [50] And Jesus cried again with a loud voice and yielded up his spirit.

51 And behold, the curtain of the temple was torn in two, from top to bottom; and the earth shook, and the rocks were split; [52] the tombs also were opened, and many bodies of the saints who had fallen asleep were raised, [53] and coming out of the tombs after his resurrection they went into the holy city and appeared to many. [54] When the centurion and those who were with him, keeping watch over Jesus, saw the earthquake and what took place, they were filled with awe, and said, "Truly this was the Son of God!"

55 There were also many women there, looking on from afar, who had followed Jesus from Galilee, ministering to him; [56]among whom were Mary Mag′dalene, and Mary the mother of James and Joseph, and the mother of the sons of Zeb′edee.

57 When it was evening, there came a rich man from Arimathe′a, named Joseph, who also was a disciple of Jesus. [58]He went to Pilate and asked for the body of Jesus. Then Pilate ordered it to be given to him. [59]And Joseph took the body, and wrapped it in a clean linen shroud, [60]and laid it in his own new tomb, which he had hewn in the rock; and he rolled a great stone to the door of the tomb, and departed. [61]Mary Mag′dalene and the other Mary were there, sitting opposite the sepulchre.

62 Next day, that is, after the day of Preparation,[e] the chief priests and the Pharisees gathered before Pilate [63]and said, "Sir, we remember how that impostor said, while he was still alive, 'After three days I will rise again.' [64]Therefore order the sepulchre to be made secure until the third day, lest his disciples go and steal him away, and tell the people, 'He has risen from the dead,' and the last fraud will be worse than the first." [65]Pilate said to them, "You have a guard of soldiers; go, make it as secure as you can." [66]So they went and made the sepulchre secure by sealing the stone and setting a guard.

**28** Now after the sabbath, toward the dawn of the first day of the week, Mary Mag′dalene and the other Mary went to see the sepulchre. [2]And behold, there was a great earthquake; for an angel of the Lord descended from heaven and came and rolled back the stone, and sat upon it. [3]His appearance was like lightning, and his raiment white as snow. [4]And for fear of him the guards trembled and became like dead men. [5]But the angel said to the women, "Do not be afraid; for I know that you seek Jesus who was crucified. [6]He is not here; for he has risen, as he said. Come, see the place where he lay. [7]Then go quickly and tell his disciples that he has risen from the dead, and behold, he is going before you to Galilee; there you will see him. Lo, I have told you." [8]So they departed quickly from the tomb with fear and great joy, and ran to tell his disciples. [9]And behold, Jesus met them and said, "Hail!" And they came up and took hold of his feet and worshiped him. [10]Then Jesus said to them, "Do not be afraid; go and tell my brethren to go to Galilee, and there they will see me."

11 While they were going, behold, some of the guard went into the city and told the chief priests all that had taken place. [12]And when they had assembled with the elders and taken counsel, they gave a sum of money to the soldiers [13]and said, "Tell people, 'His disciples came by night and stole him away while we were asleep.' [14]And if this comes to the governor's ears, we will satisfy him and keep you out of trouble." [15]So they took the money and did as they were directed; and this story has been spread among the Jews to this day.

16 Now the eleven disciples went to Galilee, to the mountain to which Jesus had directed them. [17] And when they saw him they worshiped him; but some doubted. [18] And Jesus came and said to them, "All authority in heaven and on earth has been given to me." [19] Go therefore and make disciples of all nations, baptizing them in the name of the Father and of the Son and of the Holy Spirit, [20] teaching them to observe all that I have commanded you; and lo, I am with you always, to the close of the age."

## Notes

[a] A talent is a measure of weight. This indicates considerable value, as a talent of silver would be worth about $1,900 in today's money, a talent of gold almost $30,000.

[b] One of the major Jewish holidays, commemorating God's deliverance of the Israelites from Egyptian captivity.

[c] This may mean a military headquarters or the governor's residence.

[d] A bitter substance.

[e] The day before Passover.

# The New Testament:
# The Acts of the Apostles

The Gospel of Luke, one of the three "synoptic gospels," begins with an address to a certain Theophilus (the name means "lover of God") and explains that "Inasmuch as many have undertaken to compile a narrative of the things which have been accomplished among us"—i.e., the Christian story—he proposes to provide an "orderly account" so that Theophilus may know the truth. The Gospel of Luke ends with the resurrected Jesus appearing to his disciples, whom he blesses; the disciples "returned to Jerusalem with great joy, and were continually in the temple blessing God."

The Book of Acts is by the same author and addressed to Theophilus, again, and begins by referring to "the first book." The Acts of the Apostles picks up the account of what happened in the Christian community after Jesus's departure. It focuses on two main stories: the beginnings of the church in Palestine and its separation from Judaism, followed by the movement of the gospel westward and its extension to the Gentiles. The main figure in the first story is Peter; the main figure in the second is Paul. It begins with an account of the resurrected Jesus and is followed by an account of the institutionalization of the church, including arrangements for leadership and support for Christian families in the face of disapproval and persecution by the religious authorities.

Though early manuscripts of the Gospel of Luke (and by implication The Acts of the Apostles) are anonymous, the author became identified with Luke, who is mentioned in Paul's letter to the Colossians as "the beloved physician."

MM

# from The New Testament:
## The Acts of the Apostles

**1** In the first book, O The-oph´ilus, I have dealt with all that Jesus began to do and teach, [2] until the day when he was taken up, after he had given commandment through the Holy Spirit to the apostles whom he had chosen. [3] To them he presented himself alive after his passion by many proofs, appearing to them during forty days, and speaking of the kingdom of God. [4] And while staying with them he charged them not to depart from Jerusalem, but to wait for the promise of the Father, which, he said, "you heard from me, [5] for John baptized with water, but before many days you shall be baptized with the Holy Spirit."

6 So when they had come together, they asked him, "Lord, will you at this time restore the kingdom to Israel?" [7] He said to them, "It is not for you to know times or seasons which the Father has fixed by his own authority. [8] But you shall receive power when the Holy Spirit has come upon you; and you shall be my witnesses in Jerusalem and in all Judea and Sama´ria and to the end of the earth." [9] And when he had said this, as they were looking on, he was lifted up, and a cloud took him out of their sight. [10] And while they were gazing into heaven as he went, behold, two men stood by them in white robes, [11] and said, "Men of Galilee, why do you stand looking into heaven? This Jesus who was taken up from you into heaven, will come in the same way as you saw him go into heaven."

12 Then they returned to Jerusalem from the mount called Olivet, which is near Jerusalem, a sabbath day's journey away; [13] and when they had entered, they went up to the upper room, where they were staying, Peter and John and James and Andrew, Philip and Thomas, Bartholomew and Matthew, James the son of Alphaeus and Simon the Zealot and Judas the son of James. [14] All these with one accord devoted themselves to prayer, together with the women and Mary the mother of Jesus, and with his brothers.

15 In those days Peter stood up among the brethren (the company of persons was in all about a hundred and twenty), and said, [16] "Brethren, the scripture had to be fulfilled, which the Holy Spirit spoke beforehand by the mouth of David, concerning Judas who was guide to those who arrested Jesus. [17] For he was numbered among us, and was allotted his share in this ministry. [18] (Now this man bought a field with the reward of his wickedness; and falling headlong he burst open in the middle and all his bowels gushed out. [19] And it

became known to all the inhabitants of Jerusalem, so that the field was called in their language Akel´dama, that is, Field of Blood.) [20] For it is written in the book of Psalms,

'Let his habitation become desolate,
and let there be no one to live in it';

and

'His office let another take.'

[21] So one of the men who have accompanied us during all the time that the Lord Jesus went in and out among us, [22] beginning from the baptism of John until the day when he was taken up from us—one of these men must become with us a witness to his resurrection. [23] And they put forward two, Joseph called Barsab´bas, who was surnamed Justus, and Matthi´as. [24] And they prayed and said, "Lord, who knowest the hearts of all men, show which one of these two thou hast chosen [25] to take the place in this ministry and apostleship from which Judas turned aside, to go to his own place." [26] And they cast lots for them, and the lot fell on Matthi´as; and he was enrolled with the eleven apostles.

**2** When the day of Pentecost had come, they were all together in one place. [2] And suddenly a sound came from heaven like the rush of a mighty wind, and it filled all the house where they were sitting. [3] And there appeared to them tongues as of fire, distributed and resting on each one of them. [4] And they were all filled with the Holy Spirit and began to speak in other tongues, as the Spirit gave them utterance.

5 Now there were dwelling in Jerusalem Jews, devout men from every nation under heaven. [6] And at this sound the multitude came together, and they were bewildered, because each one heard them speaking in his own language. [7] And they were amazed and wondered, saying, "Are not all these who are speaking Galileans? [8] And how is it that we hear, each of us in his own native language? [9] Par´thians and Medes and E´lamites and residents of Mesopota´mia, Judea and Cappado´cia, Pontus and Asia, [10] Phryg´ia and Pamphyl´ia, Egypt and the parts of Libya belonging to Cyre´ne, and visitors from Rome, both Jews and proselytes, [11] Cretans and Arabians, we hear them telling in our own tongues the mighty works of God." [12] And all were amazed and perplexed, saying to one another, "What does this mean?" [13] But others mocking said, "They are filled with new wine."

14 But Peter, standing with the eleven, lifted up his voice and addressed them, "Men of Judea and all who dwell in Jerusalem, let this be known to you, and give ear to my words. [15] For these men are not drunk, as you suppose, since it is only the third hour of the day; [16] but this is what was spoken by the prophet Joel:

[17] 'And in the last days it shall be, God declares,
that I will pour out my Spirit upon all flesh,
and your sons and your daughters shall prophesy,
and your young men shall see visions,
and your old men shall dream dreams;
[18] yea, and on my menservants and my maidservants in those days
I will pour out my Spirit; and they shall prophesy.
And I will show wonders in the heaven above
and signs on the earth beneath,
blood, and fire, and vapor of smoke;
the sun shall be turned into darkness
and the moon into blood,
before the day of the Lord comes,
the great and manifest day.
[21] And it shall be that whoever calls on the name of the Lord shall
be saved.'

22 "Men of Israel, hear these words: Jesus of Nazareth, a man attested to you by God with mighty works and wonders and signs which God did through him in your midst, as you yourselves know—[23] this Jesus, delivered up according to the definite plan and foreknowledge of God, you crucified and killed by the hands of lawless men. [24] But God raised him up, having loosed the pangs of death, because it was not possible for him to be held by it. [25] For David says concerning him,

'I saw the Lord always before me,
for he is at my right hand that I may
not be shaken;
[26] therefore my heart was glad, and my tongue rejoiced;
moreover my flesh will dwell in hope.
[27] For thou wilt not abandon my soul to Hades,
nor let thy Holy One see corruption.
[28] Thou hast made known to me the
ways of life;
thou wilt make me full of gladness
with thy presence.'

29 "Brethren, I may say to you confidently of the patriarch David that he both died and was buried, and his tomb is with us to this day. [30] Being therefore a prophet, and knowing that God had sworn with an oath to him that he would set one of his descendants upon his throne, [31] he foresaw and spoke of the resurrection of the Christ, that he was not abandoned to Hades, nor did his flesh see corruption. [32] This Jesus God raised up, and of that we all are wit-

nesses. [33] Being therefore exalted at the right hand of God, and having received from the Father the promise of the Holy Spirit, he has poured out this which you see and hear. [34] For David did not ascend into the heavens; but he himself says,

> 'The Lord said to my Lord, Sit at my
>> right hand,
> [35] till I make thy enemies a stool for
>> thy feet.'

[36] Let all the house of Israel therefore know assuredly that God has made him both Lord and Christ, this Jesus whom you crucified."

37 Now when they heard this they were cut to the heart, and said to Peter and the rest of the apostles, "Brethren, what shall we do?" [38] And Peter said to them, "Repent, and be baptized every one of you in the name of Jesus Christ for the forgiveness of your sins; and you shall receive the gift of the Holy Spirit. [39] For the promise is to you and to your children and to all that are far off, every one whom the Lord our God calls to him." [40] And he testified with many other words and exhorted them, saying, "Save yourselves from this crooked generation." [41] So those who received his word were baptized, and there were added that day about three thousand souls. [42] And they devoted themselves to the apostles' teaching and fellowship, to the breaking of bread and the prayers.

43 And fear came upon every soul; and many wonders and signs were done through the apostles. [44] And all who believed were together and had all things in common; [45] and they sold their possessions and goods and distributed them to all, as any had need. [46] And day by day, attending the temple together and breaking bread in their homes, they partook of food with glad and generous hearts, [47] praising God and having favor with all the people. And the Lord added to their number day by day those who were being saved.

3 Now Peter and John were going up to the temple at the hour of prayer, the ninth hour. [2] And a man lame from birth was being carried, whom they laid daily at that gate of the temple which is called Beautiful to ask alms of those who entered the temple. [3] Seeing Peter and John about to go into the temple, he asked for alms. [4] And Peter directed his gaze at him, with John, and said, "Look at us." [5] And he fixed his attention upon them, expecting to receive something from them. [6] But Peter said, "I have no silver and gold, but I give you what I have; in the name of Jesus Christ of Nazareth, walk." [7] And he took him by the right hand and raised him up; and immediately his feet and ankles were made strong. [8] And leaping up he stood and walked and entered the temple with them, walking and leaping and praising God. [9] And all the people saw him walking and praising God, [10] and recognized him as the one who sat for alms at the Beautiful Gate of the temple; and they were filled with wonder and amazement at what had happened to him.

11 While he clung to Peter and John, all the people ran together to them in the portico called Solomon's, astounded. [12] And when Peter saw it he addressed the people, "Men of Israel, why do you wonder at this, or why do you stare at us, as though by our own power or piety we had made him walk? [13] The God of Abraham and of Isaac and of Jacob, the God of our fathers, glorified his servant Jesus, whom you delivered up and denied in the presence of Pilate, when he had decided to release him. [14] But you denied the Holy and Righteous One, and asked for a murderer to be granted to you, [15] and killed the Author of life, whom God raised from the dead. To this we are witnesses. [16] And his name, by faith in his name, has made this man strong whom you see and know; and the faith which is through Jesus has given the man this perfect health in the presence of you all.

17 "And now, brethren, I know that you acted in ignorance, as did also your rulers. [18] But what God foretold by the mouth of all the prophets, that his Christ should suffer, he thus fulfilled. [19] Repent therefore, and turn again, that your sins may be blotted out, that times of refreshing may come from the presence of the Lord, [20] and that he may send the Christ appointed for you, Jesus, [21] whom heaven must receive until the time for establishing all that God spoke by the mouth of his holy prophets from of old. [22] Moses said, 'The Lord God will raise up for you a prophet from your brethren as he raised me up. You shall listen to him in whatever he tells you. [23] And it shall be that every soul that does not listen to that prophet shall be destroyed from the people.' [24] And all the prophets who have spoken, from Samuel and those who came afterwards, also proclaimed these days. [25] You are the sons of the prophets and of the covenant which God gave to your fathers, saying to Abraham, 'And in your posterity shall all the families of the earth be blessed.' [26] God, having raised up his servant, sent him to you first, to bless you in turning every one of you from your wickedness."

**4** And as they were speaking to the people, the priests and the captain of the temple and the Sad´ducees came upon them, [2] annoyed because they were teaching the people and proclaiming in Jesus the resurrection from the dead. [3] And they arrested them and put them in custody until the morrow, for it was already evening. [4] But many of those who heard the word believed; and the number of the men came to about five thousand.

5 On the morrow their rulers and elders and scribes were gathered together in Jerusalem, [6] with Annas the high priest and Ca´iaphas and John and Alexander, and all who were of the high-priestly family. [7] And when they had set them in the midst, they inquired, "By what power or by what name did you do this?" [8] Then Peter, filled with the Holy Spirit, said to them, "Rulers of the people and elders, [9] if we are being examined today concerning a good

deed done to a cripple, by what means this man has been healed, [10] be it known to you all, and to all the people of Israel, that by the name of Jesus Christ of Nazareth, whom you crucified, whom God raised from the dead, by him this man is standing before you well. [11] This is the stone which was rejected by you builders, but which has become the head of the corner. [12] And there is salvation in no one else, for there is no other name under heaven given among men by which we must be saved."

13 Now when they saw the boldness of Peter and John, and perceived that they were uneducated, common men, they wondered; and they recognized that they had been with Jesus. [14] But seeing the man that had been healed standing beside them, they had nothing to say in opposition. [15] But when they had commanded them to go aside out of the council, they conferred with one another, [16] saying, "What shall we do with these men? For that a notable sign has been performed through them is manifest to all the inhabitants of Jerusalem, and we cannot deny it. [17] But in order that it may spread no further among the people, let us warn them to speak no more to any one in this name." [18] So they called them and charged them not to speak or teach at all in the name of Jesus. [19] But Peter and John answered them, "Whether it is right in the sight of God to listen to you rather than to God, you must judge; [20] for we cannot but speak of what we have seen and heard." [21] And when they had further threatened them, they let them go, finding no way to punish them, because of the people; for all men praised God for what had happened. [22] For the man on whom this sign of healing was performed was more than forty years old.

23 When they were released they went to their friends and reported what the chief priests and the elders had said to them. [24] And when they heard it, they lifted their voices together to God and said, "Sovereign Lord, who didst make the heaven and the earth and the sea and everything in them, [25] who by the mouth of our father David, thy servant, didst say by the Holy Spirit,

'Why did the Gentiles rage,
and the peoples imagine vain things?
[26] The kings of the earth set themselves
in array,
and the rulers were gathered
together,
against the Lord and against his
Anointed'—

[27] for truly in this city there were gathered together against thy holy servant Jesus, whom thou didst anoint, both Herod and Pontius Pilate, with the Gentiles and the peoples of Israel, [28] to do whatever thy hand and thy plan had

predestined to take place. [29] And now, Lord, look upon their threats, and grant to thy servants to speak thy word with all boldness, [30] while thou stretchest out thy hand to heal, and signs and wonders are performed through the name of thy holy servant Jesus." [31] And when they had prayed, the place in which they were gathered together was shaken; and they were all filled with the Holy Spirit and spoke the word of God with boldness.

32 Now the company of those who believed were of one heart and soul, and no one said that any of the things which he possessed was his own, but they had everything in common. [33] And with great power the apostles gave their testimony to the resurrection of the Lord Jesus, and great grace was upon them all. [34] There was not a needy person among them, for as many as were possessors of lands or houses sold them, and brought the proceeds of what was sold [35] and laid it at the apostles' feet; and distribution was made to each as any had need. . . .

5 . . . 12 Now many signs and wonders were done among the people by the hands of the apostles. And they were all together in Solomon's Portico. [13] None of the rest dared join them, but the people held them in high honor. [14] And more than ever believers were added to the Lord, multitudes both of men and women, [15] so that they even carried out the sick into the streets, and laid them on beds and pallets, that as Peter came by at least his shadow might fall on some of them. [16] The people also gathered from the towns around Jerusalem, bringing the sick and those afflicted with unclean spirits, and they were all healed.

17 But the high priest rose up and all who were with him, that is, the party of the Sad´ducees, and filled with jealousy [18] they arrested the apostles and put them in the common prison. [19] But at night an angel of the Lord opened the prison doors and brought them out and said, [20] "Go and stand in the temple and speak to the people all the words of this Life." [21] And when they heard this, they entered the temple at daybreak and taught.

Now the high priest came and those who were with him and called together the council and all the senate of Israel, and sent to the prison to have them brought. [22] But when the officers came they did not find them in the prison, and they returned and reported, [23] "We found the prison securely locked and the sentries standing at the doors, but when we opened it we found no one inside." [24] Now when the captain of the temple and the chief priests heard these words, they were much perplexed about them, wondering what this would come to. [25] And some one came and told them, "The men whom you put in prison are standing in the temple and teaching the people." [26] Then the captain with the officers went and brought them, but without violence, for they were afraid of being stoned by the people.

27 And when they had brought them, they set them before the council. And the high priest questioned them, [28] saying, "We strictly charged you not to teach in this name, yet here you have filled Jerusalem with your teaching and you intend to bring this man's blood upon us." [29] But Peter and the apostles answered, "We must obey God rather than men. [30] The God of our fathers raised Jesus whom you killed by hanging him on a tree. [31] God exalted him at his right hand as Leader and Savior, to give repentance to Israel and forgiveness of sins. [32] And we are witnesses to these things, and so is the Holy Spirit whom God has given to those who obey him."

33 When they heard this they were enraged and wanted to kill them. [34] But a Pharisee in the council named Gama′li-el, a teacher of the law, held in honor by all the people, stood up and ordered the men to be put outside for a while. [35] And he said to them, "Men of Israel, take care what you do with these men. [36] For before these days Theu′das arose, giving himself out to be somebody, and a number of men, about four hundred, joined him; but he was slain and all who followed him were dispersed and came to nothing. [37] After him Judas the Galilean arose in the days of the census and drew away some of the people after him; he also perished, and all who followed him were scattered. [38] So in the present case I tell you, keep away from these men and let them alone; for if this plan or this undertaking is of men, it will fail; [39] but if it is of God, you will not be able to overthrow them. You might even be found opposing God!"

40 So they took his advice, and when they had called in the apostles, they beat them and charged them not to speak in the name of Jesus, and let them go. [41] Then they left the presence of the council, rejoicing that they were counted worthy to suffer dishonor for the name. [42] And every day in the temple and at home they did not cease teaching and preaching Jesus as the Christ.

# The New Testament: 1 Corinthians

Saul, a Jew from Tarsus in Asia Minor, became under his new name of Paul the second most important figure in Christianity. Beginning as an active persecutor of the small Christian group (see the account of his role in the Book of Acts [chapters 8–9], where he was present at the first Christian martyrdom, of Stephen, and went on "breathing threats and murder against the disciples of the Lord,") he experienced a spectacular conversion on the road to Damascus. He was struck blind and heard the voice of Jesus speaking to him; three days later he was miraculously healed and became a follower of Christ. Understandably suspicious, the other disciples eventually granted Paul a role in the early church. He became the apostle to the Gentiles, traveling throughout the Greco-Roman world carrying the gospel, establishing churches, disputing with enemies, and laying the theological groundwork for the Christian religion.

His letters are the earliest documents in the New Testament. (It is worth remembering that Paul did not have the gospels as a source of information on Jesus.) Probably written around 54 C.E., Paul's first letter to the Corinthians was sent from Ephesus to a Christian group in a city where he had lived for a year and a half. It is not his first letter to the Corinthians— an earlier one seems to be lost—and is part of an ongoing discussion with the church about Christian belief and practice. He is clearly responding to questions the church has sent to him. Paul's churches were sometimes troubled or led astray, once he had departed, by internal factions or by other Christian teachers (of whom there were many in the early years of the new religion) offering a message at variance with Paul's understanding of the new religion.

Corinth was a major city, with important temples to Apollo and many other Greco-Roman gods and goddesses and a well-established cult of Isis with initiation rites. Since private citizens, as well as priests serving in temples, sacrificed to the gods, the question of eating meat thus sacrificed was an important one to the Corinthian Christians. This would have been both a social problem and an economic one, since meat was expensive and meat free from the taint of sacrifice would have been scarce.

1 Corinthians also contains Paul's eloquent celebration of love (*agape*), his explanation of the gifts of the spirit and their relation to missionary activity, and an account of the Resurrection.

MM

# from The New Testament: 1 Corinthians

**6** When one of you has a grievance against a brother, does he dare go to law before the unrighteous instead of the saints? [2] Do you not know that the saints will judge the world? And if the world is to be judged by you, are you incompetent to try trivial cases? [3] Do you not know that we are to judge angels? How much more, matters pertaining to this life! [4] If then you have such cases, why do you lay them before those who are least esteemed by the church? [5] I say this to your shame. Can it be that there is no man among you wise enough to decide between members of the brotherhood, [6] but brother goes to law against brother, and that before unbelievers?

7 To have lawsuits at all with one another is defeat for you. Why not rather suffer wrong? Why not rather be defrauded? [8] But you yourselves wrong and defraud, and that even your own brethren.

9 Do you not know that the unrighteous will not inherit the kingdom of God? Do not be deceived; neither the immoral, nor idolaters, nor adulterers, nor homosexuals, [10] nor thieves, nor the greedy, nor drunkards, nor revilers, nor robbers will inherit the kingdom of God. [11] And such were some of you. But you were washed, you were sanctified, you were justified in the name of the Lord Jesus Christ and in the Spirit of our God.

12 "All things are lawful for me," but not all things are helpful. "All things are lawful for me," but I will not be enslaved by anything. [13] "Food is meant for the stomach and the stomach for food"—and God will destroy both one and the other. The body is not meant for immorality, but for the Lord, and the Lord for the body. [14] And God raised the Lord and will also raise us up by his power. [15] Do you not know that your bodies are members of Christ? Shall I therefore take the members of Christ and make them members of a prostitute? Never! [16] Do you not know that he who joins himself to a prostitute becomes one body with her? For, as it is written, "The two shall become one." [17] But he who is united to the Lord becomes one spirit with him. [18] Shun immorality. Every other sin which a man commits is outside the body; but the immoral man sins against his own body. [19] Do you not know that your body is a temple of the Holy Spirit within you, which you have from God? You are not your own; [20] you were bought with a price. So glorify God in your body.

7 Now concerning the matters about which you wrote. It is well for a man not to touch a woman. [2] But because of the temptation to immorality,

each man should have his own wife and each woman her own husband. [3] The husband should give to his wife her conjugal rights, and likewise the wife to her husband. [4] For the wife does not rule over her own body, but the husband does; likewise the husband does not rule over his own body, but the wife does. [5] Do not refuse one another except perhaps by agreement for a season, that you may devote yourselves to prayer; but then come together again, lest Satan tempt you through lack of self-control. [6] I say this by way of concession, not of command. [7] I wish that all were as I myself am. But each has his own special gift from God, one of one kind and one of another.

8 To the unmarried and the widows I say that it is well for them to remain single as I do. [9] But if they cannot exercise self-control, they should marry. For it is better to marry than to be aflame with passion.

10 To the married I give charge, not I but the Lord, that the wife should not separate from her husband [11] (but if she does, let her remain single or else be reconciled to her husband)—and that the husband should not divorce his wife.

12 To the rest I say, not the Lord, that if any brother has a wife who is an unbeliever, and she consents to live with him, he should not divorce her. [13] If any woman has a husband who is an unbeliever and he consents to live with her, she should not divorce him. [14] For the unbelieving husband is consecrated through his wife, and the unbelieving wife is consecrated through her husband. Otherwise, your children would be unclean, but as it is they are holy. [15] But if the unbelieving partner desires to separate, let it be so; in such a case the brother or sister is not bound. For God has called us to peace. [16] Wife, how do you know whether you will save your husband? Husband, how do you know whether you will save your wife?

17 Only, let every one lead the life which the Lord has assigned to him, and in which God has called him. This is my rule in all the churches. [18] Was any one at the time of his call already circumcised? Let him not seek to remove the marks of circumcision. Was any one at the time of his call uncircumcised? Let him not seek circumcision. [19] For neither circumcision counts for anything nor uncircumcision, but keeping the commandments of God. [20] Every one should remain in the state in which he was called. [21] Were you a slave when called? Never mind. But if you can gain your freedom, avail yourself of the opportunity. [22] For he who was called in the Lord as a slave is a freedman of the Lord. Likewise he who was free when called is a slave of Christ. [23] You were bought with a price; do not become slaves of men. [24] So, brethren, in whatever state each was called, there let him remain with God.

25 Now concerning the unmarried, I have no command of the Lord, but I give my opinion as one who by the Lord's mercy is trustworthy. [26] "I think

that in view of the impending distress it is well for a person to remain as he is. [27] Are you bound to a wife? Do not seek to be free. Are you free from a wife? Do not seek marriage. [28] But if you marry, you do not sin, and if a girl marries she does not sin. Yet those who marry will have worldly troubles, and I would spare you that. [29] I mean, brethren, the appointed time has grown very short;[a] from now on, let those who have wives live as though they had none, [30] and those who mourn as though they were not mourning, and those who rejoice as though they were not rejoicing, and those who buy as though they had no goods, [31] and those who deal with the world as though they had no dealings with it. For the form of this world is passing away.

32 I want you to be free from anxieties. The unmarried man is anxious about the affairs of the Lord, how to please the Lord; [33] but the married man is anxious about worldly affairs, how to please his wife, [34] and his interests are divided. And the unmarried woman or girl is anxious about the affairs of the Lord, how to be holy in body and spirit; but the married woman is anxious about worldly affairs, how to please her husband. [35] I say this for your own benefit, not to lay any restraint upon you, but to promote good order and to secure your undivided devotion to the Lord.

36 If any one thinks that he is not behaving properly toward his betrothed, if his passions are strong, and it has to be, let him do as he wishes: let them marry—it is no sin. [37] But whoever is firmly established in his heart, being under no necessity but having his desire under control, and has determined this in his heart, to keep her as his betrothed, he will do well. [38] So that he who marries his betrothed does well; and he who refrains from marriage will do better.

39 A wife is bound to her husband as long as he lives. If the husband dies, she is free to be married to whom she wishes, only in the Lord. [40] But in my judgment she is happier if she remains as she is. And I think that I have the Spirit of God.

**8** Now concerning food offered to idols: we know that "all of us possess knowledge." "Knowledge" puffs up, but love builds up. [2] If any one imagines that he knows something, he does not yet know as he ought to know. [3] But if one loves God, one is known by him.

4 Hence, as to the eating of food offered to idols, we know that "an idol has no real existence," and that "there is no God but one." [5] For although there may be so-called gods in heaven or on earth—as indeed there are many "gods" and many "lords"— [6] yet for us there is one God, the Father, from whom are all things and for whom we exist, and one Lord, Jesus Christ, through whom are all things and through whom we exist.

7 However, not all possess this knowledge. But some, through being hitherto accustomed to idols, eat food as really offered to an idol; and their conscience, being weak, is defiled. [8] Food will not commend us to God. We are no worse off if we do not eat, and no better off if we do. [9] Only take care lest this liberty of yours somehow become a stumbling block to the weak. [10] For if any one sees you, a man of knowledge, at table in an idol's temple, might he not be encouraged, if his conscience is weak, to eat food offered to idols? [11] And so by your knowledge this weak man is destroyed, the brother for whom Christ died. [12] Thus, sinning against your brethren and wounding their conscience when it is weak, you sin against Christ. [13] Therefore, if food is a cause of my brother's falling, I will never eat meat, lest I cause my brother to fall.

**9** Am I not free? Am I not an apostle? Have I not seen Jesus our Lord? Are not you my workmanship in the Lord? [2] If to others I am not an apostle, at least I am to you; for you are the seal of my apostleship in the Lord.

3 This is my defense to those who would examine me. [4] Do we not have the right to our food and drink? [5] Do we not have the right to be accompanied by a wife, as the other apostles and the brothers of the Lord and Cephas?[b] [6] Or is it only Barnabas and I who have no right to refrain from working for a living? [7] Who serves as a soldier at his own expense? Who plants a vineyard without eating any of its fruit? Who tends a flock without getting some of the milk?

8 Do I say this on human authority? Does not the law say the same? [9] For it is written in the law of Moses, "You shall not muzzle an ox when it is treading out the grain." Is it for oxen that God is concerned? [10] Does he not speak entirely for our sake? It was written for our sake, because the plowman should plow in hope and the thresher thresh in hope of a share in the crop. [11] If we have sown spiritual good among you, is it too much if we reap your material benefits? [12] If others share this rightful claim upon you, do not we still more?

Nevertheless, we have not made use of this right, but we endure anything rather than put an obstacle in the way of the gospel of Christ. [13] Do you not know that those who are employed in the temple service get their food from the temple, and those who serve at the altar share in the sacrificial offerings? [14] In the same way, the Lord commanded that those who proclaim the gospel should get their living by the gospel.

15 But I have made no use of any of these rights, nor am I writing this to secure any such provision. For I would rather die than have any one deprive me of my ground for boasting. [16] For if I preach the gospel, that gives me no ground for boasting. For necessity is laid upon me. Woe to me if I do not preach the gospel! [17] For if I do this of my own will, I have a reward; but if not of my own will, I am entrusted with a commission. [18] What then is my reward?

Just this: that in my preaching I may make the gospel free of charge, not making full use of my right in the gospel.

19 For though I am free from all men, I have made myself a slave to all, that I might win the more. $^{20}$To the Jews I became as a Jew, in order to win Jews; to those under the law I became as one under the law—though not being myself under the law—that I might win those under the law. $^{21}$To those outside the law I became as one outside the law—not being without law toward God but under the law of Christ—that I might win those outside the law. $^{22}$To the weak I became weak, that I might win the weak. I have become all things to all men, that I might by all means save some. $^{23}$I do it all for the sake of the gospel, that I may share in its blessings.

24 Do you not know that in a race all the runners compete, but only one receives the prize? So run that you may obtain it. $^{25}$Every athlete exercises self-control in all things. They do it to receive a perishable wreath, but we an imperishable. $^{26}$Well, I do not run aimlessly, I do not box as one beating the air; $^{27}$but I pommel my body and subdue it, lest after preaching to others I myself should be disqualified. . . .

**13** If I speak in the tongues of men and of angels, but have not love, I am a noisy gong or a clanging cymbal. $^{2}$And if I have prophetic powers, and understand all mysteries and all knowledge, and if I have all faith, so as to remove mountains, but have not love, I am nothing. $^{3}$If I give away all I have, and if I deliver my body to be burned," but have not love, I gain nothing.

4 Love is patient and kind; love is not jealous or boastful; $^{5}$it is not arrogant or rude. Love does not insist on its own way; it is not irritable or resentful; $^{6}$it does not rejoice at wrong, but rejoices in the right. $^{7}$Love bears all things, believes all things, hopes all things, endures all things.

8 Love never ends; as for prophecies, they will pass away; as for tongues, they will cease; as for knowledge, it will pass away. $^{9}$For our knowledge is imperfect and our prophecy is imperfect; $^{10}$but when the perfect comes, the imperfect will pass away. $^{11}$When I was a child, I spoke like a child, I thought like a child, I reasoned like a child; when I became a man, I gave up childish ways. $^{12}$For now we see in a mirror dimly, but then face to face. Now I know in part; then I shall understand fully, even as I have been fully understood. $^{13}$So faith, hope, love abide, these three; but the greatest of these is love.

**14** Make love your aim, and earnestly desire the spiritual gifts, especially that you may prophesy. $^{2}$For one who speaks in a tongue speaks not to men but to God; for no one understands him, but he utters mysteries in the Spirit. $^{3}$On the other hand, he who prophesies speaks to men for their upbuilding and encouragement and consolation. $^{4}$He who speaks in a tongue edifies himself, but he who prophesies edifies the church. $^{5}$Now I want you all to speak in tongues, but even more to prophesy. He who prophesies is greater than he who speaks in tongues, unless some one interprets, so that the church may be edified. . . .

26 What then, brethren? When you come together, each one has a hymn, a lesson, a revelation, a tongue, or an interpretation. Let all things be done for edification. [27] If any speak in a tongue, let there be only two or at most three, and each in turn; and let one interpret. [28] But if there is no one to interpret, let each of them keep silence in church and speak to himself and to God. [29] Let two or three prophets speak, and let the others weigh what is said. [30] If a revelation is made to another sitting by, let the first be silent. [31] For you can all prophesy one by one, so that all may learn and all be encouraged; [32] and the spirits of prophets are subject to prophets. [33] For God is not a God of confusion but of peace.

As in all the churches of the saints, [34] the women should keep silence in the churches. For they are not permitted to speak, but should be subordinate, as even the law says. [35] If there is anything they desire to know, let them ask their husbands at home. For it is shameful for a woman to speak in church. [36] What! Did the word of God originate with you, or are you the only ones it has reached?

37 If any one thinks that he is a prophet, or spiritual, he should acknowledge that what I am writing to you is a command of the Lord. [38] If any one does not recognize this, he is not recognized. [39] So, my brethren, earnestly desire to prophesy, and do not forbid speaking in tongues; [40] but all things should be done decently and in order.

**15** Now I would remind you, brethren, in what terms I preached to you the gospel, which you received, in which you stand, [2] by which you are saved, if you hold it fast—unless you believed in vain.

3 For I delivered to you as of first importance what I also received, that Christ died for our sins in accordance with the scriptures, [4] that he was buried, that he was raised on the third day in accordance with the scriptures, [5] and that he appeared to Cephas, then to the twelve. [6] Then he appeared to more than five hundred brethren at one time, most of whom are still alive, though some have fallen asleep. [7] Then he appeared to James, then to all the apostles. [8] Last of all, as to one untimely born, he appeared also to me. [9] For I am the least of the apostles, unfit to be called an apostle, because I persecuted the church of God. [10] But by the grace of God I am what I am, and his grace toward me was not in vain. On the contrary, I worked harder than any of them, though it was not I, but the grace of God which is with me. [11] Whether then it was I or they, so we preach and so you believed.

12 Now if Christ is preached as raised from the dead, how can some of you say that there is no resurrection of the dead? [13] But if there is no resurrection of the dead, then Christ has not been raised; [14] if Christ has not been raised, then our preaching is in vain and your faith is in vain. [15] We are even found to be misrepresenting God, because we testified of God that he raised Christ, whom he did not raise if it is true that the dead are not raised. [16] For if the dead are not raised, then Christ has not been raised. [17] If Christ has not been raised, your faith is futile and you are still in your sins. [18] Then those also who have fallen asleep in Christ have perished. [19] If for this life only we have hoped in Christ, we are of all men most to be pitied.

20 But in fact Christ has been raised from the dead, the first fruits of those who have fallen asleep. [21] For as by a man came death, by a man has come also the resurrection of the dead. [22] For as in Adam all die, so also in Christ shall all be made alive. [23] But each in his own order: Christ the first fruits, then at his coming those who belong to Christ. [24] Then comes the end, when he delivers the kingdom to God the Father after destroying every rule and every authority and power. [25] For he must reign until he has put all his enemies under his feet. [26] The last enemy to be destroyed is death. [27] "For God has put all things in subjection under his feet." But when it says, "All things are put in subjection under him," it is plain that he is excepted who put all things under him. [28] When all things are subjected to him, then the Son himself will also be subjected to him who put all things under him, that God may be everything to every one.

29 Otherwise, what do people mean by being baptized on behalf of the dead? If the dead are not raised at all, why are people baptized on their behalf? [30] Why am I in peril every hour? [31] I protest, brethren, by my pride in you which I have in Christ Jesus our Lord, I die every day! [32] What do I gain if, humanly speaking, I fought with beasts at Ephesus? If the dead are not raised, "Let us eat and drink, for tomorrow we die." [33] Do not be deceived: "Bad company ruins good morals." [34] Come to your right mind, and sin no more. For some have no knowledge of God. I say this to your shame.

35 But some one will ask, "How are the dead raised? With what kind of body do they come?" [36] You foolish man! What you sow does not come to life unless it dies. [37] And what you sow is not the body which is to be, but a bare kernel, perhaps of wheat or of some other grain. [38] But God gives it a body as he has chosen, and to each kind of seed its own body. [39] For not all flesh is alike, but there is one kind for men, another for animals, another for birds, and another for fish. [40] There are celestial bodies and there are terrestrial bodies; but the glory of the celestial is one, and the glory of the terrestrial is another.

[41] There is one glory of the sun, and another glory of the moon, and another glory of the stars; for star differs from star in glory.

42 So is it with the resurrection of the dead. What is sown is perishable, what is raised is imperishable. [43] It is sown in dishonor, it is raised in glory. It is sown in weakness, it is raised in power. [44] It is sown a physical body, it is raised a spiritual body. If there is a physical body, there is also a spiritual body. [45] Thus it is written, "The first man Adam became a living being"; the last Adam became a life-giving spirit. [46] But it is not the spiritual which is first but the physical, and then the spiritual. [47] The first man was from the earth, a man of dust; the second man is from heaven. [48] As was the man of dust, so are those who are of the dust; and as is the man of heaven, so are those who are of heaven. [49] Just as we have borne the image of the man of dust, we shall also bear the image of the man of heaven. [50] I tell you this, brethren: flesh and blood cannot inherit the kingdom of God, nor does the perishable inherit the imperishable.

51 Lo! I tell you a mystery.[c] We shall not all sleep, but we shall all be changed, [52] in a moment, in the twinkling of an eye, at the last trumpet. For the trumpet will sound, and the dead will be raised imperishable, and we shall be changed. [53] For this perishable nature must put on the imperishable, and this mortal nature must put on immortality. [54] When the perishable puts on the imperishable, and the mortal puts on immortality, then shall come to pass the saying that is written:

"Death is swallowed up in victory."
[55] "O death, where is thy victory?
O death, where is thy sting?"

[56] The sting of death is sin, and the power of sin is the law. [57] But thanks be to God, who gives us the victory through our Lord Jesus Christ.

58 Therefore, my beloved brethren, be steadfast, immovable, always abounding in the work of the Lord, knowing that in the Lord your labor is not in vain.

## Notes

[a] I.e., before the Second Coming.

[b] Peter.

[c] A confidential fact or secret, not something hard to understand.

# The New Testament:
# The Letter of Paul to Titus

The letter to Titus, like the two letters to Timothy also found in the New Testament, is thought of as a "pastoral letter" of Paul. These three books testify to the beginnings of the institutional church, being ostensibly directed to two of Paul's traveling companions who had been assigned leadership roles in Pauline churches—Timothy at Ephesus and Titus at Crete. Many scholars believe Titus was written after Paul's lifetime and thus consider it a "pseudo-Pauline epistle."

Titus is encouraged to resist false and dangerous ideas, including some about dietary practices, and false teachers—an ever-present problem in an age when Christian belief was still very diverse and there was no canon of Scripture to set boundaries to orthodoxy—whom Paul accuses of being motivated by greed.

MM

# The New Testament: The Letter of Paul to Titus

**1** Paul, a servant of God and an apostle of Jesus Christ, to further the faith of God's elect and their knowledge of the truth which accords with godliness, [2] in hope of eternal life which God, who never lies, promised ages ago [3] and at the proper time manifested in his word through the preaching with which I have been entrusted by command of God our Savior;

4 To Titus, my true child in a common faith:

Grace and peace from God the Father and Christ Jesus our Savior.

5 This is why I left you in Crete, that you might amend what was defective, and appoint elders in every town as I directed you, [6] if any man is blameless, the husband of one wife, and his children are believers and not open to the charge of being profligate or insubordinate. [7] For a bishop, as God's steward, must be blameless; he must not be arrogant or quick-tempered or a drunkard or violent or greedy for gain, [8] but hospitable, a lover of goodness, master of himself, upright, holy, and self-controlled; [9] he must hold firm to the sure word as taught, so that he may be able to give instruction in sound doctrine and also to confute those who contradict it. [10] For there are many insubordinate men, empty talkers and deceivers, especially the circumcision party; [11] they must be silenced, since they are upsetting whole families by teaching for base gain what they have no right to teach. [12] One of themselves, a prophet of their own, said, "Cretans are always liars, evil beasts, lazy gluttons." [13] This testimony is true. Therefore rebuke them sharply, that they may be sound in the faith, [14] instead of giving heed to Jewish myths or to commands of men who reject the truth. [15] To the pure all things are pure, but to the corrupt and unbelieving nothing is pure; their very minds and consciences are corrupted. [16] They profess to know God, but they deny him by their deeds; they are detestable, disobedient, unfit for any good deed.

**2** But as for you, teach what befits sound doctrine. [2] Bid the older men be temperate, serious, sensible, sound in faith, in love, and in steadfastness. [3] Bid the older women likewise to be reverent in behavior, not to be slanderers or slaves to drink; they are to teach what is good, [4] and so train the young women to love their husbands and children, [5] to be sensible, chaste, domestic, kind, and submissive to their husbands, that the word of God may not be discredited. [6] Likewise urge the younger men to control themselves. [7] Show yourself in all respects a model of good deeds, and in your teaching show integrity, gravity, [8] and sound speech that cannot be censured, so that an opponent may be put to shame, having nothing evil to say of us. [9] Bid slaves to be submissive to their masters and to give satisfaction in every respect; they are not to be refractory, [10] nor to pilfer, but to show entire and true fidelity, so that in everything they may adorn the doctrine of God our Savior.

11 For the grace of God has appeared for the salvation of all men, [12] training us to renounce irreligion and worldly passions, and to live sober, upright, and godly lives in this world, [13] awaiting our blessed hope, the appearing of the glory of our great God and Savior Jesus Christ, [14] who gave himself for us to redeem us from all iniquity and to purify for himself a people of his own who are zealous for good deeds.

15 Declare these things; exhort and reprove with all authority. Let no one disregard you.

**3** Remind them to be submissive to rulers, and authorities, to be obedient, to be ready for any honest work, [2] to speak evil of no one, to avoid quarreling, to be gentle, and to show perfect courtesy toward all men. [3] For we ourselves were once foolish, disobedient, led astray, slaves to various passions and pleasures, passing our days in malice and envy, hated by men and hating one another; [4] but when the goodness and loving kindness of God our Savior appeared, [5] he saved us, not because of deeds done by us in righteousness, but in virtue of his own mercy, by the washing of regeneration and renewal in the Holy Spirit, [6] which he poured out upon us richly through Jesus Christ our Savior, [7] so that we might be justified by his grace and become heirs in hope of eternal life. [8] The saying is sure.

I desire you to insist on these things, so that those who have believed in God may be careful to apply themselves to good deeds; these are excellent and profitable to men. [9] But avoid stupid controversies, genealogies, dissensions, and quarrels over the law, for they are unprofitable and futile. [10] As for a man who is factious, after admonishing him once or twice, have nothing more to do with him, [11] knowing that such a person is perverted and sinful; he is self-condemned.

12 When I send Artemas or Tych´icus to you, do your best to come to me at Nicop´olis, for I have decided to spend the winter there. [13] Do your best to speed Zenas the lawyer and Apol´los on their way; see that they lack nothing. [14] And let our people learn to apply themselves to good deeds, so as to help cases of urgent need, and not to be unfruitful.

15 All who are with me send greetings to you. Greet those who love us in the faith.

Grace be with you all.

# Josephus

## ca. 37–110 C.E.

Josephus (ca. 37–110 C.E.) was a Jewish aristocrat and military officer who commanded a contingent of Jewish insurgents during the Great Revolt (66–70 C.E.). He surrendered to the Romans, was taken to Rome, and there became a proponent of the Flavian Dynasty during the reign of Emperor Titus. Josephus achieved renown as a historian, and of his four surviving works, two are excerpted here: *Bellum Judaicum (The Jewish War)* and *Antiquitates Judaicae (Jewish Antiquities)*. In these works, he tackled the history of the Great Revolt and the history of the Jewish people respectively. He is known as an apologist because his work is sympathetic rather than objective as he explains to his audience (1) his own role in the Great Revolt, (2) Jewish sentiments toward the Great Revolt and (3) the history of the Jews.

The writings of Josephus must be considered against the backdrop of Jewish history circa 325 B.C.E.–80 C.E. For these four centuries, the Jews of Syria-Palestine experienced an almost continuous cycle of foreign domination and oppression. The cycle was briefly broken with the founding of the Jewish Hasmonean State (164 B.C.). When the fledgling independent nation fell to the Romans after only 133 years,[1] the Jews once again found themselves under persecution. They were subjected to oppressive taxation, harassment and demonstrated disregard toward their religious tenets. In 4 B.C.E., Herod the Great erected a golden eagle (the standard of Rome) on the Jerusalem Temple. In 26 C.E., Pontius Pilate surreptitiously installed the standards of emperor Tiberius in Jerusalem. Both Pilate and a later official, Florus (64 C.E.), confiscated the temple treasury. But perhaps the most notorious events took place during the reign of Caligula (37–41 C.E.), when first the emperor authorized a massacre of the Jews of Alexandria (the capital of Egypt) and then attempted to erect a golden statue of himself in the Jerusalem Temple. Social, political and religious tensions all fuelled rebellion and eventually ignited The Great Revolt against Rome (66–70 C.E.). Though the Jews made some initial headway in the war, ultimately the Romans crushed the rebellion, took Jerusalem and destroyed the temple.

In the *Jewish War*, Josephus offers an account of the Great Revolt based upon his own memory of events, court documents and other various sources. His intended audience is the Jewish Diaspora, that is, Jews living outside of Palestine in places such as Roman Persia, Egypt and Syria. Josephus actually defends the actions of the Romans to these Jews and depicts the insurgents as a radical fringe movement that did not reflect the sentiment or support of the majority of Jews. In the selection that follows, you read of the famous clash between the Jewish insurgents and the Roman army at Masada in 72–74 C.E. The engagement took place in the wake of the destruction of Jerusalem by the Romans, when a group of approximately one thousand rebels fled to a desert fortress on the high plateau of Masada. Once there, the group managed to hold the Roman army at bay for nearly two years. According to Josephus, the rebels realized that given the impending completion of a siege ramp, the Romans would soon breach the fortress walls. Our selection picks up at this point, with an address to the rebels by one of their leaders (Eleazar) who offers a dramatic plan to avoid surrender and conquest. Historically speaking, Josephus' account has been challenged by the archaeological findings at the site; his portrayal of events is considered to lack a high level of accuracy. Nonetheless, the narrative quality of his account of the Jewish Revolt stands shoulder to shoulder with the account of the Peloponnesian War by the Greek historian Thucydides. Indeed, compare Eleazar's speech with that of Pericles' Funeral Oration.

Our second selection from the works of Josephus is the Prologue to *Jewish Antiquities*, a book in which Josephus offers a history of the Jews from the creation to the initial stages of the Revolt. Though the narrative oftentimes merely retells the stories of the biblical Pentateuch,[2] the Prologue is distinctive, for it is there that Josephus outlines his philosophy of history and examines the motivations behind the historiography (lit. "history writing") of his peers. Rarely in ancient writings outside the works of Greek and Roman authors do we find such articulated self-analysis; indeed, Josephus' debt to Greco-Roman literary traditions may be most apparent in this work.

As a client of the imperial family, Josephus curried favor with the Flavian dynasty in an attempt to alleviate the punishment inflicted upon the Jews empire-wide during the decades immediately following the Great Revolt. Josephus intends for *Jewish Antiquities* to educate the Roman world about Judaism and expects the Roman world, once armed with this knowledge, to exonerate Jews from charges of sedition, treason, and impiety. The works of Josephus are indispensable for their literary merit and as the only surviving account of many events in Jewish history of the Greco-Roman periods.

KP

## Notes

[1] For a brief history of the Hasmonean period, please see the Introduction to 1 Maccabees 1–4.

[2] Pentateuch is the Greek designation for the first five books of the Hebrew Bible: Genesis, Exodus, Numbers, Leviticus, and Deuteronomy. The Hebrew word for these five books is Torah ("Law").

# from *The Jewish War* and *Jewish Antiquities*

from *The Wars of the Jews*

*Book 7, Chapter 8*

3. There was a rock not small in circumference, and very high. It was encompassed with valleys of such vast depth downward that the eye could not reach their bottoms; they were abrupt, and such as no animal could walk upon, excepting at two places of the rock, where it subsides, in order to afford a passage for ascent, though not without difficulty. Now, of the ways that lead to it, one is that from the lake Asphaltitis, towards the sun-rising, and another on the west where the ascent is easier: the one of these ways is called the *Serpent*, as resembling that animal in its narrowness and its perpetual windings; for it is broken off at the prominent precipices of the rock, and returns frequently into itself, and lengthening again by little and little, hath much ado to proceed forward; and he that would walk along it must first go on one leg and then on the other: there is also nothing but destruction in case your feet slip, for on each side there is a vastly deep chasm and precipice, sufficient to quell the courage of everybody by the terror it infuses into the mind. When, therefore, a man hath gone along this way for thirty furlongs,[1] the rest is the top of the hill,—not ending at a small point, but is no other than a plain upon the highest part of the mountain. Upon this top of the hill, Jonathan the high-priest first of all built a fortress, and called it *Masada*; after which the building of this place employed the care of king Herod to a great degree: he also built a wall round about the entire top of the hill, seven furlongs long; it was composed of white stone; its height was twelve, and its breadth eight cubits:[2] there were also erected upon that wall thirty-eight towers, each of them fifty cubits high; out of which you might pass into lesser edifices, which were built on the inside, round the entire wall; for the king reserved the top of the hill, which was of a fat soil and better mould than any valley, for agriculture, that such as committed themselves to this fortress for their preservation might not even there be quite destitute of food, in case they should ever be in want of it from abroad. Moreover, he built a palace therein at the western ascent: it was within and beneath the walls of the citadel, but inclined to its north side. Now the wall of this palace was very high and strong, and had at its four corners towers sixty cubits high. The furniture also of the edifices, and of the cloisters, and of the baths, was of great variety, and very costly; and these buildings were supported by pillars of single stones on every side: the walls also and the floors of

the edifices were paved with stones of several colors. He also had cut many and great pits, as reservoirs for water, out of the rocks, at every one of the places that were inhabited, both above and round about the palace, and before the wall; and by this contrivance he endeavored to have water for several uses, as if there had been fountains there. Here was also a road digged from the palace, and leading to the very top of the mountain, which yet could not be seen by such as were without [the walls]; nor indeed could enemies easily make use of the plain roads; for the road on the east side, as we have already taken notice, could not be walked upon by reason of its nature; and for the western road, he built a large tower at its narrowest place, at no less a distance from the top of the hill than a thousand cubits; which tower could not possibly be passed by, nor could it be easily taken; nor indeed could those that walked along it without any fear (such was its contrivance) easily get to the end of it: and after such a manner was this citadel fortified, both by nature and by the hands of men, in order to frustrate the attacks of enemies.

4. As for the furniture that was within this fortress, it was still more wonderful on account of its splendor and long continuance; for here was laid up corn in large quantities, and such as would subsist men for a long time; here was also wine and oil in abundance, with all kinds of pulse[3] and dates heaped up together: all which Eleazar found there when he and his *Sicarii*[4] got possession of the fortress by treachery. These fruits were also fresh and full ripe, and no way inferior to such fruits newly laid in, although they were little short of a hundred years from the laying in these provisions [by Herod] till the place was taken by the Romans: nay, indeed, when the Romans got possession of those fruits that were left, they found them not corrupted all that while: nor should we be mistaken if we supposed that the air was here the cause of their enduring so long, this fortress being so high, and so free from the mixture of all terrene[5] and muddy particles of matter. There was also found here a large quantity of all sorts of weapons of war, which had been treasured up by that king, and were sufficient for ten thousand men; there was cast iron, and brass, and tin, which show that he had taken much pains to have all things here ready for the greatest occasions; for the report goes how Herod thus prepared this fortress on his own account, as a refuge against two kinds of danger: the one for fear of the multitude of the Jews, lest they should depose him and restore their former kings to the government; the other danger was greater and more terrible, which arose from Cleopatra, queen of Egypt, who did not conceal her intentions, but spoke often to Antony, and desired him to cut off Herod, and entreated him to bestow the kingdom of Judea upon her. And certainly it is a great wonder that Antony did never comply with her commands in this point, as he was so miserably enslaved to his passion for her; nor should any one have

been surprised if she had been gratified in such her request. So the fear of these dangers made Herod rebuild Masada, and thereby leave it for the finishing-stroke of the Romans in this Jewish war.

5. Since, therefore, the Roman commander Silva had now built a wall on the outside, round about this whole place, as we have said already, and had thereby made a most accurate provision to prevent any one of the besieged running away, he undertook the siege itself, though he found but one single place that would admit of the banks he was to raise; for behind that tower which secured the road that led to the palace, and to the top of the hill from the west, there was a certain eminency of the rock, very broad and very prominent, but three hundred cubits beneath the highest part of Masada; it was called the White Promontory. Accordingly he got upon that part of the rock, and ordered the army to bring earth; and when they fell to that work with alacrity, and abundance of them together, the bank was raised, and became solid for two hundred cubits in height. Yet was not this bank thought sufficiently high for the use of the engines that were to be set upon it; but still another elevated work of great stones compacted together was raised upon that bank: this was fifty cubits, both in breadth and height. The other machines that were now got ready were like to those that had been first devised by Vespasian, and afterward by Titus, for sieges. There was also a tower made of the height of sixty cubits, and all over plated with iron, out of which the Romans threw darts and stones from the engines, and soon made those that fought from the walls of the place to retire, and would not let them lift up their heads above the works. At the same time Silva ordered that great battering-ram which he had made, to be brought thither, and to be set against the wall, and to make frequent batteries against it, which with some difficulty broke down a part of the wall, and quite overthrew it. However, the *Sicarii* made haste, and presently built another wall within that, which should not be liable to the same misfortune from the machines with the other: it was made soft and yielding, and so was capable of avoiding the terrible blows that affected the other. It was framed after the following manner:—They laid together great beams of wood lengthways, one close to the end of another, and the same way in which they were cut: there were two of these rows parallel to one another, and laid at such a distance from each other, as the breadth of the wall required, and earth was put into the space between those rows. Now, that the earth might not fall away upon the elevation of this bank to a greater height, they farther laid other beams over across them, and thereby bound those beams together that lay lengthways. This work of theirs was like a real edifice; and when the machines were applied, the blows were weakened by its yielding; and as the materials by such concussion were shaken closer together, the pile by that means becamer

firmer than before. When Silva saw this, he thought it best to endeavor the taking of this wall by setting fire to it; so he gave order that the soldiers should throw a great number of burning torches upon it: accordingly, as it was chiefly made of wood, it soon took fire; and when it was once set on fire, its hollowness made that fire spread to mighty flame. Now, at the very beginning of this fire, a north wind that then blew proved terrible to the Romans: for by bringing the flame downward, it drove it upon them, and they were almost in despair of success, as fearing their machines would be burnt: but after this, on a sudden the wind changed into the south, as if it were done by divine Providence; and blew strongly the contrary way, and carried the flame, and drove it against the wall, which was now on fire through its entire thickness. So the Romans, having now assistance from God, returned to their camp with joy, and resolved to attack their enemies the very next day; on which occasion they set their watch more carefully that night, lest any of the Jews should run away from them without being discovered.

6. However, neither did Eleazar once think of flying away, nor would he permit any one else to do so; but when he saw their wall burnt down by the fire, and could devise no other way of escaping, or room for their farther courage, and setting before their eyes what the Romans would do to them, their children, and their wives, if they got them into their power, he consulted about having them all slain. Now, as he judged this to be the best thing they could do in their present circumstances, he gathered the most courageous of his companions together, and encouraged them to take that course by a speech which he made to them in the manner following:—"Since we, long ago, my generous friends, resolved never to be servants to the Romans, nor to any other than to God himself, who alone is the true and just Lord of mankind, the time is now come that obliges us to make that resolution true in practice. And let us not at this time bring a reproach upon ourselves for self-contradiction, while we formerly would not undergo slavery, though it were then without danger, but must now, together with slavery, choose such punishments also as are intolerable; I mean this, upon the supposition that the Romans once reduce us under their power while we are alive. We were the very first that revolted from them, and we are the last that fight against them; and I cannot but esteem it as a favor that God hath granted us, that it is still in our power to die bravely, and in a state of freedom, which hath not been the case of others, who were conquered unexpectedly. It is very plain that we shall be taken within a day's time; but it is still an eligible thing to die after a glorious manner, together with our dearest friends. This is what our enemies themselves cannot by any means hinder, although they be very desirous to take us alive. Nor can we propose to ourselves any more to fight them, and beat them: It had been proper indeed for us to have

conjectured at the purpose of God much sooner, and at the very first, when we were so desirous of defending our liberty, and when we received such sore treatment from one another, and worse treatment from our enemies, and to have been sensible that the same God, who had of old taken the Jewish nation into his favor, had now condemned them to destruction; for had he either continued favorable, or been but in a lesser degree displeased with us, he had not overlooked the destruction of so many men, or delivered his most holy city to be burnt and demolished by our enemies. To be sure, we weakly hoped to have preserved ourselves, and ourselves alone, still in a state of freedom, as if we had been guilty of no sins ourselves against God, nor been partners with those of others; we also taught other men to preserve their liberty. Wherefore, consider how God hath convinced us that our hopes were in vain, by bringing such distress upon us in the desperate state we are now in, and which is beyond all our expectations; for the nature of this fortress, which was in itself unconquerable, hath not proved a means of our deliverance; and even while we have still great abundance of food and a great quantity of arms, and other necessaries more than we want, we are openly deprived by God himself of all hope of deliverance; for that fire which was driven upon our enemies did not, of its own accord, turn back upon the wall which we had built: this was the effect of God's anger against us for our manifold sins, which we have been guilty of in a most insolent and extravagant manner with regard to our own countrymen; the punishments of which let us not receive from the Romans, but from God himself, as executed by our own hands, for these will be more moderate than the other. Let our wives die before they are abused, and our children before they have tasted of slavery; and after we have slain them, let us bestow that glorious benefit upon one another mutually and preserve ourselves in freedom, as an excellent funeral monument for us. But first let us destroy our money and the fortress by fire; for I am well assured that this will be a great grief to the Romans, that they shall not be able to seize upon our bodies, and shall fail of our wealth also: and let us spare nothing but our provisions; for they will be a testimonial when we are dead that we are not subdued for want of necessaries; but that, according to our original resolution, we have preferred death before slavery."

7. This was Eleazar's speech to them. Yet did not the opinions of all the auditors, acquiesce therein; but although some of them were very zealous to put his advice in practice, and were in a manner filled with pleasure at it, and thought death to be a good thing, yet had those that were most effeminate a commiseration for their wives and families; and when these men were especially moved by the prospect of their own certain death, they looked wistfully at one another, and by the tears that were in their eyes, declared their dissent from his opinion. When Eleazar saw these people in such fear, and that their

souls were dejected at so prodigious a proposal, he was afraid lest perhaps these effeminate persons should, by their lamentations and tears, enfeeble those that heard what he had said courageously; so he did not leave off exhorting them, but stirred up himself, and recollecting proper arguments for raising their courage, he undertook to speak more briskly and fully to them, and that concerning the immortality of the soul. So he made a lamentable groan, and fixing his eyes intently on those that wept, he spake thus:—"Truly, I was greatly mistaken when I thought to be assisting to brave men who struggle hard for their liberty, and to such as were resolved either to live with honor, or else to die; but I find that you are such people as are no better than others, either in virtue or in courage, and are afraid of dying, though you be delivered thereby from the greatest miseries, while you ought to make no delay in this matter, nor to await any one to give you good advice; for the laws of our country, and of God himself, have, from ancient times, and as soon as ever we could use our reason, continually taught us, and our forefathers have corroborated the same doctrine by their actions and by their bravery of mind, that it is life that is a calamity to men, and not death; for this last affords our souls their liberty, and sends them by a removal into their own place of purity, where they are to be insensible of all sorts of misery; for while souls are tied down to a mortal body, they are partakers of its miseries; and really, to speak the truth, they are themselves dead; for the union of what is divine to what is mortal is disagreeable. It is true, the power of the soul is great, even when it is imprisoned in a mortal body; for by moving it after a way that is invisible, it makes the body a sensible instrument, and causes it to advance farther in its actions than mortal nature could otherwise do. However, when it is freed from that weight which draws it down to the earth and is connected with it, it obtains its own proper place, and does then become a partaker of that blessed power, and those abilities, which are then every way incapable of being hindered in their operations. It continues invisible, indeed to the eyes of men, as does God himself; for certainly it is not itself seen, while it is in the body; for it is there after an invisible manner, and when it is freed from it, it is still not seen. It is this soul which hath one nature, and that an incorruptible one also; but yet is it the cause of the change that is made in the body; for whatsoever it be which the soul touches, that lives and flourishes; and from whatsoever it is removed, that withers away and dies: such a degree is there in it of immortality. Let me produce the state of sleep as a most evident demonstration of the truth of what I say; wherein souls, when the body does not distract them, have the sweetest rest depending on themselves, and conversing with God, by their alliance to him; they then go everywhere, and foretell many futurities, beforehand; and why are we afraid of death, while we are pleased with the rest that we have in sleep? and how absurd a thing is it to pursue after liberty while we are alive, and yet to envy it to our-selves where it will be eternal! We, therefore, who have been brought up in a discipline of our own, ought to become an example to others of our readiness to die; yet if we do not stand in need of foreigners to support us in this mat-ter, let us regard those Indians who profess the exercise of philosophy; for these good men do but unwillingly undergo the time of life, and look upon it as a necessary servitude, and make haste to let their souls loose from their bodies; nay, when no misfortune presses them to it, nor drives them upon it, these have such a desire of a life of immortality, that they tell other men beforehand that they are about to depart; and nobody hinders them, but every one thinks them happy men, and gives them letters to be carried to their familiar friends [that are dead]; so firmly and certainly do they believe that souls converse with one another [in the other world]. So when these men have heard all such commands that were to be given them, they deliver their body to the fire; and, in order to their getting their soul a separation from the body, in the greatest purity, they die in the midst of hymns of commendations made to them; for their dearest friends conduct them to their death more readily than do any of the rest of mankind conduct their fellow-citizens when they are going a very long jour-ney, who, at the same time, weep on their own account, but look upon the others as happy persons, as so soon to be made partakers of the immortal order of beings. Are not we, therefore, ashamed to have lower notions than the Indians? and by our own cowardice to lay a base reproach upon the laws of our country, which are so much desired and imitated by all mankind? But put the case that we had been brought up under another persuasion and taught that life is the greatest good which men are capable of, and that death is a calami-ty; however, the circumstances we are now in ought to be an inducement to us to bear such calamity courageously, since it is by the will of God, and by neces-sity, that we are to die; for it now appears that God hath made such a decree against the whole Jewish nation, that we are to be deprived of this life which [he knew] we would not make a due use of; for do not you ascribe the occa-sion of your present condition to yourselves, nor think the Romans are the true occasion that this war we have had with them is become so destructive to us all: these things have not come to pass by their power, but a more powerful cause hath intervened, and made us afford them an occasion of their appear-ing to be conquerors over us.

What Roman weapons, I pray you, were those by which the Jews of Cesarea were slain? On the contrary, when they were no way disposed to rebel, but were all the while keeping their seventh day festival, and did not so much as lift up their hands against the citizens of Cesarea, yet did those citizens run upon them in great crowds, and cut their throats, and the throats of their wives and children, and this without any regard to the Romans themselves, who never took us for their enemies till we revolted from them. But some may be ready to say, that truly the people of Cesarea had always a quarrel against those that lived among them, and that when an opportunity offered itself, they only satisfied the old rancor they had against them. What then shall we say to those of Scythopolis, who ventured to wage war with us on account of the Greeks? Nor did they do it by way of revenge upon the Romans, when they acted in concert with our countrymen. Wherefore you see how little our good-will and fidelity to them profited us, while they were slain, they and their whole families after the most inhuman manner, which was all the requital that was made them for the assistance they had afforded the others; for that very same destruction which they had prevented from falling upon the others, did they suffer themselves from them, as if they had been ready to be the actors against them. It would be too long for me to speak at this time of every destruction brought upon us; for you cannot but know that there was not any one Syrian city which did not slay their Jewish inhabitants, and were not more bitter enemies to us than were the Romans themselves: nay, even those of Damascus, when they were able to allege no tolerable pretence against us, filled their city with the most barbarous slaughter of our people, and cut the throats of eighteen thousand Jews, with their wives and children. And as to the multitude of those that were slain in Egypt, and that with torments also, we have been informed they were more than sixty thousand; those, indeed, being in a foreign country, and so naturally meeting with nothing to oppose against their enemies, were killed in the manner forementioned. As for all those of us who have waged war against the Romans in our own country, had we not sufficient reason to have sure hopes of victory? For we had arms, and walls, and fortresses so prepared as not to be easily taken, and courage not to be moved by any dangers in the cause of liberty, which encouraged us all to revolt from the Romans. But then, these advantages sufficed us but for a short time, and only raised our hopes, while they really appeared to be the origin of our miseries; for all we had hath been taken from us, and all hath fallen under our enemies, as if these advantages were only to render their victory over us the more glorious, and were not disposed for the preservation of those by whom these preparations were made. And as for those that are already dead in the war, it is reasonable we should esteem them blessed, for they are dead in defending, and not in betraying their liberty; but as to the multitude of those that are now under the Romans, who would not pity their condition? and who would not make haste to die, before he would suffer the same miseries with them? Some of them have been put upon the rack, and tortured with fire and whippings, and so died. Some have been half-devoured by wild beasts, and yet have been reserved alive to be devoured by them a second time, in order to afford laughter and sport to our enemies; and such of those as are alive still are to be looked on as the most miserable, who, being so desirous of death, could not come at it. And where is now that great city, the metropolis of the Jewish nation, which was fortified by so many walls round about, which had so many fortresses and large towers to defend it, which could hardly contain the instruments prepared for the war, and which had so many ten thousands of men to fight for it? Where is this city that was believed to have God himself inhabiting therein? It is now demolished to the very foundations; and hath nothing but that monument of it preserved, I mean the camp of those that have destroyed it, which still dwells upon its ruins; some unfortunate old men also lie upon the ashes of the temple, and a few women are there preserved alive by the enemy, for our bitter shame and reproach. Now, who is there that revolves these things in his mind, and yet is able to bear the sight of the sun, though he might live out of danger? Who is there so much his country's enemy, or so unmanly, and so desirous of living, as not to repent that he is still alive? And I cannot but wish that we had all died before we had seen that holy city demolished by the hands of our enemies, or the foundations of our holy temple dug up after so profane a manner. But since we had a generous hope that deluded us, as if we might perhaps have been able to avenge ourselves on our enemies on that account, though it be now become vanity, and hath left us alone in this distress, let us make haste to die bravely. Let us pity ourselves, our children, and our wives, while it is in our power to show pity to them; for we are born to die, as well as those were whom we have begotten; nor is it in the power of the most happy of our race to avoid it. But for abuses and slavery, and the sight of our wives let away after an ignominious manner, with their children, these are not such evils as are natural and necessary among men; although such as do not prefer death before those miseries, when it is in their power so to do, must undergo even them, on account of their own cowardice. We revolted from the Romans with great pretensions to courage; and when, at the very last, they invited us to preserve ourselves, we would not comply with them. Who will not, therefore, believe that they will certainly be in a rage at us, in case they can take us alive? Miserable will then be the young men, who will be strong enough in their bodies to sustain many torments! miserable also will be those of elder years, who will not be able to bear those calamities which young men might sustain. One man will be obliged to hear the voice of his son imploring help of his father, when his hands are bound! But certainly our hands are still at liberty, and have a sword in them: let them be subservient to us in our glorious design; let us die before we become slaves under our enemies, and let us go out of the world, together with our children and our wives, in a state of freedom.

This it is that our laws command us to do; this it is that our wives and children crave at our hands; nay, God himself hath brought this necessity upon us; while the Romans desire the contrary, and are afraid lest any of us should die before we are taken. Let us therefore make haste, and instead of affording them so much pleasure, as they hope for in getting us under their power, let us leave them an example which shall at once cause their astonishment at our death, and their admiration of our hardiness therein."

## Antiquities of the Jews.

### *Preface*

1. Those who undertake to write histories do not, I perceive, take that trouble on one and the same account, but for many reasons, and those such as are very different one from another; for some of them apply themselves to this part of learning to show their skill in composition, and that they may therein acquire a reputation for speaking finely; others of them there are who write histories, in order to gratify those that happened to be concerned in them, and on that account have spared no pains, but rather go beyond their own abilities in the performance; but others there are, who, of necessity and by force, are driven to write history, because they are concerned in the facts, and so cannot excuse themselves from committing them to writing, for the advantage of posterity; nay, there are not a few who are induced to draw their historical facts out of darkness into light, and to produce them for the benefit of the public on account of the great importance of the facts themselves with which they have been concerned. Now of these several reasons for writing history, I must profess the two last were my own reasons also; for since I was myself interested in that war which we Jews had with the Romans, and knew myself its particular actions, and what conclusion it had, I was forced to give the history of it, because I saw that others perverted the truth of those actions in their writings.

2. Now I have undertaken the present work, as thinking it will appear to all the Greeks worthy of their study; for it will contain all our antiquities, and the constitution of our government, as interpreted out of the Hebrew Scriptures; and indeed I did formerly intend, when I wrote of the war,[6] to explain who the Jews originally were,—what fortunes they had been subjected to,—and by what legislator they had been instructed in piety, and the exercise of other virtues,—what wars also they had made in remote ages, till they were unwillingly engaged in this last with the Romans; but because this work would take up a great compass, I separated it into a set treatise by itself, with a beginning of its own, and its own conclusion; but in process of time, as usually happens to such as undertake great things, I grew weary, and went on slowly, it being a large subject, and a difficult thing to translate our history into a

foreign, and to us unaccustomed, language. However, some persons there were who desired to know our history, and so exhorted me to go on with it; and, above all the rest, Epaphroditus, a man who is a lover of all kind of learning, but is principally delighted with the knowledge of history; and this on account of his having been himself concerned in great affairs, and many turns of fortune, and having shown a wonderful vigor of an excellent nature, and an immovable virtuous resolution in them all. I yielded to this man's persuasions, who always excites such as have abilities in what is useful and acceptable, to join their endeavors with his. I was also ashamed myself to permit any laziness of disposition to have a greater influence upon me than the delight of taking pains in such studies as were very useful: I thereupon stirred up myself, and went on with my work more cheerfully. Besides the foregoing motives, I had others which I greatly reflected on; and these were, that our forefathers were willing to communicate such things to others; and that some of the Greeks took considerable pains to know the affairs of our nation.

3. I found, therefore, that the second of the Ptolemies was a king who was extraordinarily diligent in what concerned learning and the collection of books; that he was also peculiarly ambitious to procure a translation of our law, and of the constitution of our government therein contained, into the Greek tongue. Now Eleazar, the high priest, one not inferior to any other of that dignity among us, did not envy the forenamed king the participation of that advantage, which otherwise he would for certain have denied him, but that he knew the custom of our nation was, to hinder nothing of what we esteemed ourselves from being communicated to others. Accordingly, I thought it became me both to imitate the generosity of our high priest, and to suppose there might even now be many lovers of learning like the king; for he did not obtain all our writings at that time; but those who were sent to Alexandria as interpreters, gave him only the books of the law, while there were a vast number of other matters in our sacred books. They indeed contain in them the history of five thousand years; in which time happened many strange accidents, many chances of war, and great actions of the commanders, and mutations of the form of our government. Upon the whole, a man that will peruse this history, may principally learn from it, that all events succeed well, even to an incredible degree, and the reward of felicity is proposed by God; but then it is to those that follow his will, and do not venture to break his excellent laws;— and that so far as men any way apostatize from the accurate observation of them, what was practicable before, becomes impracticable; and whatsoever they set about as a good thing is converted into an incurable calamity;—and now I exhort all those that peruse these books to apply their minds to God; and to examine the mind of our legislator, whether he hath not understood his

nature in a manner worthy of him; and hath not ever ascribed to him such operations as become his power, and hath not preserved his writings from those indecent fables which others have framed, although, by the great distance of time when he lived, he might have securely forged such lies; for he lived two thousand years ago; at which vast distance of ages the poets themselves have not been so hardy as to fix even the generations of their gods, much less the actions of their men, or their own laws. As I proceed, therefore, I shall accurately describe what is contained in our records, in the order of time that belongs to them; for I have already promised so to do throughout this undertaking, and this without adding anything to what is therein contained, or taking away anything therefrom.

4. But because almost all our constitution depends on the wisdom of Moses, our legislator, I cannot avoid saying somewhat concerning him beforehand, though I shall do it briefly; I mean, because otherwise those that read my book may wonder how it comes to pass that my discourse, which promises an account of laws and historical facts, contains so much of philosophy. The reader is therefore to know, that Moses deemed it exceeding necessary, that he who would conduct his own life well, and give laws to others, in the first place should consider the divine nature, and upon the contemplation of God's operations, should thereby imitate the best of all patterns, so far as it is possible for human nature to do, and to endeavor to follow after it, neither could the legislator himself have a right mind without such a contemplation; nor would anything he should write tend to the promotion of virtue in his readers; I mean, unless they be taught first of all, that God is the father and Lord of all things, and sees all things, and that thence he bestows a happy life upon those that follow him; but plunges such as do not walk in the paths of virtue into inevitable miseries. Now when Moses was desirous to teach this lesson to his countrymen, he did not begin the establishment of his laws after the same manner that other legislators did; I mean, upon contracts and other rites between one man and another, but by raising their minds upwards to regard God, and his creation of the world; and by persuading them, that we men are the most excellent of the creatures of God upon earth. Now when once he had brought them to submit to religion, he easily persuaded them to submit in all other things; for, as to other legislators, they followed fables, and, by their discourses, transferred the most reproachful of human vices unto the gods, and so afforded wicked men the most plausible excuses for their crimes; but, as for our legislator, when he had once demonstrated that God was possessed of perfect virtue, he supposed that man also ought to strive after the participation of it; and on those who did not so think and so believe he inflicted the severest punishments. I exhort, therefore, my readers to examine this whole undertak-

ing in that view; for thereby it will appear to them that there is nothing therein disagreeable either to the majesty of God, or to his love to mankind; for all things have here a reference to the nature of the universe; while our legislator speaks some things wisely, but enigmatically, and others under a decent allegory, but still explains such things as required a direct explication plainly and expressly. However those that have a mind to know the reason of everything, may find here a very curious philosophical theory, which I now indeed shall waive the explication of; but if God afford me time for it, I will set about writing it after I have finished the present work. I shall now betake myself to the history before me, after I have first mentioned what Moses says of the creation of the world, which I find described in the sacred books after the manner following.

## Notes

[1] A furlong is about 200 meters.

[2] A cubit is about 18 inches.

[3] Peas and beans.

[4] Nationalist Jewish followers of Eleazer; the name comes from *sicae*, meaning daggers.

[5] Earthy.

[6] A reference to his book on *The Wars of the Jews*.

# The Apostles' Creed

This creed (from *credo*, Latin for "I believe") is one of the most widely used statements of Christian faith. Its title is based on a legend that it was composed by the Apostles on the tenth day after Jesus ascended into heaven. In fact it was developed over a number of centuries. The first written form may be the Interrogatory Creed of Hippolytus (ca. 215 C.E.).

The function of a creed is to define and delimit what is orthodox (meaning "correct teaching or doctrine"), and thus what is heretical (heretical beliefs, or heresies—the word comes from the Greek *haireisthai*, "to choose," and in this context means to make the wrong choice of what to believe—are Christian beliefs at variance with those considered authoritative or orthodox). The statement that Jesus suffered and died contrasts with the views of some early Christians that Jesus never really took human form and thus could not suffer pain or death.

As currently used by Protestants, the Apostles' Creed often omits the assertion that Jesus descended into hell, and usually glosses the phrase "holy catholic church," pointing out that this does not refer to the Roman Catholic church, but means that the church is universal.

MM

# The Apostles' Creed

I believe in God the Father Almighty, Maker of heaven and earth.

And in Jesus Christ his only Son our Lord; who was conceived by the Holy Ghost, born of the Virgin Mary, suffered under Pontius Pilate, was crucified, dead, and buried; he descended into hell; the third day he rose again from the dead; he ascended into heaven, and sitteth on the right hand of God the Father Almighty; from thence he shall come to judge the quick and the dead.

I believe in the Holy Ghost; the holy catholic Church; the communion of saints; the forgiveness of sins; the resurrection of the body; and the life everlasting. AMEN.

# II. Ancient North Africa

## INTRODUCTION

The development of literature in North Africa follows much the same evolutionary path as the literature of Southwest Asia. Scholars believe that the Egyptians borrowed the notion of writing from the Sumerians, but for some reason did not adopt cuneiform script. Instead, around 2600 B.C.E. the Egyptians created hieroglyphics, a writing system characterized by almost a thousand signs representing specific objects. Eventually, the language developed to the point that the signs represented sounds. Whereas the Semitic languages of Southwest Asia are read from right to left, Egyptian hieroglyphics could be arranged to read vertically, right to left, or left to right. From Egypt, the Kushites then adopted the hieroglyphic script, but just as we saw with the spread of cuneiform, the Kushites simplified the signs to a more manageable number—23, which represented the alphabet. Like the Semitic languages, it was read from right to left. This second oldest language of Africa is known as Meroitic, after one of the most prominent cities of ancient Kush, Meroë. Both Egypt and Kush eventually developed cursive script, a system much less cumbersome than hieroglyphics.

The Egyptian language was deciphered in the early nineteenth century when a trilingual inscription (the Rosetta Stone) was discovered by Napoleon's soldiers. On the Stone, the same passage was inscribed in three scripts: Greek, demotic (the Egyptian cursive script) and hieroglyphic. Because scholars could translate the Greek, they soon cracked the code for deciphering the Egyptian scripts. Meroitic is still largely undeciphered, and so much of the literature of ancient Kush remains a mystery. The texts we do have were those that the Kushites composed in Egyptian, their second language.

The literature of ancient North Africa was written on wood and papyrus; it was inscribed on the stone of temples and painted on tomb walls. Papyrus was readily available and inexpensive, but both wood and papyrus are perishable and susceptible to decay. The scribal class produced libraries of literature but again few survived. Indeed, tombs and temples preserved most of our current collection of ancient Egyptian literature. Tombs kept the papyrus and frescoes in a relatively stable, climate controlled environment while the temple inscriptions, buried along with the stone blocks upon which they were carved, were preserved by the sand that covered them.

Because tombs and temples are our two main sources for literature, religious themes predominate. From the poetic Book of the Dead to the prosaic Story of Sinuhe, we read theological reflections on death and afterlife. Because both the body and spirit of an individual were thought to carry over into the afterlife, we find many examples of autobiography and biography, literature intended to emphasize the virtuous life of the deceased and ensure a good reception in the netherworld. Many prayers survived, and as the Hymn to Hapy (the Nile River) demonstrates, the Egyptians could be effusive in their thanks for the stable and benevolent land in which they lived. Lastly, we find prophetic literature, though this genre is not as widely attested from North Africa as it is in Southwest Asia. The most prominent example is the Prophecies of Neferti, a text which in its predictions of civil unrest and dynastic change appears to be a work of political propaganda written well after the time period depicted in the story.

Literature of a more secular nature has also survived, thanks in part to learned elite who had their personal libraries entombed along with them. The *Instruction of Amenemope*, often compared to the biblical book of Proverbs, is an Egyptian contribution to the genre of wisdom literature. Couched as the advice of a father to a son, it is a guide to right living with an emphasis on just behavior and honesty. Scholars believe that the ethical teachings of North African didactic literature, like the *Instruction of Amenemope*, influenced later Israelite wisdom and prophetic literature. Several Love Songs, found in the excavated domestic quarters of an Egyptian village, give voice to women and lovers. The Songs touch on personal relationships in a way rarely found in national literature. Moreover, their provenance bespeaks the literary predilections of the working class.

Of course, the temple complex was central to the dissemination of royal edicts and propaganda. Battle chronicles and memorial accounts were inscribed in verse, with accompanying relief, on temple edifices so that both the literate and the illiterate could perceive royal power. From the Temple of Amun in Nubia, the *Election Stela of Aspelta* documents political aspects of the king's reign.

Over the course of millennia, North Africa became less isolated from the rest of the Mediterranean world. Egyptian and Meroitic eventually gave way to Greek as the *lingua franca*. North African deities and theology merged with those of the Greco-Roman world. The distinctive flavor of North Africa was lost to the cosmopolitan world of the Mediterranean by the third century C.E.

Fortunately, that distinctive flavor is preserved in literature to be appreciated anew by students of the humanities.

KP

# The Story of Sinuhe

The Story of Sinuhe is the most popular prose work to survive from the Middle Kingdom, 2050–1785 B.C.E. This period saw central authority reestablished in the figure of the pharaoh; Egypt was a united kingdom once again. This political success was fragile, however; its tenuousness is hinted at by the Story of Sinuhe itself. While the Story relates key events in the life of its title character, Sinuhe, because of his political position as a high court official (of the harem) the Story necessarily relates, and is perhaps most fundamentally concerned with, broader themes of political stability and political loyalty. The Story is autobiographical, told in the first person by Sinuhe himself. But it is a political autobiography of a traitor returned home. Three times Sinuhe "explains" why he fled Egypt, first to the reader, then to his host and father-in-law, Ammunenshi, and finally to the new pharaoh, Sesostris.

The Story of Sinuhe draws many contrasts between Egyptian life and the life Sinuhe leads abroad in Syria. The pharaoh Sesostris himself points to these differences as a lure to get Sinuhe to return to Egypt. With the closing of the Story it becomes clear that Sinuhe is home in his own tomb and that the entire story is a tomb inscription. In this ancient Egyptian story you *can* go home again, for your tomb in your homeland is the proper and true home for your immortal soul. The Story is propagandistic, praising the kindly concerned pharaoh, the shepherd of his people.

This piece of literature is not the only one from the Ancient World that relates how a main character leaves his home, has adventures, then returns home: e.g., *The Epic of Gilgamesh* and Homer's *Odyssey* use this narrative structure.

JM

148

# The Story of Sinuhe

(R, 1) The Prince, Count, Governor of the domains of the sovereign in the lands of the Asiatics,[1] true and beloved Friend of the King, the Attendant Sinuhe, says:

I was an attendant who attended his lord, a servant of the royal harem, waiting on the Princess, the highly praised Royal Wife of King Sesostris[2] in Khenemsut, the daughter of King Amenemhet in Kanefru, Nefru, the revered.

Year 30, third month of the inundation, day 7: the god ascended to his horizon. The King of Upper and Lower Egypt, *Sehetepibre*,[3] flew to heaven and united with the sun-disk, the divine body merging with its maker. Then the residence was hushed; hearts grieved; the great portals were shut; (10) the courtiers were head-on-knee; the people moaned.

His majesty, however, had despatched an army to the land of the Tjemeh, with his eldest son as its commander, the good god Sesostris. He had been sent to smite the foreign lands and to punish those of Tjehenu.[4] (15) Now he was returning, bringing captives of the Tjehenu and cattle of all kinds beyond number. The officials of the palace sent to the western border to let the king's son know the event that had occurred at the court. The messengers met him on the road, (20) reaching him at night. Not a moment did he delay. The falcon flew with his attendants, without letting his army know it.

But the royal sons who had been with him on this expedition had also been sent for. (B, 1) One of them was summoned while I was standing (there). I heard his voice, as he spoke, while I was in the near distance. My heart fluttered, my arms spread out, a trembling befell all my limbs. I removed myself in leaps, to seek a hiding place. I put (5) myself between two bushes, so as to leave the road to its traveler.

I set out southward.[5] I did not plan to go to the residence. I believed there would be turmoil and did not expect to survive it. I crossed Maaty near Sycamore; I reached Isle-of-Snefru. I spent the day there at the edge (10) of the cultivation. Departing at dawn I encountered a man who stood on the road. He saluted me while I was afraid of him. At dinner time I reached "Cattle-Quay." I crossed in a barge without a rudder, by the force of the westwind. I passed to the east of the quarry, (15) at the height of "Mistress of the Red Mountain." Then I made my way northward. I reached the "Walls of the Ruler," which were made to repel the Asiatics and to crush the Sand-farers. I crouched in a bush for fear of being seen by the guard on duty upon the wall.

I set out (20) at night. At dawn I reached Peten. I halted at "Isle-of-Kem-Wer." An attack of thirst overtook me; I was parched, my throat burned. I said, "This is the taste of death." I raised my heart and collected myself when I heard the lowing sound of cattle (25) and saw Asiatics. One of their leaders, who had been in Egypt, recognized me. He gave me water and boiled milk for me. I went with him to his tribe. What they did for me was good.

Land gave me to land. I traveled to Byblos; I returned to Qedem. I spent (30) a year and a half there. Then Ammunenshi, the ruler of Upper Retenu, took me to him, saying to me: "You will be happy with me; you will hear the language of Egypt." He said this because he knew my character and had heard of my skill, Egyptians who were with him having borne witness for me. He said to me: "Why (35) have you come here? Has something happened at the residence?" I said to him: "King Sehetepibre departed to the horizon, and one did not know the circumstances." But I spoke in half-truths: "When I returned from the expedition to the land of the Tjemeh, it was reported to me and my heart grew faint. It carried (40) me away on the path of flight, though I had not been talked about; no one had spat in my face; I had not heard a reproach; my name had not been heard in the mouth of the herald. I do not know what brought me to this country; it is as if planned by god. As if a Delta-man saw himself in Yebu, a marsh-man in Nubia."

Then he said to me: "How then is that land without that excellent god, fear of whom was throughout (45) the lands like Sakhmet in a year of plague?" I said to him in reply: "Of course his son has entered into the palace, having taken his father's heritage.

> He is a god without peer,
> No other comes before him;
> He is lord of knowledge, wise planner, skilled leader,
> One goes and comes by (50) his will.
>
> He was the smiter of foreign lands,
> While his father stayed in the palace,
> He reported to him on commands carried out.
>
> He is a champion who acts with his arm,
> A fighter who has no equal,
> When seen engaged in archery,
> When joining the melee.
>
> Horn-curber who makes hands turn weak,
> His foes (55) can not close ranks;
> Keen-sighted he smashes foreheads,
> None can withstand his presence.

Wide-striding he smites the fleeing,
No retreat for him who turns him his back;
Steadfast in time of attack,
He makes turn back and turns not his back.

Stouthearted when he sees the mass,
He lets not slackness fill his heart;
(60) Eager at the sight of combat,
Joyful when he works his bow.

Clasping his shield he treads under foot,
No second blow needed to kill;
None can escape his arrow,
None turn aside his bow.

The Bowmen flee before him,
As before the might of the goddess;
As he fights he plans the goal,
(65) Unconcerned about all else.

Lord of grace, rich in kindness,
He has conquered through affection;
His city loves him more than itself,
Acclaims him more than its own god.

Men outdo women in hailing him,
Now that he is king;
Victor while yet in the egg,
Set to be ruler since his birth.

Augmenter of those born with him,
(70) He is unique, god-given;
Happy the land that he rules!

Enlarger of frontiers,
He will conquer southern lands,
While ignoring northern lands,
Though made to smite Asiatics and tread on Sand-farers!

"Send to him! Let him know your name as one who inquires while being far from his majesty. He will not fail to do (75) good to a land that will be loyal to him."

He said to me: "Well then, Egypt is happy knowing that he is strong. But you are here. You shall stay with me. What I shall do for you is good."

He set me at the head of his children. He married me to his eldest daughter. He let me choose for myself of his land, (80) of the best that was his, on his border with another land. It was a good land called Yaa. Figs were in it and grapes. It had more wine than water. Abundant was its honey, plentiful its oil. All kinds of fruit were on its trees. Barley was there and emmer, and no end of cattle of all kinds.

(85) Much also came to me because of the love of me; for he had made me chief of a tribe in the best part of his land. Loaves were made for me daily, and wine as daily fare, cooked meat, roast fowl, as well as desert game. (90) For they snared for me and laid it before me, in addition to the catch of my hounds. Many sweets were made for me, and milk dishes of all kinds.

I passed many years, my children becoming strong men, each a master of his tribe. The envoy who came north or went south to the residence (95) stayed with me. I let everyone stay with me. I gave water to the thirsty; I showed the way to him who had strayed; I rescued him who had been robbed. When Asiatics conspired to attack the Rulers of Hill-Countries, I opposed their movements. For this ruler of (100) Retenu made me carry out numerous missions as commander of his troops. Every hill tribe against which I marched I vanquished, so that it was driven from the pasture of its wells. I plundered its cattle, carried off its families, seized their food, and killed people (105) by my strong arm, by my bow, by my movements and my skillful plans. I won his heart and he loved me, for he recognized my valor. He set me at the head of his children, for he saw the strength of my arms.

> There came a hero of Retenu,
> To challenge me (110) in my tent.
> A champion was he without peer,
> He had subdued it all.
> He said he would fight with me,
> He planned to plunder me,
> He meant to seize my cattle
> At the behest of his tribe.

The ruler conferred with me and I said: "I do not know him; I am not his ally, (115) that I could walk about in his camp. Have I ever opened his back rooms or climbed over his fence? It is envy, because he sees me doing your commissions. I am indeed like a stray bull in a strange herd, whom the bull of the herd charges, (120) whom the longhorn attacks. Is an inferior beloved when he becomes a superior? No Asiatic makes friends with a Delta-man. And what would make papyrus cleave to the mountain? If a bull loves combat, should a champion bull retreat for fear of being equaled? (125) If he wishes to fight, let him declare his wish. Is there a god who does not know what he has ordained, and a man who knows how it will be?"

At night I strung my bow, sorted my arrows, practiced with my dagger, polished my weapons. When it dawned Retenu came. (130) It had assembled its tribes; it had gathered its neighboring peoples; it was intent on this combat.

He came toward me while I waited, having placed myself near him. Every heart burned for me; the women jabbered. All hearts ached for me thinking: "Is there another champion who could fight him?" He <raised> his battle-axe and shield, (135) while his armful of missiles fell toward me. When I had made his weapons attack me, I let his arrows pass me by without effect, one following the other. Then, when he charged me, I shot him, my arrow sticking in his neck. He screamed; he fell on his nose; (140) I slew him with his axe. I raised my war cry over his back, while every Asiatic shouted. I gave praise to Mont, while his people mourned him. The ruler Ammunenshi took me in his arms.

Then I carried off his goods; I plundered his cattle. What he had meant to do (145) to me I did to him. I took what was in his tent; I stripped his camp. Thus I became great, wealthy in goods, rich in herds. It was the god who acted, so as to show mercy to one with whom he had been angry, whom he had made stray abroad. For today his heart is appeased.

> A fugitive fled (150) his surroundings—
>  I am famed at home.
> A laggard lagged from hunger—
>  I give bread to my neighbor.
> A man left his land in nakedness—
>  I have bright clothes, fine linen.
> A man ran for lack of one to send—
>  I am (155) rich in servants.
> My house is fine, my dwelling spacious—
>  My thoughts are at the palace!

Whichever god decreed this flight, have mercy, bring me home! Surely you will let me see the place in which my heart dwells! What is more important than that my corpse be buried in the land (160) in which I was born! Come to my aid! What if the happy event should occur! May god pity me! May he act so as to make happy the end of one whom he punished! May his heart ache for one whom he forced to live abroad! If he is truly appeased today, may he hearken to the prayer of one far away! May he return one whom he made roam the earth to the place from which he carried him off!

(165) May Egypt's king have mercy on me, that I may live by his mercy! May I greet the mistress of the land who is in the palace! May I hear

the commands of her children! Would that my body were young again! For old age has come; feebleness has overtaken me. My eyes are heavy, my arms weak; (170) my legs fail to follow. The heart is weary; death is near. May I be conducted to the city of eternity! May I serve the Mistress of All! May she speak well of me to her children; may she spend eternity above me!

Now when the majesty of King Kheperkare[6] was told of the condition in which I was, his majesty sent word (175) to me with royal gifts, in order, to gladden the heart of this servant like that of a foreign ruler. And the royal children who were in his palace sent me their messages. Copy of the decree brought to this servant concerning his return to Egypt:

Horus: Living in Births; the Two Ladies: Living in Births; the King of Upper and Lower Egypt: *Kheperkare*; the Son of Re: (180) *Sesostris*, who lives forever. Royal decree to the Attendant Sinuhe:

This decree of the King if brought to you to let you know: that you circled the foreign countries, going from Qedem to Retenu and giving you to land, was the counsel of your own heart. What had you done that one should act against you? You had not cursed, so that your speech would be reproved. You had not spoken against the counsel of the nobles, that your words should have been rejected. (185) This matter—it carried away your heart. It was not in my heart against you. This your heaven in the palace lives and prospers to this day. Her head is adorned with the kingship of the land; her children are in the palace. You will store riches which they give you; you will live on their bounty. Come back to Egypt! See the residence in which you lived! Kiss the ground at the great portals, mingle with the courtiers! For today (190) you have begun to age. You have lost a man's strength. Think of the day of burial, the passing into reveredness.

A night is made for you with ointments and wrappings from the hand of Tait.[7] A funeral procession is made for you on the day of burial; the mummy case is of gold, its head of lapis lazuli. The sky is above you as you lie in the hearse, oxen drawing you, musicians going before you. The dance of (195) the *mww*-dancers is done at the door of your tomb; the offering-list is read to you; sacrifice is made before your offering-stone. Your tomb-pillars, made of white stone, are among (those of) the royal children. You shall not die abroad! Not shall Asiatics inter you. You shall not be wrapped in the skin of a ram to serve as your coffin. Too long a roaming of the earth! Think of your corpse, come back!

This decree reached me while I was standing (200) in the midst of my tribe. When it had been read to me, I threw myself on my belly. Having touched the soil, I spread it on my chest. I strode around my camp shouting: "What compares with this which is done to a servant whom his heart led astray to alien lands? Truly good is the kindness that saves me from death! Your *ka* will grant me to reach my end, my body being at home!"

Copy of the reply to this decree:

The servant of the Palace, Sinuhe, (205) says: In very good peace! Regarding the matter of this flight which this servant did in his ignorance. It is your *ka*, O good god, lord of the Two Lands, which Re loves and which Mont lord of Thebes favors; and Amun lord of Thrones-of-the-Two-Lands, and Sobk-Re lord of Sumenu, and Horus, Hathor, Atum with his Ennead, and Sopdu-Neferbau-Semseru the Eastern Horus, and the Lady of Yemet—may she enfold your head—and the conclave upon the flood, and Min-Horus of the hill-countries, and Wereret lady of (210) Punt, Nut, Haroeris-Re, and all the gods of Egypt and the isles of the sea—may they give life and joy to your nostrils, may they endue you with their bounty, may they give you eternity without limit, infinity without bounds! May the fear of you resound in lowlands and highlands, for you have subdued all that the sun encircles! This is the prayer of this servant for his lord who saves from the West.

The lord of knowledge who knows people knew (215) in the majesty of the palace that this servant was afraid to say it. It is like a thing too great to repeat. The great god, the peer of Re, knows the heart of one who has served him willingly. This servant is in the hand of one who thinks about him. He is placed under his care. Your Majesty is the conquering Horus; your arms vanquish all lands. May then your Majesty command to have brought to you the prince of Meki from Qedem, (220) the mountain chiefs from Keshu, and the prince of Menus from the lands of the Fenkhu. They are rulers of renown who have grown up in the love of you. I do not mention Retenu—it belongs to you like your hounds.

Lo, this flight which the servant made—I did not plan it. It was not in my heart; I did not devise it. I do not know what removed me from my place. It was like (225) a dream. As if a Delta-man saw himself in Yebu, a marsh-man in Nubia. I was not afraid; no one ran after me. I had not heard a reproach; my name was not heard in the mouth of the herald. Yet my flesh crept, my feet hurried, my heart drove me; the god who had willed this flight (230) dragged me away. Nor am I a haughty man. He who knows his land respects men. Re has set the fear of you throughout the land, the dread of you in every foreign country. Whether I am at the residence, whether I am in this place, it is you who covers this horizon. The sun rises at your pleasure. The water in the river is drunk when you wish. The air of heaven is breathed at your bidding. This servant will hand over (235) to the brood which this servant begot in this place! This servant has been sent for! Your Majesty will do as he wishes! One lives by the breath which you give. As Re, Horus, and Hathor love your august nose, may Mont lord of Thebes wish it to live forever!

I was allowed to spend one more day in Yaa, handing over my possessions to my children, my eldest son taking charge of my tribe; (240) all my possessions became his—my serfs, my herds, my fruit, my fruit trees. This servant departed southward. I halted at Horus-ways. The commander in charge of the garrison sent a message to the residence to let it be known. Then his majesty sent a trusted overseer of the royal domains with whom were loaded ships, (245) bearing royal gifts for the Asiatics who had come with me to escort me to Horusways. I called each one by his name, while every butler was at his task. When I had started and set sail, there was kneading and straining beside me, until I reached the city of Itj-tawy.

When it dawned, very early, they came to summon me. Ten men came and ten men went to usher me into the palace. My forehead touched the ground between the sphinxes, (250) and the royal children stood in the gateway to meet me. The courtiers who usher through the forecourt set me on the way to the audience-hall. I found his majesty on the great throne in a kiosk of gold. Stretched out on my belly, I did not know myself before him, while this god greeted me pleasantly. I was like a man seized by darkness. (255) My *ba*[8] was gone, my limbs trembled; my heart was not in my body, I did not know life from death.

His majesty said to one of the courtiers: "Lift him up, let him speak to me." Then his majesty said: "Now you have come, after having roamed foreign lands. Flight has taken its toll of you. You have aged, have reached old age. It is no small matter that your corpse will be interred without being escorted by Bowmen. But don't act thus, don't act thus, speechless (260) though your name was called!" Fearful of punishment I answered with the answer of a frightened man: "What has my lord said to me, that I might answer it? It is not disrespect to the god! It is the terror which is in my body, like that which caused the fateful flight! Here I am before you. Life is yours. May your Majesty do as he wishes!"

Then the royal daughters were brought in, and his majesty said to the queen: "Here is Sinuhe, (265) come as an Asiatic, a product of nomads!" She uttered a very great cry, and the royal daughters shrieked all together. They said to his majesty: "Is it really he, O king, our lord?" Said his majesty: "It is really he!" Now having brought with them their necklaces, rattles, and sistra, they held them out to his majesty:

Your hands (270) upon the radiance, eternal king,
Jewels of heaven's mistress!

The Gold gives life to your nostrils,
The Lady of Stars enfolds you!

Southcrown fared north, northcrown south,
Joined, united by your majesty's word.
While the Cobra decks your brow,
You deliver the poor from harm.
Peace to you from Re, Lord of Lands!
Hail to you and the Mistress of All!

Slacken your bow, lay down your arrow,
(275) Give breath to him who gasps for breath!
Give us our good gift on this good day,
Grant us the son of northwind, Bowman born in Egypt!

He made the flight in fear of you,
He left the land in dread of you!
A face that sees you shall not pale,
Eyes that see you shall not fear!

His majesty said: "He shall not fear, he shall not (280) dread!" He shall
be a Companion among the nobles. He shall be among the courtiers. Proceed
to the robing-room to wait on him!"

I left the audience-hall, the royal daughters giving me their hands. (285)
We went through the great portals, and I was put in the house of a prince. In
it were luxuries: a bathroom and mirrors. In it were riches from the treasury;
clothes of royal linen, myrrh, and the choice perfume of the king and of his
favorite courtiers were in every (290) room. Every servant was at his task. Years
were removed from my body. I was shaved; my hair was combed. Thus was my
squalor returned to the foreign land, my dress to the Sand-farers. I was clothed
in fine linen; I was anointed with fine oil. I slept on a bed. I had returned the
sand to those who dwell in it, (295) the tree-oil to those who grease themselves
with it.

I was given a house and garden that had belonged to a courtier. Many
craftsmen rebuilt it, and all its woodwork was made anew. Meals were brought
to me from the palace three times, four times a day, apart from what the royal
children gave without a moment's pause.

(300) A stone pyramid was built for me in the midst of the pyramids. The
masons who build tombs constructed it. A master draughtsman designed in it.
A master sculptor carved in it. The overseers of construction in the necropolis[9] busied themselves with it. All the equipment that is placed in (305) a
tomb-shaft was supplied. Mortuary priests were given me. A funerary domain

was made for me. It had fields and a garden in the right place, as is done for a Companion of the first rank. My statue was overlaid with gold, its skirt with electrum.[10] It was his majesty who ordered it made. There is no commoner for whom the like has been done. I was in (310) the favor of the king, until the day of landing came.

*Colophon*: It is done from beginning to end as it was found in writing.

## Notes

[1] The Egyptians referred to the general population of Syria-Palestine as Asiatics.

[2] Sesostris I (a.k.a. Senusret I) was the second king of the 12th Dynasty of the Middle Kingdom, who ruled Egypt from 1960–1916 B.C.E. Ten of those years, 1960–1950 B.C.E., Sesostris ruled as a co-regent with his father, Amunemhat I (ca. 1980–1950 B.C.E.).

[3] Sehetepibre is the titulary praenomen of Amunemhat I, father of Sesostris I. Sehetepibre means "satisfied is Re."

[4] The Tjemeh and Tjehenu were two of the population groups that occupied the region of Libya. Throughout Egyptian history, Libyans pressured the western Egyptian frontier and harassed the lucrative caravan routes.

[5] Sinuhe begins his journey by heading south along the western edge of Egypt, on the frontier that bordered the Libyan Desert. He eventually heads east, crossing the Nile, and then turns north. He crosses the border from Egypt and heads in the direction of Syria-Palestine. He travels up the Phoenician coast, through the port city of Byblos, and settles in Retenu, the land of Syria.

[6] Kheperkare is the titular praenomen of Sesostris I.

[7] Tait is one of the many aspects of Isis. In her manifestation as Tait, Isis weaves fate.

[8] According to Egyptian theology, human beings had two distinct entities or aspects that accompanied an individual through life and death—the *ka* and the *ba*. They inhabited a realm outside of the human body, but were constrained by the material world insofar as they needed food (or food offerings) to survive. To the best of our understanding, the *ka* was a parallel personality combining both the intellect and the spiritual essence of a person. The *ba* embodied power one of mobility and action, one that could transport the *ba* between this world and the netherworld, one that could smite one's enemies long after the human being passed on. Statues of both the *ka* and the *ba* were included in burial chambers to ensure that an individual would live on, despite the natural decay of the human form.

[9] Necropolis is literally the "city of the dead" and denotes the main cemetery for a city. Generally speaking, in the ancient world only the elite could afford burials as typify such city cemeteries.

[10] Electrum is an alloy of silver and gold. It is not manmade but occurs in nature.

# The Hymn to Hapy

Hapy is the personification, or deification, of the flooding of the Nile River, which was the most crucial feature of natural (and supernatural) life for Egyptians. The Nile's regular inundation fertilized the land on either side of its channel by depositing a rich silt, permitting agriculture in a country essentially without rainfall and providing an example of divine benevolence. The Nile was also useful for transportation and hunting and fishing.

The hymn dates from the Middle Kingdom (2040–1650 B.C.E.). Scholars believe there may have been religious festivals celebrating the inundation of the Nile with sacrificial offerings, and such festivals would have included singing of hymns. There are several sources for the Hymn to Hapy, all recorded in the New Kingdom period.

MM

# The Hymn to the Nile Inundation (Hapy)

Adoration of Hapy:
Hail to you, Hapy, Sprung from earth,
Come to nourish Egypt!
Of secret ways,
A darkness by day,
To whom his followers sing!
Who floods the fields that Re[1] has made,
To nourish all who thirst;
Lets drink the waterless desert,
His dew descending from the sky.

Friend of Geb, lord of Nepri,
Promoter of the arts of Ptah.[2]
Lord of the fishes,
He makes fowl stream south,
No bird falling down from heat.
Maker of barley, creator of emmer,
He lets the temples celebrate.

When he is sluggish noses clog,
Everyone is poor;
As the sacred loaves are pared,
A million perish among men.
When he plunders, the whole land rages,
Great and small roar;
People change according to his coming,
When Khnum[3] has fashioned him.
When he floods, earth rejoices,
Every belly jubilates,
Every jawbone takes on laughter,
Every tooth is bared.

Food provider, bounty maker,
Who creates all that is good!
Lord of awe, sweetly fragrant,
Gracious when he comes.
Who makes herbage for the herds,
Gives sacrifice for every god.

160

Dwelling in the netherworld,
He controls both sky and earth.
Conqueror of the Two Lands,
He fills the stores,
Makes bulge the barns,
Gives bounty to the poor.

Grower of all delightful trees—
He has no revenue;
Barges exist by his might—
He is not hewn in stone.
Mountains cleave by his surge—
One sees no workmen, no leader,
He carries off in secrecy.

No one knows the place he's in,
His cavern is not found in books.
He has no shrines, no portions,
No service of his choice;
But youths, his children, hail him,
One greets him like a king.
Lawful, timely, he comes forth,
Filling Egypt, South and North;
As one drinks, all eyes are on him,
Who makes his bounty overflow.

He who grieved goes out in joy,
Every heart rejoices;
Sobk, Neith's child, bares his teeth,
The Nine Gods exult.
As he spouts, makes drink the fields,
Everyone grows vigorous.
Rich because another toils,
One has no quarrel with him;
Maker of food he's not defied,
One sets no limits for him.

Light-maker who comes from dark,
Fattener of herds,
Might that fashions all,
None can live without him.
People are clothed with the flax of his fields,
For he made Hedj-hotep [i.e., the weaver-god] serve him;

He made anointing with his unguents,
For he is the like of Ptah.
All kinds of crafts exist through him,
All books of godly words,
His produce from the sedges [i.e., the papyrus plant from which books
    were made].

Entering the cavern,
Coming out above,
He wants his coming secret.
If he is heavy [i.e., sluggish and insufficient], the people dwindle,
A year's food supply is lost.
The rich man looks concerned,
Everyone is seen with weapons,

Friend does not attend to friend.
Cloth is wanting for one's clothes,
Noble children lack their finery;
There's no eye-paint to be had,
No one is anointed.

This truth is fixed in people's hearts:
Want is followed by deceit.
He who consorts with the sea,
Does not harvest grain.
Though one praises all the gods,
Birds will not come down to deserts.
No one beats his hand with gold,
No man can get drunk on silver,
One can not eat lapis lazuli,
Barley is foremost and strong!

Songs to the harp are made for you,
One sings to you with clapping hands;
The youths, your children hail you,
Crowds adorn themselves for you,
Who comes with riches, decks the land,
Makes flourish every body;
Sustains the pregnant woman's heart,
And loves a multitude of herds.

When he rises at the residence,
Men feast on the meadows' gifts,

Decked with lotus for the nose,
And all the things that sprout from earth.
Children's hands are filled with herbs,
They forget to eat.
Good things are strewn about the houses,
The whole land leaps for joy.

When you overflow, O Hapy,
Sacrifice is made for you;
Oxen are slaughtered for you,
A great oblation is made to you.
Fowl is fattened for you,
Desert game snared for you,
As one repays your bounty.

One offers to all the gods
Of that which Hapy has provided,
Choice incense, oxen, goats,
And birds in holocaust.[4]

Mighty is Hapy in his cavern [i.e., the source of the Nile]
His name unknown to those below,
For the gods do not reveal it.
You people who extol the gods,
Respect the awe his son has made,
The All-Lord who sustains the shores!
Oh joy when you come!
Oh joy when you come, O Hapy,
Oh joy when you come!
You who feed men and herds
With your meadow gifts!
Oh joy when you come!
Oh joy when you come, O Hapy,
Oh joy when you come!

## Notes

[1] Re is one of the names for the Egyptian sun god. Re was the patron deity of the city of Heliopolis (the City of the Sun). Eventually, Re is combined with Amun, the patron god Thebes who was the god of light. By the Middle of the New Kingdoms the sun god is predominantly referred to as Amun-Re.

[2] Ptah was a creator god whose cult was centered in Memphis. Ptah created the world by speaking; through his words, all things came into existence.

[3] Khnum was another creator god, one who fashioned both humans and divinities on a potter's wheel.

[4] Holocaust denotes a burnt offering to the divine. Burnt offerings were a type of sacrifice common in ancient temple rituals. The term "holocaust" was later applied to the victims of Hitler's death camps, for their bodies were often incinerated.

# Egyptian Love Poems

The New Kingdom period of Egyptian history (ca. 1550–1080 B.C.E.) saw the introduction and development of several literary genres. Though lyric poetry had been known in the Middle Kingdom (ca. 2040–1650 B.C.E.), no examples of love poetry (or songs) have been found dating earlier than the New Kingdom. The cycle of love poems presented here comprises seven lyrics contained in the Papyrus Chester Beatty I (there are two other collections of love poems on the same papyrus). The standard form for such lyrics is the first-person speech of a young man or woman addressed, as a monologue, to the speaker's own heart.

These poems should be understood as being spoken, alternatively, by male and female speakers. Though they speak of the beloved as "brother" and "sister," these are terms of endearment only and do not imply a family relationship. The poems compare the beloved to divinities. For instance, at the end of the first stanza, "that other One" is the sun; "the Golden," mentioned in stanza five, is Hathor, the patroness of love. Love lyrics often touch on the same themes despite the period or place of their composition, and the poems of the New Kingdom are no exception: note the praise of the beloved one's appearance and movements; the young person's doubt about being understood by parents; and love-sickness.

MM

# From Papyrus Chester Beatty I

## I.a  A Cycle of Seven Stanzas

### *Beginning of the sayings of the great happiness*

The *One*, the sister without peer,
The handsomest of all!
She looks like the rising morning star
At the start of a happy year.
Shining bright, fair of skin,
Lovely the look of her eyes,
Sweet the speech of her lips,
She has not a word too much.
Upright neck, shining breast,
Hair true lapis lazuli;
Arms surpassing gold,
Fingers like lotus buds.
Heavy thighs, narrow waist,
Her legs parade her beauty;
With graceful step she treads the ground,
Captures my heart by her movements.
She causes all men's necks
To turn about to see her;
Joy has he whom she embraces,
He is like the first of men!
When she steps outside she seems
Like that other *One*!

### *Second Stanza*

My *brother* torments my heart with his voice,
He makes sickness take hold of me;
He is neighbor to my mother's house,
And I cannot go to him!
Mother is right in charging him thus:
"Give up seeing her!"
It pains my heart to think of him,
I am possessed by love of him.
Truly, he is a foolish one,

166

But I resemble him;
He knows not my wish to embrace him,
Or he would write to my mother.
Brother, I am promised to you
By the Gold of women!
Come to me that I see your beauty,
Father, Mother will rejoice!
My people will hail you all together,
They will hail you, O my *brother*!

### Third Stanza

My heart *devised* to see her beauty
While sitting down in her house;
On the way I met Mehy[1] on his chariot,
With him were his young men.
I knew not how to avoid him:
Should I stride on to pass him?
But the river was the road,
I knew no place for my feet.
My heart, you are very foolish,
Why accost Mehy?
If I pass before him,
I tell him my movements;
Here, I'm yours, I say to him,
Then he will shout my name,
And assign me to the first . . .
Among his *followers*.

### Fourth Stanza

My heart *flutters* hastily,
When I think of my love of you;
It lets me not act sensibly,
It leaps (from) its place.
It lets me not put on a dress,
Nor wrap my scarf around me;
I put no paint upon my eyes,
I'm even not anointed.
"Don't wait, go there," says it to me,
As often as I think of him;
My heart, don't act so stupidly,

Why do you play the fool?
Sit still, the brother comes to you,
And many eyes as well!
Let not the people say of me:
"A woman fallen through love!"
Be steady when you think of him,
My heart, do not *flutter*!

### Fifth Stanza

I *praise* the Golden, I worship her majesty,
I extol the Lady of Heaven;
I give adoration to Hathor,[2]
Laudations to my Mistress!
I called to her, she heard my plea,
She sent my mistress to me;
She came by herself to see me,
O great wonder that happened to me!
I was joyful, exulting, elated,
When they said: "See, she is here!"
As she came, the young men bowed,
Out of great love for her.
I make devotions to my goddess,
That she grant me my sister as gift;
Three days now that I pray to her name,
*Five* days since she went from me!

### Sixth Stanza

I *passed* before his house,
I found his door ajar;
My brother stood by his mother,
And all his brothers with him.
Love of him captures the heart
Of all who tread the path;
Splendid youth who has no peer,
Brother outstanding in virtues!
He looked at me as I passed by,
And I, by myself, rejoiced;
How my heart exulted in gladness,
My brother, at your sight!
If only the mother knew my heart,

She would have understood by now;
O Golden, put it in her heart,
Then will I hurry to my brother!
I will kiss him before his companions,
I would not weep before them;
I would rejoice at their understanding
That you acknowledge me!
I will make a feast for my goddess,
My heart leaps to go;
To let me see my brother tonight,
O happiness in *passing*!

### Seventh Stanza

*Seven* days since I saw my sister,
And sickness invaded me;
I am heavy in all my limbs,
My body has forsaken me.
When the physicians come to me,
My heart rejects their remedies;
The magicians are quite helpless,
My sickness is not discerned.
To tell me "She is here" would revive me!
Her name would make me rise;
Her messenger's coming and going,
That would revive my heart!
My sister is better than all prescriptions,
She does more for me than all medicines;
Her coming to me is my amulet,
The sight of her makes me well!
When she opens her eyes my body is young,
Her speaking makes me strong;
Embracing her expels my malady—
*Seven* days since she went from me!

## Notes

1  By some accounts Mehy was a fictional character, by others a historical figure. Recent archaeological investigations indicate that he was indeed a historical personage. Debate continues, though, as some scholars argue that he was a commoner, others a prince. We do know that Mehy served as a military commander under the New Kingdom King Seti I (ca. 1295–1280 B.C.E.). In literature, Mehy becomes a romantic hero.

Eventually however, he becomes a villain, for Ramses II, the successor of Seti, hated Mehy and did his best to eradicate him from the annals of Egyptian history.

[2] Though Hathor is best known as the goddess of the sky, she was also the goddess of music, beauty, and love.

# The Instruction of Amenemope

## ca. 1100–1000 B.C.

The *Instruction of Amenemope* was composed during the Ramesside era of the late New Kingdom, probably around 1100–1000 B.C., though some sources date it as late as 600 B.C.E. This was the beginning of a protracted period of political decline for Egypt, from domestic unity and empire building to internal struggle between the nobility and priests and, finally, invasion; Libyan rulers took the Egyptian throne in 945 B.C.E., the Nubians in 720, followed by Assyrians, Persians, Macedonians and Greeks under Alexander, and finally Rome. Egypt's golden age of independence was over. Despite these political changes, the *Instruction* continued the tradition of Egyptian "wisdom literature" whose purpose was, as the title indicates, to offer moral instruction to the reader. Dating this particular "instruction" within a broad time frame is possible because of its similarity with the Hebrew book of Proverbs. Scholars for a long time have believed that the *Instruction of Amenemope* must have influenced the writing of Proverbs not only in its tone and purpose, but also as an explicit, direct guide for how to write such literature; the Hebrew text refers to its own "thirty sayings" (Prov 22:20) which follow the structure of the thirty chapters of the *Instruction*.

The *Instruction* instructs one about relationships, of all sorts. It is about how one should try to get along with other people, with the gods, and with oneself. How should one behave? The *Instruction's* answer is: honestly. Though the gods favor honesty, one's primary motivation should not be the things that one may acquire from having an honest reputation. Rather, the true goal is contentment: to be calm and patient, to be, literally, silent. This ideal of quietude and internal calm, the "truly quiet," is the opposite of the "heated man." This person "tears down, he builds up with his tongue, When he makes hurtful speech. . . . He is the ferryman of snaring words, He goes and comes with quarrels. . . . His lips are sweet, his tongue is bitter." (Chapter 9). He is "heated" because he covets whatever it is that he does not have, from the rich or the poor, "he is like a young wolf in the farmyard. . . ." (Chapter 9).

To maintain a peaceful life one should avoid contact with such a "heated" man. But the *Instruction of Amenemope* has another lesson: do not *be* a "heated man." This is the fundamental instruction. How one treats others is linked to how one treats oneself.

JM

# The Instruction of Amenemope

## Prologue

| | |
|---|---|
| Beginning of the teaching for life, | I,1 |
| The instructions for well-being, | |
| Every rule for relations with elders, | |
| For conduct toward magistrates; | |
| Knowing how to answer one who speaks, | 5 |
| To reply to one who sends a message. | |
| So as to direct him on the paths of life, | |
| To make him prosper upon earth; | |
| To let his heart enter its shrine, | |
| Steering clear of evil; | 10 |
| To save him from the mouth of strangers, | |
| To let (him) be praised in the mouth of people. | |
| Made by the overseer of fields, experienced in his office, | |
| The offspring of a scribe of Egypt, | |
| The overseer of grains who controls the measure, | 15 |
| Who sets the harvest-dues for his lord, | |
| Who registers the islands of new land, | |
| In the great name of his majesty, | |
| Who records the markers on the borders of fields, | |
| Who acts for the king in his listing of taxes, | II,1 |
| Who makes the land-register of Egypt; | |
| The scribe who determines the offerings for all the gods. | |
| Who gives land-leases to the people, | |
| The overseer of grains, [provider of] foods, | 5 |
| Who supplies the granary with grains; | |
| The truly silent in This of Ta-wer,[1] | |
| The justified in Ipu, | |
| Who owns a tomb on the west of Senu, | |
| Who has a chapel at Abydos, | 10 |
| Amenemope, the son of Kanakht, | |
| The justified in Ta-wer. | |
| (For) his son, the youngest of his children, | |
| The smallest of his family, | |

The devotee of Min-Kamutef,[2]                                        15
The water-pourer of Wennofer,[3]
Who places Horus on his father's throne,
Who guards him in his noble shrine,
Who ———
The guardian of the mother of god,                                   III,1
Inspector of the black cattle of the terrace of Min,
Who protects Min in his shrine:
Hor-em-maakher is his true name,
The child of a nobleman of Ipu,                                        5
The son of the sistrum-player of Shu and Tefnut,
And chief songstress of Horus, Tawosre.

He says: Chapter I
Give your ears, hear the sayings,
Give your heart to understand them;                                   10
It profits to put them in your heart,
Woe to him who neglects them!
Let them rest in the casket of your belly,
May they be bolted in your heart;
When there rises a whirlwind of words,                                15
They'll be a mooring post for your tongue.
If you make your life with these in your heart,
You will find it a success;
You will find my words a storehouse for life,                         IV,1
Your being will prosper upon earth.

## Chapter 2

Beware of robbing a wretch,
Of attacking a cripple;                                                5
Don't stretch out your hand to touch an old man,
Nor ⌐open your mouth⌐ to an elder.
Don't let yourself be sent on a mischievous errand,
Nor be friends with him who does it.
Don't raise an outcry against one who attacks you,                    10
Nor answer him yourself.
He who does evil, the shore rejects him,
Its floodwater carries him away.
The northwind descends to end his hour,
It mingles with the thunderstorm.                                     15

The storm cloud is tall, the crocodiles are vicious,
You heated man, how are you now?
He cries out, his voice reaches heaven,
It is the Moon who declares his crime.
Steer, we will ferry the wicked,                                                    V,1
We do not act like his kind;
Lift him up, give him your hand,
Leave him <in> the hands of the god;
Fill his belly with bread of your own,                                              5
That he be sated and weep.
Another thing good in the heart of the god:
To pause before speaking.

## Chapter 3

Don't start a quarrel with a hot-mouthed man,                                       10
Nor needle him with words.
Pause before a foe, bend before an attacker,
Sleep (on it) before speaking.
A storm that bursts like fire in straw,
Such is the heated man in his hour.                                                 15
Withdraw from him, leave him alone,
The god knows how to answer him.
If you make your life with these (words) in your heart,
Your children will observe them.

## Chapter 4

As for the heated man in the temple,                                                VI,1
He is like a tree growing ⌐indoors⌐;
A moment lasts its growth of ⌐shoots⌐,
Its end comes about in the ⌐woodshed⌐;
It is floated far from its place,                                                   5
The flame is its burial shroud.
The truly silent, who keeps apart,
He is like a tree grown in a meadow.
It greens, it doubles its yield,
It stands in front of its lord.                                                     10
Its fruit is sweet, its shade delightful,
Its end comes in the garden.

## Chapter 5

Do not falsify the temple rations,
Do not grasp and you'll find profit.                                    15
Do not remove a servant of the god,
So as to do favors to another.
Do not say: "Today is like tomorrow,"
How will this end?
Comes tomorrow, today has vanished,                                     VII,1
The deep has become the water's edge.
Crocodiles are bared, hippopotami stranded,
The fish crowded together.
Jackals are sated, birds are in feast,                                  5
The fishnets have been drained.
But all the silent in the temple,
They say: "Re's blessing is great."
Cling to the silent, then you find life,
Your being will prosper upon earth.                                     10

## Chapter 6

Do not move the markers on the borders of fields,
Nor shift the position of the measuring-cord.
Do not be greedy for a cubit of land,
Nor encroach on the boundaries of a widow.                              15
The trodden furrow worn down by time,
He who disguises it in the fields,
When he has snared (it) by false oaths,
He will be caught by the might of the Moon.
Recognize him who does this on earth:                                   VIII,1
He is an oppressor of the weak,
A foe bent on destroying your being,
The taking of life is in his eye.
His house is an enemy to the town,                                      5
His storage bins will be destroyed;
His wealth will be seized from his children's hands,
His possessions will be given to another.
Beware of destroying the borders of fields,
Lest a terror carry you away;                                           10
One pleases god with the might of the lord
When one discerns the borders of fields.
Desire your being to be sound,

Beware of the Lord of All;
Do not erase another's furrow,                                   15
It profits you to keep it sound.
Plow your fields and you'll find what you need,
You'll receive bread from your threshing-floor.
Better is a bushel given you by the god,
Than five thousand through wrongdoing.                          20
They stay not a day in bin and barn,                            IX,1
They make no food for the beer jar;
A moment is their stay in the granary,
Comes morning they have vanished.
Better is poverty in the hand of the god,                        5
Than wealth in the storehouse;
Better is bread with a happy heart
Than wealth with vexation.

## Chapter 7

Do not set your heart on wealth,                                10
There is no ignoring Fate and Destiny;
Do not let your heart go straying,
Every man comes to his hour.
Do not strain to seek increase,
What you have, let it suffice you.                              15
If riches come to you by theft,
They will not stay the night with you.
Comes day they are not in your house,
Their place is seen but they're not there;
Earth opened its mouth, leveled them, swallowed them,          20
And made them sink into *dat*.                                  X,1
They made a hole as big as their size,
And sank into the netherworld;
They made themselves wings like geese,
And flew away to the sky.                                        5
Do not rejoice in wealth from theft,
Nor complain of being poor.
If the leading archer presses forward,
His company abandons him;
The boat of the greedy is left <in> the mud,                   10
While the bark of the silent sails with the wind.
You shall pray to the Aten when he rises,

Saying: "Grant me well-being and health";
He will give you your needs for this life,
And you will be safe from fear.                                    15

## Chapter 8

Set your goodness before people,
Then you are greeted by all;
One welcomes the Uraeus,
One spits upon Apopis.[4]                                          20
Guard your tongue from harmful speech,
Then you will be loved by others.                                  XI,1
You will find your place in the house of god,
You will share in the offerings of your lord.
When you're revered and your coffin conceals you,
You will be safe from the power of god.                            5
Do not shout "crime" against a man,
When the cause of (his) flight is hidden.
Whether you hear something good or evil,
Do it outside where it is not heard.
Put the good remark on your tongue,                                10
While the bad is concealed in your belly.

## Chapter 9

Do not befriend the heated man,
Nor approach him for conversation.
Keep your tongue from answering your superior,                     15
And take care not to insult him.
Let him not cast his speech to catch you,
Nor give free rein to your answer.
Converse with a man of your own measure,
And take care not to ⌐offend⌐ him.                                 20
Swift is the speech of one who is angered,                         XII,1
More than wind ⌐over⌐ water.
He tears down, he builds up with his tongue,
When he makes his hurtful speech.
He gives an answer worthy of a beating,                            5
For its weight is harm.
He hauls freight like all the world,
But his load is falsehood.
He is the ferryman of snaring words,

He goes and comes with quarrels.                                    10
When he eats and drinks inside,
His answer is (heard) outside.
The day he is charged with his crime
Is misfortune for his children.
If only Khnum came to him,                                          15
The Potter to the heated man,
So as to knead the ⌐faulty⌐ heart.
He is like a young wolf in the farmyard,
He turns one eye against the other,
He causes brothers to quarrel.                                      XIII,1
He runs before every wind like clouds,
He dims the radiance of the sun;
He flips his tail like the crocodile's young,
⌐He draws himself up so as to strike.⌐                              5
His lips are sweet, his tongue is bitter,
A fire burns in his belly.
Don't leap to join such a one,
Lest a terror carry you away.

## Chapter 10                                                       10

Don't force yourself to greet the heated man,
For then you injure your own heart;
Do not say "greetings" to him falsely,
While there is terror in your belly.
Do not speak falsely to a man,                                      15
The god abhors it;
Do not sever your heart from your tongue,
That all your strivings may succeed.
You will be weighty before the others,
And secure in the hand of the god.                                  XIV,1
God hates the falsifier of words,
He greatly abhors the dissembler.

## Chapter 11

Do not covet a poor man's goods,                                    5
Nor hunger for his bread;
A poor man's goods are a block in the throat,
It makes the gullet vomit.
He who makes gain by lying oaths,

His heart is misled by his belly; 10
Where there is fraud success is feeble,
The bad spoils the good.
You will be guilty before your superior,
And confused in your account;
Your pleas will be answered by a curse, 15
Your prostrations by a beating.
The big mouthful of bread—you swallow, you vomit it,
And you are emptied of your gain.
Observe the overseer of the poor,
When the stick attains him; XV,1
All his people are bound in chains,
And he is led to the executioner.
If you are released before your superior,
You are yet hateful to your subordinates; 5
Steer away from the poor man on the road,
Look at him and keep clear of his goods.

## Chapter 12

Do not desire a noble's wealth,
Nor make free with a big mouthful of bread; 10
If he sets you to manage his property,
Shun his, and yours will prosper.
Do not converse with a heated man,
So as to befriend a hostile man.
If you are sent to transport straw, 15
Stay away from its container.
If a man is observed on a fraudulent errand,
He will not be sent on another occasion.

## Chapter 13

Do not cheat a man <through> pen on scroll, 20
The god abhors it;
Do not bear witness with false words, XVI,1
So as to brush aside a man by your tongue.
Do not assess a man who has nothing,
And thus falsify your pen.
If you find a large debt against a poor man, 5
Make it into three parts;
Forgive two, let one stand,

You will find it a path of life.
After sleep, when you wake in the morning,
You will find it as good news.                                    10
Better is praise with the love of men
Than wealth in the storehouse;
Better is bread with a happy heart
Than wealth with vexation.

## Chapter 14                                                     15

Do not recall yourself to a man,
Nor strain to seek his hand.
If he says to you: "Here is a gift,
⌐No have-not⌐ will refuse it,"
Don't blink at him, nor bow your head,                            20
Nor turn aside your gaze.
Salute him with your mouth, say, "Greetings,"
He will desist, and you succeed.                                  XVII,1
Do not rebuff him in his approach,
⌐Another time he'll be taken away.⌐

## Chapter 15

Do the good and you will prosper,                                 5
Do not dip your pen to injure a man.
The finger of the scribe is the beak of the Ibis,[5]
Beware of brushing it aside.
The Ape dwells in the House of Khmun,
His eye encircles the Two Lands;                                  10
When he sees one who cheats with his finger,
He carries his livelihood off in the flood.
The scribe who cheats with his finger,
His son will not be enrolled.
If you make your life with these (words) in your heart,          15
Your children will observe them.

## Chapter 16

Do not move the scales nor alter the weights,
Nor diminish the fractions of the measure;
Do not desire a measure of the fields,                           20
Nor neglect those of the treasury.

The Ape sits by the balance,
His heart is in the plummet;                    XVIII,1
Where is a god as great as Thoth,
Who invented these things and made them?
Do not make for yourself deficient weights,
They are rich in grief through the might of god.    5
If you see someone who cheats,
Keep your distance from him.
Do not covet copper,
Disdain beautiful linen;
What good is one dressed in finery,                 10
If he cheats before the god?
Faience[6] disguised as gold,
Comes day, it turns to lead.

## Chapter 17

Beware of disguising the measure,                   15
So as to falsify its fractions;
Do not force it to overflow,
Nor let its belly be empty.
Measure according to its true size,
Your hand clearing exactly.                         20
Do not make a bushel of twice its size,
For then you are headed for the abyss.
The bushel is the Eye of Re,
It abhors him who trims;                            XIX,1
A measurer who indulges in cheating,
His Eye seals (the verdict) against him.
Do not accept a farmer's dues
And then assess him so as to injure him;            5
Do not conspire with the measurer,
So as to defraud the share of the Residence.
Greater is the might of the threshing floor
Than an oath by the great throne.

## Chapter 18                                        10

Do not lie down in fear of tomorrow:
"Comes day, how will tomorrow be?"
Man ignores how tomorrow will be;
God is ever in his perfection,

Man is ever in his failure.     15
The words men say are one thing,
The deeds of the god are another.
Do not say: "I have done no wrong,"
And then strain to seek a quarrel;
The wrong belongs to the god,     20
He seals (the verdict) with his finger.
There is no perfection before the god,
But there is failure before him;
If one strains to seek perfection,     XX,1
In a moment he has marred it.
Keep firm your heart, steady your heart,
Do not steer with your tongue;
If a man's tongue is the boat's rudder,     5
The Lord of All is yet its pilot.

## Chapter 19

Do not go to court before an official
In order to falsify your words;
Do not vacillate in your answers,     10
When your witnesses accuse.
Do not strain <with> oaths by your lord,
<With> speeches at the hearing;
Tell the truth before the official,
Lest he lay a hand on you.     15
If another day you come before him,
He will incline to all you say;
He will relate your speech to the Council of Thirty,
It will be observed on another occasion.

## Chapter 20     20

Do not confound a man in the law court,
In order to brush aside one who is right.
Do not incline to the well-dressed man,     XXI,1
And rebuff the one in rags.
Don't accept the gift of a powerful man,
And deprive the weak for his sake.
*Maat*[7] is a great gift of god,     5
He gives it to whom he wishes.
The might of him who resembles him,

It saves the poor from his tormentor.
Do not make for yourself false documents,
They are a deadly provocation;                                    10
They (mean) the great restraining oath,
They (mean) a hearing by the herald.
Don't falsify the oracles in the scrolls,
And thus disturb the plans of god;
Don't use for yourself the might of god,                          15
As if there were no Fate and Destiny.
Hand over property to its owners,
Thus do you seek life for yourself;
Don't raise your desire in their house,
Or your bones belong to the execution-block.                      20

## Chapter 21

Do not say: "Find me a strong superior,                           XXII,1
For a man in your town has injured me";
Do not say: "Find me a protector,
For one who hates me has injured me."
Indeed you do not know the plans of god,                          5
And should not weep for tomorrow;
Settle in the arms of the god,
Your silence will overthrow them.
The crocodile that makes no sound,
Dread of it is ancient.                                           10
Do not empty your belly to everyone,
And thus destroy respect of you;
Broadcast not your words to others,
Nor join with one who bares his heart.
Better is one whose speech is in his belly                        15
Than he who tells it to cause harm.
One does not run to reach success,
One does not move to spoil it.

## Chapter 22

Do not provoke your adversary,                                    20
So as to <make> him tell his thoughts;
Do not leap to come before him,
When you do not see his doings.                                   XXIII,1
First gain insight from his answer,

Then keep still and you'll succeed.
Leave it to him to empty his belly,
Know how to sleep, he'll be found out.                                    5
⌐Grasp his legs¬, do not harm him,
Be wary of him, do not ignore him.
Indeed you do not know the plans of god,
And should not weep for tomorrow;
Settle in the arms of the god,                                           10
Your silence will overthrow them.

## Chapter 23

Do not eat in the presence of an official
And then set your mouth before <him>;
If you are sated pretend to chew,                                        15
Content yourself with your saliva.
Look at the bowl that is before you,
And let it serve your needs.
An official is great in his office,
As a well is rich in drawings of water.                                  20

## Chapter 24

Do not listen to an official's reply indoors
In order to repeat it to another outside.                               XXIV,1
Do not let your word be carried outside,
Lest your heart be aggrieved.
The heart of man is a gift of god,
Beware of neglecting it.                                                  5
The man at the side of an official,
His name should not be known.

## Chapter 25

Do not laugh at a blind man,
Nor tease a dwarf,
Nor cause hardship for the lame.                                         10
Don't tease a man who is in the hand of the god,
Nor be angry with him for his failings.
Man is clay and straw,
The god is his builder.
He tears down, he builds up daily,                                       15

He makes a thousand poor by his will,
He makes a thousand men into chiefs,
When he is in his hour of life.
Happy is he who reaches the west,
When he is safe in the hand of the god. 20

## Chapter 26

Do not sit down in the beer-house
In order to join one greater than you, XXV,1
Be he a youth great through his office,
Or be he an elder through birth.
Befriend a man of your own measure,
Re is helpful from afar. 5
If you see one greater than you outdoors,
Walk behind him respectfully;
Give a hand to an elder sated with beer,
Respect him as his children would.
The arm is not hurt by being bared, 10
The back is not broken by bending it.
A man does not lose by speaking sweetly,
Nor does he gain if his speech bristles.
The pilot who sees from afar,
He will not wreck his boat. 15

## Chapter 27

Do not revile one older than you,
He has seen Re before you;
Let <him> not report you to the Aten at his rising,
Saying: "A youth has reviled an old man." 20
Very painful before Pre[8]
Is a youth who reviles an elder. XXVI,1
Let him beat you while your hand is on your chest,
Let him revile you while you are silent;
If next day you come before him,
He will give you food in plenty. 5
A dog's food is from its master,
It barks to him who gives it.

## Chapter 28

Do not pounce on a widow when you find her in the fields
And then fail to be patient with her reply.                    10
Do not refuse your oil jar to a stranger,
Double it before your brothers.
God prefers him who honors the poor
To him who worships the wealthy.

## Chapter 29                                                  15

Do not prevent people from crossing the river,
If you stride freely in the ferry.
When you are given an oar in the midst of the deep,
Bend your arms and take it.
It is no crime before the god,                                 20
⌐If the passenger is not passed up⌐                            XXVII,1
Don't make yourself a ferry on the river
And then strain to seek its fare;
Take the fare from him who is wealthy,
And let pass him who is poor.                                  5

## Chapter 30

Look to these thirty chapters,
They inform, they educate;
They are the foremost of all books,
They make the ignorant wise.                                   10
If they are read to the ignorant,
He is cleansed through them.
Be filled with them, put them in your heart,
And become a man who expounds them,
One who expounds as a teacher.                                 15
The scribe who is skilled in his office,
He is found worthy to be a courtier.

## *Colophon*

That is its end.
Written by Senu, son of the divine father Pemu.               XXVIII,1

# Notes

[1] This of Ta-wer, meaning "Nome of the Exalted Land," is the name of the Egyptian province (nome) encompassing the city of Abydos in Upper Egypt.

[2] Min was the god of fertility and sexuality. Kamutef translates literally "Bull of the Mother" and is associated with creation. It could be appended to the name of multiple deities (we read of Amun-Kamutef, for example).

[3] Wennofer was one of the many names of Osiris.

[4] Apopis was a snake demon associated with Seth (the god of the desert) and representing darkness. Apopis threatened the barge of the sun-god as it navigated through the night.

[5] The god Thoth is variously depicted as an ibis (a marsh bird common in Lower Egypt) and a baboon. He was the inventor of writing and is the scribe of the gods.

[6] Faience is glazed earthenware. Egypt is famous for the manufacture of vivid blue faience.

[7] *Maat*, personified as a goddess with an ostrich feather resting upright on her head, embodies truth and cosmic order or balance.

[8] Pre is a less frequently used name for the sun-god.

# Aspelta

## Sixth Century B.C.E.

This selection belongs to the Kushite king Aspelta, who ruled Kush from 593–568 B.C.E.; the selection finds its origins in the history of ancient Northeast Africa, an area generally encompassing Nubia and Egypt. Ancient Nubia was the region along the Nile Valley just south of Upper Egypt, and though the ancient territorial boundaries were quite fluid, for our purposes Nubia began at the 1st Cataract and traditionally extended to the 6th Cataract. Its modern equivalents are the southern portions of Egypt and the whole of the Sudan. "Kush" is an ancient, seemingly indigenous term used by its inhabitants in reference to both the land and themselves, though politically speaking Kush refers to the ancient state whose distinguished story archaeologists are able to trace back to 5000 B.C.E. The heyday of Kush was 750–650 B.C.E., when Kushite kings ruled all of Egypt as the 25th Dynasty. It is of this Kushite Empire that Derek Welsby wrote:

> At the time when Rome was a small village on the banks of the Tiber and the Greek city states held sway over minuscule territories, the Kushites ruled an empire stretching from the central Sudan to the borders of Palestine. The Kingdom of Kush outlived the Greek city states and the period of Macedonian hegemony over vast tracts of the ancient world, and co-existed with the rise, heyday and much of the period of the decline of the Roman Empire.[1]

Although Kush had a long and distinguished history, we know comparatively little of it. The language of the Kushites was Meriotic, one of the oldest written languages of Africa. Meriotic used an alphabet of 23 letters, and could be written in both cursive and hieroglyphics, but it remains largely undecipherable. Therefore, most of what we know comes from the enemies of Kush, particularly the Egyptians, and from a few of the Kushites' own inscriptions that they wrote in Egyptian.

For millennia, political power in Northeast Africa shifted between Kush and Egypt. Early Dynastic Egypt (3000–2710 B.C.E.) depended on the mineral rich land of Kush for gold, copper, and stone. Concomitant with the Egyptian Middle Kingdom (2040–1650 B.C.E.) a powerful Kushite kingdom controlled the flow of trade along the cataracts of the Nile, and thereby monopolized the exchange of goods from inner and Southern Africa into

Egypt and ultimately to the Mediterranean world. The Kushites' position as the merchant middlemen for all of African trade made Egypt increasingly hostile to Kushite power. Egypt therefore built fortresses to control the movement of Nubians, and Northern Nubia was effectively subjugated. During the Second Intermediate Period (1760–1560 B.C.E.), when Egypt was dominated by outside invaders known as the Hyksos, Kushite kings took advantage of Egypt's weakness. They reasserted their independence, and renewed the strength of their kingdom by establishing diplomatic relations with the Hyksos.[2] Then in 1540, a new phase of Egyptian hegemony began, when the Egyptian governor Ahmose expelled the Hyksos, reunified Egypt, and ushered in the New Kingdom (1550–1220 B.C.E.). Though there was little military activity during the remainder of his reign, Ahmose did create a new administrative position, that of the Vizier (or Governor) of Kush, with the intent of directly controlling Egypt's southern neighbor. Such was the ebb and flow of centuries of Nilotic history. When Egypt was strong, the Egyptians dominated Kush; when Egypt was weak, the Kushites reasserted their independence and created empire. The most notable phase of Kushite strength was from the mid-eighth–mid-seventh centuries, when a Kushite king ushered in the 25th Egyptian Dynasty and ruled as "Pharaoh of Egypt."[3]

The political ties between Kush and Egypt signify cultural ties. While the Pharaohs of the Middle Kingdom were intent on dominating Kush militarily, Pharaohs of the New Kingdom merged military action with the cultural Egyptianization of Kushite society.[4] The material assemblage of excavated sites in Iron Age Kush indicates that Egyptian style goods and gods were imported (or imposed) and embraced by the Kushites.[5] In religious spheres, Egyptian gods such as Amun appear in the pantheon.[6] By the time of the 25th Dynasty, Kushite kings patronized the traditional Egyptian gods at Egyptian temples in the Egyptian capital cities of Thebes and Memphis. Eventually, the Egyptians regained strength and expelled the Kushites from Egypt in 650 B.C.E.

Sixty years after the 25th Dynasty came to an end, Aspelta (593–568 B.C.E. ) was crowned King of Kush and ruled from the city of Napata, near the 4th Cataract. Archaeologists have discovered many records of his reign, including inscriptional evidence, his sarcophagus, and temples constructed under his auspices. For this reason, the reign of Aspelta is one of the better-known periods of Kushite history. From the temple of Amun-Re at Gebel Barkal comes Aspelta's *Election Stela*, upon which is inscribed the story of his coronation. The account can be broken down into discrete sections. It begins with the Queen Mother prayerfully petitioning Amun-Re for her son's accession to the throne. Attention then turns to the representatives of the people, who go to the temple seeking a divine oracle from Amun-Re; only Amun-Re can determine the next king. The representatives present all eligible princes before the god (literally his statue), and, through oracular means, Amun-Re chooses Aspelta for the throne. At this point, the representatives and the princes fade from the scene, and a private dialogue between god and newly crowned king ensues. Eventually, Aspelta is presented to the people and the army amidst great acclamation. A description of the coronation festival marks the end of the account. The story serves as propaganda as much as it serves as history, for the *Election Stela* asserts that Aspelta was handpicked by Amun-Re and therefore ruled by divine sanction as the Son of Amun-Re. Historically, from this stela and other sources, we are able to piece together a scenario in which there were numerous other princes (brothers?) vying for the throne, but Aspelta came out on top. The propagandistic nature of the text, with its emphasis on divine legitimation, suggests that there was some contention over his selection. This suspicion is supported by Aspelta's purge of the temple and its "false priests" shortly after his election.

Perhaps one of the most distinguishing characteristics of the *Election Stela* is the prominence of Aspelta's female relatives within the account. Kushite queens traditionally had a preeminent role in government, a fact contributing to the hypothesis that Kushite royal succession was matrilineal, though this is far from proven. Even so, in the *Election Stela* Aspelta traces his ancestry back through seven generations of women. It is his mother who intercedes on his behalf, and his mother who appears by his side in both textual and artistic renderings of his reign. In the relief that accompanies the *Election Stela*, Aspelta's mother is depicted as the high priestess of Amun-Re, and this is further attestation of her importance.

Aspelta's accession to the throne was marked by renewed tensions with Egypt. In 593 B.C.E., the Egyptian army under Psamtik II (a.k.a. Psammetichus II) invaded Kush. Aspelta was forced to abandon Napata for the city of Meroë, further south. Aspelta continued to rule a much-diminished kingdom for another twenty-five years. The Kingdom of Kush continued on towards a slow, progressive demise characterized by agricultural depletion, deforestation, and population pressures which culminated in the conquest of Kush in 277 C.E. by a new regional power, the Kingdom of Aksum.

Though archaeologists are still in the initial stages of Nubian exploration, the discovery of texts such as Aspelta's *Election Stela* contributes significantly to our understanding of this vital region of the ancient world.

KP

## Notes

[1] Derek Welsby, *The Kingdom of Kush, the Napatan and Meroitic Empires* (Princeton, NJ: Markus Weiner Publishers, 1998), 9.

[2] Welsby, 12.

[3] William Adams, "The Kingdom and Civilization of Kush in Northeast Africa," in *Civilizations of the Ancient Near East*, vol. 2, ed. J. Sasson, J. Baines, G. Beckman, K. Rubinson (New York: Charles Scribner's Sons, 1995), 779.

[4] Jen Leclant, "Egypt in Nubia during the Old, Middle, and New Kingdoms" in *Africa in Antiquity*, ed. S. Hochfield, E. Riefstahl (New York: The Brooklyn Museum, 1978), 64–70.

[5] See for example, Adams, 781; Welsby, 72–136.

[6] See Welsby, 72–98. Amun was originally a primordial creator god associated with wind and water, but who over time became assimilated with the sun god.

# Election Stela of Aspelta
## from Year 1, from the Amûn temple
## at Gebel Barkal

**Scene at Top**
**Speech of King's Mother (five columns, reading from left to right)**

> (1) Utterance by the king's sister, the king's mother, mistress of Kush,
> [Nasalsa]:
> "I am come to you, Amen-Rê,[1] lord of the Thrones of Two-lands,
> the great god, (2) who is in front of his harem, whose name is known,
> who gives bravery <to> him who is loyal to him,
> establish your son whom you love, (3) [Aspelta], may he live for ever,
> in the highest office of Rê, that he may be great(er) in it (4) than all
> gods.
> Make numerous his years of life on ⌐<earth>⌐ like Aton of Napata.[2]
> Give him all life and dominion from you, all happiness from you,
> and appearing on the throne of Horus for ever."

**Speech of Amen-Re (eight columns, reading from right to left)**

> (1) Utterance by Amûn of Napata:
> "My beloved son, (2) [Aspelta],
> I give you the crown (4) of Rê, his kingship on ⌐your⌐ father's throne.
> (5) I have fixed the Two-Ladies[3] on your head
> (even) as heaven is fixed on four posts,
> (6) you being alive, strong, renewed, youthful, like Rê (7) for ever,
> every land and every foreign country collected under (8) your sandals."

**In Front of Mut (two columns, reading from right to left)**

> (1) Utterance by Mut, Lady of Heaven,
> "Grant (him) (2) all life and dominion, all health, all happiness, for
> ever."

**Main Text**

> (1) Regnal year 1, 2nd month of Winter, day 15, under the majesty of

Horus: "Whose-appearances-are-beautiful",
the Two-Ladies: "Whose-appearances-are-beautiful",
Golden-Horus: "Whose-heart-is-strong",
the King-of-Upper-and-Lower-Egypt, lord of Two-lands: ["Rê-is-One-
    whose-ka-is-loved"],
Son-of-Rê, lord of crowns: [Aspelta],
beloved of Amen-Rê, lord of the Thrones of Two-lands, who is upon
    Pure-mountain (Gebel Barkal).
Now (2) His Majesty's entire army was in the town named Pure-moun-
    tain (Gebel Barkal),
the god in which is Dedwen, the foremost of Bow-land (Nubia),
—he is a god of Kush—
after the Falcon had settled on his (3) throne.
Now there were trusted commanders in the midst of His Majesty's army,
    six men,
while there were (also) trusted commanders and overseers of fortresses,
    six men.
Moreover, there (4) were trusted overseers of documents, six men,
while there were officials, overseers of seals of the estate of the king,
    seven men.
Then they said to the entire army,
"Come, let us cause our lord (5) to appear (in procession),
(for we are) like a herd of cattle without their herdsman."
Then this army was very very concerned, saying,
"Our lord is here with us, (but) we do not know him!
(6) Would that we might know him, that we might enter under him
and serve him, as Two-lands served Horus son of Isis,
after he rested upon the throne of his father Osiris,
and give praise to his (7) Two Uraei.[4]
Then one said to his companion among them,
"There is no one that knows him, excepting it is Rê himself.
He drives away all evil from him in every place in which he is."
Then one said (8) to his companion among them,
"Rê rests in (the Place of) Life, he will crown him from amongst us."
Then said one to his companion among them,
"That is right.
It has been the work of Rê since heaven (9) came into being
and (ever) since crowning the king came into being.
He has (always) given it to his son whom he loves
because the king among the living is the image of Rê.

Rê is the one who places him in this land in the desire that this land be
    set in order."
Then one (10) said to his companion among them,
"Rê will not enter heaven, while his throne is bereft of a ruler,
(for) his excellent office is (still) here in his hands.
He has given it to his son whom he loves
because Rê knows that he will make good laws on his throne."
(11) Then this entire army was concerned, saying,
"Our lord is here with us, (but) we do not know him!"
Then His Majesty's entire army said with one voice,
"But there is (still) this god Amen-Rê,
lord of the Thrones of Two-lands, who resides in Pure-mountain (Gebel
    Barkal)
—he is a god of Kush.
Come, (12) let us go to him.
We cannot accomplish anything without him;
(for) an affair carried out without him cannot be good,
while an event in the hand of the god is successful.
He has been the god of the kings of Kush since the time of Rê.
It is he that guides us.
(13) The kings of Kush have (always) been in his hands.
He has (always) given (it) to (his) son whom he loves.
Let us give praise to him, kiss the ground on their (sic) bellies,
and say in his presence, 'We are come to you, O Amûn,
that you may give us our lord to vivify us,
to build temples for all the gods and goddesses of South-land and
    North-land,
and to institute their endow(14)ments.
We cannot accomplish anything without you.
It is you that guides us.
An affair carried out without you cannot be fortunate.'"
Then this entire army said, "This is truly very good statement indeed!"
Off went His Majesty's commanders (15) and the "friends" of the
    palace
to the temple-compound of Amûn.
They found the prophets and the major *wâb*-priests standing outside
    the temple.
They said to them (the priests),
"O may this god Amen-Rê, who resides in Pure-mountain (Gebel
    Barkal) come

to cause that he give us our lord, to vivify us,

to build temples (16) for all the gods and goddesses of South-land and
     North-land,

and to institute their endowments.

We cannot accomplish anything without this god.

It is he that guides us."

In went the prophets and the major *wâb*-priests into the temple-com-
     pound

that every man might perform his purification and his censing.

In entered His Majesty's comman(17)ders and the officials of the palace
into the temple-compound,

placed themselves on their bellies before this god, and said,

"We have come to you, O Amen-Rê,

lord of the Thrones of Two-lands, who resides in Pure-mountain (Gebel
     Barkal),

that you may give us a lord to vivify us,

to build temples for the gods of South-land and North-land,

and to institute endowments.

That (18) beneficent office is in your hands.

Give it to your son whom you love."

The they placed the king's brothers before this god,

(but) he did not take one of them.

Placing a second time the king's brother,

the son of Amûn, the child of Mut, Lady of Heaven,

the Son-of-Rê: Aspelta, may he live for ever.

Then this (19) god, Amen-Rê, lord of the Thrones of Two-lands, said,

"It is he that is the king, your lord.

It is he that vivifies you.

It is he that builds every temple of South-land and North-land.

He is the one who institutes their endowments.

His father was my son, the Son-of-Rê, [. . .], justified;

and his mother is king's sister, king's mother, mistress of Kush,

(20) the Daughter of Rê, [. . .], may she live for ever,

whose mother (again) was king's sister,

divine adoratrix of Amen-Rê, king of the gods of Dominion (Thebes),
     [. . .], justified;

whose mother (again) was king's sister [. . .], justified;

whose mother (again) was king's sister [. . .], justified;

whose mother (again) was king's sister [. . .], justified;

whose mother (again) was king's sister [. . .], (21), justified;

whose mother (again) was king's sister, mistress of Kush, [. . .], justified;
It is he that is your lord."
Then those commanders of His Majesty and the officials of the palace
placed themselves on their bellies before this god,
kissing the ground over and over again, and giving praise to this god
because of (22) the mighty thing he did to his son whom he loves,
the King-of-Upper-and-Lower-Egypt: [Aspelta], may he live for ever.
In entered His Majesty to appear before his father,
Amen-Rê, lord of the Thrones of Two-lands,
and found all the crowns of the king's of Kush and their dominion-
    scepters
set before this god.
His Majesty kept saying in the presence of this (23) god,
"Come to me, Amen-Rê,
lord of the Thrones of Two-lands, who resides in Pure-mountain (Gebel
    Barkal),
that you may here give me the office, the beneficent one,
(even though) it was not in my heart,
through the greatness of your love,
and that you may give me the crown according to your heart's desire,
    together with the dominion-scepter.
Then this god said,
"Yours is the crown of your brother,
the King-of-Upper-and-Lower-Egypt: [Anlamani], triumphant (24)
    {triumphant}.
It shall remain on your head
(even) as the double crown remains on your head,
his dominion-scepter being in your grasp
so that it may overthrow all your enemies."
Then His Majesty appeared in [— — — Anlamani], triumphant.
the dominion-scepter being placed in his grasp.
Then His Majesty placed himself on his belly before this (25) god,
kissing the ground over and over again, and said,
"Come to me, Amen-Rê,
lord of the Thrones of Two-lands, who resides in Pure-mountain (Gebel
    Barkal),
eldest god, whose love is sweet,
who hearkens to him who petitions him at once [— — — — — —]
that you may grant life, stability, and all dominion,
health and all happiness, like Rê (has), for ever,

and a long, good old age,
(26) that you may grant that . . . be sated in my time
without ⌐your letting . . lie down in it⌐,
that you may grant . . . them as a serpent,
that you may put love in Kush—
this is (27) the awe of North-land . . . which he desires—
and that you may grant love . . . they being . . .”
Then this god said, “[. . .] you, all of them,
without your saying, ‘Would that I had’, about it, for ever and ever.”
(28) Out came His Majesty [from] the temple-compound into the
  midst of his army,
(even) as [Rê] shines [in heaven].
Then this entire army raised a very loud cry
. . . ,        their hearts being exceeding glad,
giving praise to His Majesty,    and said,
(29) “Welcome, ⌐lord⌐ [- — — — —] ⌐-⌐ [-]
— — — —] ⌐-⌐ [-]        like the years of Horus
in the midst of your army, appearing on the throne of Horus like Rê,
  for ever.”
In this year of His Majesty's appearance:
then he instituted festivals (30) [— — — —] them
[. . .] winter [. . .] his ⌐majesty⌐ [— . . . —]
. . . beer, . . -jugs, 40; *shu*-jugs, 100;    total: beer 140.

[RHP]

## Notes

[1]  Amen is an alternative spelling of Amun, Re an alternative spelling of Ra.

[2]  Aton was another manifestation of the sun god and was depicted as the solar disc.
  The title of "Aton of Napata" demonstrates the Kushite kings adoption of Aton as
  the patron deity of their capital city.

[3]  The Two-Ladies are the goddesses of Upper Egypt (Nekhbet) and Lower Egypt
  (Wadjet). The reference to fixing them upon one's head has to do with the use of
  their images, the vulture and cobra, respectively, on the crown of Egyptian kings. A
  crown adorned with these symbols signifies dominion over the two parts of Egypt.
  Though Egyptian kings inaugurated this design, Kushite kings adopted it as part of
  their royal insignia.

[4]  The uraeus originated in Egypt and is the depiction of a snake, typically a cobra,
  that signifies kingship. Uraei is the plural of uraeus.

# III. Ancient China

## INTRODUCTION

There are many reasons to read ancient Chinese philosophy today. The ideas are intriguing in themselves, the concepts are still extremely influential in East Asia (home to a quarter of the world's population), and the approaches to life advocated by early Chinese thinkers can be surprisingly relevant to our modern world. But in addition, it is also interesting to compare intellectual life in ancient China with that of India and the Mediterranean. Similarities may help us think about universal truths or human nature since there was almost no contact between ancient China and other advanced civilizations of the time. The Greeks and the Romans knew nothing of China, and the Chinese in turn had never heard of Homer and Plato, Moses and Asoka, or Alexander and Caesar. Nevertheless, across the Eurasian continent thoughtful people tried to understand how to deal with suffering, social inequities, and desire. They wrestled with questions of duty and family obligations.

Yet the differences are striking as well. Chinese philosophers tended to focus on issues of social relations and politics. There was some concern with metaphysics—the ultimate nature of reality—but the Chinese looked for orderly, cyclical processes rather than identifying key elements or substances. There was also a sense among many Chinese thinkers that balance and harmony were the ideal, so that binary oppositions like Heaven/Earth could not be reduced to Good/Bad. Both parts were equally valued and necessary (though in practice one might be higher than the other). There was less emphasis in China on individual founders of schools. Indeed, nearly all early Chinese texts seem to be the work of several generations of authors and compilers rather than single authors. Confucius was certainly a historical person, but the same cannot be said of Laozi (whose name simply means "the Old Master"). Laozi did not found Daoism, and even in the case of Confucius, there was no ancient philosophy called "Confucianism" in Chinese; Confucius was simply the most prominent practitioner of an already existing tradition called Ru-ism, which was composed of professional ritualists. And finally, religion—as we think of it—played a smaller role in Chinese thought. The primary religion of China was (and is) ancestor worship. There were local divinities as well, but no universal gods. In fact, there was no creation story in ancient China; the Chinese simply assumed that the world as we know it had always existed.

The golden age of Chinese philosophy, roughly 500–200 B.C.E., came out of a remarkable social context. At a time when scores of semi-independent Chinese kingdoms were fighting each other incessantly with ever more destructive results, clever, eloquent men wandered from state to state looking for positions as advisors to various rulers. Nearly all the Chinese philosophers of the time fit this description, and they often came from the lower levels of the aristocracy; that is, they were men who either by birth or political maneuvering were shut out of the ordinary avenues to power. As A. C. Graham has noted:

> Their whole thinking is a response to the breakdown of the moral and political order which had claimed the authority of Heaven; and the crucial question for all of them is not the Western Philosopher's "What is the truth?" but "Where is the Way?", the way to order the state and conduct personal life. From the viewpoint of the rulers who listen at least to the more practical of them, they are men with new answers to the problem of how to run a state in these changing times; and this problem is indeed central to all of them, whether they have practical answers (the Legalists), or ponder the moral basis of social order and its relation to the ruling power of Heaven (Confucians), or as defenders of private life who think the proper business of the state is to leave everyone alone (Zhuangzi).

Chinese philosophical texts generally take the form of advice offered to a ruler rather than treatises written for students or for other intellectuals. And for all the attention given to the proper organization of society, no Chinese thinker entertained the notion of democracy; everyone accepted the inevitability of a political system based on authoritarian rule.

The search for political, social and economic stability in the Warring States Era fueled the creation of the "Hundred Schools of Philosophy," and there really was no end to the proposals that those wandering debaters put forward. Some were agriculturalists, who claimed new techniques for increasing the farm yields crucial to supporting large armies in the field; others knew how to construct canals; and still others were military strategists (the most famous of these was Sunzi [or Sun Tzu], whose *Art of War* can still be found today in most American bookstores). There were cosmologists who promised to reveal how to harness the forces of nature, logicians who analyzed argumentation itself, and there were even some who suggested that what the world really needed was more love (they did not last very long). Among these many competing philosophies, three schools of thought stand out as particularly significant: Confucianism, Daoism, and Legalism.

Selections from each appear below, but as you read keep in mind three caveats. First, only a small portion of the literature of early China survives. We now have less than a quarter of the texts that were listed in an imperial bibliography in the first century C.E., and every few years newly excavated Chinese tombs yield books that no one has heard of for thousands of years (along with variant copies of favorites like the *Daodejing*). Second, our handy categorization of philosophers into various schools was a creation of Han dynasty (202 B.C.E.–C.E. 220) librarians trying to make sense of hundreds of texts. In pre-imperial China, there were only two distinct schools—the Ru-ists (Confucians) and the Mo-ists (advocates of universal love). Other thinkers were very eclectic as they analyzed and argued. We're not sure that even Laozi would have called himself a Daoist. And third, be wary of translations. Words and terms that we use unselfconsciously have histories, and English is very connected to the Western classical tradition. For instance, the word *xin* in Chinese carries the meanings of both our words "heart" and "mind," and many translators today render it as "heart/mind." This means that the distinction we make so readily between emotion and reason would not have easily occurred to Chinese philosophers. Or think of what is implied when the standard Chinese translation of the Bible translated the philosophically rich Greek term *logos* [the Word] in John 1:1 with an equally philosophically rich Chinese term: "In the beginning was the Dao [the Way], and the Dao was with God and the Dao was God." The concepts that Chinese thinkers had in mind ("heart/mind") when they used words translated into English as "self," "truth," "nature," "god" or even "exists" may not be what you assume those terms to mean.

The selection also includes some lyric poems, a genre which developed very early in Chinese history and which constituted an important part of the reading of educated people, including not just sages but government officers, for over two thousand years. The *Book of Songs* eventually became one of the five Confucian Classics and thus, even though it was originally a literary anthology with poems about courtship, marriage, feasting, sacrifices to the ancestors, was subject to intense study and philosophical analysis.

GH

# Book of Songs

## ca. 1000–600 B.C.E.

The *Shih-jing*, variously translated as *The Classic of Poetry*, *The Book of Odes* or the *Book of Songs* (*Shih-jing* means "poetry scripture") is a collection of some 300 poems. They were written under the Zhou dynasty, which ruled after ca. 1045 B.C.E., when it replaced the Shang. The contents of the *Book of Songs* are varied, including hymns and odes closely related to religious rites, narratives of the founding of the Zhou dynasty, love poems, descriptions of natural processes, moral commentary, and poems about war. Some of them seem to have a peasant, or folk, origin; others are clearly of courtly authorship. They appear to have been written between 1000 and 600 B.C.E.

The *Book of Songs* is sometimes referred to as a Confucian classic, both because of early traditions that Confucius was either the author or the editor of the text (neither of which seems to be true) and because, more importantly, he praised its study in his own teachings. In his *Analects* (XVII, 9) he suggests to his followers:

> My sons, my disciples, why do you not study the poets? Poetry is able to stimulate the mind, it can train to observation, it can encourage social intercourse, it can modify the vexations of life; from it the student learns to fulfil his more immediate duty to his parents, and his remoter duty to the prince; and in it he may become widely acquainted with the names of birds and beasts, plants and trees.[1]

Because Confucius insisted on the morally improving results of studying the *Shih-jing*, the poems have been exhaustively annotated and interpreted, often by supplying allegorical readings.

The current selection includes examples of several genres included in the *Book of Songs*. Selection 1 is a mythical account of the birth of Lord Millet, a miraculous benefactor who was considered the ancestor of the Zhou dynasty. "She Bore the Folk" serves to explain an agriculturally significant ritual. Selection 2 refers to the selection of courtiers to undergo human sacrifice and be buried with their king or lord and laments the loss of three of them. Selections 3, 4, 6, 7, 9 and 10 are on the perennial themes of love, courtship, and loss. Selection 11 is a tribute to a royal bride, including praise of her beauty. Selection 5 is a paean to the prince, while selection 8 is a tribute to friendship and comradeship in time of war.

MM

# Note

[1] Confucius, *The Analects* (trans. William Edward Soothill) 1910; rpt. New York: Dover 1995: 107.

# Selections from *Book of Songs*

## Dynastic Legends

*238*

She who in the beginning gave birth to the people,
This was Chiang Yüan.
How did she give birth to the people?
Well she sacrificed and prayed
That she might no longer be childless.
She trod on the big toe of God's footprint,
Was accepted and got what she desired.
Then in reverence, then in awe
She gave birth, she nurtured;
And this was Hou Chi.

Indeed, she had fulfilled her months,
And her first-born came like a lamb
With no bursting or rending,
With no hurt or harm.
To make manifest His magic power
God on high gave her ease.
So blessed were her sacrifice and prayer
That easily she bore her child.

Indeed, they put it in a narrow lane;
But oxen and sheep tenderly cherished it.
Indeed, they put it in a far-off wood;
But it chanced that woodcutters came to this wood.
Indeed, they put it on the cold ice;
But the birds covered it with their wings.
The birds at last went away,
And Hou Chi began to wail.

Truly far and wide
His voice was very loud.
Then sure enough he began to crawl;
Well he straddled, well he reared,
To reach food for his mouth.

He planted large beans;
His beans grew fat and tall.
His paddy-lines[1] were close set,
His hemp and wheat grew thick,
His young gourds teemed.

Truly Hou Chi's husbandry
Followed the way that had been shown.
He cleared away the thick grass,
He planted the yellow crop.
It failed nowhere, it grew thick,
It was heavy, it was tall,
It sprouted, it eared,
It was firm and good,
It nodded, it hung—
He made house and home in T'ai.

Indeed, the lucky grains were sent down to us,
The black millet, the double-kernelled,
Millet pink-sprouted and white.
Far and wide the black and the double-kernelled
He reaped and acred;
Far and wide the millet pink and white
He carried in his arms, he bore on his back,
Brought them home, and created the sacrifice.

Indeed, what are they, our sacrifices?
We pound the grain, we bale it out,
We sift, we tread,
We wash it—soak, soak;
We boil it all steamy.
Then with due care, due thought
We gather southernwood, make offering of fat,
Take lambs for the rite of expiation,
We roast, we broil,
To give a start to the coming year.

High we load the stands,
The stands of wood and of earthenware.
As soon as the smell rises
God on high is very pleased:
'What smell is this, so strong and good?'

Hou Chi founded the sacrifices,
And without blemish or flaw
They have gone on till now.

## Blessings on Gentle Folk

### *163*

In the south is a tree with drooping boughs;
The cloth-creeper[2] binds it.
Oh, happy is our lord;
Blessings and boons secure him!

In the south is a tree with drooping boughs;
The cloth-creeper covers it.
Oh, happy is our lord;
Blessings and boons protect him!

In the south is a tree with drooping boughs;
The cloth-creeper encircles it.
Oh, happy is our lord;
Blessings and boons surround him!

## Lamentations

### *278*

'Kio' sings the oriole
As it lights on the thorn-bush.
Who went with Duke Mu to the grave?
Yen-hsi of the clan Tzŭ-chü.
Now this Yen-hsi
Was the pick of all our men;
But as he drew near the tomb-hole
His limbs shook with dread.
That blue one, Heaven,
Takes all our good men.
Could we but ransom him
There are a hundred would give their lives.

'Kio' sings the oriole
As it lights on the mulberry-tree.
Who went with Duke Mu to the grave?

Chung-hang of the clan Tzŭ-chü.
Now this Chung-hang
Was the sturdiest of all our men;
But as he drew near the tomb-hole
His limbs shook with dread.
That blue one, Heaven,
Takes all our good men.
Could we but ransom him
There are a hundred would give their lives.

'Kio' sings the oriole
As it lights on the brambles.
Who went with Duke Mu to the grave?
Ch'ien-hu of the clan Tzŭ-chü.
Now this Ch'ien-hu
Was the strongest of all our men.
But as he drew near the tomb-hole
His limbs shook with dread.
That blue one, Heaven,
Takes all our good men.
Could we but ransom him
There are a hundred would give their lives.

## Warriors and Battles

### 148

How can you plead that you have no wraps?
I will share my rug with you.
The king is raising an army;
I have made ready both axe and spear;
You shall share them with me as my comrade.

How can you plead that you have no wraps?
I will share my under-robe with you.
The king is raising an army,
I have made ready both spear and halberd;
You shall share them with me when we start.

How can you plead that you have no wraps?
I will share my skirt with you.
The king is raising an army,

I have made ready both armour and arms;
You shall share them with me on the march.

## Marriage

### *86*

A splendid woman and upstanding;
Brocade she wore, over an unlined coat.
Daughter of the Lord of Ch'i,
Wife of the Lord of Wei,
Sister of the Crown Prince of Ch'i,
Called sister-in-law by the Lord of Hsing,
Calling the Lord of T'an her brother-in-law.

Hands white as rush-down,
Skin like lard,
Neck long and white as the tree-grub,
Teeth like melon seeds,
Lovely head, beautiful brows.
Oh, the sweet smile dimpling,
The lovely eyes so black and white.

This splendid lady takes her ease;
She rests where the fields begin.
Her four steeds prance,
The red trappings flutter.
Screened by fans of pheasant-feather she is led to Court.
Oh, you Great Officers, retire early,
Do not fatigue our lord.

Where the water of the river, deep and wide,
Flows northward in strong course,
In the fish-net's swish and swirl
Sturgeon, snout-fish leap and lash.
Reeds and sedges tower high.
All her ladies are tall-coiffed;
All her knights, doughty men.

## Courtship

*17*

Plop fall the plums; but there are still seven.
Let those gentlemen that would court me
Come while it is lucky!

Plop fall the plums; there are still three.
Let any gentleman that would court me
Come before it is too late!

Plop fall the plums; in shallow baskets we lay them.
Any gentleman who would court me
Had better speak while there is time.

*63*

In the wilds there is a dead doe;
With white rushes we cover her.
There was a lady longing for the spring;
A fair knight seduced her.

In the wood there is a clump of oaks,
And in the wilds a dead deer
With white rushes well bound;
There was a lady fair as jade.

'Heigh, not so hasty, not so rough;
Heigh, do not touch my handkerchief.
Take care, or the dog will bark.'

*24*

I beg of you, Chung Tzu,
Do not climb into our homestead,
Do not break the willows we have planted.
Not that I mind about the willows,
But I am afraid of my father and mother.
Chung Tzu I dearly love;
But of what my father and mother say
Indeed I am afraid.

I beg of you, Chung Tzu,
Do not climb over our wall,

Do not break the mulberry-trees we have planted.
Not that I mind about the mulberry-trees,
But I am afraid of my brothers.
Chung Tzu I dearly love;
But of what my brothers say
Indeed I am afraid.

I beg of you, Chung Tzu,
Do not climb into our garden,
Do not break the hard-wood we have planted.
Not that I mind about the hard-wood,
But I am afraid of what people will say.
Chung Tzu I dearly love;
But of all that people will say
Indeed I am afraid.

## 10

That the mere glimpse of a plain cap
Could harry me with such longing,
Cause pain so dire!

That the mere glimpse of a plain coat
Could stab my heat with grief!
Enough! Take me with you to your home.

That a mere glimpse of plain leggings
Could tie my heart in tangles!
Enough! Let us two be one.

## 12

In the ten-acre field
A mulberry-picker stands idle,
Says: 'If you're going, I will come back with you.'

Beyond the ten-acre field
A mulberry-picker has strayed,
Says: 'If you're going, I will stroll with you.'

*39*

If you tenderly love me,
Gird our loins and wade across the Chên;[3]
But if you do not love me—
There are plenty of other men,
Of madcaps maddest, oh!

If you tenderly love me,
Gird our loins and wade across the Wei;
But if you do not love me—
There are plenty of other knights,
Of madcaps maddest, oh!

## Notes

[1] In a rice paddy.

[2] A brambly vine.

[3] The Chen and Wei were rivers in north-central Honan.

# Confucius

## 551–479 B.C.

Confucius considered himself a failure in life. Tradition has it that his pleas for employment were rejected by some seventy different rulers. When he failed to gain office he became a teacher, and the ideas that he developed were later widely adopted in China. Basically, he thought that the problems of the age—increasing violence and the breakup of society—could be countered with a return to the morality of the past, by which he meant the aristocratic ways of the early Zhou dynasty. He urged his students to study ancient history and literature, and he felt that if a ruler lived according to high ethical standards the people would naturally follow his example. Confucius taught the importance of ritual and music in shaping moral sensibilities, and he advocated a benevolent sort of hierarchical social order. When the Duke of Qi asked him about government, he replied "Let rulers be rulers, ministers be ministers, fathers fathers, and sons sons" (*Analects* 12:11). The idea is that if everyone knew their place in society and acted in accordance with their position, then things would run smoothly. If, for example, every father acted as a true father—caring for the welfare of his children, protecting, educating, and supporting them—and every son showed proper respect and obedience, families would be more stable and successful. Similarly rulers and ministers should work together in a relationship that was unequal, but nevertheless was characterized by generosity and mutual concern.

Key terms in Confucian thought include *ren*, sometimes translated as "perfect virtue," "human-heartedness" or "humanity"; *li* or ritual, which included not only ceremonial correctness, but also proper etiquette and demeanor; and *xiao*, usually rendered as "filial piety" and referring to a respect for parents so strong that there is no already-existing equivalent term in English. In fact, Confucius believed that filial piety was the foundation of a well-ordered society.

In Chinese, Confucius is referred to as *Kongzi*, or "Master Kong" ("Confucius" is a Latinized form introduced by Jesuit missionaries) and his school was called Ruism. The word *ru* meant something like "soft or weak" and referred to scholars and officials who had no military responsibilities. Confucius became the foremost teacher in this school, and he and his students gathered together the heritage of Chinese literary culture and became experts in their transmission and interpretation. The five "Confucian Classics" were the *Classic of History*, the *Classic of Poetry*, the *Classic of Change* (otherwise known as the *Yijing*—a divination text), the *Record of Ritual*, and the *Spring and Autumn Annals*—a laconic history of Confucius' native state of Lu from 722 to 480 B.C.E. These texts were thought to have been edited by Confucius, but although modern scholars dispute this, there is broad consensus that our best source for Confucius' ideas is the *Analects*, a collection of short sayings of Confucius put together after his death by his disciples (in this way, our knowledge of Confucius is like our understanding of Socrates and Jesus, neither of whom wrote anything themselves).

As presented in the *Analects*, Confucius makes no attempt at systematic philosophy. He responds to specific inquiries from students or rulers (sometimes we get just the answers without the questions), and his primary concern seems to be inspiring and motivating his disciples. Different students sometimes get different answers to the same question, and Confucius is not overly concerned with contractions. Perhaps he is still trying to figure things himself as he engages in ongoing conversation about the issues that really matter in life. The *Analects* include twenty chapters that treat a variety of topics in a haphazard, even random order. I have organized the following selections by theme, but the original is much more diffuse. Through it all comes a portrait of a teacher—patient usually, frustrated sometimes, curious, dedicated, generous, judgmental, and above all committed to identifying true virtue and putting it into practice.

GH

# Selections from the *Analects*

## Education

1.1  The Master said, "Is it not pleasant to learn with a constant perseverance and application? Is it not delightful to have friends coming from distant quarters? Is he not a man of complete virtue, who feels no discomposure though men may take no note of him?"

2.15  The Master said, "Learning without thought is labor lost; thought without learning is perilous."

2.17  The Master said, "Zilu [one of Confucius' students], shall I teach you what knowledge is? When you know a thing, to hold that you know it; and when you do not know a thing, to allow that you do not know it;— this is knowledge."

5.13  When Zilu heard anything, if he had not yet succeeded in carrying it into practice, he was only afraid lest he should hear something else.

6.18  The Master said, "They who know the truth are not equal to those who love it, and they who love it are not equal to those who delight in it."

7.8  The Master said, "I do not open up the truth to one who is not eager to get knowledge, nor help out any one who is not anxious to explain himself. When I have presented one corner of a subject to any one, and he cannot from it learn the other three, I do not repeat my lesson."

15.38  The Master said, "In teaching there should be no distinction of classes."

17.2  The Master said, "By nature, men are nearly alike; by practice, they get to be wide apart."

## Government

2.3  The Master said, "If the people be led by laws, and uniformity sought to be given them by punishments, they will try to avoid the punishment, but have no sense of shame. If they be led by virtue, and uniformity sought to be given them by the rules of propriety [*li*], they will have the sense of shame, and moreover will become good."

2.20  Lord Ji Kang asked how to cause the people to reverence their ruler, to be faithful to him, and to go on to nerve themselves to virtue. The Master said, "Let him preside over them with gravity;—then they will reverence him. Let him be final and kind to all;—then they will be faithful to him. Let him advance the good and teach the incompetent;—then they will eagerly seek to be virtuous."

12.7  Zigong [a student] asked about government. The Master said, "The requisites of government are that there be sufficiency of food, sufficiency of military equipment, and the confidence of the people in their ruler." Zigong said, "If it cannot be helped, and one of these must be dispensed with, which of the three should be foregone first?" "The military equipment," said the Master. Zigong again asked, "If it cannot be helped, and one of the remaining two must be dispensed with, which of them should be foregone?" The Master answered, "Part with the food. From of old, death has been the lot of men; but if the people have no faith in their rulers, there is no standing for the state."

12.11  Duke Jing, of Qi, asked Confucius about government. Confucius replied, "There is government, when the prince is prince, and the minister is minister; when the father is father, and the son is son." "Good!" said the duke; "if, indeed, the prince be not prince, the minister not minister, the father not father, and the son not son, although I have my revenue, can I enjoy it?"

12.18  Lord Ji Kang, distressed about the number of thieves in the state, inquired of Confucius how to do away with them. Confucius said, "If you, sir, were not covetous, although you should reward them to do it, they would not steal."

12.19  Lord Ji Kang asked Confucius about government, saying, "What do you say to killing the unprincipled for the good of the principled?" Confucius replied, "Sir, in carrying on your government, why should you use killing at all? Let your evinced desires be for what is good, and the people will be good. The relation between superiors and inferiors is like that between the wind and the grass. The grass must bend, when the wind blows across it."

13.9  When the Master went to Wei, Ran Qiu acted as driver of his carriage. The Master observed, "How numerous are the people!" Ran Qiu said, "Since they are thus numerous, what more shall be done for them?" "Enrich them," was the reply. "And when they have been enriched, what more shall be done?" The Master said, "Teach them."

## The Superior Man (or Gentleman)

2.13  Zigong asked what constituted the superior man. The Master said, "He acts before he speaks, and afterwards speaks according to his actions."

4.5  The Master said, "Riches and honors are what men desire. If it cannot be obtained in the proper way, they should not be held. Poverty and meanness are what men dislike. If it cannot be avoided in the proper way, they should not be avoided. If a superior man abandons virtue [*ren*], how can he fulfill the requirements of that name? The superior man does not, even for the space of a single meal, act contrary to virtue. In moments of haste, he cleaves to it. In seasons of danger, he cleaves to it."

4.16 The Master said, "The mind of the superior man is conversant with righteousness; the mind of the mean man is conversant with gain."

7.36 The Master said, "The superior man is satisfied and composed; the mean man is always full of distress."

9.13 The Master was wishing to go and live among the nine wild tribes of the east. Some one said, "They are rude. How can you do such a thing?" The Master said, "If a superior man dwelt among them, what rudeness would there be?"

15.20 The Master said, "What the superior man seeks, is in himself. What the mean man seeks, is in others."

16.7 Confucius said, "There are three things which the superior man guards against. In youth, when the physical powers are not yet settled, he guards against lust. When he is strong and the physical powers are full of vigor, he guards against quarrelsomeness. When he is old, and the animal powers are decayed, he guards against covetousness."

## Morality

4.17 The Master said, "When we see men of worth, we should think of equaling them; when we see men of a contrary character, we should turn inwards and examine ourselves."

5.19 Lord Ji Wen thought thrice, and then acted. When the Master was informed of it, he said, "Twice may do."

13.18 The Duke of She informed Confucius, saying, "Among us here there are those who may be styled upright in their conduct. If their father have stolen a sheep, they will bear witness to the fact." Confucius said, "Among us, in our part of the country, those who are upright are different from this. The father conceals the misconduct of the son, and the son conceals the misconduct of the father. Uprightness is to be found in this."

13.24 Zigong asked, saying, "What do you say of a man who is loved by all the people of his neighborhood?" The Master replied, "We may not for that accord our approval of him." "And what do you say of him who is hated by all the people of his neighborhood?" The Master said, "We may not for that conclude that he is bad. It is better than either of these cases that the good in the neighborhood love him, and the bad hate him."

14.36 Some one said, "What do you say concerning the principle that injury should be recompensed with kindness?" The Master said, "With what then will you recompense kindness? Recompense injury with justice, and recompense kindness with kindness."

15.23 Zigong asked, saying, "Is there one word which may serve as a rule of practice for all one's life?" The Master said, "Is not *reciprocity* such a word? What you do not want done to yourself, do not do to others."

16.10 Confucius said, "The superior man has nine things which are subjects with him of thoughtful consideration. In regard to the use of his eyes, he is anxious to see clearly. In regard to the use of his ears, he is anxious to hear distinctly. In regard to his countenance, he is anxious that it should be benign. In regard to his demeanor, he is anxious that it should be respectful. In regard to his speech, he is anxious that it should be sincere. In regard to his doing of business, he is anxious that it should be reverently careful. In regard to what he doubts about, he is anxious to question others. When he is angry, he thinks of the difficulties (his anger may involve him in). When he sees gain to be got, he thinks of righteousness."

## Humanity

3.3 The Master said, "If a man be without the virtues proper to humanity [*ren*], what has he to do with the rites of propriety [*li*]? If a man be without the virtues proper to humanity, what has he to do with music?"

4.2 The Master said, "Those who are without virtue [*ren*] cannot abide long either in a condition of poverty and hardship, or in a condition of enjoyment. The virtuous rest in virtue; the wise desire virtue."

4.3 The Master said, "It is only the (truly) virtuous man [*ren*], who can love, or who can hate, others."

6.21 The Master said, "The wise find pleasure in water; the virtuous [*ren*] find pleasure in hills. The wise are active; the virtuous are tranquil. The wise are joyful; the virtuous are long-lived."

## Filial Piety

1.11 The Master said, "While a man's father is alive, look at the bent of his will; when his father is dead, look at his conduct. If for three years he does not alter from the way of his father, he may be called filial."

2.6 Ziyou [a student] asked what filial piety was. The Master said, "The filial piety nowadays means the support of one's parents. But dogs and horses likewise are able to do something in the way of support;—without reverence, what is there to distinguish the one support given from the other?"

4.18 The Master said, "In serving his parents, a son may remonstrate with them, but gently; when he sees that they do not incline to follow his advice, he shows an increased degree of reverence, but does not abandon his purpose; and should they punish him, he does not allow himself to murmur."

4.19 The Master said, "While his parents are alive, the son may not go abroad to a distance. If he does go abroad, he must have a fixed place to which he goes."

## Ritual/Music

8.2 The Master said, "Respectfulness, without the rules of propriety [*li*], becomes laborious bustle; carefulness, without the rules of propriety, becomes timidity; boldness, without the rules of propriety, becomes insubordination; straightforwardness, without the rules of propriety, becomes rudeness. When those who are in high stations perform well all their duties to their relations, the people are aroused to virtue. When old friends are not neglected by them, the people are preserved from meanness."

8.8 The Master said, "It is by the *Classic of Poetry* that the mind is aroused. It is by the rules of propriety that the character is established. It is from music that the finish is received."

11.12 Zilu asked about serving the spirits of the dead. The Master said, "While you are not able to serve men, how can you serve their spirits?" Zilu added, "I venture to ask about death?" He was answered, "While you do not know life, how can you know about death?"

12.1 1. Yan Hui [Confucius' favorite student] asked about perfect virtue [*ren*]. The Master said, "To subdue one's self and return to propriety, is perfect virtue. If a man can for one day subdue himself and return to propriety, all under heaven will ascribe perfect virtue to him. Is the practice of perfect virtue from a man himself, or is it from others?" Yen Hui said, "I beg to ask the steps of that process." The Master replied, "Look not at what is contrary to propriety; listen not to what is contrary to propriety; speak not what is contrary to propriety; make no movement which is contrary to propriety." Yen Hui then said, "Though I am deficient in intelligence and vigor, I will make it my business to practice this lesson."

17.25 The Master said, "Of all people, girls and servants are the most difficult to behave to. If you are familiar with them, they lose their humility. If you maintain a reserve towards them, they are discontented."

## Confucius the Man

2.4 The Master said, "At fifteen, I had my mind bent on learning. At thirty, I stood firm. At forty, I had no doubts. At fifty, I knew the decrees of Heaven. At sixty, my ear was an obedient organ for the reception of truth. At seventy, I could follow what my heart desired, without transgressing what was right."

2.21 Some one addressed Confucius, saying, "Sir, why are you not engaged in the government?" The Master said, "What does the *Classic of Poetry* say of filial piety?—'You are filial, you discharge your brotherly duties. These qualities are displayed in government.' This then also constitutes the exercise of government. Why must there be THAT—making one be in the government?"

5.27 The Master said, "In a hamlet of ten families, there may be found one honorable and sincere as I am, but not so fond of learning."

7.18 The Duke of She asked Zilu about Confucius, and Zilu did not answer him. The Master said, "Why did you not say to him,—He is simply a man, who in his eager pursuit of knowledge forgets his food, who in the joy of its attainment forgets his sorrows, and who does not perceive that old age is coming on?"

7.19 The Master said, "I am not one who was born in the possession of knowledge; I am one who is fond of antiquity, and earnest in seeking it there."

7.31 When the Master was in company with a person who was singing, if he sang well, he would make him repeat the song, while he accompanied it with his own voice.

7.33 The Master said, "The sage and the man of perfect virtue [*ren*];—how dare I rank myself with them? It may simply be said of me, that I strive to become such without satiety, and teach others without weariness." Gongxi Chi said, "This is just what we, the disciples, cannot imitate you in."

10.8 Although his food might be coarse rice and vegetable soup, he would offer a little of it in sacrifice with a grave, respectful air.

11.8 When Yan Hui [Confucius' favorite student] died, the Master said, "Alas! Heaven is destroying me! Heaven is destroying me!"

13.10 The Master said, "If there were (any of the princes) who would employ me, in the course of twelve months, I should have done something considerable. In three years, the government would be perfected."

[Some spellings have been modified, ed.]

# Laozi[1]

If Confucius comes across as a real person, Laozi (Master Lao) is a mystery. His name may not even be a name, for it might simply mean "The Old Master." We have no idea when he lived, or even if he lived. What we do have is a book, sometimes called the Laozi, and sometimes referred to as the *Daodejing* (The Way and Integrity Classic). This short text of about 5,000 Chinese characters has proven endlessly fascinating to both Chinese and foreigners alike, and it is easily the most translated Chinese book ever. The Confucian *Analects* seem fairly straightforward and commonsensical in comparison to the *Daodejing*, which is cryptic, paradoxical, poetic, and provocative. There are eighty-one short chapters, many of which seem quite jumbled. In fact, a silk manuscript found in a tomb in 1973 starts with Chapters 38–82 (the Integrity section) and ends with Chapters 1–37 (the Way section). In any event, the text seems to date to the third century B.C.E.

The author (or authors, but we can follow convention and call this writer Laozi) appears to be dealing with the same social problems that vexed Confucius, but his answer was to return to the *Dao*—often translated as "the Way." The *Dao* is a bit hard to describe since Laozi taught that it was beyond words, but it has something to do with nature and it encompasses all opposites (this is the concept behind the famous yin/yang symbol). So although we tend to judge things as being weak or strong, hard or soft, desirable or repugnant, from the perspective of nature these artificial, human distinctions don't mean much. For instance, gold and dirt are both natural products and both have their uses, but because we think that gold is more valuable, people are willing to lie and steal and even murder to get it (even though it would be impossible to grow crops in a field of gold). If people could ignore such common value judgments, everyone would be happier.

According to Laozi, the best society would be one made up of small villages whose inhabitants were basically content with what they had. It is desire and ambition that get us into trouble, and they are hardly ever worth it. Even more strikingly, Laozi suggests that many opposites are illusory. Thus water appears soft and weak, but for wearing away mountains and digging canyons, there is nothing like it. And opposites always come in pairs, so that when we praise someone as being beautiful, we are also implying that everyone who looks different is ugly. So also, Laozi complains that whenever the Confucians emphasize a virtue, they also highlight a vice. For example, the only reason they speak so much about filial piety is because the lack of respect for parents is already a major problem. Some listeners might respond, "You mean, not everyone obeys their parents? There's an idea!"

Laozi offers advice for individuals, but he also has suggestions for rulers. In political terms, the best government is one that doesn't do much, because trying to change things too quickly will always bring a backlash of resentment. Laozi promotes a vision of simplicity, contentment, and quietism, and he specifically advocates *wu-wei,* or "non-action." This probably does not literally mean doing nothing. Rather, we should avoid doing anything that takes too much effort. Relax. Go with the flow. Don't worry, be happy. Such sentiments still resonate with people today.

Most Chinese traditionally have been both Confucian and Daoist to some degree. When times are good and hard work seems to pay off, Confucianism provides direction and encouragement to make things even better. But when times are bad and the government is corrupt, Daoism functions as a sort of safety valve, an ideology that allows one to withdraw from public life and concentrate on simple pleasures. To summarize, Confucianism is associated with hierarchy, order, social responsibility, service, and conformity. It is moralistic, activist, and serious. Daoism, on the other hand, values individualism, freedom, nonconformity, nature, retirement, wit, and mysticism. But Confucius and Laozi were not exactly opposites, since they shared many assumptions. They both rejected competition and strife, they were suspicious of attempts to pin down ideas in exact language, and they believed that an intuitive, spontaneous sort of harmony would naturally arise from their principles.

[Note that in the excerpt below, the translator sometimes refers to sages and rulers in the feminine form. This does not reflect any Chinese traditions of governance nor is it in the Chinese original. But then again, Laozi does say "Know the masculine, but keep to the feminine" (ch. 28), so perhaps even gender distinctions are lost from the perspective of the Dao. But this would occur much more readily to us than to the ancient Chinese.]

GH

## Note

[1] You will notice that the translator of the following selection offered variant spellings for Laozi (Lao Tzu) and *Daodejing* (*Tao Te Ching*). The discrepancy reflects different transliteration and translation systems used in a process we call "Romanization": the process of converting non-Latin scripts (such as Chinese) to the Roman alphabetic system (A, B, C . . .). There are two prominent Romanization stems—Wade Giles, used by the translator, and Pinyin, used in the introduction. Pinyin has been officially

adopted by the People's Republic of China and in recent years has come to be used by most scholars and libraries.

# from *Tao Te Ching*

## I

1 The way that can be spoken of
Is not the constant way;
The name that can be named
Is not the constant name.

2 The nameless was the beginning of heaven and earth;
The named was the mother of the myriad creatures.

3 Hence always rid yourself of desires in order to observe its secrets;
But always allow yourself to have desires in order to observe
　　its manifestations.

32 These two are the same
But diverge in name as they issue forth.
Being the same they are called mysteries,
Mystery upon mystery—
The gateway of the manifold secrets.

## II

4 The whole world recognizes the beautiful as the beautiful,
yet this is only the ugly; the whole world recognizes the
good as the good, yet this is only the bad.

5 　　Thus Something and Nothing produce each other;
　　The difficult and the easy complement each other;
　　The long and the short offset each other;
　　The high and the low incline towards each other;
　　Note and sound harmonize with each other;
　　Before and after follow each other.

6 Therefore the sage keeps to the deed that consists in taking
no action and practises the teaching that uses no words.

7 　　The myriad creatures rise from it yet it claims no authority;
　　It gives them life yet claims no possession;
　　It benefits them yet exacts no gratitude;
　　It accomplishes its task yet lays claim to no merit.

7a It is because it lays claim to no merit
　　That its merit never deserts it.

# III

8   Not to honour men of worth will keep the people from contention; not to value goods which are hard to come by will keep them from theft; not to display what is desirable will keep them from being unsettled of mind.

9   Therefore in governing the people, the sage empties their minds but fills their bellies, weakens their wills but strengthens their bones. He always keeps them innocent of knowledge and free from desire, and ensures that the clever never dare to act.

10   Do that which consists in taking no action, and order will prevail.

# IX

23   Rather than fill it to the brim by keeping it upright
Better to have stopped in time;
Hammer it to a point
And the sharpness cannot be preserved for ever;
There may be gold and jade to fill a hall
But there is none who can keep them.
To be overbearing when one has wealth and position
Is to bring calamity upon oneself.
To retire when the task is accomplished
Is the way of heaven.

# XVIII

42   When the great way falls into disuse
There are benevolence and rectitude;
When cleverness emerges
There is great hypocrisy;
When the six relations are at variance
There are filial children;
When the state is benighted
There are loyal ministers.

## XXXVI

79  If you would have a thing shrink,
You must first stretch it;
If you would have a thing weakened,
You must first strengthen it;
If you would have a thing laid aside,
You must first set it up;
If you would take from a thing,
You must first give to it.

79a  This is called subtle discernment:
The submissive and weak will overcome the hard and strong.

80  The fish must not be allowed to leave the deep;
The instruments of power in a state must not be revealed to anyone.

## XLVII

106  Without stirring abroad
One can know the whole world;
Without looking out of the window
One can see the way of heaven.
The further one goes
The less one knows.

107  Therefore the sage knows without having to stir,
Identifies without having to see,
Accomplishes without having to act.

## LXXXI

194  Truthful words are not beautiful; beautiful words are not
truthful. Good words are not persuasive; persuasive words
are not good. He who knows has no wide learning; he
who has wide learning does not know.

195  The sage does not hoard.
Having bestowed all he has on others, he has yet more;
Having given all he has to others, he is richer still.

196  The way of heaven benefits and does not harm; the way of
the sage is bountiful and does not contend.

# Zhuangzi

## Third Century B.C.E.

Zhuangzi, or Master Zhuang, can be reliably dated to the beginning of the 3rd century B.C.E. His book, also called the *Zhuangzi*, was probably augmented by later writers, but the first seven chapters seem to be by the same person. Because his ideas are similar to those of Laozi (he may, in fact, have been earlier than Laozi), Chinese scholars in the first century B.C.E. categorized both of them as Daoists. Their styles, however, are very different. Zhuangzi wrote long, fantastic narratives and dialogues that humorously poke holes in our everyday notions of value and truth. Perspective is everything, he seems to say, and he delights in language games that leave readers both exhilarated and a bit confused.

Zhuangzi is unlike Lao Tzu, who argues that there is no real difference between opposites like weak and strong, but in the end shows a clear preference as he gives advice to rulers. Take the weaker position (like water), he suggests, because then you will survive longer. Zhuangzi, by contrast, really seems to have no preferences. Dream and reality; power and powerlessness; even life and death are all the same to him. A few excerpts, particularly on this last theme, will illustrate this.

GH

# Selections from the *Zhuangzi*

## Chapter 2: "The Adjustment of Controversies"

"How do I know that the love of life is not a delusion? and that the dislike of death is not like a young person's losing his way, and not knowing that he is really going home? Lady Li was a daughter of the border Warden of Ai. When the ruler of the state of Jin first got possession of her, she wept till the tears wetted all the front of her dress. But when she came to the place of the king, shared with him his luxurious couch, and ate his grain-and-grass-fed meat, then she regretted that she had wept. How do I know that the dead do not repent of their former craving for life?

"Those who dream of the pleasures of drinking may in the morning wail and weep; those who dream of wailing and weeping may in the morning be going out to hunt. When they were dreaming they did not know it was a dream; in their dream they may even have tried to interpret it; but when they awoke they knew that it was a dream. And there is the great awaking, after which we shall know that this life was a great dream. All the while, the stupid think they are awake, and with nice discrimination insist on their knowledge; now playing the part of rulers, and now of grooms. Bigoted was that Confucius! He and you are both dreaming. I who say that you are dreaming am dreaming myself. These words seem very strange; but if after ten thousand ages we once meet with a great sage who knows how to explain them, it will be as if we met him unexpectedly some morning or evening.

"Since you made me enter into this discussion with you, if you have got the better of me and not I of you, are you indeed right, and I indeed wrong? If I have got the better of you and not you of me, am I indeed right and you indeed wrong? Is the one of us right and the other wrong? are we both right or both wrong? Since we cannot come to a mutual and common understanding, men will certainly continue in darkness on the subject.

"Whom shall I employ to adjudicate in the matter? If I employ one who agrees with you, how can he, agreeing with you, do so correctly? And the same may be said, if I employ one who agrees with me. It will be the same if I employ one who differs from us both or one who agrees with us both. In this way I and you and those others would all not be able to come to a mutual understanding; and shall we then wait for that great sage? We need not do so. To wait on others to learn how conflicting opinions are changed is simply like not so waiting at all. The harmonising of them is to be found in the invisible operation of

227

Heaven, and by following this on into the unlimited past. It is by this method that we can complete our years without our minds being disturbed.

• • •

"Formerly, I, Zhuang Chou (Zhuangzi), dreamt that I was a butterfly, a butterfly flying about, feeling that it was enjoying itself. I did not know that it was Zhuang Chou. Suddenly I awoke, and was myself again, the veritable Zhuang Chou. I did not know whether it had formerly been Zhuang Chou dreaming that he was a butterfly, or it was now a butterfly dreaming that it was Zhuang Chou. But between Zhuang Chou and a butterfly there must be a difference. This is a case of what is called the Transformation of Things."

## Chapter 17: "The Floods of Autumn"

Zhuangzi was once fishing in the river Pu, when the king of Chu sent two great officers to him, with the message, "I wish to trouble you with the charge of all within my territories." Zhuangzi kept on holding his rod without looking round, and said, "I have heard that in Chu there is a spirit-like tortoise-shell, the wearer of which died 3000 years ago, and which the king keeps, in his ancestral temple, in a hamper covered with a cloth. Was it better for the tortoise to die, and leave its shell to be thus honoured? Or would it have been better for it to live, and keep on dragging its tail through the mud?" The two officers said, "It would have been better for it to live, and draw its tail after it over the mud." "Go your ways. I will keep on drawing my tail after me through the mud."

• • •

Zhuangzi and Huizi were walking on the dam over the Hao River, when the former said, "These minnows come out, and play about at their ease;— that is the enjoyment of fishes." The other said, "You are not a fish; how do you know what constitutes the enjoyment of fishes?" Zhuangzi rejoined, "You are not I. How do you know that I do not know what constitutes the enjoyment of fishes?" Huizi said, "I am not you; and though indeed I do not fully know you, you certainly are not a fish, and the argument is complete against your knowing what constitutes the happiness of fishes." Zhuangzi replied, "Let us keep to your original question. You said to me, '*How* do you know what constitutes the enjoyment of fishes?' You knew that I knew it, and yet you put your question to me;—well, I know it from our enjoying ourselves together over the River Hao."

## Chapter 18: "Perfect Enjoyment"

When Zhuangzi's wife died, Huizi went to condole with him, and, finding him squatted on the ground, drumming on the basin, and singing, said to him, "When a wife has lived with her husband, and brought up children, and then dies in her old age, not to wail for her is enough. When you go on to drum on this basin and sing, is it not an excessive and strange demonstration?" Zhuangzi replied, "It is not so. When she first died, was it possible for me to be singular and not affected by the event? But I reflected on the commencement of her being. She had not yet been born to life; not only had she no life, but she had no bodily form; not only had she no bodily form, but she had no breath. During the intermingling of the waste and dark chaos, there ensued a change, and there was breath; another change, and there was the bodily form; another change, and there came birth and life. There is now a change again, and she is dead. The relation between these things is like the procession of the four seasons from spring to autumn, from winter to summer. There now she lies with her face up, sleeping in the Great Chamber; and if I were to fall sobbing and going on to wail for her, I should think that I did not understand what was appointed for all. I therefore restrained myself!"

• • •

When Zhuangzi went to Chu, he saw an empty skull, bleached indeed, but still retaining its shape. Tapping it with his horse-switch, he asked it, saying, "Did you, Sir, in your greed of life, fail in the lessons of reason, and come to this? Or did you do so, in the service of a perishing state, by the punishment of the axe? Or was it through your evil conduct, reflecting disgrace on your parents and on your wife and children? Or was it through your hard endurances of cold and hunger? Or was it that you had completed your term of life?"

Having given expression to these questions, he took up the skull, and made a pillow of it when he went to sleep. At midnight the skull appeared to him in a dream, and said, "What you said to me was after the fashion of an orator. All your words were about the entanglements of men in their lifetime. There are none of those things after death. Would you like to hear me, Sir, tell you about death?" "I should," said Zhuangzi, and the skull resumed: "In death there are not the distinctions of ruler above and minister below. There are none of the phenomena of the four seasons. Tranquil and at ease, our years are those of heaven and earth. No king in his court has greater enjoyment than we have."

Zhuangzi did not believe it, and said, "If I could get the Ruler of our Destiny to restore your body to life with its bones and flesh and skin, and to give you back your father and mother, your wife and children, and all your village acquaintances, would you wish me to do so?" The skull stared fixedly at him, knitted its brows, and said, "How should I cast away the enjoyment of my royal court, and undertake again the toils of life among mankind?"

[The spelling of names has been modified.]

—Translated by James Legge

# Han Feizi

## Third Century B.C.E.

Some Chinese thinkers saw both Confucianism and Daoism as hopelessly idealistic. The Legalists had ideas that were much more direct. You don't motivate people with vague concepts of morality or visions of a simpler world; you get them to do what you want through punishments and rewards. Legalist scholars would approach an anxious ruler and rather than saying "you first need to shape up your own life" (as did Confucians) or "relax and don't worry so much" (the Daoist line), they would suggest that if they were allowed to set up the laws of a state, the ruler could enjoy himself while the country pretty much ran itself. Laws, they argued, should be objective—quantifiable, if possible—applied equally, widely publicized, and strict. If a ruler wanted his people to fight hard in battle, he should offer a reward—say, a piece of gold for each enemy head the soldier brought in. In fact, in the Legalist state of Qin, one way to get ahead was precisely "getting a head." It might be a gruesome method of accounting, but it had the advantage of being clear-cut and easily administered. And family background was irrelevant; whether someone's father was a general or a peasant, four heads were worth four pieces of gold. On the other hand, running away in battle would be punishable by death. If the laws were consistently and forcefully applied, people could be made to do almost anything.

Legalists are often regarded as the villains of Chinese philosophy because they taught techniques of government that relied on raw power and came with no moral justifications. By applying rewards and punishments they could make people do whatever the ruler wanted—good or bad—and most rulers were interested in success in war. Legalists therefore increased the power of the state, and they disdained history and philosophy as a waste of time, though that did not prevent Han Feizi (d. 233 B.C.E.), one of the most famous of Legalist philosophers, from appealing to historical precedent to argue that rulers need not appeal to historical precedent. A native of the state of Han, he studied under Xunzi—a Confucian philosopher. Unfortunately, Han's stuttering made it impossible to for him gain the attention of the king, so he set his ideas down in written form. Some of these essays made it to the king of Qin, who was impressed but nevertheless invaded the state of Han. In a desperate attempt to appease Qin, the king of Han sent Han Feizi as a gift. The king of Qin was delighted, but some of his other advisors grew jealous and argued that

Han Feizi could not be trusted to give sound advice since his loyalties still lay, undoubtedly, with his native state. Eventually the king of Qin had Han thrown in prison. Not long thereafter Han received a package of poison and a suicide-order. The king later regretted his decision, but he did adopt the sort of harsh realistic approach to social problems that Han had advocated. In fact, had Han Feizi lived another dozen years, he would have seen the king go on to become the First Emperor as the Legalist state of Qin unified all of China.

GH

# from *The Five Vermin*

Past and present have different customs; new and old adopt different measures. To try to use the ways of a generous and lenient government to rule the people of a critical age is like trying to drive a runaway horse without using reigns or whip. This is the misfortune that ignorance invites.

Now the Confucians and Mo-ists all praise the ancient kings for their universal love of the world, saying that they looked after the people as parents look after a beloved child. And how do they prove this contention? They say, "Whenever the minister of justice administered some punishment, the ruler would purposely cancel all musical performances; and whenever the ruler learned that the death sentence had been passed on someone, he would shed tears." For this reason they praise the ancient kings.

Now if ruler and subject must become like father and son before there can be order, then we must suppose that there is no such thing as an unruly father or son. Among human affections none takes priority over the love of parents for their children. But though all parents may show love for their children, the children are not always well behaved. And though the parents may love them even more, will this prevent the children from becoming unruly? Now the love of the ancient kings for their people was no greater than the love of parents for their children. And if such love cannot prevent children from becoming unruly, then how can it bring the people to order?

As for the ruler's shedding tears when punishments are carried out in accordance with the law—this is a fine display of benevolence but contributes nothing to the achievement of order. Benevolence may make one shed tears and be reluctant to apply penalties; but law makes it clear that such penalties must be applied. The ancient kings allowed law to be supreme and did not give in to their tearful longings. Hence it is obvious that benevolence cannot be used to achieve order in the state.

Moreover, the people will bow naturally to authority, but few of them can be moved by righteousness. Confucius was one of the greatest sages of the world. He perfected his conduct, made clear the Way, and traveled throughout the area within the four seas, but in all that area those who rejoiced in his benevolence, admired his righteousness, and were willing to become his disciples numbered only seventy. For to honor benevolence is a rare thing, and to adhere to righteousness is hard. Therefore within the vast area of the world only seventy men became his disciples, and only one man—he himself—was truly benevolent and righteous.

Duke Ai of Lu was a mediocre ruler, yet when he ascended the throne and faced south as sovereign of the state, there was no one within its boundaries who did not acknowledge allegiance to him. The people will bow naturally to authority, and he who wields authority may easily command men to submit; therefore Confucius remained a subject and Duke Ai continued to be his ruler. It was not that Confucius was won by the duke's righteousness; he simply bowed before his authority. On the basis of righteousness alone, Confucius would never have bowed before Duke Ai; but because the duke wielded authority, he was able to make Confucius acknowledge his sovereignty.

Nowadays, when scholars counsel a ruler, they do not urge him to wield authority, which is the certain way to success, but instead insist that he must practice benevolence and righteousness before he can become a true king. This is, in effect, to demand that the ruler rise to the level of Confucius, and that all the ordinary people of the time be like Confucius' disciples. Such a policy is bound to fail.

Now here is a young man of bad character. His parents rail at him but he does not reform; the neighbors scold but he is unmoved; his teachers instruct him but he refuses to change his ways. Thus, although three fine influences are brought to bear on him—the love of his parents, the efforts of the neighbors, the wisdom of his teachers—yet he remains unmoved and refuses to change so much as a hair on his shin. But let the local magistrate send out the government soldiers to enforce the law and search for evil-doers, and then he is filled with terror, reforms his conduct, and changes his ways. Thus the love of parents is not enough to make children learn what is right, but must be backed up by the strict penalties of the local officials; for people by nature grow proud on love, but they listen to authority.

Even the nimble Lou-chi could not climb a city wall ten spans high, because it is too precipitous; but lame sheep may easily graze up and down a mountain a hundred times as high, because the slope is gradual. Therefore the enlightened ruler makes his laws precipitous and his punishments severe. Ordinary people are unwilling to discard a few feet of cloth, but even Robber Chih would not pick up a hundred taels of molten gold. As long as there is no harm involved, people will not discard a few feet of cloth, but because they are certain to hurt their hands they refuse to pick up a hundred taels of molten gold. Therefore the enlightened ruler makes his punishments certain.

For this reason, the best rewards are those which are generous and predictable, so that the people may profit by them. The best penalties are those which are severe and inescapable, so that the people will fear them. The best laws are those which are uniform and inflexible, so that the people can understand them. Therefore the ruler should never delay in handing out rewards, nor be merciful in administering punishments. If praise accompanies the reward, and censure follows on the heels of punishment, then worthy and unworthy men alike will put forth their best efforts.

# IV. Ancient India

## INTRODUCTION

The earliest civilization that flourished in the Indian subcontinent was called the 'Indus Valley civilization' since it developed along the banks of the river Indus (*Sindhu*) and its many tributaries in the northwest side of modern India. However, we will not be reading any Indus Valley literature since the alphabets of Indus valley writings remain largely undeciphered. The people of the Indus valley—the Harappans, as they are called after one of the earliest excavated sites of Harappa in modern Pakistan—were conquered by groups of nomadic tribes who invaded from the northwest. These Indo-European tribes called themselves Aryans. Both Hinduism and the Vedas are often believed to have been imported to India by the Aryans. As an evidence for this one may point to that fact that the language of the most classical literature of ancient India including the Vedas was Sanskrit, a language that Aryans brought with them. It is also generally believed that the Vedas—the most sacred texts of the Hindu religion—were brought by the Aryans. However, there is little literal truth in this assertion. First, most Indologists accept that some of the principal gods of the Hindu pantheon, for example, Shiva, were not brought with them by the Aryans but are contributions of the indigenous Harappans. Second, historically speaking it is not accurate to say that the Aryans brought the Vedas to India since the Aryan invasion happened between 2000 and 1500 B.C.E. while the last parts of the Vedas, namely, the Upanisads, were composed between 800 and 200 B.C.E. The sense in which the Vedas as well as Hinduism were an import of the Aryans is that they brought the main structure of a sacrificial system which eventually evolved into the complex Vedic religion and literature.

The term "Veda" is derived from the Sanskrit root *vid* which means "to know." Thus the term "Veda" is often taken to mean knowledge. The term "Vedas" signifies the fact that there are four major texts each considered an independent Veda. The oldest among these Vedas, which is called the Rig Veda, is a collection of the earliest Aryan hymns. Many of these hymns were chanted by the *hotri* priests while invoking the gods during elaborate ritual sacrificial practices which were common during the early parts of the development of the Vedic religion. The other three Vedas are *Sama*, *Yajur* and *Atharva*.

237

Though the Rig Veda is the most prominent of all the Vedas, each of the other three Vedas played an important role in the Vedic sacrifice as well.

Each of the four Vedas has parts, which are a result of the gradual evolution of the themes and ideas of the Vedic canon. The first and oldest part of each Veda consists of the hymns for invoking and inviting the gods during sacrificial rituals and is called the Mantras or the chants. The later parts of the Vedas are commentaries that were added later to the Mantras. The first commentaries to be added are called the Brahmanas, which are sets of passages that explain and elucidate the Mantras. Further, they also provide detailed and specific instructions on how to perform various sacrificial rituals. Each Brahmana has two sets of appendices, the Aranyakas and the Upanisads. The Aranyakas contain rules and procedures of meditation for the forest dwellers; the Upanisads are the concluding parts of the Vedas that focus on the more philosophical questions of self-quest, etc. Thus, not only does the Mantras section of each Veda have its own Brahmanas, but each Brahmana has its own Aranyakas and Upanisads. For example, the Kausitaki and the Aitareya Upanisads are appended to the Brahmanas of the Rig Veda.

What is interesting to note in this regard is the correlation between the four parts of each Veda and four stages of life that a traditional Hindu male is supposed to go through in his life. These four stages are *Brahmacarya* (student life), *Garhastya* (householder), *Banaprastha* (forest dweller) and *Sanyasa* (renunciation). While a student, a Hindu male focuses on learning the Mantras of the various Vedas; while a householder he focuses on the Brahmanas since they explain specific sacrificial rituals for the attainment of various worldly goals like winning a battle or getting a male child. *Banaprastha* refers to that stage where a Hindu male retires from the hustle and bustle of the householder's everyday life to the quietude of the forest. The final stage is that of renunciation, in which a Hindu male meditates intently on the questions about self-realization; here the Upanisads provide the perfect guidance and direction. Thus though it is difficult to argue that the four parts of the Vedas developed in response to the four stages of life, their clear correlation does point to at least some relation between the development and evolution of these two systems.

The reasons for selecting samples from the *Mantras* of the Rig Veda and Upanisads are two-fold. First, being the oldest Veda, Rig Veda is one of the most fascinating pieces of ancient literature both in its beauty and its cosmological mystery. Second, the Mantras and the Upanisads represent two distinct stages in the development of the principal Vedic theme. While the Rig Vedic hymns and mantras represent man's quest to achieve power by controlling his world with the help of the Vedic gods, the Upanisadic poems represent man's quest for the ultimate truth through self-knowledge and self-understanding. Thus while the mantras and early Vedic brahmanical literature represent an outward orientation where the human mind is focused on mastering the external world, the Upanisads represent an inward orientation where the human mind is focused on mastering itself in introspective reflection. The evolution of the basic Vedic theme from outward orientation to inward orientation not only captures the immense diversity and complexity within the Vedic literature but also represents two distinct ways of achieving happiness as pursued by the Vedic writers. Herman usefully identifies these two ways of conceptualizing the relation between man and the world as the "Epicurean way" and the "Stoic way."[1] While the Epicurean way focuses on the world, by making it smaller and less threatening by conquering it, the Stoic way focuses on the individual and especially the inner world of contemplation as a way to arriving at the truth in the relation between man and the world. Thus, while the Brahmanical Vedic thinkers adopted their own version of the Epicurean way to human happiness, the Upanisadic thinkers adopted their own version of the Stoic way to human happiness. In this way, the Upanisadic sages not only focused on the self but also made it their entire world—not only their *explanandum*—the thing needing to be explained but also their *explanans*—the thing that does the explaining.

This section also includes some Buddhist texts. Buddhism arose in India as a development out of classic Hinduism, before spreading, primarily eastward, and becoming a world religion. It was eventually to become more powerful and influential in East Asian than in its Indian homeland.

KM

## Note

[1] Herman, A. L. (1976). *An Introduction to Indian Thought*. Upper Saddle River, NJ: Prentice-Hall.

# Rig Veda

## ca. 1800–1400 B.C.E.

Since every selected hymn from the Rig Veda is accompanied by the translator's brief introduction here, I want to focus on a few general themes of the Rig Veda.

As the oldest Veda the Rig Veda constitutes the most significant part of what is called the sruti literature. The term "*sruti*" signifies something that is not really authored but something that is heard or is being revealed. In this capacity the Rig Vedic Mantras are most revered. The hymns (1028 in total) of the Rig Veda can be divided into two periods: the first period consisting of the earlier hymns of Book I (verse 51 to 191) and Book II through IX; the second and more recent period consists of the remaining hymns of Book I (1 through 50) and all of the Book X. The first period reflects the Aryan commitment to polytheism where certain major deities seem to share power equally as evidenced in hymns in praise of Indra, Agni, Usas, etc. The second period, on the other hand, reflects a move from polytheism towards a modified polytheism called "henotheism" and there is also a gradual development of the concept of life after death.

The Rig Veda is also unique in containing the "Creation hymn" (X: 90) which includes the very first reference to the *varna dharma* or the "law of color" or what is more commonly known as the caste system. The four castes are *Brahmin* (the priest caste), *Kshatriya* (warrior and royal caste), *Vaisya* (business class) and *Sudra* (servants) which were originally supposed to have been divided along occupational lines. Though the rationale for introducing the caste system and its exact date remain a topic of passionate debate even today, one of the common reasons often offered is fear of the indigenous Harappans and a desire to maintain separation from them.

The basic structure of Rig Vedic religious system can be captured in terms of the following formula: (a) There are gods with power; (b) Man wants and needs power; (c) There is a way to power; and (d) The Rig Veda Mantras describe that way. This "formula for power" constitutes the key theme of the Rig Vedic religious life and the conclusion about the performance of Rig Vedic mantras and the associated sacrifices as a way to power follows necessarily and obviously from this formula. Thus, one of the major characteristics of the Rig Vedic religion is its "power-oriented" nature. Other major characteristics include "excessively ritualistic," "priest or Brahmin caste dominated," "aristocratic," and "pragmatic or practical." As we have noted in the general intro-duction, most of these outward-oriented characteristics came under attack from the inward-looking Upanisadic sages.

KM

# from Rig Veda

## 7.104 The Demons in Hell

*In banishing all evil spirits to a dark hole (a place that may prefigure the post-Vedic hell of the demons, the poet also takes the opportunity to wish evils upon the head of his rival priest, a 'sorcerer' who apparently accuses the author of the hymn of being a sorcerer.*

. . . 8 Whoever has spoken against me with false words when I was acting with a pure heart, O Indra, let him become nothing even as he talks about nothing, like water grasped in one's fist.

9 Those who casually seduce the man of pure heart or who wilfully make the good man bad, let Soma deliver them over to the serpent, or let him set them in the lap of Destruction.

10 Agni, whoever wants to injure the sap of our drink, of our horses, of our cows, of our own bodies, he is our enemy, a thief and a robber; let him fall upon hard times; let him perish with his own body and his offspring.

11 Let him with his own body and his offspring be beyond, let him be below all three earths. Gods, dry up the glory of the one who wants to injure us by day or by night.

12 For the clever man it is easy to distinguish: true and false words fight against one another. Soma favours the one of them that is true, that is straight; he kills the false.

13 Surely Soma does not push forward the one who is dishonest, nor the ruler who holds power falsely. He kills the demon, he kills the one who speaks lies. Both of these lie in Indra's snare.

14 As if I worshipped false gods, or considered the gods useless—why, Agni knower of creatures, why are you angry with us? Gather into your destruction those who speak hateful words. . . .

## 10.85 The Marriage of Sūryā

*The divine prototype for human marriages is the hierogamy of Sūryā (daughter of Sūryā, the sun) and Soma (here, for the only time in the* Rig Veda, *regarded as the moon, as well as the sacred plant and its expressed juice). Later marriages are modelled upon this one, and the bride is called Sūryā. The first nineteen verses refer to the myth of the marriage of Sūryā and Soma; subsequent verses also refer back to Sūryā (vv. 20, 35 and 38) and to Soma (40–41), though*

*the former seems merely to designate the bride and the latter is a reference to*
*Soma in his other aspect, his* droit de seigneur *over all brides. Verses 20–47 pres-*
*ent formulaic verses, some of a highly magical nature, to be recited at a wedding.*

1 The earth is propped up by truth; the sky is propped up by the sun.
Through the Law the Ādityas stand firm and Soma is placed in the sky.

2 Through Soma the Ādityas are mighty; through Soma the earth is
great. And in the lap of these constellations Soma has been set.

3 One thinks he has drunk Soma when they press the plant. But the
Soma that the Brahmins know—no one ever eats that.

4 Hidden by those charged with veiling you, protected by those who live
on high, O Soma, you stand listening to the pressing-stones. No earthling eats
you.

5 When they drink you who are a god, then you are filled up again. Vāyu
is the guardian of Soma; the moon is the one that shapes the years.

6 The Raibhī metre was the woman who gave her away; the Nārāśaṁsī
metre was the girl who accompanied her. The fine dress of Sūryā was adorned
by the songs.

7 Intelligence was the pillow; sight was the balm. Heaven and Earth were
the hope-chest when Sūryā went to her husband.

8 The hymns of praise were the shafts and metre was the diadem and
coiffure. The Aśvins were the suitors of Sūryā, and Agni was the one who went
in front.

9 Soma became the bridegroom and the two Aśvins were the suitors, as
Savitṛ gave Sūryā to her husband and she said 'Yes' in her heart.

10 Thought was her chariot and the sky was its canopy. The two luminaries were the two carriage animals when Sūryā went to the house.

11 Your two cattle, yoked with the verse and the chant, went with the
same accord. You had hearing for your two wheels. In the sky the path
stretched on and on.

12 The two luminaries were your wheels as you journeyed; the outward
breath was made into the axle. Sūryā mounted a chariot made of thought as
she went to her husband.

13 The wedding procession of Sūryā went forward as Savitṛ sent it off.
When the sun is in Aghā they kill the cattle, and when it is in Arjunī she is
brought home.

14 When you Aśvins came to the wedding in your three-wheeled chariot, asking for Sūryā for yourselves, all the gods gave you their consent, and
Pūṣan, the son, chose you as his two fathers.

15 When you two husbands of beauty came as suitors for Sūryā, where
was your single wheel? Where did you two stand to point the way?

16 Your two-wheels, Sūryā, the Brahmins know in their measured rounds. But the one wheel that is hidden, only the inspired know that.

17 To Sūryā, to the gods, to Mitra and Varuṇa, who are provident for all creation, to them I have bowed down.

18 These two change places through their power of illusion, now forward, now backward. Like two children at play they circle the sacrificial ground. The one gazes upon all creatures, and the other is born again and again marking the order of the seasons.

19 He becomes new and again new as he is born, going in front of the dawns as the banner of the days. As he arrives he apportions to the gods their share. The moon stretches out the long span of life.

20 Mount the world of immortality, O Sūryā, that is adorned with red flowers and made of fragrant wood, carved with many forms and painted with gold, rolling smoothly on its fine wheels. Prepare an exquisite wedding voyage for your husband.

21 'Go away from here! For this woman has a husband.' Thus I implore Viśvāvasu with words of praise as I bow to him. 'Look for another girl who is ripe and still lives in her father's house. That is your birthright; find it.

22 'Go away from here, Viśvāvasu, we implore you as we bow. Look for another girl, willing and ready. Leave the wife to unite with her husband.'

23 May the roads be straight and thornless on which our friends go courting. May Aryaman and Bhaga united lead us together. O Gods, may the united household be easy to manage.

24 I free you from Varuṇa's snare, with which the gentle Savitṛ bound you. In the seat of the Law, in the world of good action, I place you unharmed with your husband.

25 I free her from here, but not from there. I have bound her firmly there, so that through the grace of Indra she will have fine sons and be fortunate in her husband's love.

26 Let Pūṣan lead you from here, taking you by the hand; let the Aśvins carry you in their chariot. Go home to be mistress of the house with the right to speak commands to the gathered people.

27 May happiness be fated for you here through your progeny. Watch over this house as mistress of the house. Mingle your body with that of your husband, and even when you are grey with age you will have the right to speak to the gathered people.

28 The purple and red appears, a magic spirit; the stain is imprinted. Her family prospers, and her husband is bound in the bonds.

29 Throw away the gown, and distribute wealth to the priests. It becomes a magic spirit walking on feet, and like the wife it draws near the husband.

30 The body becomes ugly and sinisterly pale, if the husband with evil desire covers his sexual limb with his wife's robe.

31 The diseases that come from her own people and follow after the glorious bridal procession, may the gods who receive sacrifices lead them back whence they have come.

32 Let no highwaymen, lying in ambush, fall upon the wedding couple. Let the two of them on good paths avoid the dangerous path. Let all demonic powers run away.

33 This bride has auspicious signs; come and look at her. Wish her the good fortune of her husband's love, and depart, each to your own house.

34 It burns, it bites, and it has claws, as dangerous as poison is to eat. Only the priest who knows the Sūryā hymn is able to receive the bridal gown.

35 Cutting, carving, and chopping into pieces—see the colours of Sūryā, which the priest alone purifies.

36 I take your hand for good fortune, so that with me as your husband you will attain a ripe old age. Bhaga, Aryaman, Savitṛ, Purandhi—the gods have given you to me to be mistress of the house.

37 Pūṣan, rouse her to be most eager to please, the woman in whom men sow their seed, so that she will spread her thighs in her desire for us and we, in our desire, will plant our penis in her.

38 To you first of all they led Sūryā, circling with the bridal procession. Give her back to her husbands, Agni, now as a wife with progeny.

39 Agni has given the wife back again, together with long life and beauty. Let her have a long life-span, and let her husband live for a hundred autumns.

40 Soma first possessed her, and the Gandharva possess her second. Agni was your third husband, and the fourth was the son of a man.

41 Soma give her to the Gandharva, and the Gandharva gave her to Agni. Agni gave me wealth and sons—and her.

42 Stay here and do not separate. Enjoy your whole life-span playing with sons and grandsons and rejoicing in your own home.

43 Let Prajāpati create progeny for us; let Aryaman anoint us into old age. Free from evil signs, enter the world of your husband. Be good luck for our two-legged creatures and good luck for our four-legged creatures.

44 Have no evil eye; do not be a husband-killer. Be friendly to animals, good-tempered and glowing with beauty. Bringing forth strong sons, prosper as one beloved of the gods and eager to please. Be good luck for our two-legged creatures and good luck for our four-legged creatures.

45 Generous Indra, give this woman fine sons and the good fortune of her husband's love. Place ten sons in her and make her husband the eleventh.

46 Be an empress over your husband's father, an empress over your husband's mother; be an empress over your husband's sister and an empress over your husband's brothers.

47 Let all the gods and the waters together anoint our two hearts together. Let Mātariśvan together with the Creator and together with her who shows the way join the two of us together.

## 1.92 Dawn and the Aśvins

*The central and recurring metaphor in this hymn to Uṣas (personification of dawn) is that of harnessing tawny cows or bay horses to her chariot, in which she is to bring all riches to the men who worship her. The chariot is both a simple instrument of portage, a kind of cosmic Wells Fargo wagon, and symbolic of the victory chariot by which all riches are won. The metaphor is complicated and enriched by the fact that the lights of dawn themselves are regarded as cows or mothers, who come of their own accord to be milked at dawn.*

1 See how the dawns have set up their banner in the eastern half of the sky, adorning and anointing themselves with sunlight for balm. Unleashing themselves like impetuous heroes unsheathing their weapons, the tawny cows, the mothers, return.

2 The red-gold lights have flown up freely; they have yoked the tawny cows who let themselves be yoked. The dawns have spread their webs in the ancient way; the tawny ones have set forth the glowing light.

3 They sing like women busy at their tasks, coming from a distant place with a single harnessed team, bringing refreshing food day after day to the man of good actions, the man of generosity, the man who sacrifices and presses the Soma.

4 Like a dancing girl, she puts on bright ornaments; she uncovers her breast as a cow reveals her swollen udder. Creating light for the whole universe, Dawn has opened up the darkness as cows break out from their enclosed pen.

5 Her brilliant flame has become visible once more; she spreads herself out, driving back the formless black abyss. As one sets up the stake in the sacrifice, anointing and adorning it with coloured ornaments, so the daughter of the sky sets up her many-coloured light.

6 We have crossed to the farther bank of this darkness; radiant Dawn spreads her webs. Smiling like a lover who wishes to win his way, she shines forth and with her lovely face awakens us to happiness.

7 The shining daughter of the sky, bringing rich gifts, is praised by the Gotamas. Measure out offspring and strong men as the victory prizes, Dawn, the rewards that begin with cattle and culminate in horses.

8 Let me obtain great riches of glory and heroic men, Dawn, riches that begin with slaves and culminate in heroes. Fortunate in your beauty, incited by the victory prize you shine forth with the fame of great achievements.

9 Gazing out over all creatures, the goddess shines from the distance facing straight towards every eye. Awakening into motion everything that lives, she has found the speech of every inspired poet.

10 The ancient goddess, born again and again dressed in the same colour, causes the mortal to age and wears away his life-span, as a cunning gambler carries off the stakes.

11 She has awakened, uncovering the very edges of the sky; she pushes aside her sister. Shrinking human generations, the young woman shines under her lover's gaze.

12 Spreading out her rays like cattle, like a river in full flood the brightly coloured one shines from the distance. The fortunate goddess does not break the laws of the gods but becomes visible, appearing by the rays of the sun.

13 Dawn, you who hold the victory prize, bring us that brightly coloured power by which we establish children and grandchildren.

14 Dawn, rich in cows, rich in horses, resplendent giver of gifts, shine your riches upon us here and now.

15 Harness your red-gold horses now, O prize-giving Dawn, and bring all good fortunes to us.

16 O Aśvins who work wonders, turn your chariot that brings cattle, that brings gold, and with one mind come back to us.

17 You Aśvins who gave a shout from heaven and made light for mankind, bring us strength.

18 May those who wake at dawn bring here to drink the Soma the two gods who work wonders and give joy, moving on paths of gold.

## 2.12 'Who is Indra?'

*As if to answer the challenges of the atheists, or at least of those who question the divinity of Indra (v. 5), the poet insists that Indra is indeed the god who did what he is said to have done. These concerns, and the verbal patterns used to express them, are repeated in a later hymn about the Creator (10.121).*

1 The god who had insight the moment he was born, the first who protected the gods with his power of thought, before whose hot breath the two world-halves tremble at the greatness of his manly powers—he, my people, is Indra.

2 He who made fast the tottering earth, who made still the quaking mountains, who measured out and extended the expanse of the air, who propped up the sky—he, my people, is Indra.

3 He who killed the serpent and loosed the seven rivers, who drove out the cows that had been pent up by Vala, who gave birth to fire between two stones, the winner of booty in combats—he, my people, is Indra.

4 He by whom all these changes were rung, who drove the race of Dāsas down into obscurity, who took away the flourishing wealth of the enemy as a winning gambler takes the stake—he, my people, is Indra.

5 He about whom they ask, 'Where is he?', or they say of him, the terrible one, 'He does not exist', he who diminishes the flourishing wealth of the enemy as gambling does—believe in him! He, my people, is Indra.

6 He who encourages the weary and the sick, and the poor priest who is in need, who helps the man who harnesses the stones to press Soma, he who has lips fine for drinking—he, my people, is Indra.

7 He under whose command are horses and cows and villages and all chariots, who gave birth to the sun and the dawn and led out the waters, he, my people, is Indra.

8 He who is invoked by both of two armies, enemies locked in combat, on this side and that side, he who is even invoked separately by each of two men standing on the very same chariot, he, my people, is Indra.

9 He without whom people do not conquer, he whom they call on for help when they are fighting, who became the image of everything, who shakes the unshakeable—he, my people, is Indra.

10 He who killed with his weapon all those who had committed a great sin, even when they did not know it, he who does not pardon the arrogant man for his arrogance, who is the slayer of the Dasyus, he, my people, is Indra.

11 He who in the fortieth autumn discovered Śambara living in the mountains, who killed the violent serpent, the Dānu, as he lay there, he, my people, is Indra.

12 He, the mighty bull who with his seven reins let loose the seven rivers to flow, who with his thunderbolt in his hand hurled down Rauhina as he was climbing up to the sky, he, my people, is Indra.

13 Even the sky and the earth bow low before him, and the mountains are terrified of his hot breath; he who is known as the Soma-drinker, with the thunderbolt in his hand, with the thunderbolt in his palm, he, my people, is Indra.

14 He who helps with his favour the one who presses and the one who cooks, the praiser and the preparer, he for whom prayer is nourishment, for whom Soma is the special gift, he, my people, is Indra.

15 You who furiously grasp the prize for the one who presses and the one who cooks, you are truly real. Let us be dear to you, Indra, all our days, and let us speak as men of power in the sacrificial gathering.

## 1.50 The Sun, Sūryā

*The Sun in this hymn drives a chariot whose rays (also called banners) are said to be seven mares. In his fiery aspect, he is identified with Agni 'Knower of Creatures' (Jātavedas), and through the recurrent image of seeing and being seen and giving light that allows others to see he is further identified with Varuṇa, the eye of the gods.*

1 His brilliant banners draw upwards the god who knows all creatures, so that everyone may see the sun.

2 The constellations, along with the nights, steal away like thieves, making way for the sun who gazes on everyone.

3 The rays that are his banners have become visible from the distance, shining over mankind like blazing fires.

4 Crossing space, you are the maker of light, seen by everyone, O sun. You illumine the whole, wide realm of space.

5 You rise up facing all the groups of gods, facing mankind, facing everyone, so that they can see the sunlight.

6 He is the eye with which, O Purifying Varuṇa, you look upon the busy one among men.

7 You cross heaven and the vast realm of space, O sun, measuring days by nights, looking upon the generations.

8 Seven bay mares carry you in the chariot, O sun god with hair of flame, gazing from afar.

9 The sun has yoked the seven splendid daughters of the chariot; he goes with them, who yoke themselves.

10 We have come up out of darkness, seeing the higher light around us, going to the sun, the god among gods, the highest light.

11 As you rise today, O sun, you who are honoured as a friend, climbing to the highest sky, make me free of heartache and yellow pallor.

12 Let us place my yellow pallor among parrots and thrushes, or let us place my yellow pallor among other yellow birds in yellow trees.

13 This Āditya has risen with all his dominating force, hurling my hateful enemy down into my hands. Let me not fall into my enemy's hands!

## 1.1 I Pray to Agni

*Appropriately placed at the very beginning of the* Rig Veda, *this hymn invites Agni, the divine priest, to come to the sacrifice.*

1 I pray to Agni, the household priest who is the god of the sacrifice, the one who chants and invokes and brings most treasure.

2 Agni earned the prayers of the ancient sages, and of those of the present, too; he will bring the gods here.

3 Through Agni one may win wealth, and growth from day to day, glorious and most abounding in heroic sons.

4 Agni, the sacrificial ritual that you encompass on all sides—only that one goes to the gods.

5 Agni, the priest with the sharp sight of a poet, the true and most brilliant, the god will come with the gods.

6 Whatever good you wish to do for the one who worships you, Agni, through you, O Angiras, that comes true.

7 To you, Agni, who shine upon darkness, we come day after day, bringing our thoughts and homage

8 To you, the king over sacrifices, the shining guardian of the Order, growing in your own house.

9 Be easy for us to reach, like a father to his son. Abide with us, Agni, for our happiness.

## 10.14 Yama and the Fathers

*This funeral hymn centres upon Yama, king of the dead, the first mortal to have reached the other world and the pathmaker for all who came after him. Verses 1 and 2 address the mourners and describe this ancient path; 4 and 5 invoke Yama to come to the funeral in order that he may lead the dead man to heaven. Verses 3 and 6 invoke famous ancestors already in the world beyond; 7, 8 and 10 speed the dead man on his way, and 9 speeds the evil spirits on their way. Yama and his two dogs are addressed in 11 and 12; these dogs are regarded (like many Vedic gods) as dangerous because they kill you (verses 10 and 12 ) but also as potentially benevolent, because they lead you to heaven (verse 11). Verses 13–15 call upon the priests to offer Soma to Yama, and the final verse recapitulates the two main themes: the farewell to the dead man on the path of Yama, and the offerings of Soma and praise to Yama.*

1 The one who has passed beyond along the great, steep straits, spying out the path for many, the son of Vivasvan, the gatherer of men, King Yama—honour him with the oblation.

2 Yama was the first to find the way for us, this pasture that shall not be taken away. Where our ancient fathers passed beyond, there everyone who is born follows, each on his own path.

3 Mātalī made strong by the Kavyas, and Yama, by the Angirases, and Bṛhaspati by the Ṛkvans—both those whom the gods made strong and those who strengthen the gods: some rejoice in the sacrificial call, others in the sacrificial drink.

4 Sit upon this strewn grass, O Yama, together with the Angirases, the fathers. Let the verses chanted by the poets carry you here. O King, rejoice in this oblation.

5 Come, Yama, with the Angirases worthy of sacrifice: rejoice here with the Vairūpas, sitting on the sacred grass at this sacrifice. I will invoke Vivasvan, who is your father.

6 Our fathers, the Angirases, and the Navagvas, Atharvans, and Bṛhgus, all worthy of Soma—let us remain in favour with them, as they are worthy of sacrifice, and let them be helpful and kind.

7 [*To the dead man*:] Go forth, go forth on those ancient paths on which our ancient fathers passed beyond. There you shall see the two kings, Yama and Varuṇa, rejoicing in the sacrificial drink.

8 Unite with the fathers, with Yama, with the rewards of your sacrifices and good deeds, in the highest heaven. Leaving behind all imperfections, go back home again; merge with a glorious body.

9 [*To demons*:] Go away, get away, crawl away from here. The fathers have prepared this place for *him*. Yama gives him a resting-place adorned by days, and waters, and nights.

10 [*To the dead man*:] Run on the right path, past the two brindled, four-eyed dogs, the sons of Saramā, and then approach the fathers, who are easy to reach and who rejoice at the same feast as Yama.

11 Yama, give him over to your two guardian dogs, the four-eyed keepers of the path, who watch over men. O king, grant him happiness and health.

12 The two dark messengers of Yama with flaring nostrils wander among men, thirsting for the breath of life. Let them give back to us a life of happiness here and today, so that we may see the sun.

13 For Yama press the Soma; to Yama offer the oblation; to Yama goes the well-prepared sacrifice, with Agni as its messenger.

14 Offer to Yama the oblation rich in butter, and go forth. So may he intercede for us among the gods, so that we may live out a long life-span.

15 Offer to Yama, to the king, the oblation most rich in honey. We bow down before the sages born in the ancient times, the ancient path-makers.

16 All through the three Soma days, he flies to the six broad spaces and the one great one. Triṣṭubh, Gāyatrī, the metres—all these are placed in Yama.

## 10.90 Paruṣa-Sūkta, or The Hymn of Man

*In this famous hymn, the gods create the world by dismembering the cos-mic giant, Puruṣa, the primeval male who is the victim in a Vedic sacrifice. Though the theme of the cosmic sacrifice is a widespread mythological motif, this hymn is part of a particularly Indo-European corpus of myths of dismem-*

*berment. The underlying concept is, therefore, quite ancient; yet the fact that this is one of the latest hymns in the* Rig Veda *is evident from its reference to the three Vedas (v. 9) and to the four social classes or* varṇas *(v. 12, the first time that this concept appears in Indian civilization), as well as from its generally monistic worldview.*

1 The Man has a thousand heads, a thousand eyes, a thousand feet. He pervaded the earth on all sides and extended beyond it as far as ten fingers.

2 It is the Man who is all this, whatever has been and whatever is to be. He is the ruler of immortality, when he grows beyond everything through food.

3 Such is his greatness, and the Man is yet more than this. All creatures are a quarter of him; three quarters are what is immortal in heaven.

4 With three quarters the Man rose upwards, and one quarter of him still remains here. From this he spread out in all directions, into that which eats and that which does not eat.

5 From him Virāj was born, and from Virāj came the Man. When he was born, he ranged beyond the earth behind and before.

6 When the gods spread the sacrifice with the Man as the offering, spring was the clarified butter, summer the fuel, autumn the oblation.

7 They anointed the Man, the sacrifice born at the beginning, upon the sacred grass. With him the gods, Sādhyas, and sages sacrificed.

8 From that sacrifice in which everything was offered, the melted fat was collected, and he made it into those beasts who live in the air, in the forest, and in villages.

9 From that sacrifice in which everything was offered, the verses and chants were born, the metres were born from it, and from it the formulas were born.

10 Horses were born from it, and those other animals that have two rows of teeth; cows were born from it, and from it goats and sheep were born.

11 When they divided the Man, into how many parts did they apportion him? What do they call his mouth, his two arms and thighs and feet?

12 His mouth became the Brahmin; his arms were made into the Warrior, his thighs the People, and from his feet the Servants were born.

13 The moon was born from his mind; from his eye the sun was born. Indra and Agni came from his mouth, and from his vital breath the Wind was born.

14 From his navel the middle realm of space arose; from his head the sky evolved. From his two feet came the earth, and the quarters of the sky from his ear. Thus they set the worlds in order.

15 There were seven enclosing-sticks for him, and thrice seven fuel-sticks, when the gods, spreading the sacrifice, bound the Man as the sacrificial beast.

16 With the sacrifice the gods sacrificed to the sacrifice. These were the first ritual laws. These very powers reached the dome of the sky where dwell the Sādhyas, the ancient gods.

## 10.129 Creation Hymn (Nāsadīya)

*This short hymn, though linguistically simple (with the exception of one or two troublesome nouns), is conceptually extremely provocative and has, indeed, provoked hundreds of complex commentaries among Indian theologians and Western scholars. In many ways, it is meant to puzzle and challenge, to raise unanswerable questions, to pile up paradoxes.*

1 There was neither non-existence nor existence then; there was neither the realm of space nor the sky which is beyond. What stirred? Where? In whose protection? Was there water, bottomlessly deep?

2 There was neither death nor immortality then. There was no distinguishing sign of night nor of day. That one breathed, windless, by its own impulse. Other than that there was nothing beyond.

3 Darkness was hidden by darkness in the beginning; with no distinguishing sign, all this was water. The life force that was covered with emptiness, that one arose through the power of heat.

4 Desire came upon that one in the beginning; that was the first seed of mind. Poets seeking in their heart with wisdom found the bond of existence in non-existence.

5 Their cord was extended across. Was there below? Was there above? There were seed-placers; there were powers. There was impulse beneath; there was giving-forth above.

6 Who really knows? Who will here proclaim it? Whence was it produced? Whence is this creation? The gods came afterwards, with the creation of this universe. Who then knows whence it has arisen?

7 Whence this creation has arisen—perhaps it formed itself, or perhaps it did not—the one who looks down on it, in the highest heaven, only he knows—or perhaps he does not know.

# Katha Upanisad

## Fourth–Third Centuries B.C.E.

The word *"Upanisad"* comes from the Sanskrit root *"sad"* which means to sit. With *"upa"* which means under and *'ni'* which means beneath, the complete meaning of *"upanisad"* can be taken as an instruction while sitting at the feet of a master. The Katha Upanisad formally belongs to the Kathaka school of Black Yajurveda but appears to be a late addition to the Brahmana of that school. According to many scholars, it is the most philosophical of all the Upanisads. Its important features include "the dialogue between Naciketas and Yama (the god of the world of departed spirits) on the question of the immortality of the self, in which Naciketas chooses knowledge above all worldly blessings; the theory of the superiority of the good (*sreyas*) over the pleasant (*preyas*); the view that the Atman cannot be known by the senses, by reason, or by much learning, but only by intuitive insight or direct realization; and the doctrine of the body as the chariot of the self—a reminder of a similar figure used by Plato."[1]

One of the concepts essential to understanding this and any other Upanisad is the idea of the Brahman or Atman. It is understood as the sole principle of truth and reality. Using this essential concept, all Upanisads make the further point that everything in the universe—big and small, animate and inanimate—has a representation of this pure principle in them. This concept also characterizes the monism of the Upanisads. The Upanisadic goal for human life can be identified as two-fold: first, to realize that one is the same as the Brahman and second, to realize that everything and everyone is the same as oneself since they are same as the single principle of truth, i.e., the Brahman.

KM

## Note

[1] S. Radhakrishnan and C. A. Moore (eds.) (1957). *A Source Book in Indian Philosophy*. Princeton, NJ: Princeton University Press: 42–43.

# from Katha Upanishad

## Part I

Vajasravasa gave away all his possessions at a sacrifice; but it was out of desire for heaven.

He had a son called Nachiketas who, although he was only a boy, had a vision of faith when the offerings were given and thus he thought:

'This poor offering of cows that are too old to give milk and too weak to eat grass or drink water must lead to a world of sorrow.'

And he thought of offering himself, and said to his father: 'Father, to whom will you give me?' He asked once, and twice, and three times; and then his father answered in anger: 'I will give you to Death!'

*Nachiketas.* At the head of many I go, and I go in the midst of many. What may be the work of Death that today must be done through me?

Remember how the men of old passed away, and how those of days to come will also pass away: a mortal ripens like corn, and like corn is born again.

Nachiketas had to wait three nights without food in the abode of YAMA, the god of death.

*A Voice.* As the spirit of fire a Brahmin comes to a house: bring the offering of water, O god of Death.

How unwise is the man who does not give hospitality to a Brahmin! He loses his future hopes, his past merits, his present possessions: his sons and his all.

*Death.* Since you have come as a sacred guest to my abode, and you have had no hospitality for three nights, choose then three boons.

*Nachiketas.* May my father's anger be appeased, and may he remember me and welcome me when I return to him. Let this be my first boon.

*Death.* By my power your father will remember you and love you as before; and when he sees you free from the jaws of death, sweet will be his sleep at night.

*Nachiketas.* There is no fear in heaven: old age and death are not there. The good, beyond both, rejoice in heaven, beyond hunger and thirst and sorrow.

And those in heaven attain immortality. You know, O Death, that sacred fire which leads to heaven. Explain it to me, since I have faith. Be this my second boon.

*Death.* I know, Nachiketas, that sacred fire which leads to heaven. Listen. That fire which is the means of attaining the infinite worlds, and is also their foundation, is hidden in the sacred place of the heart.

And Death told him of the fire of creation, the beginning of the worlds, and of the altar of the fire-sacrifice, of how many bricks it should be built and how they should be placed. Nachiketas repeated the teaching. Death was pleased and went on:

A further boon I give you today. This fire of sacrifice shall be known by your name. Take also from me this chain of many forms.

One who lights three times this sacred fire, and attains union with the Three, and performs the three holy actions, passes beyond life and death; for then he knows the god of fire, the god who knows all things, and through knowledge and adoration he attains the peace supreme.

He who, knowing the Three, builds up the altar of fire-sacrifice and performs three times the sacrifice of Nachiketas, casts off the bonds of death and, passing beyond sorrow, finds joy in the regions of heaven.

This is the fire that leads to heaven which you chose as the second gift. Men will call it the fire-sacrifice of Nachiketas. Choose now the third boon.

*Nachiketas.* When a man dies, this doubt arises: some say 'he is' and some say 'he is not'. Teach me the truth.

*Death.* Even the gods had this doubt in times of old; for mysterious is the law of life and death. Ask for another boon. Release me from this.

*Nachiketas.* This doubt indeed arose even to the gods, and you say, O Death, that it is difficult to understand; but no greater teacher than you can explain it, and there is no other boon so great as this.

*Death.* Take horses and gold and cattle and elephants; choose sons and grandsons that shall live a hundred years. Have vast expanses of land, and live as many years as you desire.

Or choose another gift that you think equal to this, and enjoy it with wealth and long life. Be a ruler of this vast earth. I will grant you all your desires.

Ask for any wishes in the world of mortals, however hard to obtain. To attend on you I will give you fair maidens with chariots and musical instruments. But ask me not, Nachiketas, the secrets of death.

*Nachiketas.* All these pleasures pass away, O End of all! They weaken the power of life. And indeed how short is all life! Keep thy horses and dancing and singing.

Man cannot be satisfied with wealth. Shall we enjoy wealth with you in sight? Shall we live whilst you are in power? I can only ask for the boon I have asked.

When a mortal here on earth has felt his own immortality, could he wish for a long life of pleasures, for the lust of deceitful beauty?

Solve then the doubt as to the great beyond. Grant me the gift that unveils the mystery. This is the only gift Nachiketas can ask.

## Part 2

*Death*. There is the path of joy, and there is the path of pleasure. Both attract the soul. Who follows the first comes to good; who follows pleasure reaches not the End.

The two paths lie in front of man. Pondering on them, the wise man chooses the path of joy; the fool takes the path of pleasure.

You have pondered, Nachiketas, on pleasures and you have rejected them. You have not accepted that chain of possessions wherewith men bind themselves and beneath which they sink.

There is the path of wisdom and the path of ignorance. They are far apart and lead to different ends. You are, Nachiketas, a follower of the path of wisdom: many pleasures tempt you not.

Abiding in the midst of ignorance, thinking themselves wise and learned, fools go aimlessly hither and thither, like blind led by the blind.

What lies beyond life shines not to those who are childish, or careless, or deluded by wealth. 'This is the only world: there is no other', they say; and thus they go from death to death.

Not many hear of him; and of those not many reach him. Wonderful is he who can teach about him; and wise is he who can be taught. Wonderful is he who knows him when taught.

He cannot be taught by one who has not reached him; and he cannot be reached by much thinking. The way to him is through a Teacher who has seen him: He is higher than the highest thoughts, in truth above all thought.

This sacred knowledge is not attained by reasoning; but it can be given by a true Teacher. As your purpose is steady you have found him. May I find another pupil like you!

I know that treasures pass away and that the Eternal is not reached by the transient. I have thus laid the fire of sacrifice of Nachiketas, and by burning in it the transient I have reached the Eternal.

Before your eyes have been spread, Nachiketas, the fulfilment of all desire, the dominion of the world, the eternal reward of ritual, the shore where there is no fear, the greatness of fame and boundless spaces. With strength and wisdom you have renounced them all.

When the wise rests his mind in contemplation on our God beyond time, who invisibly dwells in the mystery of things and in the heart of man, then he rises above pleasures and sorrow.

When a man has heard and has understood and, finding the essence, reaches the Inmost, then he finds joy in the Source of joy. Nachiketas is a house open for thy Atman, thy God.

*Nachiketas.* Tell me what you see beyond right and wrong, beyond what is done or not done, beyond past and future.

*Death.* I will tell you the Word that all the *Vedas* glorify, all self-sacrifice expresses, all sacred studies and holy life seek. That Word is OM.

That Word is the everlasting Brahman: that Word is the highest End. When that sacred Word is known, all longings are fulfilled.

It is the supreme means of salvation: it is the help supreme. When that great Word is known, one is great in the heaven of Brahman.

Atman, the Spirit of vision, is never born and never dies. Before him there was nothing, and he is ONE for evermore. Never-born and eternal, beyond times gone or to come, he does not die when the body dies.

If the slayer thinks that he kills, and if the slain thinks that he dies, neither knows the ways of truth. The Eternal in man cannot kill: the Eternal in man cannot die.

Concealed in the heart of all beings is the Atman, the Spirit, the Self; smaller than the smallest atom, greater than the vast spaces. The man who surrenders his human will leaves sorrows behind, and beholds the glory of the Atman by the grace of the Creator.

Resting, he wanders afar; sleeping, he goes everywhere. Who else but my Self can know that God of joy and of sorrows?

When the wise realize the omnipresent Spirit, who rests invisible in the visible and permanent in the impermanent, then they go beyond sorrow.

Not through much learning is the Atman reached, not through the intellect and sacred teaching. It is reached by the chosen of him—because they choose him. To his chosen the Atman reveals his glory.

Not even through deep knowledge can the Atman be reached, unless evil ways are abandoned, and there is rest in the senses, concentration in the mind and peace in one's heart.

Who knows in truth where he is? The majesty of his power carries away priests and warriors, and death itself is carried away.

## Part 3

In the secret high place of the heart there are two beings who drink the wine of life in the world of truth. Those who know Brahman, those who keep the five sacred fires and those who light the three-fold fire of Nachiketas call them 'light' and 'shade'.

May we light the sacred fire of Nachiketas, the bridge to cross to the other shore where there is no fear, the supreme everlasting Spirit!

Know the Atman as Lord of a chariot; and the body as the chariot itself. Know that reason is the charioteer; and the mind indeed is the reins.

The horses, they say, are the senses; and their paths are the objects of sense. When the soul becomes one with the mind and the senses he is called 'one who has joys and sorrows'.

He who has not right understanding and whose mind is never steady is not the ruler of his life, like a bad driver with wild horses.

But he who has right understanding and whose mind is ever steady is the ruler of his life, like a good driver with well-trained horses.

He who has not right understanding, is careless and never pure, reaches not the End of the journey; but wanders on from death to death.

But he who has understanding, is careful and ever pure, reaches the End of the journey, from which he never returns.

The man whose chariot is driven by reason, who watches and holds the reins of his mind, reaches the End of the journey, the supreme everlasting Spirit.

Beyond the senses are their objects, and beyond the objects is the mind. Beyond the mind is pure reason, and beyond reason is the Spirit in man.

Beyond the Spirit in man is the Spirit of the universe, and beyond is Purusha, the Spirit Supreme. Nothing is beyond Purusha: He is the End of the path.

The light of the Atman, the Spirit, is invisible, concealed in all beings. It is seen by the seers of the subtle, when their vision is keen and is clear.

The wise should surrender speech in mind, mind in the knowing self, the knowing self in the Spirit of the universe, and the Spirit of the universe in the Spirit of peace.

Awake, arise! Strive for the Highest, and be in the Light! Sages say the path is narrow and difficult to tread, narrow as the edge of a razor.

The Atman is beyond sound and form, without touch and taste and perfume. It is eternal, unchangeable, and without beginning or end: indeed above reasoning. When consciousness of the Atman manifests itself, man becomes free from the jaws of death.

The wise who can learn and can teach this ancient story of Nachiketas, taught by Yama, the god of death, finds glory in the world of Brahman.

He who, filled with devotion, recites this supreme mystery at the gathering of Brahmins, or at the ceremony of the Sradha for the departed, prepares for Eternity, he prepares in truth for Eternity.

## Part 4

The Creator made the senses outward-going: they go to the world of matter outside, not to the Spirit within. But a sage who sought immortality looked within himself and found his own Soul.

The foolish run after outward pleasures and fall into the snares of vast-embracing death. But the wise have found immortality, and do not seek the Eternal in things that pass away.

This by which we perceive colours and sounds, perfumes and kisses of love; by which alone we attain knowledge; by which verily we can be conscious of anything:
This in truth is That.

When the wise knows that it is through the great and omnipresent Spirit in us that we are conscious in waking or in dreaming, then he goes beyond sorrow.

When he knows the Atman, the Self, the inner life, who enjoys like a bee the sweetness of the flowers of the senses, the Lord of what was and of what will be, then he goes beyond fear:
This in truth is That.

The god of creation, who in the beginning was born from the fire of thought before the waters were; who appeared in the elements and rests, having entered the heart:
This in truth is That.

The goddess of Infinity who comes as Life-power and Nature; who was born from the elements and rests, having entered the heart:
This in truth is That.

Agni, the all-knowing god of fire, hidden in the two friction fire-sticks of the holy sacrifice, as a seed of life in the womb of a mother, who receives the morning adoration of those who follow the path of light or the path of work:
This in truth is That.

Whence the rising sun does come, and into which it sets again; wherein all the gods have their birth, and beyond which no man can go:
This in truth is That

What is here is also there, and what is there is also here. Who sees the many and not the ONE, wanders on from death to death.

Even by the mind this truth is to be learned: there are not many but only ONE. Who sees variety and not the unity wanders on from death to death.

The soul dwells within us, a flame the size of a thumb. When it is known as the Lord of the past and the future, then ceases all fear:

This in truth is That.

Like a flame without smoke, the size of a thumb, is the soul; the Lord of the past and the future, the same both today and tomorrow:

This in truth is That.

As water raining on a mountain-ridge runs down the rocks on all sides, so the man who only sees variety of things runs after them on all sides.

But as pure water raining on pure water becomes one and the same, so becomes, O Nachiketas, the soul of the sage who knows.

## Part 5

The pure eternal Spirit dwells in the castle of eleven gates of the body. By ruling this castle, man is free from sorrows and, free from all bondage, attains liberation.

'In space he is the sun, and he is the wind and the sky; at the altar he is the priest, and the Soma wine in the jar. He dwells in men and in gods, in righteousness and in the vast heavens. He is in the earth and the waters and in the rocks of the mountains. He is Truth and Power.'

The powers of life adore that god who is in the heart, and he rules the breath of life, breathing in and breathing out.

When the ties that bind the Spirit to the body are unloosed and the Spirit is set free, what remains then?

This in truth is That.

A mortal lives not through that breath that flows in and that flows out. The source of his life is another and this causes the breath to flow.

I will now speak to you of the mystery of the eternal Brahman; and of what happens to the soul after death.

The soul may go to the womb of a mother and thus obtain a new body. It even may go into trees or plants, according to its previous wisdom and work.

There is a Spirit who is awake in our sleep and creates the wonder of dreams. He is Brahman, the Spirit of Light. who in truth is called the Immortal. All the worlds rest on that Spirit and beyond him no one can go:

This in truth is That.

As fire, though one, takes new forms in all things that burn, the Spirit, though one, takes new forms in all things that live. He is within all, and is also outside.

As the wind, though one, takes new forms in whatever it enters, the Spirit, though one, takes new forms in all things that live. He is within all, and is also outside.

As the sun that beholds the world is untouched by earthly impurities, so the Spirit that is in all things is untouched by external sufferings.

There is one Ruler, the Spirit that is in all things, who transforms his own form into many. Only the wise who see him in their souls attain the joy eternal.

He is the Eternal among things that pass away, pure Consciousness of conscious beings, the ONE who fulfils the prayers of many. Only the wise who see him in their souls attain the peace eternal.

'This is That'—thus they realize the ineffable joy supreme. How can 'This' be known? Does he give light or does he reflect light?

There the sun shines not, nor the moon, nor the stars; lightnings shine not there and much less earthly fire. From his light all these give light, and his radiance illumines all creation.

## Part 6

The Tree of Eternity has its roots in heaven above and its branches reach down to earth. It is Brahman, pure Spirit, who in truth is called the Immortal. All the worlds rest on that Spirit and beyond him no one can go:

This in truth is That.

The whole universe comes from him and his life burns through the whole universe. In his power is the majesty of thunder. Those who know him have found immortality.

From fear of him fire burns, and from fear of him the sun shines. From fear of him the clouds and the winds, and death itself, move on their way.

If one sees him in this life before the body passes away, one is free from bondage; but if not, one is born and dies again in new worlds and new creations.

Brahman is seen in a pure soul as in a mirror clear, and also in the Creator's heaven as clear as light; but in the land of shades as remembrance of dreams, and in the world of spirits as reflections in trembling waters.

When the wise man knows that the material senses come not from the Spirit, and that their waking and sleeping belong to their own nature, then he grieves no more.

Beyond the senses is the mind, and beyond mind is reason, its essence. Beyond reason is the Spirit in man, and beyond this is the Spirit of the universe, the evolver of all.

And beyond is Purusha, all-pervading, beyond definitions. When a mortal knows him, he attains liberation and reaches immortality.

His form is not in the field of vision: no one sees him with mortal eyes. He is seen by a pure heart and by a mind and thoughts that are pure. Those who know him attain life immortal.

When the five senses and the mind are still, and reason itself rests in silence, then begins the Path supreme.

This calm steadiness of the senses is called Yoga. Then one should become watchful, because Yoga comes and goes.

Words and thoughts cannot reach him and he cannot be seen by the eye. How can he then be perceived except by him who says 'He is'?

In the faith of 'He is' his existence must be perceived, and he must be perceived in his essence. When he is perceived as 'He is', then shines forth the revelation of his essence.

When all desires that cling to the heart are surrendered, then a mortal becomes immortal, and even in this world he is one with Brahman.

When all the ties that bind the heart are unloosened, then a mortal becomes immortal. This is the sacred teaching.

One hundred and one subtle ways come from the heart. One of them rises to the crown of the head. This is the way that leads to immortality; the others lead to different ends.

Always dwelling within all beings is the Atman, the Purusha, the Self, a little flame in the heart. Let one with steadiness withdraw him from the body even as an inner stem is withdrawn from its sheath. Know this pure immortal light; know in truth this pure immortal light.

And Nachiketas learnt the supreme wisdom taught by the god of afterlife, and he learnt the whole teaching of inner-union, of Yoga. Then he reached Brahman, the Spirit Supreme, and became immortal and pure. So in truth will anyone who knows his Atman, his higher Self.

# Selected Buddhist Texts

Buddhism is one of the three most successful "missionary religions" in history (along with Christianity and Islam), meaning that it was able to spread far from its place of origin, among vastly different cultures and ethnic groups. Today there are about as many Buddhists in the world as Protestants, and the Buddhist *Sangha*—the community of monks and nuns—is probably the oldest continuously-lasting social institution in the world. Buddhism began with Siddartha Gautama (either ca. 560–480 B.C.E. or ca. 440–360 B.C.E.), a prince in northern India who became dissatisfied with his pampered lifestyle and left home to find out for himself the truth about life; in particular he wanted an answer to the problem of the pervasive suffering he had discovered in three trips outside the palace grounds. After several years spent in asceticism—neglecting, as much as possible, bodily needs such as food and shelter in order to concentrate on spiritual refinement—he decided that this was not the right path. Instead he combined moderate self-discipline with meditation and eventually he gained enlightenment while sitting under a Bodhi tree. In this way he became the Buddha, or the "Awakened One." This story can be found in the *Buddha-karita*, one of the first biographies of the Buddha, written in Sanskrit poetry by Asvaghosa in the second century C.E. (the long time-lapse between the Buddha's life and his biographies is part of the reason his dates are so uncertain).

The Buddha's basic insight was that nothing lasts forever, and suffering is the result of ignorance of this fact, along with the desire for impermanent things. One of the most important expressions of Buddhist teaching is the "Four Holy Truths" from his first sermon. The Buddha also argued that that the temporariness of all things includes you and me. This means that, despite the fact that Buddhists believe in reincarnation and karma, the ultimate truth is that there is no such thing as a soul—no self that has an eternal, independent existence—and when we truly realize this, we will pass into nirvana, a state of neither existence nor non-existence. If someday existence as we know it will come to an end for each of us, then our current life is an illusion. From this perspective the Buddha can claim in the *Diamond Sutra* that he has not saved any being, for there were never really any beings in need of salvation in the first place.

In the centuries after the death of the Buddha, three major traditions developed. Theravada ("ancient") Buddhism teaches that the Buddha was a man who no longer exists and thus should not be worshipped as a god. This is the oldest form of Buddhism, and adherents believe that enlightenment is available only to monks and nuns, that is, those who can devote their lives to meditation and the study of the voluminous Buddhist sutras (scriptures). It is the predominant form of Buddhism in Southeast Asia and Sri Lanka, and its scriptures are written in Pali—an ancient dialect of South India.

Mahayana ("Large Vehicle") Buddhism arose around the first century B.C.E. with new scriptures written in Sanskrit—the classical language of India—and a more open approach to salvation in which enlightenment was within the reach of everyone. These Buddhists believe that the Buddha was a god and that there are other enlightened beings called bodhisattvas to which one can pray and ask for spiritual and temporal aid. Mahayana Buddhism is found primarily in East Asia, and in America its most visible sect is Zen.

Mantrayana Buddhism is mainly found in Tibet and Nepal. It offers shortcuts to enlightenment through ritual gestures and words of power ("mantras"), and it combines traditional Buddhism with the worship of local divinities and a sophisticated philosophy. The Dalai Lama is a key figure in this type of Buddhism.

In general, Buddhism offers the "middle way" between extreme self-denial and extreme self-indulgence. Through its teachings and practices, Buddhism leads its followers to a calmer, more integrated, more compassionate way of living. From there they can become enlightened and pass into nirvana, leaving the cares and sorrows of this world behind.

GH

# from *The Buddha-karita of Asvaghosha*

## Second Century C.E.

The king, having learned the character of the wish thus expressed by his son, ordered a pleasure-party to be prepared, worthy of his own affection and his son's beauty and youth. He prohibited the encounter of any afflicted common person in the highroad; 'heaven forbid that the prince with his tender nature should even imagine himself to be distressed.' Then having removed out of the way with the greatest gentleness all those who had mutilated limbs or maimed senses, the decrepit and the sick and all squalid beggars, they made the highway assume its perfect beauty. . . .

But then the gods, dwelling in pure abodes, having beheld the city thus rejoicing like heaven itself, created an old man to walk along on purpose to stir the heart of the king's son. The prince having beheld him thus overcome with decrepitude and different in form from other men, with his gaze intently fixed on him, thus addressed his driver with simple confidence: 'Who is this man that has come here, O charioteer, with white hair and his hand resting on a staff, his eyes hidden beneath his brows, his limbs bent down and hanging loose,—is this a change produced in him or his natural state or an accident?

Thus addressed, the charioteer revealed to the king's son the secret that should have been kept so carefully, thinking no harm in his simplicity, for those same gods had bewildered his mind: 'That is old age by which he is broken down,—the ravisher of beauty, the ruin of vigour, the cause of sorrow, the destruction of delights, the bane of memories, the enemy of the senses. He too once drank milk in his childhood, and in course of time he learned to grope on the ground; having step by step become a vigorous youth, he has step by step in the same way reached old age.'

Being thus addressed, the prince, starting a little, spoke these words to the charioteer, 'What! will this evil come to me also?' and to him again spoke the charioteer: 'It will come without doubt by the force of time through multitude of years even to the long-lived lord; all the world knows thus that old age will destroy their comeliness and they are content to have it so.'

Then he, the great-souled one, who had his mind purified by the impressions of former good actions, who possessed a store of merits accumulated through many preceding aeons, was deeply agitated when he heard of old age, like a bull who has heard the crash of a thunderbolt close by. Drawing a long sigh and shaking his head, and fixing his eyes on that decrepit old man, and looking round on that exultant multitude he then uttered these distressed words: 'Old age thus strikes down all alike, our memory, comeliness, and valour; and yet the world is not disturbed, even when it sees such a fate visibly impending. Since such is our condition, O charioteer, turn back the horses,— go quickly home; how can I rejoice in the pleasure-garden, when the thoughts arising from old age overpower me?

Then the charioteer at the command of the king's son turned the chariot back, and the prince lost in thought entered even that royal palace as if it were empty. But when he found no happiness even there, as he continually kept reflecting, 'old age, old age.' Then once more, with the permission of the king, he went out with the same arrangement as before.

Then the same deities created another man with his body all afflicted by disease; and on seeing him the son of Suddhodana addressed the charioteer, having his gaze fixed on the man: 'Yonder man with a swollen belly, his whole frame shaking as he pants, his arms and shoulders hanging loose, his body all pale and thin, uttering plaintively the word "mother," when he embraces a stranger,—who, pray, is this?'

The his charioteer answered, 'Gentle Sir, it is a very great affliction called sickness, that has grown up, caused by the inflammation of the (three) humours, which has made even this strong man no longer master of himself.'

• • •

But as the king's son was thus going on his way, the very same deities created a dead man, and only the charioteer and the prince, and none else, beheld him as he was carried dead along the road. Then spoke the prince to the charioteer, 'Who is this borne by four men, followed by mournful companions, who is bewailed, adorned but no longer breathing?'

Then the driver,—having his mind overpowered by the gods who possess pure minds and pure dwelling,—himself knowing the truth, uttered to his lord this truth also which was not to be told: 'This is some poor man who, bereft of his intellect, senses, vital airs and qualities, lying asleep and unconscious, like mere wood or straw, is abandoned alike by friends and enemies after they have carefully swathed and guarded him'. . . .

Then the king's son, sedate though he was, as soon as he heard of death, immediately sank down overwhelmed, and pressing the end of the chariot-pole with his shoulder spoke with a loud voice, 'Is this end appointed to all creatures, and yet the world throws off all fear and is infatuated! Hard indeed, I think, must the hearts of men be, who can be self-composed in such a road. Therefore, O charioteer, turn back our chariot, this is not time or place for a pleasure-excursion; how can a rational being, who knows what destruction is, stay heedless here, in the hour of calamity?'

# The Four Noble Truths from *The Mahavagga*

And the Blessed One thus addressed the five Bhikkhus [wandering ascetics]: 'There are two extremes, O Bhikkhus, which he who has given up the world, ought to avoid. What are these two extremes? A life given to pleasures, devoted to pleasures and lusts: this is degrading, sensual, vulgar, ignoble, and profitless; and a life given to mortifications: this is painful, ignoble, and profitless. By avoiding these two extremes, O Bhikkhus, the Tathagata has gained the knowledge of the Middle Path which leads to insight, which leads to wisdom, which conduces to calm, to knowledge, to the Sambodhi [enlightenment], to Nirvana. . . .

'This, O Bhikkhus, is the Noble Truth of Suffering: Birth is suffering; decay is suffering; illness is suffering; death is suffering. Presence of objects we hate, is suffering; Separation from objects we love, is suffering; not to obtain what we desire, is suffering. Briefly, the fivefold clinging to existence is suffering.

'This, O Bhikkhus, is the Noble Truth of the Cause of suffering: Thirst, that leads to re-birth, accompanied by pleasure and lust, finding its delight here and there. (This thirst is threefold), namely, thirst for pleasure, thirst for existence, thirst for prosperity.

'This, O Bhikkhus, is the Noble Truth of the Cessation of suffering: (it ceases with) the complete cessation of this thirst,—a cessation which consists in the absence of every passion,—with the abandoning of this thirst, with the doing away with it, with the deliverance from it, with the destruction of desire.

'This, O Bhikkhus, is the Noble Truth of the Path which leads to the cessation of suffering: that holy eightfold Path, that is to say, Right Belief, Right Aspiration, Right Speech, Right Conduct, Right Means of Livelihood, Right Endeavour, Right Memory, Right Meditation.'

# from *The Diamond Sutra*

## Third–Fourth Century C.E.

'What do you think then, O Subhuti, does a Tathagata [a Buddha] think in this wise: Beings have been delivered by me? You should not think so, O Subhuti. And why? Because there is no being, O Subhuti, that has been delivered by the Tathagata. And, if there were a being, O Subhuti, that has been delivered by the Tathagata, then the Tathagata would believe in self, believe in a being, believe in a living being, and believe in a person. And what is called a belief in self, O Subhuti, that is preached as no-belief by the Tathagata. And this is learned by children and ignorant persons; and they who were preached as children and ignorant persons, O Subhuti, were preached as no-persons by the Tathagata, and therefore they are called children and ignorant persons.' (25)

# V. Ancient Greece

## INTRODUCTION

No brief introduction to Greek literature can hope to offer anything comprehensive or worthy of its subject. Fortunately, Greek literature needs no introduction to make it accessible: most of the literature of ancient Greece still reaches modern readers in immediate and powerful ways. Many of the figures of Greek epic and drama still inhabit our language and patterns of thought: we still speak of an "Achilles heel" and a "Trojan Horse" and a "Herculean task." Greek mythology appeals to readers young and old for its apparent simplicity—many myths seem appropriate for children's books or comic books—that belies its complex symbolism and function in Greek society. And perhaps most indicative of all, the majority of our words for naming or categorizing literature come directly from the Greeks: epic, lyric, drama, tragedy, comedy, philosophy, even poet, poem, and poetry, are words and forms all inherited from Greek literature and Greek language.

Familiar connections like these can be drawn for hundreds of pages. Instead, this short essay will be used to point out a few things that may not be familiar, but are important in considering Greek literature in its original contexts and in its present state for us. We will target three things:

1.  Performance was the primary context for most of Greek literature.
2.  Writers imitated and borrowed from their predecessors even across generic lines, creating dense patterns of reference and allusion.
3.  The vast bulk of the Greek literature that existed has not survived.

1) We usually approach Greek literature as readers, and we assume that the Greeks did, too. In fact, most of the literature that we have was experienced by Greek audiences in some type of performance. Even before Homer, stories and myths circulated orally and widely. The earliest examples of Greek literature, and arguably the greatest, the *Iliad* and the *Odyssey*, borrow and build on this oral tradition. The store of myths and tales was widely held; consider that Homer begins the *Iliad*, as Horace says, *in medias res*, with no explanation of the principal characters or the background of his story. These myths, tales, and episodes were conveyed by professional singers, bards, such as appear in the characters of Demodocus and Phemius in the *Odyssey*, and such as Homer him-

self might have been. The texts of Homer became the material for professional singers, some of whom devoted themselves to his epics and delivered them at contests and festivals. We can glean some aspects of such a performance from Plato's short dialogue *Ion*, which is named for such a professional Homerist. Ion says that he weeps himself during his delivery; he apparently also added gesticulation, and modulated his voice. He says that his audience was moved to tears, or anger, or amazement—for a story that they already knew.

The term "lyric poetry" implies poetry that is set to music and sung, but it encompasses a wide variety of poems, only a few of which are represented in our anthology. Some lyric poetry was expressly choral, and though we do not know the exact circumstances of its performance, we know that it was performed with dance and, sometimes, call and response between the leader and the chorus. The music and dance are lost to us, but vase paintings exist which give meager representations of such performances. Some lyric poems, such as victory songs, were performed at games and festivals. The venue of individual lyric poetry is more difficult to assess. Some lyric poems, such as the elegaic poems of Tyrtaeus or Solon, clearly address the public, and probably were recited to the Spartans or Athenians. And some lyric poetry, like that of Sappho, addresses individuals or divinities and concerns emotions, and seems intended for a smaller, more private audience, perhaps those gathered for a *symposium*, a "drinking together," at home.

Thanks to archeological remains, artistic representations, and copious textual evidence, we know much more about the performances of tragedy and comedy, much more than can be repeated here. We know less of drama's origins, but the hints that we have of professional bards performing Homer, and of choral song and dance in lyric modes, provide possible sources for what became dramatic performance in Athens in the early sixth century B.C.E. Tragedy and comedy, of course, are much more than chorus and recited story. The dramas were performed at festivals in honor of Dionysus, and they were performed in competition with other dramas. Male actors played all parts, including female parts; all were citizens, and were taught by the tragedian himself, who served as the "director" and occasionally one of the actors. All the actors were masked and often elaborately costumed. Among the elements of tragedy, Aristotle lists music (and with it dance or movement) and spectacle, which are not available from the texts themselves. Aristotle says that Sophocles introduced scene-painting; scenes were frequently palaces but could also be groves or caves. Stage-effects probably did not aim at realism as we might think of it, but plots include an earthquake and the collapse of a palace, as in Euripides' *Bacchae*. Some sort of crane also allowed the entrance of gods (or comic parody of such an entrance). The texts of comedy are more explicit than those of tragedy in describing action, costume, dance, and song, but both genres still lose much of their vibrancy if left to languish as words on a page. Even after Athens fell at the end of the fifth century B.C.E. and tragedy and comedy changed so profoundly, the plays of Aeschylus, Sophocles, and Euripides continued to be performed, and guilds of professional actors, the *technitai* of Dionysus, carried performances through the Hellenistic world.

History is probably the genre furthest removed from the context of performance, but it is almost certain that the first audiences of Herodotus and Thucydides experienced their histories as things heard rather than read. Herodotus' history can be broken down into smaller narrative sections (*logoi*) which may indicate that he was able to present parts, just as the bard could present a scene from Homer.

Only in the Hellenistic age do we begin to find the idea of the "text" in a sense resembling our own, that is, as words on a page and separate from a larger performative context. Literature written during the period, however, still must have had an imagined audience who would receive the text as something read to them out loud, often in the company of others. Rather than public festivals or competitions, the locations of these readings might have been a royal court, or a scholarly or artistic enclave. The western world would wait centuries before it arrived at the silent, solitary reader: in the late fourth century C.E., St. Augustine notes the strange habit of St. Ambrose, who read without making a sound.

2) A quick reference of the relative dates of Greek epic, lyric, drama, and other genres might lead to the conclusion that these genres developed one after the other, and perhaps in response to one another. This conclusion would neither be entirely accurate nor inaccurate. Genres coexisted simultaneously and influenced each other, and later writers borrowed from their predecessors in varieties of ways. Homer refers to various types of lyric expression in the context of epic: wedding songs, hymns to gods, funeral dirges, and other lyric forms existed contemporaneously with epic. After the material of the Homeric epics became familiar throughout the Greek world, however, its influence was pervasive. Even extant lyric poetry, that addresses the present and the private and has little in common with the grandeur and remoteness of epic, seems occasionally to define itself in opposition to epic. Sappho claims that the most beautiful thing in the world is not soldiers or horses or ships, but one's love.

Drama's debt to epic can scarcely be exhausted. The tragedian Aeschylus is said to have called his tragedies "slices from the banquet of Homer," and modern scholars see the Iliadic Achilles, solitary and disaffected, as one of the principal sources for the Sophoclean hero or heroine. Tragedy's debt to epic is not principally located in setting or subject matter—relatively few of the tragedies are set at Troy—but rather in view, tone, action, and character. Comedy also borrows from Homer, though more indirectly. The crafty, amoral hero of Athenian comedy is sometimes viewed as a descendent of "versatile" Odysseus, surviving challenges not from cannibals and witches but from politicians and horny husbands. Comedy more frequently alludes to its dramatic sibling, tragedy, usually in parody but sometimes with respect. Euripides is a frequent target of Aristophanes' jokes; Euripidean plots form the basis for several comedic scenes, and Euripides himself appears in three surviving Aristophanic comedies.

Aristotle makes provocative statements about the evolution of tragedy and comedy from certain choral lyric forms. Tragic and comic choruses are always written in lyric meters, that is, they were sung and sometimes danced; occasionally, especially in early tragedy, the chorus functioned more integrally, sometimes as one character. Lyric continued to develop as well in tandem with drama, and some later dramas of Euripides and Aristophanes reveal more lyric expression by the principal characters, which might have resembled arias in opera.

Tragedy also informs the historical worldview, and sometimes the composition, of Herodotus and Thucydides. Herodotus and Sophocles were contemporaries and reputedly acquainted, and several passages bear such similarity (for example, Herodotus 3.119 and *Antigone* 905–912) that it seems improbable that one did not know the other, even though we cannot know who might have borrowed from whom. Certainly, Herodotus' story of Croesus (1.1–91) and his misinterpretation of the Delphic oracle seems like a tragic reversal and recognition. Thucydides' account of the debate between Athens and Melos and the fate of the Melians (5.85–113) resembles the events described in Euripides' *Trojan Women*.

In addition to Euripides, Socrates was a target of Aristophanes' comedy; one of his jokes suggests that Socrates helped Euripides compose his tragedies. Even though Socrates attacked the teachings and practices of the Sophists, Aristophanes characterizes Socrates as one of those immoral intellectuals in the *Clouds*; Plato has Socrates name that comedy specifically as one of the sources of popular opinion against him, even though the *Clouds* was first produced almost 25 years before Socrates' trial. The influence of epic and tragedy on Plato was enormous: a later writer says that Plato first wrote tragedies, and when he met Socrates, he threw his tragedies into the flames. Plato's complex interaction with Homer and tragedy seems to involve both adoration and rejection. Plato offers us Socrates as a hero greater than Hercules or Achilles in the *Apology of Socrates*, and in his *Republic* he famously banishes Homer and the tragedians from his ideal state, because they tell lies about the gods, among other things.

These imitations, parodies, adaptations, allusions, borrowings, and rejections are more than inside messages or jokes of artists to other artists. They reveal the vital and vibrant role that these forms of literature had in public, civic, political, intellectual, and religious life in Greece generally and in Athens especially in the fifth century B.C.E. They were the "popular culture," which made little if any distinction between high and low forms. During Alexander's campaign, Greek culture, including Greek literature, was disseminated more broadly to places where it had not been before, where knowledge of it became an element of "culturedness." Hellenistic authors continued to write in response to earlier Greek literature. Separate from the original contexts, their results often took on a more learned tone but were free to develop in new directions. Nevertheless, it is doubtful that any author writing in Greek, even during the Hellenistic period, imagined himself or herself to be doing something unique and entirely original, free from all influence.

3) Only a very small percentage of all ancient Greek literature has survived into the present. Some of the losses are astonishing: according to ancient sources, Aeschylus wrote 80 dramas, Sophocles 123, and Euripides 90. Of these totals, seven plays of Aeschylus, seven of Sophocles, and 19 of Euripides have survived. The canonization of these three playwrights, which had begun already in the fifth century, as Aristophanes' *Frogs* shows, helped guarantee their survival but probably factored into the disappearance of all other tragedians who are mentioned in our sources, some of whom—Phrynichus, Agathon—were quite famous.

From alternative versions of myths and from the mentions of authors and works in other sources, we catch a glimpse of what we do not have. There were many more epics than Homer's *Iliad* and *Odyssey* (some also attributed to him); there were countless lyric poems and poets; as mentioned above, there were many, many more tragedies and comedies than we have; there were historical accounts, philosophical treatises, orations, and much more, that have not survived to our day. Works like Hesiod's *Theogony* and the *Library* attributed to Apollodorus reveal many versions of myths current at the same time, and for many of them, no literary sources are extant.

The more amazing fact is that any has survived at all. The process by which what we have has come down to us is as varied as history itself. The Greek texts that we now consider canonical were generally regarded as such by the scholars working in the great Hellenistic library in Alexandria, and these scholars devoted a great deal of attention to preserving and editing these texts. The canonical texts, then as now, were taught in schools, and this helped ensure their survival through popular interest and the number of copies available. The Romans also preserved Greek literature; in the early second century C.E., for example, Trajan's Forum contained a library with two wings, one for Greek works. Based on Greek and Roman authors from the late Roman Empire, it seems that the bulk of Greek literature survived into sixth century C.E. After that, however, a few periods of relative indifference or hostility contributed to the small selection we now possess. The famous library at Alexandria seems to have suffered destruction several times. After the "fall" of the Roman Empire, the Eastern Roman capital of Constantinople (present day Istanbul) became the center of learning and preservation, but the texts suffered during the period of Iconoclasm (726–842 C.E.). After several centuries of renewed interest in classical learning, the city fell to the Crusaders during the Fourth Crusade (1204 C.E.), with irreparable loss of classical material. When the Ottoman Turks captured Constantinople in 1453 C.E., some of the scholars fled to Europe, especially to Italy, taking texts with them, where they contributed to the Renaissance. Aldus Manutius of Venice produced the first printed editions of Greek texts in the 1490s. Since that time, new texts have come to light through improved technology, manuscript research, and papyrus discoveries in Egypt, but it is nearly impossible that the world will ever recover another tragedy of Sophocles or a book of Sappho's poems.

BSH

# Pre-Socratic Philosophers

The earliest Greek philosophers are conventionally called the pre-Socratics, though in fact some of the later ones were contemporary with Socrates and knew him. While they devoted thought to a wide variety of topics, including medicine, mathematics, ethics, and epistemology, they are now thought of perhaps mostly in connection with their ideas on physics. Many of them wrote works called *Peri Phuseos*, which means "On Nature"—so that our modern word "physics" comes from the Greek word for nature—and most of the philosophers themselves were *phusikoi*, that is, students of nature or natural philosophers.

Almost none of the works written by the pre-Socratics is available for the modern reader. Most of what we know about them comes from paraphrases or summaries contained in later books (sometimes as much as a thousand years later), though there is good reason to believe that many of these later writers *did* have the original texts to consult. All such materials must be treated with a bit of skepticism because, in addition to such sources of corruption as bad manuscripts or mistaken ascription of beliefs, many of the quotations occur in books written in order to refute what the later authors thought of as error. Several of the sources are written by early Christians who regarded pagan philosophy as heretical.

MM

# Early Greek Philosophy

## Thales (ca. 625–ca. 545 B.C.E.)

Most of the first philosophers thought that principles in the form of matter were the only principles of all things. For they say that the element and first principle of the things that exist is that from which they all are and from which they first come into being and into which they are finally destroyed, its substance remaining and its properties changing . . . There must be some nature—either one or more than one—from which the other things come into being, it being preserved. But as to the number and form of this sort of principle, they do not all agree. Thales, the founder of this kind of philosophy, says that it is water (that is why he declares that the earth rests on water). He perhaps came to acquire this belief from seeing that the nourishment of everything is moist and that heat itself comes from this and lives by this (for that from which anything comes into being is its first principle)—he came to his belief both for this reason and because the seeds of everything have a moist nature, and water is the natural principle of moist things.

(Aristotle, *Metaphysics* 983b 6–11, 17–27)

Aristotle and Hippias say that he ascribed souls to lifeless things too, taking the magnet and amber as his evidence. Pamphila says that he learned geometry from the Egyptians and was the first to inscribe a right-angled triangle inside a circle, for which he sacrificed an ox. . . . He is also thought to have given excellent advice in political affairs. . . . No-one taught him, although he went to Egypt and spent time with the priests there. Heironymus says that he actually measured the pyramids from their shadows, having observed the time when <our shadows> are the same size as we are. . . . Hermippus in his Lives ascribes to Thales what others say of Socrates. He used to say, they report, that he thanked Fortune for three things: first, that I am a human and not a beast; secondly, that I am a man and not a woman; thirdly, that I am a Greek and not a foreigner. . . . The Sage died of heat and thirst and weakness while watching a gymnastic contest. He was by then an old man. On his tomb is inscribed:

> His tomb is small, his fame is heaven-high
> behold the grave of the wise and ingenious Thales.

(Diogenes Laertius, *Lives of the Philosophers* I 22–28, 33–40)

# Pythagoras (ca. 570 B.C.E.–?)

Pythagoras acquired a great reputation: he won many followers in the city of Croton itself (both men and women, one of whom, Theano, achieved some fame), and many from the nearby foreign territory, both kings and noblemen. What he said to his associates no-one can say with any certainty; for they preserved no ordinary silence. But it became very well known to everyone that he said, first, that the soul is immortal; then, that it changes into other kinds of animals; and further, that at certain periods whatever has happened happens again, there being nothing absolutely new; and that all living things should be considered as belonging to the same kind. Pythagoras seems to have been the first to introduce these doctrines into Greece.

(Porphyry, *Life of Pythagoras* 19)

Pythagoras believed in metempsychosis[1] and thought that eating meat was an abominable thing, saying that the souls of all animals enter different animals after death. He himself used to say that he remembered being, in Trojan times, Euphorbus, Panthus's son, who was killed by Menelaus.

(Diodorus, *Universal History* X vi 1–3)

# Xenophanes (ca. 580–480 B.C.E.)

Xenophanes of Colophon, claiming that god is one and incorporeal, says:

There is one god, greatest among gods and men,
similar to mortals neither in shape nor in thought. [B 23]

And again:

But mortals think that the gods are born,
and have clothes and speech and shape like their own. [B 14]

And again:

But if cows and horses or lions had hands
or could draw with their hands and make the things men can make,
then horses would draw the forms of gods like horses,
cows like cows, and they would make their bodies
similar in shape to those which each had themselves. [B15]

(Clement, *Miscellanies* V xiv 109.1–3)

He [Xenophanes] says that nothing comes into being or is destroyed or changes, and that the universe is one and changeless. He also says that god is eternal and unique and homogenous in every way and limited and spherical and capable of perception in all his parts.

The sun comes into existence each day from small sparks which congregated. The earth is infinite and surrounded neither by air nor by the heavens. There are infinitely many suns and moons. Everything is made from earth.

He said that the sea is salty because many mixtures flow together in it. (Metrodorus holds that it is salty because it is filtered in the earth, but Xenophanes thinks that the earth mixes with the sea.) He holds that the earth in time is dissolved by the moisture, urging as proof the fact that shells are found in the middle of the land and on mountains; and he says that in the quarries of Syracuse there were found impressions of fish and of seaweed, on Paros the impression of a bay-leaf deep in the rock, and on Malta shapes of all sea-creatures. He says that these were formed long ago when everything was covered in mud—the impressions dried in the mud. All men are destroyed when the earth is carried down into the sea and becomes mud; they they begin to be born again—and this is the foundation of all the worlds.

(Hippolytus, *Refutation of All Heresies* I xiv 2–6)

## Heraclitus (flourished about 500 B.C.E.)

The path up and down is one and the same.

(Quoted in Hippolytus, *Refutation of all Heresies*)

To be temperate is the greatest excellence. And wisdom is speaking the truth and acting with knowledge in accordance with nature.

(Quoted in John Stobaeus, *Anthology*)

Thinking is common to all.

(Stobaeus, *Anthology*)

Gods are mortal, humans immortal, living their death, dying their life.

(Quoted in Heraclitus, *Homeric Questions*)

We step and do not step into the same rivers, we are and we are not.

(Heraclitus, *Homeric Questions*)

His views, in general, were the following: All things are constituted from fire and resolve into fire. All things come about in accordance with fate, and the things that exist are fitted together by the transformation of opposites. All things are full of souls and spirits. He spoke also about all the events that occur in the world, and he said that the sun is the size it appears. . . . He also said

If you travel every path, you will not find the limits of the soul, so deep is its account. [B 45]

He said that conceit is a sort of epilepsy, and that sight is fallacious [B 46]. . . . In detail, his doctrines are these. Fire is an element, and all things are an exchange for fire, coming about by rarefaction and condensation. (But he expresses nothing clearly.) All things come about through opposition, and the universe flows like a river. The universe is finite, and there is one world. It is generated from fire and is consumed in fire again, alternating in fixed periods throughout the whole of time. And this happens by fate. . . .

Of the opposites, that which leads to generation is called war and strife, and that which leads to conflagration is called agreement and peace. The change is a path up and down, and the world is generated in accordance with it. For fire as it is condensed becomes moist, and as it coheres becomes water; water as it solidified turns into earth—this is the path downwards. Then again the earth dissolves, and water comes into being from it, and everything else from water (he refers pretty well everything to the exhalation given off by the sea)—this is the path upwards.

(Diogenes Laertius, Lives of the Philosophers, IX)

For it is not possible to step twice into the same river, according to Heraclitus, nor to touch mortal substance twice in any condition: by the swiftness and speed of its change, it scatters and collects itself again—or rather, it is not again and later but simultaneously that it comes together and departs, approaches and retires.

(Plutarch, On the E at Delphi 392B)

Always remember Heraclitus' view that the death of earth is to become water, and the death of water to become air, and of air fire, and the reverse.

(Marcus Aurelius, Meditations IV)

## Zeno (??)

Zeno's argument seemed to do away with the existence of place. It was propounded as follows: If places exist, they will be in something; for everything that exists is in something. But what is in something is in a place. Therefore places are in places—and so on ad infinitum.

(Simplicius, Commentary on the Physics 562.3–6)

Aristotle [in his Physics] thus solves the problem which Zeno of Elea put to Protagoras the sophist. "Tell me, Protagoras," he said, "does one millet-seed—or the ten-thousandth part of a seed—make a sound when it falls?" Protagoras said that it did not. "But," he said, "does a bushel of millet make a sound when it falls or not?" When he replied that a bushel does make a sound, Zeno said: "Well, then, isn't there a ratio between the bushel of millet-seed and the single seed—or the ten-thousandth part of a single seed?" He agreed. "Well, then," said Zeno, "will there not be similar ratios between the sounds?

For as are the sounders so are the sounds. And if that is the case, then if the bushel of millet-seed makes a sound, the single seed—and the ten-thousandth part of a single seed—will also make a sound." That was Zeno's argument.

(Ibid, 1108.14–28)

## Empedocles (ca. 495–ca. 435 B.C.E.)

In the first book of his *Physics*, Empedocles talks about the one and the finitely many and the periodic recreation and generation and destruction by association and dissociation in the following way:

> I will tell a two-fold story. At one time they grew to be one alone
> from being many, and at another they grew apart again to be many from
> being one.
> Double is the generation of mortal things, double their passing away:
> one is born and destroyed by the congregation of everything,
> the other is nurtured and flies apart as they grow apart again
> And these never cease their continual change,
> now coming together by Love all into one,
> now again all being carried away by the hatred of Strife.
> <Thus insofar as they have learned to become one from many>
> and again become many as the one grows apart,
> to that extent they come into being and have no lasting life;
> but insofar as they never cease their continual change,
> to that extent they exist forever, unmoving in a circle.
>   But come, hear my words; for learning enlarges the mind.
> As I said before when I revealed the limits of my words,
> I will tell a two-fold story. At one time they grew to be one alone
> from being many, and at another they grew apart again to be many from
>     being one—
> fire and water and earth and the endless height of air,
> and curses Strife apart from them, balanced in every way,
> and Love among them, equal in length and breadth.
>
> (Simplicius, *Commentary on the Physics* 157–161)

## Democritus (ca. 460 B.C.E.–?)

If the same atoms endure, being impassive, it is clear that [the Democriteans] too will say the worlds are altered rather than destroyed—just as Empedocles and Heraclitus seem to think. An extract from Aristotle's work *On Democritus* will show what the view of these men was:

> Democritus thinks that the nature of eternal things consists in small substances, infinite in quantity, and for them he posits a place, distinct from then and infinite in extent. He calls place by the names "void," "nothing"

and "infinite," and each of the substances he calls "thing," "solid" and "being." He thinks that the substances are so small that they escape our senses, and that they possess all sorts of forms and all sorts of shapes and differences in magnitude. From them, as from elements, he was able to generate and compound visible and perceptible bodies. The atoms struggle and are carried about in the void because of their dissimilarities and the other differences mentioned, and as they are carried about they collide and are bound together in a binding which makes them touch and be contiguous with one another but which does not genuinely produce any other single nature whatever from them; for it is utterly silly to think that two or more things could ever become one. He explains how the substances remain together in terms of the ways in which the bodies entangle with and grasp hold of one another; for some of them are uneven, some hooked, some concave, some convex, and others have innumerable other differences. So he thinks that they hold on to one another and remain together up to the time when some stronger force reaches them from their environment and shakes them and scatters them apart. He speaks of generation and its contrary, dissolution, not only in connection with animals but also in connection with plants and worlds—and in general with all perceptible bodies [Aristotle, fragment 208]

(Simplicius, *Commentary on the Heavens* 294.30–295.22)

Democritus sometimes does away with what appears to the senses and says that nothing of this sort appears in truth but only in opinion, truth among the things that exist lying in the fact that there are atoms and void. For he says:

By convention sweet and by convention bitter, by convention hot, by convention cold, by convention colour: in reality atoms and void.

That is to say, objects of perception are thought and believed to exist but they do not exist in truth—only atoms and void do.

(Sextus Empiricus, *Against the Mathematicians* VII)

Flavours [according to Democritus] are sharp if their shapes [i.e., their constituent atoms] are angular and crinkled and small and fine. . . . Sweet flavour is constituted by round shapes which are not too small. That is why they relax the body completely without doing so violently or quickly passing through all of it. . . . Sour flavour is constituted by large shapes with many angles and as little roundness as possible. . . Bitter flavour is constituted by small, smooth, rounded shapes, where the roundness also contains crinkles. That is why it is viscous and sticky. Salty flavour is constituted by large shapes which are not rounded nor yet uneven but angular and crinkled . . . Pungent flavour is small, rounded and angular, but not uneven.

(Theophrastus, *On the Senses* 65–67)

Democritus and Plato both place happiness in the soul. Democritus writes thus:

> Happiness and unhappiness belong to the soul. [B 170]
> Happiness does not dwell in herds, nor yet in gold: the soul is the dwelling place of a man's lot. [B 171]

He calls happiness contentment, well-being, harmony, orderliness, tranquillity. It is constituted by distinguishing and discriminating among pleasures, and this is the noblest and most advantageous thing for men.

(Stobaeus, Anthology II vii 31)

## Note

[1] Transmigration of souls.

# Lyric Poetry

## Tyrtaeus, Solon, Sappho

### Tyrtaeus of Sparta (fl. 640 B.C.E.)

Little about Tyrtaeus' life and work is known. He seems to have flourished during the second half of the seventh century B.C.E., and his poems provide an important source for early Spartan history. Around the end of the eighth century B.C.E., Sparta conquered and enslaved the inhabitants of neighboring Messene, to their north; about 50 years later, the enslaved Messenians revolted. Some scholars think that the fragment "To the Soldiers, after a defeat" refers to a battle from this "Second Messenian War." When the Spartans finally won, they apparently transformed themselves into the strict military society that they became. David Campbell writes "(The Spartans) decided that they could maintain their position only by submitting to a rigorous military discipline, and life in Sparta became spartan. The crafts of vase-painters, ivory-carvers, and poets, which had all flourished, now died." (*Greek Lyric Poetry* 1967:169). Tyrtaeus composed his poems in elegiac meter (a couplet consisting of one dactylic hexameter and one dactylic pentameter), but used Homeric vocabulary almost exclusively. The method of fighting, however, is not Iliadic. (Translations by Richmond Lattimore)

### Solon of Athens (ca. 630?–559? B.C.E.)

Solon was an Athenian politician and poet, the first Athenian poet of note before the tragedian Aeschylus. Probably born noble, Solon nevertheless worked on behalf of the poor, abolishing debt-slavery, organizing the Athenians into property classes, and revising the law code. Solon allegedly traveled away from Athens for 10 years after enacting his measures, during which time the Athenians were not to change them. Solon came to be regarded as one of the Seven Sages of Greece by later generations; in the first book of Herodotus' *Histories* he appears to give wise advice to the Lydian king Croesus. Solon composed most of his poems in elegiac meter (a couplet consisting of one dactylic hexameter and one dactylic pentameter), but he depends on Homeric vocabulary and style much less heavily than his elegiac predecessors. (Translations by John Porter)

## Sappho of Lesbos, ca. 620–555 B.C.E.

Though Sappho's output was reputedly large—Hellenistic editors are said to have collected her poems in nine volumes organized by metrical type—we have very little, and all of it apparently fragmentary. What we have, however, is often striking. As David Campbell notes, "Clarity of language and simplicity of thought are everywhere evident in our fragments; wit and rhetoric, so common in English love-poetry and not quite absent from Catullus' love poems, are nowhere to be found. Her images are sharp—the arrows that draw Aphrodite's chariot, the full moon in the starry sky, the solitary red apple at the tree-top—and she sometimes lingers over them to elaborate them for their own sake . . . the music to which she sang them is gone, but the spoken sounds may still enchant" (*Greek Lyric Poetry* 1967:261–262). Many of her poems are in a meter and stanza form that bears her name, Sapphics, though she wrote in other meters as well, including dactylic hexameter, in which fragments 105a and c are composed. (Translations by Richmond Lattimore)

BSH

# Greek Lyric Poetry

## Tyrtaeus of Sparta

*Frontiers*

> You should reach the limits of virtue
> before you cross the border of death.

## *To the Soldiers, after a defeat*

Now, since you are the seed of Heracles the invincible,
courage! Zeus has not yet turned away from us. Do not
fear the multitude of their men, nor run away from them.
Each man should bear his shield straight at the foremost ranks
and make his heart a thing full of hate, and hold the black flying
spirits of death as dear as he holds the flash of the sun.

You know what havoc is the work of the painful War God,
you have learned well how things go in exhausting war,
for you have been with those who ran and with the pursuers,
O young men, you have had as much of both as you want.

Those who, standing their ground and closing their ranks together,
endure the onset at close quarters and fight in the front,
they lose fewer men. They also protect the army behind them.
Once they flinch, the spirit of the whole army falls apart.
And no man could count over and tell all the number of evils,
all that can come to a man, once he gives way to disgrace.
For once a man reverses and runs in the terror of battle,
he offers his back, a tempting mark to spear from behind,
and it is a shameful sight when a dead man lies in the dust there,
driven through from behind by the stroke of an enemy spear.

No, no, let him take a wide stance and stand up strongly against them,
digging both heels in the ground, biting his lip with his teeth,
covering thighs and legs beneath, his chest and his shoulders
under the hollowed-out protection of his broad shield,
while in his right hand he brandishes the powerful war-spear,
and shakes terribly the crest high above his helm.
Our man should be disciplined in the work of the heavy fighter,

287

and not stand out from the missiles when he carries a shield,
but go right up and fight at close quarters and, with his long spear
or short sword, thrust home and strike his enemy down.
Let him fight toe to toe and shield against shield hard driven,
crest against crest and helmet on helmet, chest against chest;
let him close hard and fight it out with his opposite foeman,
holding tight to the hilt of his sword, or to his long spear.
And you, O light-armed fighters, from shield to shield of your fellows,
dodge for protection and keep steadily throwing great stones,
and keep on pelting the enemy with your javelins, only
remember always to stand near your own heavy-armed men.

## *Spartan Soldier*

It is beautiful when a brave man of the front ranks,
falls and dies, battling for his homeland,
and ghastly when a man flees planted fields and city
and wanders begging with his dear mother,
aging father, little children and true wife.
He will be scorned in every new village,
reduced to want and loathsome poverty; and shame
will brand his family line, his noble
figure. Derision and disaster will hound him.
A turncoat gets no respect or pity;
so let us battle for our country and freely give
our lives to save our darling children.

Young men, fight shield to shield and never succumb
to panic or miserable flight,
but steel the heart in your chests with magnificence
and courage. Forget your own life
when you grapple with the enemy. Never run
and let an old soldier collapse
whose legs have lost their power. It is shocking when
an old man lies on the front line
before a youth: an old warrior whose head is white
and beard gray, exhaling his strong soul
into the dust, clutching his bloody genitals
into his hands: an abominable vision,
foul to see: his flesh naked. But in a young man
all is beautiful when he still

possesses the shining flower of lovely youth.
Alive he is adored by men,
desired by women, and finest to look upon
when he falls dead in the forward clash.
Let each man spread his legs, rooting them in the ground,
bite his teeth into his lips, and hold.

## Solon of Athens

### Fragment 5 (West)

For to the *demos*[1] I gave so much honor as is sufficient,
neither diminishing their *timê*[2] nor adding to it in profusion.
As for those who held power and were admired for their wealth,
I saw to it that they, also, had nothing shameful.
I took my stand, covering both in the protection of my mighty shield,
nor did I allow either side to win unjustly.

### Fragment 36 (West)

Of all the purposes for which I gathered the *demos* together,
which of them had I not achieved when I quit?
On this point the greatest mother of the
Olympian spirits, black Earth, might best bear
witness in the court of Time, she from whom I once
lifted the boundary stones that had been fixed everywhere:
before she was in slavery, now she is free.
And many Athenians sold into slavery—some justly, some not—
did I bring home to their god-founded land, while others,
having fled their debts under Necessity's compulsion, no longer
spoke the Attic tongue (since they wandered to all parts of the earth),
and others here, bound in shameful servitude and trembling before the
    harsh
character of their masters, I set free. I achieved these things,
forcefully yoking force and justice together,
and I proceeded on the course that I had promised.
I composed ordinances for base and noble alike,
fitting straight justice for each. But another taking the goad of state in
    hand
as had I—particularly one who was thoughtless and greedy—
would not have restrained the *demos*. For if I then had been willing
to effect what was pleasing to one faction,

or, in turn, what their enemies counseled,
this city would have been bereaved of many men.
For this reason, fashioning a defense on all sides,
I wheeled about like a wolf among the hounds.

## Fragment 7 (West)

In undertakings of great import, it is difficult to please all.

## Fragment 6 (West)

In this way would the *demos* best follow the rule of its leaders,
neither being given too free a rein nor subjected to excessive force.
For *koros*³ breeds *hybris*, whenever great *olbos*⁴ should attend
men whose minds are not firm and sound.

# Sappho of Lesbos

## Fragment 96 (A poem of consolation)

When we lived all as one, she adored you as
symbol of some divinity,
Arignóta, delighted in your dancing.

Now she shines among Lydian women as
into dark when the sun has set
the moon, pale-handed, at last appeareth,

making dim all the rest of the stars, and light
spreads afar on the deep, salt sea,
spreading likewise across the flowering cornfields;

and the dew rinses glittering from the sky;
roses spread, and the delicate
antherisk, and the lotus spreads her petals.

So she goes to and fro there, remembering
Atthis and her compassion, sick
the tender mind, and the heart with grief is eaten.

## Fragments 105a and 105c (Part of an epithalamium?)

Like the sweet apple turning red on the branch top, on the
top of the topmost branch, and the gatherers did not notice it,
rather, they did notice, but could not reach up to take it.

Like the hyacinth in the hills which the shepherd people
step on, trampling into the ground the flower in its purple.

## Notes

[1] People.

[2] Honor.

[3] Excess.

[4] Wealth.

# Herodotus

## ca. 480 B.C.E.–ca. 425 B.C.E.)

The historian Herodotus was a native of Halicarnassus in Caria, on the southwest coast of modern Turkey, born in the 480s B.C.E. Otherwise, very little about his life is known. Tradition, based on Aristotle (*Rhet.* 3.9.2), relates that Herodotus became a citizen of Thurii, an Athenian colony in south Italy, sometime around its foundation in 444 B.C.E. Based on the internal evidence of his work, Herodotus must have died sometime after 429 B.C.E., shortly after the start of the Peloponnesian War. Anything else about Herodotus must be deduced from what he tells us in his famous *Histories*.

And Herodotus tells us quite a bit. The ostensible subject of his nine books of history is the wars between Persia and Greece, which took place in 490 under Darius I and again in 480–479 under Darius' son Xerxes. To tell this story, however, Herodotus backs up to the rule of Croesus, king of Lydia, who fell to Cyrus in 545 B.C.E. Herodotus then traces Cyrus and his successor Cambyses, and the latter's exploits against Egypt, and the accession of Darius I and his campaigns in Scythia. Along the way, Herodotus reports some history of Egypt, which he has apparently visited, along with Egyptian customs, religion, architecture, even dress. He does the same with the Scythians and other peoples who enter his narrative. Herodotus does not begin the account of the first Persian expedition against Greece until Book 6, and from that point his narrative follows the wars continuously.

In a conscious rebuke to Herodotus, the later historian Thucydides claims to weigh every piece of evidence for probability, not to write for the "taste of an immediate public" (I.22). Herodotus, however, lacks that element of judiciousness, and he reports essentially what he has heard and seen. In this regard, Herodotus' style may be considered more journalistic and ethnographic, sharing something too of the tourist's travelogue. But Herodotus' achievement can only be appreciated with the realization that he had very few sources available to him other than oral tradition. He relates what the Egyptians or Persians or Spartans or Athenians have told him, even when that includes dreams, intentions, and private conversations. No comprehensive histories of the type that Herodotus was attempting were available to him; and unlike Thucydides, who wrote about events that occurred during his lifetime, Herodotus' subject preceded his birth. For this reason, Herodotus is appropriately credited with being the "Father of History," for the Greek word *historia*, which Herodotus uses of his own work, means "inquiries," not "history" as we might understand it.

Herodotus has several themes of interest to him, which probably influenced the individual narratives or *logoi* of his work. One is the character of custom, or *nomos*, as it operates among different people. Herodotus is remarkably free of prejudice in presenting non-Greek peoples, so much so that Plutarch rather narrow-mindedly calls Herodotus *philobarbaros*, essentially "unpatriotic." Another theme is the power and danger of *hybris*, excessive arrogance, which often characterizes the actions of the Persian kings. Herodotus was motivated to make his inquiry by his wonder at the defeat of the mighty Persian empire by the cities of mainland Greece. These themes, and his apparent fondness for Athens and its political structure, reveal some of the conclusions that he reached.

BSH

# from *The Histories*

*From* BOOK II

## *The Antiquity of Egypt*

2. Now the Egyptians, before the reign of their king Psammetichus, believed themselves to be the most ancient of mankind. Since Psammetichus, however, made an attempt to discover who were actually the primitive race, they have been of opinion that while they surpass all other nations, the Phyrgians surpass them in antiquity. This king, finding it impossible to make out by dint of inquiry what men were the most ancient, contrived the following method of discovery: He took two newly born children, selected at random, and gave them over to a herdsman to bring up at his folds, strictly charging him to let no one utter a word in their presence, but to keep them in a sequestered cottage, and from time to time introduce goats to their apartment, see that they got their fill of milk, and in all other respects look after them. His object herein was to know, after the indistinct babblings of infancy were over, what word they would first articulate. It happened as he had anticipated. The herdsman obeyed his orders for two years, and at the end of that time, on his one day opening the door of their room and going in, the children both ran up to him with outstretched arms, and distinctly said, "Becos." When this first happened the herdsman took no notice; but afterwards when he observed, on coming often to see after them, that the word was constantly in their mouths, he informed his lord, and by his command brought the children into his presence. Psammetichus then himself heard them say the word, upon which he proceeded to make inquiry what people there was who called anything "becos," and hereupon he learnt that "becos" was the Phrygian name for bread. In consideration of this circumstance the Egyptians yielded their claims, and admitted the greater antiquity of the Phrygians. That these were the real facts I learnt at Memphis from the priests of Hephaestus. The Greeks, among other foolish tales, relate that Psammetichus had the children brought up by women whose tongues he had previously cut out.

3. But the priests said their bringing up was such as I have stated above. I got much other information also from conversation with these priests while I was at Memphis, and I even went to Heliopolis and to Thebes, expressly to try whether the priests of those places would agree in their accounts with the priests at Memphis. The Heliopolitans have the reputation of being the wisest of all the Egyptians. What they told me concerning their religion it is not my

intention to repeat, except the names of their deities, which I believe all men know equally. If I relate anything else concerning these matters, it will only be when compelled to do so by the course of my narrative.

4. Now with regard to mere human matters, the accounts which they gave, and in which all agreed, were the following. The Egyptians, they said, were the first to discover the solar year, and to portion out its course into twelve parts. They obtained this knowledge from the stars. (To my mind they contrive their year much more cleverly than the Greeks, for these last every other year intercalate a whole month, on account of the seasons, but the Egyptians, dividing the year into twelve months of thirty days each, add every year a space of five days besides, whereby the circuit of the seasons is made to return with uniformity.) The Egyptians, they went on to affirm, first brought into use the names of the twelve gods, which the Greeks adopted from them; and first erected altars, images, and temples to the gods; and also first engraved upon stone the figures of animals. In most of these cases they proved to me that what they said was true. And they told me that the first man who ruled over Egypt was Min, and that in his time all Egypt, except the Thebaic nome,[1] was a marsh, none of the land below Lake Moeris then showing itself above the surface of the water. This is a distance of seven days' sail from the sea up the river.

5. What they said of their country seemed to me very reasonable. For anyone who sees Egypt without having heard a word about it before must perceive, if he has only common powers of observation, that the Egypt to which the Greeks go in their ships is an acquired country, the gift of the river. . . .

## Manners and Customs

35. Concerning Egypt itself I shall extend my remarks to a great length, because there is no country that possesses so many wonders, nor any that has such a number of works which defy description. Not only is the climate different from that of the rest of the world, and the river unlike any other rivers, but the people also, in most of their manners and customs, exactly reverse the common practice of mankind. The women attend the markets and trade, while the men sit at home at the loom; and here, while the rest of the world works the woof up the warp, the Egyptians work it down; the women likewise carry burdens upon their shoulders, while the men carry them upon their heads. The women urinate standing, the men crouching. They eat their food out of doors, but retire for private purposes to their houses, giving as a reason that what is unseemly, but necessary, ought to be done in secret, but what has nothing unseemly about it, should be done openly. A woman cannot serve the priestly office, either for god or goddess, but men are priests to both. Sons need

not support their parents unless they choose, but daughters must, whether they choose or no.

36. In other countries the priests have long hair, in Egypt their heads are shaven; elsewhere it is customary, in mourning, for near relations to cut their hair close: the Egyptians, who wear no hair at any other time, when they lose a relative, let their beards and the hair of their heads grow long. All other men pass their lives separate from animals, the Egyptians have animals living with them; others make barley and wheat their food; it is a disgrace to do so in Egypt, where the grain they live on is spelt, which some call *zea*. Dough they knead with their feet; but they mix mud, and even take up dirt, with their hands. They are the only people in the world—they at least, and such as have learnt the practice from them—who do not leave their genitals in their natural state but practise circumcision. Their men wear two garments apiece, their women but one. They put on the rings and fasten the ropes to sails inside; others put them outside. When they write or calculate, instead of going, like the Greeks, from left to right, they move their hand from right to left; and they insist, notwithstanding, that it is they who go to the right, and the Greeks who go to the left. They have two quite different kinds of writing, one of which is called sacred [hieroglyphics], the other common [demotic].

37. They are religious far beyond any other race of men, and observe the following rules: They drink out of brazen cups, which they scour every day; there is no exception to this practice. They wear linen garments, which they are specially careful to have always fresh washed. They practise circumcision for the sake of cleanliness, considering it better to be cleanly than comely.

The priests shave their whole body every other day, that no lice or other impure thing may adhere to them when they are engaged in the service of the gods. Their dress is entirely of linen, and their shoes of the papyrus plant: it is not lawful for them to wear either dress or shoes of any other material. They bathe twice every day in cold water, and twice each night; besides which they observe, so to speak, thousands of ceremonies. They enjoy, however, not a few advantages. They consume none of their own property, and are at no expense for anything; but every day bread is baked for them of the sacred grain, and a plentiful supply of beef and of goose's flesh is assigned to each, and also a portion of wine made from the grape. Fish they are not allowed to eat, and beans—which none of the Egyptians ever sow, or eat, if they come up of their own accord, either raw or boiled—the priests will not even endure to look on, since they consider it an unclean kind of pulse. Instead of a single priest, each god has the attendance of a college, at the head of which is a chief priest; when one of these dies, his son is appointed in his stead.

38. Male kine are reckoned to belong to Epaphus,[2] and are therefore tested in the following manner: One of the priests appointed for the purpose searches to see if there is a single black hair on the whole body, since in that case the beast is unclean. He examines him all over, standing on his legs, and again laid upon his back; after which he takes the tongue out of his mouth, to see if it be clean in respect of the prescribed marks (what they are I will mention elsewhere); he also inspects the hairs of the tail, to observe if they grow naturally. It the animal is pronounced clean in all these various points, the priest marks him by twisting a piece of papyrus round his horns, and attaching thereto some sealing-clay, which he then stamps with his own signet ring. After this the beast is led away; and it is forbidden, under the penalty of death, to sacrifice an animal which has not been marked in this way. . . .

## The Truth about the Trojan War

113. The [Egyptian] priests, in answer to my inquiries on the subject of Helen, informed me of the following particulars. When Alexander [Paris] had carried off Helen from Sparta, he took ship and sailed homewards. On his way across the Aegean a gale arose, which drove him from his course and took him down to the sea of Egypt; hence, as the wind did not abate, he was carried on to the coast, when he went ashore, landing at the Salt Pans, in that mouth of the Nile which is now called the Canobic. At this place there stood upon the shore a temple, which still exists, dedicated to Hercules. If a slave runs away from his master, and taking sanctuary at this shrine gives himself up to the god, and receives certain sacred marks upon his person, whosoever his master may be, he cannot lay hand on him. This law still remained unchanged to my time. Hearing, therefore, of the custom of the place, the attendants of Alexander deserted him, and fled to the temple, where they sat as suppliants. While there, wishing to damage their master, they accused him to the Egyptians, narrating all the circumstances of the rape of Helen and the wrong done to Menelaus. These charges they brought not only before the priests, but also before the warden of that mouth of the river, whose name was Thonis.

114. As soon as he received the intelligence, Thonis sent a message to Proteus, who was at Memphis, to this effect: "A stranger is arrived, by race a Teucrian, and has done a wicked deed in Greece. Having seduced the wife of the man whose guest he was, he carried her away with him, and much treasure also. Compelled by stress of weather, he has now put in here. Are we to let him depart as he came, or shall we seize what he has brought?" Proteus sent a man with this reply: "Seize the man, be he who he may, that has dealt thus wickedly with his host, and bring him before me, that I may hear what he will say for himself."

115. Thonis, on receiving these orders, seized Alexander, and stopped the departure of his ships; then, taking with him Alexander, Helen, the treasures, and also the suppliant slaves, he went up to Memphis. When all were arrived, Proteus asked Alexander who he was, and whence he had come. Alexander replied by giving his descent, the name of his country, and a true account of his late voyage. Then Proteus questioned him as to where he got possession of Helen. In his reply Alexander became confused, and diverged from the truth, whereon the slaves interposed, confuted his statements, and told the whole history of the crime. Finally, Proteus delivered judgement as follows: "Did I not regard it as a matter of the utmost consequence that no stranger driven to my country by adverse winds should ever be put to death, I would certainly have avenged the Greek by slaying you. Basest of men—after accepting hospitality, to do so wicked a deed! First, you seduced the wife of your own host—then, not content therewith, you must violently excite her mind, and steal her away from her husband. Nay, even so you were not satisfied, but on leaving, you must plunder the house in which you had been a guest. Now then, as I think it of the greatest importance to put no stranger to death, I suffer you to depart; but the woman and the treasures I shall not permit to be carried away. Here they must stay, till your Greek host comes in person and takes them back with him. For yourself and your companions, I command you to begone from my land within the space of three days—and I warn you that otherwise at the end of that time you will be treated as enemies."

116. Such was the tale told me by the priests concerning the arrival of Helen at the court of Proteus. It seems to me that Homer was acquainted with this story, and, while discarding it, because he thought it less adapted for epic poetry than the version which he followed, showed that it was not unknown to him. This is evident from the travels which be assigns to Alexander in the *Iliad*—and let it be borne in mind that he has nowhere else contradicted himself—making him be carried out of his course on his return with Helen, and after divers wanderings come at last to Sidon in Phoenicia. The passage is in the Bravery of Diomedes, and the words are as follows:

> "There were the robes, many-coloured, the work of Sidonian women:
> They from Sidon had come, what time god-shaped Alexander
> Over the broad sea brought, that way, the high-born Helen."

In the *Odyssey* also the same fact is alluded to, in these words:

> "Such, so wisely prepared, were the drugs that her stores afforded,
> Excellent; gift which once Polydamna, partner of Thonis,
> Gave her in Egypt, where many the simples that grow in the meadows,
> Potent to cure in part, in part as potent to injure."

Menelaus too, in the same poem, thus addresses Telemachus:

"Much did I long to return, but the Gods still kept me in Egypt—
Angry because I had failed to pay them their hecatombs duly."

In these places Homer shows himself acquainted with the voyage of Alexander to Egypt, for Syria borders on Egypt, and the Phoenicians, to whom Sidon belongs, dwell in Syria.

117. From these various passages, and from that about Sidon especially, it is clear that Homer did not write the *Cypria*. For there it is said that Alexander arrived at Ilion with Helen on the third day after he left Sparta, the wind having been favourable, and the sea smooth; whereas in the *Iliad*, the poet makes him wander before he brings her home. Enough, however, for the present of Homer and the *Cypria*.

118. I made inquiry of the priests, whether the story which the Greeks tell about Ilion is a fable or no. In reply they related the following particulars, of which they declared that Menelaus had himself informed them. After the rape of Helen, a vast army of Greeks, wishing to render help to Menelaus, set sail for the Teucrian territory; on their arrival they disembarked, and formed their camp, after which they sent ambassadors to Ilion, of whom Menelaus was one. The embassy was received within the walls, and demanded the restoration of Helen with the treasures which Alexander had carried off, and likewise required satisfaction for the wrong done. The Teucrians gave at once the answer in which they persisted ever afterwards, backing their assertions sometimes even with oaths, to wit, that neither Helen nor the treasures claimed were in their possession; both the one and the other had remained, they said, in Egypt; and it was not just to come upon them for what Proteus, king of Egypt, was detaining. The Greeks, imagining that the Teucrians were merely laughing at them, laid siege to the town, and never rested until they finally took it. As, however, no Helen was found, and they were still told the same story, they at length believed in its truth, and despatched Menelaus to the court of Proteus.

119. So Menelaus travelled to Egypt, and on his arrival sailed up the river as far as Memphis, and related all that had happened. He was given rich gifts of hospitality, received Helen back unharmed, and recovered all his treasures. After this friendly treatment Menelaus, they said, behaved most unjustly towards the Egyptians; for as it happened that at the time when he wanted to take his departure, he was detained by the wind being contrary, and as he found this obstruction continue, he had recourse to a most impious expedient. He seized two children of the people of the country, and offered them up in sacrifice. When this became known, the indignation of the people was stirred, and they went in pursuit of Menelaus, who, however, escaped with his ships

to Libya, after which the Egyptians could not say whither he went. The rest they knew full well, partly by the inquiries which they had made, and partly from the circumstances having taken place in their own land, and therefore not admitting of doubt.

120. Such is the account given by the Egyptian priests, and I am myself inclined to regard as true all that they say of Helen from the following considerations: If Helen had been at Ilion, the inhabitants would, I think, have given her up to the Greeks, whether Alexander consented to it or no. For surely neither Priam nor his family could have been so infatuated as to endanger their own persons, their children, and their city, merely that Alexander might possess Helen. At any rate, if they determined to refuse at first, yet afterwards when so many of the Trojans fell on every encounter with the Greeks, and Priam too in each battle lost a son, or sometimes two, or three, or even more, if we may credit the epic poets, I believe that even if Priam himself had been living with her he would have delivered her up to the Achaeans, with the view of bringing the series of calamities to a close. Nor was it as if Alexander had been heir to the crown, in which case he might have had the chief management of affairs, since Priam was already old. Hector, who was his elder brother, and a far braver man, stood before him, and was the heir to the kingdom on the death of their father Priam. And it could not be Hector's interest to uphold his brother in his wrong, when it brought such dire calamities upon himself and the other Trojans. But the fact was that they had no Helen to deliver, and so they told the Greeks, but the Greeks would not believe what they said—Divine Providence, as I think, so willing, that by their utter destruction it might be made evident to all men that when great wrongs are done, the gods will surely visit them with great punishments. Such, at least, is my view of the matter. . . .

## From BOOK VII

### The Persian War after Marathon

1. Now when tidings of the battle that had been fought at Marathon [490 B.C.] reached the ears of King Darius,[3] the son of Hystaspes, his anger against the Athenians, which had been already roused by their attack upon Sardis, waxed still fiercer, and he became more than ever eager to lead an army against Greece. Instantly he sent off messengers to make proclamation through the several states that fresh levies were to be raised, and these at an increased rate, while ships, horses, provisions, and transports were likewise to be furnished. So the men published his commands; and now all Asia was in commotion by the space of three years, while everywhere, as Greece was to be attacked, the best and bravest were enrolled for the service, and had to make their preparations accordingly.

After this, in the fourth year, the Egyptians whom Cambyses had enslaved revolted from the Persians; whereupon Darius was more hot for war than ever, and earnestly desired to march an army against both adversaries.

2. Now, as he was about to lead forth his levies against Egypt and Athens, a fierce contention for the sovereign power arose among his sons, since the law of the Persians was that a king must not go out with his army until he has appointed one to succeed him upon the throne. Darius, before he obtained the kingdom, had had three sons born to him from his former wife, who was a daughter of Gobryas; while, since he began to reign, Atossa, the daughter of Cyrus, had borne him four. Artabazanes was the eldest of the first family, and Xerxes of the second. These two, therefore, being the sons of different mothers, were now at variance. Artabazanes claimed the crown as the eldest of all the children, because it was an established custom all over the world for the eldest to have the rule; while Xerxes, on the other hand, urged that he was sprung from Atossa, the daughter of Cyrus, and that it was Cyrus who had won the Persians their freedom.

3. Before Darius had pronounced on the matter, it happened that Demaratus, the son of Ariston, who had been deprived of his crown at Sparta, and had afterwards, of his own accord, gone into banishment, came up to Susa, and there heard of the quarrel of the princes. Hereupon, as report says, he went to Xerxes, and advised him, in addition to all that he had urged before, to plead that at the time when he was born Darius was already king, and bore rule over the Persians; but when Artabazanes came into the world, he was a mere private person. It would therefore be neither right nor seemly that the crown should go to another in preference to himself. "For at Sparta," said Demaratus, by way of suggestion, "the law is that if a king has sons before he comes to the throne, and another son is born to him afterwards, the child so born is heir to his father's kingdom." Xerxes followed this counsel, and Darius, persuaded that he had justice on his side, appointed him his successor. For my own part I believe that, even without this, the crown would have gone to Xerxes, for Atossa was all-powerful.

4. Darius, when he had thus appointed Xerxes his heir, was minded to lead forth his armies; but he was prevented by death while his preparations were still proceeding. He died in the year following the revolt of Egypt and the matters here related [486 B.C.], after having reigned in all six-and-thirty years, leaving the revolted Egyptians and the Athenians alike unpunished. At his death the kingdom passed to his son Xerxes.

5. Now Xerxes, on first mounting the throne, was coldly disposed towards the Grecian war, and made it his business to collect an army against Egypt. But Mardonius, the son of Gobryas, who was at the court, and had

more influence with him than any of the other Persians, being his own cousin, the child of a sister of Darius, plied him with discourses like the following:

"Master, it is not fitting that they of Athens escape scot-free, after doing the Persians such great injury. Complete the work which you now have in hand, and then, when the pride of Egypt is brought low, lead an army against Athens. So shall you yourself have good report among men, and others shall fear hereafter to attack your country."

Thus far it was of vengeance that he spoke; but sometimes he would vary the theme, and observe by the way, that Europe was a wondrous beautiful region, rich in all kinds of cultivated trees, and the soil excellent; that no one, save the king, was worthy to own such a land.

6. All this he said because he longed for adventures, and hoped to become satrap[4] of Greece under the king; and after a while he had his way, and persuaded Xerxes to do according to his desires. Other things, however, occurring about the same time, helped his persuasions. For, in the first place, it chanced that messengers arrived from Thessaly, sent by the Aleuadae, Thessalian kings, to invite Xerxes into Greece, and to promise him all the assistance which it was in their power to give. And further, the Pisistratidae, who had come up to Susa, held the same language as the Aleuadae, and worked upon him even more than they, by means of Onomacritus of Athens, an oracle-monger, and the same who set forth the prophecies of Musaeus in their order. The Pisistratidae had previously been at enmity with this man, but made up the quarrel before they removed to Susa. He was banished from Athens by Hipparchus, the son of Pisistratus, because he foisted into the writings of Musaeus a prophecy that the islands which lie off Lemnos would one day disappear in the sea. Lasus of Hermione caught him in the act of so doing. For this cause Hipparchus banished him, though till then they had been the closest of friends. Now, however, he went up to Susa with the Pisistratidae, and they talked very grandly of him to the king; while he, for his part, whenever he was in the king's company, repeated to him certain of the oracles; and while he took care to pass over all that spoke of disaster to the barbarians, brought forward the passages which promised them the greatest success. "'Twas fated," he told Xerxes, "that a Persian should bridge the Hellespont, and march an army from Asia into Greece." while Onomacritus thus plied Xerxes with his oracles, the Pisistratidae and Aleuadae did not cease to press on him their advice, till at last the king yielded, and agreed to lead forth an expedition.

7. First, however, in the year following the death of Darius, he marched against those who had revolted from him; and having reduced them, and laid all Egypt under a far harder yoke than ever his father had put upon it, he gave the government to Achaemenes, who was his own brother, and son to Darius.

This Achaemenes was afterwards slain in his government by Inaros, the son of Psammetichus, a Libyan.

8. After Egypt was subdued, Xerxes, being about to take in hand the expedition against Athens, called together an assembly of the noblest Persians, to learn their opinions, and to lay before them his own designs. So, when the men were met, the king spoke thus to them:

"Persians, I shall not be the first to bring in among you this custom—I shall but follow one which has come down to us from our forefathers. Never yet, as our old men assure me, has our race reposed itself, since the time when Cyrus overcame Astyages, and so we Persians wrested the sceptre from the Medes. Now in all this God guides us; and we, obeying his guidance, prosper greatly. What need have I to tell you of the deeds of Cyrus and Cambyses, and my own father Darius, how many nations they conquered, and added to our dominions? You know right well what great things they achieved. But for myself, I will say that, from the day on which I mounted the throne, I have not ceased to consider by what means I may rival those who have preceded me in this post of honour, and increase the power of Persia as much as any of them. And truly I have pondered upon this, until at last I have found out a way whereby we may at once win glory, and likewise get possession of a land which is as large and as rich as our own—nay, which is even more varied in the fruits it bears—while at the same time we obtain satisfaction and revenge. For this cause I have now called you together, that I may make known to you what I design to do.

"My intent is to throw a bridge over the Hellespont and march an army through Europe against Greece, that thereby I may obtain vengeance from the Athenians for the wrongs committed by them against the Persians and against my father. Your own eyes saw the preparations of Darius against these men; but death came upon him, and balked his hopes of revenge. In his behalf, therefore, and in behalf of all the Persians, I undertake the war, and pledge myself not to rest till I have taken and burnt Athens, which has dared, unprovoked, to injure me and my father. Long since they came to Sardis with Aristagoras of Miletus, who was one of our slaves, and burnt its temples and its sacred groves; again, more lately, when we made a landing upon their coast under Datis and Artaphernes, how roughly they handled us you do not need to be told.

"For these reasons, therefore, I am bent upon this war; and I see likewise therewith united no few advantages. Once let us subdue this people, and those neighbours of theirs who hold the land of Pelops the Phrygian, and we shall extend the Persian territory as far as God's heaven reaches. The sun will then shine on no land beyond our borders; for I will pass through Europe from one end to the other, and with your aid make of all the lands which it contains one country. For thus, if what I hear be true, affairs stand: the nations whereof I have spoken once swept away, there is no city, no country left in all the world which will venture so much as to withstand us in arms. By this course then we shall bring all mankind under our yoke, alike those who are guilty and those who are innocent of doing us wrong.

"For yourselves, if you wish to please me, do as follows: when I announce the time for the army to meet together, hasten to the muster with a good will, every one of you; and know that to the man who brings with him the most gallant array I will give the gifts which our people consider the most honourable. This then is what you have to do. But to show that I am not self-willed in this matter, I lay the business before you, and give you full leave to speak your minds upon it openly."

Xerxes, having so spoken, held his peace.

9. Whereupon Mardonius took the word, and said:

"Of a truth, master, you surpass not only all living Persians, but likewise those yet unborn. Most true and right is each word that you have now uttered; but best of all your resolve not to let the Ionians who live in Europe—a worthless crew—mock us any more. It were indeed a monstrous thing if, after conquering and enslaving the Sacae, the Indians, the Ethiopians, the Assyrians, and many other mighty nations, not for any wrong that they had done us, but only to increase our empire, we should then allow the Greeks, who have done us such wanton injury, to escape our vengeance. What is it that we fear in them? Not surely their numbers? Not the greatness of their wealth? We know the manner of their battle—we know how weak their power is; already have we subdued their children who dwell in our country, the Ionians, Aeolians, and Dorians. I myself have had experience of these men when I marched against them by the orders of thy father; and though I went as far as Macedonia, and came but a little short of reaching Athens itself, yet not a soul ventured to come out against me to battle. And yet, I am told, these very Greeks are wont to wage wars against one another in the most foolish way, through sheer perversity and doltishness. For no sooner is war proclaimed than they search out the smoothest and fairest plain that is to be found in all the land, and there they assemble and fight; whence it comes to pass that even the conquerors depart with great loss: I say nothing of the conquered, for they are destroyed altogether. Now surely, as they are all of one speech, they ought to interchange heralds and messengers, and make up their differences by any means rather than battle; or, at the worst, if they must needs fight one against another, they ought to post themselves as strongly as possible, and so try their quarrels. But, notwithstanding that they have so foolish a manner of warfare, yet these Greeks, when I led my army against them to the very borders of Macedonia, did not so much as think of offering me battle.

"Who then will dare, O King, to meet you in arms, when you come with all Asia's warriors at your back, and with all her ships? For my part I do not believe the Greek people will be so foolhardy. Grant, however, that I am mistaken herein, and that they are foolish enough to meet us in open fight; in that case they will learn that there are no such soldiers in the whole world as we. Nevertheless let us spare no pains; for nothing comes without trouble; but all that men acquire is got by painstaking."

When Mardonius had in this way softened the harsh speech of Xerxes, he too held his peace.

10. The other Persians were silent; for all feared to raise their voice against the plan proposed to them. But Artabanus, the son of Hystaspes, and uncle of Xerxes, trusting to his relationship, was bold to speak. "O King," he said, "it is impossible, if no more than one opinion is uttered, to make choice of the best: a man is forced then to follow whatever advice may have been given him; but if opposite speeches are delivered, then choice can be exercised. In like manner pure gold is not recognized by itself; but when we test it along with baser ore, we perceive which is the better. I counselled your father, Darius, who was my own brother, not to attack the Scyths, a race of people who had no town in their whole land. He thought however to subdue those wandering tribes, and would not listen to me, but marched an army against them, and ere he returned home lost many of his bravest warriors. You are about, O King, to attack a people far superior to the Scyths, a people distinguished above others, it is said, both by land and sea. 'Tis fit therefore that I should tell you what danger you incur hereby.

"You say that you will bridge the Hellespont, and lead your troops through Europe against Greece. Now suppose some disaster befall you by land or sea, or by both. It may be even so; for the men are reputed valiant. Indeed one may measure their prowess from what they have already done; for when Datis and Artaphernes led their huge army against Attica, the Athenians singly defeated them. But grant they are not successful on both elements. Still, if they man their ships, and, defeating us by sea, sail to the Hellespont, and there destroy our bridge—that, sire, were a fearful hazard. And here 'tis not by my own mother wit alone that I conjecture what will happen; but I remember how narrowly we escaped disaster once, when your father, after throwing bridges over the Thracian Bosporus and the Danube, marched against the Scythians, and they tried every sort of prayer to induce the Ionians, who had charge of the bridge over the Danube, to break the passage. On that day, if Histiaeus, the tyrant of Miletus, had sided with the other tyrants, and not set himself to oppose their views, the empire of the Persians would have come to nought.

Surely a dreadful thing is this even to hear said, that the king's fortunes depended wholly on one man.

"Think then no more of incurring so great a danger when no need presses, but follow the advice I tender. Break up this meeting, and when you have well considered the matter with yourself, and settled what you will do, declare to us your resolve. I know not of aught in the world that so profits a man as taking good counsel with himself; for even if things fall out against one's hopes, still one has counselled well, though fortune has made the counsel of none effect: whereas if a man counsels ill and luck follows, he has gotten a windfall, but his counsel is none the less silly. Do you see how God with His lightning smites always the bigger animals, and will not suffer them to wax insolent, while those of a lesser bulk chafe Him not? How likewise His bolts fall ever on the highest houses and the tallest trees? So plainly does He love to bring down everything that exalts itself. Thus ofttimes a mighty host is discomfited by a few men, when God in His jealousy sends fear or storm from heaven, and they perish in a way unworthy of them. For God allows no one to have high thoughts but Himself. Again, hurry always brings about disasters, from which huge sufferings are wont to arise; but in delay lie many advantages, not apparent (it may be) at first sight, but such as in course of time are seen of all. Such then is my counsel to you, O King!

"And you, Mardonius, son of Gobryas, forbear to speak foolishly concerning the Greeks, who are men that ought not to be lightly esteemed by us. For while you revile the Greeks, you encourage the king to lead his own troops against them; and this, as it seems to me, is what you are specially striving to accomplish. May that not come to pass! For slander is of all evils the most terrible. In it two men do wrong, and one man has wrong done to him. The slanderer does wrong, forasmuch as he abuses a man behind his back; and the hearer, forasmuch as he believes what he has not searched into thoroughly. The man slandered in his absence suffers wrong at the hands of both: for one brings against him a false charge, and the other thinks him an evildoer. If, however, it must needs be that we go to war with this people, at least allow the king to abide at home in Persia. Then let you and I both stake our children on the issue. Choose out your men, and, taking with you whatever number of troops you like, lead forth our armies to battle. If things go well for the king, as you say they will, let me and my children be put to death; but if they fall out as I prophesy, let your children suffer, and yourself too, if you come back alive. But should you refuse this wager, and still resolve to march an army against Greece, sure I am that some of those whom you leave behind here will one day receive the sad tidings, that Mardonius has brought a great disaster upon the Persian people, and lies a prey to dogs and birds somewhere in the land of the Athenians, or else in that of the Lacedaemonians; unless indeed you shall have perished sooner by the way, experiencing in your own person the might of those men on whom you would fain induce the king to make war."

• • •

32. Here his first care was to send off heralds into Greece, who were to prefer a demand for earth and water, and to require that preparations should be made everywhere to feast the king. To Athens indeed and to Sparta he sent no such demand; but, these cities excepted, his messengers went everywhere. Now the reason why he sent for earth and water to states which had already refused was this: he thought that although they had refused when Darius made the demand, they would now be too frightened to venture to say him nay. So he sent his heralds, wishing to know for certain how it would be.

33. Xerxes, after this, made preparations to advance to Abydos, where the bridge across the Hellespont from Asia to Europe was lately finished. Midway between Sestos and Madytus in the Hellespontine Chersonese, and right over against Abydos, there is a rocky tongue of land which runs out for some distance into the sea. This is the place where no long time afterwards [479 B.C.] the Athenians under Xanthippus, the son of Ariphron, took Artaÿctes the Persian, who was at that time governor of Sestos, and nailed him living to a plank. He was the Artaÿctes who brought women into the temple of Protesilaus at Elaeus, and there was guilty of most unholy deeds.

34. Towards this tongue of land then, the men to whom the business was assigned carried out a double bridge from Abydos; and while the Phoenicians constructed one line with cables of white flax, the Egyptians in the other used ropes made of papyrus. Now it is seven furlongs[5] across from Abydos to the opposite coast. When, therefore, the channel had been bridged successfully, it happened that a great storm arising broke the whole work to pieces, and destroyed all that had been done.

35. So when Xerxes heard of it he was full of wrath, and straightway gave orders that the Hellespont should receive three hundred lashes, and that a pair of fetters should be cast into it. Nay, I have even heard it said, that he bade the branders take their irons and therewith brand the Hellespont. It is certain that he commanded those who scourged the waters to utter, as they lashed them, these barbarian and wicked words: "You bitter water, your lord lays on you this punishment because you have wronged him without a cause, having suffered no evil at his hands. Verily King Xerxes will cross you, whether you will or no. Well do you deserve that no man should honour you with sacrifice; for you are of a truth a treacherous and unsavoury river." While the sea was thus punished by his orders, he likewise commanded that the overseers of the work should lose their heads.

• • •

60. What the exact number of the troops of each nation was I cannot say with certainty—for it is not mentioned by anyone—but the whole land army together was found to amount to one million seven hundred thousand men. The manner in which the numbering took place was the following. A body of ten thousand men was brought to a certain place, and the men were made to stand as close together as possible; after which a circle was drawn around them, and the men were let go; then where the circle had been, a fence was built about the height of a man's navel, and the enclosure was filled continually with fresh troops, till the whole army had in this way been numbered. When the numbering was over, the troops were drawn up according to their several nations.

• • •

100. Now when the numbering and marshalling of the host was ended, Xerxes conceived a wish to go himself throughout the forces, and with his own eyes behold everything. Accordingly he traversed the ranks seated in his chariot, and, going from nation to nation, made manifold inquiries, while his scribes wrote down the answers; till at last he had passed from end to end of the whole land army, both the horsemen and the foot. This done, he exchanged his chariot for a Sidonian galley, and, seated beneath a golden awning, sailed along the prows of all his vessels, while he made inquiries again, as he had done when he reviewed the land force, and caused the answers to be recorded by his scribes. The captains took their ships to the distance of about four hundred feet from the shore, and there lay to, with their vessels in a single row, the prows facing the land, and with the fighting men upon the decks accoutred as if for war, while the king sailed along in the open space between the ships and the shore, and so reviewed the fleet.

101. Now after Xerxes had sailed down the whole line and was gone ashore, he sent for Demaratus the son of Ariston, who had accompanied him in his march upon Greece, and spoke to him thus:

"Demaratus, it is my pleasure at this time to ask you certain things which I wish to know. You are a Greek, and, as I hear from the other Greeks with whom I converse, no less than from your own lips, you are a native of a city which is not the weakest or the meanest in their land. Tell me, therefore, what you think. Will the Greeks lift a hand against us? My own judgement is that even if all the Greeks and all the others of the west were gathered together in one place they would not be able to abide my onset, not being really of one mind. But I should like to know what you think."

Thus Xerxes questioned; and the other replied in his turn, "O King, is it your will that I give you a true answer, or do you wish a pleasant one?"

Then the king bade him speak the plain truth, and promised that he would not on that account hold him in less favour than heretofore.

102. So Demaratus, when he heard the promise, spoke as follows:

"O King, since you bid me at all risks speak the truth, and not say what will one day prove me to have lied to you, thus I answer. Want has at all times been a fellow dweller with us in our land, while valor is an ally whom we have gained by dint of wisdom and strict laws. Her aid enables us to drive out want and escape thraldom. Brave are all the Greeks who dwell in any Dorian land; but what I am about to say does not concern all, but only the Lacedaemonians. First, then, come what may, they will never accept your terms, which would reduce Greece to slavery; and further, they are sure to join battle with you, though all the rest of the Greeks should submit to your will. As for their numbers, do not ask how many they are, that their resistance should be a possible thing; for if a thousand of them should take the field, they will meet you in battle, and so will any number, be it less or more."

103. When Xerxes heard this answer of Demaratus, he laughed and answered:

"What wild words, Demaratus! A thousand men join battle with such an army as this! Come then, will you—who were once, you say, their king—engage to fight this very day against ten men? And yet, if all your fellow citizens be indeed such as you say they are, you ought, as their king, by your own country's usages, be ready to fight twice the number. If then each one of them be a match for ten of my soldiers, I may well call upon you to be a match for twenty. Thus would you assure the truth of what you have now said. If, however, you Greeks, who vaunt yourselves so much, are of a truth men like those whom I have seen about my court, like yourself, Demaratus, and the others with whom I converse—if, I say, you are really men of this sort and size, how is the speech you have uttered more than a mere empty boast? For, to go to the very verge of likelihood—how could a thousand men, or ten thousand, or even fifty thousand, particularly if they are all alike free, and not under one lord—how could such a force, I say, stand against an army like mine? Let them be five thousand, and we shall have more than a thousand men to each one of theirs. If, indeed, like our troops, they had a single master, their fear of him might make them courageous beyond their natural bent; or they might be urged by lashes against an enemy which far outnumbered them. But left to their own free choice, assuredly they will act differently. For my part, I believe that if the Greeks had to contend with the Persians only, and the numbers were equal on both sides, the Greeks would find it hard to stand their ground. We too have among us such men as those of whom you spoke—not many indeed, but still we possess a few. For instance, some of my bodyguard would be willing to engage singly with three Greeks. But you did not know this; and therefore it was that you talked so foolishly."

104. Demaratus answered him: "I knew, O King, at the outset, that if I told you the truth my speech would displease you. But as you required me to answer with all possible truthfulness, I informed you what the Spartans will do. And in this I spoke not from any love that I bear them—for none knows better than you what my love towards them is likely to be at the present time, when they have robbed me of my rank and my ancestral honours, and made me a homeless exile, whom your father received, bestowing on me both shelter and sustenance. What likelihood is there that a man of understanding should be unthankful for kindness shown him, and not cherish it in his heart? For myself, I do not pretend to cope with ten men, nor with two—nay, had I the choice, I would rather not fight even with one. But if need appeared, or if there were any great cause urging me on, I would contend with right good will against one of those persons who boast themselves a match for any three Greeks. So likewise the Lacedaemonians, when they fight singly, are as good men as any in the world, and when they fight in a body are the bravest of all. For though they be freemen, they are not in all respects free: law is the master whom they own, and this master they fear more than your subjects fear you. Whatever he commands they do; and his commandment is always the same: it forbids them to flee in battle, whatever the number of their foes, and requires them to stand firm, and either to conquer or die. If in these words, O King, I seem to you to speak foolishly, I am content from this time forward evermore to hold my peace. I had not now spoken unless compelled by you. Certainly, I pray that all may turn out according to your wishes."

105. Such was the answer of Demaratus; and Xerxes was not angry with him at all, but only laughed, and sent him away with words of kindness.

•  •  •

140. When the Athenians, anxious to consult the oracle, sent their messengers to Delphi, hardly had the envoys completed the customary rites about the sacred precinct, and taken their seats inside the sanctuary of the god, when the Pythoness,[6] Aristonice by name, thus prophesied:

"Wretches, why sit ye here? Fly, fly to the ends of creation,
    Quitting your homes, and the crags which your city crowns with
        her circlet.
Neither the head nor the body is firm in its place, nor at bottom
Firm the feet, nor the hands; nor resteth the middle uninjur'd.
All—all ruined and lost. Since fire, and impetuous Ares,
Speeding along in a Syrian chariot, hastes to destroy her.

Not alone shalt thou suffer; full many the towers he will level,
Many the shrines of the gods he will give to a fiery destruction.
Even now they stand with dark sweat horribly dripping.
Trembling and quaking for fear; and lo! from the high roofs trickleth
Black blood, sign prophetic of hard distresses impending.
Get ye away from the temple; and brood on the ills that await ye!"

141. When the Athenian messengers heard this reply, they were filled with the deepest affliction: whereupon Timon, the son of Androbulus, one of the men of most mark among the Delphians, seeing how utterly cast down they were at the gloomy prophecy, advised them to take an olive branch, and entering the sanctuary again, consult the oracle as suppliants. The Athenians followed this advice, and going in once more, said, "O Lord, we pray thee reverence these boughs of supplication which we bear in our hands, and deliver to us something more comforting concerning our country. Else we will not leave thy sanctuary, but will stay here till we die." Upon this the priestess gave them a second answer, which was the following:

"Pallas has not been able to soften the lord of Olympus,
Though she has often prayed him, and urged him with excellent counsel.
Yet once more I address thee in words than adamant firmer.
When the foe shall have taken whatever the limit of Cecrops
Holds within it, and all which divine Cithaeron shelters,
Then far-seeing Zeus grants this to the prayers of Athena;
Safe shall the wooden wall continue for thee and thy children.
Wait not the tramp of the horse, nor the footmen mightily moving
Over the land, but turn your back to the foe, and retire ye.
Yet shall a day arrive when ye shall meet him in battle.
Holy Salamis, thou shalt destroy the offspring of women,
When men scatter the seed, or when they gather the harvest."

142. This answer seemed, as indeed it was, gentler than the former one; so the envoys wrote it down, and went back with it to Athens. When, however, upon their arrival, they produced it before the assembly, many and various were the interpretations which men put on it; two, more especially, seemed to be directly opposed to one another. Certain of the old men were of opinion that the god meant to tell them the Acropolis would escape; for this was anciently defended by a palisade; and they supposed that barrier to be the "wooden wall" of the oracle. Others maintained that the fleet was what the god pointed at; and their advice was that nothing should be thought of except the ships, which had best be at once got ready. Still such as said the "wooden wall" meant the fleet were perplexed by the last two lines of the oracle—

"Holy Salamis, thou shalt destroy the offspring of women,
When men scatter the seed, or when they gather the harvest."

These words caused great disturbance among those who took the wooden wall to be the ships; since the interpreters understood them to mean that, if they made preparations for a seafight, they would suffer a defeat off Salamis.

143. Now there was at Athens a man who had lately made his way into the first rank of citizens: his name was Themistocles; but he was known more generally as the son of Neocles. This man came forward and said that the interpreters had not explained the oracle altogether aright—"For if," he argued, "the clause in question had really referred to the Athenians, it would not have been expressed so mildly; the phrase used would have been 'Luckless Salamis,' rather than 'Holy Salamis,' had those to whom the island belonged been about to perish in its neighbourhood. Rightly taken, the response of the god threatened the enemy, and not the Athenians." He therefore counselled his countrymen to make ready to fight on board their ships, since *they* were the wooden wall in which the god told them to trust. When Themistocles had thus cleared the matter, the Athenians embraced his view, preferring it to that of the interpreters. The advice of these last had been against engaging in a seafight; all the Athenians could do, they said was, without lifting a hand in their defence, to quit Attica, and make a settlement in some other country.

144. Themistocles had before this given a counsel which prevailed very seasonably. The Athenians, having a large sum of money in their treasury, the produce of the mines at Laureium, were about to share it among the citizens, who would have received ten drachmas apiece, when Themistocles persuaded them to forbear the distribution, and build with the money two hundred ships, to help them in their war against the Aeginetans. It was the breaking out of the Aeginetan war which was at this time the saving of Greece; for hereby were the Athenians forced to become a maritime power. The new ships were not used for the purpose for which they had been built, but became a help to Greece in her hour of need. And the Athenians had not only these vessels ready before the war, but they likewise set to work to build more; while they determined, in a council which was held after the debate upon the oracle, that, according to the advice of the god, they would embark their whole force aboard their ships, and, with such Greeks as chose to join them, give battle to the barbarian invader. Such, then, were the oracles which had been received by the Athenians.

•  •  •

207. Such accordingly were the intentions of the allies. The Greek forces at Thermopylae, when the Persian army drew near to the entrance of the pass, were seized with fear; and a council was held to consider about a retreat. It was

the wish of the Peloponnesians generally that the army should fall back upon the Peloponnesus, and there guard the Isthmus. But Leonidas, who saw with what indignation the Phocians and Locrians heard of this plan, gave his voice for remaining where they were, while they sent envoys to the several cities to ask for help, since they were too few to make a stand against an army like that of the Medes.

208. While this debate was going on, Xerxes sent a mounted spy to observe the Greeks, and note how many they were, and see what they were doing. He had heard, before he came out of Thessaly, that a few men were assembled at this place, and that at their head were certain Lacedaemonians,[7] under Leonidas, a descendant of Hercules. The horseman rode up to the camp, and looked about him, but did not see the whole army; for such as were on the farther side of the wall (which had been rebuilt and was now carefully guarded) it was not possible for him to behold; but he observed those on the outside, who were encamped in front of the rampart. It chanced that at this time the Lacedaemonians held the outer guard, and were seen by the spy, some of them engaged in gymnastic exercises, others combing their long hair. At this the spy greatly marvelled, but he counted their number, and when he had taken accurate note of everything he rode back quietly; for no one pursued after him, nor paid any heed to his visit. So he returned, and told Xerxes all that he had seen.

209. Upon this Xerxes, who had no means of surmising the truth—namely, that the Spartans were preparing to die manfully—but thought it laughable that they should be engaged in such employments, sent and called to his presence Demaratus the son of Ariston, who still remained with the army. When he appeared, Xerxes told him all that he had heard, and questioned him concerning the news, since he was anxious to understand the meaning of such behaviour on the part of the Spartans. Then Demaratus said:

"I spoke to you concerning these men long since, when we had just begun our march upon Greece; you, however, only laughed at my words, when I told you of all this, which I saw would come to pass. Earnestly do I struggle at all times to speak truth to you, O King, and now listen to it once more. These men have come to dispute the pass with us; and it is for this that they are now making ready. It is their custom, when they are about to hazard their lives, to adorn their heads with care. Be assured, however, that if you can subdue the men who are here and the Lacedaemonians who remain in Sparta, there is no other nation in all the world which will venture to lift a hand against you. You have now to deal with the first kingdom in Greece, and with the bravest men."

Then Xerxes, to whom what Demaratus said seemed altogether to surpass belief, asked further how it was possible for so small an army to contend with his.

"O King," Demaratus answered, "let me be treated as a liar if matters fall not out as I say."

210. But Xerxes was not persuaded any the more. Four whole days he suffered to go by, expecting that the Greeks would run away. When, however, he found on the fifth that they were not gone, thinking that their firm stand was mere impudence and recklessness, he grew wroth, and sent against them the Medes and Cissians, with orders to take them alive and bring them into his presence. Then the Medes rushed forward and charged the Greeks, but fell in vast numbers: others however took the places of the slain, and would not be beaten off, though they suffered terrible losses. In this way it became clear to all, and especially to the king, that though he had plenty of combatants, he had but very few warriors. The struggle, however, continued during the whole day.

211. Then the Medes, having met so rough a reception, withdrew from the fight; and their place was taken by the band of Persians under Hydarnes, whom the king called his "Immortals"; they, it was thought, would soon finish the business. But when they joined battle with the Greeks, it was with no better success than the Median detachment—things went much as before—the two armies fighting in a narrow space, and the barbarians using shorter spears than the Greeks, and having no advantage from their numbers. The Lacedaemonians fought in a way worthy of note, and showed themselves far more skilful in fight than their adversaries, often turning their backs and making as though they were all flying away, on which the barbarians would rush after them with much noise and shouting, when the Spartans at their approach would wheel round and face their pursuers, in this way destroying vast numbers of the enemy. Some Spartans likewise fell in these encounters, but only a very few. At last the Persians, finding that all their efforts to gain the pass availed nothing, and that, whether they attacked by divisions or in any other way, it was to no purpose, withdrew to their own quarters.

212. During these assaults, it is said that Xerxes, who was watching the battle, thrice leaped from his throne. Thus they fought. Next day the barbarians had no better success. The Greeks were so few that the barbarians hoped to find them disabled, by reason of their wounds, from offering any further resistance; and so they once more attacked them. But the Greeks were drawn up in detachments according to their cities, and bore the brunt of the battle in turns—all except the Phocians, who had been stationed on the mountain to guard the pathway. So, when the Persians found no difference between that day and the preceding, they again retired to their quarters.

213. Now, as the king was in a great strait, and knew not how he should deal with the emergency, Ephialtes, the son of Eurydemus, a man of Malis, came to him and was admitted to a conference. Stirred by the hope of receiving a rich reward at the king's hands, he had come to tell him of the pathway

which led across the mountain to Thermopylae; by which disclosure he brought destruction on the band of Greeks who had there withstood the barbarians. . . .

217. The Persians took this path, and, crossing the Asopus, continued their march through the whole of the night, having the mountains of Oeta on their right hand, and on their left those of Trachis. At dawn of day they found themselves close to the summit. . . .

219. The Greeks at Thermopylae received the first warning of the destruction which the dawn would bring on them from the seer Megistias, who read their fate in the victims as he was sacrificing. After this deserters came in, and brought the news that the Persians were marching round by the hills: it was still night when these men arrived. Last of all, the scouts came running down from the heights, and brought in the same accounts, when the day was just beginning to break. Then the Greeks held a council to consider what they should do, and here opinions were divided: some were strong against quitting their post, while others contended to the contrary. So when the council had broken up, part of the troops departed and went their ways homeward to their several states; part however resolved to remain, and to stand by Leonidas to the last.

220. It is said that Leonidas himself sent away the troops who departed, because he tendered their safety, but thought it unseemly that either he or his Spartans should quit the post which they had been especially sent to guard. For my own part, I incline to think that Leonidas gave the order, because he perceived the allies to be out of heart and unwilling to encounter the danger to which his own mind was made up. He therefore commanded them to retreat, but said that he himself could not draw back with honour; knowing that, if he stayed, glory awaited him, and that Sparta in that case would not lose her prosperity. For when the Spartans, at the very beginning of the war, sent to consult the oracle concerning it, the answer which they received from the Pythoness was that either Sparta must be overthrown by the barbarians, or one of her kings must perish. The prophecy was delivered in hexameter verse, and ran thus:

> "O ye men who dwell in the streets of broad Lacedaemon!
> Either your glorious town shall be sacked by the children of Perseus,
> Or, in exchange, must all through the whole Laconian country
> Mourn for the loss of a king, descendant of great Heracles.
> HE cannot be withstood by the courage of bulls nor of lions,
> Strive as they may; he is mighty as Zeus; there is nought that shall
>     stay him,
> Till he have got for his prey your king, or your glorious city."

The remembrance of this answer, I think, and the wish to secure the whole glory for the Spartans, caused Leonidas to send the allies away. This is more likely than that they quarrelled with him and took their departure in such unruly fashion.

221. To me it seems no small argument in favour of this view that the seer also who accompanied the army, Megistias, the Acarnanian—said to have been of the blood of Melampus, and the same who was led by the appearance of the victims to warn the Greeks of the danger which threatened them—received orders to retire (as it is certain he did) from Leonidas, that he might escape the coming destruction. Megistias, however, though bidden to depart, refused, and stayed with the army; but he had an only son present with the expedition, whom he now sent away.

222. So the allies, when Leonidas ordered them to retire, obeyed him and forthwith departed. Only the Thespians and the Thebans remained with the Spartans; and of these the Thebans were kept back by Leonidas as hostages, very much against their will. The Thespians, on the contrary, stayed entirely of their own accord, refusing to retreat, and declaring that they would not forsake Leonidas and his followers. So they abode with the Spartans, and died with them. Their leader was Demophilus, the son of Diadromes.

223. At sunrise Xerxes made libations, after which he waited until the time when the Agora is wont to fill, and then began his advance. Ephialtes had instructed him thus, as the descent of the mountain is much quicker, and the distance much shorter, than the way round the hills, and the ascent. So the barbarians under Xerxes began to draw nigh; and the Greeks under Leonidas, as they now went forth determined to die, advanced much farther than on previous days until they reached the more open portion of the pass. Hitherto they had held their station within the wall, and from this had gone forth to fight at the point where the pass was the narrowest. Now they joined battle beyond the defile, and carried slaughter among the barbarians, who fell in heaps. Behind them the captains of the squadrons, armed with whips, urged their men forward with continual blows. Many were thrust into the sea, and there perished; a still greater number were trampled to death by their own soldiers; no one heeded the dying. For the Greeks, reckless of their own safety and desperate, since they knew that, as the mountain had been crossed, their destruction was nigh at hand, exerted themselves with the most furious valour against the barbarians.

224. By this time the spears of the greater number were all shivered, and with their swords they hewed down the ranks of the Persians; and here, as they strove, Leonidas fell fighting bravely, together with many other famous Spartans, whose names I have taken care to learn on account of their great worthiness, as indeed I have those of all the three hundred. . . .

226. Thus nobly did the whole body of Lacedaemonians and Thespians behave; but nevertheless one man is said to have distinguished himself above all

the rest, to wit, Dieneces the Spartan. A speech which he made before the Greeks engaged the Medes remains on record. One of the Trachinians told him that such was the number of the barbarians that when they shot forth their arrows the sun would be darkened by their multitude. Dieneces, not at all frightened at these words, but making light of the Median numbers, answered, "Our Trachinian friend brings us excellent tidings. If the Medes darken the sun, we shall have our fight in the shade." Other sayings too of a like nature are reported to have been left for posterity by Dieneces the Lacedaemonian. . . .

## *From* BOOK VIII

74. So the Greeks at the Isthmus toiled unceasingly, as though in the greatest peril, since they never imagined that any great success would be gained by the fleet. The Greeks at Salamis, on the other hand, when they heard what the rest were about, felt greatly alarmed; but their fear was not so much for themselves as for the Peloponnesus. At first they conversed together in low tones, each man with his fellow, secretly, and marvelled at the folly shown by Eurybiades; but presently the smothered feeling broke out, and another assembly was held, whereat the old subjects provoked much talk from the speakers, one side maintaining that it was best to sail to the Peloponnesus and risk battle for that, instead of abiding at Salamis and fighting for a land already taken by the enemy; while the other, which consisted of the Athenians, Aeginetans, and Megarians, was urgent to remain and have the battle fought where they were.

75. Then Themistocles, when he saw that the Peloponnesians would carry the vote against him, went out secretly from the council, and, instructing a certain man what he should say, sent him on board a ship to the camp of the Medes. The man's name was Sicinnus; he was one of Themistocles' household slaves, and acted as tutor to his sons; in after times, when the Thespians were admitting persons to citizenship, Themistocles made him a Thespian, and a rich man to boot. The ship brought Sicinnus to the Persian fleet, and there he delivered his message to the barbarian leaders in these words:

"The Athenian commander has sent me to you privily, without the knowledge of the other Greeks. He is a wellwisher to the king's cause, and would rather success should attend on you than on his countrymen; wherefore he bids me tell you that fear has seized the Greeks and they are meditating a hasty flight. Now then it is open to you to achieve the best work that ever you wrought, if only you will hinder their escaping. They no longer agree among themselves, so that they will not now make any resistance—nay, it is likely you may see a fight already begun between such as favour and such as oppose your cause." The messenger, when he had thus expressed himself, departed and was seen no more.

76. Then the captains, believing all that the messenger had said, proceeded to land a large body of Persian troops on the islet of Psyttaleia, which lies between Salamis and the mainland; after which, about the hour of midnight, they advanced their western wing towards Salamis, so as to inclose the Greeks. At the same time the force stationed about Ceos and Cynosura moved forward, and filled the whole strait as far as Munychia with their ships. This advance was made to prevent the Greeks from escaping by flight, and to block them up in Salamis, where it was thought that vengeance might be taken upon them for the battles fought near Artemisium. The Persian troops were landed on the islet of Psyttaleia, because, as soon as the battle began, the men and wrecks were likely to be drifted thither, as the isle lay in the very path of the coming fight, and they would thus be able to save their own men and destroy those of the enemy. All these movements were made in silence, that the Greeks might have no knowledge of them; and they occupied the whole night, so that the men had no time to get their sleep.

77. I cannot say that there is no truth in oracles, or feel inclined to call in question those which speak with clearness, when I think of the following:

> "When they shall bridge with their ships to the sacred strand of Artemis
> Girt with the golden falchion, and eke to marine Cynosura,
> Mad hope swelling their hearts at the downfall of beautiful Athens—
> Then shall godlike Right extinguish haughty Presumption,
> Insult's furious offspring, who thinketh to overthrow all things.
> Brass with brass shall mingle, and Ares with blood shall empurple
> Ocean's waves. Then—then shall the day of Greece's freedom
> Come from Victory fair, and Cronos' son all-seeing."

When I look to this, and perceive how clearly Bacis spoke, I neither venture myself to say anything against prophecies, nor do I approve of others impugning them.

78. Meanwhile, among the captains at Salamis, the strife of words grew fierce. As yet they did not know that they were encompassed, but imagined that the barbarians remained in the same places where they had seen them the day before.

79. In the midst of their contention, Aristides, the son of Lysimachus, who had crossed from Aegina, arrived in Salamis. He was an Athenian, and had been ostracized by the commonalty, yet I believe, from what I have heard concerning his character, that there was not in all Athens a man so worthy or so just as he. He now came to the council, and, standing outside, called for Themistocles. Now Themistocles was not his friend, but his most determined enemy. However, under the pressure of the great dangers impending, Aristides forgot their feud, and called Themistocles out of the council, since he wished

to confer with him. He had heard before his arrival of the impatience of the Peloponnesians to withdraw the fleet to the Isthmus. As soon therefore as Themistocles came forth, Aristides addressed him in these words:

"Our rivalry at all times, and especially at the present season, ought to be a struggle, which of us shall most advantage our country. Let me then say to you, that so far as regards the departure of the Peloponnesians from this place, much talk and little will be found precisely alike. I have seen with my own eyes that which I now report: that, however much the Corinthians or Eurybiades himself may wish it, they cannot now retreat; for we are enclosed on every side by the enemy. Go in to them, and make this known."

80. "Your advice is excellent," answered the other; "and your tidings are also good. That which I earnestly desired to happen, your eyes have beheld accomplished. Know that what the Medes have now done was at my instance; for it was necessary, as the Greeks would not fight here of their own free will, to make them fight whether they would or no. But come now, as you have brought the good news, go in and tell it. For if I speak to them, they will think it a feigned tale, and will not believe that the barbarians have inclosed us around. Therefore you go to them, and inform them how matters stand. If they believe you, it will be for the best; but if otherwise, it will not harm. For it is impossible that they should now flee away, if we are indeed shut in on all sides, as you say."

81. Then Aristides entered the assembly, and spoke to the captains; he had come, he told them, from Aegina, and had but barely escaped the blockading vessels—the Greek fleet was entirely inclosed by the ships of Xerxes—and he advised them to get themselves in readiness to resist the foe. Having said so much, he withdrew. And now another contest arose, for the greater part of the captains would not believe the tidings.

82. But while they still doubted, a Tenian trireme, commanded by Panaetius the son of Sosimenes, deserted from the Persians and joined the Greeks, bringing full intelligence. For this reason the Tenians were inscribed upon the tripod at Delphi among those who overthrew the barbarians. With this ship, which deserted to their side at Salamis, and the Lemnian vessel which came over before at Astemisium, the Greek fleet was brought to the full number of three hundred and eighty ships; otherwise it fell short by two of that amount.

83. The Greeks now, not doubting what the Tenians told them, made ready for the coming fight. At the dawn of day, all the men-at-arms were assembled together, and speeches were made to them, of which the best was that of Themistocles; who throughout contrasted what was noble with what was base, and bade them, in all that came within the range of man's nature and constitution, *always* to make choice of the nobler part. Having thus wound up

his discourse, he told them to go at once on board their ships, which they accordingly did; and about this time the trireme, that had been sent to Aegina for the Aeacidae, returned; whereupon the Greeks put to sea with all their fleet.

84. The fleet had scarce left the land when they were attacked by the barbarians. At once most of the Greeks began to back water, and were about touching the shore, when Ameinias of Pallene, an Athenian, darted forth in front of the line and charged a ship of the enemy. The two vessels became entangled, and could not separate, whereupon the rest of the fleet came up to help Ameinias and engaged with the Persians. Such is the account which the Athenians give of the way in which the battle began; but the Aeginetans maintain that the vessel which had been to Aegina for the Aeacidae was the one that brought on the fight. It is also reported that a phantom in the form of a woman appeared to the Greeks, and, in a voice that was heard from end to end of the fleet, cheered them on to the fight, first, however, rebuking them and saying, "Strange men, how long are you going to back water?"

85. Against the Athenians, who held the western extremity of the line towards Eleusis, were placed the Phoenicians; against the Lacedaemonians, whose station was eastward towards the Piraeus, the Ionians. Of these last a few only followed the advice of Themistocles, to fight backwardly; the greater number did far otherwise. I could mention here the names of many trierarchs who took vessels from the Greeks, but I shall pass over all excepting Theomestor, the son of Androdamas, and Phylacus, the son of Histiaeus, both Samians. I show this preference to them, inasmuch as for this service Theomestor was made tyrant of Samos by the Persians, while Phylacus was enrolled among the king's benefactors and presented with a large estate in land. In the Persian tongue the king's benefactors are called *Orosangs*.

86. Far the greater number of the Persian ships engaged in this battle were disabled, either by the Athenians or by the Aeginetans. For as the Greeks fought in order and kept their line, while the barbarians were in confusion and had no plan in anything that they did, the issue of the battle could scarce be other than it was. Yet the Persians fought far more bravely here than at Euboea, and indeed surpassed themselves; each did his utmost through fear of Xerxes, for each thought that the king's eye was upon himself.

87. What part the several contingents, whether Greek or barbarian, took in the combat, I am not able to say for certain; Artemisia, however, I know, distinguished herself in such a way as raised her even higher than she stood before in the esteem of the king. For after confusion had spread throughout the whole of the king's fleet, and her ship was closely pursued by an Athenian trireme, she, having no way to fly, since in front of her were a number of friendly vessels, and she was nearest of all the Persians to the enemy, resolved on a measure which in fact proved her safety. Pressed by the Athenian pursuer,

she bore straight against one of the ships of her own party, a Calyndian, which had Damasithymus, the Calyndian king, himself on board. I cannot say whether she had had any quarrel with the man while the fleet was at the Hellespont, or no—neither can I decide whether she of set purpose attacked his vessel, or whether it merely chanced that the Calyndian ship came in her way—but certain it is that she bore down upon his vessel and sank it, and that thereby she had the good fortune to procure herself a double advantage. For the commander of the Athenian trireme, when he saw her bear down on one of the enemy's fleet, thought immediately that her vessel was a Greek, or else had deserted from the Persians, and was now fighting on the Greek side; he therefore gave up the chase, and turned away to attack others.

88. Thus in the first place she saved her life by the action, and was enabled to get clear off from the battle; while further, it fell out that in the very act of doing the king an injury she raised herself to a greater height than ever in his esteem. For as Xerxes beheld the fight, he remarked (it is said) the destruction of the vessel, whereupon the bystanders observed to him—"Do you see, master, how well Artemisia fights, and how she has just sunk a ship of the enemy?" Then Xerxes asked if it were really Artemisia's doing; and they answered, certainly, for they knew her ensign; while all were sure that the sunken vessel belonged to the opposite side. Everything, it is said, conspired to prosper the queen—it was especially fortunate for her that not one of those on board the Calyndian ship survived to become her accuser. Xerxes, they say, in reply to the remarks made to him, observed, "My men have behaved like women, my women like men!" This is what Xerxes is supposed to have said.

## Notes

[1] Province or district.

[2] Legendary king, son of Zeus and Io, who founded the city of Memphis.

[3] King Darius of Persia.

[4] Persian governor.

[5] About 1,400 meters.

[6] Priestess of Apollo at Delphi.

[7] Citizens of Sparta.

# Thucydides

## ca. 460–400 B.C.E.

Thucydides' *The History of the Peloponnesian War* is his version of the conflict between Athens and Sparta for domination of the Greek world in the last third of the fifth century; the war lasted from 431 to 404. The war in Thucydides' account is not just a military conflict, though he spends much time on the details of battles, tactics, general international strategies and the human and material costs for both sides. Rather, for Thucydides the war is a conflict most crucially of ideas, the basic cultural principles and values brought to the struggle. The Peloponnesian war is a "culture war." To Thucydides the ideas of the parties involved, what they really are, what they say that they are, and the differences between the two, generate an inevitable conflict.

Thucydides was an Athenian, an aristocrat, and a general for Athens. Blamed for a defeat relatively early in the war, he was, in the Athenian manner, exiled. He did not return to Athens until 404. As an historian, he has two approaches by which to relate the war. He writes "history" as a straightforward narrative of events. But this narrative he often interrupts with speeches and dialogues wherein the pertinent actors speak for themselves, explaining, arguing, and most importantly justifying their actions, past and future. Often these speeches, which can be dialogues between opposing speakers, are "philosophical." Thucydides' book is a history, but a philosophical one where ideas are presented and defended with arguments.

The following selection reports the events at Melos, an island that was at the time a city state of free and originally neutral colonists from Sparta, until they were provoked by Athens. The Greek world of Thucydides' day was not only the homeland, Greece herself. Given the long-term commitment to colonization, Greeks were literally all over the Mediterranean. Thus the war occurred from Sicily to the Black Sea, as well as throughout the Aegean. Melos is north of Crete.

In the dialogue representatives from Athens express clearly their determination for Melos to submit. If Melos refuses, they intend to destroy her. The Melians refuse. The Athenians do destroy her, killing all the men and selling the women and children into slavery. That is the bare outline of the events.

Consideration of the Melian episode raises such questions as: Why does Athens take such a seemingly intractable hard line? Are they "just" reasons, or rather is justice not relevant to them?

In the Funeral Oration of Pericles as recorded by Thucydides much earlier in the war, Pericles stated all that was special about Athens: democracy, openness, intellect, beauty, pleasure. And empire, too. Pericles reconciled Athens being a democracy, at home, with having an empire, overseas, by claiming Athens as the legitimate educator for the rest of Greece. Athens' power is for good: the spread of democracy and culture. But by the time of the events at Melos, Pericles was long dead. *The History of the Peloponnesian War* is the story of the rise, then fall, of Athens; she eventually loses the war. Perhaps her actions at Melos help to explain why. This dialogue has become a classic discussion for subsequent "just war" theory in the West.

JM

# from *The History of the Peloponnesian War*

## Chapter XVII

*Sixteenth Year of the War—The Melian Conference—Fate of Melos*

B.C. 416: Athenian expedition to Melos—Discussion of envoys—Melians refuse to submit—Siege of Melos—Melians massacred and made slaves.

The next summer Alcibiades sailed with twenty ships to Argos and seized the suspected persons still left of the Lacedæmonian faction[1] to the number of three hundred, whom the Athenians forthwith lodged in the neighbouring islands of their empire. The Athenians also made an expedition against the isle of Melos with thirty ships of their own, six Chian, and two Lesbian vessels, sixteen hundred heavy infantry, three hundred archers, and twenty mounted archers from Athens, and about fifteen hundred heavy infantry from the allies and the islanders. The Melians are a colony of Lacedæmon that would not submit to the Athenians like the other islanders, and at first remained neutral and took no part in the struggle, but afterwards upon the Athenians using violence and plundering their territory, assumed an attitude of open hostility. Cleomedes, son of Lycomedes, and Tisias, son of Tisimachus, the generals, encamping in their territory with the above armament, before doing any harm to their land, sent envoys to negotiate. These the Melians did not bring before the people, but bade them state the object of their mission to the magistrates and the few; upon which the Athenian envoys spoke as follows:—

*Athenians.*—'Since the negotiations are not to go on before the people, in order that we may not be able to speak straight on without interruption, and deceive the ears of the multitude by seductive arguments which would pass without refutation (for we know that this is the meaning of our being brought before the few), what if you who sit there were to pursue a method more cautious still! Make no set speech yourselves, but take us up at whatever you do not like, and settle that before going any farther. And first tell us if this proposition of ours suits you.'

The Melian commissioners answered:—

*Melians.*—'To the fairness of quietly instructing each other as you propose there is nothing to object; but your military preparations are too far advanced to agree with what you say, as we see you are come to be judges in your own cause, and that all we can reasonably expect from this negotiation is

324

war, if we prove to have right on our side and refuse to submit, and in the contrary case, slavery.'

*Athenians*—'If you have met to reason about presentiments of the future, or for anything else than to consult for the safety of your state upon the facts that you see before you, we will give over; otherwise we will go on.'

*Melians.*—'It is natural and excusable for men in our position to turn more ways than one both in thought and utterance. However, the question in this conference is, as you say, the safety of our country; and the discussion, if you please, can proceed in the way which you propose.'

*Athenians.*—'For ourselves, we shall not trouble you with specious pretences—either of how we have a right to our empire because we overthrew the Mede,[2] or are now attacking you because of wrong that you have done us—and make a long speech which would not be believed; and in return we hope that you, instead of thinking to influence us by saying that you did not join the Lacedæmonians, although their colonists, or that you have done us no wrong, will aim at what is feasible, holding in view the real sentiments of us both; since you know as well as we do that right, as the world goes, is only in question between equals in power, while the strong do what they can and the weak suffer what they must.'

*Melians.*—'As we think, at any rate, it is expedient—we speak as we are obliged, since you enjoin us to let right alone and talk only of interest—that you should not destroy what is our common protection, the privilege of being allowed in danger to invoke what is fair and right, and even to profit by arguments not strictly valid if they can be got to pass current. And you are as much interested in this as any, as your fall would be a signal for the heaviest vengeance and an example for the world to meditate upon.'

*Athenians.*—'The end of our empire, if end it should, does not frighten us: a rival empire like Lacedæmon, even if Lacedæmon was our real antagonist, is not so terrible to the vanquished as subjects who by themselves attack and overpower their rulers. This, however, is a risk that we are content to take. We will now proceed to show you that we are come here in the interest of our empire, and that we shall say what we are now going to say, for the preservation of your country; as we would fain exercise that empire over you without trouble, and see you preserved for the good of us both.'

*Melians.*— 'And how, pray, could it turn out as good for us to serve as for you to rule?'

*Athenians.*—'Because you would have the advantage of submitting before suffering the worst, and we should gain by not destroying you.'

*Melians.*—'So that you would not consent to our being neutral, friends instead of enemies, but allies of neither side.'

*Athenians.*—'No; for your hostility cannot so much hurt us as your friendship will be an argument to our subjects of our weakness, and your enmity of our power.'

*Melians.*—'Is that your subjects' idea of equity, to put those who have nothing to do with you in the same category with peoples that are most of them your own colonists, and some conquered rebels?'

*Athenians.*—'As far as right goes they think one has as much of it as the other, and that if any maintain their independence it is because they are strong, and that if we do not molest them it is because we are afraid; so that besides extending our empire we should gain in security by your subjection; the fact that you are islanders and weaker than others rendering it all the more important that you should not succeed in baffling the masters of the sea.'

*Melians.*—'But do you consider that there is no security in the policy which we indicate? For here again if you debar us from talking about justice and invite us to obey your interest, we also must explain ours, and try to persuade you, if the two happen to coincide. How can you avoid making enemies of all existing neutrals who shall look at our case and conclude from it that one day or another you will attack them? And what is this but to make greater the enemies that you have already, and to force others to become so who would otherwise have never thought of it?'

*Athenians.*—'Why, the fact is that continentals generally give us but little alarm; the liberty which they enjoy will long prevent their taking precautions against us; it is rather islanders like yourselves, outside our empire, and subjects smarting under the yoke, who would be the most likely to take a rash step and lead themselves and us into obvious danger.'

*Melians,*—'Well then, if you risk so much to retain your empire, and your subjects to get rid of it, it were surely great baseness and cowardice in us who are still free not to try everything that can be tried, before submitting to your yoke.'

*Athenians.*—'Not if you are well advised, the contest not being an equal one, with honour as the prize and shame as the penalty, but a question of self-preservation and of not resisting those who are far stronger than you are.'

*Melians.*—'But we know that the fortune of war is sometimes more impartial than the disproportion of numbers might lead one to suppose; to submit is to give ourselves over to despair, while action still preserves for us a hope that we may stand erect.'

*Athenians.*—'Hope, danger's comforter, may be indulged in by those who have abundant resources, if not without loss at all events without ruin; but its nature is to be extravagant, and those who go so far as to put their all upon the venture see it in its true colours only when they are ruined; but so long as the discovery would enable them to guard against it, it is never found wanting. Let not this be the case with you, who are weak and hang on a single turn of the scale; nor be like the vulgar, who, abandoning such security as human means may still afford, when [the] visible hopes fail them in extremity, turn to invisible, to prophecies and oracles, and other such inventions that delude men with hopes to their destruction.'

*Melians.*—'You may be sure that we are as well aware as you of the difficulty of contending against your power and fortune, unless the terms be equal. But we trust that the gods may grant us fortune as good as yours, since we are just men fighting against unjust, and that what we want in power will be made up by the alliance of the Lacedæmonians, who are bound, if only for very shame, to come to the aid of their kindred. Our confidence, therefore, after all is not so utterly irrational.'

*Athenians.*—'When you speak of the favour of the gods, we may as fairly hope for that as yourselves; neither our pretensions nor our conduct being in any way contrary to what men believe of the gods, or practise among themselves. Of the gods we believe, and of men we know, that by a necessary law of their nature they rule wherever they can. And it is not as if we were the first to make this law, or to act upon it when made: we found it existing before us, and shall leave it to exist for ever after us; all we do is to make use of it, knowing that you and everybody else, having the same power as we have, would do the same as we do. Thus, as far as the gods are concerned, we have no fear and no reason to fear that we shall be at a disadvantage. But when we come to your notion about the Lacedæmonians, which leads you to believe that shame will make them help you, here we bless your simplicity but do not envy your folly. The Lacedæmonians, when their own interests or their country's laws are in question, are the worthiest men alive; of their conduct towards others much might be said, but no clearer idea of it could be given than by shortly saying that of all the men we know they are most conspicuous in considering what is agreeable honourable, and what is expedient just. Such a way of thinking does not promise much for the safety which you now unreasonably count upon.'

*Melians.*—'But it is for this very reason that we now trust to their respect for expediency to prevent them from betraying the Melians, their colonists, and thereby losing the confidence of their friends in Hellas and helping their enemies.'

*Athenians.*—'Then you do not adopt the view that expediency goes with security, while justice and honour cannot be followed without danger; and danger the Lacedæmonians generally court as little as possible.'

*Melians.*—'But we believe that they would be more likely to face even danger for our sake, and with more confidence than for others, as our nearness to [the] Peloponnese makes it easier for them to act, and our common blood insures our fidelity.'

*Athenians.*—'Yes, but what an intending ally trusts to, is not the goodwill of those who ask his aid, but a decided superiority of power for action; and the Lacedæmonians look to this even more than others. At least, such is their distrust of their home resources that it is only with numerous allies that they attack a neighbour; now is it likely that while we are masters of the sea they will cross over to an island?'

*Melians.*—'But they would have others to send. The Cretan sea is a wide one, and it is more difficult for those who command it to intercept others, than for those who wish to elude them to do so safely. And should the Lacedæmonians miscarry in this, they would fall upon your land, and upon those left of your allies whom Brasidas[3] did not reach; and instead of places which are not yours, you will have to fight for your own country and your own confederacy.'

*Athenians.*—'Some diversion of the kind you speak of you may one day experience, only to learn, as others have done, that the Athenians never once yet withdrew from a siege for fear of any. But we are struck by the fact, that after saying you would consult for the safety of your country, in all this discussion you have mentioned nothing which men might trust in and think to be saved by. Your strongest arguments depend upon hope and the future, and your actual resources are too scanty, as compared with those arrayed against you, for you to come out victorious. You will therefore show great blindness of judgment, unless, after allowing us to retire, you can find some counsel more prudent than this. You will surely not be caught by that idea of disgrace, which in dangers that are disgraceful, and at the same time too plain to be mistaken, proves so fatal to mankind; since in too many cases the very men that have their eyes perfectly open to what they are rushing into, let the thing called disgrace, by the mere influence of a seductive name, lead them on to a point at which they become so enslaved by the phrase as in fact to fall wilfully into hopeless disaster, and incur disgrace more disgraceful as the companion of error, than when it comes as the result of misfortune. This, if you are well advised, you will guard against; and you will not think it dishonourable to submit to the greatest city in Hellas, when it makes you the moderate offer of becoming its tributary ally, without ceasing to enjoy the country that belongs to you; nor when you have the choice given you between war and security, will you be so blinded as to choose the worse. And it is certain that those who do not yield to their equals, who keep terms with their superiors, and are moderate towards their inferiors, on the whole succeed best. Think over the matter, therefore, after our withdrawal, and reflect once and again that it is for your country that you are consulting, that you have not more than one, and that upon this one deliberation depends its prosperity or ruin.'

The Athenians now withdrew from the conference; and the Melians, left to themselves, came to a decision corresponding with what they had maintained in the discussion, and answered, 'Our resolution, Athenians, is the same as it was at first. We will not in a moment deprive of freedom a city that has been inhabited these seven hundred years; but we put our trust in the fortune by which the gods have preserved it until now, and in the help of men, that is, of the Lacedæmonians; and so we will try and save ourselves. Meanwhile we invite you to allow us to be friends to you and foes to neither party, and to retire from our country after making such a treaty as shall seem fit to us both.'

Such was the answer of the Melians. The Athenians now departing from the conference said, 'Well, you alone, as it seems to us, judging from these resolutions, regard what is future as more certain than what is before your eyes, and what is out of sight, in your eagerness, as already coming to pass; and as you have staked most on, and trusted most in, the Lacedæmonians, your fortune, and your hopes, so will you be most completely deceived.'

The Athenian envoys now returned to the army; and the Melians showing no signs of yielding, the generals at once betook themselves to hostilities, and drew a line of circumvallation[4] round the Melians, dividing the work among the different states. Subsequently the Athenians returned with most of their army, leaving behind them a certain number of their own citizens and of the allies to keep guard by land and sea. The force thus left stayed on and besieged the place.

About the same time the Argives invaded the territory of Phlius and lost eighty men cut off in an ambush by the Phliasians and Argive exiles. Meanwhile the Athenians at Pylos took so much plunder from the Lacedæmonians that the latter, although they still refrained from breaking off the treaty and going to war with Athens, yet proclaimed that any of their people that chose might plunder the Athenians. The Corinthians also commenced hostilities with the Athenians for private quarrels of their own; but the rest of the Peloponnesians stayed quiet. Meanwhile the Melians attacked by night and took the part of the Athenian lines over against the market, and killed some of the men, and brought in corn and all else that they could find useful to them, and so returned and kept quiet, while the Athenians took measures to keep better guard in future.

Summer was now over. The next winter the Lacedæmonians intended to invade the Argive territory, but arriving at the frontier found the sacrifices for crossing unfavourable, and went back again. This intention of theirs gave the Argives suspicions of certain of their fellow-citizens, some of whom they arrested; others, however, escaped them. About the same time the Melians again took another part of the Athenian lines which were but feebly garrisoned. Reinforcements afterwards arriving from Athens in consequence, under the command of Philocrates, son of Demeas, the siege was now pressed vigorously; and some treachery taking place inside, the Melians surrendered at discretion to the Athenians, who put to death all the grown men whom they took, and sold the women and children for slaves, and subsequently sent out five hundred colonists and inhabited the place themselves.

## Notes

[1] Those who supported Sparta.

[2] The Persians.

[3] A Spartan general.

[4] A wall or fortification.

# Gorgias

## Fifth Century B.C.E.

Gorgias was a native of Leontini in eastern Sicily. When his town was attacked in 427 B.C.E. by its larger neighbor Syracuse (cf. Thucydides 3.86), Gorgias was selected by his fellow citizens to travel to Athens to ask for aid; Syracuse and other cities in Sicily were allies of Sparta. Gorgias' oratory amazed the Athenians, who had apparently heard nothing comparable before him. Athens sent ships to Leontini, and Gorgias returned home. Sometime after that, Gorgias left Leontini and traveled throughout the Greek world, offering to teach rhetoric to others for pay. He spent most of his time in Thessaly, but he was famous enough in Athens for Plato to make him the title character of a dialogue with Socrates. Gorgias was also famous in antiquity for his longevity: though we know no dates for his birth or death, sources report that he lived well past the age of 100.

Gorgias is generally considered to be a Sophist, one of the philosophers against whom Socrates directed so much of his effort. That association, however, is made largely on the basis of his public displays and his charging fees. Unlike other Sophists, Gorgias is not reported to have claimed the ability to teach virtue. Rather, he taught his pupils how to speak as he did. He focused everything on style rather than on the facts or—as Plato would say—the truth. Gorgias himself points out in the *Encomium of Helen* 13 that a speech can "please and persuade a crowd because it was written with artfulness, not spoken with truth." The *Encomium of Helen*, one of only two works of Gorgias to survive, demonstrates that artfulness which Gorgias taught, which E. R. Dodds (*Plato: Gorgias*, 1959) aptly terms "dazzling insincerity." In it, Gorgias sets out to defend Helen from all charges against her, specifically, the charge of infidelity, and more generally, the Trojan War. He does so by naming four potential causes for her elopement with Paris—Chance or divine necessity, force, persuasion, and love—and claiming that none could be resisted.

Gorgias' insincerity should not be confused with insignificance. Gorgias himself recognized that rhetoric is "a powerful ruler" and, like magic, can have an incantatory effect on its hearers (*Encomium of Helen* 8, 10). The amorality of this power is Plato's chief concern, and in his writings he argues through Socrates that it is necessary to subordinate rhetoric to the truth of what is right and good.

BSH

# Encomium of Helen

(1) What is becoming to a city is manpower, to a body beauty, to a soul wisdom, to an action virtue, to a speech truth, and the opposites of these are unbecoming. Man and woman and speech and deed and city and object should be honored with praise if praiseworthy and incur blame if unworthy, for it is an equal error and mistake to blame the praisable and to praise the blamable.

(2) It is the duty of one and the same man both to speak the needful rightly and to refute the unrightfully spoken. Thus it is right to refute those who rebuke Helen, a woman about whom the testimony of inspired poets has become univocal and unanimous as has the ill omen of her name, which has become a reminder of misfortunes. For my part, by introducing some reasoning into my speech, I wish to free the accused of blame and, having reproved her detractors as prevaricators and proved the truth, to free her from their ignorance.

(3) Now it is not unclear, not even to a few, that in nature and in blood the woman who is the subject of this speech is preeminent among preeminent men and women. For it is clear that her mother was Leda, and her father was in fact a god, Zeus, but allegedly a mortal, Tyndareus, of whom the former was shown to be her father because he was and the latter was disproved because he was said to be, and the one was the most powerful of men and the other the Lord of all. (4) Born from such stock, she had godlike beauty, which taking and not mistaking, she kept. In many did she work much desire for her love, and her one body was the cause of bringing together many bodies of men thinking great thoughts for great goals, of whom some had greatness of wealth, some the glory of ancient nobility, some the vigor of personal agility, some command of acquired knowledge. And all came because of a passion which loved to conquer and a love of honor which was unconquered. (5) Who it was and why and how he sailed away, taking Helen as his love, I shall not say. To tell the knowing what they know shows it is right but brings no delight.

Having gone beyond the time once set for my speech, I shall go on to the beginning of my future speech, and I shall set forth the causes through which it is likely that Helen's voyage to Troy should take place. (6) For either by will of Fate and decision of the gods and vote of Necessity did she do what she did, or by force reduced or by words seduced or by love possessed.

Now if through the first, it is right for the responsible one to be held responsible; for god's predetermination cannot be hindered by human premeditation. For it is the nature of things, not for the strong to be hindered by the weak, but for the weaker to be ruled and drawn by the stronger, and for the stronger to lead and the weaker to follow. God is a stronger force than man in might and in wit and in other ways. If then one must place blame on Fate and on a god, one must free Helen from disgrace.

(7) But if she was raped by violence and illegally assaulted and unjustly insulted, it is clear that the raper, as the insulter, did the wronging, and the raped, as the insulted, did the suffering. It is right then for the barbarian who undertook a barbaric undertaking in word and law and deed to meet with blame in word, exclusion in law, and punishment in deed. And surely it is proper for a woman raped and robbed of her country and deprived of her loved ones to be pitied rather than pilloried. He did the dread deeds; she suffered them. It is just therefore to pity her but to hate him.

(8) But if it was speech which persuaded her and deceived her heart, not even to this is it difficult to make an answer and to banish blame as follows. Speech is a powerful lord, which by means of the finest and most invisible body effects the divinest works: it can stop fear and banish grief and create joy and nurture pity. I shall show how this is the case, since (9) it is necessary to offer proof to the opinion of my hearers: I both deem and define all poetry as speech with meter. Fearful shuddering and tearful pity and grievous longing come upon its hearers, and at the actions and physical sufferings of others in good fortunes and in evil fortunes, through the agency of words, the soul is wont to experience a suffering of its own. But come, I shall turn from one argument to another. (10) Sacred incantations sung with words are bearers of pleasure and banishers of pain, for, merging with opinion in the soul, the power of the incantation is wont to beguile it and persuade it and alter it by witchcraft. There have been discovered two arts of witchcraft and magic: one consists of errors of soul and the other of deceptions of opinion. (11) All who have and do persuade people of things do so by molding a false argument. For if all men on all subjects had both memory of things past and awareness of things present and foreknowledge of the future, speech would not be similarly similar, since as things are now it is not easy for them to recall the past nor to consider the present nor to predict the future. So that on most subjects most men take opinion as counselor to their soul, but since opinion is slippery and insecure it casts those employing it into slippery and insecure successes. (12) What cause then prevents the conclusion that Helen similarly, against her will, might have come under the influence of speech, just as if ravished by the force of the mighty? For it was possible to see how the force of persuasion prevails; persuasion has the form of necessity, but it does not have the same power. For speech constrained the soul, persuading it which it persuaded, both to believe

the things said and to approve the things done. The persuader, like a constrainer, does the wrong and the persuaded, like the constrained, in speech is wrongly charged. (13) To understand that persuasion, when added to speech, is wont also to impress the soul as it wishes, one must study: first, the words of Astronomers who, substituting opinion for opinion, taking away one but creating another, make what is incredible and unclear seem true to the eyes of opinion; then, second, logically necessary debates in which a single speech, written with art but not spoken with truth, bends a great crowd and persuades; and, third, the verbal disputes of philosophers in which the swiftness of thought is also shown making the belief in an opinion subject to easy change. (14) The effect of speech upon the condition of the soul is comparable to the power of drugs over the nature of bodies. For just as different drugs dispel different secretions from the body, and some bring an end to disease and others to life, so also in the case of speeches, some distress, others delight, some cause fear, others make the hearers bold, and some drug and bewitch the soul with a kind of evil persuasion.

(15) It has been explained that if she was persuaded by speech she did not do wrong but was unfortunate. I shall discuss the fourth cause in a fourth passage. For if it was love which did all these things, there will be no difficulty in escaping the charge of the sin which is alleged to have taken place. For the things we see do not have the nature which we wish them to have, but the nature which each actually has. Through sight the soul receives an impression even in its inner features. (16) When belligerents in war buckle on their warlike accouterments of bronze and steel, some designed for defense, others for offense, if the sight sees this, immediately it is alarmed and it alarms the soul, so that often men flee, panic stricken from future danger as though it were present. For strong as is the habit of obedience to the law, it is ejected by fear resulting from sight, which coming to a man causes him to be indifferent both to what is judged honorable because of the law and to the advantage to be derived from victory. (17) It has happened that people, after having seen frightening sights, have also lost presence of mind for the present moment; in this way fear extinguishes and excludes thought. And many have fallen victim to useless labor and dread diseases and hardly curable madnesses. In this way the sight engraves upon the mind images of things which have been seen. And many frightening impressions linger, and what lingers is exactly analogous to what is spoken. (18) Moreover, whenever pictures perfectly create a single figure and form from many colors and figures, they delight the sight, while the creation of statues and the production of works of art furnish a pleasant sight to the eyes. Thus it is natural for the sight to grieve for some things and to long for others, and much love and desire for many objects and figures is engraved

in many men. (19) If, therefore, the eye of Helen, pleased by the figure of Alexander, presented to her soul eager desire and contest of love, what wonder? If, being a god, Love has the divine power of the gods, how could a lesser being reject and refuse it? But if it is a disease of human origin and a fault of the soul, it should not be blamed as a sin, but regarded as an affliction. For she came, as she did come, caught in the net of Fate, not by the plans of the mind, and by the constraints of love, not by the devices of art.

(20) How then can one blame of Helen as unjust, since she is utterly acquitted of all charge, whether she did what she did through falling in love or persuaded by speech or ravished by force or constrained by divine constraint?

(21) I have by means of speech removed disgrace from a woman; I have observed the procedure which I set up at the beginning of the speech; I have tried to end the injustice of blame and the ignorance of opinion; I wished to write a speech which would be a praise of Helen and a diversion to myself.

# Aristotle

## 384–322 B.C.E.

Aristotle was born in Stagira in Thrace. His father, Nicomachus, was a court physician to the Macedonian king Amyntas, and his father's practice may have influenced the son's keen interest in observation and description. After his father's death, Aristotle was sent to Athens, where he began his study with Plato in his school, the Academy, when he was seventeen. His association with Plato lasted twenty years, until Plato's death in 347 B.C.E. After Plato, the leadership of the Academy went to Speusippus, Plato's nephew, rather than to Aristotle, whose thought diverged from his master's too much. Aristotle went to the court of Hermeas, a ruler in Asia, for three years, and shortly afterwards was recruited by Philip of Macedon to serve as a tutor for his son, Alexander. Philip died—or was murdered—in 336 B.C.E., and Alexander began plans for his conquest of Persia; Aristotle returned to Athens, and founded his own school at a place called the Lyceum. Aristotle's habit of walking around while he taught gave his philosophy the name of *Peripatetic* (from the Greek *peripateîn* "to walk around"). Aristotle spent the next thirteen years lecturing and writing. In 323, Alexander the Great died, and there was a general backlash in Athens against all things Macedonian. Aristotle fled, allegedly in his words "to prevent the Athenians from sinning a second time against philosophy" after they had killed Socrates; he retired to Chalcis in Euboia, where he died the next year, in 322 B.C.E.

Aristotle wrote systematically and exhaustively on all branches of human knowledge, both theoretical and practical: logic, physics, psychology, natural science, theology, ethics, politics, rhetoric, poetics. He is said to have written dialogues like Plato's, which Cicero, who read them, described as "a golden flow"; but such dialogues have not survived for us. The many works that have survived seem more like lecture notes than polished works, and modern scholars are still challenged by the tasks of editing and interpreting Aristotle's work.

Aristotle, like Plato, was concerned with establishing what was true and real, but unlike Plato, Aristotle did not locate reality in ideal Forms. Rather, Aristotle argues for the reality of particular objects, claiming that true being exists in the actual material object, not in its abstract form. In this, Aristotle capitalizes on Plato's vagueness about the relation between the Forms and particular things. In the excerpts below, Aristotle famously defines virtue as a kind of moderation, and its cultivation as a "habituation" through action. In this,

Aristotle differs from his teacher. Plato defines virtue variously as a state of soul, or as knowledge, or as psychological balance, but never as a kind of action or a set of actions. Aristotle sees that a "state of soul" can be reached through the "discipline of action," to borrow a phrase from the Bhagavad-Gita, and that knowledge need not precede virtuous action. Aristotle's examination of friendship is a compelling example of his process of observation and deduction, and of his view that virtue is to be sought rather than happiness—and that the virtuous person will choose virtuous friends not for utility or pleasure, but for a kind of completeness. Hence, in Aristotle's view, a friend is "another self."

BSH

# from *Nicomachean Ethics*

## 4.5 Magnanimity

### *4.51 The virtue compared with the vices contrary to it*

Magnanimity seems, even going by the name alone, to be concerned with great things. Let us see first the sorts of things it is concerned with. It does not matter whether we consider the state itself or the person who expresses it.

The magnanimous person, then, seems to be the one who thinks himself worthy of great things and is really worthy of them. For if someone is not worthy of them but thinks he is, he is foolish, and no virtuous person is foolish or senseless; hence the magnanimous person is the one we have mentioned. Someone who is worthy of little and thinks so is temperate, but not magnanimous; for magnanimity is found in greatness, just as beauty is found in a large body, and small people can be attractive and well-proportioned, but not beautiful.

Someone who thinks he is worthy of great things when he is not is vain; but not everyone who thinks he is worthy of greater things than he is worthy of is vain.

Someone who thinks he is worthy of less than he is worthy of is pusillanimous, whether he is worthy of great or of moderate things; and even if he is worthy of little, he thinks he is worthy of still less than that. The one who seems most pusillanimous is the one who is worthy of great things; for consider how little he would think of himself if he were worthy of less.

The magnanimous person, then, is at the extreme in so far as he makes great claims. But in so far as he makes them rightly, he is intermediate; for what he thinks he is worthy of reflects his real worth, while the others are excessive or deficient. The pusillanimous person is deficient both in relation to himself [i.e. his worth] and in relation to the magnanimous person's estimate of his own worth, while the vain person makes claims that are excessive for himself, but not for the magnanimous person.

### *4.52 The scope of magnanimity: Honour*

If, then, he thinks he is worthy of great things, and is worthy of them, especially of the greatest things, he has one concern above all. Worth is said to

[make one worthy of] external goods; and we would suppose that the greatest
20 of these is the one we award to the gods, the one above all that is the aim of
people with a reputation for worth, the prize for the finest [achievements]. All
this is true of honour, since it is called the greatest of the external goods. Hence
the magnanimous person has the right concern with honours and dishonours.

And even without argument it appears that magnanimous people are
concerned with honour. For the great think themselves worthy of honour most
of all, and honour befits their worth.

## 4.53 The state of the magnanimous person

### Magnanimity requires complete virtue

Since the magnanimous person is worthy of the greatest things, he is the
best person. For in every case the better person is worthy of something greater,
and the best person is worthy of the greatest things; and hence the truly magnanimous person must be good.

30 Greatness in each virtue also seems proper to the magnanimous person.
And surely it would not at all fit a magnanimous person to run away [from
danger when a coward would], swinging his arms [to get away faster], or to do
injustice. For what goal will make him do shameful actions, when none [of
their goals] is great to him? And examination of particular cases makes the
magnanimous person appear altogether ridiculous if he is not good.

35 Nor would he be worthy of honour if he were base. For honour is the
prize of virtue, and is awarded to good people.

24a Magnanimity, then, looks like a sort of adornment of the virtues; for it
makes them greater, and it does not arise without them. Hence it is hard to be
truly magnanimous, since it is not possible without being fine and good.

### Hence he has a discriminating attitude to honour . . .

5 The magnanimous person, then, is concerned especially with honours
and dishonours. And when he receives great honours from excellent people, he
will be moderately pleased, thinking he is getting what is proper to him, or
even less. For there can be no honour worthy of complete virtue; but still he
will accept [excellent people's] honours, since they have nothing greater to
award him.

10 But if he is honoured by just anyone, or for something small, he will
entirely disdain it; for that is not what he is worthy of. And similarly he will
disdain dishonour; for it will not be justly attached to him.

## . . . And to other goods of fortune

As we have said, then, the magnanimous person is concerned especially
with honours. Still, he will also have a moderate attitude to riches and power
and every sort of good and bad fortune, however it turns out. He will be nei- 15
ther excessively pleased by good fortune nor excessively distressed by ill fortune, since he does not even regard honour as the greatest good.

For positions of power and riches are choiceworthy for their honour; at
any rate their possessors wish to be honoured on account of them. Hence the
magnanimous person who counts honour for little will also count these other
goods for little, which is why he seems arrogant. 20

The results of good fortune, however, seem to contribute to magnanimity. For the well-born and the powerful or rich are thought worthy of honour,
since they are in a superior position, and everything superior in some good is
more honoured. Hence these things also make people more magnanimous,
since some people honour their possessors for these goods.

In reality, however, it is only the good person who is honourable. Still, 25
anyone who has both virtue and these goods is more readily thought worthy
of honour.

## This attitude distinguishes him from pretenders to magnanimity

Those who lack virtue but have these other goods are not justified in
thinking themselves worthy of great things, and are not correctly called magnanimous; that is impossible without complete virtue. However, they become
arrogant and wantonly aggressive when they have these other goods. For with- 30
out virtue it is hard to bear the results of good fortune suitably, and when these
people cannot do it, but suppose they are superior to other people, they despise 112
everyone else, and do whatever they please.

They do this because they are imitating the magnanimous person though
they are not really like him. They imitate him where they can; hence they do
not do actions expressing virtue, but they despise other people. For the mag- 5
nanimous person is justified when he despises, since his beliefs are true; but the
many despise with no good reason.

## His attitude to danger

He does not face dangers in a small cause, and does not face them frequently, since he honours few things, and is no lover of danger. But he faces
them in a great cause, and whenever he faces them he is unsparing of his life,
since he does not think life at all costs is worthwhile.

### His attitude to giving and receiving benefits

10     He is the sort of person who does good but is ashamed when he receives it; for doing good is proper to the superior person, and receiving it to the inferior. He returns more good than he has received; for in this way the original giver will be repaid, and will also have incurred a new debt to him, and will be the beneficiary.

    Magnanimous people seem to remember the good they do, but not what they receive, since the recipient is inferior to the giver, and the magnanimous
15  person wishes to be superior. And they seem to find pleasure in hearing of the good they do, and none in hearing what they receive—that also seems to be why Thetis[1] does not tell Zeus of the good she has done him, and the Spartans do not tell of the good they have done the Athenians, but only of the good received from them.

    Again, it is proper to the magnanimous person to ask for nothing, or hardly anything, but to help eagerly.

### His attitude to other people

    When he meets people with good fortune or a reputation for worth, he
20  displays his greatness, since superiority over them is difficult and impressive, and there is nothing ignoble in trying to be impressive with them. But when he meets ordinary people he is moderate, since superiority over them is easy, and an attempt to be impressive among inferiors is as vulgar as a display of strength against the weak.

    He stays away from what is commonly honoured, and from areas where
25  others lead; he is inactive and lethargic except for some great honour or achievement. Hence his actions are few, but great and renowned.

    Moreover, he must be open in his hatreds and his friendships, since concealment is proper to a frightened person. He is concerned for the truth more than for people's opinion. He is open in his speech and actions, since his dis-
30  dain makes him speak freely. And he speaks the truth, except [when he speaks less than the truth] to the many, [because he is moderate], not because he is self-deprecating.

25a     He cannot let anyone else, except a friend, determine his life. For that would be slavish; and this is why all flatterers are servile and inferior people are flatterers.

    He is not prone to marvel, since he finds nothing great; or to remember evils, since it is not proper to a magnanimous person to nurse memories, espe-
5  cially not of evils, but to overlook them.

He is no gossip. For he will not talk about himself or about another, since he is not concerned to have himself praised or other people blamed. Nor is he given to praising people. Hence he does not speak evil even of his enemies, except [when he responds to their] wanton aggression.

He especially avoids laments or entreaties about necessities or small matters, 10 since these attitudes are proper to someone who takes these things seriously.

He is the sort of person whose possessions are fine and unproductive rather than productive and advantageous, since that is more proper to a self-sufficient person.

The magnanimous person seems to have slow movements, a deep voice and calm speech. For since he takes few things seriously, he is in no hurry, and since he counts nothing great, he is not strident; and these [attitudes he avoids] 15 are the causes of a shrill voice and hasty movements.

This, then, is the character of the magnanimous person.

## 4.54 The vices of excess and deficiency

The deficient person is pusillanimous, and the person who goes to excess is vain. [Like the vulgar and the niggardly person) these also seem not to be evil people, since they are not evil-doers, but to be in error.

### Pusillanimity

For the pusillanimous person is worthy of goods, but deprives himself of 20 the goods he is worthy of, and would seem to have something bad in him because he does not think he is worthy of the goods. Indeed he would seem not to know himself; for if he did, he would aim at the things he is worthy of, since they are goods. For all that, such people seem hesitant rather than foolish.

But this belief of theirs actually seems to make them worse. For each sort of person seeks what [he thinks] he is worth; and these people hold back from 25 fine actions and practices, and equally from external goods, because they think they are unworthy of them.

### Vanity

Vain people, on the other hand, are foolish and do not know themselves; and they make this obvious. For they undertake commonly honoured exploits, but are not worthy of them, and then they are found out. They adorn them- 30 selves with clothes and ostentatious style and that sort of thing; and since they both wish for good fortune and wish it to be evident, they talk about it, think-ing it will bring them honour.

Pusillanimity is more opposed than vanity to magnanimity; for it arises more often, and is worse. . . .

## 4.11 Shame

### 4.111 It is a feeling, not a virtue

Shame is not properly regarded as a virtue, since it would seem to be more like a feeling than like a state [of character]. It is defined, at any rate, as a sort of fear of disrepute, and its expression is similar to that of fear of something terrifying; for a feeling of disgrace makes people blush, and fear of death makes them turn pale. Hence both [types of fear] appear to be in some way bodily [reactions], which seem to be more characteristic of feelings than of states.

### 4.112 It is suitable for young people

Further, the feeling of shame is suitable for youth, not for every time of life. For we think it right for young people to be prone to shame, since they live by their feelings, and hence often go astray, but are restrained by shame; and hence we praise young people who are prone to shame. No one, by contrast, would praise an older person for readiness to feel disgrace, since we think it wrong for him to do any action that causes a feeling of disgrace.

### 4.113 But it is not suitable for a virtuous person

For a feeling of disgrace is not proper to the decent person either, if it is caused by base actions; for these should not be done. And if some actions are really disgraceful and others are base [only] in [his] belief, that does not matter, since neither should be done, and so he should not feel disgrace. It is proper to a base person to have a character that makes him do disgraceful action.

Further, if someone is in a state that would make him feel disgrace if he were to do a disgraceful action, and because of this thinks he is decent, that is absurd. For shame is concerned with what is voluntary, and the decent person will never willingly do base actions. Shame might, however, be decent on an assumption; for if [the decent person] were to do [these disgraceful actions], he would feel disgrace; but this does not apply to the virtues.

And if we grant that it is base to feel no disgrace or shame at disgraceful actions, it still does not follow that to do such actions and then to feel disgrace at them is decent. . . .

## 9.2 General Account of Friendship

### 9.21 The object of friendship: What is lovable

Perhaps these questions will become clear once we find out what it is that viii
is lovable. For, it seems, not everything is loved, but [only] what is lovable, and
this is either good or pleasant or useful. However, it seems that what is useful
is the source of some good or some pleasure; hence what is good and what is 20
pleasant are lovable as ends.

Do people love what is good, or what is good for them? For sometimes
these conflict; and the same is true of what is pleasant. Each one, it seems, loves
what is good for him; and while what is good is lovable unconditionally, what
is lovable for each one is what is good for him. In fact each one loves not what 25
*is* good for him, but what *appears* good for him; but this will not matter, since
[what appears good for him] will be what appears lovable.

Hence there are these three causes of love.

### 9.22 Necessary conditions for friendship

#### There is no friendship for soulless things

Love for a soulless thing is not called friendship, since there is no mutual loving, and you do not wish good to it. For it would presumably be ridiculous to wish good things to wine; the most you wish is its preservation so that 30
you can have it. To a friend, however, it is said, you must wish goods for his
own sake.

#### Friendship is not mere goodwill . . .

If you wish good things in this way, but the same wish is not returned by
the other, you would be said to have [only] goodwill for the other. For friendship is said to be *reciprocated* goodwill.

#### And not mere reciprocated goodwill

But perhaps we should add that friends are aware of the reciprocated
goodwill. For many a one has goodwill to people whom he has not seen but 35
supposes to be decent or useful, and one of these might have the same good- 115
will towards him. These people, then, apparently have goodwill to each other,
but how could we call them friends when they are unaware of their attitude to
each other?

Hence, [to be friends] they must have goodwill to each other, wish goods 5
and be aware of it, from one of the causes mentioned above.

## 9.3 The Three Types of Friendship

### 9.31 Complete and incomplete species of friendship correspond to the different objects

ii 3     Now since these causes differ in species, so do the types of loving and types of friendship. Hence friendship has three species, corresponding to the three objects of love. For each object of love has a corresponding type of mutual loving, combined with awareness of it, and those who love each other wish
10  goods to each other in so far as they love each other.

### 9.32 Friendships for utility and pleasure are incomplete

Those who love each other for utility love the other not in himself, but in so far as they gain some good for themselves from him. The same is true of those who love for pleasure; for they like a witty person not because of his character, but because he is pleasant to themselves.

And so those who love for utility or pleasure are fond of a friend because
15  of what is good or pleasant for themselves, not in so far as the beloved is who he is, but in so far as he is useful or pleasant.

Hence these friendships as well [as the friends] are coincidental, since the beloved is loved not in so far as he is who he is, but in so far as he provides some good or pleasure.

And so these sorts of friendships are easily dissolved, when the friends do
20  not remain similar [to what they were]; for if someone is no longer pleasant or useful, the other stops loving him.

### 9.33 Friendship for utility

What is useful does not remain the same, but is different at different times. Hence, when the cause of their being friends is removed, the friendship is dissolved too, on the assumption that the friendship aims at these [useful results]. This sort of friendship seems to arise especially among older people,
25  since at that age they pursue what is advantageous, not what is pleasant, and also among those in their prime or youth who pursue what is expedient.

Nor do such people live together very much. For sometimes they do not even find each other pleasant. Hence they have no further need to meet in this way if they are not advantageous [to each other]; for each finds the other pleas-
30  ant [only] to the extent that he expects some good from him. The friendship of hosts and guests is taken to be of this type too.

## 9.34 Friendships for pleasure

The cause of friendship between young people seems to be pleasure. For their lives are guided by their feelings, and they pursue above all what is pleasant for themselves and what is near at hand. But as they grow up [what they find] pleasant changes too. Hence they are quick to become friends, and quick 35 to stop; for their friendship shifts with [what they find] pleasant, and the change in such pleasure is quick. Young people are prone to erotic passion, 115 since this mostly follows feelings, and is caused by pleasure; that is why they love and quickly stop, often changing in a single day.

These people wish to spend their days together and to live together; for 5 this is how they gain [the good things) corresponding to their friendship.

## 9.35 Complete friendship is the friendship of good people

But complete friendship is the friendship of good people similar in virtue; for they wish goods in the same way to each other in so far as they are good, and they are good in themselves. [Hence they wish goods to each other for each other's own sake.] Now those who wish goods to their friend for the 10 friend's own sake are friends most of all; for they have this attitude because of the friend himself, not coincidentally. Hence these people's friendship lasts as long as they are good; and virtue is enduring.

Each of them is both good unconditionally and good for his friend, since good people are both unconditionally good and advantageous for each other. They are pleasant in the same ways too, since good people are pleasant both 15 unconditionally and for each other. [They are pleasant for each other] because each person finds his own actions and actions of that kind pleasant, and the actions of good people are the same or similar.

It is reasonable that this sort of friendship is enduring, since it embraces in itself all the features that friends must have. For the cause of every friend- 20 ship is good or pleasure, either unconditional or for the lover; and every friendship reflects some similarity. And all the features we have mentioned are found in this friendship because of [the nature of] the friends themselves. For they are similar in this way [i.e. in being good]. Moreover, their friendship also has the other things—what is unconditionally good and what is unconditionally pleasant; and these are lovable most of all. Hence loving and friendship are found most of all and at their best in these friends.

These kinds of friendships are likely to be rare, since such people are few. 25 Moreover, they need time to grow accustomed to each other; for, as the proverb says, they cannot know each other before they have shared the traditional [peck of] salt, and they cannot accept each other or be friends until each appears lovable to the other and gains the other's confidence. Those who are

30 quick to treat each other in friendly ways wish to be friends, but are not friends, unless they are also lovable, and know this. For though the wish for friendship comes quickly, friendship does not.

## 9.4 Differences and Similarities Between Complete and Incomplete Friendship

### 9.41 The incomplete friendships resemble the complete

ii 4     This sort of friendship, then, is complete both in time and in the other ways. In every way each friend gets the same things and similar things from
35 each, and this is what must be true of friends. Friendship for pleasure bears
57a some resemblance to this complete sort, since good people are also pleasant to each other. And friendship for utility also resembles it, since good people are also useful to each other.

**Incomplete friendships endure to the extent that they resemble complete friendships**

    With these [incomplete friends] also, the friendships are most enduring
5 when they get the same thing—e.g. pleasure—from each other, and, moreover, get it from the same source, as witty people do. They must not be like the erotic lover and the boy he loves. For these do not take pleasure in the same things; the lover takes pleasure in seeing his beloved, while the beloved takes pleasure in being courted by his lover. When the beloved's bloom is fading, sometimes the friendship fades too; for the lover no longer finds pleasure in seeing his
10 beloved, while the beloved is no longer courted by the lover.

    Many, however, remain friends if they have similar characters and come to be fond of each other's characters from being accustomed to them. Those who exchange utility rather than pleasure in their erotic relations are friends to a lesser extent and less enduring friends.

    Those who are friends for utility dissolve the friendship as soon as the
15 advantage is removed; for they were never friends of each other, but of what was expedient for them.

### 9.42 But the character of the friends in complete friendship makes it more enduring

    Now it is possible for bad people as well [as good] to be friends to each other for pleasure or utility, for decent people to be friends to base people, and for someone with neither character to be a friend to someone with any character. Clearly, however, only good people can be friends to each other because

of the other person himself; for bad people find no enjoyment in one another    20
if they get no benefit.

Moreover, it is only the friendship of good people that is immune to slander. For it is hard to trust anyone speaking against someone whom we ourselves have found reliable for a long time; and among good people there is trust, the belief that he would never do injustice [to a friend], and all the other things expected in a true friendship. But in the other types of friendship [distrust] may easily arise.    25

### 9.43 Hence incomplete friendships are friendships only to a limited extent

[These must be counted as types of friendship.] For people include among friends [not only the best type, but] also those who are friends for utility, as cities are—since alliances between cities seem to aim at expediency— and those who are fond of each other, as children are, for pleasure. Hence we must presumably also say that such people are friends, but say that there are    30 more species of friendship than one.

On this view, the friendship of good people in so far as they are good is friendship in the primary way, and to the full extent; and the others are friendships by similarity. They are friends in so far as there is something good, and [hence] something similar to [what one finds in the best kind]; for what is pleasant is good to lovers of pleasure, But these [incomplete] types of friendship are not very regularly combined, and the same people do not become friends for both utility and pleasure. For things that [merely] coincide with    35 each other are not very regularly combined.

Friendship has been assigned, then, to these species. Base people will be    115 friends for pleasure or utility, since they are similar in that way. But good people will be friends because of themselves, since they are friends in so far as they are good. These, then, are friends unconditionally; the others are friends coin-    5 cidentally and by being similar to these. . . .

### 9.53 The value of friendship consists in loving more than in being loved

**The many might seem to value being loved simply as a means to honour**

It is because they love honour that the many seem to prefer being loved    viii to loving; that is why they love flatterers. For the flatterer is a friend in an infe-    15 rior position, or [rather] pretends to be one, and pretends to love more than he is loved; and being loved seems close to being honoured, which the many do indeed pursue.

**But in fact they also value friendship apart from honour**

20 It would seem, however, that they choose honour coincidentally, not in itself. For the many enjoy being honoured by powerful people because they expect to get whatever they need from them, and so enjoy the honour as a sign of this good treatment. Those who want honour from decent people with knowledge are seeking to confirm their own view of themselves, and so they are pleased because the judgment of those who say they are good makes them confident that they are good.

25 Being loved, on the contrary, they enjoy in itself. Hence it seems to be better than being honoured, and friendship seems choiceworthy in itself.

**And loving, not being loved, is the more valuable aspect of friendship**

But friendship seems to consist more in loving than in being loved. A sign of this is the enjoyment a mother finds in loving. For sometimes she gives her
30 child away to be brought up, and loves him as long as she knows about him; but she does not seek the child's love, if she cannot both [love and be loved]. She would seem to be satisfied if she sees the child doing well, and she loves the child even if ignorance prevents him from according to her what befits a mother.

Friendship, then, consists more in loving; and people who love their
35 friends are praised; hence, it would seem, loving is the virtue of friends. And so friends whose love corresponds to their friends' worth are enduring friends
59a and have an enduring friendship. This above all is the way for unequals as well as equals to be friends, since this is the way for them to be equalized.

**This explains why virtuous friendships endure**

Equality and similarity, and above all the similarity of those who are similar in being virtuous, is friendship. For virtuous people are enduringly [virtu-
5 ous] in themselves, and enduring [friends] to each other. They neither request nor provide assistance that requires base actions, but, you might even say, prevent this. For it is proper to good people to avoid error themselves and not to permit it in their friends.

Vicious people, by contrast, have no firmness, since they do not even remain similar to what they were, but become friends for a short time, enjoy-
10 ing each other's vice.

Useful or pleasant friends, however, last longer, for as long as they supply each other with pleasures or benefits. . . .

## 11. The Sources and Justification of Friendship

### 11.1 Friendship May Be Understood by Reference to Self-love

### 11.11 The features of friendship

The defining features of friendship that are found in friendships to one's neighbours would seem to be derived from features of friendship towards oneself.

For a friend is taken to be (1) someone who wishes and does goods or apparent goods to his friend for the friend's own sake; or (2) one who wishes the friend to be and to live for the friend's own sake—this is how mothers feel towards their children, and how friends who have been in conflict feel [towards each other]. (3) Others take a friend to be one who spends his time with his friend, and (4) makes the same choices; or (5) one who shares his friend's distress and enjoyment—and this also is true especially of mothers. And people define friendship by one of these features.

ix 4
116

5

### 11.12 These Features of Friendship Reflect the Virtuous Person's Love of Himself

Each of these features is found in the decent person's relation to himself, and it is found in other people in so far as they suppose they are decent. As we have said, virtue and the excellent person would seem to be the standard in each case.

10

(4) The excellent person is of one mind with himself, and desires the same things in his whole soul.

(1) Hence he wishes goods and apparent goods to himself, and does them in his actions, since it is proper to the good person to achieve the good. He wishes and does them for his own sake, since he does them for the sake of his thinking part, and that is what each person seems to be.

15

(2) He wishes himself to live and to be preserved. And he wishes this for the part by which he has intelligence more than for any other part. For being is a good for the good person, and each person wishes for goods for himself. And no one chooses to become another person even if that other will have every good when he has come into being; for, as it is, the god has the good [but no one chooses to be replaced by a god]. Rather [each of us chooses goods] on condition that he remains whatever he is; and each person would seem to be the understanding part, or that most of all. [Hence the good person wishes for goods for the understanding part.]

20

(3) Further, such a person finds it pleasant to spend time with himself, and so wishes to do it. For his memories of what he has done are agreeable,

25

and his expectations for the future are good, and hence both are pleasant. And besides, his thought is well supplied with topics for study.

(5) Moreover, he shares his own distresses and pleasures, more than other people share theirs. For it is always the same thing that is painful or pleasant, not different things at different times. This is because he practically never regrets [what he has done].

30     The decent person, then, has each of these features in relation to himself, and is related to his friend as he is to himself, since the friend is another himself. Hence friendship seems to be one of these features, and people with these features seem to be friends.

Is there friendship towards oneself, or is there not? Let us dismiss that
35   question for the present. However, there seems to be friendship in so far as someone is two or more parts. This seems to be true from what we have said,
56b   and because an extreme degree of friendship resembles one's friendship to oneself.

## 11.13 Vicious people are not capable of the same self-love

The many, base though they are, also appear to have these features. But perhaps they share in them only in so far as they approve of themselves and
5   suppose they are decent. For no one who is utterly bad and unscrupulous either has these features or appears to have them.

Indeed, even base people hardly have them.

(4) For they are at odds with themselves, and, like incontinent people, have an appetite for one thing and a wish for another.

(1) For they do not choose things that seem to be good for them, but instead choose pleasant things that are actually harmful. And cowardice or lazi-
10   ness causes others to shrink from doing what they think best for themselves.

(2) Those who have done many terrible actions hate and shun life because of their vice, and destroy themselves.

(3) Besides, vicious people seek others to pass their days with, and shun themselves. For when they are by themselves they remember many disagree-
15   able actions, and expect to do others in the future; but they manage to forget these in other people's company. These people have nothing lovable about them, and so have no friendly feelings for themselves.

(5) Hence such a person does not share his own enjoyments and distresses. For his soul is in conflict, and because he is vicious one part is distressed
20   at being restrained, and another is pleased [by the intended action]; and so each part pulls in a different direction, as though they were tearing him apart. Even if he cannot be distressed and pleased at the same time, still he is soon

distressed because he was pleased, and wishes these things had not become
pleasant to him; for base people are full of regret.                                    25

## 11.14 Both self-love and friendship require virtue

Hence the base person appears not to have a friendly attitude even
towards himself, because he has nothing lovable about him.

If this state is utterly miserable, everyone should earnestly shun vice and
try to be decent; for that is how someone will have a friendly relation to himself and will become a friend to another. . . .

## 11.5 Self-love is a Component of Friendship

### 11.51 The common view identifies self-love with selfishness

There is also a puzzle about whether one ought to love oneself or some-      ix 8
one else most of all; for those who like themselves most are criticized and      30
denounced as self-lovers, as though this were something shameful.

Indeed, the base person does seem to go to every length for his own sake,
and all the more the more vicious he is; hence he is accused, e.g., of doing
nothing of his own accord. The decent person, on the contrary, acts for what
is fine, all the more the better he is, and for his friend's sake, disregarding his      35
own good.

### 11.52 But facts about friendship justify self-love

The facts, however, conflict with these claims, and that is not unreason-      116
able.

For it is said that we must love most the friend who is most a friend; and
one person is most a friend to another if he wishes goods to the other for the
other's sake, even if no one will know about it. But these are features most of
all of one's relation to oneself; and so too are all the other defining features of      116
a friend, since we have said that all the features of friendship extend from oneself to others.

All the proverbs agree with this too, e.g. speaking of 'one soul', 'what
friends have is common', 'equality is friendship' and 'the knee is closer than the
shin'. For all these are true most of all in someone's relations with himself, since
one is a friend to himself most of all. Hence he should also love himself most      10
of all.

### 11.53 Hence we must distinguish good and bad forms of self-love

It is not surprising that there is a puzzle about which view we ought to follow, since both inspire some confidence; hence we must presumably divide these sorts of arguments, and distinguish how far and in what ways those on each side are true.

15 Perhaps, then, it will become clear, if we grasp how those on each side understand self-love.

### 11.54 The bad form of self-love is selfish, resting on an incorrect view of the self

Those who make self-love a matter for reproach ascribe it to those who award the biggest share in money, honours and bodily pleasures to themselves. For these are the goods desired and eagerly pursued by the many on the assumption that they are best; and hence they are also contested.

20 Those who are greedy for these goods gratify their appetites and in general their feelings and the non-rational part of the soul; and since this is the character of the many, the application of the term ['self-love'] is derived from the most frequent [kind of self-love], which is base. This type of self-lover, then, is justifiably reproached.

And plainly it is the person who awards himself these goods whom the 25 many habitually call a self-lover. For if someone is always eager to excel everyone in doing just or temperate actions or any others expressing the virtues, and in general always gains for himself what is fine, no one will call him a self-lover or blame him for it.

### 11.55 But the good form of self-love rests on a correct view of the self

However, it is this more than the other sort of person who seems to be a 30 self-lover. At any rate he awards himself what is finest and best of all, and gratifies the most controlling part of himself, obeying it in everything. And just as a city and every other composite system seems to be above all its most controlling part, the same is true of a human being; hence someone loves himself most if he likes and gratifies this part.

Similarly, someone is called continent or incontinent because his under- 35 standing is or is not the master, on the assumption that this is what each per- 116 son is. Moreover, his own voluntary actions seem above all to be those involving reason. Clearly, then, this, or this above all, is what each person is, and the decent person likes this most of all.

Hence he most of all is a self-lover, but a different kind from the self-lover who is reproached, differing from him as much as the life guided by reason dif-

fers from the life guided by feelings, and as much as the desire for what is fine 5
differs from the desire for what seems advantageous.

## 11.56 Hence it leads to virtuous action

Those who are unusually eager to do fine actions are welcomed and
praised by everyone. And when everyone competes to achieve what is fine and
strains to do the finest actions, everything that is right will be done for the 10
common good, and each person individually will receive the greatest of goods,
since that is the character of virtue.

Hence the good person must be a self-lover, since he will both help himself and benefit others by doing fine actions. But the vicious person must not
love himself, since he will harm both himself and his neighbours by following
his base feelings.

For the vicious person, then, the right actions conflict with those he does. 15
The decent person, however, does the right actions, since every understanding
chooses what is best for itself and the decent person obeys his understanding.

## 11.57 It even leads to costly sacrifices

Besides, it is true that, as they say, the excellent person labours for his
friends and for his native country, and will die for them if he must; he will sac- 20
rifice money, honours and contested goods in general, in achieving what is fine
for himself. For he will choose intense pleasure for a short time over mild pleasure for a long time; a year of living finely over many years of undistinguished
life; and a single fine and great action over many small actions. 25

This is presumably true of one who dies for others; he does indeed choose
something great and fine for himself. He is ready to sacrifice money as long as
his friends profit; for the friends gain money, while he gains what is fine, and
so he awards himself the greater good. He treats honours and offices the same
way; for he will sacrifice them all for his friends, since this is fine and praise- 30
worthy for him. It is not surprising, then, that he seems to be excellent, when
he chooses what is fine at the cost of everything. It is also possible, however, to
sacrifice actions to his friend, since it may be finer to be responsible for his
friend's doing the action than to do it himself. In everything praiseworthy,
then, the excellent person awards himself what is fine. 35

In this way, then, we must be self-lovers, as we have said. But in the way 11(
the many are, we ought not to be.

## Note

[1] In the *Iliad*, Book I, lines 668 ff., when she solicits Zeus's help on behalf of her son
Achilles.

# Epicurus

## 341–271 B.C.E.

Perhaps no philosopher has been less well served by his adjective; even Plato is more "platonic" than Epicurus is "epicurean." Although Epicurus does teach that "pleasure is our first and kindred good," he does not advocate self-indulgent hedonism (from *hêdonê*, Greek for "pleasure"), as "epicurean" suggests in English. Rather, Epicurus defines "the magnitude of pleasure" as "the removal of all pain" (Diogenes Laertius 10.139), and he holds pain of the mind, e.g., anguish and fear, to be worse than physical pain. Injustice and lack of virtue are sources of mental pain, Epicurus holds, and therefore virtue is held to be a pleasure. The goal of life, as Epicurus describes it, is untroubledness, or tranquillity of mind, which is the equivalent of happiness.

Epicurus was born on the island of Samos. His father was an Athenian citizen, and Epicurus first went to Athens when he was eighteen, about the time that Aristotle was leaving it. We know little of his next fifteen years—he seems to have traveled back to Asia and taught there—but he returned to Athens around 307, bought a house and garden, and remained there for the rest of his life. He formed a community rather than a school, which was known as the "Garden" (*kêpos* in Greek); it was marked by its acceptance of women and slaves and the deep friendship between members that is one of the most admirable aspects of Epicurus' teaching. Epicurus seems not to have sought a highly public and visible life, but cultivated the kind of tranquillity that characterizes his teaching. He wrote voluminously, but we have very little of his writings. His works, however, remained canonical for his followers. One of our best sources of Epicureanism is the Roman writer Lucretius (99?–55? B.C.E.), who speaks of his devotion to Epicurus' "golden words" and lays out Epicurean doctrine in the six books of his didactic epic *De Rerum Natura*, "On the Nature of the Universe."

Like Stoicism, the other principal Hellenistic philosophy, Epicureanism is a materialist philosophy. Epicurus held that everything was composed of atoms and void, including the gods, mental perceptions, and the human soul. Since the human soul was corporeal, it would die with the body, and hence Epicurus taught that "death is nothing," simply a dissolution of the atoms that compose soul and body, and that humans should therefore have no fear of it. This fearlessness of death, however, was not to lead to rashness or the satisfaction of all bodily pleasures, because such pursuits lead to mental anguish. As

355

Epicurus says below, the "greatest good is prudence" and the best life is the one that accommodates itself to the simplest satisfactions of body and mind.

BSH

# Letter to Menoeceus, On Happiness

"Epicurus to Menoeceus, greeting.

"Let no one be slow to seek wisdom when he is young nor weary in the search thereof when he is grown old. For no age is too early or too late for the health of the soul. And to say that the season for studying philosophy has not yet come, or that it is past and gone, is like saying that the season for happiness is not yet or that it is now no more. Therefore, both old and young ought to seek wisdom, the former in order that, as age comes over him, he may be young in good things because of the grace of what has been, and the latter in order that, while he is young, he may at the same time be old, because he has no fear of the things which are to come. So we must exercise ourselves in the things which bring happiness, since, if that be present, we have everything, and, if that be absent, all our actions are directed toward attaining it.

"Those things which without ceasing I have declared unto thee, those do, and exercise thyself therein, holding them to be the elements of right life. First believe that God is a living being immortal and blessed, according to the notion of a god indicated by the common sense of mankind; and so believing, thou shalt not affirm of him aught that is foreign to his immortality or that agrees not with blessedness, but shalt believe about him whatever may uphold both his blessedness and his immortality. For verily there are gods, and the knowledge of them is manifest; but they are not such as the multitude believe, seeing that men do not steadfastly maintain the notions they form respecting them. Not the man who denies the gods worshipped by the multitude, but he who affirms of the gods what the multitude believes about them is truly impious. For the utterances of the multitude about the gods are not true preconceptions but false assumptions; hence it is that the greatest evils happen to the wicked and the greatest blessings happen to the good from the hand of the gods, seeing that they are always favourable to their own good qualities and take pleasure in men like unto themselves, but reject as alien whatever is not of their kind.

"Accustom thyself to believe that death is nothing to us, for good and evil imply sentience, and death is the privation of all sentience; therefore a right understanding that death is nothing to us makes the mortality of life enjoyable, not by adding to life an illimitable time, but by taking away the yearning after immortality. For life has no terrors for him who has thoroughly apprehended that there are no terrors for him in ceasing to live. Foolish, therefore, is the man who says that he fears death, not because it will pain when it comes, but because it pains in the prospect. Whatsoever causes no annoyance when it is present, causes only a groundless pain in the expectation. Death, therefore, the most awful of evils, is nothing to us, seeing that, when we are, death is not come, and, when death is come, we are not. It is nothing, then, either to the living or to the dead, for with the living it is not and the dead exist no longer. But in the world, at one time men shun death as the greatest of all evils, and at another time choose it as a respite from the evils in life. The wise man does not deprecate life nor does he fear the cessation of life. The thought of life is no offence to him, nor is the cessation of life regarded as an evil. And even as men choose of food not merely and simply the larger portion, but the more pleasant, so the wise seek to enjoy the time which is most pleasant and not merely that which is longest. And he who admonishes the young to live well and the old to make a good end speaks foolishly, not merely because of the desirableness of life, but because the same exercise at once teaches to live well and to die well. Much worse is he who says that it were good not to be born, but when once one is born to pass with all speed through the gates of Hades. For if he truly believes this, why does he not depart from life? It were easy for him to do so, if once he were firmly convinced. If he speaks only in mockery, his words are foolishness, for those who hear believe him not.

"We must remember that the future is neither wholly ours nor wholly not ours, so that neither must we count upon it as quite certain to come nor despair of it as quite certain not to come.

"We must also reflect that of desires some are natural, others are groundless; and that of the natural some are necessary as well as natural, and some natural only. And of the necessary desires some are necessary if we are to be happy, some if the body is to be rid of uneasiness, some if we are even to live. He who has a clear and certain understanding of these things will direct every preference and aversion toward securing health of body and tranquillity of mind, seeing that this is the sum and end of a blessed life. For the end of all our actions is to be free from pain and fear, and, when once we have attained all this, the tempest of the soul is laid; seeing that the living creature has no need to go in search of something that is lacking, nor to look for anything else by which the good of the soul and of the body will be fulfilled. When we are pained because of the absence of pleasure, then, and then only, do we feel the need of pleasure. Wherefore we call pleasure the alpha and omega of a blessed life. Pleasure is our first and kindred good. It is the starting-point of every choice and of every aversion, and to it we come back, inasmuch as we make feeling the rule by which to judge of every good thing. And since pleasure is our first and native good, for that reason we do not choose every pleasure whatsoever, but ofttimes pass over many pleasures when a greater annoyance ensues from them. And ofttimes we consider pains superior to pleasures when submission to the pains for a long time brings us as a consequence a greater pleasure. While therefore all pleasure because it is naturally akin to us is good, not all pleasure is choiceworthy, just as all pain is an evil and yet not all pain is to be shunned. It is, however, by measuring one against another, and by looking at the conveniences and inconveniences, that all these matters must be judged. Sometimes we treat the good as an evil, and the evil, on the contrary, as a good. Again, we regard independence of outward things as a great good, not so as in all cases to use little, but so as to be contented with little if we have not much, being honestly persuaded that they have the sweetest enjoyment of luxury who stand least in need of it, and that whatever is natural is easily procured and only the vain and worthless hard to win. Plain fare gives as much pleasure as a costly diet, when once the pain of want has been removed, while bread and water confer the highest possible pleasure when they are brought to hungry lips. To habituate one's self, therefore, to simple and inexpensive diet supplies all that is needful for health, and enables a man to meet the necessary requirements of life without shrinking, and it places us in a better condition when we approach at intervals a costly fare and renders us fearless of fortune.

"When we say, then, that pleasure is the end and aim, we do not mean the pleasures of the prodigal or the pleasures of sensuality, as we are understood to do by some through ignorance, prejudice, or wilful misrepresentation. By pleasure we mean the absence of pain in the body and of trouble in the soul. It is not an unbroken succession of drinking-bouts and of revelry, not sexual love, not the enjoyment of the fish and other delicacies of a luxurious table, which produce a pleasant life; it is sober reasoning, searching out the grounds of every choice and avoidance, and banishing those beliefs through which the greatest tumults take possession of the soul. Of all this the beginning and the greatest good is prudence. Wherefore prudence is a more precious thing even than philosophy; from it spring all the other virtues, for it teaches that we cannot lead a life of pleasure which is not also a life of prudence, honour, and justice; nor lead a life of prudence, honour, and justice, which is not also a life of pleasure. For the virtues have grown into one with a pleasant life, and a pleasant life is inseparable from them.

"Who, then, is superior in thy judgement to such a man? He holds a holy belief concerning the gods, and is altogether free from the fear of death. He has diligently considered the end fixed by nature, and understands how easily the limit of good things can be reached and attained, and how either the duration or the intensity of evils is but slight. Destiny, which some introduce as sovereign over all things, he laughs to scorn, affirming rather that some things happen of necessity, others by chance, others through our own agency. For he sees that necessity destroys responsibility and that chance or fortune is inconstant; whereas our own actions are free, and it is to them that praise and blame naturally attach. It were better, indeed, to accept the legends of the gods than to bow beneath that yoke of destiny which the natural philosophers have imposed. The one holds out some faint hope that we may escape if we honour the gods, while the necessity of the naturalists is deaf to all entreaties. Nor does he hold chance to be a god, as the world in general does, for in the acts of a god there is no disorder; nor to be a cause, though an uncertain one, for he believes that no good or evil is dispensed by chance to men so as to make life blessed, though it supplies the starting-point of great good and great evil. He believes that the misfortune of the wise is better than the prosperity of the fool. It is better, in short, that what is well judged in action should not owe its successful issue to the aid of chance.

"Exercise thyself in these and kindred precepts day and night, both by thyself and with him who is like unto thee; then never, either in waking or in dream, wilt thou be disturbed, but wilt live as a god among men. For man loses all semblance of mortality by living in the midst of immortal blessings."

# Callimachus

## Third Century B.C.E.

Along with Theocritus and Apollonius of Rhodes, Callimachus was one of the predominant figures in Hellenistic poetry. Unlike the works of his contemporaries, however, little of Callimachus' work survives. Although he is credited with over 800 "books" in ancient sources, we now have only six hymns, about sixty epigrams, and many fragments.

Callimachus was born in Cyrene, a city near the coast in modern Libya, perhaps around 310 B.C.E. He won the patronage of Ptolemy II Philadelphus in Alexandria, Egypt, which had become the principal cultural center of the Hellenistic world. Callimachus' statements about poetry represent a new development in the creation of art. Poetry no longer necessarily connects to or has a function in civic life, as the city-state yielded to the Hellenistic kingdom, and books begin to be written from books. Callimachus champions scholarly precision, refinement of style, and manipulation and innovation of generic categories, all of which characterize Hellenistic poetry in general. Some of Callimachus' fragments reveal his poetic principles: shorter poems, a "slender Muse," are better than longer poems, or as Callimachus famously says, "a big book is a big evil"; he writes not for the masses but for the few who understand; as he says in Epigram XVIII below, he does "not rejoice in the path that takes the many to and fro." His is almost an early version of "Art for art's sake." Callimachus did not convince everyone—his student Apollonius disagreed with his teacher and revived the epic form in his *Argonautica*—but the influence of Callimachean precision and refinement was considerable, especially on Roman poets such as Horace, Vergil, and Propertius, and through them, on us.

To our modern tastes, Callimachus' principles are most pleasantly revealed in his epigrams, modelled on funerary inscriptions. His variation, his lightness of touch, his wit, and his interest in emotion are clearly on display.

BSH

# Epigrams

## II (2)

Someone told me, Heracleitus,
that you were dead and brought me
close to tears, for I remembered
how often in our talk we put
the sun to bed. You, I suppose,
my Halicarnassian friend,
are ashes four times long ago,
but your nightingales still live.
On them Hades who snatches all
away shall not cast his hand.

## IV (5)

Timon, for you exist no more,
which do you hate more,
the darkness or the light?
"The dark, for the Great Majority
of you reside in Hades."

## XIX (21)

Here Philip the father buried
his twelve-year-old son
Nicoteles, his great hope.

## XX (22)

At dawn we buried Melanippus. At sunset
his sister Basilo died by her own hand.
She could not bear to place her brother upon
the pyre and live. The house of Aristippus,
their father, saw a double catastrophe,
and all Cyrene bowed her head when she saw
the house, once blessed in its children, thus bereft.

# XVII (19)

Would that there had never been swift ships!
We would not be mourning Sopolis, Diocleides' son.
But now his corpse floats in the sea somewhere, and we
pass by, instead of him, a name and an empty tomb.

# III (4)

Do not say "Godspeed" to me, wicked heart,
but pass on by. It will be Godspeed to me
if only you do not laugh.

# XXXI (33)

On the mountain, Epicydes the hunter seeks
every hare and the track of the roe deer, though chilled
by frost and snow. But if someone says, "Here,
this wild beast is shot," he refuses it.
Such is my love. It can follow all that flees,
but passes by what lies at its very side.

# XXVIII (30)

I hate the cyclic poem, nor do I rejoice
in the path that takes the many to and fro.
I loathe the roaming lover, nor do I drink
from every spring. I detest all common things.
Lysanius, you are comely, yes, comely. Before
Echo repeats, someone says, "Another's."

# XXXVIII (39)

These gifts to Aphrodite
did the fickle Simon
dedicate: a portrait
of herself, the band
that kissed her breasts,
her torch, and the wands
that the wretched girl
used to carry about.

## XXI (23, II 1–6)

Whoever passes by my tomb, know
that I am son and sire of Callimachus
of Cyrene. You would know them both, for once
the one led his fatherland in arms. The other
composed songs surpassing the strength of envy.
No wonder, for whom the Muses look upon
as children, not askance, they do not put
aside as friends, once their locks are white.
"Goodbye, O sun," said Cleombrotus of Ambracia
and jumped from a high wall into Hades. He'd seen
no evil worthy of death but had read one work
of Plato, that dialogue on the immortal soul.

# Theocritus

## Third Century B.C.E.

Theocritus worked in the first half of the third century B.C.E. He was born in Syracuse in Sicily, but was also active on the Greek island of Cos and in Egypt in Alexandria. He is best known for writing pastoral poetry set in an idealized countryside. *Idyll* 11 is one of his most enjoyable poems. Its humor centers on the contrast between the unsophisticated Polyphemus and his conventional romantic feelings towards the nymph Galatea. Theocritus portrays him not as the ferocious epic monster of the *Odyssey* but as an ordinary herdsman: we are amused by, yet sympathetic towards, a creature who ardently hopes that in a Cyclops with such splendid economic prospects, his one eye surrounded with the shaggy eyebrow will not be an insuperable barrier to love. The cheery, practical "plenty more fish in the sea" ending is quite characteristic of Theocritus' general outlook as a poet, as is his tendency to mix epic (the figure of the Cyclops) with other genres (such as the pastoral scene).

Theocritus' poetic range extends beyond purely pastoral poetry to other subjects, such as the myth of Heracles and Hylas (*Idyll* 13): whereas his contemporary Apollonius handles such a story in a traditional epic style, Theocritus' narrative concentrates on small details and is typical of the branch of Hellenistic poetry most famously represented by Callimachus, who championed such small-scale writing over epic. Theocritus was an influence on Bion and remained popular in the ancient world after his death. Vergil took Theocritus as the inspiration for his *Eclogues* which, in their turn, inspire a long tradition of European pastoral poetry. There is a famous representation of the story of Hylas and the nymphs by the pre-Raphaelite painter J. W. Waterhouse.

SJVM

# from *Idylls*

## XI  Cyclops

For love there is no other drug, Nicias,
it seems to me, neither unguent nor salve,
than the Muses. This remedy is delicate
and sweet for mortal men, but not easy to find.
You know this well, of course, as a doctor and one
whom the nine Muses love exceedingly well.
So at least the Cyclops, my countryman,
Polyphemus of old, got along quite well when he loved
Galatea and the down was just showing
on his temples and chin. He didn't woo her
with apples or roses or ringlets, but with sheer madness.
He counted everything else beside the point.
Often his sheep would come back to the fold themselves
from the green pastures while he, alone, would sing
from dawn of Galatea, wasting away
upon the shore where the seaweed lay. He had
beneath his heart a most angry wound, where
the mighty Cyprian goddess[1] had fixed her shaft.
But he found the cure. He'd sit upon a cliff
and gaze out to sea while he sang songs like these:
O white Galatea, why do you spurn your lover?
Galatea—whiter than curd to see, more tender
than the lamb, more skittish than the calf,
more glistening than the unripe grape. Why
do you come when sweet sleep embraces me
and go when sweet sleep releases me—
as the ewe goes when she glimpses the gray wolf?
I fell in love with you, girl, when first
you came with your mother to pick the hyacinths
that grow upon the hill and I showed you the path.
Once I'd seen you, I couldn't stop—not then
or later or even now. But you don't care.
No, by Zeus, no, you don't care at all.
I know, my charming girl, why you shun me.

It's because a single shaggy eyebrow stretches
from ear to ear across my whole forehead.
There is just one eye beneath and the nose
is broad above my lip. But still, such
that I am, I tend a thousand head of cattle.
From them I draw and drink the best of milk.
I never lack for cheese, neither in summer
nor autumn nor in the worst of winter. My racks
are always weighted down. No other Cyclops
can pipe as I can, singing of me and you,
my darling sweet apple, many times
in the depths of night. I raise eleven fawns
with collars for you and four bear cubs.
Come to me and you'll have no less than these.
Leave the gray sea to gasp on the shore.
You'll sleep more sweetly here in my cave with me.
There are bays there and slender cypresses.
There is dark ivy and the vine with its sweet fruit.
There is cool water, which heavily wooded Aetna
sheds from her white snows, an ambrosial drink
for me. Who would choose the waves of the sea
rather than these? But if I myself seem
too shaggy to you, I have logs of oak and beneath
the ash an everlasting fire. With these
you may burn my soul and even my single eye—
for there is nothing sweeter than that to me.
O dear, I wish that my mother had borne me with gills—
I could have dived down to you and kissed
your hand if you won't allow me to kiss your mouth.
I'd have brought you white lilies or soft poppies
with petals of scarlet. But one grows in summer,
the other in winter. I couldn't have brought them both
together. Now, my girl, I'll learn straightway
at least to swim, if only some stranger would come,
sailing here in his ship, so that I could know
what pleasure you find to dwell there in the depths.
Come out, Galatea, and when you've come out,
forget, as I do, to go home again.
Shepherd with me and milk and set the cheese
with acid drops of rennet. My mother alone

does me wrong and I blame her. For never
once has she said a kind word for me
to you, though she sees that I grow thinner
day by day. I shall tell her that my head
throbs and my feet throb so that she may suffer—
since I suffer. O Cyclops, Cyclops, where
have your wits flown? You'd show much better sense
if you'd go out and weave crates for your cheese
and gather and bring fresh green shoots for your lambs.
Milk the ewe that's here. Why chase the one
that's gone? Perhaps you'll find another Galatea
lovelier than this. Many girls ask me
to play by night and giggle too when I listen.
It's obvious that on land I am someone.

So did the Cyclops shepherd his love with song
and fared better than if he'd spent gold.

## XIII Hylas

Not for us alone did the god, Nicias,
as once we thought, beget that child Love,
not for us did the fair first seem fair,
for we are mortal and do not see tomorrow.
But even Amphitryon's son[2] of brazen heart
who survived the savage lion loved a boy,
the charming Hylas who wore his hair long.
He taught him all, as a father his own son,
that had made him noble and worthy of song.
He never parted from him, not even at noon,
nor when Dawn drove her white steeds to the sky,
nor when the twittering chicks looked to their roost
and their mother ruffled her wings on her sooty perch.
He wanted the boy to be shaped to his taste, and become
in his companionship a true man.
But when Jason sailed in search of the golden fleece,
Aeson's son, and the nobles joined his crew,
chosen from all the cities that could be of use,
there came to rich Iolcus the laboring man,
son of Alcmena,[3] heroine of Midea.
With him Hylas embarked on the well-benched Argo.

The ship kept free of the clashing dark blue rocks
and at running speed rushed into Phasis' deep—
like an eagle—a great gulf. Since then the rocks
stand well apart. But when the Pleiades rose
and the farthest fields pastured the young lambs,
in spring, the godlike band remembered their trip,
and the heroes sat down in Argo, the hollow ship,
and anchored the third day of a south wind
at the Hellespont within Propontis where Cian
oxen made wide the furrows with worn plow.
Stepping upon the shore, in pairs, they dined
at evening, and many made a single couch,
for the meadow supplied a great bed of leaves,
and they cut deep galingale and flowering rush,
and blond Hylas set off with brazen pail
to fetch water for dinner for Heracles
and sturdy Telamon, those comrades who feasted
always at one table. He soon found a spring
in low-lying ground. Rushes grew around
and dark swallowwort, green maidenhair,
pliant parsley, and creeping dog's tooth.
Amid the water the nymphs were beginning their dance—
they never sleep, are dread to countryfolk—
Eunice and Malis and Nycheia with glances of spring.
The boy held forth his wide-mouthed pail for drink,
reaching to dip. The nymphs all grasped at his hand,
for love had fluttered the wits of all of them
for the Argive boy. Into the black water
he fell headlong, as when a fiery star
falls into the sea and a sailor cries,
"Make your tackle tight, my boys—it's a sailing wind!"
The nymphs held the lad upon their knees and tried
with tender words to comfort him while he wept.
But Amphitryon's son, frantic at loss of the boy,
was gone with his bow bent in the Scythian way
and his club, which he always kept in his right hand.
Three times "Hylas" he called from the depths of his throat.
Three times the boy replied, but his voice came faint
from the spring. Though very near, he seemed far,
as when a carnivorous lion hears the voice

of a fawn and speeds from his lair for a ready meal,
so Heracles amid the untrodden thorns
was wracked by his love for the boy. He covered much ground—
lovers are wretched—wandering over hills
and oak groves, and Jason he quite forgot.
The ship had its rig aloft, its crew on hand,
but at midnight the heroes took down the sails again
awaiting him who went where his feet led,
crazed, for a god had cruelly torn his heart.
And so the lovely Hylas is counted among
the blest, and the heroes mocked Heracles
because he deserted the Argo of sixty oars
and went to Colchis and unfriendly Phasis on foot.

## Notes

[1] Aphrodite.
[2] Heracles.
[3] Heracles.

# Cleanthes

## 331–232 B.C.E.

Cleanthes was the second head of the Stoa, the school begun in Athens by Zeno of Kitium (Cyprus) around 330 B.C.E., which we know as Stoicism. Cleanthes was a student of Zeno, and like his teacher, Cleanthes came to Athens from the east, from Assos on the coast of Asia Minor across from Lesbos. His biographical details are sketchy and anecdotal—Diogenes Laertius says that Cleanthes was a boxer by trade, lived a very ascetic life, and starved himself to death—and few of his writings survive. From his extant fragments and the writings of others, Cleanthes seems principally to have expounded Zeno's doctrines and innovated little, especially in relation to his successor, Chrysippus. In his most substantial fragment, the *Hymn to Zeus*, Cleanthes exhibits a nearly religious fervor. He follows Zeno in associating Zeus with Nature (*phusis*), with fire (*pneuma*), and with divine and perfect rationality (*logos*), the principle that governs all that is. The *Hymn to Zeus*, written in dactylic hexameter, follows a tripartite structure. The middle third is concerned with a central problem in Stoicism, namely, human evil in a divinely governed world. Cleanthes solves this with a solution reminiscent of the Pre-Socratic Heraclitus: Zeus incorporates even evil into his good plan, and "makes the odd even" (line 18), and "harmonizes all the good with the bad into one" (line 20). The Stoics were always interested in poetry and its interpretation, and several wrote poetry themselves, but this is certainly the best poetic expression of Stoic physics, theology, and ethics to have reached us from antiquity.

BSH

# Hymn to Zeus

Most glorious of the immortals, called by many names, ever all-mighty
Zeus, leader of nature, guiding everything with law
Hail! For it is right that all mortals should address you,
since all are descended from you and imitate your voice,
alone of all the mortals which live and creep upon the earth.
So I will sing your praises and hymn your might always.
This entire cosmos which revolves around the earth obeys you,
wherever you might lead it, and is willingly ruled by you;
such is [the might of] your thunderbolt, a two-edged helper
in your invincible hands, fiery and everliving;
for by its blows all deeds in nature are <accomplished>.
By it you straighten the common rational principle which penetrates
all things, being mixed with lights both great and small.
By it you have become such a lofty power and king forever.
Nor does any deed occur on earth without you, god,
neither in the aithereal divine heaven nor on the sea,
except for the deeds of the wicked in their folly.
But you know how to set straight what is crooked,
and to put in order what is disorderly; for you, what is not dear is dear.
For thus you have fitted together all good things with the bad,
so that there is one eternal rational principle for them all—
and it is this which the wicked flee from and neglect,
ill-fated, since they always long for the possession of good things
and do not see the common law of god, nor do they hear it;
and if they obeyed it sensibly they would have a good life.
But fools they be, impelled each to his own evil,
some with a strife-torn zeal for glory,
others devoted to gain in undue measure,
others devoted to release and the pleasures of the body.
. . . they are swept off in pursuit of different things at different times
while rushing to acquire the exact opposites of these things above all.
But Zeus, giver of all, you of the dark clouds, of the blazing thunderbolt,
save men from their baneful inexperience
and disperse it, father, far from their souls; grant that they may achieve
the wisdom with which you confidently guide all with justice
so that we may requite you with honour for the honour you give us

praising your works continually, as is fitting
for mortals; for there is no greater prize, neither for mortals
nor for gods, than to praise with justice the common law forever.

# Bion

## Second Century B.C.E.

About Bion very little is known apart from his birthplace, Smyrna, and his assignment in antiquity as the third pastoral poet after Theocritus and Moschus. He probably lived around the end of the second century B.C.E. In all, only about 200 verses ascribed to him survive; his most important work is the "Lament for Adonis."

The stylized lament is not a Hellenistic Greek invention. The *Iliad* ends with laments for Hector, and tragedy easily incorporates lamentation. In these earlier literary examples, ritual lamentation belongs to women, as it apparently did in Greek life. The ritualization of expressions of grief, some scholars suggest, kept grief (and thus the women) in check, and prevented it from becoming a powerful and unrestrained force. The Hellenistic lament seems to go in the opposite direction. The Hellenistic poets, with their profound interest in the emotions and their artistic representation, explored the emotion of grief in new ways, connecting it with love and loss, attributing it to the natural world, even finding a kind of aesthetic beauty in death and dying. And they represent men as participating in the lament. Theocritus' *Idyll* I, which is not presented in this anthology, seems to be the first example of this sub-genre, pastoral elegy. Bion's "Lament for Adonis," as the translator Barbara Hughes Fowler notes, has "gone beyond Theocritean sensuousness to a startling sensuality" (1990:xvi). Bion lavishes details of dress and gesture and color; Adonis' death effects the entire world.

As artificial as this example may feel to us, the Hellenistic pastoral elegies have influenced several notable successors, among them several of Vergil's *Eclogues*, Milton's *Lycidas*, Shelley's *Adonais* (for Keats), and Matthew Arnold's *Thyrsis*.

BSH

# Lament for Adonis

I weep for Adonis, "The lovely Adonis is dead."
"Dead the lovely Adonis," the Loves weep too.

No longer in crimson cover, Cypris, sleep.
Arise in dark robes, and beat your breasts
and say to all, "The lovely Adonis is dead."

I weep for Adonis. The Loves weep too.

The lovely Adonis lies in the hills, his thigh
struck with the tusk, white against white,
and Cypris grieves as he breathes his delicate last.
His black blood drips down his snowy flesh,
his eyes are numb beneath his brows, and the rose
flees from his lips. The kiss dies too. Cypris
will have it never again. The kiss of the dead
is enough, but Adonis knows not that she's kissed him dead.

I weep for Adonis. The Loves weep too.

Savage the wound that Adonis has in his thigh.
Cythereia[1] bears a greater wound in her heart.
His own hounds howl for that boy. The Oread
nymphs bewail him too, and Aphrodite
unbraids her hair, and through the oak woods
she wails, distraught, disheveled, unsandaled, and the wild
brambles tear and cull her sacred blood.
Shrilling through the long glens she goes,
calling her Assyrian lord, her child.
The black blood spouted about his navel.
His chest was crimsoned from his thighs. His breasts,
white as snow before, were scarlet now.

Alas for Cythereia. The Loves wail too.

She lost her lovely man. She lost her sacred
beauty, the beauty she had while Adonis lived.
Her beauty died with Adonis. "Alas for Cypris,"[2]
all the mountains say, and the oaks, "For Adonis woe,"
and the rivers weep for Aphrodite's grief,

and the springs in the hills shed tears for Adonis,
and the blossoms blush red from grief. Cythera
through all its vales, through every glen, sings,
"Alas for Cythereia. The lovely Adonis is dead."

And Echo replies, "The lovely Adonis is dead."
Who would not have wept for Cypris' dreadful
love? When she saw Adonis' fatal wound,
when she saw the crimson blood around his wasting
thigh, spreading her arms, she cried, "Wait,
Adonis, allow me to touch you one last time.
I want to embrace you, press my lips to yours.

"Adonis, stay, kiss me one last time.
Kiss me just so long as the kiss lives.
Until you breathe your life away into
my mouth, your breath into my heart, your sweet
kiss I'll milk. I'll drain your love. I'll keep
this kiss as I do Adonis himself since you
abandon me and go to far-off Acheron,[3]
to its grim and hateful king, while I, alas
a goddess, must live and cannot follow you.
Persephone, take my spouse. You're stronger than I.
All that is lovely comes to you, but I
am ill-fated. I have insatiable grief,
and I weep for Adonis who's dead to me. I'm afraid
of you. You die, O thrice-desired. Like a dream
my love has fluttered away, and Cythereia
is widowed now. Bereft are the Loves in her house.
Her embroidered sash is lost too. Oh, why
were you so bold? Why did you hunt? Why,
being fair, were you so mad to wrestle the beast?"
So did Cypris lament. The Loves wailed too.
Alas Cythereia, the lovely Adonis is dead.

The Paphian sheds as many tears as Adonis
shed blood and every drop becomes a bud;
the blood bears roses; the tears, anemones.

I weep for Adonis, "The lovely Adonis is dead."

No longer in the oak thickets mourn your man,
Cypris. The lonely leaves make no bed

for Adonis. Let Adonis, now dead, share
your bed, Cythereia. He is a lovely corpse,
a lovely corpse, just as though he slept.
Lay him in soft coverlets in which
he spent the night in sacred sleep with you.
On the golden couch lay the disheveled Adonis.
Cover him with garlands and flowers. As he
died, so also all the blossoms withered.
Sprinkle him with Syrian ointments and myrrh.
Let all the perfumes die. Your perfume is dead.
Delicate Adonis lies in robes
of purple. Around him the Loves moan and wail.
They cut their hair for Adonis. One
cast arrows, another a bow, a quiver, a feather.
One loosed Adonis' sandal. One bore water
in a golden pitcher, another washed his thighs.
One, behind, fanned the lad with his wings.

"Alas, Cythereia," the Loves wail too.

Hymen[4] has quenched every lamp at the door
and scattered the bridal wreath. No longer
does he sing the wedding song but more
"Woe for Adonis." The Graces weep for the son
of Cinyras, "Lovely Adonis is dead." More
shrilly they cry "Woe" than they sing the Paean.
Even the Fates weep and wail, "Adonis,"
and sing a spell to bring him back, but he
can't hear them. It's not that he's not willing
but that the Maiden will not let him go.

Cease your grieving today, Cythereia, cease
beating your breasts. You must wail again,
weep again, come another year.

## Notes

[1] Aphrodite.

[2] Aphrodite.

[3] The river crossed by the souls of the departed; here refers to Hades.

[4] The god of marriage.

# Polybius

## ca. 200–118 B.C.E.

From the fourth–second centuries B.C.E., the work of no Hellenistic historian survives, except for Polybius. His methodology, which he called *pragmatike historia*, was based on documents and written memoirs, eyewitness accounts, and his own first-hand knowledge of geography and certain historical events. Even so, his history is not free from speculation, subjectivity, and error; it is however, worthy of study not only because it is one of few written sources for this period of history in Greece and Rome, but also because, despite his shortcomings, Polybius attempted something new: a history that would describe and explain Rome's rise to world dominion.

Perhaps you are wondering why a Greek would write about the power of Rome? We must turn to Polybius' personal history for the answer, which competes in interest with the works he wrote. During Rome's conquest of Greece, a certain Greek diplomat submitted to Rome a list of one thousand Greeks whom he considered to be "unfriendly" to Roman interests. Polybius was on that list. The thousand were arrested and brought to Rome, and were subsequently detained in various towns in Italy without a trial, because Rome believed them to be a potential danger to the state. Luckily for Polybius, a Roman nobleman befriended him and he was allowed to stay in Rome. Because of this friendship, Polybius remained in Rome after his release and became part of the literary elite of his day. Like other "Romanized" Greeks of his time, he supported the settlement of Greece as a Roman province and at the same time advocated philhellenism in Roman culture. The story goes that he died at the ripe old age of 82 after suffering a fall from his horse.

This excerpt from Book 6 is a pivotal study of "The Roman Constitution." Polybius formulates a unique theory of Roman government: the secret of its success was its "mixed constitution," a blend of aristocracy (the consuls), oligarchy (the Senate), and democracy (the popular assemblies). His view has remained influential in Western civilization, and probably helped to shape some aspects of the American Constitution.

LH

# from *The Histories*

11. . . . I am fully conscious that to those who have been brought up under the Roman constitution I shall appear to give an inadequate account of it by the omission of certain details. Knowing accurately every portion of it from personal experience, and from having been bred up in its customs and laws from childhood, they will not be struck so much by the accuracy of the description as annoyed by its omissions; nor will they believe that the historian has purposely omitted unimportant distinctions, but will attribute his silence upon the origin of existing institutions or other important facts to ignorance. What is told they depreciate as insignificant or beside the purpose, what is omitted they desiderate as vital to the question, their object being to appear to know more than the writers. But a good critic should judge a writer not by what he leaves unsaid, but from what he says; if he detects misstatements in the latter, he may then feel certain that ignorance accounts for the former; but if what he says is accurate, his omissions ought to be attributed to deliberate judgement and not to ignorance. So much for those whose criticisms are prompted by personal ambition rather than by justice. . . .

As for the Roman constitution, it had the three elements controlling the constitution which I have mentioned before; and their respective share of power in the whole state had been regulated with such a scrupulous regard to equality and equilibrium that no one could say for certain, not even a native, whether the constitution as a whole were an aristocracy or democracy or monarchy. And no wonder, for if we confine our observation to the power of the consuls we should be inclined to regard it as monarchic and kingly; if to that of the Senate, as aristocratic; and if finally one looks at the power possessed by the people it would seem a clear case of a democracy. What the exact powers of these several parts were and still, with slight modifications, are, I will now state.

12. The consuls, before leading out the legions, remain in Rome and are supreme masters of the administration. All other magistrates, except the tribunes, are under them and take their orders. They introduce foreign ambassadors to the Senate, bring matters requiring deliberation before it, and see to the execution of its decrees. If, again, there are any matters of state which require the authorization of the people, it is their business to see to them, to summon the assemblies, to bring the proposals before them, and to carry out the decrees of the people. In the preparations for war also, and in a word in the entire administration of a campaign, they have all but absolute power. It is compe-

tent to them to impose on the allies such levies as they think good, to appoint the military tribunes, to make up the roll for soldiers and select those that are suitable. Besides they have absolute power of inflicting punishment on all who are under their command while on active service; and they have authority to expend as much of the public money as they choose, being accompanied by a quaestor who is entirely at their orders. A survey of these powers alone would in fact justify our describing the constitution as purely monarchic and royal. Nor will it affect the truth of my description if any of the institutions I have described are changed in our time, or in that of our posterity, and the same remarks apply to what follows.

13. The Senate has first of all the control of the treasury, and regulates the receipts and disbursements alike. For the quaestors[1] cannot issue any public money for the various departments of the state without a decree of the Senate, except for the service of the consuls. The Senate controls also what is by far the largest and most important expenditure, that, namely, which is made by the censors every five years for the repair or construction of public buildings; this money cannot be obtained by the censors except by the grant of the Senate. Similarly all crimes committed in Italy requiring a public investigation, such as treason, conspiracy, poisoning, or willful murder, are in the hands of the Senate. Besides, if any individual or state among the Italian allies requires a controversy to be settled, a penalty to be assessed, help or protection to be afforded—all this is the province of the Senate. Or again, outside Italy, if it is necessary to send an embassy to reconcile warring communities, or to remind them of their duty, or sometimes to impose requisitions upon them, or to receive their submission, or finally to proclaim war against them—this too is the business of the Senate. In like manner the reception to be given to foreign ambassadors in Rome, and the answer to be returned to them, are decided by the Senate. With such business the people have nothing to do. Consequently, if one were staying at Rome when the consuls were not in town, one would imagine the constitution to be a complete aristocracy: and this has been the idea entertained by many Greeks, and by many kings as well, from the fact that nearly all the business they had with Rome was settled by the Senate.

14. After this one would naturally be inclined to ask what part is left for the people in the constitution, when the Senate has these various functions, especially the control of the receipts and expenditures of the exchequer; and when the consuls, again, have absolute power over the details of military preparation and an absolute authority in the field. There is, however, a part left the people, and it is a most important one. For the people is the sole fountain of honour and of punishment, and it is by these two things and these alone that dynasties and constitutions and, in a word, human society are held together;

for where the distinction between them is not sharply drawn both in theory and practice, there no undertaking can be properly administered—as indeed we might expect when good and bad are held in exactly the same honour. The people then are the only court to decide matters of life and death, and even in cases where the penalty is money, if the sum to be assessed is sufficiently serious, and especially when the accused have held the higher magistracies. And in regard to this arrangement there is one point deserving especial commendation and record. Men who are on trial for their lives at Rome, while sentence is in process of being voted—if even only one of the tribes whose votes are needed to ratify the sentence has not voted—have the privilege of openly departing and condemning themselves to a voluntary exile. Such men are safe at Naples, Praeneste, or Tibur, and at the other towns with which this arrangement has been duly ratified on oath.

Again, it is the people who bestow offices on the deserving, which are the most honourable rewards of virtue. It has also the absolute power of passing or repealing laws, and, most important of all, it is the people who deliberate on the question of war or peace. And when provisional terms are made for alliance, suspension of hostilities, or treaties, it is the people who ratify them or the reverse. These considerations again would lead one to say that the chief power in the state was the people's, and that the constitution was a democracy.

15. Such, then, is the distribution of power between the several parts of the state. I must now show how these several parts can, when they choose, oppose or support each other.

The consul, then, when he has started on an expedition with the powers I have described, is to all appearance absolute in the administration of the business in hand; still he has need of the support both of people and Senate, and without them is quite unable to bring the matter to a successful conclusion. For it is plain that he must have supplies sent to his legions from time to time, but without a decree of the Senate they can be supplied neither with food nor clothes nor pay, so that all the plans of a commander must be futile if the Senate is resolved either to shrink from danger or hamper his plans. And again, whether a consul shall bring any undertaking to a conclusion or not depends entirely upon the Senate, for it has absolute authority at the end of a year to send another consul to supersede him, or to continue the existing one in his command. Again, even to the successes of the generals the Senate has the power to add distinction and glory, and on the other hand to obscure their merits and lower their credit. For these high achievements are brought in tangible form before the eyes of the citizens by what are called "triumphs." But these triumphs the commanders can not celebrate with proper pomp, or in some cases celebrate at all, unless the Senate concurs and grants the necessary money. As for the people, the consuls are pre-eminently obliged to court their favour, however distant from home may be their field of operations, for it is the people, as I have said before, that ratifies, or refuses to ratify, terms of peace and treaties, but most of all because when laying down their office they have to give an account of their administration before it. Therefore in no case is it safe for the consuls to neglect either the Senate or the good will of the people.

16. As for the Senate, which possesses the immense power I have described, in the first place it is obliged in public affairs to take the multitude into account, and respect the wishes of the people; and it cannot put into execution the penalty for offences against the republic which are punishable with death, unless the people first ratify its decrees. Similarly even in matters which directly affect the senators—for instance, in the case of a law diminishing the Senate's traditional authority, or depriving senators of certain dignities and offices, or even actually cutting down their property—even in such cases the people have the sole power of passing or rejecting the law. But most important of all is the fact that if a single tribune interposes his veto, the Senate not only is unable to pass a decree, but cannot even hold a meeting at all, whether formal or informal. Now, the tribunes are always bound to carry out the decree of the people, and above all things to have regard to their wishes; therefore, for all these reasons the Senate stands in awe of the multitude, and cannot neglect the feelings of the people.

17. In like manner the people on its part is far from being independent of the Senate, and is bound to take its wishes into account both collectively and individually. For contracts, too numerous to count, are given out by the censors in all parts of Italy for the repair or construction of public buildings; there is also the collection of revenue from many rivers, harbours, gardens, mines, and land—everything, in a word, that comes under the control of the Roman government—and in all these the people at large are engaged, so that there is scarcely a man, so to speak, who is not interested in these contracts and the profits from them. For some purchase the contracts from the censors for themselves, and others go partners with them, while others again go surety for these contractors, or actually pledge their property to the treasury for them. Now over all these transactions the Senate has absolute control. It can grant an extension of time, and in case of unforeseen accident can relieve the contractors from a portion of their obligation, or release them from it altogether if they are absolutely unable to fulfill it. And there are many details in which the Senate can inflict great hardship, or, on the other hand, grant great indulgences to the contractors, for in every case the appeal is to it. But the most important point of all is that the judges are taken from its members in the majority of trials, whether public or private, in which the charges are

heavy. Consequently all citizens are much at its mercy and, being alarmed at the uncertainty as to when they may need its aid, are cautious about resisting or actively opposing its will. And for a similar reason men do not rashly resist the wishes of the consuls, because one and all may become subject to their absolute authority on a campaign.

18. The result of this power of the several estates for mutual help or harm is a union sufficiently firm for all emergencies, and a constitution than which it is impossible to find a better. For whenever any danger from without compels them to unite and work together, the strength which is developed by the state is so extraordinary that everything required is unfailingly carried out by the eager rivalry shown by all classes to devote their whole minds to the needs of the hour, and to secure that any determination come to should not fail for want of promptitude; while each individual works, privately and publicly allke, for the accomplishment of the business at hand. Accordingly, the peculiar constitution of the state makes it irresistible, and certain of obtaining whatever it determines to attempt. Nay, even when these external alarms are past, and the people are enjoying their good fortune and the fruits of their victories, and, as usually happens, growing corrupted by flattery and idleness, show a tendency to violence and arrogance—it is in these circumstances more than ever that the constitution is seen to possess within itself the power of correcting abuses. For when any one of the three classes becomes puffed up, and manifests an inclination to be contentious and unduly encroaching, the mutual interdependence of all the three, and the possibility of the pretensions of any being checked and thwarted by the others, must plainly check this tendency; and so the proper equilibrium is maintained by the impulsiveness of the one part being checked by its fear of the other. . . .

## Note

[1] Holders of the lowest annual magistracy, responsible for the Treasury, Quaestors became Senators for life.

# Epictetus

## ca. 50–130 C.E.

According to his somewhat confused biographical tradition, Epictetus was born in Hieropolis in Phrygia (mentioned by St. Paul in Colossians 4:13) and became a slave of Epaphroditus, one of Nero's former slaves and administrators. Eventually freed, Epictetus became a student of Stoicism under Musonius Rufus, and later taught in Rome until he was expelled by the emperor Domitian around 89 C.E. Epictetus set up a school in Nicopolis, near the Bay of Actium in northwestern Greece, and there he attracted wealthy Romans. Among his students was Arrian, who recorded Epictetus' oral teachings. Two works survive: four books of *Discourses* (there may originally have been eight books) and a smaller collection distilled from the *Discourses*, called the *Encheiridion*, or the *Handbook*. The *Discourses* reveal more of Epictetus' personality and his relationship with students, but the *Handbook* conveys the essential thought of Epictetus. Stoicism adapted to challenges from other philosophies (e.g., the Skeptics and Academics) and to new social circumstances (the dominance of Rome), and modern scholars identify early, middle, and late periods of Stoic philosophy.

Epictetus, along with the Romans Seneca (ca. 4 B.C.E.–65 C.E.) and Marcus Aurelius (121–180 C.E.), represents the late Stoa, and theirs are the only works to reach us from antiquity. Nevertheless, much of Epictetus' Stoicism is consistent with the teachings of Zeno, Cleanthes, and Chrysippus, the early Stoics, who lived nearly four centuries before him.

For all Stoics, virtue (*aretê* in Greek) is the sole good, and it consists in "living according to Nature." Epictetus repeatedly distinguishes the things that are "up to us"—our judgments, impulses, desires, and aversions—from those things that are not "up to us"—our health, wealth, reputation, and status (Chapter 1). The Stoic moral progressor disciplines herself to identify good and bad only with what is up to her; everything else that is out of her control, she regards as indifferent and immaterial to happiness. This teaching occasionally seems inhuman, as when Epictetus suggests that one regard the loss of a spouse or child as one would a broken jug (Chapter 3), and its deterministic outlook (e.g., Chapter 8) offers little hope to persons in difficult social or familial situations. But the goal of Stoicism is not simply self-discipline, but rather inner tranquillity and happiness, and Epictetus' essential insight, that our happiness is bound up with our valuation of things, seems indisputably right. Like a good teacher, Epictetus makes liberal use of analogies (e.g., traveler, Chapter 7; actor, Chapter 17; athlete, Chapter 29) and provides examples, especially in the figure of Socrates (Chapters 5, 33, 46). The *Handbook* ends with several quotations, two of which are Socratic; the first is from Cleanthes' *Hymn to Zeus*.

BSH

# from *Handbook of Epictetus*

1. Some things are up to us and some are not up to us. Our opinions are up to us, and our impulses, desires, aversions—in short, whatever is our own doing. Our bodies are not up to us, nor are our possessions, our reputations, or our public offices, or, that is, whatever is not our own doing. The things that are up to us are by nature free, unhindered, and unimpeded; the things that are not up to us are weak, enslaved, hindered, not our own. So remember, if you think that things naturally enslaved are free or that things not your own are your own, you will be thwarted, miserable, and upset, and will blame both gods and men. But if you think that only what is yours is yours, and that what is not your own is, just as it is, not your own, then no one will ever coerce you, no one will hinder you, you will blame no one, you will not accuse anyone, you will not do a single thing unwillingly, you will have no enemies, and no one will harm you, because you will not be harmed at all.

As you aim for such great goals, remember that you must not undertake them by acting moderately, but must let some things go completely and postpone others for the time being. But if you want both those great goals and also to hold public office and to be rich, then you may perhaps not get even the latter just because you aim at the former too; and you certainly will fail to get the former, which are the only things that yield freedom and happiness.

From the start, then, work on saying to each harsh appearance,[1] "You are an appearance, and not at all the thing that has the appearance." Then examine it and assess it by these yardsticks that you have, and first and foremost by whether it concerns the things that are up to us or the things that are not up to us. And if it is about one of the things that is not up to us, be ready to say, "You are nothing in relation to me."

2. Remember, what a desire proposes is that you gain what you desire, and what an aversion proposes is that you not fall into what you are averse to. Someone who fails to get what he desires is *un*fortunate, while someone who falls into what he is averse to has met *mis*fortune. So if you are averse only to what is against nature among the things that are up to you, then you will never fall into anything that you are averse to; but if you are averse to illness or death or poverty, you will meet misfortune. So detach your aversion from everything not up to us, and transfer it to what is against nature among the things that are up to us. And for the time being eliminate desire completely, since if you desire something that is not up to us, you are bound to be unfortunate, and at the same time none of the things that are up to us, which it would be good

386

to desire, will be available to you. Make use only of impulse and its contrary, rejection, though with reservation, lightly, and without straining.

3. In the case of everything attractive or useful or that you are fond of, remember to say just what sort of thing it is, beginning with the least little things. If you are fond of a jug, say "I am fond of a jug!" For then when it is broken you will not be upset. If you kiss your child or your wife, say that you are kissing a human being; for when it dies you will not be upset. . . .

5. What upsets people is not things themselves but their judgments about the things. For example, death is nothing dreadful (or else it would have appeared dreadful to Socrates), but instead the judgment about death that it is dreadful—*that* is what is dreadful. So when we are thwarted or upset or distressed, let us never blame someone else but rather ourselves, that is, our own judgments. An uneducated person accuses others when he is doing badly; a partly educated person accuses himself, an educated person accuses neither someone else nor himself. . . .

7. On a voyage when your boat has anchored, if you want to get fresh water you may pick up a small shellfish and a vegetable by the way, but you must keep your mind fixed on the boat and look around frequently in case the captain calls. If he calls you must let all those other things go so that you will not be tied up and thrown on the ship like livestock. That is how it is in life too: if you are given a wife and a child instead of a vegetable and a small shellfish, that will not hinder you; but if the captain calls, let all those things go and run to the boat without turning back; and if you are old, do not even go very far from the boat, so that when the call comes you are not left behind.

8. Do not seek to have events happen as you want them to, but instead want them to happen as they do happen, and your life will go well. . . .

15. Remember, you must behave as you do at a banquet. Something is passed around and comes to you: reach out your hand politely and take some. It goes by: do not hold it back. It has not arrived yet: do not stretch your desire out toward it, but wait until it comes to you. In the same way toward your children, in the same way toward your wife, in the same way toward public office, in the same way toward wealth, and you will be fit to share a banquet with the gods. But if when things are set in front of you, you do not take them but despise them, then you will not only share a banquet with the gods but also be a ruler along with them. For by acting in this way Diogenes and Heraclitus[2] and people like them were deservedly gods and were deservedly called gods. . . .

17. Remember that you are an actor in a play, which is as the playwright wants it to be: short if he wants it short, long if he wants it long. If he wants you to play a beggar, play even this part skillfully, or a cripple, or a public offi-

cial, or a private citizen. What is yours is to play the assigned part well. But to choose it belongs to someone else. . . .

21. Let death and exile and everything that is terrible appear before your eyes every day, especially death; and you will never have anything contemptible in your thoughts or crave anything excessively. . . .

23. If it ever happens that you turn outward to want to please another person, certainly you have lost your plan of life. Be content therefore in everything to be a philosopher, and if you want to seem to be one, make yourself appear so to yourself, and you will be capable of it. . . .

29. For each action, consider what leads up to it and what follows it, and approach it in the light of that. Otherwise you will come to it enthusiastically at first, since you have not borne in mind any of what will happen next, but later when difficulties turn up you will give up disgracefully. You want to win an Olympic victory? I do too, by the gods, since that is a fine thing. But consider what leads up to it and what follows it, and undertake the action in the light of that. You must be disciplined, keep a strict diet, stay away from cakes, train according to strict routine at a fixed time in heat and in cold, not drink cold water, not drink wine when you feel like it, and in general you must have turned yourself over to your trainer as to a doctor, and then in the contest "dig in," sometimes dislocate your hand, twist your ankle, swallow a lot of sand, sometimes be whipped, and, after all that, lose. Think about that and then undertake training, if you want to. Otherwise you will be behaving the way children do, who play wrestlers one time, gladiators another time, blow trumpets another time, then act a play. In this way you too are now an athlete, now a gladiator, then an orator, then a philosopher, yet you are nothing wholeheartedly, but like a monkey you mimic each sight that you see, and one thing after another is to your taste, since you do not undertake a thing after considering it from every side, but only randomly and half-heartedly.

In the same way when some people watch a philosopher and hear one speaking like Euphrates (though after all who can speak like him?), they want to be philosophers themselves. Just you consider, as a human being, what sort of thing it is; then inspect your own nature and whether you can bear it. You want to do the pentathlon, or to wrestle? Look at your arms, your thighs, inspect your loins. Different people are naturally suited for different things. Do you think that if you do those things you can eat as you now do, drink as you now do, have the same likes and dislikes? You must go without sleep, put up with hardship, be away from your own people, be looked down on by a little slave boy, be laughed at by people who meet you, get the worse of it in everything, honor, public office, law course, every little thing. Think about whether you want to exchange these things for tranquillity, freedom, calm. If not, do not embrace philosophy, and do not like children be a philosopher at one time, later a tax-collector, then an orator, then a procurator of the emperor. These things do not go together. You must be one person, either good or bad. You must either work on your ruling principle, or work on externals, practice the art either of what is inside or of what is outside, that is, play the role either of a philosopher or of a non-philosopher.

30. Appropriate actions[3] are in general measured by relationships. He is a father: that entails taking care of him, yielding to him in everything, putting up with him when he abuses you or strikes you. "But he is a bad father." Does nature then determine that you have a good father? No, only that you have a father. "My brother has done me wrong." Then keep your place in relation to him; do not consider his action, but instead consider what you can do to bring your own faculty of choice into accord with nature. Another person will not do you harm unless you wish it; you will be harmed at just that time at which you take yourself to be harmed. In this way, then, you will discover the appropriate actions to expect from a neighbor, from a citizen, from a general, if you are in the habit of looking at relationships.

31. The most important aspect of piety toward the gods is certainly both to have correct beliefs about them, as beings that arrange the universe well and justly, and to set yourself to obey them and acquiesce in everything that happens and to follow it willingly, as something brought to completion by the best judgment. For in this way you will never blame the gods or accuse them of neglecting you. And this piety is impossible unless you detach the good and the bad from what is not up to us and attach it exclusively to what is up to us, because if you think that any of what is not up to us is good or bad, then when you fail to get what you want and fall into what you do not want, you will be bound to blame and hate those who cause this. For every animal by nature flees and turns away from things that are harmful and from what causes them, and pursues and admires things that are beneficial and what causes them. There is therefore no way for a person who thinks he is being harmed to enjoy what he thinks is harming him, just as it is impossible to enjoy the harm itself. Hence a son even abuses his father when the father does not give him a share of things that he thinks are good; and thinking that being a tyrant was a good thing is what made enemies of Polyneices and Eteocles.[4] This is why the farmer too abuses the gods, and the sailor, and the merchant, and those who have lost their wives and children. For wherever someone's advantage lies, there he also shows piety. So whoever takes care to have desires and aversions as one should also in the same instance takes care about being pious. And it is always appropriate to make libations and sacrifices and give firstfruits according to the custom of one's forefathers, in a manner that is pure and neither slovenly nor careless, nor indeed cheaply nor beyond one's means. . . .

33. Set up right now a certain character and pattern for yourself which you will preserve when you are by yourself and when you are with people. Be silent for the most part, or say what you have to in a few words. Speak rarely, when the occasion requires speaking, but not about just any topic that comes up, not about gladiators, horse-races, athletes, eating or drinking—the things that always come up; and especially if it is about people, talk without blaming or praising or comparing. Divert by your own talk, if you can, the talk of those with you to something appropriate. If you happen to be stranded among strangers, do not talk. Do not laugh a great deal or at a great many things or unrestrainedly. Refuse to swear oaths, altogether if possible, or otherwise as circumstances allow. Avoid banquets given by those outside philosophy. But if the appropriate occasion arises, take great care not to slide into their ways, since certainly if a person's companion is dirty the person who spends time with him, even if he happens to be clean, is bound to become dirty too. Take what has to do with the body to the point of bare need, such as food, drink, clothing, house, household slaves, and cut out everything that is for reputation or luxury. As for sex stay pure as far as possible before marriage, and if you have it do only what is allowable. But do not be angry or censorious toward those who do engage in it, and do not always be making an exhibition of the fact that you do not.

If someone reports back to you that so-and-so is saying bad things about you, do not reply to them but answer, "Obviously he didn't know my other bad characteristics, since otherwise he wouldn't just have mentioned these."

For the most part there is no need to go to public shows, but if ever the right occasion comes do not show your concern to be for anything but yourself; that is to say, wish to have happen only what does happen, and for the person to win who actually does win, since that way you will not be thwarted. But refrain completely from shouting or laughing at anyone or being very much caught up in it. After you leave, do not talk very much about what has happened, except what contributes to your own improvement, since that would show that the spectacle had impressed you.

Do not go indiscriminately or readily to people's public lectures, but when you do be on guard to be dignified and steady and at the same time try not to be disagreeable.

When you are about to meet someone, especially someone who seems to be distinguished, put to yourself the question, "What would Socrates or Zeno have done in these circumstances?" and you will not be at a loss as to how to deal with the occasion. When you go to see someone who is important, put to yourself the thought that you will not find him at home, that you will be shut out, that the door will be slammed, that he will pay no attention to you. If it is appropriate to go even under these conditions, go and put up with what happens, and never say to yourself, "It wasn't worth all that!" For that is the way of a non-philosopher, someone who is misled by externals.

In your conversations stay away from making frequent and longwinded mention of what you have done and the dangers that you have been in, since it is not as pleasant for others to hear about what has happened to you as it is for you to remember your own dangers.

Stay away from raising a laugh, since this manner slips easily into vulgarity and at the same time is liable to lessen your neighbors' respect for you. It is also risky to fall into foul language. So when anything like that occurs, if a good opportunity arises, go so far as to criticize the person who has done it, and otherwise by staying silent and blushing and frowning you will show that you are displeased by what has been said.

34. Whenever you encounter some kind of apparent pleasure, be on guard, as in the case of other appearances, not to be carried away by it, but let the thing wait for you and allow yourself to delay. Then bring before your mind two times, both the time when you enjoy the pleasure and the time when after enjoying it you later regret it and berate yourself; and set against these the way you will be pleased and will praise yourself if you refrain from it. But if the right occasion appears for you to undertake the action, pay attention so that you will not be overcome by its attractiveness and pleasantness and seductiveness, and set against it how much better it is to be conscious of having won this victory against it. . . .

46. Never call yourself a philosopher and do not talk a great deal among non-philosophers about philosophical propositions, but do what follows from them. For example, at a banquet do not say how a person ought to eat, but eat as a person ought to. Remember that Socrates had so completely put aside ostentation that people actually went to him when they wanted to be introduced to philosophers, and he took them. He was that tolerant of being overlooked. And if talk about philosophical propositions arises among non-philosophers, for the most part be silent, since there is a great danger of your spewing out what you have not digested. And when someone says to you that you know nothing and you are not hurt by it, then you know that you are making a start at your task. Sheep do not show how much they have eaten by bringing the feed to the shepherds, but they digest the food inside themselves, and outside themselves they bear wool and milk. So in your case likewise do not display propositions to non-philosophers but instead the actions that come from the propositions when they are digested. . . .

48. The position and character of a non-philosopher: he never looks for benefit or harm to come from himself but from things outside. The position and character of a philosopher: he looks for all benefit and harm to come from himself.

Signs of someone's making progress:[5] he censures no one; he praises no one; he blames no one; he never talks about himself as a person who amounts to something or knows something. When he is thwarted or prevented in something, he accuses himself. And if someone praises him he laughs to himself at the person who has praised him; and if someone censures him he does not respond. He goes around like an invalid, careful not to move any of his parts that are healing before they have become firm. He has kept off all desire from himself, and he has transferred all aversion onto what is against nature among the things that are up to us. His impulses toward everything are diminished. If he seems foolish or ignorant, he does not care. In a single phrase, he is on guard against himself as an enemy lying in wait. . . .

50. Abide by whatever task is set before you as if it were a law, and as if you would be committing sacrilege if you went against it. But pay no attention to whatever anyone says about you, since that falls outside what is yours. . . .

53. On every occasion you must have these thoughts ready:

Lead me, Zeus, and you too, Destiny,
Wherever I am assigned by you;
I'll follow and not hesitate,
But even if I do not wish to,
Because I'm bad, I'll follow anyway.

Whoever has complied well with necessity
Is counted wise by us, and understands divine affairs.

Well, Crito, if it is pleasing to the gods this way, then let it happen this way.

Anytus and Meletus can kill me, but they can't harm me.[6]

## Notes

[1] In Greek, *phantasia*, which may also be translated impression or presentation; that is, something perceptible to the senses.

[2] Both Greek philosophers—a Cynic and a pre-Socratic, respectively—admired by the Stoics.

[3] Actions in accordance with nature.

[4] Sons of Oedipus who killed each other in a battle over who would rule in Thebes.

[5] Epictetus uses this phrase to mean someone behaving in accordance with nature; being a philosopher.

[6] Sources: Cleanthes, a Greek Stoic; tragic playwright Euripides; Plato's *Crito*; Plato's *Apology*.

# Plutarch

## ca. 46–120 C.E.

Plutarch was a Greek, living in the Roman world. He lived from about 46 C.E. to sometime after 120 C.E. A philosopher (in the Platonic tradition, and a critic of Stoicism and Epicureanism), a priest at Delphi, and a man of the world, he wrote essays and dialogues on many subjects including science and philosophy. M. E. Finley calls him "a brilliant, erudite and widely ranging essayist and biographer, who succeeded in recapturing something of the zest and depth of the long-dead classical civilization. . . ." He is best known for his *Parallel Lives*; in each of these he writes about an eminent Roman and an eminent Greek. In the beginning of his life of Alexander he gives some idea of what he thinks the point of biography is.

It is important to remember that Plutarch was writing almost four hundred years after the death of Alexander. Others had written about the conqueror and his life had already accumulated a thick layer of legend and mythologizing, which Plutarch tries to subject to critical scrutiny in order to arrive at the truth about Alexander, both of events and character. In his life of Pericles, Plutarch wrote: "It is so hard to find out the truth of anything by looking at the record of the past. The process of time obscures the truth of former times, and even contemporaneous writers disguise and twist the truth out of malice or flattery."

Twenty-two pairs of biographies and four without their parallel lives are extant, though references from the ancient world identify other lives by Plutarch which have not survived.

MM

# from *The Life of Alexander*

My subject in this book is the life of Alexander, the king, and of Julius
Caesar, the conqueror of Pompey. [The parallel life of Julius Caesar is omitted.] The careers of these men embrace such a multitude of events that my pre-
amble shall consist of nothing more than this one plea: if I do not record all
their most celebrated achievements or describe any of them exhaustively, but
merely summarize for the most part what they accomplished, I ask my readers not to regard this as a fault. For I am writing biography, not history, and
the truth is that the most brilliant exploits often tell us nothing of the virtues
or vices of the men who performed them, while on the other hand a chance
remark or a joke may reveal far more of a man's character than the mere feat
of winning battles in which thousands fall, or of marshalling great armies, or
laying siege to cities. When a portrait painter sets out to create a likeness, he
relies above all upon the face and the expression of the eyes and pays less attention to the other parts of the body: in the same way it is my task to dwell upon
those actions which illuminate the workings of the soul, and by this means to
create a portrait of each man's life. I leave the story of his greatest struggles and
achievements to be told by others.

2. On his father's side Alexander was descended from Hercules through
Caranus, and on his mother's from Aeacus through Neoptolemus[1]: so much is
accepted by all authorities without question. It is said that his father Philip fell
in love with Olympias, Alexander's mother, at the time when they were both
initiated into the mysteries at Samothrace. He was then a young man and she
an orphan, and after obtaining the consent of her brother Arybbas, Philip
betrothed himself to her.[2] On the night before the marriage was consummat-
ed, the bride dreamed that there was a crash of thunder, that her womb was
struck by a thunderbolt, and that there followed a blinding flash from which
a great sheet of flame blazed up and spread far and wide before it finally died
away. Then, some time after their marriage, Philip saw himself in a dream in
the act of sealing up his wife's womb, and upon the seal he had used there was
engraved, so it seemed to him, the figure of a lion. The soothsayers treated this
dream with suspicion, since it seemed to suggest that Philip needed to keep a
closer watch on his wife. The only exception was Aristander of Telmessus, who
declared that the woman must be pregnant, since men do not seal up what is
empty, and that she would bring forth a son whose nature would be bold and
lion-like. At another time a serpent was seen stretched out at Olympias' side
as she slept, and it was this more than anything else, we are told, which weak-

ened Philip's passion and cooled his affection for her, so that from that time on he seldom came to sleep with her. The reason for this may either have been that he was afraid she would cast some evil spell or charm upon him or else that he recoiled from her embrace because he believed that she was the consort of some higher being.

· · ·

4. The best likeness of Alexander which has been preserved for us is to be found in the statues sculpted by Lysippus,[3] the only artist whom Alexander considered worthy to represent him. Alexander possessed a number of individual features which many of Lysippus' followers later tried to reproduce, for example the poise of the neck which was tilted slightly to the left, or a certain melting look in his eyes, and the artist has exactly caught these peculiarities. On the other hand when Apelles painted Alexander wielding a thunderbolt, he did not reproduce his colouring at all accurately. He made Alexander's complexion appear too dark-skinned and swarthy, whereas we are told that he was fair-skinned, with a ruddy tinge that showed itself especially upon his face and chest. Aristoxenus also tells us in his memoirs that Alexander's skin was fresh and sweet-smelling, and that his breath and the whole of his body gave off a peculiar fragrance which permeated the clothes he wore.

The cause of this may have been the blend of hot and dry elements which were combined in his constitution, for fragrance, if we are to believe Theophrastus,[4] is generated by the action of heat upon moist humours. This is why the hottest and driest regions of the earth produce the finest and most numerous spices, for the sun draws up the moisture which abounds in vegetable bodies and causes them to decay. In Alexander's case it was this same warmth of temperament which made him fond of drinking, and also prone to outbursts of choleric[5] rage.

Even while he was still a boy, he gave plenty of evidence of his powers of self-control. In spite of his vehement and impulsive nature, he showed little interest in the pleasures of the senses and indulged in them only with great moderation, but his passionate desire for fame implanted in him a pride and a grandeur of vision which went far beyond his years. And yet it was by no means every kind of glory that he sought, and, unlike his father, he did not seek it in every form of action. Philip, for example, was as proud of his powers of eloquence as any sophist, and took care to have the victories won by his chariots at Olympia stamped upon his coins. But Alexander's attitude is made clear by his reply to some of his friends when they asked him whether he would be willing to compete at Olympia, since he was a fine runner. 'Yes,' he answered, 'if I have kings to run against me.' He seems in fact to have disapproved of the whole race of trained athletes. At any rate although he founded a great many contests of other kinds, including not only the tragic drama and performances on the flute and the lyre, but also the reciting of poetry, fighting with the quarter-staff and various forms of hunting, yet he never offered prizes either for boxing or for the *pancration*.[6]

• • •

7. Philip had noticed that his son was self-willed, and that while it was very difficult to influence him by force, he could easily be guided towards his duty by an appeal to reason, and he therefore made a point of trying to persuade the boy rather than giving him orders. Besides this he considered that the task of training and educating his son was too important to be entrusted to the ordinary run of teachers of poetry, music and general education: it required, as Sophocles puts it

The rudder's guidance and the curb's restraint,

and so he sent for Aristotle,[7] the most famous and learned of the philosophers of his time, and rewarded him with the generosity that his reputation deserved. Aristotle was a native of the city of Stageira, which Philip had himself destroyed. He now repopulated it and brought back all the citizens who had been enslaved or driven into exile.

He gave Aristotle and his pupil the temple of the Nymphs near Mieza as a place where they could study and converse, and to this day they show you the stone seats and shady walks which Aristotle used. It seems clear too that Alexander was instructed by his teacher not only in the principles of ethics and politics, but also in those secret and more esoteric studies which philosophers do not impart to the general run of students, but only by word of mouth to a select circle of the initiated.

• • •

8. It was Aristotle, I believe, who did more than anyone to implant in Alexander his interest in the art of healing as well as that of philosophy. He was not merely attracted to the theory of medicine, but was in the habit of tending his friends when they were sick and prescribing for them various courses of treatment or diet, as we learn from his letters. He was also devoted by nature to all kinds of learning and was a lover of books. He regarded the *Iliad* as a handbook of the art of war and took with him on his campaigns a text annotated by Aristotle, which became known as 'the casket copy', and which he always kept under his pillow together with his dagger. When his campaigns had taken him far into the interior of Asia and he could find no other books, he ordered his treasurer Harpalus to send him some. Harpalus sent him the

histories of Philistus, many of the tragedies of Aeschylus, Sophocles and Euripides, and the dithyrambic poems of Telestes and Philoxenus.

At first Alexander greatly admired Aristotle and became more attached to him than to his father, for the one, he used to say, had given him the gift of life, but the other had taught him how to live well. But in later years he came to regard Aristotle with suspicion. He never actually did him any harm, but his friendship for the philosopher lost its original warmth and affection, and this was a clear proof of the estrangement which developed between them. At the same time Alexander never lost the devotion to philosophy which had been innate in him from the first, and which matured as he grew older: he proved this on many occasions, for example by the honours which he paid to Anaxarchus, the fifty talents which he presented to Xenocrates, and the encouragement which he lavished upon Dandamis and Calanus.

•  •  •

11. Alexander was only twenty years old when he inherited his kingdom, which at that moment was beset by formidable jealousies and feuds, and external dangers on every side. The neighbouring barbarian tribes were eager to throw off the Macedonian yoke and longed for the rule of their native kings: as for the Greek states, although Philip had defeated them in battle, he had not had time to subdue them or accustom them to his authority. He had swept away the existing governments, and then, having prepared their peoples for drastic changes, had left them in turmoil and confusion, because he had created a situation which was completely unfamiliar to them. Alexander's Macedonian advisers feared that a crisis was at hand and urged the young king to leave the Greek states to their own devices and refrain from using any force against them. As for the barbarian tribes, they considered that he should try to win them back to their allegiance by using milder methods, and forestall the first signs of revolt by offering them concessions. Alexander, however, chose precisely the opposite course, and decided that the only way to make his kingdom safe was to act with audacity and a lofty spirit, for he was certain that if he were seen to yield even a fraction of his authority, all his enemies would attack him at once. He swiftly crushed the uprisings among the barbarians by advancing with his army as far as the Danube, where he overcame Syrmus, the king of the Triballi, in a great battle. Then when the news reached him that the Thebans had revolted and were being supported by the Athenians, he immediately marched south through the pass of Thermopylae. 'Demosthenes',[8] he said, 'called me a boy while I was in Illyria and among the Triballi, and a youth when I was marching through Thessaly; I will show him I am a man by the time I reach the walls of Athens.'

When he arrived before Thebes,[9] he wished to give the citizens the opportunity to repent of their actions, and so he merely demanded the surrender of their leaders Phoenix and Prothytes, and offered an amnesty to all the rest if they would come over to his side. The Thebans countered by demanding the surrender of Philotas and Antipater and appealing to all who wished to liberate Greece to range themselves on their side, and at this Alexander ordered his troops to prepare for battle. The Thebans, although greatly outnumbered, fought with a superhuman courage and spirit, but when the Macedonian garrison which had been posted in the citadel of the Cadmeia made a sortie and fell upon them from the rear, the greater part of their army was encircled, they were slaughtered where they stood, and the city was stormed, plundered and razed to the ground. Alexander's principal object in permitting the sack of Thebes was to frighten the rest of the Greeks into submission by making a terrible example. But he also put forward the excuse that he was redressing the wrongs done to his allies, for the Plataeans and Phocians had both complained of the actions of the Thebans against them. As for the population of Thebes, he singled out the priests, a few citizens who had friendly connections with Macedonia, the descendants of the poet Pindar, and those who had opposed the revolt to be spared: all the rest were publicly sold into slavery to the number of twenty thousand. Those who were killed in the battle numbered more than six thousand.

●　　●　　●

14. In the previous year[10] a congress of the Greek states had been held at the Isthmus of Corinth: here a vote had been passed that the states should join forces with Alexander in invading Persia and that he should be commander-in-chief of the expedition. Many of the Greek statesmen and philosophers visited him to offer their congratulations, and he hoped that Diogenes of Sinope,[11] who was at that time living in Corinth, would do the same. However since he paid no attention whatever to Alexander, but continued to live at leisure in the suburb of Corinth which was known as Craneion, Alexander went in person to see him and found him basking at full length in the sun. When he saw so many people approaching him, Diogenes raised himself a little on his elbow and fixed his gaze upon Alexander. The king greeted him and inquired whether he could do anything for him. 'Yes,' replied the philosopher, 'you can stand a little to one side out of my sun.' Alexander is said to have been greatly impressed by this answer and full of admiration for the hauteur and independence of mind of a man who could look down on him with such condescension. So much so that he remarked to his followers, who were laughing and mocking the philosopher as they went away, 'You may say what you like, but if I were not Alexander, I would be Diogenes.'

• • •

[Having invaded Asia, Alexander's army conquered many cities and, at the battle of Issus, routed the army of Darius, the Persian emperor. Though Darius escaped, Alexander captured his wife and two daughters, whom he treated kindly.]

22. When Philoxenus, the commander of his forces on the sea coast, wrote to say that he had with him a slave merchant from Tarentum named Theodorus who was offering exceptionally handsome boys for sale and asked whether Alexander wished to buy them, the king was furious and angrily demanded of his friends what signs of degeneracy Philoxenus had ever noticed in him that he should waste his time procuring such debased creatures. He wrote a letter to Philoxenus telling him what he thought of him and ordering him to send Theodorus and his merchandise to the devil. He also sharply rebuked Hagnon, who had written that he wanted to buy as a present for him a young man named Crobylus, whose good looks were famous in Corinth. And when he discovered that Damon and Timotheus, two Macedonian soldiers who were serving under Parmenio, had seduced the wives of some of the Greek mercenaries, he sent orders to Parmenio that if the two men were found guilty, they should be put to death as wild beasts which are born to prey upon mankind. In the same letter he wrote of himself: 'In my own case it will be found not only that I have never seen nor wished to see Darius' wife, but that I have not even allowed her beauty to be mentioned in my presence.' He also used to say that it was sleep and sexual intercourse which more than anything else, reminded him that he was mortal; by this he meant that both exhaustion and pleasure proceed from the same weakness of human nature.

He was exceptionally temperate in what he ate, as he showed in many different ways, but above all in the answer he gave to Queen Ada, whom he honoured with the official title of Mother and made Queen of Caria. To show her affection for him she had formed the habit of sending him delicacies and sweetmeats every day, and finally offered him bakers and cooks who were supposed to be the most skilful in the country. Alexander's reply was that he did not need them, because his tutor Leonidas had provided him with better cooks than these, that is a night march to prepare him for breakfast, and a light breakfast to give him an appetite for supper. 'This same Leonidas,' he went on, 'would often come and open my chests of bedding and clothes, to see whether my mother had not hidden some luxury inside.'

23. Alexander was also more moderate in his drinking than was generally supposed. The impression that he was a heavy drinker arose because when he had nothing else to do, he liked to linger over each cup, but in fact he was

usually talking rather than drinking: he enjoyed holding long conversations, but only when he had plenty of leisure. Whenever there was urgent business to attend to, neither wine, nor sleep, nor sport, nor sex, nor spectacle, could ever distract his attention, as they did for other generals. The proof of this is his life-span, which although so short, was filled to overflowing with the most prodigious achievements. When he was at leisure, his first act after rising was to sacrifice to the gods, after which he took his breakfast sitting down. The rest of the day would be spent in hunting, administering justice, planning military affairs or reading. If he were on a march which required no great haste, he would practise archery as he rode, or mounting and dismounting from a moving chariot, and he often hunted foxes or birds, as he mentions in his journals. When he had chosen his quarters for the night and while he was being refreshed with a bath or rubbed down, he would ask his cooks and bakers whether the arrangements for supper had been suitably made.

His custom was not to begin supper until late, as it was growing dark. He took it reclining on a couch, and he was wonderfully attentive and observant in ensuring that his table was well provided, his guests equally served, and none of them neglected. He sat long over his wine, as I have remarked, because of his fondness for conversation. And although at other times his society was delightful and his manner full of charm beyond that of any prince of his age, yet when he was drinking he would sometimes become offensively arrogant and descend to the level of a common soldier, and on these occasions he would allow himself not only to give way to boasting but also to be led on by his flatterers. These men were a great trial to the finer spirits among his companions, who had no desire to compete with them in their sycophancy, but were unwilling to be outdone in praising Alexander. The one course they thought shameful, but the other was dangerous. When the drinking was over it was his custom to take a bath and sleep, often until midday, and sometimes for the whole of the following day.

As for delicacies, Alexander was so restrained in his appetite that often when the rarest fruits or fish were brought him from the sea coast, he would distribute them so generously among his companions that there would be nothing left for himself. His evening meal, however, was always a magnificent affair, and as his successes multiplied, so did his expenditure on hospitality until it reached the sum of ten thousand drachmae. At this point he fixed a limit and those who entertained Alexander were told that they must not exceed this sum.

• • •

26. One day a casket was brought to him which was regarded by those who were in charge of Darius' baggage and treasure as the most valuable item of all, and so Alexander asked his friends what he should keep in it as his own

most precious possession. Many different suggestions were put forward, and finally Alexander said that he intended to keep his copy of the *Iliad* there. This anecdote is supported by many reliable historians, and if the tradition which has been handed down by the Alexandrians on the authority of Heracleides is true, then certainly the poems of Homer were by no means an irrelevant or an unprofitable possession to accompany him on his campaigns. According to this story, after Alexander had conquered Egypt, he was anxious to found a great and populous Greek city there, to be called after him. He had chosen a certain site on the advice of his architects, and was on the point of measuring and marking it out. Then as he lay asleep he dreamed that a grey-haired man of venerable appearance stood by his side and recited these lines from the *Odyssey*:

> Out of the tossing sea where it breaks on the beaches of Egypt
> Rises an isle from the waters: the name that men give it is Pharos[12]

Alexander rose the next morning and immediately visited Pharos: at that time it was still an island near the Canopic mouth of the Nile, but since then it has been joined to the mainland by a causeway. When he saw what wonderful natural advantages the place possessed—for it was a strip of land resembling a broad isthmus, which stretched between the sea and a great lagoon, with a spacious harbour at the end of it—he declared that Homer, besides his other admirable qualities, was also a very far-seeing architect, and he ordered the plan of the city to be designed so that it would conform to this site.[13] There was no chalk to mark the ground plan, so they took barley meal, sprinkled it on the dark earth and marked out a semi-circle, which was divided into equal segments by lines radiating from the inner arc to the circumference: the shape was similar to that of the *chlamys* or military cloak, so that the lines proceeded, as it were, from the skirt, and narrowed the breadth of the area uniformly. While the king was enjoying the symmetry of the design, suddenly huge flocks of birds appeared from the river and the lagoon, descended upon the site and devoured every grain of the barley. Alexander was greatly disturbed by this omen, but the diviners urged him to take heart and interpreted the occurrence as a sign that the city would not only have abundant resources of its own but would be the nurse of men of innumerable nations, and so he ordered those in charge of the work to proceed while he himself set out to visit the temple of Ammon.[14]

• • •

The great battle that was fought against Darius [331 B.C.E. This follows several years of campaigning in Asia Minor and Alexander's pursuit of Darius into the upper Tigris region] did not take place at Arbela, as the majority of writers say, but at Gaugamela. The word signifies 'the house of the camel': one of the ancient kings of this country escaped the pursuit of his enemies on a swift camel and gave the animal a home there, setting aside various revenues and the produce of several villages to maintain it. It happened that in the month of Boedromion, about the same time as the beginning of the festival of the mysteries at Athens, there was an eclipse of the moon. On the eleventh night after this, by which time the two armies were in sight of one another, Darius kept his troops under arms and held a review of them by torchlight. Alexander allowed his Macedonians to sleep, but himself spent the night in front of his tent in the company of his diviner Aristander, with whom he performed certain mysterious and sacred ceremonies and offered sacrifice to the god Fear. Meanwhile some of the older of his companions[15] and Parmenio in particular looked out over the plain between the river Niphates and the Gordyaean mountains and saw the entire plain agleam with the watch-fires of the barbarians, while from their camp there arose the confused and indistinguishable murmur of myriads of voices, like the distant roar of a vast ocean. They were filled with amazement at the sight and remarked to one another that it would be an overwhelmingly difficult task to defeat an enemy of such strength by engaging him by day. They therefore went to the king as soon as he had performed his sacrifice and tried to persuade him to attack by night, so as to conceal from his men the most terrifying element in the coming struggle, that is the odds against them. It was then that Alexander gave them his celebrated answer, 'I will not steal my victory.' Some of his companions thought this an immature and empty boast on the part of a young man who was merely joking in the presence of danger. But others interpreted it as meaning that he had confidence in his present situation and that he had correctly judged the future. In other words he was determined that if Darius were defeated, he should have no cause to summon up courage for another attempt: he was not to be allowed to blame darkness and night for his failure on this occasion, as at Issus he had blamed the narrow mountain passes and the sea. Certainly Darius would never abandon the war for lack of arms or of troops, when he could draw upon such a vast territory and such immense reserves of man-power. He would only do so when he had lost courage and become convinced of his inferiority in consequence of an unmistakable defeat suffered in broad daylight.

32. When his friends had gone, Alexander lay down in his tent and is said to have passed the rest of the night in a deeper sleep than usual. At any rate when his officers came to him in the early morning, they were astonished to find him not yet awake, and on their own responsibility gave out orders for the soldiers to take breakfast before anything else was done. Then, as time was pressing, Parmenio entered Alexander's tent, stood by his couch and called him two or three times by name: when he had roused him, he asked how he could

possibly sleep as if he were already victorious, instead of being about to fight the greatest battle of his life. Alexander smiled and said, 'Why not? Do you not see that we have already won the battle, now that we are delivered from roving around these endless devastated plains, and chasing this Darius, who will never stand and fight?' And indeed not only beforehand, but at the very height of the battle Alexander displayed the supremacy and steadfastness of a man who is confident of the soundness of his judgement.

As the action developed, the left wing under Parmenio was driven back and found itself hard pressed, first by a violent charge from the Bactrian cavalry, and later by an outflanking movement when Mazaeus sent a detachment of horsemen to ride round the line and attack the troops who were guarding the Macedonian baggage. Parmenio, who was disconcerted by both these manoeuvres, sent messengers to warn Alexander that his camp and his baggage train were lost, unless he could immediately move strong reinforcements from the front to protect his rear. It so happened that at that moment Alexander was about to give the signal to the right wing, which he commanded, to attack: when he received this message, he exclaimed that Parmenio must have lost his wits and forgotten in his agitation that the victors will always take possession of their enemy's baggage in any event, and that the losers must not concern themselves with their property or their slaves, but only with how to fight bravely and die with honour.

After he had sent this message to Parmenio, he put on his helmet. He was already wearing the rest of his armour when he left his tent, a tunic made in Sicily which was belted around his waist and over this a thickly quilted linen corslet, which had been among the spoils captured at Issus. His helmet, the work of Theophilus, was made of steel which gleamed like polished silver, and to this was fitted a steel gorget set with precious stones. His sword, which was a gift from the king of Citium, was a marvel of lightness and tempering, and he had trained himself to use this as his principal weapon in hand-to-hand fighting. He also wore a cloak which was more ornate than the rest of his armour. It had been made by Helicon, an artist of earlier times, and presented to Alexander as a mark of honour by the city of Rhodes, and this too he was in the habit of wearing in battle. While he was drawing up the phalanx in formation, reviewing the troops, or giving out orders, he rode another horse to spare Bucephalas,[16] who was by now past his prime: but when he was about to go into action Bucephalas would be led up, and he would mount him and at once begin the attack.

33. On this occasion Alexander gave a long address to the Thessalians and the rest of the Greeks. They acclaimed by shouting for him to lead them against the barbarians, and at this he shifted his lance into his left hand, so Callisthenes

tells us, and raising his right he called upon the gods and prayed that if he were really the son of Zeus they should protect and encourage the Greeks. Then Aristander the diviner, who was wearing a white robe and a crown of gold, rode along the ranks and pointed out to the men an eagle which hovered for a while over Alexander's head and then flew straight towards the enemy. The sight acted as an immediate inspiration to the watching troops, and with shouts of encouragement to one another the cavalry charged the enemy at full speed and the phalanx rolled forward like a flood. Before the leading ranks could engage, the barbarians began to fall back, hotly pursued by Alexander, who drove the retreating enemy towards the centre, where Darius was stationed.

Alexander had sighted his adversary through the ranks of the royal squadron of cavalry, as they waited drawn up in deep formation in front of him. Darius was a tall and handsome man and he towered conspicuously above this large and superbly equipped body of horsemen, who were closely massed to guard the lofty chariot in which he stood. But the horseguards were seized with panic at the terrible sight of Alexander bearing down upon them and driving the fugitives before him against those who still held their ground, and the greater number of them broke and scattered. The bravest and most highly born, however, stood fast and were slaughtered in front of their king: they fell upon one another in heaps, and in their dying struggles they clung to the legs of horses and riders, entwining themselves about them so as to hinder the pursuit. As for Darius, all the horrors of the battle were now before his eyes. The forces which had been stationed in the centre for his protection had now been driven back upon him: it had become difficult to turn his chariot round and drive it away, since the wheels were encumbered and entangled with heaps of bodies, and the horses which were surrounded and almost covered by the dead began to rear and plunge so that the charioteer could not control them. In this extremity the king abandoned his chariot and his armour, mounted a mare which, so the story goes, had recently foaled, and rode away. It is believed that he would not have escaped at that moment, had not Parmenio sent another party of horsemen begging Alexander to come to his rescue, because he was engaged with a strong enemy force which still held together and would not give way. In this battle Parmenio is generally accused of having been sluggish and lacking in spirit, either because old age had dulled his courage, or because he had become envious of the authority and pomp, to use Callisthenes' words, which Alexander now displayed. Alexander was vexed by this appeal for help, but at the time he did not reveal to his men the fact that it had been made. Instead he ordered the recall to be sounded on the ground that it was growing dark and that he wished to bring the slaughter to an end. Then as he rode back to the part of the field where Parmenio's troops were supposedly threatened, he learned on his way that the enemy had been utterly defeated and put to flight.

34. After the battle had ended in this way, the authority of the Persian empire was regarded as having been completely overthrown. Alexander was proclaimed king of Asia and after offering splendid sacrifices to the gods, he proceeded to reward his friends with riches, estates and governorships. As he wished to increase his prestige in the Greek world, he wrote to the states saying that all tyrannies were now abolished and that henceforth they might live under their own laws: to the Plataeans in particular he wrote that he would rebuild their city because their ancestors had allowed the Greeks to make their territory the seat of war in the struggle for their common freedom.[17] He also sent a share of the spoils to the people of Croton in Italy in honour of the spirit and valour shown by their athlete Phaÿllus: this man, when the rest of the Greeks in Italy had refused to give any help to their compatriots in the Persian wars, had fitted out a ship at his own expense and sailed with it to Salarnis to share in the common danger. Such was Alexander's desire to pay tribute to any manifestation of courage and to prove himself the friend and guardian of noble actions.

35. He then advanced through the province of Babylonia which immediately surrendered to him.

• • •

From this point [after further conquests in Persia, Media, Parthia, Scythia, etc., etc. he began to adapt his own style of living more closely to that of the country and tried to reconcile Asiatic and Macedonian customs: he believed that if the two traditions could be blended and assimilated in this way his authority would be more securely established when he was far away, since it would rest on goodwill rather than on force. For this reason he selected thirty thousand boys and gave orders that they should be taught to speak the Greek language and to use Macedonian weapons, and he appointed a large number of instructors to train them. His marriage to Roxane[18] was a love match, which began when he first saw her at the height of her youthful beauty taking part in a dance at a banquet, but it also played a great part in furthering his policy of reconciliation. The barbarians were encouraged by the feeling of partnership which their alliance created, and they were completely won over by Alexander's moderation and courtesy and by the fact that without the sanction of marriage he would not approach the only woman who had ever conquered his heart.

• • •

[Alexander advanced as far as the River Indus, captured Indian philoso-phers, and fought a great winning battle in 326 B.C.E. against King Porus and his war elephants. Finally his army refused to go any further and Alexander turned back toward Mesopotamia, while part of his army under Nearchus traveled back via the Indian Ocean and the Persian Gulf.]

72. In the spring he left Susa for Ecbatana in Media and there, after he had dealt with the most pressing of his concerns, he once more turned his attention to plays and spectacles, since three thousand players had arrived from Greece. At this time it happened that Hephaestion had caught a fever, and being a young man who was accustomed to a soldier's life, he could not bear to remain on a strict diet. No sooner had his physician Glaucus gone off to the theatre, than he sat down to breakfast, devoured a boiled fowl and washed it down with a great cooler-full of wine. His fever quickly mounted and soon afterwards he died. Alexander's grief was uncontrollable. As a sign of mourn-ing he gave orders that the manes and tails of all horses should be shorn, demolished the battlements of all the neighbouring cities, crucified the unlucky physician and forebade the playing of flutes or any other kind of music for a long time until finally an oracle was announced from the temple of Ammon, commanding him to honour Hephaestion and sacrifice to him as a hero. To lighten his sorrow he set off on a campaign, as if the tracking down and hunting of men might console him, and he subdued the tribe of the Cossaeans, massacring the whole male population from the youths upwards: this was termed a sacrifice to the spirit of Hephaestion. He determined to spend ten thousand talents on the funeral and the tomb for his friend, and as he wished the ingenuity and originality of the design to surpass the expense he was especially anxious to employ Stasicrates, as this artist was famous for his innovations, which combined an exceptional degree of magnificence, audaci-ty and ostentation.

•  •  •

73. Towards the end of the year Alexander travelled to Babylon. Before he arrived he was joined by Nearchus, who had sailed through the ocean and up the Euphrates: Nearchus told him that he had met some Chaldaeans who had advised the king to stay away from Babylon. Alexander paid no attention to this warning and continued his journey, but when he arrived before the walls of the city, he saw a large number of ravens flying about and pecking one another, and some of them fell dead in front of him. Next he received a report that Apollodorus the governor of Babylon had offered up a sacrifice to try to discover what fate held in store for Alexander, and he then sent for Pythagoras, the diviner who had conducted the sacrifice. Pythagoras admitted that this was

true, and Alexander then asked him in what condition he had found the victim. 'The liver,' Pythagoras told him, 'had no lobe.' 'Indeed,' replied Alexander, 'that is a threatening omen.' He did Pythagoras no harm and he began to regret that he had not taken Nearchus' advice, and so he spent most of his time outside the walls of Babylon, either in his tent or in boats on the Euphrates. Many more omens now occurred to trouble him. A tame ass attacked the finest lion in his menagerie and kicked it to death. On another occasion Alexander took off his clothes for exercise and played a game of ball. When it was time to dress again, the young men who had joined him in the game suddenly noticed that there was a man sitting silently on the throne and wearing Alexander's diadem and royal robes. When he was questioned, he could say nothing for a long while, but later he came to his senses and explained that he was a citizen of Messenia named Dionysius. He had been accused of some crime, brought to Babylon from the coast, and kept for a long time in chains. Then the god Serapis had appeared to him, cast off his chains and brought him to this place, where he had commanded him to put on the king's robe and diadem, take his seat on the throne and hold his peace.

74. When he had heard the man's story, Alexander had him put to death, as the diviners recommended. But his confidence now deserted him, he began to believe that he had lost the favour of the gods, and he became increasingly suspicious of his friends. It was Antipater and his sons whom he feared most of all. One of them named Iolas was his chief cup-bearer. The other, Cassander, had only lately arrived in Babylon, and when he saw some of the barbarians prostrate themselves before the king, he burst into loud and disrespectful laughter, for he had been brought up as a Greek and had never seen such a spectacle in his life. Alexander was furious at this insult, seized him by the hair with both hands and dashed his head against the wall. On another occasion when Cassander wished to reply to some men who were making accusations against his father Antipater, Alexander interrupted him and said, 'What do you mean? Are you really saying that these men have suffered no wrong, but have travelled all this way just to bring a false accusation?' When Cassander replied that the very fact of their having travelled so far from those who could contradict them might point to the charges being false, Alexander laughed and said, 'This reminds me of some of Aristotle's sophisms, which can be used equally well on either side of a question: but if any of you are proved to have done these men even the smallest wrong, you will be sorry for it.' In general, we are told, this fear was implanted so deeply and took such hold of Cassander's mind that even many years later, when he had become king of Macedonia and master of Greece, and was walking about one day looking at the sculptures at Delphi, the mere sight of a statue of Alexander struck him with horror, so that

he shuddered and trembled in every limb, his head swam and he could scarcely regain control of himself.

75. Meanwhile Alexander had become so much obsessed by his fears of the supernatural and so overwrought and apprehensive in his own mind, that he interpreted every strange or unusual occurrence, no matter how trivial, as a prodigy or a portent, with the result that the palace was filled with soothsayers, sacrificers, purifiers and prognosticators. Certainly it is dangerous to disbelieve or show contempt for the power of the gods, but it is equally dangerous to harbour superstition, and in this case just as water constantly gravitates to a lower level, so unreasoning dread filled Alexander's mind with foolish misgivings, once he had become a slave to his fears. However, when the verdict of the oracle concerning Hephaestion was brought to him, he laid aside his grief and allowed himself to indulge in a number of sacrifices and drinking-bouts. He gave a splendid banquet in honour of Nearchus, after which he took a bath as his custom was, with the intention of going to bed soon afterwards. But when Medius invited him, he went to his house to join a party, and there after drinking all through the next day, he began to feel feverish. This did not happen 'as he was drinking from the cup of Hercules', nor did he become conscious of a sudden pain in the back as if he had been pierced by a spear: these are details with which certain historians felt obliged to embellish the occasion, and thus invent a tragic and moving finale to a great action. Aristobulus tells us that he was seized with a raging fever, that when he became very thirsty he drank wine which made him delirious, and that he died on the thirtieth day of the month Daesius.

76. According to his journals, the course of his sickness was as follows. On the eighteenth day of the month Daesius[19] he slept in the bathroom because he was feverish. On the next day, after taking a bath, he moved into the bedchamber and spent the day playing dice with Medius. He took a bath late in the evening, offered sacrifice to the gods, dined and remained feverish throughout the night. On the twentieth he again bathed and sacrificed as usual, and while he was lying down in the bathroom he was entertained by listening to Nearchus' account of his voyage, and his exploration of the great sea. On the twenty-first he passed the time in the same way, but the fever grew more intense: he had a bad night and all through the following day his fever was very high. He had his bed moved and lay in it by the side of the great plunge-bath, and there he discussed with his commanders the vacant posts in the army and how to fill them with experienced officers. On the twenty-fourth his fever was still worse and he had to be carried outside to offer sacrifice. He gave orders to the senior commanders to remain on call in the courtyard of the

palace and to the commanders of companies and regiments to spend the night outside. On the twenty-fifth day he was moved to the palace on the other side of the river, and there he slept a little, but his fever did not abate. When his commanders entered the room he was speechless and remained so on the twenty-sixth. The Macedonians now believed that he was dead: they thronged the doors of the palace and began to shout and threaten the Companions, who were at last obliged to let them in. When the doors had been thrown open they all filed slowly past his bedside one by one, wearing neither cloak nor armour. In the course of this day too Python and Seleucus were sent to the temple of Serapis to ask whether Alexander should be moved there, and the god replied that they should leave him where he was. On the twenty-eighth towards evening he died.

## Notes

[1] Caranus was supposedly the founder of the Macedonian dynasty; Aeacus was a legendary king of Aegina and the grandfather of Achilles.

[2] They married in 357 B.C.E.; Olympias was Philip's third wife.

[3] The most famous of Hellenistic sculptors.

[4] A student of Aristotle's and his designated successor.

[5] Choler, or yellow bile, is one of the four humours; according to the theory of humours, a balance or imbalance produces personal characteristics. A surplus of choler produces anger.

[6] A combination of wrestling and boxing.

[7] When Alexander was thirteen.

[8] Famous Athenian orator, an outspoken opponent of Alexander's father Philip and of Macedonian ascendancy.

[9] 335 B.C.E.

[10] 334 B.C.E.

[11] The famous Cynic philosopher.

[12] *Odyssey* iv, 354–55.

[13] This describes the founding of Alexandria in Egypt.

[14] Ammon, or, in a syncretic development, Ammon-Zeus, was the chief Egyptian god; various accounts suggest that Alexander was greeted at the temple as the son of Zeus.

[15] The "companions" were a group of men with whom Alexander had been reared, most of them his contemporaries (though not Parmenio, apparently) who formed his inner circle.

[16] Alexander's famous horse. When he was about fourteen, he tamed Bucephalas when his father and other observers considered him wild and unmanageable.

[17] During the Persian wars of the previous century.

[18] 327 B.C.E.

[19] This was in June 323 B.C.E.

# Plotinus

## 204/5–270 C.E.

Plotinus is considered the founder of what is now called Neoplatonism, the last school of non-Christian philosophy in the classical period of the West. He was probably born in Egypt when it was a part of the Roman Empire, but his parentage is obscure. He certainly studied in Alexandria, the center of Hellenistic culture prior to the rise of Rome. Given the cosmopolitan character of Alexandria, he may have been of Greek or Roman or Egyptian roots. After well over a decade of study there, he eventually established his own school in the city of Rome itself at the age of 40. In Rome he acquired many pupils and admirers, including a Roman emperor, Gallienus, and his wife. Plotinus became a fashionable philosopher, with many patrons and friends from the upper classes in addition to the emperor. He never left Italy and died on a follower's estate outside of Rome at about the age of 66.

Plotinus is a Platonist in that he accepts the idea that the material world, and how we "know'" it via our senses, is not in fact ultimate reality. Nevertheless, what is "beautiful" in that world provides a path towards understanding true reality, if one reasons what Beauty is and what Beauty does. With Plato, Plotinus believes that reason is crucial for understanding that Ideas are ultimately real. Ideas are most Beautiful. Their source is the ONE.

What is The ONE? To answer that question the reader needs to appreciate that Plotinus, though a follower of Plato, is unlike Plato in at least two essential ways: (1) Plotinus is a monist, not a dualist. Rather than understanding reality as made up of two realms—ideas and matter—he believes that there is only one realm, The ONE, in which everything participates in a connected hierarchy. Everything is really one, The ONE, which is the source and destination of everything. The ONE is the totality of everything. You cannot see this totality; you cannot reason its infinity. Thus (2) Though reason (intellect) is required for understanding, it is not enough. Reason should lead to introspection, intuition, and finally what sounds like a mystical connection with supreme reality, The ONE. To attempt to understand with the senses alone, or even reason, reveals only parts of The ONE, distorting its completeness. To "connect" is to contemplate.

If the Neoplatonism of Plotinus sounds like a religion, it is a religion. Plotinus' philosophy uses reason, not against itself, but to embrace transcendence with the supernatural ONE as most perfect truth.

Plotinus' philosophy coincides with the rise of Christianity; St. Augustine was influenced by it. But Neoplatonism does not vanish with the rise of Christianity. Its approach to beauty and ultimate truth reoccurs in the West, notably during the Italian Renaissance.

JM

# from *The Enneads*

1. Beauty addresses itself chiefly to sight; but there is a beauty for the hearing too, as in certain combinations of words and in all kinds of music, for melodies and cadences are beautiful; and minds that lift themselves above the realm of sense to a higher order are aware of beauty in the conduct of life, in actions, in character, in the pursuits of the intellect; and there is the beauty of the virtues. What loftier beauty there may be, yet, our argument will bring to light.

What, then, is it that gives comeliness to material forms and draws the ear to the sweetness perceived in sounds, and what is the secret of the beauty there is in all that derives from Soul?

Is there some One Principle from which all take their grace, or is there a beauty peculiar to the embodied and another for the bodiless? Finally, one or many, what would such a Principle be?

Consider that some things, material shapes for instance, are gracious not by anything inherent but by something communicated, while others are lovely of themselves, as, for example, Virtue.

The same bodies appear sometimes beautiful, sometimes not; so that there is a good deal between being body and being beautiful.

What, then, is this something that shows itself in certain material forms? This is the natural beginning of our inquiry.

What is it that attracts the eyes of those to whom a beautiful object is presented, and calls them, lures them, towards it, and fills them with joy at the sight? If we possess ourselves of this, we have at once a standpoint for the wider survey.

Almost everyone declares that the symmetry of parts towards each other and towards a whole, with, besides, a certain charm of colour, constitutes the beauty recognized by the eye, that in visible things, as indeed in all else, universally, the beautiful thing is essentially symmetrical, patterned.

But think what this means.

Only a compound can be beautiful, never anything devoid of parts; and only a whole; the several parts will have beauty, not in themselves, but only as working together to give a comely total. Yet beauty in an aggregate demands beauty in details: it cannot be constructed out of ugliness; its law must run throughout.

All the loveliness of colour and even the light of the sun, being devoid of parts and so not beautiful by symmetry, must be ruled out of the realm of

413

beauty. And how comes gold to be a beautiful thing? And lightning by night, and the stars, why are these so fair?

In sounds also the simple must be proscribed, though often in a whole noble composition each several tone is delicious in itself.

Again since the one face, constant in symmetry, appears sometimes fair and sometimes not, can we doubt that beauty is something more than symmetry, that symmetry itself owes its beauty to a remoter principle?

Turn to what is attractive in methods of life or in the expression of thought; are we to call in symmetry here? What symmetry is to be found in noble conduct, or excellent laws, in any form of mental pursuit?

What symmetry can there be in points of abstract thought?

The symmetry of being accordant with each other? But there may be accordance or entire identity where there is nothing but ugliness: the proposition that honesty is merely a generous artlessness chimes in the most perfect harmony with the proposition that morality means weakness of will; the accordance is complete.

Then again, all the virtues are a beauty of the Soul, a beauty authentic beyond any of these others; but how does symmetry enter here? The Soul, it is true, is not a simple unity, but still its virtue cannot have the symmetry of size or of number: what standard of measurement could preside over the compromise or the coalescence of the Soul's faculties or purposes?

Finally, how by this theory would there be beauty in the Intellectual-Principle, essentially the solitary?

2. Let us, then, go back to the source, and indicate at once the Principle that bestows beauty on material things.

Undoubtedly this Principle exists; it is something that is perceived at the first glance, something which the Soul names as from an ancient knowledge and, recognizing, welcomes it, enters into unison with it.

But let the Soul fall in with the Ugly and at once it shrinks within itself, denies the thing, turns away from it, not accordant, resenting it.

Our interpretation is that the Soul—by the very truth of its nature, by its affiliation to the noblest Existents in the hierarchy of Being—when it sees anything of that kin, or any trace of that kinship, thrills with an immediate delight, takes its own to itself, and thus stirs anew to the sense of its nature and of all its affinity.

But, is there any such likeness between the loveliness of this world and the splendours in the Supreme? Such a likeness in the particulars would make the two orders alike: but what is there in common between beauty here and beauty There?

We hold that all the loveliness of this world comes by communion in Ideal-Form.

All shapelessness whose kind admits of pattern and form, as long as it remains outside of Reason and Idea, is ugly by that very isolation from the Divine Reason-Principle. And this is the Absolute Ugly: an ugly thing is something that has not been entirely mastered by pattern, that is by Reason, the Matter not yielding at all points and in all respects to Ideal-Form.

But where the Ideal-Form has entered, it has grouped and co-ordinated what from a diversity of parts was to become a unity: it has rallied confusion into cooperation: it has made the sum one harmonious coherence: for the Idea is a unity and what it moulds must come to unity as far as multiplicity may.

And on what has thus been compacted to unity, Beauty enthrones itself, giving itself to the parts as to the sum: when it lights on some natural unity, a thing of like parts, then it gives itself to that whole. Thus, for an illustration, there is the beauty, conferred by craftsmanship, of all a house with all its parts, and the beauty which some natural quality may give to a single stone.

This, then, is how the material thing becomes beautiful—by communicating in the Reason-Principle that flows from the Divine.

3. And the Soul includes a faculty peculiarly addressed to Beauty—one incomparably sure in the appreciation of its own, when Soul entire is enlisted to support its judgement.

Or perhaps the faculty acts immediately, affirming the Beautiful where it finds something accordant with the Ideal-Form within itself, using this Idea as a canon of accuracy in its decision.

But what accordance is there between the material and that which antedates all Matter?

On what principle does the architect, when he finds the house standing before him correspondent with his inner ideal of a house, pronounce it beautiful? Is it not that the house before him, the stones apart, is the inner idea stamped upon the mass of exterior matter, the indivisible exhibited in diversity?

So with the perceptive faculty: discerning in certain objects the Ideal-Form which has bound and controlled shapeless matter, opposed in nature to Idea, seeing further stamped upon the common shapes some shape excellent above the common, it gathers into unity what still remains fragmentary, catches it up and carries it within, no longer a thing of parts, and presents it to the inner Ideal-Principle as something concordant and congenial, a natural friend: the joy here is like that of a good man who discerns in a youth the early signs of a virtue consonant with the achieved perfection within his own soul.

The beauty of colour is also the outcome of a unification: it derives from shape, from the conquest of the darkness inherent in Matter by the pouring-in of light, the unembodied, which is a Rational-Principle and an Ideal-Form.

Hence it is that Fire itself is splendid beyond all material bodies, holding the rank of Ideal-Principle to the other elements, making ever upwards, the subtlest and sprightliest of all bodies, as very near to the unembodied; itself alone admitting no other, all the others penetrated by it: for they take warmth but this is never cold; it has colour primally; they receive the Form of colour from it: hence the splendour of its light, the splendour that belongs to the Idea. And all that has resisted and is but uncertainly held by its light remains outside of beauty, as not having absorbed the plenitude of the Form of colour.

And harmonies unheard in sound create the harmonies we hear and wake the Soul to the consciousness of beauty, showing it the one essence in another kind: for the measures of our sensible music are not arbitrary but are determined by the Principle whose labour is to dominate Matter and bring pattern into being.

Thus far of the beauties of the realm of sense, images and shadow-pictures, fugitives that have entered into Matter—to adorn, and to ravish, where they are seen.

4. But there are earlier and loftier beauties than these. In the sense-bound life we are no longer granted to know them, but the Soul, taking no help from the organs, sees and proclaims them. To the vision of these we must mount, leaving sense to its own low place.

As it is not for those to speak of the graceful forms of the material world who have never seen them or known their grace—men born blind, let us suppose—in the same way those must be silent upon the beauty of noble conduct and of learning and all that order who have never cared for such things, nor may those tell of the splendour of virtue who have never known the face of Justice and of Moral-Wisdom beautiful beyond the beauty of Evening and of Dawn.

Such vision is for those only who see with the Soul's sight—and at the vision, they will rejoice, and awe will fall upon them and a trouble deeper than all the rest could ever stir, for now they are moving in the realm of Truth.

This is the spirit that Beauty must ever induce, wonderment and a delicious trouble, longing and love and a trembling that is all delight. For the unseen all this may be felt as for the seen; and this the Souls feel for it, every Soul in some degree, but those the more deeply that are the more truly apt to this higher love—just as all take delight in the beauty of the body but all are not stung as sharply, and those only that feel the keener wound are known as Lovers.

5. These Lovers, then, lovers of the beauty outside of sense, must be made to declare themselves.

What do you feel in presence of the grace you discern in actions, in manners, in sound morality, in all the works and fruits of virtue, in the beauty of Souls? When you see that you yourselves are beautiful within, what do you feel? What is this Dionysiac exultation that thrills through your being, this straining upwards of all your soul, this longing to break away from the body and live sunken within the veritable self?

These are no other than the emotions of Souls under the spell of love.

But what is it that awakens all this passion? No shape, no colour, no grandeur of mass: all is for a Soul, something whose beauty rests upon no colour, for the moral wisdom the Soul enshrines and all the other hueless splendour of the virtues. It is that you find in yourself, or admire in another, loftiness of spirit; righteousness of life; disciplined purity, courage of the majestic face; gravity, modesty that goes fearless and tranquil and passionless; and, shining down upon all, the light of godlike Intellection.

All these noble qualities are to be reverenced and loved, no doubt, but what entitles them to be called beautiful?

They exist: they manifest themselves to us: anyone that sees them must admit that they have reality of Being; and is not Real-Being really beautiful?

But we have not yet shown by what property in them they have wrought the Soul to loveliness: what is this grace, this splendour as of Light, resting upon all the virtues?

Let us take the contrary, the ugliness of the Soul, and set that against its beauty: to understand, at once, what this ugliness is and how it comes to appear in the Soul will certainly open our way before us.

Let us then suppose an ugly Soul, dissolute, unrighteous: teeming with all the lusts; torn by internal discord; beset by the fears of its cowardice and the envies of its pettiness; thinking, in the little thought it has, only of the perishable and the base; perverse in all its impulses; the friend of unclean pleasures; living the life of abandonment to bodily sensation and delighting in its deformity.

What must we think but that all this shame is something that has gathered about the Soul, some foreign bane outraging it, soiling it, so that, encumbered with all manner of turpitude, it has no longer a clean activity or a clean sensation, but commands only a life smouldering dully under the crust of evil; that, sunk in manifold death, it no longer sees what a Soul should see, may no longer rest in its own being, dragged ever as it is towards the outer, the lower, the dark?

An unclean thing, I dare to say, flickering hither and thither at the call of objects of sense, deeply infected with the taint of body, occupied always in Matter, and absorbing Matter into itself, in its commerce with the Ignoble it has trafficked away for an alien nature its own essential form.

If a man has been immersed in filth or daubed with mud, his native comeliness disappears and all that is seen is the foul stuff besmearing him: his ugly condition is due to alien matter that has encrusted him, and if he is to win back his grace it must be his business to scour and purify himself and make himself what he was.

So, we may justly say, a Soul becomes ugly—by something foisted upon it, by sinking itself into the alien, by a fall, a descent into body, into Matter. The dishonour of the Soul is in its ceasing to be clean and apart. Gold is degraded when it is mixed with earthy particles; if these be worked out, the gold is left and is beautiful, isolated from all that is foreign, gold with gold alone. And so the Soul; let it be but cleared of the desires that come by its too intimate converse with the body, emancipated from all the passions, purged of all that embodiment has thrust upon it, withdrawn, a solitary, to itself again— in that moment the ugliness that came only from the alien is stripped away.

6. For, as the ancient teaching was, moral-discipline and courage and every virtue, not even excepting Wisdom itself, all is purification.

Hence the Mysteries with good reason adumbrate the immersion of the unpurified in filth, even in the Nether-World, since the. unclean loves filth for its very filthiness, and swine foul of body find their joy in foulness.

What else is Sophrosyny, rightly so-called, but to take no part in the pleasures of the body, to break away from them as unclean and unworthy of the clean? So too, Courage is but being fearless of the death which is but the parting of the Soul from the body, an event which no one can dread whose delight is to be his unmingled self. And Magnanimity is but disregard for the lure of things here. And Wisdom is but the Act of the Intellectual-Principle withdrawn from the lower places and leading the Soul to the Above.

The Soul thus cleansed is all Idea and Reason, wholly free of body, intellective, entirely of that divine order from which the wellspring of Beauty rises and all the race of Beauty.

Hence the Soul heightened to the Intellectual-Principle is beautiful to all its power. For Intellection and all that proceeds from Intellection are the Soul's beauty, a graciousness native to it and not foreign, for only with these is it truly Soul. And it is just to say that in the Soul's becoming a good and beautiful thing is its becoming like to God, for from the Divine comes all the Beauty and all the Good in beings.

We may even say that Beauty is the Authentic-Existents and Ugliness is the Principle contrary to Existence: and the Ugly is also the primal evil; therefore its contrary is at once good and beautiful, or is Good and Beauty: and hence the one method will discover to us the Beauty-Good and the Ugliness-Evil.

And Beauty, this Beauty which is also The Good, must be posed as The First: directly deriving from this First is the Intellectual-Principle which is preeminently the manifestation of Beauty; through the Intellectual-Principle Soul is beautiful. The beauty in things of a lower order—actions and pursuits for instance—comes by operation of the shaping Soul which is also the author of the beauty found in the world of sense. For the Soul, a divine thing, a fragment as it were of the Primal Beauty, makes beautiful to the fullness of their capacity all things whatsoever that it grasps and moulds.

7. Therefore we must ascend again towards the Good, the desired of every Soul. Anyone that has seen This, knows what I intend when I say that it is beautiful. It is desired as the goal of desire. To attain it is for those that will take the upward path, who will set all their forces towards it, who will divest themselves of all that we have put on in our descent: so, to those that approach the Holy Celebrations of the Mysteries, there are appointed purifications and the laying aside of the garments worn before, and the entry in nakedness—until, passing, on the upward way, all that is other than the God, each in the solitude of himself shall behold that solitary-dwelling Existence, the Apart, the Unmingled, the Pure, that from Which all things depend, for Which all look and live and act and know, the Source of Life and of Intellection and of Being.

And one that shall know this vision—with what passion of love shall he not be seized, with what pang of desire, what longing to be molten into one with This, what wondering delight! If he that has never seen this Being must hunger for It as for all his welfare, he that has known must love and reverence It as the very Beauty; he will be flooded with awe and gladness, stricken by a salutary terror; he loves with a veritable love, with sharp desire; all other loves than this he must despise, and disdain all that once seemed fair.

This, indeed, is the mood even of those who, having witnessed the manifestation of Gods or Supernals, can never again feel the old delight in the comeliness of material forms: what then are we to think of one that contemplates Absolute Beauty in Its essential integrity, no accumulation of flesh and matter, no dweller on earth or in the heavens—so perfect Its purity—far above all such things in that they are nonessential, composite, not primal but descending from This?

Beholding this Being—the Choragus of all Existence, the Self-Intent that ever gives forth and never takes—resting, rapt, in the vision and possession of so lofty a loveliness, growing to Its likeness, what Beauty can the Soul yet lack? For This, the Beauty supreme, the absolute, and the primal, fashions Its lovers to Beauty and makes them also worthy of love.

And for This, the sternest and the uttermost combat is set before the Souls; all our labour is for This, lest we be left without part in this noblest vision, which to attain is to be blessed in the blissful sight, which to fail of is to fail utterly.

For not he that has failed of the joy that is in colour or in visible forms, not he that has failed of power or of honours or of kingdom has failed, but only he that has failed of only This, for Whose winning he should renounce kingdoms and command over earth and ocean and sky, if only, spurning the world of sense from beneath his feet, and straining to This, he may see.

8. But what must we do? How lies the path? How come to vision of the inaccessible Beauty, dwelling as if in consecrated precincts, apart from the common ways where all may see, even the profane?

He that has the strength, let him arise and withdraw into himself, foregoing all that is known by the eyes, turning away for ever from the material beauty that once made his joy. When he perceives those shapes of grace that show in body, let him not pursue: he must know them for copies, vestiges, shadows, and hasten away towards That they tell of. For if anyone follow what is like a beautiful shape playing over water—is there not a myth telling in symbol of such a dupe, how he sank into the depths of the current and was swept away to nothingness? So too, one that is held by material beauty and will not break free shall be precipitated, not in body but in Soul, down to the dark depths loathed of the Intellective-Being, where, blind even in the Lower-World, he shall have commerce only with shadows, there as here.

'Let us flee then to the beloved Fatherland': this is the soundest counsel. But what is this flight? How are we to gain the open sea? For Odysseus is surely a parable to us when he commands the flight from the sorceries of Circe or Calypso—not content to linger for all the pleasure offered to his eyes and all the delight of sense filling his days.

The Fatherland to us is There whence we have come, and There is The Father.

What then is our course, what the manner of our flight? This is not a journey for the feet; the feet bring us only from land to land; nor need you think of coach or ship to carry you away; all this order of things you must set aside and refuse to see: you must close the eyes and call instead upon another vision which is to be waked within you, a vision, the birth-right of all, which few turn to use.

9. And this inner vision, what is its operation?

Newly awakened it is all too feeble to bear the ultimate splendour. Therefore the Soul must be trained—to the habit of remarking, first, all noble pursuits, then the works of beauty produced not by the labour of the arts but by the virtue of men known for their goodness: lastly, you must search the souls of those that have shaped these beautiful forms.

But how are you to see into a virtuous Soul and know its loveliness?

Withdraw into yourself and look. And if you do not find yourself beautiful yet, act as does the creator of a statue that is to be made beautiful: he cuts away here, he smoothes there, he makes this line lighter, this other purer, until a lovely face has grown upon his work. So do you also: cut away all that is excessive, straighten all that is crooked, bring light to all that is overcast, labour to make all one glow of beauty and never cease chiselling your statue, until there shall shine out on you from it the godlike splendour of virtue, until you shall see the perfect goodness surely established in the stainless shrine.

When you know that you have become this perfect work, when you are self-gathered in the purity of your being, nothing now remaining that can shatter that inner unity, nothing from without clinging to the authentic man, when you find yourself wholly true to your essential nature, wholly that only veritable Light which is not measured by space, not narrowed to any circumscribed form nor again diffused as a thing void of term, but ever unmeasurable as something greater than all measure and more than all quantity—when you perceive that you have grown to this, you are now become very vision: now call up all your confidence, strike forward yet a step—you need a guide no longer—strain, and see.

This is the only eye that sees the mighty Beauty. If the eye that adventures the vision be dimmed by vice, impure, or weak, and unable in its cowardly blenching to see the uttermost brightness, then it sees nothing even though another point to what lies plain to sight before it. To any vision must be brought an eye adapted to what is to be seen, and having some likeness to it. Never did eye see the sun unless it had first become sun-like, and never can the Soul have vision of the First Beauty unless itself be beautiful.

Therefore, first let each become godlike and each beautiful who cares to see God and Beauty. So, mounting, the Soul will come first to the Intellectual-Principle and survey all the beautiful Ideas in the Supreme and will avow that this is Beauty, that the Ideas are Beauty. For by their efficacy comes all Beauty else, by the offspring of Being and of the Intellectual-Principle. What is beyond the Intellectual-Principle we affirm to be the nature of Good radiating Beauty before it. So that, treating the Intellectual-Cosmos as one, the first is the Beautiful: if we make distinction there, the Realm of Ideas constitutes the

Beauty of the Intellectual Sphere; and The Good, which lies beyond, is the Fountain at once and Principle of Beauty: the Primal Good and the Primal Beauty have the one dwelling-place and, thus, always, Beauty's seat is There.

# VI. Ancient Rome

## INTRODUCTION

As with Greek literature, no short account can do justice to the breadth of Roman literature, or measure its influence on the literatures which emerged after Rome's fall. It is probably true, however, that most of us know less about Roman literature than Greek literature, and that the Romans most familiar to us are not authors, such as Vergil or Ovid, but political leaders, such as Julius Caesar or Augustus. Because of this, this introduction will address three related areas that are important in interpreting Roman literature:

1. Roman literature was not a simple derivation of Greek literature; at its best it adapted Greek elements in complex and ingenious ways.
2. Roman literature can and often should be read within its political context.
3. Roman literature was often written under a system of patronage.

1) It is often said that the Greeks were theoretical and imaginative, and the Romans were practical and imitative. As with nearly all such sweeping assessments, this one has a tiny kernel of truth to it. Rome rose as a military and political power in the Mediterranean relatively late in comparison with the Assyrian, Phoenician, and Greek cultures. When the Romans came into contact with Greek culture, especially through conquest, they were struck by the relative lack of variety and sophistication of their own art and literature, and they began to borrow and copy Greek forms and works as models for their own. Greek culture "conquered" its Roman conquerors, as Horace said. Some of the earliest creations were translations from Greek to Latin: we hear of a rough translation of the *Odyssey* by a Livius Andronicus in the third century B.C.E. which was still used as a school text two centuries later. Nearly every Greek genre—epic, tragedy, comedy, lyric—was undertaken by Roman authors, sometimes successfully, sometimes not. Native Italian and Roman performances and histories, such as Atellan farces and historical annals kept by priests, continued and influenced this new "high" literature, but it was still the classical heights represented by Greek literature that set the standards for Roman literature to follow. This led to an idea of creative originality that is quite different

from our own, but is essential to understanding Roman literature: originality is viewed as innovation within the context of recognized traditions.

The earliest attempts at epic, tragedy, and history are known to us only by names and fragments. The works of Ennius, Accius, Lucilius, Fabius Pictor, and many others were the foundations that Vergil, Horace, and Livy built on, but they took from their predecessors sparingly, and not without criticism. Horace describes Lucilius, his precedent for satire, as "a muddy river" (*Sat.* I.4.11), and the first century B.C.E. orator Cicero characterizes the third century oratory of the elder Cato as "rough and shaggy," but very appropriately adds that "nothing is found and perfected at the same time." Perfection, at least in the eyes of those who came afterwards, was reached by Cicero in oratory, by Vergil in epic, and by Horace in lyric. But these authors kept Greek models in mind as well as their Roman predecessors. The educated members of their audience were expected to know their Greek models. Vergil's *Aeneid* has one of the most complex interactions with its Greek precedents, Homer's *Iliad* and *Odyssey*. To give one example of Vergil's use and revision of Homer, consider the character of Dido in the first half of the *Aeneid*. As Aeneas travels from Troy to Italy, he follows the pattern of Odysseus in his wanderings; and like Odysseus, Aeneas is impeded in his progress by a woman. Odysseus is held for one year by a witch, Circe, and for seven by a divine nymph, Calypso, who loves him, as he makes his way toward his faithful wife, Penelope. Aeneas is detained for a swift year of love by Dido, who loves him. But Dido is very human, devoted to the memory of her first husband, and surrounded by suitors, like Penelope in the *Odyssey*. By mingling parallels to Circe, Calypso, and Penelope in the character of Dido, Vergil complicates the question of Dido's place in Aeneas' heart and in his destiny. Put another way, Dido is used to distinguish Aeneas from Odysseus, to characterize him as a different kind of hero.

The Romans are not inclined to hide their influences: Horace borrows lines as well as rhythms from Greek lyric poets; Propertius adapts a whole poem of Theocritus, making only a few important changes. Even satire, the one genre the Romans claimed as *tota nostra*, "all ours," acknowledges its debt to Greek comedy and Hellenistic diatribe. Roman authors advertised their debts, so that their audience could recognize not only what they had borrowed, but how they had reapplied, changed, and perhaps even surpassed it. Roman literature can certainly be read without a knowledge of its Greek influences, just as action movies can be enjoyed without knowing Westerns, as rock music can be enjoyed without a knowledge of the blues—but a layer of understanding and appreciation will be undetected.

Roman poets continued to build layer upon layer, mindful of everything that had gone before them. The idea of *auctoritas* is both political and literary;

the Latin word provides English with both "authority" and "author." Vergil serves as the best example. All epic after Vergil is cognizant of following the *Aeneid*. Statius, who lived from 48–96 C.E., ends his epic *Thebaid* with a direct address to his work: "do not rival the divine *Aeneid*, but follow at a distance, with reverence for its steps" (XII.815–816). Not all works explicitly chose reverence over rivalry, but your understanding of nearly all Roman literature will be enhanced by observing how similar these two motivations and their effects can be.

2) The political dimension of Roman literature is expressed in several ways. First, a few of the most noted Roman authors were also important political figures themselves. Cicero and Julius Caesar are probably the most famous of this class, but the emperors Augustus, Nero, and Marcus Aurelius also belong on this list. Most of the earliest historians of Rome were members of powerful families who wrote to record their families' contributions to Rome, and many later historians were also politically active, including Asinius Pollio, to whom Vergil addresses his *Fourth Eclogue*, and Tacitus, who served as a senator. (Livy, in this regard, is the exception.) The political motivatons and affiliations of these authors are usually obvious, but must always be kept in mind: Caesar is writing not simply as a historian of the wars in Gaul, for example, but as the victorious general keeping his distant audience informed of his military and diplomatic successes.

Writers who were themselves not politically active still wrote under the patronage of those in power. The system of patronage will be discussed below, but its political nature is more complicated than might appear. In its most direct form, writers wrote works favorable to their patrons, or critical of their patrons' enemies. But this is not always the case: the so-called Golden Age of Roman literature began with the rise of Augustus, who supported Vergil, Horace, Propertius and others, but it is not possible to see praise of Augustus in every Horatian ode or Propertian elegy. Other elements can be seen as the results of political influence, such as the genre, the choice or avoidance of subjects and themes, the tone or characterization of the poetic voice. These influences were in place during the Republic, but more important during the Empire, when the Emperor's disfavor could bring banishment or death. Ovid spent the last nine years of his life in exile on the coast of the Black Sea, petitioning for his return; and we have very little literature from the reigns of Tiberius, Caligula, or Claudius (14–54 C.E.), when out of fear little seems to have been written.

The Romans themselves seem to have been a very politically inclined audience, looking for political messages in seemingly unrelated places. Cicero reports that an audience saw a reference to Mark Antony and Brutus in a performance of a tragedy by Accius—even though it was the restaging of a play that was first produced 60 years earlier! (*Philippics* I.36) Of course, the theme of the play, which dealt with a vicious tyrant and his downfall, and the probable organizer of the performance, Brutus, influenced the audience's response, but it gives some indication of the potential political charge that ran beneath the surface of both the writing and the reception of many works in their original context. It also gives an indication of the potential danger of writing a work that could be read, or misread, as a political statement, even if none was intended. Probably for this reason, literature did not always flourish under the Emperors, whose suspicion could be fatal for any author.

3) All of Roman society was structured by a hierarchical system of patrons and clients, who felt and exercised a variety of obligations for each other: financing, legal defense, political support, even marital advice. Not surprisingly, this dense web of mutual obligation also included poets and authors. Some of the early Latin literature was written by non-Romans who attached themselves to important Romans and enjoyed their support. In return, the literary clients praised their patrons explicitly, not only for their support but for their refinement and culture. Some families seem to have had an "in house" poet. One Greek poet, Archias, was hauled into court on a specious charge by the enemies of the Luculli, his patrons, where Cicero defended him. There may have been some competition for the services of the accomplished poets. Cicero himself offered his patronage to poets to write about him, and he seems to have been unsuccessful.

During the Republic, there were multiple, and occasionally conflicting, lines of patronage, but under the Empire, the Emperor stood at the head of all clients. Consequently, literary patronage under the Empire took a more obvious, and yet less explicitly expressed, form. Poets cite other patrons (especially Maecenas), but Maecenas was an associate of Augustus, and it is clear that Augustus' favor lay behind all poetic support. The support presumably took the form of substantial gifts—Horace constantly thanks Maecenas for the gift of a small farm—but obligates the poets in ways that are not always apparent. The writers themselves were also thought to offer something substantial in return: immortal renown. Perhaps for this reason, the relationship between poet and patron in the early Empire is not always expressed as a subordinate one. Horace talks about his introduction to Maecenas through Vergil and others, and after several meetings, Horace tells us that Maecenas included him in *amicorum numero*, "among his friends" (*Sat.* I.6.62).

BSH

# Catullus

## 84–54 B.C.E.

Gaius Valerius Catullus is probably the Roman poet whose work is most readily accessible to modern readers, young and old. His output consists of 116 poems in a variety of meters, including Sapphics and elegaic meters, and the subjects tend to be drawn from the private and daily world of Catullus. He has poems—not included here—that wittily invite a friend to dinner, sing the praises of his hometown, Sirmio, and tweak a rival for his body odor. Catullus' tone can vary from the nearly pornographic to the poignant: poem 101, left as a grave offering at his brother's tomb, mixes palpable grief with a ritual farewell. Catullus also wrote several longer refined poems that demonstrate Hellenistic learning and polish. The poems that we include below, however, are those for which Catullus is most well-known, and they tell of his love for Lesbia, and the suffering that it brings.

Catullus was probably born in 84 and died in 54 B.C.E. As a young man, he came to Rome and met the woman whom he calls Lesbia. A later writer, Apuleius, tells us that Catullus' Lesbia was in fact Clodia, the notorious young wife of Metellus Celer who was consul in 60 B.C.E. In Catullus' poems, Lesbia at first betrays her husband with him, and later betrays him for another, and the anguish that attends her unfaithfulness is torture to him. Catullus' poetry is marked by its apparent spontaneity and the immediacy of its passions, but it is dangerous to read his poems as the spontaneous creations of an emotional whirlwind. By renaming his beloved "Lesbia" Catullus signals that he is writing poetry in the mode of Sappho of Lesbos, and his poems reveal the highest degree of metrical and linguistic refinement.

To give a simple example of the depth of Catullus which is not often obvious at the first reading, consider the 85th poem. The translation could be mistaken for any run-of-the-mill rock song of the last 20 years:

> I hate and I love. Why do I do this, maybe you ask.
> I don't know, but I sense it happening—and I'm tortured.

The Latin is also deceptively simple:

> *Odi et amo. Quare id faciam, fortasse requiris.*
> *Nescio, sed fieri sentio, et excrucior.*

One key comes in the words *faciam* and *fieri*. Both occur before the significant pauses in each line; and they are lexically the opposite of each other. *Facio* is the active form of the verb "to do", and *fieri* is the passive of the same verb. With that prompt, we see that the two lines flow by degrees from active to passive: "I do," "you ask," "I don't know," "I sense," "it happening," "I am tortured." The poem poses questions: is love an action or passion? is hate something you do or you suffer? And it proceeds to confound the answer by conflating experience with grammar: they are both, they are neither, they are a category unto themselves. Out of specific events and common experience, Catullus produces artful poems that give the impression of simplicity.

BSH

# from *Poems* (*Carmina*)

## 5

Live, my Lesbia, and love—let's do it!
and austere old men's aspersions,
all of them, value at ten for a penny.
The sun, new each day, can sink and return,
but we—? once sunk, our brief light's                                    5
night, endless, one we're bound to sleep through.
Give me a thousand kisses. Then a hundred.
Then another thousand. Then a second hundred.
Then a further thousand. Then a hundred.
Then, when we've achieved untold thousands,                              10
we'll jumble them all up, so *we won't know*—and
no one spiteful can evil-eye us, since he
won't know either!—the Grand Total of kisses.

## 8

*Poor dear Catullus!*—would you please stop this foolishness?
Get this and get it right:
if you see that a thing has died? it's dead. Gone. *LOST.*
The sun shone, once, radiant, all yours each day,
when you went wandering right where she led you,                        5
the maid we loved as no other shall ever be loved.
Then, when first those many amusements saw the light,
the ones you so wanted and the maid did not *not* want,
the sun did shine (truly!) radiant, all yours each day . . .

Now she does not want: you too, weakling, stop wanting!                 10
if she runs off, don't chase her, don't *be* 'poor dear,'
but, iron-willed, plan to get past it. Be firm.
Good-bye, little maid! Catullus has now become firm.
He won't plead or invite you out, Ms. Don't-think-I-will!
But you'll fret when you find yourself uninvited!                       15
Sorry bitch! shove off! What kind of life awaits you?
Who now will go near you? who'll find you appealing?
what man will you love now? whose will they call you?

429

whom will you kiss? whose lips will you bite?
But *you*, Catullus! stick to your plan: BE FIRM.                    20

## 11

Furius and Aurelus, Catullus's comrades
whether he makes tracks for the wilds of India
where the sunrise surf, far resounding, gives the
       shoreline a pounding,

or if he treks off to effete Arabia,                                5
or to Parthian backcountry[1] thick with bowmen,
or to seas stained black where the seven Nile-streams
       empty their waters,

or if he sets out to traverse the high Alps,
touring Caesar's trophies, his trail of glory,                      10
namely, Gaulish Rhine and the Britons (fierce, re-
       motest of races)—

you two, though you're ready to face these hazards
with me, face "whatever is Heaven's pleasure,"
take my *Little Maiden* a message, short but                        15
       not sweetly-worded:

*Live it up. Farewell. Hope you like your lovers,*
*hug and squeeze them tight—all three hundred jointly—*
*true to none but, matter-of-factly, help them*
       *all get their rocks off.*                         20

Tell her *she can look someplace else for my love*
*which she, by her crime, cut to pieces—like a*
*flower at meadow's edge that the plow, in passing,*
       *brushed and left broken.*

## 51

He appears, to me, to be God's own equal,
he (may God forgive me!) surpasses all Gods,
he that sits so matter-of-factly near you,
    watching and hearing

your delicious laughter—a thing which (ah me!)            5
rips out all my senses for, when I see you,

Lesbia, I disintegrate, nothing's left of
    [me, I am speechless.]

Yes, my tongue goes numb, tender fire is
seeping down through bone marrow; ears re-echo,         10
belling their own notes; over both bright eyes, night
    knots double blindfolds.

(Idle ways, Catullus—they cause you trouble.
Idling turns you on—and you've grown addicted.
Idle ways have left bygone kings and wealthy         15
    nations in ruins.)

## 72

You used to say, once, that you knew only Catullus,
    Lesbia, that you'd not take Jove before me.
I cherished you then, not the way men do their sweethearts,
    but as a father cherishes sons and sons-in-law.
Now *I* know *you*: so, though the burn's deeper and costs me more,     5
    still I find you cheaper and much more trifling.
How can that be, you ask? Simple. This kind of wrong
    makes a lover *love* more but *like* less.

## 75

To this has my mind been reduced, Lesbia, by your crime,
    and by its own devotion so doomed itself,
that now it *can*not like you—though you change for the best,
    nor cease to love you—though you do your worst.

## 76

If a person feels any pleasure in recalling
    past kindnesses when he thinks, with clear conscience,
that he has shattered no hallowed faith nor broken
    any true allegiance to play someone false,
much is in store for you in the long years ahead, Catullus—     5
    joy on joy derived from this thankless love:
for whatever one person can in kindness say or
    do for another, that have you said and done.

Everything you entrusted to a thankless mind is lost—
    so why put yourself through further torment?         10

why not stiffen your will and pull back from where you are now
　　and, as God is against it, don't *be* 'poor dear.'

No easy thing, to set old love aside of a sudden. . .
　　No easy thing but, somehow, you've *got to do it.*
This is your one hope, this is a fight you must win,　　　　　　　　15
　　you've just **got** to, possible or not.

O God, if mercy is Thine, or if Thou hast ever
　　succored mortals at the last—even in death—
look upon me (poor me!) and, if I have led a pure life,
　　rip from my flesh this poisonous putrefaction　　　　　　　　20
which, creeping like cancer into my deepest marrow,
　　has squeezed all happiness out of my heart.

No more do I pray either that *she* should cherish *me*
　　or—since it's not possible—want to be true:
I yearn to be well and to set this loathsome illness aside:　　　　25
　　God, grant me this, for I am a man of good conscience!

## 85

I loathe and I love. Why do it, perhaps you ask?
*I don't know*—I just feel it happening,
needle-jab in the vein.

## Note

[1] The Parthian Empire stretched from present day Iran into Turkey. Catullus' Latin also mentions Hyrcanians, who lived at the southern end of the Caspian Sea, in modern Iran and Turkmenistan.

# Cicero

## 106–43 B.C.E.

According to Quintilian, a scholar of the later first century C.E., the name of Cicero was considered synonymous with eloquence itself. And thanks to the more than 900 correspondences of his which survive, we know more about Marcus Tullius Cicero (106–43 B.C.E.) than about any other individual in antiquity. In his final speeches against Mark Antony, Cicero neatly equated himself with the Roman Republic; as it happens, modern readers nearly do the same.

In addition to his forensic and deliberative speeches and his letters, Cicero also wrote philosophical, rhetorical, and political dialogues and treatises. Some scholars fault Cicero for the derivative nature of his philosophy and his lack of originality, but in truth many of his sources do not survive, and we are often incapable of judging the degrees of Cicero's borrowing and his innovation. He is certainly eclectic in his sources. The immediate model for his work *On the Republic*—and for the *Laws* which followed—was Plato. For Plato, however, as for Aristotle, the city-state was still the political unit that defined citizenship and political life. A huge change had taken place since the death of Aristotle in 323 B.C.E.: the city-state had largely been replaced by Hellenistic kingdoms, and citizenship gave way to cosmopolitanism. For Cicero, Rome was the model city-state which governed an empire, and ruled it justly, and held the favor of the gods. We can identify many elements of Rome's governance that lent it stability; elsewhere Polybius (see selection) extolled the balance of monarchy, aristocracy and democracy in the Roman constitution. Here Cicero focuses on the laws, which stand at the heart of Rome's political structure and religious observances.

BSH

# from *On the Laws (De Legibus)*

*M.* There you are mistaken, Quintus, for it is rather ignorance of the law than knowledge of it that leads to litigation. But that will come later; now let us investigate the origins of Justice.

Well then, the most learned men have determined to begin with Law, and it would seem that they are right, if, according to their definition, Law is the highest reason, implanted in Nature, which commands what ought to be done and forbids the opposite. This reason, when firmly fixed and fully developed in the human mind, is Law. And so they believe that Law is intelligence, whose natural function it is to command right conduct and forbid wrongdoing. They think that this quality has derived its name in Greek from the idea of granting to every man his own, and in our language I believe it has been named from the idea of choosing. For as they have attributed the idea of fairness to the word law, so we have given it that of selection, though both ideas properly belong to Law. Now if this is correct, as I think it to be in general, then the origin of Justice is to be found in Law, for Law is a natural force; it is the mind and reason of the intelligent man, the standard by which Justice and Injustice are measured. But since our whole discussion has do with the reasoning of the populace, it will sometimes be necessary to speak in the popular manner, and give the name of law to that which in written form decrees whatever it wishes, either by command or prohibition. For such is the crowd's definition of law. But in determining what Justice is, let us begin with that supreme Law which had its origin ages before any written law existed or any State had been established.

*Q.* Indeed that will be preferable and more suitable to the character of the conversation we have begun.

*M.* Well, then, shall we seek the origin of Justice itself at its fountain-head? For when that is discovered we shall undoubtedly have a standard by which the things we are seeking may be tested.

*Q.* I think that is certainly what we must do.

*A.* Put me down also as agreeing with your brother's opinion.

*M.* Since, then, we must retain and preserve that constitution of the State which Scipio[1] proved to be the best in the six books I devoted to the subject, and all our laws must be fitted to that type of State, and since we must also inculcate good morals, and not prescribe everything in writing, I shall seek the root of Justice in Nature, under whose guidance our whole discussion must be conducted.

*A.* Quite right. Surely with her as our guide, it will be impossible for us to go astray.

VII. *M.* Do you grant us, then, Pomponius (for I am aware of what Quintus thinks), that it is by the might of the immortal gods, or by their nature, reason, power, mind, will, or any other term which may make my meaning clearer, that all Nature is governed? For if you do not admit it, we must begin our argument with this problem before taking up anything else.

*A.* Surely I will grant it, if you insist upon it, for the singing of the birds about us and the babbling of the streams relieve me from all fear that I may be overheard by any of my comrades in the School.[2]

*M.* Yet you must be careful; for it is their way to become very angry at times, as virtuous men will; and they will not tolerate your treason, if they hear of it, to the opening passage of that excellent book, in which the author has written, "God troubles himself about nothing, neither his own concerns nor those of others."

*A.* Continue, if you please, for I am eager to learn what my admission will lead to.

*M.* I will not make the argument long. Your admission leads us to this: that animal which we call man, endowed with foresight and quick intelligence, complex, keen, possessing memory, full of reason and prudence, has been given a certain distinguished status by the supreme God who created him; for he is the only one among so many different kinds and varieties of living beings who has a share in reason and thought, while all the rest are deprived of it. But what is more divine, I will not say in man only, but in all heaven and earth, than reason? And reason, when it is full grown and perfected, is rightly called wisdom. Therefore, since there is nothing better than reason, and since it exists both in man and God, the first common possession of man and God is reason. But those who have reason in common must also have right reason in common. And since right reason is Law, we must believe that men have Law also in common with the gods. Further, those who share Law must also share Justice; and those who share these are to be regarded as members of the same commonwealth. If indeed they obey the same authorities and powers, this is true in a far greater degree; but as a matter of fact they do obey this celestial system, the divine mind, and the God of transcendent power. Hence we must now conceive of this whole universe as one commonwealth of which both gods and men are members.

And just as in States distinctions in legal status are made on account of the blood relationships of families, according to a system which I shall take up in its proper place, so in the universe the same thing holds true, but on a scale much vaster and more splendid, so that men are grouped with Gods on the basis of blood relationship and descent. VIII. For when the nature of man is examined, the theory is usually advanced (and in all probability it is correct) that through constant changes and revolutions in the heavens, a time came which was suitable for sowing the seed of the human race. And when this seed was scattered and sown over the earth, it was granted the divine gift of the soul. For while the other elements of which man consists were derived from what is mortal, and are therefore fragile and perishable, the soul was generated in us by God. Hence we are justified in saying that there is a blood relationship between ourselves and the celestial beings; or we may call it a common ancestry or origin. Therefore among all the varieties of living beings there is no creature except man which has any knowledge of God, and among men themselves there is no race either so highly civilized or so savage as not to know that it must believe in a god, even if it does not know in what sort of god it ought to believe. Thus it is clear that man recognizes God because, in a way, he remembers and recognizes the source from which he sprang.

Moreover, virtue exists in man and God alike, but in no other creature besides; virtue, however, is nothing else than Nature perfected and developed to its highest point; therefore there is a likeness between man and God. As this is true, what relationship could be closer or clearer than this one? For this reason, Nature has lavishly yielded such a wealth of things adapted to man's convenience and use that what she produces seems intended as a gift to us, and not brought forth by chance; and this is true, not only of what the fertile earth bountifully bestows in the form of grain and fruit, but also of the animals; for it is clear that some of them have been created to be man's slaves, some to supply him with their products, and others to serve as his food. Moreover innumerable arts have been discovered through the teachings of Nature; for it is by a skilful imitation of her that reason has acquired the necessities of life. IX. Nature has likewise not only equipped man himself with nimbleness of thought, but has also given him the senses, to be, as it were, his attendants and messengers; she has laid bare the obscure and none too [obvious] meanings of a great many things, to serve as the foundations of knowledge, as we may call them; and she has granted us a bodily form which is convenient and well suited to the human mind. For while she has bent the other creatures down toward their food, she has made man alone erect and has challenged him to look up toward heaven, as being, so to speak, akin to him, and his first home. In addition, she has so formed his features as to portray therein the character that lies hidden deep within him; for not only do the eyes declare with exceeding clearness the innermost feelings of our hearts, but also the countenance, as we Romans call it, which can be found in no living thing save man, reveals the character. (The Greeks are familiar with the meaning which this word "countenance" conveys, though they have no name for it.) I will pass over the special faculties and aptitudes of the other parts of the body, such as the varying tones of the voice and the power of speech, which is the most effective promoter of human intercourse; for all these things are not in keeping with our present discussion or the time at our disposal; and besides, this topic has been adequately treated, as it seems to me, by Scipio in the books which you have read. But, whereas God has begotten and equipped man, desiring him to be the chief of all created things, it should now be evident, without going into all the details, that Nature, alone and unaided, goes a step farther; for, with no guide to point the way, she starts with those things whose character she has learned through the rudimentary beginnings of intelligence, and, alone and unaided, strengthens and perfects faculty of reason.

. . . From this point of view it can be readily understood that those who formulated wicked and unjust statutes for nations, thereby breaking their promises and agreements, put into effect anything but "laws." It may thus be clear that in the very definition of the term "law" there inheres the idea and principle of choosing what is just and true. I ask you then, Quintus, according to the custom of the philosophers: if there is a certain thing, the lack of which in a State compels us to consider it no State at all, must we consider this thing a good?

*Q.* One of the greatest goods, certainly.

*M.* And if a State lacks Law, must it for that reason be considered no State at all?

*Q.* It cannot be denied.

*M.* Then Law must necessarily be considered one of the greatest goods.

*Q.* I agree with you entirely.

*M.* What of the many deadly, the many pestilential statutes which nations put in force? These no more deserve to be called laws than the rules a band of robbers might pass in their assembly. For if ignorant and unskilful men have prescribed deadly poisons instead of healing drugs, these cannot possibly be called physicians' prescriptions; neither in a nation can a statute of any sort be called a law, even though the nation, in spite of its being a ruinous regulation, has accepted it. Therefore Law is the distinction between things just and unjust, made in agreement with that primal and most ancient of all things, Nature; and in conformity to Nature's standard are framed those human laws which inflict punishment upon the wicked but defend and protect the good.

VI. *Q.* I understand you completely, and believe that from now on we must not consider or even call anything else a law.

*M.* Then you do not think the Titian or Apuleian Laws[3] were really laws at all?

*Q.* No; nor the Livian Laws either.

*M.* And you are right, especially as the Senate repealed them in one sentence and in a single moment. But the Law whose nature I have explained can neither be repealed nor abrogated.

*Q.* Then the laws you intend to propose will, of course, be the kind that will never be repealed?

*M.* Certainly, if only they are accepted by both of you. But I think that I should follow the same course as Plato, who was at the same time a very learned man and the greatest of all philosophers, and who wrote a book about the Republic first, and then in a separate treatise described its Laws. Therefore, before I recite the law itself, I will speak in praise of that law. I note that Zaleucus and Charondas[4] did the same thing, though they wrote their laws, not for the interest and pleasure of doing so, but for actual use in their own States. Clearly Plato agreed with their opinion that it was also the function of Law to win some measure of approval, and not always compel by threats of force.

*Q.* What do you think of Timaeus' denial of Zaleucus' existence?

*M.* Well, Theophrastus[5] affirms it, and he is just as trustworthy an authority, in my opinion (indeed, many rate him higher); and, in fact, my protégés, the Locrians, his own fellow-citizens, still tell of Zaleucus. But whether he ever existed or has nothing to do with the case; my statement merely follows the tradition.

VII. So in the very beginning we must persuade our citizens that the gods are the lords and rulers of all things, and that what is done, is done by their will and authority; that they are likewise great benefactors of man, observing the character of every individual, what he does, of what wrong he is guilty, and with what intentions and with what piety he fulfils his religious duties; and that they take note of the pious and the impious. For surely minds which are imbued with such ideas will not fail to form true and useful opinions. Indeed, what is more true than that no one ought to be so foolishly proud as to think that, though reason and intellect exist in himself, they do not exist in the heavens and the universe, or that those things which can hardly be understood by the highest reasoning powers of the human intellect are guided by no reason at all? In truth, the man that is not driven to gratitude by the orderly courses of the stars, the regular alternation of day and night, the gentle progress of the seasons, and the produce of the earth brought forth for our sustenance—how can such an one be accounted a man at all? And since all things that possess reason stand above those things which are without reason, and since it would be sacrilege to say that anything stands above universal Nature, we must admit that reason is inherent in Nature. Who will deny that such beliefs are useful when he remembers how often oaths are used to confirm agreements, how important to our well-being is the sanctity of treaties, how many persons are deterred from crime by the fear of divine punishment, and how sacred an association of citizens becomes when the immortal gods are made members of it, either as judges or as witnesses?

There you have the proem to the law; for that is the name given to it by Plato.

*Q.* There it is indeed, brother, and I am particularly pleased that you have taken up different subjects and presented different ideas from his. For nothing could be more unlike his treatment than your previous remarks, and also this preface in regard to the gods. In just one thing you do seem to me to imitate him—in the style of your language.

*M.* Wish to do so, possibly; for who can or ever will be able to imitate him in this? It is very easy to translate another man's ideas, and I might do that, if I did not fully wish to be myself. For what difficulty is there in presenting the same thoughts rendered in practically the same phrases?

*Q.* I agree with you entirely. I certainly prefer that you be independent, as you have just said. But, if you please, let us hear your laws concerning religion.

*M.* I will present them as well as I can, and, since the place and the conversation are private, I will recite my laws in the legal style.

*Q.* What do you mean by that?

*M.* There is a certain legal language, Quintus, not so antiquated as that of our ancient Twelve Tables and Sacred Laws, and yet, to give greater authority, a little more archaic than the language of the present day. That style, together with its brevity, I will follow as far as I can. But I shall not present my laws in complete form, for that would be an infinite task, but shall give only the gist and substance of their provisions.

*Q.* That is the only possible way: therefore let us hear them.

*VIII. M. They shall approach the gods in purity, bringing piety, and leaving riches behind. Whoever shall do otherwise, God Himself will deal out punishment to him.*

*No one shall have gods to himself, either new gods or alien gods, unless recognized by the State. Privately they shall worship those gods whose worship they have duly received from their ancestors.*

*In cities they shall have shrines; they shall have groves in the country and homes for the Lares.*

*They shall preserve the rites of their families and their ancestors.*

*They shall worship as gods both those who have always been regarded as dwellers in heaven, and also those whose merits have admitted them to heaven; Hercules, Liber, Aesculopius, Castor, Pollux, Quirinus; also those qualities through which an ascent to heaven is granted to mankind: Intellect, Virtue, Piety, Good Faith. To their praise there shall be shrines, but none for the vices.*

*They shall perform the established rites.*

*On holidays they shall refrain from law-suits; these they shall celebrate together with their slaves after their tasks are done. Let holidays be so arranged as to fall at regularly recurring breaks in the year. The priest shall offer on behalf of the State the prescribed grains and the prescribed fruits; this shall be done according to prescribed rites and on prescribed days; likewise for other days they shall reserve the plenteous offerings of the milk and the offspring. And so that no violation of these customs shall take place, the priests shall determine the mode and the annual circuit of such offerings; and they the shall prescribe the victims which are proper and pleasing to each of the gods.*

*The several gods shall have their several priests, the gods all together their pontiffs, and the individual gods their flamens. The Vestal Virgins[6] shall guard the eternal fire on the public hearth of the city.*

*Those who are ignorant as to the methods and rites suitable to these public and private sacrifices shall seek instruction from the public priests. Of them there shall be three kinds: one to have charge of ceremonies and sacred rites; another to interpret those obscure sayings of soothsayers and prophets which shall be recognized by the Senate and the people; and the interpreters of Jupiter the Best and Greatest, namely the public augurs, shall foretell the future from portents and auspices, and maintain their art. And the priests shall observe the omens in regard to vineyards and orchards and the safety of the people; those who carry on war or affairs of State shall be informed by them beforehand of the auspices and shall obey them; the priests shall foresee the wrath of the gods and yield to it; they shall observe flashes of lightning in fixed regions of the sky, and shall keep free and unobstructed the city and fields and their places of observation. Whatever an augur shall declare to be unjust, unholy, pernicious, or ill-omened, shall be null and void; and whosoever yields not obedience shall be put to death.*

*IX. The fetial priests shall be judges and messengers for treaties, peace and war, truces, and embassies; they shall make the decisions in regard to war.*

*Prodigies and portents shall be referred to the Etruscan soothsayers, if the Senate so decree; Etruria shall instruct her leading men in this art. They shall make expiatory offerings to whatever gods they decide upon, and shall perform expiations for flashes of lightning and for whatever shall be struck by lightning.*

*No sacrifices shall be performed by women at night except those offered for the people in proper form;[7] nor shall anyone be initiated except into the Greek rites of Ceres,[8] according to the custom.*

*Sacrilege which cannot be expiated shall be held to be impiously committed; that which can be expiated shall be atoned for by the public priests.*

*At the public games which are held without chariot races or the contest of body with body, the public pleasure shall be provided for with moderation by song to the music of harp and flute, and this shall be combined with honour to the gods.*

*Of the ancestral rites the best shall be preserved.*

*No one shall ask for contributions except the servants of the Idean Mother,[9] and they only on the appointed days.*

*Whoever steals or carries off what is sacred or anything entrusted to what is sacred shall be considered as equal in guilt to a parricide.*

*For the perjurer the punishment from the gods is destruction; the human punishment shall be disgrace.*

*The pontiffs shall inflict capital punishment on those guilty of incest.*

*No wicked man shall dare to appease the wrath of the gods with gifts.*

*Vows shall be scrupulously performed; there shall be a penalty for the violation of the law.*

*No one shall consecrate a field; the consecration of gold, silver, and ivory shall be confined to reasonable limits.*

*The sacred rites of families shall remain for ever.*

*The rights of the gods of the lower world shall be sacred. Kinsfolk who are dead shall be considered gods; the expenditure and mourning for them shall be limited.*

X. *Q.* My dear brother, how quickly you have completed this important body of law! However, it seems to me that this religious system of yours does not differ a great deal from the laws of Numa and our own customs.

*M.* Do you not think, then, since Scipio in my former work on the Republic offered a convincing proof that our early State was the best in the world, that we must provide that ideal State with laws which are in harmony with its character?

*Q.* Certainly I think so.

*M.* Then you must expect such laws as will establish that best type of State. And if I chance to propose any provisions to-day which do not exist now and never have existed in our State, they will nevertheless be found for the most part among the customs of our ancestors, which used to have the binding force of law. . . .

Having established these facts, we shall now proceed to the statement of the laws themselves, if that plan meets with your approval.

*A.* Indeed I approve not merely of that, but of your whole order of treatment.

III. *M. Commands shall be just, and the citizens shall obey them dutifully and without protest. Upon the disobedient or guilty citizen the magistrate shall use compulsion by means of fines, imprisonment, or stripes, unless an equal or higher authority, or the people, forbid it; the citizen shall have the right of appeal to them. After the magistrate has pronounced sentence, either of death or fine, there shall be a trial before the people for the final determination of the fine or other penalty.*

*There shall be no appeal from orders given by a commander in the field; while a magistrate is waging war his commands shall be valid and binding.*

*There shall be minor magistrates with partial authority, who shall be assigned to special functions. In the army they shall command those over whom they are placed, and be their tribunes; in the city they shall be custodians of public moneys; they shall have charge of the confinement of criminals; they shall inflict capital punishment; they shall coin bronze, silver, and gold money; they shall decide lawsuits; they shall do whatsoever the Senate shall decree.*

*There shall be aediles, who shall be curators of the city, of the markets, and of the customary games. This magistracy shall be their first step in the advancement to higher office.*

*Censors shall make a list of the citizens, recording their ages, families, and slaves and other property. They shall have charge of the temples, streets, and aqueducts within the city, and of the public treasury and the revenues. They shall make a division of the citizens into tribes, and other divisions according to wealth, age, and rank. They shall enrol the recruits for the cavalry and infantry; they shall prohibit celibacy; they shall regulate the morals of the people; they shall allow no one guilty of dishonourable conduct to remain in the Senate. They shall be two in number, and shall hold office for five years. The other magistrates shall hold office for one year. The office of censor shall never be vacant.*

*The administrator of justice, who shall decide or direct the decision of civil cases, shall be called praetor; he shall be the guardian of the civil law. There shall be as many praetors, with equal powers, as the Senate shall decree, or the people command.*

*There shall be two magistrates with royal powers. Since they lead, judge, and confer, from these functions they shall be called praetors, judges, and consuls. In the field they shall hold the supreme military power; they shall be subject to no one; the safety of the people shall be their highest law.*

*No one shall hold the same office a second time except after an interval of ten years. They shall observe the age limits fixed by a law defining the year.*

*But when a serious war or civil dissensions arise, one man shall hold, for not longer than six months, the power which ordinarily belongs to the two consuls, if the Senate shall so decree. And after being appointed under favourable auspices, he shall be master of the people.*[10] *He shall have an assistant to command the cavalry, whose rank shall be equal to that of the administrator of justice.*

*But when there are neither consuls nor a master of the people, there shall be no other magistrates, and the auspices shall be in the hands of the Senate, which shall appoint one of its number to conduct the election of consuls in the customary manner.*

*Officials with and without imperium*[11] *and ambassadors shall leave the city when the Senate shall so decree or the people so command; they shall wage just wars justly; they shall spare the allies; they shall hold themselves and their subordinates in check; they shall increase the national renown; they shall return home with honour.*

*No one shall be made an ambassador for the purpose of attending to his own personal affairs.*

*The ten officials whom the plebeians shall elect to protect them from violence shall be their tribunes. Their prohibitions and resolutions passed by the plebeians under their presidency shall be binding. Their persons shall be inviolable. They shall not leave the plebeians without tribunes.*

*All magistrates shall possess the right of taking the auspices, and the judicial power. The Senate shall consist of those who have held magistracies. Its decrees shall be binding. But in case an equal or higher authority than the presiding officer shall veto a decree of the Senate, it shall nevertheless be written out and preserved.*

*The senatorial order shall be free from dishonour, and shall be a model for the rest of the citizens.*

*When elective, judicial, and legislative acts of the people are performed by vote, the voting shall not be concealed from citizens of high rank, and shall be free to the common people.*

*IV. But if any acts of administration shall be necessary in addition to those done by the regular magistrates, the people shall elect officials to perform them, and give them the authority to do so.*

*Consuls, praetors, masters of the people, masters of the horse, and those officials whom the Senate shall appoint to conduct the election of consuls shall have the right to preside over meetings of the people and the Senate. The tribunes chosen by the plebeians shall have the right to preside over the Senate, and shall also refer whatever is necessary to the plebeians.*

*Moderation shall be preserved in meetings of the people and the Senate.*

*A senator's absence from a meeting of the Senate shall be either for cause or culpable. A senator shall speak in his turn and at moderate length. He shall be conversant with public affairs.*

*No violence shall be used at meetings of the people. An equal or higher authority shall have the greater power. But the presiding officer shall be responsible for any disorder which may occur. He who vetoes a bad measure shall be deemed a citizen of distinguished service.*

*Presiding officers shall observe the auspices and obey the State augur. They shall see that bills, after being read, are filed among the archives in the State treasury. They shall not take the people's vote on more than one question at a time. They shall instruct the people in regard to the matter in hand, and allow them to be instructed by other magistrates and by private citizens.*

*No law of personal exception shall be proposed. Cases in which the penalty is death or loss of citizenship shall be tried only before the greatest assembly and by those whom the censors have enrolled among the citizens.*

*No one shall give or receive a present, either during a candidacy or during or after a term of office.*

*The punishment for violation of any of these laws shall fit the offence.*

*The censors shall have charge of the official text of the laws. When officials go out of office, they shall refer their official acts to the censors, but shall not receive exemption from prosecution thereby.*

## Notes

[1] Cicero refers to Publius Cornelius Scipio Africanus (185–129 B.C.E.). Cicero presents him as the ideal Roman statesman, and used him as the principal interlocutor in his dialogue *On the Republic*, as Plato had used Socrates.

[2] Titus Pomponius Atticus, one of Cicero's closest friends, was a student of Epicurean philosophy. Epicurus held that the gods did not trouble themselves with political matters; Atticus jokes that Epicureans listening to this conversation would consider him a traitor.

[3] Laws proposed by the tribunes Sextus Titus (99 B.C.E.), Lucius Apuleius Saturninus (100 B.C.E.), and Marcus Livius Drusus (91 B.C.E.) respectively. These laws redistributed land or offered free grain, and contributed to civic violence. Cicero views them as partisan and manipulative.

[4] Ancient lawgivers of Greek colonies in southern Italy in the seventh (Zaleucus) and sixth (Charondas) centuries B.C.E. Zaleucus established laws for Locri, and Charondas for Catana and Rhegium.

[5] Aristotle's student and successor as head of Peripatetic school after Aristotle's death in 323 B.C.E. Theophrastus wrote several works on laws and constitutions, but none has survived.

[6] Celibate priestesses of Vesta, goddess of the hearth, whose circular temple stood in the Forum.

[7] The sacrifices allowed are the rites of the Bona Dea, or "Good Goddess," from which men were strictly forbidden.

[8] Mystery religion centered at Eleusis, 15 miles northwest of Athens, here presumably practiced at Rome. Roman religion was generally public; these exceptions reveal the Roman squeamishness about initiations and "private" religions.

[9] Cybele (or Cybebe), the Great Goddess, whose worship was imported from Asia Minor to Rome in 204 B.C.E. Roman citizens were not allowed to enter her priesthood, and her worship was usually ecstatic. See Catallus 63.

[10] The usual Latin term for this position is *dictator*.

[11] *Imperium* here means "the authority to command an army." It can also mean "command" or "empire."

# Livy

## ca. 59 B.C.E.–17 C.E.

Titus Livius (ca. 59 B.C.E.–17 C.E.), whom we call Livy, was a native of Padua in northern Italy. Relatively little is known of his life, but he seems to have come to Rome about the time of Octavian's victory over Antony at the Battle of Actium in 31 B.C.E., or in other words, just as the Roman Republic was giving way to the Roman Empire. Livy began to write a massive history of Rome, from its beginnings down to his own day, and possibly through this endeavor, he gained the friendship of Octavian, who in 27 B.C.E. became Augustus Caesar. He completed 142 books, of which 35 survive, namely books 1–10 and 21–45. Ancient summaries of nearly all the rest also survive. Livy brought his history, which he titled *Ab Urbe Condita* (*From the Foundation of the City*), down to 9 B.C.E.; the final books may have been published after his death.

The scope of Livy's accomplishment appears even greater when measured against his predecessors writing in Latin. Only two such historians survive, and neither writer attempted anything like the scale and vividness of Livy. Julius Caesar's *Commentaries* on the wars in Gaul and the Roman Civil War are focused narrowly on campaigns and military strategy; and from Sallust we have two historical monographs, on Jugurtha and Catiline, that target particular crises in recent Roman history. Of the many Roman historians whose works did not survive, some of whom Livy consulted, none seems to have written a comprehensive history along the lines that Livy set out. It is noteworthy that no Roman historian after Livy seems to have tried to rewrite the history of the Republic. Tacitus, the great historian of the Roman Empire, begins his *Annals* roughly where Livy ends.

Rome's historical record was largely kept by religious officials on a year by year basis, hence the words "annals," and Livy also writes in this annalistic tradition. But these records were spare, and for Rome's earliest history, not available, a loss that Livy himself laments. Livy relies on early legends which he fleshes out with dramatic flair; scholars have suggested that Roman historical dramas may be the source for some of Livy's episodes and characterizations. Livy is fond of direct speeches, and his characters tend to exemplify one or another trait—modesty (*pudicitia*), arrogance (*superbia*), dignity (*gravitas*)—that Livy wishes to showcase. Livy proclaims a great nostalgia for the supposed virtues of the early Republic, which he feels were the source of Rome's rise to power in the Mediterranean, and which he also feels are in decline in his own day, when, as he states in the preface to his entire work, "we can endure neither our vices nor their remedies."

Books 21-30 of Livy's history cover the second Punic War (218–202 B.C.E.), also known as the War with Hannibal. Rome waged three wars with Carthage, a Phoenician colony in modern day Tunisia, and won them all (*Poenus* is the Latin word for "Phoenician," hence "Punic"). The Carthaginian general Hannibal famously marched through Spain, over the Alps, and into Italy to attack the Romans on their home soil. At three battles, Trebia (218), Lake Trasimene (217) and Cannae (216), he inflicted devastating losses on the Romans, and his subsequent victories led to secessions from Rome among southern Italians. Hannibal stayed in Italy on the offensive until 203, but he never attacked Rome, and he failed to encourage the mass defections of Rome's allies that he had expected, nor did he receive the reinforcements from Carthage that he hoped for. He was recalled to Carthage when the Roman Scipio Africanus attacked it, and he was defeated at Zama in 202. Livy does not offer particular insights into the political or economic causes of the war. He is more interested in the psychology of Hannibal, who represents the anti-Roman, despite his military brilliance, and in the moral excellence of Scipio Africanus.

Livy's moral vision of the Roman growth and domination, on the obligation to rule that belongs to the "good" men, has had influence on later writers and politicians including Dante and Machiavelli in Renaissance Italy. Historians and politicians of Victorian England also studied Livy closely, and he was a favored author of some of the "neoconservative" advisors of the presidential administration of George W. Bush.

BSH

# from *From the Foundation of the City*
## *(Ab Urbe Condita)*

## Book XXI

1. Most historians have prefaced their work by stressing the importance of the period they propose to deal with; and I may well, at this point, follow their example and declare that I am now about to tell the story of the most memorable war in history: that, namely, which was fought by Carthage under the leadership of Hannibal against Rome.

A number of things contributed to give this war its unique character: in the first place, it was fought between peoples unrivalled throughout previous history in material resources, and themselves at the peak of their prosperity and power; secondly, it was a struggle between old antagonists, each of whom had learned, in the first Punic War,[1] to appreciate the military capabilities of the other; thirdly, the final issue hung so much in doubt that the eventual victors came nearer to destruction than their adversaries. Moreover, high passions were at work throughout, and mutual hatred was hardly less sharp a weapon than the sword; on the Roman side there was rage at the unprovoked attack by a previously beaten enemy; on the Carthaginian, bitter resentment at what was felt to be the grasping and tyrannical attitude of their conquerors. The intensity of the feeling is illustrated by an anecdote of Hannibal's boyhood: his father Hamilcar, after the campaign in Africa, was about to carry his troops over into Spain, when Hannibal, then about nine years old, begged, with all the childish arts he could muster, to be allowed to accompany him; whereupon Hamilcar, who was preparing to offer sacrifice for a successful outcome, led the boy to the altar and made him solemnly swear, with his hand upon the sacred victim, that as soon as he was old enough he would be the enemy of the Roman people. Hamilcar was a proud man and the loss of Sicily and Sardinia was a cruel blow to his pride; he remembered, moreover, that Sicily had been surrendered too soon, before the situation had become really desperate, and that Rome, taking advantage of internal troubles in Africa, had tricked Carthage into the loss of Sardinia, and then had added insult to injury by the imposition of a tribute. 2. All this rankled in his mind, and his conduct of affairs during the five years of the war in Africa, following hard upon the signature of peace with Rome, and subsequently during the nine years he spent in extending Carthaginian influence in Spain, made it clear enough that his ultimate object was an enterprise of far greater moment, and that if he had

447

lived the invasion of Italy would have taken place under Hamilcar's leadership, instead of, as actually happened, under Hannibal's. That the war was postponed was due to Hamilcar's timely death and the fact that Hannibal was still too young to assume command.

The interval between father and son was filled by Hasdrubal, who commanded the Carthaginian armies for some eight years. . . .

. . . Hannibal was sent to Spain, where the troops received him with unanimous enthusiasm, the old soldiers feeling that in the person of this young man Hamilcar himself was restored to them. In the features and expression of the son's face they saw the father once again, the same vigour in his look, the same fire in his eyes. Very soon he no longer needed to rely upon his father's memory to make himself beloved and obeyed: his own qualities were sufficient. Power to command and readiness to obey are rare associates; but in Hannibal they were perfectly united, and their union made him as much valued by his commander as by his men. Hasdrubal preferred him to all other officers in any action which called for vigour and courage, and under his leadership the men invariably showed to the best advantage both dash and confidence. Reckless in courting danger, he showed superb tactical ability once it was upon him. Indefatigable both physically and mentally, he could endure with equal ease excessive heat or excessive cold; he ate and drank not to flatter his appetites but only so much as would sustain his bodily strength. His time for waking, like his time for sleeping, was never determined by daylight or darkness: when his work was done, then, any then only, he rested, without need, moreover, of silence or a soft bed to woo sleep to his eyes. Often he was seen lying in his cloak on the bare ground amongst the common soldiers on sentry or picket duty. His accoutrement, like the horses he rode, was always conspicuous, but not his clothes, which were like those of any other officer of his rank and standing. Mounted or unmounted he was unequalled as a fighting man, always the first to attack, the last to leave the field. So much for his virtues—and they were great; but no less great were his faults: inhuman cruelty, a more than Punic perfidy, a total disregard of truth, honour, and religion, of the sanctity of an oath and of all that other men hold sacred. Such was the complex character of the man who for three years served under Hasdrubal's command, doing and seeing everything which could help to equip him as a great military leader.

5. From the very first day of his command Hannibal acted as if he had definite instructions to take Italy as his sphere of operations and to make war on Rome. . . .

On the ninth day the army reached the summit. Most of the climb had been over trackless mountain-sides; frequently a wrong route was taken—

sometimes through the deliberate deception of the guides, or, again, when some likely-looking valley would be entered by guess-work, without knowledge of whither it led. There was a two days' halt on the summit, to rest the men after the exhausting climb and the fighting. Some of the pack-animals which had fallen amongst the rocks managed, by following the army's tracks, to find their way into camp. The troops had indeed endured hardships enough; but there was worse to come. It was the season of the setting of the Pleiades: winter was near—and it began to snow. Getting on the move at dawn, the army struggled slowly forward over snow-covered ground, the hopelessness of utter exhaustion in every face. Seeing their despair, Hannibal rode ahead and at a point of vantage which afforded a prospect of a vast extent of country, he gave the order to halt, pointing to Italy far below, and the Po Valley beyond the foothills of the Alps. 'My men,' he said, 'you are at this moment passing the protective barrier of Italy—nay more, you are walking over the very walls of Rome. Henceforward all will be easy going—no more hills to climb. After a fight or two you will have the capital of Italy, the citadel of Rome, in the hollow of your hands.'

The march continued, more or less without molestation from the natives, who confined themselves to petty raids when they saw a chance of stealing something. Unfortunately, however, as in most parts of the Alps the descent on the Italian side, being shorter, is correspondingly steeper, the going was much more difficult than it had been during the ascent. The track was almost everywhere precipitous, narrow, and slippery; it was impossible for a man to keep his feet; the least stumble meant a fall, and a fall a slide, so that there was indescribable confusion, men and beasts stumbling and slipping on top of each other.

36. Soon they found themselves on the edge of a precipice—a narrow cliff falling away so sheer that even a lightly-armed soldier could hardly have got down it by feeling his way and clinging to such bushes and stumps as presented themselves. It must always have been a most awkward spot, but a recent landslide had converted it on this occasion to a perpendicular drop of nearly a thousand feet. On the brink the cavalry drew rein—their journey seemed to be over. Hannibal, in the rear, did not yet know what had brought the column to a halt; but when the message was passed to him that there was no possibility of proceeding, he went in person to reconnoitre. It was clear to him that a detour would have to be made, however long it might prove to be, over the trackless and untrodden slopes in the vicinity. But even so he was no luckier; progress was impossible, for though there was good foothold in the quite shallow layer of soft fresh snow which had covered the old snow underneath, nevertheless as soon as it had been trampled and dispersed by the feet of all those

men and animals, there was left to tread upon only the bare ice and liquid slush of melting snow underneath. The result was a horrible struggle, the ice affording no foothold in any case, and least of all on a steep slope; when a man tried by hands or knees to get on his feet again, even those useless supports slipped from under him and let him down; there were no stumps or roots anywhere to afford a purchase to either foot or hand; in short, there was nothing for it but to roll and slither on the smooth ice and melting snow. Sometimes the mules' weight would drive their hoofs through into the lower layer of old snow; they would fall and, once down, lashing savagely out in their struggles to rise, they would break right through it, so that as often as not they were held as in a vice by a thick layer of hard ice.

37. When it became apparent that both men and beasts were wearing themselves out to no purpose, a space was cleared—with the greatest labour because of the amount of snow to be dug and carted away—and camp was pitched, high up on the ridge. The next task was to construct some sort of passable track clown the precipice, for by no other route could the army proceed. It was necessary to cut through rock, a problem they solved by the ingenious application of heat and moisture; large trees were felled and lopped, and a huge pile of timber erected; this, with the opportune help of a strong wind, was set on fire, and when the rock was sufficiently heated the men's rations of sour wine were flung upon it, to render it friable. They then got to work with picks on the heated rock, and opened a sort of zigzag track, to minimize the steepness of the descent, and were able, in consequence, to get the pack animals, and even the elephants, down it.

Four days were spent in the neighborhood of this precipice; the animals came near to dying of starvation, for on most of the peaks nothing grows, or, if there is any pasture, the snow covers it. Lower down there are sunny hills and valleys and woods with streams flowing by: country, in fact, more worthy for men to dwell in. There the beasts were put out to pasture, and the troops given three days' rest to recover from the fatigue of their road-building. Thence the descent was continued to the plains—a kindlier region, with kindlier inhabitants. . . .

52. The whole military strength of Rome, and both consuls, were now facing Hannibal. It was therefore clear that unless that strength proved adequate, there was no hope of saving the Roman dominion. None the less, counsels were divided: one consul influenced, no doubt, by his wound and by his ill success in the cavalry engagement, urged caution and delay; the other, feeling, as he did, fresh and ready for anything, demanded instant action. The Gallic tribes between the Trebia and the Po were, in the present circumstances, sitting on the fence: a struggle being imminent between two mighty nations,

they were unwilling to declare their allegiance outright, and looked for the favour of the winning side. The Romans accepted readily enough this attitude, provided no actually hostile move was made, but Hannibal, on the contrary, violently resented it, urging that it was the Gauls themselves who had invited him into Italy to liberate them. His indignation against them, combined with the need to get provisions for his men, induced him to send out a force of 2,000 infantry and 1,000 cavalry, mostly Numidians[2] with an admixture of Gauls, to raid the whole district as far as the Po. The Gauls, unable to resist, were driven by this act of aggression to make up their minds; accordingly they at once turned their sympathies towards the party they hoped would defend them, sent a delegation to Roman headquarters and begged aid for their unfortunate country which was suffering only for its inhabitants' excessive loyalty to Rome. Scipio, however, found the request untimely, and disliked the matter of it; he had no reason to trust the Gauls, remembering, as he did, their many acts of treachery, in particular, not to mention others which time might have obliterated, the recent perfidy of the Boii. Sempronius, on the other hand, expressed the opinion that to offer assistance to the first who asked for it would prove the strongest possible bond for keeping the Gallic tribes loyal to Rome. Then, while his colleague was still hesitating, he despatched his own cavalry, supported by about a thousand infantry spearmen, with orders to protect Gallic territory on the other side of the Trebia. This force surprised Hannibal's raiders while they were scattered about over the countryside and mostly quite unfit for action as they were loaded with plunder and in no sort of order. They were thrown into complete confusion, many were killed and the remnants driven in flight right up to the outposts of the Carthaginian camp. From the camp the enemy came pouring out in force, and Sempronius's[3] men were compelled to retire, until with the arrival of reinforcements they were able to renew the offensive. After that there was a ding-dong struggle, the Romans now advancing, now giving ground. It ended with the honours more or less even, though report favoured, on the whole, a Roman victory.

53. To Sempronius, however, there was no doubt about the matter at all. He was beside himself with delight. He had won a famous victory—and with his cavalry, the very arm in which Scipio had suffered defeat. He was convinced that the morale of the troops was now fully restored; that there was not a man apart from his colleague who wished to delay a general engagement. As for Scipio, it was his mind that was sick rather than his body—the mere memory of his wound made him shrink from the thought of blood and battle. But because one man was sick, was that a reason for the rest to behave like dotards? No, no: further procrastination and shilly-shallying were out of the question. Were they waiting for a third consul and yet another army? The enemy camp

was on Italian soil—almost within sight of Rome; the enemy objective was not the recovery of Sicily and Sardinia, nor of Spain north of the Ebro—it was the expulsion of the Romans from the land where they had been born and bred. 'Can you not hear,' he cried, 'the groans of our fathers who were wont to fight around the walls of Carthage, at the sight of their sons cowering here, in Italy, behind their defences, though two consuls and two consular armies are in the field? What would those brave men feel at the thought of all the country between the Alps and the Apennines being controlled by Hannibal?'

So Sempronius went on, urging his point of view by the sick-bed of his colleague and passionately haranguing the officers at headquarters as if addressing the troops. An additional reason for his urgency was, no doubt, the approach of the consular elections; for he had no desire that the fighting should be put off until new consuls were in control, and he himself, while his colleague lay sick, should lose the chance of gaining the glory. Scipio continued to protest, but to no purpose; the order was given to prepare for action without delay.

Hannibal was well aware of what the proper Roman strategy ought to have been, and he had hardly dared to hope that the consuls would make any rash or ill-considered move. Now, however, that facts had confirmed the report that one of them was a proud and passionate man, rendered even more so by his recent success against the raiders, he was convinced that luck was with him and that a battle was imminent. He took every possible measure to ensure that he should not lose his chance; now was the moment, while the Roman troops were still raw, and the better of their two commanders was still incapacitated by his wound. The Gauls moreover were still full of fight, and he knew that thousands of them would lose their enthusiasm for his cause in proportion as they were drawn further and further from their homes. For these and similar reasons he both expected that a fight was coming, and was determined, should the Romans hold back, to provoke one; accordingly, when his Gallic spies (it was safer to use Gauls in this capacity, as they were serving in both camps) reported that the Romans were ready for action, he began to look around for a suitable place to set a trap.

54. Between the armies was the stream, running between high banks and edged for some distance by a dense growth of marsh plants, together with the brambles and scrub which usually cover waste ground. Hannibal rode round on his horse minutely examining the terrain, and when he found a place which afforded adequate concealment for cavalry, he summoned his brother Mago. 'This,' he said, 'is the spot you must occupy. Choose a hundred men from the infantry, and a hundred from the cavalry, and bring them to me early tonight. Meanwhile the troops may rest!' The staff meeting was then dismissed, and

soon Mago reported with the men he had picked. 'I can see,' said Hannibal, 'that you have brought me some tough fellows; but as you will all need quantity as well as quality, I want each of you to select nine others like yourselves from the cavalry squadrons and infantry companies. Mago will show you where to set your trap. The enemy, you will find, has no eye for this sort of stratagem.'

Mago's thousand horse and thousand foot were in this way sent off, and Hannibal issued orders to the Numidian cavalry to cross the Trebia at dawn, advance to the enemy position, and lure him to engage by an attack with missiles on his guardposts; then, once the fight was on, they were to give ground gradually and so draw him to cross the river. The orders to the commanders of other units, infantry and cavalry, were to see that all their men had a good meal, after which they were to arm, saddle their horses, and await the signal.

Sempronius was thirsting for action: to meet the Numidians' raid on his guard-posts he at once led out his whole cavalry force—the arm in which he felt the greatest confidence; these were followed first by 6,000 infantry and finally by the entire army, and stationed in the spot previously determined upon.

There, between Alps and Apennines, it was a snowy winter's day, and the cold was increased by the proximity of rivers and marsh; men and horses had left the shelter of camp without a moment's warning—they had eaten nothing, taken no sort of precautions against the cold. There was not a spark of warmth in their bodies; and the nearer they approached the chilling breath of the water, the more bitterly cold it became. But worse was to come, for when in pursuit of the Numidians they actually entered the river—it had rained in the night and the water was up to their breasts—the cold so numbed them that after struggling across they could hardly hold their weapons. In fact, they were exhausted and, as the day wore on, hunger was added to fatigue.

55. Meanwhile Hannibal's troops were warming themselves by great fires in front of their tents. Rations of oil had been distributed for the men to rub themselves with, to keep them supple; they had all breakfasted at leisure; so that when word came that the Romans were across the river, it was a fresh and eager army that ran to its stations in the line.

In the van of his force Hannibal posted the Baliares and the light-armed foot, about 8,000 strong; supporting them were the heavier infantry—the flower of his troops. On the wings were 10,000 mounted troops, with the elephants beyond them—half on the right, half on the left. Sempronius posted his cavalry on the flanks of his infantry—having recalled them for the purpose; for in their disorderly chase after the Numidian raiding-party they had received an unexpected check from a sudden rally of the enemy. The total Roman strength at the beginning of this battle was 18,000 legionaries, 20,000 allied troops of the Latin name, and certain contingents provided by the Cenomani, the only Gallic nation to remain loyal.

The action was opened by Hannibal's Baliares. They were met by the superior weight of the Roman legionaries and quickly withdrawn to the wings, where they greatly increased the pressure on the Roman cavalry, which was already fighting against odds—for they were tired men, while their antagonists were fresh, and more than double their number. Now, however, on top of that, the Baliares almost overwhelmed them with a cloud of javelins. The elephants, too, on the extreme wings caused wide-spread confusion, as the horses were terrified by the sight and smell of these strange beasts they had never seen before. As for the infantry, the Roman foot showed no lack of spirit, but they were physically weak compared with the enemy, who had entered the fight refreshed with food and rest, unlike themselves, half frozen as they were, and faint with hunger. None the less sheer courage might have carried them through if they had had only the Carthaginian infantry to contend with; but as it was, the Baliares, after the repulse of the Roman mounted troops, were attacking them on the flanks with missiles, and the elephants had by now forced a way right into their line. Finally, Mago and his Numidians, once the line had—all unaware—moved forward beyond their place of concealment, appeared suddenly in their rear with almost shattering effect. Yet even in this terrible situation the Roman line for some time held firm—even, what was least of all to be expected, against the elephants. The light-armed foot, specially brought in to deal with them, drove them off with their javelins, followed up, and pierced them again in the soft skin under their tails. 56. Under this treatment the brutes were getting out of hand and looked like turning in panic against their own masters, so Hannibal had them removed from the centre and transferred to the left wing, against the Gallic auxiliaries. The auxiliaries promptly broke and fled, thus adding a fresh cause of alarm for the hardpressed Romans.

In these circumstances a body of some 10,000 Romans—who were now completely encircled—took the only way of escape they could find and hacked a passage with the edge of the sword right through the African centre, supported, as it was, by its allied Gallic contingents. The river barred the way back to camp, and it was raining so hard that they could not see at what point in the mêlée they could best help their friends, so they took the shortest route to Placentia. Subsequently a number of other groups, at various points, succeeded in breaking out; those who made for the river were either drowned or cut down as they hesitated on the brink; others, scattered in flight over the countryside, made for Placentia on the tracks of the retreating column. A few, emboldened by sheer terror of death by the sword to plunge into the water, got across and reached the camp.

Rain, sleet, and intolerable cold carried off many of the pack-animals and nearly all the elephants. At the river-bank the Carthaginians ceased their pursuit, and on their return to camp the men were so benumbed with cold that they could hardly feel pleasure in their victory. Accordingly the following night they allowed the garrison in Scipio's camp and most of the remaining troops to cross the Trebia on rafts unmolested: either they were unaware of the movement because of the noise of the torrential rain, or else too exhausted for further effort, and suffering from wounds, as many were, they pretended to have noticed nothing. Scipio led his force quietly to Placentia. There was no opposition. From Placentia he crossed the Po and proceeded to Cremona, to spare one town the heavy burden of two armies wintering in it.

57. In Rome the news of this disastrous defeat caused such panic that people fancied that at any moment Hannibal would be at the city gates. There was no hope, it seemed, nothing to help them defend the gates and walls from assault. One consul had been beaten at the Ticinus, the other recalled from Sicily, and now the two together, with the combined force of both consular armies, had been defeated too. What other commanders, what other troops could be summoned to their defence? Such was the state of feeling when Sempronius himself arrived in Rome. . . .

## Book XXII

. . . The region (the Etruscan plains between Faesulae and Arretium)[4] was amongst the most productive in Italy, rich in cattle, grain, and everything else. Flaminius,[5] still remembering his former consulship, was as arrogant as ever, with but scant respect even for the gods, let alone the laws of his country or the majesty of the Senate. His innate recklessness had been further nourished by the successes he had achieved in war and politics, so it was pretty clear that, on the present occasion, he would act with headlong impetuosity and with no thought of restraint by God or man. Hannibal, in order to foster for his own advantage Flaminius's defects of character, prepared to bait him and prick him to action; leaving the Roman camp on his left he made for Faesulae, harrying and devastating Etruscan territory with the intention of forcing upon Flaminius the spectacle of as much damage as fire and sword could produce. Flaminius, for his part, could never have remained inactive even had the enemy done so, still less now that everything his friends possessed was being ruined or carried off almost before his eyes. It was, he felt, the gravest reflection upon himself that a Carthaginian army should be roaming at large through central Italy, marching without any attempt at resistance to attack the very walls of Rome. At a meeting of his staff all his officers urged a policy of caution; any spectacular move would, they declared, be dangerous; he should wait for the other consul, so that the two of them might join forces and cooperate in the coming campaign—two heads, two hearts being better than one. Meanwhile they suggested that the cavalry and light auxiliaries might be used to check the widespread enemy depredations. Flaminius was furious; he precipitately left the meeting and gave the order to march and to prepare for immediate action. 'So be it!' he exclaimed with bitter irony; 'let us stay here before the walls of Arretium where our country is, and the guardian spirits of our homes! Hannibal is at liberty to escape us and make Italy a desert—let him march to Rome leaving fire and ruin behind him! We have no intention of moving until the Senate summons Flaminius from Arretium as once it summoned Camillus from Veii!'

In the act of giving the order to have the standards lifted, and just as he had sprung into the saddle, his horse stumbled and threw him. All who saw the accident were much alarmed by the bad omen; but there was more to come, for at that moment word was brought that one of the standards, despite every effort of the standard-bearer to pull it out of the ground, refused to budge. Flaminius turned to the man who brought the message and asked him if he also, perchance, had a letter from the Senate in his pocket, forbidding him to engage. 'Be off with you,' he cried; 'tell them to *dig* it out, if they are too weak with fright to pull it up.'

Thereupon the column began to move. The officers, in addition to the fact that they disapproved of Flaminius's policy, were greatly disheartened by the two bad omens; the men, on the contrary, thoroughly appreciated their commander's independence and audacity, buoyed up, as they were, by hope, however baseless.

4. Hannibal, determined to inflame his antagonist and drive him to avenge the sufferings of his allies, left nothing undone to reduce to a desert the whole stretch of country between Cortona and Lake Trasimene. His army had now reached a place which nature herself had made a trap for the unwary. Between the mountains of Cortona, where they slope down to the lake, and the lake itself there is only a very narrow path, an opening just wide enough to get through—deliberately designed, it would seem, for its sinister purpose. Further on is a somewhat wider area of level ground, and at the eastern end rises the barrier of the mountains. Here, at the eastern exit, Hannibal took up a position, in full view, with his African and Spanish veterans; his light troops, including the Baliares, he concealed amongst the mountains north of the lake, and stationed his cavalry, also hidden by hills, close to the narrow western entrance, so that they could block it the instant the Romans had passed with-

in. Thus, with the lake on one side and the mountains on the other, all egress would be barred.

Flaminius had reached the lake at sunset the previous day. On the day following, in the uncertain light of early dawn, he entered the narrow pass. No sort of reconnaissance had been made. When his column began to open out on reaching the wider area of level ground north of the lake, he was aware only of those enemy units which were in the direct line of his advance; of the units concealed in his rear and in the hills above him he had no inkling whatever. Hannibal had achieved his object: as soon as he had his antagonist penned in by the lake and the mountains and surrounded, front, rear, and flank, by his own men, he gave the order for a simultaneous attack by all units. Down they came from the hills, each man by the nearest way, taking the Romans totally unprepared. The unexpectedness of the attack was, moreover, increased by the morning mist from the lake, lying thicker on the low ground than on the hills; the units on the hills could see each other well enough, and were able, in consequence, the better to coordinate their attack.

By the battle-cry which arose on every side of them the Romans knew they were surrounded before they could see that the trap had closed. Fighting began in front and on their flanks before the column had time to form into line of battle, before even their weapons could be made ready, or swords drawn. 5. In the general shock and confusion Flaminius, so far as such an emergency permitted, kept a cool head, and tried as well as time and place allowed to reduce the chaos in the ranks to some sort of order, as each man swung this way or that to face the shouts of triumph or calls for help that met his ears. Wherever he could make his voice heard, or force a way through the press, he encouraged his men and urged them to stand firm, crying out that no prayers would save them now, but only their own strength and their own valour. They must cut their way through with the sword, and the greater their courage the less would be their peril. But the din of the mêlée was so great that not a word either of exhortation or command could be heard. In the chaos that reigned not a soldier could recognize his own standard or knew his place in the ranks—indeed, they were almost too bemused to get proper control over their swords and shields, while to some their very armour and weapons proved not a defence but a fatal encumbrance. In that enveloping mist ears were a better guide than eyes: it was sounds, not sights, they turned to face—the groans of wounded men, the thud or ring of blows on body or shield, the shout of onslaught, the cry of fear. Some, flying for their lives, found themselves caught in a jam of their own men still standing their ground; others, trying to return to the fight, were forced back again by a crowd of fugitives. In every direction attempts to break out failed. The mountains on one flank, the lake on the other, hemmed them in, while in front of them and behind stood the formations of the enemy. When at last it was clear to all that the one hope of life lay in their own individual swords, the nature of the struggle was transformed: no man now waited for orders or exhortation: each became his own commander, dependent on his own efforts alone. Familiar tactics, the well-known disposition of forces, were flung to the winds; legion, cohort, company no longer had any significance; if formations there were, chance alone made them, to fight in front or rear was a matter for the spirit in each breast to decide. So great was the fury of the struggle, so totally absorbed was every man in its grim immediacy, that no one even noticed the earthquake which ruined large parts of many Italian towns, altered the course of swift rivers, brought the sea flooding into estuaries and started avalanches in the mountains.

6. For three long and bloody hours the fight continued, and most furiously of all around the person of Flaminius. His best troops kept constantly at his side, and he was always quick to bring support to any point where he saw his men in trouble or likely to be overwhelmed. His dress and equipment made him a conspicuous figure, and the enemy attacks were as determined as the efforts to save him; and so it continued, until a mounted trooper, an Insubrian named Ducarius, recognized his face. Calling to his fellow-tribesmen, 'There is the consul,' he cried, 'who destroyed our legions and laid our town and our fields in ruin! I will offer him as a sacrifice to the ghosts of our people foully slain!' Putting spurs to his horse he galloped through the thickest of the press, cut down the armour-bearer who had tried to check his murderous intent, and drove his lance through Flaminius's body. Only the shields of some veterans of the reserve prevented him from stripping the corpse.

For a large part of the Roman army the consul's death was the beginning of the end. Panic ensued, and neither lake nor mountains could stop the wild rush for safety. Men tried blindly to escape by any possible way, however steep, however narrow; arms were flung away, men fell and others fell on top of them; many, finding nowhere to turn to save their skins, plunged into the edge of the lake till the water was up to their necks, while a few in desperation tried to swim for it—a forlorn hope indeed over that broad lake, and they were either drowned, or, struggling back exhausted into shallow water were butchered wholesale by the mounted troops who rode in to meet them.

Some 6,000 of the leading column succeeded by a vigorous effort in breaking through and got clear of the pass without knowing anything of the situation in their rear; they halted on an eminence, whence they could hear shouts and the clash of arms, but the mist was too thick for them to see the progress of the battle or to know what was happening. All was nearly over when at last the heat of the sun dispersed the mist, and in the clear morning light hills and plain revealed to their eyes the terrible truth that the Roman army was almost totally destroyed. Hurriedly, lest the enemy cavalry should see them and give chase, they plucked the standards from the ground and made off with all the speed they could muster. Next day they surrendered to Maharbal, who with the Carthaginian cavalry had overtaken them before dawn; hunger was by then staring them in the face, and Maharbal had promised to let them go with a garment apiece on condition of giving up their arms. Hannibal, however, with a truly Punic disregard for the sanctity of a promise, put them all into chains.

7. Such was the famous fight at Lake Trasimene, one of the few memorable disasters to Roman arms. The Roman dead amounted to 15,000; 10,000, scattered in flight throughout Etruria, found their way back to Rome by various ways. Of the enemy 2,500 were killed; many on both sides died of wounds. Some writers have estimated the casualties, both our own and the enemy's, at many times the number; I myself, apart from my unwillingness to exaggerate on insufficient evidence, that all too common vice of historians, have based my account on Fabius, a contemporary witness of these events. All prisoners of the Latin name Hannibal liberated without ransom; Roman prisoners he put in chains. He then gave orders that the bodies of his own men should be picked out from the heaps of enemy dead and given burial. He also wished to honour Flaminius with burial, but, though his body was searched for with all diligence, it was never found. . . .

Near the village of Cannae[6] Hannibal had taken up a position facing away from the prevailing wind from the hills, which drives clouds of dust over that stretch of parched and level ground. This was a great convenience to his men in camp, and it would be especially advantageous once the action began, as his own men would be fighting with their backs to the wind against an enemy blinded by the flying dust.

44. In their pursuit of the Carthaginians the consuls spared no pains in reconnoitring the route. Arrived at Cannae, where they had the Carthaginian position full in view, they fortified two separate camps about the same distance apart as at Gereonium, dividing the forces as before. The river Aufidus, flowing between the two camps, could be reached by watering-parties, as opportunity arose, though not without opposition; but parties from the smaller camp, on the further (or southern) side of the river, could water more freely, as the bank on that side was not guarded. Hannibal hoped that the consuls would offer to engage him on ground peculiarly suited to cavalry, the arm in which he was invincible; and with this in view he formed his line and sent his Numidian horse to provoke the enemy by small-scale, rapid charges. At this, the old trouble broke out again in the Roman lines: the men threatened

mutiny; the consuls were at loggerheads. Paullus faced Varro with the reckless conduct of Sempronius and Flaminius; Varro replied by holding up Fabius as a specious example for commanders who wanted to conceal their own timidity and lack of spirit. Varro called gods and men to witness that it was no fault of his that Hannibal now owned Italy by right of possession—his hands had been tied by his colleague; his angry men, spoiling for a fight, were being robbed of their swords. Paullus, in his turn, declared that if the legions were recklessly betrayed into an ill-advised and imprudent battle and suffered a reverse, he would himself be free of all blame for the disaster, though he would share its consequences. It was up to Varro, he added, to see that their readiness to use bold words was matched, when it came to action, by the vigour of their hands.

45. Thus in the Roman camp the time was passed in altercation rather than in planning for the coming fight. Meanwhile Hannibal began to withdraw the main body of his men from the battle-positions they had occupied during the greater part of the day, and at the same time sent his Numidians across the river to attack the Roman watering-parties from the smaller of their two camps. The watering-parties were mere unorganized groups, and the Numidians sent them flying in much noise and confusion almost before they were over the river, and then continued their advance to a guard-post in front of the Roman defences, carrying on almost to the very gates of the camp. That their camp should be threatened by what was only a small skirmishing force of auxiliary troops was felt by the Romans as an insult; and the only thing that prevented them from immediately crossing the river in force and offering battle was the fact that it was Paullus's day of command. Varro's turn was on the day following, and he used it as was to be expected: without in any way consulting his colleague he gave the order for battle, marshalled the troops, and led them across the river. Paullus followed, for he could not but lend his aid, deeply though he disapproved of what was done.

Once over the river, they joined up with the troops in the smaller camp, forming their line with the Roman cavalry on the right wing, nearer the river, and the Roman legionaries on their left; on the other wing were stationed, first—on the extreme flank—the allied cavalry, then the allied foot extending inwards till they joined the legionaries in the centre. The javelins and other light auxiliaries formed the front line. The consuls commanded the wings, Varro the left, Paullus the right. The task of controlling the centre was assigned to Servilius.

46. At dawn Hannibal first sent his light contingents, including the Baleares, across the river, then followed with his main force, drawing up in their battle positions the various contingents as they reached the other side. On

his left, near the river bank, were the Gallic and Spanish horse, facing their Roman counterparts; on his right were the Numidians, and his centre was strongly held by infantry, so disposed as to have Gauls and Spaniards in the centre and African troops on each flank. To look at them, one might have thought the Africans were Roman soldiers—their arms were largely Roman, having been part of the spoils at Trasimene, and some, too, at the Trebia. The Gallic and Spanish contingents carried shields of similar shape, but their swords were of different pattern, those of the Gauls being very long and not pointed, those of the Spaniards, who were accustomed to use them for piercing rather than cutting, being handily short and sharply pointed. One must admit, too, that the rest of the turn-out of these peoples, combined with their general appearance and great stature, made an awesome spectacle: the Gauls naked from the navel upwards; the Spaniards ranged in line in their dazzling white linen tunics bordered with purple. The total number of infantry in the battle-line was 40,000; of cavalry 10,000. The left wing was commanded by Hasdrubal, the right by Maharbal; Hannibal in person, supported by his brother Mago, held the centre. The Roman line faced south, the Carthaginian north; and luckily for both the early morning sun (whether they had taken up their positions by accident or design) shone obliquely on each of them; but a wind which had got up—called locally the Volturnus—was a disadvantage to the Romans as it carried clouds of dust into their eyes and obscured their vision.

47. The battle-cry rang out; the auxiliaries leapt forward, and with the light troops the action began. Soon the Gallic and Spanish horse on the Carthaginian left were engaged with the Roman right. Lack of space made it an unusual cavalry encounter: the antagonists were compelled to charge head-on, front to front; there was no room for outflanking manoeuvres, as the river on one side and the massed infantry on the other pinned them in, leaving them no option but to go straight ahead. The horses soon found themselves brought to a halt, jammed close together in the inadequate space, and the riders set about dragging their opponents from the saddle, turning the contest more or less into an infantry battle. It was fierce while it lasted, but that was not for long; the Romans were forced to yield and hurriedly withdrew. Towards the end of this preliminary skirmish, the regular infantry became engaged; for a time it was an equal struggle, but at last the Romans, after repeated efforts, maintaining close formation on a broad front, drove in the opposing Gallic and Spanish troops, which were in wedge formation, projecting from the main body, and too thin to be strong enough to withstand the pressure. As these hurriedly withdrew, the Romans continued their forward thrust, carrying straight on through the broken column of the enemy now fly-

ing for their lives, until they reached the Carthaginian centre, after which, with little or no resistance, they penetrated to the position held by the African auxiliaries. These troops held the two Carthaginian wings, drawn back a little, while the centre, held by the Gauls and Spaniards, projected somewhat forward. The forcing back of the projecting wedge soon levelled the Carthaginian front; then, as under increasing pressure the beaten troops still further retired, the front assumed a concave shape, leaving the Africans on, as it were, the two projecting ends of the crescent. Recklessly the Romans charged straight into it, and the Africans on each side closed in. In another minute they had further extended their wings and closed the trap in the Roman rear.

The brief Roman success had been in vain. Now, leaving the Gauls and Spaniards on whom they had done much execution as they fled, they turned to face the Africans. This time the fight was by no means on equal terms: the Romans were surrounded, and—which was worse—they were tired men matched against a fresh and vigorous enemy.

48. Meanwhile the Roman left, where the allied horse confronted the Numidians, was also engaged. For a while things went slowly, owing to a Carthaginian ruse right at the outset. About 500 Numidians pretended to desert: in addition to their regular weapons they concealed swords under their tunics and rode up to the Roman line with their shields slung behind their backs. Suddenly dismounting, and flinging their shields and javelins on the ground, they were taken into the line by the Romans, and then conducted to the rear, where they were ordered to remain. While the general action was developing, they kept quiet enough; but as soon as no one in their vicinity had eyes or thoughts for anything but the progress of the battle, they picked up their shields from where they lay scattered around amongst the heaps of dead, and attacked the Roman line in the rear, striking at the soldiers' backs, hamstringing them, and causing terrible destruction, and even more panic and disorder.

It was at this juncture, when in one part of the field the Romans had little left but to try to save their skins, while in another, though hope was almost gone, they continued to fight with dogged determination, that Hasdrubal withdrew the Numidians from the centre, where they were not being used to much advantage, and sent them in pursuit of the scattered fugitives, at the same time ordering the Spaniards and Gauls to move to the support of the Africans, who by now were almost exhausted by what might be called butchery rather than battle.

49. Paullus, on the other wing, had been severely wounded by a slingstone right at the start of the fight; none the less, at the head of his men in close order, he continued to make a number of attempts to get at Hannibal, and in

several places succeeded in pulling things together. He had with him a guard of Roman cavalry, but the time came when Paullus was too weak even to control his horse, and they were obliged to dismount. Someone, it is said, told Hannibal that the consul had ordered his cavalry to dismount, and Hannibal, knowing they were therefore done for, replied that he might as well have delivered them up to him in chains.

The enemy's victory was now assured, and the dismounted cavalry fought in the full knowledge of defeat; they made no attempt to escape, preferring to die where they stood; and their refusal to budge, by delaying total victory even for a moment, further incensed the triumphant enemy, who unable to drive them from their ground, mercilessly cut them down. Some few survivors did indeed turn and run, wounded and worn out though they were.

The whole force was now broken and dispersed. Those who could, recovered their horses, hoping to escape. Lentulus, the military tribune, as he rode by saw the consul Paullus sitting on a stone and bleeding profusely. 'Lucius Aemilius,' he said, 'you only, in the sight of heaven, are guiltless of this day's disaster; take my horse, while you still have some strength left, and I am here to lift you up and protect you. Do not add to the darkness of our calamity by a consul's death. Without that, we have cause enough for tears!' 'God bless your courage,' Paullus answered, 'but you have little time to escape; do not waste it in useless pity—get you gone, and tell the Senate to look to Rome and fortify it with strong defences before the victorious enemy can come. And take a personal message too: tell Quintus Fabius that while I lived I did not forget his counsel, and that I remember it still in the hour of death. As for me, let me die here amongst my dead soldiers: I would not a second time stand trial after my consulship, nor would I accuse my colleague, to protect myself by incriminating another.' The two men were still speaking when a crowd of fugitives swept by. The Numidians were close on their heels. Paullus fell under a shower of spears, his killers not even knowing whom they killed. In the confusion Lentulus's horse bolted, and carried him off.

After that, there was nothing but men flying for their lives. 7,000 got away into the smaller camp, 10,000 into the larger; about 2,000 sought refuge in Cannae, but the village had no sort of defences and they were immediately surrounded by Carthalo and his cavalry. Varro, whether by chance or design, managed to keep clear of the fugitives and reached Venusia alive, with some seventy horsemen. The total number of casualties is said to have been 45,500 infant men and 2,700 cavalrymen killed—about equally divided between citizens and allies. Amongst the dead were the consuls' two quaestors, Lucius Atilius and Lucius Furius Bibaculus, twenty-nine military tribunes, a number of ex-consuls and of men who had the rank of praetor or aedile—amongst them are numbered Gnaeus Servilius Geminus and Marcus Minicius (who had been master of Horse the previous year and consul some years earlier)— eighty distinguished men who were either members of the Senate, or had held offices which qualified for membership, and had, on this occasion, volunteered for service in the legions. The number of prisoners amounted to 3,000 infantry and 1,500 cavalry.

50. Such is the story of Cannae, a defeat no less famous than the defeat on the Allia;[7] for the enormous losses involved, it was the more dreadful of the two, through less serious in its results, as Hannibal did not follow up his victory. The rout at the Allia lost Rome, but it left the army still in existence; at Cannae hardly seventy men got away with Varro, and almost the whole army shared the fate of Paullus. . . .

## Book XXVI

. . . 18. Meanwhile the Spanish peoples who had revolted from Rome after the defeat of the Scipios were not returning to their allegiance, nor were any new ones coming to join her. In Rome, moreover, now Capua was recovered, both Senate and people were as much concerned about Spain as about Italy. It was the intention that the army should be reinforced and a commander-in-chief sent out; but there was less agreement upon whom to send than upon the obvious fact that, where two most eminent generals had perished within thirty days, their successor needed to be chosen with extraordinary care. Various names were put forward and rejected, until the Senate finally had recourse to holding an election for a proconsul to take over Spanish affairs, and the consuls announced the date.

Up to now people had been waiting for anyone who thought himself good enough for so important a command to hand in his name; and when nobody did so, the loss of the two dead generals seemed to make itself felt afresh, together with distress at the defeat of their armies. The City was in mourning, and had no clear idea of the next step to take. Nevertheless, on election day, everyone went down to the Campus. People turned towards the magistrates and watched the faces of the leading citizens, the likely candidates: they were exchanging glances with one another. A murmur arose that things were desperate, that hope of saving the country had been so utterly lost that no one dared accept the Spanish command. Such was the general feeling when suddenly Publius Cornelius Scipio, son of the Publius Scipio who had been killed in Spain and still a young man of about twenty-four, announced his candidature for the command. He then moved to a spot where the ground rose a little, and stood there, visible to the whole assembly. All eyes were turned upon him, and the crowd by their roar of approval unanimously predicted good luck for him and every success. Bidden to record their votes, not only all the centuries, but every individual man, supported him for the Spanish command. However, once that was done and the first sudden impulse had had time to cool, there was an awkward silence and people began to ask themselves if what they had done had not been prompted by personal feeling rather than by common sense. It was Scipio's youth which, more than anything, gave them pause, though some were chilled by the evil destiny of his house and dreaded the name of this man who belonged to two mourning families and was about to leave for a field of action where he would be forced to fight by the graves of his father and his uncle.

19. Scipio was quick to observe the anxious concern which followed that over-impulsive vote. He called an assembly, and discoursed of his youth, of his appointment to the command, and of the coming war in such lofty and magnanimous terms that he kindled afresh the cooling ardour of the populace, and filled everybody with a more confident hope than is usually inspired by trust in a mere promise or even by a reasoned deduction from facts. For Scipio was a remarkable man not only by virtue of his actual attainments; he had also from his early youth practised their display by certain deliberate devices. For instance, he used to present most of his public actions as inspired by nocturnal visions or by warnings from heaven, perhaps because he was himself of a superstitious turn of mind, perhaps to get his orders carried out promptly in the belief that they came from some sort of oracular response. Moreover, to prepare men's minds, from the earliest days when he first came of age he never on any day performed any public or private business until he had first gone to the Capitol, where, taking his seat in the temple, he watched and waited, apart and usually alone. This habit, continued throughout his life, confirmed in some men the belief (which may or may not have been deliberately spread) that he was a man of divine race, and revived the old tale once told of Alexander the Great, and equally empty and absurd, that his conception came from the embraces of a huge snake, a monster that was often seen in his mother's bedroom, only to glide away and vanish when anyone came in. Scipio himself never said a word to diminish belief in these marvels; on the contrary, he tended to strengthen it by skilfully and deliberately refusing either to deny or openly to affirm their truth. Many other similar things, some true, some fictitious, had set the young Scipio on a sort of pinnacle, above the heads of mere men; and that was the reason why the citizens of Rome entrusted the heavy burden of this important command to a man who had by no means reached full maturity.

To the old army in Spain and the forces which sailed with Nero from Puteoli were added 10,000 foot and 1,000 horse, and the pro-praetor Marcus

Junius Silanus was appointed as an assistant in the conduct of operations. So with a fleet of thirty ships, all quinqueremes, Scipio sailed from Ostia at the mouth of the Tiber along the Etruscan coast, past the Alps, and across the Gallic gulf, and thence round the promontory of the Pyrenees, finally disembarking his troops at Emporiae, a Greek settlement originally founded by men from Phocaea. Then, after ordering the fleet to follow, he proceeded by land to Tarraco, where he summoned representatives of all the allies to meet him, for at the news of his approach delegations had come thronging from everywhere in the province to attend upon him. There he had the ships beached after sending back four triremes from Massilia which had escorted him from their home-port to show their respect. That done he proceeded to answer the delegations, who were in great anxiety owing to the recent ups-and-downs of fortune in the war. Supremely confident in his own abilities, he spoke with a studied and lofty pride, yet without allowing a single arrogant word to escape his lips, and informing all he said with overwhelming authority and sincerity. . . .

41. In Spain at the beginning of spring Scipio got his ships afloat again; then, having summoned the allied auxiliaries to Tarraco, he ordered the fleet, warships and transports, to the mouth of the Ebro. The legions were ordered to leave their winter quarters and assemble at the same point, and Scipio himself with 5,000 allied troops marched in Tarraco to join them. On his arrival, wishing particularly to speak a word to the veterans who had survived such grave defeats, he had them paraded and delivered the following address: 'I am the first newly appointed commander-in-chief who has been in a position to express deserved and justifiable thanks to his men before he has experienced what they can do for him. Even before I saw the camp or the country in which my duties were to lie, Fortune had made a bond between you and me: I was grateful, first for the devotion you showed to my father and my uncle both before and after their deaths; and secondly, for your soldierly qualities in holding intact for me, their successor, and for the Roman people the possession of this province which had been so disastrously lost. But since now, by God's blessing, the object before us is not to stay in Spain ourselves but to push the Carthaginians out of it—not to stand in front of the Ebro and keep the enemy from crossing it, but to cross it ourselves and take the initiative on the other side—I fear that some of you may feel that such a plan is beyond the capacity of a commander so young as I am, and too bold when we remember those recent defeats. No one could be less able than I am to forget our defeats in Spain: within thirty days my father and my uncle were killed, two grievous losses in succession for my family to bear. But though, as an individual, to be all but orphaned and left desolate is enough to break my spirit, yet the Fortune of our country and her valour forbid me to despair of the final issue. The des-

tiny granted us by some inscrutable providence is, that in all our great wars we have emerged victorious from defeat.

'I will not speak of the distant past, of Porsenna, the Gauls, the Samnites—let me begin with Carthage. How many fleets, generals, armies were lost in the first Punic war? And what of the present one? I was present myself at all our defeats, or if I was not, they touched me more closely than anyone else. Trebia, Trasimene, Cannae, what are those names but records of the destruction of Roman armies and the deaths of consuls? Then think of the defection of a large part of Italy and Sicily and of Sardinia, and then of that moment of ultimate horror when the Carthaginians lay in camp between the Anio and Rome, and victorious Hannibal was seen almost within the gates. When everything, it seemed, was falling about us in ruin, one thing alone stood firm—the inviolable, the unshakeable courage of the Roman people. This it was that raised up again the scattered fragments of our fallen fortunes. You, soldiers, under the auspices of your general my father, were the first to check the advance of Hasdrubal to the Alps and Italy, after the defeat at Cannae; and if Hasdrubal had joined forces with his brother, the Roman name would now have ceased to exist. This success of yours was the prop to sustain us in our reverses; and now, by the favour of the gods, all our affairs in Italy and Sicily are prospering, and the news is more cheerful and better every day. In Sicily, Syracuse and Agrigentum have been taken, the enemy has been expelled from the island, the province is restored to the control of Rome. In Italy Arpi has been recovered, Capua has fallen. Hannibal has been sent scurrying back along the road from Rome and driven into the remotest corner of Bruttium, where now he prays for nothing better than leave to escape with his life from his enemies' territory. What then, my soldiers, could be more unreasonable than that you should be faint-hearted now, when everything in Italy smiles upon our triumphs, you, who with my parents—let them share that honourable name—upheld the tottering fortunes of the Roman people when disaster after disaster was being heaped upon them and the gods themselves, it seemed, fought on Hannibal's side? . . .

'And now the immortal gods, guardians of our empire, who at the elections inspired the people to vote unanimously for my appointment to the command, are by auguries an auspices and visions in the night foreshowing nothing but prosperity and success. My own mind too, always my most trusted seer, foresees that Spain is ours and that every Carthaginian will soon be gone, their fleeing armies covering the land as their ships the sea. What the mind of itself divines is suggested no less by sound reasoning: their allies are weary of their burdens and are beginning to beg for our protection; their three army-commanders are so much at odds that each is almost a traitor to his colleagues, and the three divisions of their force are widely separated. The ill fortune which so short a time ago crushed us is now gathering its strength against them: they are being deserted by their friends, as we were by the Celtiberians; they have divided their forces, the very thing that brought disaster upon my father and uncle; their private differences will not let them unite, while separately none of them will be able to stand against us. All I ask you, my men, is that you give your loyalty to the name of Scipio, to the scion of your lost commanders, growing again from the lopped branch. Come, my veterans, take with you across the Ebro a new army and a new commander; take them into territory you have so often trod, fighting like the brave men you are. Already you recognize in me something of my father and uncle, in my face, my look, the turn of my body; soon I shall strive to give you back an image of their hearts as well, of their loyalty and courage, so that each of you may say that Scipio, his beloved general, has risen from the dead or been born again.' . . .

## Book XXX

. . . At any rate it is certain that nothing further was done by Hannibal in Italy; for it so happened that the emissaries from Carthage came to recall him to Africa just about the same time as they came to Mago. 20. The story goes that he groaned and gnashed his teeth and could hardly refrain from tears when he heard what the emissaries had to say. When their message was delivered, he said, 'For years past they have been trying to force me back by refusing me reinforcements and money; but now they recall me no longer by indirect means, but in plain words. Hannibal has been conquered not by the Roman people whom he defeated so many times in battle and put to flight, but by the envy and continual disparagement of the Carthaginian senate. At this unlovely and shameful return of mine it will not be Scipio who will be wild with triumph and delight, but rather Hanno, whose only way of ruining me and my house has been by ruining Carthage.'

Hannibal had already foreseen his recall and in consequence had his ships in readiness. All his troops which were unfit for service he distributed, ostensibly for garrison duty amongst the few Bruttian towns which fear rather than loyalty kept on his side, and all who were still serviceable he transported to Africa. Before he went, he had many Italians who had refused to go with him and had taken refuge in the hitherto inviolate shrine of Juno Lacinia brutally butchered in the very precincts of the temple.

Seldom, we are told, has any exile left his native land with so heavy a heart as Hannibal's when he left the country of his enemies; again and again he looked back at the shores of Italy, accusing gods and men and calling down curses on his own head for not having led his armies straight to Rome when they were still bloody from the victorious field of Cannae. Scipio, who in his consulship had never seen a Carthaginian enemy in Italy, had had the audacity to march on Carthage, while he—when a hundred thousand Roman soldiers had been killed at Trasimene and Cannae—had been content to grow old in idleness at Casilinum and Cumae and Nola! Such were his self-accusations and expressions of distress as he was forced to surrender his long occupation of Italy. . . .

28. Meanwhile there was a growing conflict in men's minds between anxiety and hope. Which should take precedence—joy that Hannibal after sixteen years was gone at last and had left the Roman people in undisputed possession of Italy, or fear because he had reached Africa with his army still intact? The danger remained—it was only the place which was changed. In the mighty struggle still to come, the late Quintus Fabius,[8] with prophetic words, often and not without reason foretold that Hannibal would prove a more terrible enemy in his own country than he had been in Italy; nor would Scipio have to deal with Syphax, king of a mob of undisciplined savages, whose armies used to be led by Statorius, a sort of army-cook, or with Syphax's father-in-law Hasdrubal,[9] a general who showed his speed chiefly in retreat, or with irregulars hurriedly gathered together from a half-armed mob of country bumpkins. No, he would have Hannibal as his antagonist, Hannibal, who, one might say, was born at the headquarters of his father the mighty Hamilcar, was nursed amongst arms through his childhood years, and became a soldier while yet a boy and a commander in earliest manhood, and now, grown old by victories, had filled Italy from the Alps to the Straits of Messana and the provinces of Spain and Gaul with monuments of his tremendous campaigns. Hannibal, moreover, was in command of an army which had been with him through all his years of fighting, an army toughened by hardships almost beyond human endurance, drenched a thousand times with Roman blood, and carrying with it the spoils not of soldiers only, but of generals. Many a man who would encounter Scipio in battle had with his own hand killed a praetor, a general, a Roman consul: many would be heroes decorated with the Mural or Vallarian Crown,[10] men who had strolled at their ease through captured Roman camps and cities. The *fasces* of all Roman magistrates put together at that moment would not equal in number those which Hannibal had captured from dead Roman generals and could proudly bear before him.

These were grim thoughts, and by brooding over them people only increased their fears and anxieties. There was another reason too, for whereas for years past they had grown accustomed to war being waged before their eyes now here, now there throughout the length of Italy—a war which raised no immediate hopes of any swift conclusion—now everyone was on tiptoe with excitement at the thought of Scipio and Hannibal facing one another for what would surely be the final struggle. Even those whose supreme confidence in Scipio assured them of victory were racked with anxiety in proportion to their longing that the victory should not be delayed. At Carthage, too, there were mixed feelings, and conflicting hopes and fears. Now, when they thought of Hannibal and the magnitude of his achievements, they regretted having sued for peace; and again, when they looked back on their two defeats in the field, on the capture of Syphax and the expulsion of their armies from Spain and Italy and knew that all this was the result of the brave and brilliant generalship of Scipio, they dreaded him as a man of destiny born to destroy them.

29. Hannibal had now reached Hadrumetum.[11] After a few days spent there to allow his troops to recover from the effects of their voyage, alarmist reports of the occupation of all the country round Carthage forced him to move, and he hurried with all possible speed to Zama,[12] which lies five days' march south-west of Carthage. Scouts who had been sent from Zama ahead of the army were caught and brought by their Roman guards to Scipio, who handed them over to an officer and, telling them to have a good look at everything without fear of consequences, gave orders that they should be taken round the camp and shown whatever they wished to see. He then asked them if their investigations had been both comfortable and adequate, furnished them with an escort, and sent them back to Hannibal.

Nothing in the men's report gave Hannibal any pleasure to hear: for amongst other things they told him that Masinissa had joined Scipio that very day with 6,000 foot and 4,000 horse, though what he found most alarming was the enemy's confidence, which could hardly be entirely without foundation. Accordingly he sent to Scipio, and asked to be allowed a personal conference—in spite of the fact that he was himself responsible for the war, and by his arrival in Africa had violated the armistice and wrecked the hope of a treaty of peace. However, it seemed to him likely that he would get better terms from Scipio if he approached him while his army was still intact than after a defeat. Whether Hannibal took this step on his own initiative or by the instructions of his government, I cannot say with confidence; Valerius Antias related that he was beaten by Scipio in the first battle, in which he lost 12,000 men killed and 1,700 taken prisoner, and after that visited Scipio in his camp as an envoy of his government in company with ten others.

Scipio acceded to Hannibal's request for a conference, and the two generals agreed to advance the position of their respective camps so as to facilitate their meeting. Scipio established himself near Naraggara in a favourable position within javelin-range of water; Hannibal occupied a hill four miles away, safe and convenient enough except for its distance from water. Between the two positions a spot in full view from every side was chosen for the meeting, to ensure against a treacherous attack.

30. Exactly half-way between the opposing ranks of armed men, each attended by an interpreter, the generals met. They were not only the two greatest soldiers of their time, but the equals of any king or commander in the whole history of the world. For a minute mutual admiration struck them dumb, and they looked at each other in silence. Hannibal was the first to speak. 'If fate,' he said, 'has decreed that I who was the aggressor in the war with Rome, and so many times have had victory almost within my grasp, should of my own will come to ask for peace, I rejoice at least that destiny has given me you, and no other, from whom to ask it. You have many titles to honour, and amongst them, for you too, it will not be the least to have received the submission of Hannibal, to whom the gods gave victory over so many Roman generals, and to have brought to an end this war which was made memorable by your defeats before ever it was marked by ours. May it not also be a pretty example of the irony of fate that I took up arms when your father was consul, fought against him my first battle with a Roman general, and now come, unarmed, to his son to sue for peace? Assuredly it would have been best if the gods had given our fathers contentment with what was their own—you with ruling Italy, us with ruling Africa. Not even you can find Sicily and Sardinia adequate compensation for the loss of so many fleets and armies and the deaths of so many fine officers: but what is done is done—it may be censured, but it cannot be altered.

'Though we sought to win what did not belong to us, we are now fighting to defend our own, and the war has not been, for us, fought only in Italy, any more than for you it has been only in Africa. You too have seen the arms and standards of the enemy almost at your gates, just as now we can hear from Carthage the mutter and stir of a Roman camp. So in discussing terms of peace, it is you who can negotiate from strength—which is precisely what *you* most want, and *we* find most unfortunate. You and I have the most to gain by peace, and our respective governments will ratify whatever terms we decide on; the one essential thing is that we preserve in our negotiations a calm and rational temper.

'As for myself, an old man returning to the homeland I left in boyhood, the years with their burden of success and failure have so taught me that I would rather now follow the dictates of reason than hope for what luck may bring. You are young; fortune has always favoured you; and youth—unbrokenly successful—I fear may be too intolerant for the needs of cool and rational negotiation. The man whom fortune has never deceived cannot easily weigh the changes and chances of coming' years: what I was at Trasimene and

Cannae, you are today; you accepted a command when you were barely old enough for service; you shrank at nothing—and your luck has never failed you. By avenging your father and uncle you turned a personal sorrow into an opportunity for winning a splendid reputation for valour and for devotion to your family of the highest kind; you recovered the lost provinces of Spain, driving from them four Carthaginian armies; elected consul, while others lacked courage to defend Italy, you crossed to Africa—and with what result? Two armies cut to pieces on African soil, two camps captured and burnt within an hour, the mighty Syphax taken prisoner, countless towns in his kingdom seized and as many in ours—and, to crown all, your triumph in loosening the grip which for sixteen years I maintained upon Italy and forcing me to follow you here. A man's heart may well long for victory rather than for peace; I better understand the aspiring spirit than the politic brain, and once on me, too, smiled such fortune as is yours. None the less, if in prosperity the gods also gave us wisdom, we should consider not only what has happened in the past but what might happen in the future. To ignore all else, I alone am sufficient warning of what fate may bring: I, whom but yesterday you saw encamped between the Anio and Rome advancing my standards and on the point of scaling your city's walls—and whom now you see here, bereft of my two brothers—those famous generals, those valiant hearts—before the walls of my native city, already almost under siege, begging that she may be spared the terrors I so nearly inflicted upon yours.

'The greater a man's success, the less it must be trusted to endure. This is your hour of triumph, while for us all is dark; to you peace, if you grant it, will be a splendid thing and fair to look upon, but for us who sue for it, it will carry no honour but only the burden of necessity. Certain peace is better and safer than the uncertain hope of victory: the one is in your hands, the other in the hands of God. Do not stake the success of so many years upon the decision of a single hour; remember not only your own strength but the might of Fortune and the chances of war which we both must share. On both sides will be the sword, on both the bodies of mortal men—and nowhere less than in battle do results answer our hopes. If you win, you will not add as much glory to what you can have now by granting peace, as you will lose if things go against you. The luck of an hour can tumble to the ground the honours we have won, the honours we have hoped to win. In making peace, Publius Cornelius, everything is yours; refuse to make it, and you must take what the gods may please to give you. Amongst the few instances of valour rewarded by success would have been Regulus, here in Africa years ago, if only, after his victory, he granted peace when our fathers sued for it. But he set no limit to his success—his luck ran away with him and he could not draw the rein: so the higher he rose, the more shameful was his fall.

'To define terms is the privilege of him who grants a peace, not of him who sues for it; but perhaps we of Carthage are not unworthy to lay a penalty upon ourselves. We do not object to leaving you in possession of everything for which we went to war—Sicily, Sardinia, Spain, and all the islands between Africa and Italy; let us be confined within the shores of Africa, and see you, since such is God's will, extending your sway over foreign countries, both by land and by sea. I would not deny that there was some lack of sincerity in our recent request for peace and our failure to wait for it, or that therefore the honour of Carthage has become suspect to you. Confidence that a peace will be kept depends, Scipio, largely upon the persons through whom the request for it is made; and I am told that your Senate, too, refused the peace partly, at any rate, because the envoys we sent were of insufficient importance. But now it is I, Hannibal, who have come to sue—and I should not seek peace unless I thought it for our good, and for the same reason I shall keep it. I was the aggressor in this war; and just as I did what I could, till the gods envied my success, to ensure that none of my people should regret it, so shall I strive that none may regret the peace obtained through my endeavours.'

31. To Hannibal's speech the Roman general replied somewhat as follows. 'It did not escape me, Hannibal, that it was the knowledge that you would soon be with them that emboldened the Carthaginians to violate the armistice and wreck the hope of peace. Nor do you attempt to conceal this, when from the terms previously offered you leave out everything except what has long been in our possession. But just as you want your countrymen to realize how great is the burden from which you have relieved them, so I, for my part, must do my best not to reward their perfidy by omitting any of the conditions to which they formerly agreed. Though you do not deserve peace even on the same terms as before, you are actually asking to better them by your dishonesty. Our fathers were not the aggressors in the war for Sicily, nor we ourselves in the war for Spain; in the former it was the peril of our allies, the Mamertines,[13] in the latter the destruction of Saguntum which induced us to don the armour of loyalty and justice. That you were the aggressors you yourself admit, and the gods are our witnesses in that they granted for that war, even as they are granting and will grant for this, an ending in accordance with divine and human law.

'As for myself, I am aware of human infirmity; I do not ignore the might of Fortune, and I know well that all we do is subject to a thousand chances. If before you came to Africa—if while you were voluntarily evacuating Italy and had already embarked your army—you had come to me and I had turned a deaf ear to your request for peace, then, I confess, I should have been acting with outrageous insolence; but as things are, when on the brink of battle I have forced you to come here in spite of your most bitter reluctance, I am bound by no obligation to consider your feelings. If, therefore, to the terms upon which peace seemed likely to be made you wish to add some compensation for our ships which, with their cargoes, you took by force during the armistice, or for the violence you offered to our envoys, there will be something for me to bring before my council; if, on the contrary, you feel even that to be too great a burden, prepare to fight—for, evidently, you found peace intolerable.'

Negotiation had failed. The two generals after the conference returned to their armies with the news that words had been in vain and the issue must be decided by blows. Each must accept the fortune which the gods chose to give. 32. Arrived in camp, Scipio and Hannibal each urged their men to prepare both heart and hand for the supreme struggle which, if Fortune smiled, would leave them victorious, not for a day only but for ever. Before the next night they would know whether Rome or Carthage was destined to give laws to the nations, for the prize of victory would be not Italy or Africa but the whole world, while a peril as great as the prize would be theirs whom the fortune of war opposed. To the Romans, in an unknown and foreign land, no way of escape was open; Carthage, her last reserves spent, was threatened with instant destruction.

Next day, to decide this great issue, the two most famous generals and the two mightiest armies of the two wealthiest nations in the world advanced to battle, doomed either to crown or to destroy the many triumphs each had won in the past. In all hearts were mixed feelings, confidence alternating with fear. As men surveyed their own and the enemy's ranks, weighing the strength of each merely by what their eyes could tell them, thoughts of joy and of foreboding jostled for preeminence in their minds. Such grounds for confidence as did not readily occur to the rank and file were supplied by the two commanders in words of admonition and encouragement, Hannibal reminding his men of their exploits in Italy during sixteen years of campaigning, of all the Roman generals killed, all the armies wiped out, and, when he came to a man who had distinguished himself in some particular battle, of the heroic deeds of individual soldiers. Scipio, for his part, spoke of the Spanish campaigns, of the recent battles in Africa, and of the enemy's admission of weakness and guilt, in that fear had forced them to sue for a peace which their ineradicable perfidy forbade them to keep. Furthermore, he made good use of his conference with Hannibal, which, as it had taken place without witnesses, he was free to misrepresent in any way he pleased. It was a good guess, he said, that the gods had given the Carthaginians, as they went out into line, the same omens as when their fathers fought off the Aegates Islands. Soon the war and all its hardships would be over; the spoils of Carthage were within their grasp, and they would all before long be at home again with parents, children, wives, and household gods. Scipio, as he spoke, stood so erect and wore on his face an expression of such calm happiness that you might have thought the victory already won.

The Roman army was then marshalled for battle, the *hastati*[14] in the van, the *principes* behind them, and the *triarii* bringing up the rear. 33. Scipio did not mass his cohorts in the usual way, each in front of its own standards, but formed his line by maniples, leaving gaps between them to allow the enemy's elephants to pass through without breaking up the formation. Laelius, who had previously served as Scipio's second-in-command, but that year had been appointed quaestor—not by lot but by decree of the Senate—was given command of the Italian cavalry on the left wing, with Masinissa[15] and the Numidian cavalry on the right. Scipio filled the gaps between the front-line maniples with *velites* (as the light-armed troops were then called) whose orders were either to retire to the rear as soon as the elephants charged, or to split up and wheel rapidly right and left to positions immediately behind the front-line troops, either of which manoeuvres would let the elephants through and bring them, at the same time, between two fires.

Hannibal in the hope of shaking his enemy's morale put his elephants—eighty of them, more than he had had in any previous battle—right in the van of his army; behind them were the Ligurian and Gallic auxiliaries with a certain proportion of troops from Mauretania and the Balearics. In the second line he stationed his Carthaginian and African troops together with the one legion from Macedonia; then, a moderate distance to the rear of these, came a reserve line of Italians, Bruttians mostly, of whom the majority had followed Hannibal of necessity and under compulsion, and by no means of their own free will, when he left Italy. Hannibal, like Scipio, stationed the cavalry on the wings, the Carthaginian on the right, the Numidian on the left. In an army composed of men who shared neither language, customs, laws, weapons, dress, appearance, nor even a common reason for serving, the best means of arousing the fighting spirit was no simple matter; hopes and fears, to suit the case, had to be dangled before their eyes: the auxiliaries, for instance, were offered their pay not only in cash but increased by a share in the plunder; the fire to kindle the Gauls was their peculiar and ingrained detestation of the Romans; to the Ligurians was displayed the bait of the rich plains of Italy, once they had been brought down from their rugged mountains; Moors and Numidians were scared into courage by the prospect of Masinissa's tyrannical rule, while the Carthaginians were urged to keep before their eyes all they held dear—the walls of their native city, their household gods, the tombs of their ancestors, their children, parents, and trembling wives—and to remember the dread alternative, death and slavery on the one hand, world empire on the other, with no middle way, either for fear or hope, between those two extremes.

Hannibal was still addressing his Carthaginian contingent, and the various national leaders their own countrymen—mainly through interpreters because of the admixture of foreign troops—when from the Roman side the horns and trumpets blared out, and so tremendous a cheer was raised that the elephants panicked and turned against their own men, expecially against the Moors and Numidians on the left wing. The ensuing confusion was easily increased by Masinissa, who stripped that end of the line of its cavalry support. A few of the elephants, who had not panicked, did charge, and caused frightful execution amongst the Roman *velites*, though suffering severe damage themselves; for the light troops, springing back behind the maniples to let the beasts through without trampling them to death, hurled their spears from right and left simultaneously, thus catching them in a cross-fire; the javelins of the front-line troops continued meanwhile to do their work, until under a hail of missiles from every side the elephants were driven out of the Roman line and, like the others, turned against their own men and even put to flight the Carthaginian cavalry on the right wing.

34. The Carthaginian army had been stripped of cavalry support on both sides when the infantry closed, and was no longer equal to the Roman forces either in hope or in strength. There were, moreover, factors which seem trivial to recall, but proved of great importance at the time of action. The Roman war-cry was louder and more terrifying because it was in unison, whereas the cries from the Carthaginian side were discordant, coming as they did from a mixed assortment of peoples with a variety of mother-tongues. The Roman attack gained solidity as the men pressed on into the enemy by their own weight of numbers and that of their arms; on the other side, there were repeated charges with more speed than power behind them. Consequently the Romans immediately broke the enemy's line at the first attack; then they pressed on with their shoulders and shield-bosses, steadily advancing as the foe fell back, and making considerable progress as no one offered resistance. Then, as soon as they saw that the line confronting them had given way, the Roman rear line also began to press hard from behind, and this gave increased impetus to the rout of the enemy. On the other side, the second line of Africans and Carthaginians gave no support at all to the auxiliaries as they gave way; on the contrary, they fell back themselves for fear that the Romans would cut their way through those of the front line who offered firm resistance, and reach themselves. As a result, the auxiliaries suddenly turned and fled to mingle with their own men, some finding refuge in the second line, others cutting down

their fellows who refused to let them through, crying that they had been given no support before and now were refused a place in the ranks. By this time there were almost two battles in one, as the Carthaginians were forced to fight both their enemy and their own men: nevertheless they refused to admit the auxiliaries who, maddened by terror, were forcing their way into the line, but closed up their ranks and drove them out towards the wings and the open plain outside the battle. By this they hoped to keep the panic running through the routed and wounded men from spreading to the part of the army which was still intact and in formation.

But such heaps of dead men and their arms filled the place where the auxiliaries had been standing a short time before that the Romans began to find it almost more difficult to make their way through them than it had been through the dense ranks of the enemy. Consequently, the *hastati* of the front-line broke up their maniples, and ranks to pursue the enemy where they could over the piles of bodies and arms and through pools of blood. Then the maniples of the *principes* also began to break up, as they saw the first line losing formation. As soon as Scipio saw this, he ordered the recall to be sounded for the *hastati*, had the wounded men withdrawn to the rear, and led the *principes* and *triarii* out to the wings to protect and steady the centre, composed of *hastati* alone. Thus an entirely new battle began, for now the Romans had come to grips with their real enemies, the Carthaginian veterans, their equals in arms and experience of warfare, the fame of their exploits, and the extent of their hopes and perils. But the Romans had the advantage in numbers and in fighting spirit; they had already routed the Carthaginian cavalry and the elephants, and had broken up the front line, so that they were now engaged with the second.

35. Laelius and Masinissa had pursued the routed cavalry for a considerable distance; now at the right moment they wheeled round and charged into the rear of the enemy's line. It was this cavalry attack which finally defeated the Carthaginians. Many were surrounded and cut down where they stood; many were scattered in flight over the open plain, only to fall everywhere beneath the cavalry, the undisputed masters of the field. More than 20,000 of the Carthaginians and their allies were killed on that day, and about the same number captured, together with 132 military standards and eleven elephants. The Romans lost about 1,500 men.

In the confusion Hannibal escaped with a few horsemen and fled to Hadrumetum. He had tried everything he could both before and during the engagement before he withdrew from the battle, and on the admission even of Scipio as well as of all the military experts, he achieved the distinction of having drawn up his line on that day with remarkable skill. He had placed his elephants in the very front, so that their haphazard charge and irresistible weight should prevent the Romans from following their standards and keeping their ranks, tactics to which they attached the greatest importance; next came the auxiliaries, placed in front of the line of Carthaginians, so that the latter could block the possible retreat of these men drawn from the scum of any and every nation and held together by no loyal feelings but simply by the cash paid them. At the same time, the auxiliaries were to meet the first violence of the enemy's attack and to exhaust it, or, if nothing else, to blunt the enemy's swords by their own wounds. Then came the soldiers who represented Hannibal's highest hopes, the Carthaginians and Africans, a match for the Romans in every other respect, and now to have the advantage of fighting fresh against tired and wounded men. Last of all were the Italians, placed in the rear and also some distance back, since their doubtful loyalty might prove them either friend or foe. This was the last creation of Hannibal's military genius. From his refuge in Hadrumetum he was summoned to Carthage—it was thirty-five years since he had left it as a boy—and there before the senate he admitted that this defeat in the battle was also total defeat in the war. He saw no hope for the future unless Carthage asked for terms of peace and was granted them. . . .

37. On the following day the envoys were recalled and sternly rebuked for their perfidy: they were told that now that they had learned their lesson from repeated disasters, they should at long last believe in the existence of the gods and the sanctity of oaths. Terms of peace were put to them: they were to live as free men under their own laws, and to continue to hold the cities and territories which they had held before the war; the Romans from that day on would cease their raiding attacks. All deserters, runaway slaves, and prisoners-of-war were to be delivered to the Romans, all warships to be surrendered, with the exception of ten triremes, and all the trained elephants in their possession were to be handed over and no more to be trained. They were not to make war on anyone inside or outside Africa without permission from Rome; they were to make restitution to Masinissa and draw up a treaty with him; they must supply grain and pay to the allied troops until their own envoys had returned from Rome. They were to pay 10,000 talents of silver spread by equal instalments over fifty years, and hand over 100 hostages of Scipio's choosing between the ages of fourteen and thirty years. An armistice would be granted, provided that the transport ships captured during the previous time of peace were returned, together with their crews and cargoes: otherwise there would be no armistice nor any hope of peace. These then were the terms the envoys were told to take home.

When they were put before the Carthaginian assembly, a senator named Gisgo came forward to oppose the peace. The crowd listened, uneasy about the peace terms but anxious not to lose them, until Hannibal could bear it no

longer—that words like that should gain a hearing at a time of such crisis—
and pulled Gisgo down from the platform with his own hands. This was something new in a free state, and the murmur of indignation it roused left
Hannibal, the disciplined soldier, astounded at the licence of a city mob. 'I was
nine years old,' he said, 'when I left you, and after thirty-six years I have
returned. Destiny, both personal and public, since boyhood has taught me all
a soldier should know, and I think I have learned my lesson well; but it is left
to you to train me in the rights, laws, and usages of the city and the forum.'
After this apology for his ignorance, he spoke at length about the peace, showing that it was far from unfair and must be accepted. The greatest difficulty of
all the terms imposed was that of the ships captured during the truce, since
nothing was forthcoming except the ships themselves, and investigation was
made difficult by the fact that anyone accused would oppose the peace. It was
decided that the ships must be restored and the crews traced at all costs, and
that it should be left to Scipio to assess the value of what was missing so that
the Carthaginians could make restitution in cash.

Some historians say that Hannibal went straight from the battlefield to
the coast, where a ship was ready to take him at once to King Antiochus;[16] and
that when Scipio demanded Hannibal's surrender as a first essential, he was
told that Hannibal was not in Africa. . . .

The Carthaginians were accordingly dismissed, left Rome, and returned
to Africa, where they presented themselves to Scipio and made peace on the
terms I have mentioned. They surrendered their warships, elephants, deserters,
and runaway slaves, and 4,000 prisoners-of-war, amongst whom was the senator Quintus Terentius Culleo. Scipio ordered the ships to be taken out to sea
and burnt: according to some historians there were 500 of them, representing
every type of vessel propelled by oars, and the conflagration, seen without
warning, was as melancholy a sight for the Carthaginians as it would have been
if their own city were in flames. The deserters were more harshly treated than
the runaway slaves: Latin citizens were beheaded and Romans crucified.

44. It was forty years since peace[17] had last been made with Carthage, in
the year when Quintus Lutatius and Aulus Manlius were consuls. The war
which broke out twenty-three years later,[18] in the consulship of Publius
Cornelius and Tiberius Sempronius, was brought to an end in its seventeenth
year, in the consulship of Gnaeus Cornelius and Publius Aelius. Tradition has
it that later Scipio often said that it was the desire for fame, first of Tiberius
Claudius and then of Gnaeus Cornelius, which prevented him from ending
the war with the destruction of Carthage.

The raising of the first instalment of their indemnity seemed difficult to
the Carthaginians, exhausted as they were by the long war, and there was gen-

eral weeping and lamentation in the senate. On this occasion Hannibal—so the story goes—was seen to be laughing. Hasdrubal ('the Kid') rebuked him for laughing while his people wept, when he himself was the cause of their tears. 'If eyes could see the mind within,' replied Hannibal, 'as they do the expression of a face, it would soon be apparent to you that this laughter you condemn springs not from a happy heart, but from one which is almost beside itself with its misfortunes; and yet laughter is far less untimely than your own irrational and misplaced tears. The time to weep was when our arms were taken from us, our ships were burnt, and we were forbidden foreign wars; that was when we received our death blow. You have no reason to believe that the Romans had any interest in your domestic peace, for peace can never stay for long in a great country. It will find an enemy at home if it lacks one abroad, just as a powerful body appears immune from any external infection but is strained by its own strength. How true it is that we feel public misfortune only in so far as it affects our private interests! And it takes a money loss to make us feel the pinch. So when the spoils of war were being stripped from vanquished Carthage, and you saw her left naked and unarmed amidst all the many armed tribes of Africa, no one raised a moan; but today, when contributions have to be made from private property, you behave like mourners at your country's funeral. All too soon, I fear, you will realize that it is the least of your troubles which has called forth these tears today.' These were Hannibal's words to his people.

Scipio called an assembly, and there, in addition to his own kingdom, Masinissa was presented with the city of Cirta and the remaining towns and lands which had passed from the kingdom of Syphax into the power of the Roman people. Gnaeus Octavius received orders to take the fleet to Sicily and hand it over to Gnaeus Cornelius the consul, and Carthaginian envoys were told to go to Rome, so that all Scipio's acts performed on the advice of his council of ten could be confirmed by the authority of the Senate and the people's command.

45. So peace was secured on land and sea. . . .

## Notes

[1] Carthage was a colony of Phoenicia, and the Latin word for Phoenician was *Poenus*, hence our English word "Punic." Thus Punic means Phoenician or more specifically Carthaginian.

[2] Berber tribesmen who lived west and south of Carthage. They were expert cavalrymen who allied themselves with Hannibal in this war.

[3] Tiberius Sempronius Longus, one of the consuls for the year 218 B.C.E., along with Publius Cornelius Scipio. Scipio had been wounded in the first encounter with

Hannibal and saved by his son, the same Scipio who will finally defeat Hannibal in 202 B.C.E.

⁴ Etruria is essentially the modern Italian province of Tuscany; Faesulae is modern Fiesole, 5 miles north of Florence, and Arretium is Arezzo, about 40 miles southeast of Florence. The plain is that of the Arno river, the Valdarno.

⁵ Gaius Flaminius, consul of 217 B.C.E., along with Gnaeus Servilius Geminus.

⁶ Town on the river Aufidus, in the province of Apulia, on the "heel" of the boot of Italy. The year is 216 B.C.E., and the consuls are Gaius Terentius Varro, and Lucius Aemilius Paullus.

⁷ The Gauls defeated the Romans at a battle on the Allia river in 390 B.C.E., and then invaded Rome itself. See Livy Book V.34–43.

⁸ Quintus Fabius Maximus, who was made *dictator* in 217 B.C.E. after both consuls were killed at Lake Trasimeme, and elected consul in 215, 214, and 209. He was called "the Delayer" (*Cunctator*) for his tactic of avoiding direct confrontation with Hannibal. He died in 203 B.C.E., before the defeat of Hannibal.

⁹ Syphax was a Numidian king who revolted from Carthage and fought for the Romans from 214-206 B.C.E. Hasdrubal, a Carthaginian, commanded the Carthaginian forces in Spain until they were defeated by Scipio in 207. Syphax was persuaded to ally himself with the Carthaginians again in 206 by Sophonisba, the daughter of Hasdrubal, whom he wed.

¹⁰ Recognitions awarded to the first man over an enemy's walls (*murus*) or over his outer rampart (*vallum*).

¹¹ A seaport 60 miles south of Carthage.

¹² Name of several cities in the interior of modern Tunisia; the one Livy refers to is probably Zama Regia. It is the site of the defeat of Hannibal.

¹³ Southern Italy mercenaries ("sons of Mamers" or Mars) who had seized Messana and plundered northeast Sicily 70 years earlier. Their actions began a series of events that led to the First Punic War (264–241 B.C.E.).

¹⁴ The Roman legion was divided into smaller units (*maniples*) and arranged in three lines of troops, the "spearmen" (*hastati*) in front, the "leaders" (*principes*) second, and the most experienced troops (*triarii* or "third rank men") in back. In addition, light-armed troops (*velites*) could be used as needed.

¹⁵ Numidian king who fought for Carthage until 206 B.C.E., then afterwards for the Romans. He supported Rome and generally enjoyed Rome's support until his death in 148 B.C.E.

¹⁶ Antiochus III (also Antiochus the Great), king of the Seleucid Empire from 222 until his death in 187 B.C.E. Hannibal took refuge at his court, though not until 195 B.C.E. See Juvenal 10.147–167.

¹⁷ 241 B.C.E. the end of the First Punic War.

¹⁸ 218 B.C.E., the start of the Second Punic War.

# Propertius

## ca. 49–16 B.C.E.

Sextus Propertius was born around 49 B.C.E. in Assisi and died sometime after 16 B.C.E.; nothing more specific can be said. His family suffered from confiscations of property by which Octavian rewarded his soldiers, and in two poems at the end of his first book he associates with the victims of Octavian's siege of Perugia in 41 B.C.E. Nevertheless, he made his way to Rome at some point; after the publication of his first book of elegies, he gained the patronage of Maecenas, one of Octavian's most powerful associates, who also supported Vergil and Horace. Propertius published four books of elegies in all, apparently independently of each other. The first book, which is given the title of *Monobiblos* in ancient manuscripts, was published no later than 28 B.C.E. and introduces the theme for which Propertius is most remembered: his love for Cynthia.

Elegy is first a metrical form: a couplet, in dactylic meter, consisting of a hexameter and a pentameter. Archaic Greek poets wrote elegy, but with a variety of themes, including exhortation in war and political moralizing, represented by Tyrtaeus and Solon respectively in this reader. At least one Greek elegist, Mimnermus, composed love elegies, but he seems at best to have been a distant model. It is probably most accurate to say that Roman love elegy had several influences—Greek New Comedy, Hellenistic epigram, Catullus—but was largely the original creation of a few Augustan poets.

Later Roman writers recognized four elegaic poets: Gallus (of whom only a few lines survive), Tibullus, Propertius, and Ovid. Although their styles and tones vary greatly, there are a few shared traits that seem to categorize the genre. The object of the poet's love is not his wife but a mistress (*domina*), whose loyalty is questionable; his devotion to her is presented as a form of slavery (*servitium*), a disease (*morbus*), or military service (*militia*), and its sufferings outnumber its joys; and the poet often resorts to idealistic comparisons with figures of myth or the lost golden age.

Propertius begins his first book with the name of his beloved: Cynthia. The first few lines of the first elegy, presented below, reveal the circumstances of this love: it is Propertius' first love, lasted a year, was experienced as a degradation, and corrupted his ability to love "chaste women." This poem introduces several characteristics of Propertius' elegy, such as his psychologically divided *persona*, his rapid and complex leaps of thought, and his elaborate and sometimes obscure mythological allusions. The third elegy of book 1 reverses the roles and (wishfully?) casts Cynthia as the faithful one awaiting her lover's return; and in the 20th elegy of the first book, Propertius recasts Theocritus' 13th *Idyll* as an elaborate mythological warning to his friend Gallus.

Scholars have offered various reasons why Roman elegy appeared as a genre during the critical transition from the Republic to the Empire. Some look at elegy as a mirror of the sociological changes that Augustus later thought necessary to improve through legislation. Others have suggested that the uncertainty engendered by the new political dynamic, in which the old institutions were still operative but dominated by new but undefined powers, is psychologically analogous to the uncertainty of the lover in elegy. Comparisons have been drawn to the tone of poets writing during the first decades of the twentieth century, such as T. S. Eliot and Ezra Pound. The latter, perhaps recognizing the kinship, wrote an interesting adaptation of Propertius' elegies entitled "Homage to Sextus Propertius."

BSH

# from *Elegies*

## Book I

### *I.1 Cynthia prima suis miserum me cepit ocellis*

Cynthia was the first
To capture with her eyes my pitiable self:
Till then I was free from desire's contagion. Love
Then forced me to lower my gaze of steady hauteur
And trampled my head with his feet
Until, perverse, he had taught me to demur
At faithful girls and live without taking thought.
A whole year, and my frenzy does not flag,
Though I'm forced to know the gods' disapprobation.

Milanion,[1] Tullus, by not shrinking from any trial,       10
Quelled Iasus' unfeeling daughter's severity:
For once he wandered deranged in Parthenian caverns
And went to face wild hirsute beasts;
A casualty, wounded and broken by the club
Of Hylaeus, he groaned among Arcadia's rocks;
Thus he succeeded in taming the swift young woman—
So prayers and deeds well done prevail in love.

In my case Love is dull, designs no stratagems,
And forgets to tread his once accustomed ways.
But you whose trick it is to lure the moon from heaven,      20
And task to solemnize rites in magic altar-fire,
Come change my mistress' mind
And make her face blanch paler than my own!—
Then I shall believe that you can draw
The stars and rivers with Colchian[2] spells.

And, friends, that call me back from decline,
Seek out the remedies for unsound hearts:
I shall bear with fortitude cauterization and knife,
If only I'm free to speak as my anger wants.
Carry me through the farthest peoples and seas,      30
Where never a woman can follow my spoor.

Stay, to whom the god inclines a compliant ear:
Be always nicely matched in a safe love.
Our Venus plies bitter nights against me,
And at no time does Love either rest or cease.
Be warned, avoid my woe. Let each be held by
His own suit, don't change the seat of accustomed love!
But if anyone heeds my warning too late, alas,
How grievously he will recall my words.

### I.3  Qualis Thesea iacuit cedente carina

As on the lonely beach the Cnossian[3] lay
Fainting while Theseus' keel receded;
As Cepheus' Andromeda,[4] freed at last
From the rocks, reclined in her first sleep;
As one exhausted in the relentless Thracian
Ring-dance falls in a heap on Apidanus'[5] sward;
Just so, it seemed to me, did Cynthia breathe
Soft quietude, head propped on outspread hands,
When deep in wine I dragged my footsteps in
As the slaves shook up the late -night torches.          10

I, not yet quite totally deprived of all my senses,
Endeavoured softly to go to her dinted bed—
Although here Love, here Wine, each god strong
As the other, ordered me, goaded with double fire,
Lightly to pass my arm beneath her prostrate form
And seize and hold her, venturing kisses.

Yet, fearing the furious objurgations I knew so well,
I did not dare disturb my mistress' peace:
Fast I stood, with riveted eyes, like Argus
Before Inachus' daughter's strange horns.          20
Now I untied the garland from my head,
And put it, Cynthia, about your brows.
And now I joyed to arrange your straying locks,
And covertly place apples in your hands:
But I lavished all my gifts on thankless sleep—
The gifts that rolled profuse from my leaning breast!

And when you stirred at times and heaved a sigh,
I stood transfixed with empty apprehension
Lest visions brought you unaccustomed dread

And someone strove to make you, unwilling, his:　　　　　30
But then the moon, fleeting past the open shutters,
The officious moon, whose light would linger,
Opened with gentle beams your eyes becalmed.

Her elbow propped in the soft bed, then she said:
'Has another's "injustice" chased you out and shut
The doors and brought you back, at last, to me?
Where have you squandered the watches of my night,
And droop (alas for me) now the stars are put out?
If only you might endure, you shameless man, such nights
As you always enforce on my misfortune!　　　　　40

'I have eluded sleep with nitid weaving,
And then, worn out, with a song to Orpheus' lyre,
Lamented quietly in my loneliness
Your frequent long delays in love with strangers,
Until Oblivion brushed my sinking form
With his welcome wings. And that
Was my latest concern, amid my tears.'

## I.20 *Hoc pro continuo te, Galle, monemus amore*

In return for your unfailing love, Gallus, I give
This warning (let it not slip from your heedless mind):
Fortune often opposes the feckless lover—
As Ascanius, ruthless to the Minyae,[6] told.
Your love, Theodamas' boy, is very like Hylas[7]—
No less in appearance, equal in name.
So if you pick your way by shady woodland streams,
Or the ripples of Anio bathe your feet,
If you stroll on the verge of the Giants' shore,
Or wherever a wandering stream may welcome you,　　　　　10
Always beat off the snatching desires of Nymphs
(No less their love than is the Ausonian Dryads'[8]),
Lest mountains are rugged and rocks are chill,
Gallus, and you come to unattempted lakes:
Such things the wretched wanderer Hercules
Endured and deplored by untamed Ascanius' banks.

The Argo once set sail from Pagasa's yards,
Made the long voyage to Phasis, and having
Glided beyond the waves of Hellespont,

She moored her hull alongside Mysian rocks.        20
Here the band of heroes stood fast on the quiet beach,
And gathered and covered the shore with springy branches.
The comrade of the unvanquished one[9] advanced
To seek the waters of some secluded spring.

On him both brothers, the north wind's sons
(Here Zetes above, and here Calais above)
Impended, hovering palms, to cull his kisses,
Stealing his upturned kiss by turns as they flew.
Stooping, he ducks beneath a sheltering wing-tip,
And with a branch wards off their flying ambush.      30
At last Orithyia's progeny fell away—
Oh, grief!—and Hylas went, he went to forest Nymphs.

Here beneath the peak of Mount Arganthus
Was Pege, Bithynian Nymphs' dear water-home,
Above which hung from unfrequented trees
Dew-wet apples owing nothing to nurture,
And round about from water-meadows snowy
Lilies mixed with scarlet poppies sprang—
Which now he plucked with tender, childish nails,
Preferring flowers to his intended task:      40
And bent uncomprehending above the shapely wave,
He delays his straying for alluring reflections:
At length his lowered hands go to draw from the stream—
Leant on his right shoulder, he lifts full measure.

Fired by his fairness the Dryad girls
Cut short in wonder their accustomed dances—
Lightly they drew him headlong through yielding water:
Hylas cried out as his body was seized, to which
Alcides, far off, reiterated replies,
But the breeze returned him the name from farthest hills.      50

Be warned by this and protect your love, Gallus,
Whom I have seen entrust svelte Hylas to Nymphs.

## Notes

[1] The successful suitor of Atalanta ("Iasus' daughter"), a woman raised in the wild by a she-bear. The more famous version of the myth tells that Atalanta challenged her suitors to a footrace and killed the losers. Milanion won by dropping three golden

apples along her path, which Atalanta stopped to pick up. Propertius characteristically chooses a more obscure variant, in which Milanion suffers the blow of a centaur (Hylaeus, line 15) who may have threatened Atalanta.

2 Colchis was a city on the eastern coast of the Black Sea, home of Medea, and famed for its witches and spells. Propertius' Latin is corrupt here, but the reference to Colchis is appropriate.

3 Ariadne, the Cretan princess who helped Theseus defeat the Minotaur. Cnossos is a major city in Crete.

4 Cepheus was king of Egypt. Perseus rescued his daughter Andromeda from a sea-monster, to which she was offered as a sacrifice.

5 River in Thessaly, whose banks serve here as the site of Bacchic revelry.

6 The Ascanius is a river in Bithynia, near where the event happened to the Argonauts (the Minyae) which Propertius relates in this poem.

7 Hylas was the beloved of Hercules, a beautiful boy whom the Nymphs snatch when he is sent to fetch water during a stop on the Argonauts' journey. Propertius draws a long parallel between Hylas' fate and the Italian girls who will tempt Gallus' beloved in Italy in fashionable spots along "the ripples of the Anio" east of Rome or on "the verge of the Giants' shore" on the Bay of Naples.

8 Ausonia is a poetic reference to Italy, and Dryads are a type of nymph (originally tree nymphs), but Propertius generalizes. Italian girls, he says, are as amorous as the Nymphs who grabbed Hylas.

9 Hylas, comrade of Hercules, the unvanquished one.

# Horace

## 65–8 B.C.E.

The poetic output of Quintus Horatius Flaccus, whom we call Horace, defies simple categorization. He attacks in his *Epodes*; he has room for comedy, philosophy, fable, and more in his *Satires*; he offers literary criticism in his *Epistles*. But it is his *Odes* (*Carmina*, "Songs" in Latin) for which he is most well-known.

Horace tells us that he was the son of a freedman (a former slave who had bought his freedom) from Venusia, and that his father gave him the best education he could. Horace was a student in Athens when Caesar was killed, and Caesar's killers, Brutus and Cassius, fled to Greece to raise an army against the forces of Antony and Octavian. Horace joined and was given charge of a legion, but the Republican forces were routed at Philippi in 42 B.C.E.; Horace says that he threw away his shield and ran. He returned to Rome in 41 under an amnesty, but his family possessions had been confiscated. Horace became a public scribe and wrote poetry, until he was introduced by Vergil to Maecenas, one of Octavian's associates. Maecenas became Horace's patron and gave him a small farm. Horace apparently felt sincere gratitude and friendship toward Maecenas all his life; the two died within a few months of each other.

Like the other Augustan poets (e.g., Vergil and Propertius), Horace looked to Greece to find worthy precedents for the creation of a new Roman literature. For his *Odes* he took the lyric poets, especially Alcaeus and Sappho, as his models. In *Ode* 3.30 below, he boasts that he was the "first to bring Greek song to Latin measures," and it is no small feat: Greek and Latin are languages very different in sound and syllable length, and no Latin poet before or since met with Horace's success. Horace's *Odes* are masterpieces of precision, marked by simplicity of expression that betrays the complexity of their composition. Translation often serves Horace quite badly, because the rhythms and the juxtapositions of sound and meaning cannot be transferred out of Latin. (See the Essay on Translation for various attempts at one of Horace's *Odes*.)

Horace's *Odes* offer a variety of themes, many taken from his Greek models. Many poems are set as drinking songs; others celebrate love; some are hymns to gods. Horace also wrote odes on Roman themes, in celebration of Augustus and his achievements. A common motif that runs through many odes is the shortness of life, and the need, often expressed as a philosophical truism, to enjoy the moment set before you. One of the most common expressions of that sentiment still today is *carpe diem*, "seize the day", which was penned by Horace in *Ode* I.7, which appears below.

BSH

# from *Odes*

## Book I

### 5 *Quis multa gracilis*

What slender youth besprinkled with fragrant oils
now crowds you, Pyrrha, amid the roses
in some convenient grotto?
For whom do you dress that yellow hair,

so simply neat? Alas, how often he will weep
at your and the Gods' vacillations—
oh he will be flabbergasted
by rough seas and black gates,

who now enjoys the illusion your worth is golden,
who supposes you will be always available, always          10
amiable, not knowing the breeze
deceives. I pity those

for whom you blandly glitter.
A votive plaque on the temple wall
shows damp clothes (mine) hung up
to the puissant God of the sea.

### 11 *Tu ne quaesieris*

Do not inquire, we may not know, what end
the Gods will give, Leuconoe, do not attempt
Babylonian calculations. The better course
is to bear whatever will be, whether Jove allot
more winters or this is the last which exhausts
the Tuscan sea with pumice rocks opposed.
Be wise, decant the wine, prune back
your long-term hopes. Life ebbs as I speak:
so seize each day, and grant the next no credit.

## Book III

### 30 Exegi monumentum

I have achieved a monument more lasting
than bronze, and loftier than the pyramids of kings,
which neither gnawing rain nor blustering wind
may destroy, nor innumerable series of years,
nor the passage of ages. I shall not wholly die,
a large part of me will escape Libitina:[1]
while Pontiff and Vestal shall climb the Capitol Hill,
I shall be renewed and flourish in further praise.
Where churning Aufidus resounds, where Daunus[2]
poor in water governed his rustic people,                                    10
I shall be spoken of as one who was princely
though of humble birth, the first to have brought
Greek song into Latin numbers. Take hard-won pride
in your success, Melpomene,[3] and willingly
wreathe my hair with Apollo's laurel.

## Notes

[1] Roman goddess of burials, which were registered at her grove on the Esquiline hill in Rome.

[2] The Aufidus is a river in the province of Apulia, on the heel of Italy's boot (and the river on which Cannae stood), and Daunus was a mytical king of Apulia.

[3] One of the Muses.

# Laudatio Turiae
## (*A Eulogy for Turia*)

The funerary speech was considered an important genre of oratory in Roman culture, though no complete example has survived to our time. For most of the history of the Roman Republic the eulogy was reserved for men; we learn from Cicero that the first woman to be so honored was a certain Popilia, who died at the beginning of the first century B.C.E. Given the importance of the male ancestor in Roman culture, it is ironic that the most complete funeral speech we do have is the so-called *Laudatio Turiae*, written for a Roman noblewoman by her bereaved husband.

This eulogy is the longest surviving non-public Latin inscription, and dates to the end of the first century B.C.E., during the reign of the emperor Augustus. It was inscribed on two massive stone slabs, each about eight and one half feet in height and two and one half feet wide. Unfortunately, the beginning of the inscription, where the couple's names were inscribed, is lost, but it got its name from scholars who suggested, wrongly, as we now think, that it referred to a woman named Turia, who literary sources say suffered similar misfortunes in her life. It probably adorned the tomb originally, but was later broken up and reused in various parts of Rome over a long period of time; consequently, only about half of it survives today.

Funerary orations, then and now, tend to be rather flattering portraits of the dead; Turia was certainly portrayed as the perfect Roman wife in an old-fashioned sort of way. Obviously from a wealthy family, she embodied the wifely virtues of chastity, loyalty, and harmony, and she was a *univira*: a woman who had had only one husband in her lifetime. It was also considered virtuous for a woman to avoid public life; thus, Turia's efforts on her husband's behalf were all the more extraordinary because she sacrificed her privacy, and acted in ways that under normal social circumstances would have disgraced both her and her entire family. The fact that her husband praised her for these actions points to the violent and turbulent state of affairs in Rome in the decades preceding the fall of the Republic.

LH

# from *Laudatio Turiae* (*A Eulogy for Turia*)

**168. A funeral eulogy. Rome, 1st cent. BC (ILS 8393. Tr. E. Wistrand. L)**

*(heading) . . . of my wife*

*Left-hand column* (line 1) . . . through the honesty of your character . . .
(2) . . . you remained . . .
(3) You became an orphan suddenly before the day of our wedding, when both your parents were murdered together in the solitude of the countryside. It was mainly due to your efforts that the death of your parents was not left unavenged. For I had left for Macedonia, and your sister's husband Cluvius had gone to the Province of Africa.

(7) So strenuously did you perform your filial duty by your insistent demands and your pursuit of justice that we could not have done more if we had been present. But these merits you have in common with that most virtuous lady your sister.

(10) While you were engaged in these things, having secured the punishment of the guilty, you immediately left your own house in order to guard your modesty and you came to my mother's house, where you awaited my return.

(13) Then pressure was brought to bear on you and your sister to accept the view that your father's will, by which you and I were heirs, had been invalidated by his having contracted a *coemptio*[1] with his wife. If that was the case, then you together with all your father's property would necessarily come under the guardianship of those who pursued the matter; your sister would be left without any share at all of that inheritance, since she had been transferred to the *potestas*[2] of Cluvius. How you reacted to this, with what presence of mind you offered resistance, I know full well, although I was absent.

(18) You defended our common cause by asserting the truth, namely, that the will had not in fact been broken, so that we should both keep the property, instead of your getting all of it alone. It was your firm decision that you would defend your father's written word; you would do this anyhow, you declared, by sharing your inheritance with your sister, if you were unable to uphold the validity of the will. And you maintained that you would not come under the state of legal guardianship, since there was no such right against you in law, for there was no proof that your father belonged to any *gens*[3] that could by law compel you to do this. For even assuming that your father's will had

494

become void, those who prosecuted had no such right since they did not belong to the same *gens*.

(25) They gave way before your firm resolution and did not pursue the matter any further. Thus you on your own brought to a successful conclusion the defence you took up of your duty to your father, your devotion to your sister, and your faithfulness towards me.

(27) Marriages as long as ours are rare, marriages that are ended by death and not broken by divorce. For we were fortunate enough to see our marriage last without disharmony for fully 40 years. I wish that our long union had come to its final end through something that had befallen me instead of you; it would have been more just if I as the older partner had had to yield to fate through such an event.

(30) Why should I mention your domestic virtues: your loyalty, obedience, affability, reasonableness, industry in working wool, religion without superstition, sobriety of attire, modesty of appearance? Why dwell on your love for your relatives, your devotion to your family? You have shown the same attention to my mother as you did to your own parents, and have taken care to secure an equally peaceful life for her as you did for your own people, and you have innumerable other merits in common with all married women who care for their good name. It is your very own virtues that I am asserting, and very few women have encountered comparable circumstances to make them endure such sufferings and perform such deeds. Providentially Fate has made such hard tests rare for women.

We have preserved all the property you inherited from your parents under common custody, for you were not concerned to make your own what you had given to me without any restriction. We divided our duties in such a way that I had the guardianship of your property and you had the care of mine. Concerning this side of our relationship I pass over much, in case I should take a share myself in what is properly yours. May it be enough for me to have said this much to indicate how you felt and thought.

(42) Your generosity you have manifested to many friends and particularly to your beloved relatives. On this point someone might mention with praise other women, but the only equal you have had has been your sister. For you brought up your female relations who deserved such kindness in your own houses with us. You also prepared marriage-portions for them so that they could obtain marriages worthy of your family. The dowries you had decided upon Cluvius and I by common accord took upon ourselves to pay, and since we approved of your generosity we did not wish that you should let your own patrimony suffer diminution but substituted our own money and gave our own estates as dowries. I have mentioned this not from a wish to commend

ourselves but to make clear that it was a point of honour for us to execute with our means what you had conceived in a spirit of generous family affection.

(52) A number of other benefits of yours I have preferred not to mention . . . *(several lines missing)*

*Right-hand column* (2a) You provided abundantly for my needs during my flight and gave me the means for a dignified manner of living, when you took all the gold and jewellery from your own body and sent it to me and over and over again enriched me in my absence with servants, money and provisions, showing great ingenuity in deceiving the guards posted by our adversaries.

(6a) You begged for my life when I was abroad—it was your courage that urged you to this step—and because of your entreaties I was shielded by the clemency of those against whom you marshalled your words. But whatever you said was always said with undaunted courage.

(9a) Meanwhile when a troop of men collected by Milo, whose house I had acquired through purchase when he was in exile, tried to profit by the opportunities provided by the civil war and break into our house to plunder, you beat them back successfully and were able to defend our home. (*About 12 lines missing*)

(0) . . . exist . . . that I was brought back to my country by him (Caesar Augustus), for if you had not, by taking care for my safety, provided what he could save, he would have promised his support in vain. Thus I owe my life no less to your devotion than to Caesar.

(4) Why should I now hold up to view our intimate and secret plans and private conversations: how I was saved by your good advice when I was roused by startling reports to meet sudden and imminent dangers; how you did not allow me imprudently to tempt providence by an overbold step but prepared a safe hiding-place for me, when I had given up my ambitious designs, choosing as partners in your plans to save me your sister and her husband Cluvius, all of you taking the same risk? There would be no end, if I tried to go into all this. It is enough for me and for you that I was hidden and my life was saved.

(11) But I must say that the bitterest thing that happened to me in my life befell me though what happened to you. When thanks to the kindness and judgment of the absent Caesar Augustus I had been restored to my country as a citizen, Marcus Lepidus, his colleague, who was present, was confronted with your request concerning my recall, and you lay prostrate at his feet, and you were not only not raised up but were dragged away and carried off brutally like a slave. But although your body was full of bruises, your spirit was unbroken and you kept reminding him of Caesar's edict with its expression of pleasure at my reinstatement, and although you had to listen to insulting words and suffer cruel wounds, you pronounced the words of the edict in a loud voice,

so that it should be known who was the cause of my deadly perils. This matter was soon to prove harmful for him.

(19) What could have been more effective than the virtue you displayed? You managed to give Caesar an opportunity to display his clemency and not only to preserve my life but also to brand Lepidus' insolent cruelty by your admirable endurance.

(22) But why go on? Let me cut my speech short. My words should and can be brief, lest by dwelling on your great deeds I treat them unworthily. In gratitude for your great services towards me let me display before the eyes of all men my public acknowledgment that you saved my life.

(25) When peace had been restored throughout the world and the lawful political order re-established, we began to enjoy quiet and happy times. It is true that we did wish to have children, who had for a long time been denied to us by an envious fate. If it had pleased Fortune to continue to be favourable to us as she was wont to be, what would have been lacking for either of us? But Fortune took a different course, and our hopes were sinking. The courses you considered and the steps you attempted to take because of this would perhaps be remarkable and praiseworthy in some other women, but in you they are nothing to wonder at when compared to your other great qualities and I will not go into them.

(31) When you despaired of your ability to bear children and grieved over my childlessness, you became anxious lest by retaining you in marriage I might lose all hope of having children and be distressed for that reason. So you proposed a divorce outright and offered to yield our house free to another woman's fertility. Your intention was in fact that you yourself, relying on our well-known conformity of sentiment, would search out and provide for me a wife who was worthy and suitable for me, and you declared that you would regard future children as joint and as though your own, and that you would not effect a separation of our property which had hitherto been held in common, but that it would still be under my control and, if I wished so, under your administration: nothing would be kept apart by you, nothing separate, and you would thereafter take upon yourself the duties and the loyalty of a sister and a mother-in-law.

(40) I must admit that I flared up so that I almost lost control of myself; so horrified was I by what you tried to do that I found it difficult to retrieve my composure. To think that separation should be considered between us before fate had so ordained, to think that you had been able to conceive in your mind the idea that you might cease to be my wife while I was still alive, although you had been utterly faithful to me when I was exiled and practically dead!

(44) What desire, what need to have children could I have had that was so great that I should have broken faith for that reason and changed certainty for uncertainty? But no more about this! You remained with me as my wife,

for I could not have given in to you without disgrace for me and unhappiness for both of us.

(48) But on your part, what could have been more worthy of commemoration and praise than your efforts in devotion to my interests: when I could not have children from yourself, you wanted me to have them through your good offices, and since you despaired of bearing children, to provide me with offspring by my marriage to another woman.

(51) Would that the life-span of each of us had allowed our marriage to continue until I, as the older partner, had been borne to the grave—that would have been more just—and you had performed for me the last rites, and that I had died leaving you still alive and that I had had you as a daughter to myself in place of my childlessness.

(54) Fate decreed that you should precede me. You bequeathed me sorrow through my longing for you and left me a miserable man without children to comfort me. I on my part will, however, bend my way of thinking and feeling to your judgments and be guided by your admonitions.

(56) But all your opinions and instructions should give precedence to the praise you have won so that this praise will be a consolation for me and I will not feel too much the loss of what I have consecrated to immortality to be remembered for ever.

(58) What you have achieved in your life will not be lost to me. The thought of your fame gives me strength of mind and from your actions I draw instruction so that I shall be able to resist Fortune. Fortune did not rob me of everything since it permitted your memory to be glorified by praise. But along with you I have lost the tranquillity of my existence. When I recall how you used to foresee and ward off the dangers that threatened me, I break down under my calamity and cannot hold steadfastly by my promise.

(63) Natural sorrow wrests away my power of self-control and I am overwhelmed by sorrow. I am tormented by two emotions: grief and fear—and I do not stand firm against either. When I go back in thought to my previous misfortunes and when I envisage what the future may have in store for me, fixing my eyes on your glory does not give me strength to bear my sorrow with patience. Rather I seem to be destined to long mourning.

(67) The conclusions of my speech will be that you deserved everything but that it did not fall to my lot to give you everything as I ought; your last wishes I have regarded as law; whatever it will be in my power to do in addition, I shall do.

(69) I pray that your Di Manes[4] will grant you rest and protection.

# Notes

[1] "The (fictitious) sale of a woman to a man by which she passed into his *manus* or power on the occasion of marriage . . ." *Oxford Latin Dictionary.*

[2] "Power" or "authority."

[3] "(Extended) family" or "clan."

[4] Roman spirits of the dead, who were semi-deified and worshipped.

# Augustus

## 63 B.C.E.–14 C.E.

The Roman biographer Suetonius records that Augustus had given three papyrus scrolls to the Vestal Virgins for safekeeping, on which he had written his funeral instructions, a kind of "State of the Union" assessment of the Roman Empire he left behind, and an autobiographical account of his accomplishments. He wished to have the latter inscribed on bronze tablets and affixed to the entrance of the Mausoleum he had already built for himself and his family, a task which no doubt was duly executed as he had wished. The Mausoleum, however, was robbed some time in the centuries following his death, and the document was believed to have been lost forever.

In 1555 a Dutch scholar named Buysbecche saw the ruins of a temple dedicated to Rome and Augustus in Ankara, Turkey. To his delight and amazement, the walls of the temple were covered with a bilingual inscription in Latin and Greek, which he recognized as a copy of the lost *Res Gestae*, though he gave it the name *Monumentum Ancyranum* (*The Monument of Ankara*). Late in the nineteenth century the Berlin Academy had plaster casts of this "queen of Latin inscriptions" made to facilitate making a definitive text of the work. Because of the ruined state of the temple walls in Ankara, some lacunae in the text still remain, even though a few additional fragments of the Greek translation have been found in other cities. No doubt Augustus' accomplishments were published all over the Roman Empire after his death, though to date copies have only been found in Asia Minor.

Like many autobiographies, Augustus' account emphasizes his successes and glosses over shortcomings, though his terse, elegant style gives the impression of objectivity. One modern scholar has called it "a posthumous political manifesto in the retrospective form of a dignified narrative of the emperor's public career." Another has characterized it as "a combination between the *elogium* of a Roman general and the statement of accounts of a Roman magistrate." Most of it was written well before Augustus' death in 14 C.E., but when he began the writing and when he made additions and corrections remains speculative. It is a precious document, precariously rescued from oblivion, and is a most unique and important testimony of the reign of Augustus "in his own words."

LH

# from *Res Gestae*
## *(The Achievements of Augustus)*

A copy is set out below of 'The achievements of the Divine Augustus, by which he brought the world under the empire of the Roman people, and of the expenses which he bore for the state and people of Rome'; the original is engraved on two bronze pillars set up at Rome.

1 At the age of nineteen on my own responsibility and at my own expense I raised an army, with which I successfully championed the liberty of the republic when it was oppressed by the tyranny of a faction. 2 On that account the senate passed decrees in my honour enrolling me in its order in the consulship of Gaius Pansa and Aulus Hirtius, assigning me the right to give my opinion among the consulars and giving me *imperium*. 3 It ordered me as a propraetor to provide in concert with the consuls that the republic should come to no harm. 4 In the same year, when both consuls had fallen in battle, the people appointed me consul and triumvir for the organization of the republic.

2 I drove into exile the murderers of my father, avenging their crime through tribunals established by law; and afterwards, when they made war on the republic, I twice defeated them in battle.

3 I undertook many civil and foreign wars by land and sea throughout the world, and as victor I spared the lives of all citizens who asked for mercy. 2 When foreign peoples could safely be pardoned I preferred to preserve rather than to exterminate them. 3 The Roman citizens who took the soldier's oath of obedience to me numbered about 500,000. I settled rather more than 300,000 of these in colonies or sent them back to their home towns after their period of service; to all these I assigned lands or gave money as rewards for their military service. 4 I captured six hundred ships, not counting ships smaller than triremes.

4 I celebrated two ovations and three curule triumphs[1] and I was twenty-one times saluted as *imperator*. The senate decreed still more triumphs to me, all of which I declined. I laid the bay leaves with which my *fasces*[2] were wreathed in the Capitol after fulfilling all the vows which I had made in each war. 2 On fifty-five occasions the senate decreed that thanksgivings should be offered to the immortal gods on account of the successes on land and sea gained by me or by my legates acting under my auspices. The days on which thanksgivings were offered in accordance with decrees of the senate numbered

eight hundred and ninety. 3 In my triumphs nine kings or children of kings were led before my chariot. 4 At the time of writing I have been consul thirteen times and am in the thirty-seventh year of tribunician power.

5 The dictatorship was offered to me by both senate and people in my absence and when I was at Rome in the consulship of Marcus Marcellus and Lucius Arruntius, but I refused it. 2 I did not decline in the great dearth of corn to undertake the charge of the corn-supply, which I so administered that within a few days I delivered the whole city from apprehension and immediate danger at my own cost and by my own efforts. 3 At that time the consulship was also offered to me, to be held each year for the rest of my life, and I refused it.

6 In the consulship of Marcus Vinicius and Quintus Lucretius, and afterwards in that of Publius and Gnaeus Lentulus, and thirdly in that of Paullus Fabius Maximus and Quintus Tubero, the senate and people of Rome agreed that I should be appointed supervisor of laws and morals without a colleague and with supreme power, but I would not accept any office inconsistent with the custom of our ancestors. 2 The measures that the senate then desired me to take I carried out in virtue of my tribunician power. On five occasions, of my own initiative, I asked for and received from the senate a colleague in that power.

7 I was triumvir for the organization of the republic for ten consecutive years. 2 Up to the day of writing I have been *princeps senatus* for forty years. 3 I am *pontifex maximus, augur, quindecimvir sacris faciundis, septemvir epulonum, frater arvalis, sodalis Titius, fetialis.*

8 In my fifth consulship I increased the number of patricians on the instructions of the people and the senate. 2 I revised the roll of the senate three times. In my sixth consulship with Marcus Agrippa as colleague, I carried out a census of the people, and I performed a *lustrum*[3] after a lapse of forty-two years; at that *lustrum* 4,063,000 Roman citizens were registered. 3 Then a second time I performed a *lustrum* with consular *imperium* and without a colleague, in the consulship of Gaius Censorinus and Gaius Asinius; at that *lustrum* 4,233,000 citizens were registered. 4 Thirdly I performed a *lustrum* with consular *imperium*, with Tiberius Caesar, my son, as colleague, in the consulship of Sextus Pompeius and Sextus Appuleius; at that *lustrum* 4,937,000 citizens were registered. 5 By new laws passed on my proposal I brought back into use many exemplary practices of our ancestors which were disappearing in our time, and in many ways I myself transmitted exemplary practices to posterity for their imitation.

9 The senate decreed that vows should be undertaken every fifth year by the consuls and priests for my health. In fulfilment of these vows games have

frequently been celebrated in my lifetime, sometimes by the four most distinguished colleges of priests, sometimes by the consuls. 2 Moreover, all the citizens, individually and on behalf of their towns, have unanimously and continuously offered prayers at all the *pulvinaria* for my health.

10 My name was inserted in the hymn of the Salii by a decree of the senate, and it was enacted by law that my person should be inviolable for ever and that I should hold the tribunician power for the duration of my life. 2 I declined to be made *pontifex maximus* in the place of my colleague who was still alive, when the people offered me this priesthood which my father had held. Some years later, after the death of the man who had taken the opportunity of civil disturbance to seize it for himself, I received this priesthood, in the consulship of Publius Sulpicius and Gaius Valgius, and such a concourse poured in from the whole of Italy to my election as has never been recorded at Rome before that time.

11 The senate consecrated the altar of Fortuna Redux before the temples of Honour and Virtue at the Porta Capena in honour of my return, and it ordered that the *pontifices* and Vestal virgins should make an annual sacrifice there on the anniversary of my return to the city from Syria in the consulship of Quintus Lucretius and Marcus Vinicius, and it named the day the Augustalia from my *cognomen*.

12 In accordance with the will of the senate some of the praetors and tribunes of the plebs with the consul Quintus Lucretius and the leading men were sent to Campania to meet me, an honour that up to the present day has been decreed to no one besides myself. 2 On my return from Spain and Gaul in the consulship of Tiberius Nero and Publius Quintilius after successfully arranging affairs in those provinces, the senate resolved that an altar of the Augustan Peace should be consecrated next to the Campus Martius in honour of my return, and ordered that the magistrates and priests and Vestal virgins should perform an annual sacrifice there.

13 It was the will of our ancestors that the gateway of Janus Quirinus should be shut when victories had secured peace by land and sea throughout the whole empire of the Roman people; from the foundation of the city down to my birth, tradition records that it was shut only twice, but while I was the leading citizen the senate resolved that it should be shut on three occasions.

14 My sons, Gaius and Lucius Caesar, of whom Fortune bereaved me in their youth, were for my honour designated as consuls by the senate and people of Rome when they were fourteen, with the provision that they should enter on that magistracy after the lapse of five years. And the senate decreed that from the day when they were led into the forum they should take part in the councils of state. 2 Furthermore each of them was presented with silver

shields and spears by the whole body of *equites Romani* and hailed as *princeps iuventutis.*

15 To each member of the Roman plebs I paid under my father's will 300 sesterces, and in my own name I gave them 400 each from the booty of war in my fifth consulship, and once again in my tenth consulship I paid out 400 sesterces[4] as a largesse to each man from my own patrimony, and in my eleventh consulship I bought grain with my own money and distributed twelve rations apiece, and in the twelfth year of my tribunician power I gave every man 400 sesterces for the third time. These largesses of mine never reached fewer than 250,000 persons. 2 In the eighteenth year of my tribunician power and my twelfth consulship I gave 240 sesterces apiece to 320,000 members of the urban plebs. 3 In my fifth consulship I gave 1,000 sesterces out of booty to every one of the colonists drawn from my soldiers; about 120,000 men in the colonies received this largesse at the time of my triumph. 4 In my thirteenth consulship I gave 60 *denarii* apiece to the plebs who were then in receipt of public grain; they comprised a few more than 200,000 persons.

16 I paid cash to the towns for the lands that I assigned to soldiers in my fourth consulship, and later in the consulship of Marcus Crassus and Gnaeus Lentulus. The sum amounted to about 600,000,000 sesterces paid for lands in Italy, and about 260,000,000 disbursed for provincial lands. Of all those who founded military colonies in Italy or the provinces I was the first and only one to have done this in the recollection of my contemporaries. 2 Later, in the consulships of Tiberius Nero and Gnaeus Piso, of Gaius Antistius and Decimus Laelius, of Gaius Calvisius and Lucius Pasienus, of Lucius Lentulus and Marcus Messalla and of Lucius Caninius and Quintus Fabricius I paid monetary rewards to soldiers whom I settled in their home towns after completion of their service, and on this account I expended about 400,000,000 sesterces.

17 Four times I assisted the treasury with my own money, so that I transferred to the administrators of the treasury 150,000,000 sesterces. 2 In the consulship of Marcus Lepidus and Lucius Arruntius, when the military treasury was founded by my advice for the purpose of paying rewards to soldiers who had served for twenty years or more, I transferred to it from my own patrimony 170,000,000 sesterces.

18 From the consulship of Gnaeus and Publius Lentulus onwards, whenever the taxes did not suffice, I made distributions of grain and money from my own granary and patrimony, sometimes to 100,000 persons, sometimes to many more.

19 I built the Senate House, and the Chalcidicum[5] adjacent to it, the temple of Apollo on the Palatine with its porticoes, the temple of the divine

Julius, the Lupercal,[6] the portico at the Flaminian circus, which I permitted to bear the name of the portico of Octavius after the man who erected the previous portico on the same site, a *pulvinar*[7] at the Circus Maximus, (2) the temples on the Capitol of Jupiter Feretrius and Jupiter the Thunderer, the temple of Quirinus, the temples of Minerva and Queen Juno and Jupiter Libertas on the Aventine, the temple of the Lares at the top of the Sacred Way, the temple of the Di Penates in the Velia, the temple of Youth, and the temple of the Great Mother on the Palatine.

**20** I restored the Capitol and the theatre of Pompey, both works at great expense without inscribing my own name on either. **2** I restored the channels of the aqueducts, which in several places were falling into disrepair through age, and I brought water from a new spring into the aqueduct called Marcia, doubling the supply. **3** I completed the Forum Julium and the basilica between the temples of Castor and Saturn, works begun and almost finished by my father, and when that same basilica was destroyed by fire, I began to rebuild it on an enlarged site, to be dedicated in the name of my sons, and in case I do not complete it in my life time, I have given orders that it should be completed by my heirs. **4** In my sixth consulship I restored eighty-two temples of the gods in the city on the authority of the senate, neglecting none that required restoration at that time. **5** In my seventh consulship I restored the Via Flaminia from the city as far as Rimini, together with all bridges except the Mulvian and the Minucian.

**21** I built the temple of Mars the Avenger and the Forum Augustum on private ground from the proceeds of booty. I built the theatre adjacent to the temple of Apollo on ground in large part bought from private owners, and provided that it should be called after Marcus Marcellus, my son-in-law. **2** From the proceeds of booty I dedicated gifts in the Capitol and in the temples of the divine Julius, of Apollo, of Vesta and of Mars the Avenger; this cost me about 100,000,000 sesterces. **3** In my fifth consulship I remitted 35,000 lb. of *aurum coronarium*[8] contributed by the *municipia* and colonies of Italy to my triumphs, and later, whenever I was acclaimed imperator, I refused the *aurum coronarium* which the *municipia* and colonies continued to vote with the same good will as before.

**22** I gave three gladiatorial games in my own name and five in that of my sons or grandsons; at these games some 10,000 men took part in combat. Twice in my own name and a third time in that of my grandson I presented to the people displays by athletes summoned from all parts. **2** I produced shows in my own name four times and in place of other magistrates twenty-three times. On behalf of the college of *quindecimviri*,[9] as its president, with Marcus Agrippa as colleague, I produced the Secular Games in the consulship of Gaius Furnius and Gaius Silanus. In my thirteenth consulship I was the first to produce the games of Mars, which thereafter in each succeeding year have been produced by the consuls in accordance with a decree of the senate and by statute. 3 I gave beast-hunts of African beasts in my own name or in that of my sons and grandsons in the circus or forum or amphitheatre on twenty-six occasions, on which about 3,500 beasts were destroyed.

23 I produced a naval battle as a show for the people at the place across the Tiber now occupied by the grove of the Caesars, where a site 1,800 feet long and 1,200 broad was excavated. There thirty beaked triremes or biremes and still more smaller vessels were joined in battle. About 3,000 men, besides the rowers, fought in these fleets.

24 After my victory, I replaced in the temples of all the cities of the province of Asia the ornaments which my late adversary, after despoiling the temples, had taken into his private possession. 2 Some eighty silver statues of me, on foot, on horse and in chariots, had been set up in Rome; I myself removed them, and with the money that they realized I set golden offerings in the temple of Apollo, in my own name and in the names of those who had honoured me with the statues.

25 I made the sea peaceful and freed it of pirates. In that war I captured about 30,000 slaves who had escaped from their masters and taken up arms against the republic, and I handed them over to their masters for punishment. 2 The whole of Italy of its own free will swore allegiance to me and demanded me as the leader in the war in which I was victorious at Actium. The Gallic and Spanish provinces, Africa, Sicily and Sardinia swore the same oath of allegiance. 3 More than seven hundred senators served under my standards at that time, including eighty-three who previously or subsequently (down to the time of writing) were appointed consuls, and about one hundred and seventy who were appointed priests.

26 I extended the territory of all those provinces of the Roman people on whose borders lay peoples not subject to our government. 2 I brought peace to the Gallic and Spanish provinces as well as to Germany, throughout the area bordering on the Ocean from Cadiz to the mouth of the Elbe. 3 I secured the pacification of the Alps from the district nearest the Adriatic to the Tuscan sea, yet without waging an unjust war on any people. 4 My fleet sailed through the Ocean eastwards from the mouth of the Rhine to the territory of the Cimbri, a country which no Roman had visited before either by land or sea, and the Cimbri, Charydes, Semnones and other German peoples of that region sent ambassadors and sought my friendship and that of the Roman people. 5 At my command and under my auspices two armies were led almost at the same time into Ethiopia and Arabia Felix; vast enemy forces of both peoples were cut down in battle and many towns captured. Ethiopia was

penetrated as far as the town of Nabata, which adjoins Meroë; in Arabia the army advanced into the territory of the Sabaeans to the town of Mariba.

27 I added Egypt to the empire of the Roman people. 2 Greater Armenia I might have made a province after its king, Artaxes had been killed, but I preferred, following the model set by our ancestors, to hand over that kingdom to Tigranes, son of King Artavasdes and grandson of King Tigranes; Tiberius Nero, who was then my stepson, carried this out. When the same people later rebelled and went to war, I subdued them through the agency of my son Gaius and handed them over to be ruled by King Ariobarzanes, son of Artabazus King of the Medes, and after his death to his son Artavasdes. When he was killed, I sent Tigranes, a scion of the royal Armenian house, to that kingdom. 3 I recovered all the provinces beyond the Adriatic sea towards the east, together with Cyrene, the greater part of them being then occupied by kings. I had previously recovered Sicily and Sardinia which had been seized in the slave war.

28 I founded colonies of soldiers in Africa, Sicily, Macedonia, both Spanish provinces, Achaea, Asia, Syria, Gallia Narbonensis and Pisidia. 2 Italy too has twenty-eight colonies founded by my authority, which were densely populated in my lifetime.

29 By victories over enemies I recovered in Spain and in Gaul, and from the Dalmatians several standards lost by other commanders. 2 I compelled the Parthians to restore to me the spoils and standards of three Roman armies and to ask as suppliants for the friendship of the Roman people. Those standards I deposited in the innermost shrine of the temple of Mars the Avenger.

30 The Pannonian peoples, whom the army of the Roman people never approached before I was the leading citizen, were conquered through the agency of Tiberius Nero, who was then my stepson and legate; I brought them into the empire of the Roman people, and extended the frontier of Illyricum to the banks of the Danube. 2 When an army of Dacians crossed the Danube, it was defeated and routed under my auspices, and later my army crossed the Danube and compelled the Dacian peoples to submit to the commands of the Roman people.

31 Embassies from kings in India were frequently sent to me; never before had they been seen with any Roman commander. 2 The Bastarnae, Scythians and the kings of the Sarmatians on either side of the river Don, and the kings of the Albanians and the Iberians and the Medes sent embassies to seek our friendship.

32 The following kings sought refuge with me as suppliants: Tiridates, King of Parthia, and later Phraates son of King Phraates; Artavasdes, King of the Medes; Artaxares, King of the Adiabeni; Dumnobellaunus and

Tincommius, Kings of the Britons; Maelo, King of the Sugambri; . . . rus, King of the Marcomanni and Suebi. 2 Phraates, son of Orodes, King of Parthia, sent all his sons and grandsons to me in Italy, not that he had been overcome in war, but because he sought our friendship by pledging his children. 3 While I was the leading citizen very many other peoples have experienced the good faith of the Roman people which had never previously exchanged embassies or had friendly relations with the Roman people.

33 The Parthian and Median peoples sent to me ambassadors of their nobility who sought and received kings from me, for the Parthians Vonones, son of King Phraates, grandson of King Orodes, and for the Medes, Ariobarzanes, son of King Artavasdes, grandson of King Ariobarzanes.

34 In my sixth and seventh consulships, after I had extinguished civil wars, and at a time when with universal consent I was in complete control of affairs, I transferred the republic from my power to the dominion of the senate and people of Rome. 2 For this service of mine I was named Augustus by decree of the senate, and the door-posts of my house were publicly wreathed with bay leaves and a civic crown was fixed over my door and a golden shield was set in the Curia Julia,[10] which, as attested by the inscription thereon, was given me by the senate and people of Rome on account of my courage, clemency, justice and piety. 3 After this time I excelled all in influence, although I possessed no more official power than others who were my colleagues in the several magistracies.

35 In my thirteenth consulship the senate, the equestrian order and the whole people of Rome gave me the title of Father of my Country, and resolved that this should be inscribed in the porch of my house and in the Curia Julia and in the Forum Augustum below the chariot which had been set there in my honour by decree of the senate. 2 At the time of writing I am in my seventy-sixth year.

## Appendix

1 The amount of money that he gave to the treasury or to the Roman *plebs* or to discharged soldiers was 2,400,000,000 sesterces.

2 His new buildings were: the temples of Mars, of Jupiter the Thunderer and Feretrius, of Apollo, of the divine Julius, of Quirinus, of Minerva, of Queen Juno, of Jupiter Libertas, of the Lares, of the Di Penates, of Youth, of the Great Mother, the Lupercal, the shrine at the Circus, the Senate House with the Chalcidicum, the Forum Augustum, the Basilica Julia, the theatre of Marcellus, the Octavian portico, the grove of the Caesars beyond the Tiber.

3 He restored the Capitol and sacred buildings to the number of eighty-two, the theatre of Pompey, the aqueducts and the Via Flaminia.

**4** The expenditure that he devoted to dramatic shows, to gladiatorial exhibitions and athletes and hunts and the sea battle, and the money granted to colonies, *municipia*, towns destroyed by earthquake and fire or to individual friends and senators whose property qualification he made up, was beyond counting.

## Notes

1 The triumph was a procession of a victorious Roman general through Rome to the temple of Jupiter on the Capitoline. The general entered Rome in a chariot (Latin *currus*, hence "curule" triumphs), dressed elaborately, and led captives and spoils, among other things. An ovation was a lesser form of triumph—the general entered on foot or horseback, dressed less elaborately—celebrated if the margin of victory was less great or the conditions for triumph were not quite met.

2 The *fasces* were bundles of rods with an axe in the center. They were carried by officials (*lictors*) who accompanied the magistrates who held *imperium*, the authority of life and death, and symbolized the authority to punish and to kill.

3 A *lustrum* was a ceremony of purification observed by the censors after they had finished a census.

4 The Latin *sestertium* was one-fourth of a *denarius*. Comparative values are generally unhelpful, but during this time it seems that one *denarius* was the standard pay for a day's labor. See Gospel of Matthew 20:1–16.

5 A generic word whose derivation is unclear, meaning a porch or portico that forms the approach to an important building, here, the Senate House begun by Julius Caesar which Augustus completed.

6 A grotto in the Palatine hill where sacrifices were offered to commemorate the suckling of Romulus and Remus by a she-wolf (*lupa* in Latin).

7 A box on the Palatine side of the Circus Maximus, from which Augustus watched the games, or on which the symbols of the gods were set, after they had been brought in in procession.

8 Literally "gold for crowns." This comprised payments of gold (and probably silver) made by towns (*municipia*) and colonies within Italy. Colonies designated those towns which were composed of state-settled Roman citizens.

9 One of the four main colleges of priests, the *quindecemviri sacris faciundis* (see above, 7.3) were a body of fifteen men who oversaw the importation and implementation of foreign cults, especially Greek cults, in Rome.

10 The Senate House begun by Julius Caesar, which Augustus completed (see 19.1 and Appendix 2).

# Musonius Rufus

## ca. 30–101 C.E.

History provides many examples of men's (and even women's) dismissal of the intellectual capacities of women, lasting until the nineteenth and twentieth centuries when higher education for women had to overcome ridicule and pseudo-scientific opposition. While we tend to think of women's rights as a modern phenomenon, women have struggled to gain the basic right to develop their brains as they please in many world cultures, ancient and modern. Though few women's voices from antiquity have survived, fortunately there were some male advocates for women whose discourses are extant. One of these is Gaius Musonius Rufus, a Stoic philosopher who lived in Rome during the first century C.E.

Musonius seems never to have written anything himself, but in the tradition of Socrates, Jesus, and Confucius, he had pupils who recorded his words for posterity. Philosophy was his life and his passion, and his zeal for living according to his principles prompted him to go into voluntary exile along with his friend Rubellius Plautus, a young man of noble birth whom Nero banished. Musonius later returned to Rome, only to suffer exile himself, not once, but twice. The first time was for his alleged involvement in a plot to overthrow Nero. The second time he was arrested while trying to persuade the Roman army to march into Rome peacefully, and was banished by the emperor Vespasian. He was eventually allowed to return to Rome, and continued to work as a philosopher. The famous Stoic philosopher Epictetus was one of his pupils.

Stoicism and Cynicism generally were more universalist than many other philosophical schools in their acceptance of "barbarians" and women. But Musonius provides an especially eloquent testament to women's equal capacities for virtue. His stance on philosophy, education, and marriage was more consistently humane than that of many of his contemporaries, including the Christian Paul, who advocated women's submission to their husbands and silence in church.

LH

# from *Discourses*

## The study of philosophy

(3) When he was asked whether women ought to study philosophy, he began to answer the question approximately as follows. Women have received from the gods the same ability to reason that men have. We men employ reasoning in our relations with others and so far as possible in everything we do, whether it is good or bad, or noble or shameful. Likewise women have the same senses as men, sight, hearing, smell, and all the rest. Likewise each has the same parts of the body, and neither sex has more than the other. In addition, it is not men alone who possess eagerness and a natural inclination towards virtue, but women also. Women are pleased no less than men by noble and just deeds, and reject the opposite of such actions. Since that is so, why is it appropriate for men to seek out and examine how they might live well, that is, to practise philosophy, but not women? Is it fitting for men to be good, but not women?

Let us consider in detail the qualities that a woman who seeks to be good must possess, for it will be apparent that she could acquire each of these qualities from the practice of philosophy.

In the first place a woman must run her household and pick out what is beneficial for her home and take charge of the household slaves.

In these activities I claim that philosophy is particularly helpful, since each of these activities is an aspect of life, and philosophy is nothing other than the science of living, and the philosopher, as Socrates says, continually contemplates this, 'what good or evil has been done in his house'. Next, a woman must be chaste, and capable of keeping herself free from illegal love affairs, and pure in respect to the other pleasures of indulgence, and not enjoy quarrels, not be extravagant, or preoccupied with her appearance. Such is the behaviour of a chaste woman. There are still other requirements: she must control anger, and not be overcome by grief, and be stronger than every kind of emotion. That is what the philosopher's rationale entails, and the person who knows it and practises it seems to me to be perfectly controlled, whether it is a man or a woman. So much for the subject of self-control.

Now, wouldn't the woman who practises philosophy be just, and a blameless partner in life, and a good worker in common causes, and devoted in her responsibilities towards her husband and her children, and free in every way from greed or ambition? Who could be like this more than the woman who practises philosophy, so long as she truly is a philosopher, since she must inevitably think that doing wrong is worse than being wronged, because it is more disgraceful to do wrong, and to think that being inferior is preferable to being ambitious, and in addition, to love her children more than her own life? What woman would be more just than someone who behaves like that? Surely it follows that an educated woman would be more courageous than an uneducated woman and a woman who practises philosophy than a woman who is self-taught, since neither fear of death nor any apprehension about suffering would lead her to endure a disgrace, nor would she be afraid of anyone because he was well-born or powerful or rich or indeed because he was—by Zeus—a tyrant. For it is enough that she has practised being high-minded and self-reliant and enduring, since she has nursed her children at her own breast, and helps her husband with her own hands, and does without hesitation what some people would consider slave's work. Wouldn't such a woman be a great help to her husband, and an ornament to her family, and a good example to all who know her?

But, by Zeus, some people say that women who associate with philosophers are inevitably mainly headstrong and bold, if they give up their households and go about with men and practise giving speeches, and argue and attack premises, when they ought to be sitting at home spinning wool. But I would not advise women who practise philosophy or men either to abandon their required work merely to hold discussions, but that they ought to undertake discussions for the sake of the work that they do. For just as there is no need for medical discussion, unless it pertains to human health, similarly there is no need for a philosopher to hold or teach logical argument, unless it pertains to the human soul. Above all we must examine the doctrine that we think women who practise philosophy should follow, to determine if the study that shows restraint to be the greatest good makes them bold, and if the study that leads to the deportment makes them live more carelessly, and if the study that reveals that the worst evil is self-indulgence does not teach self-control, and if the study that establishes household management as a virtue does not encourage them to manage their households. And the study of philosophy encourages women to be happy and to work with their own hands.

## Education

(4) When he was asked if sons and daughters should be given the same education, he said that in the case of horses and dogs trainers of horses and of dogs make no distinction between male and female in their training.

Female dogs are trained to hunt just like male dogs, and if you expect female horses to do a horse's job effectively, you must see that they have the same training as the male horses.

In the case of human beings it would seem that males should have something in their education and upbringing distinctive in contrast to the females, as if a man and a woman were not required to have the same virtues, or as if they could aspire to the same virtues through different rather than similar educations.

But it is easy to apprehend that there are not different sets of virtues for men and women. First, men and women both need to be sensible; what need could there be for a foolish man or woman? Second, both need to live just lives. An unjust man could not be a good citizen, and a woman could not run her household well, if she did not run it justly, since if she were unjust she would do wrong to her husband, as they say Eriphyle did to hers. Third, a wife ought to be chaste, and so should a husband, for the laws punish both parties in cases of adultery. Over-indulgence in food and, drink and similar problems, excesses that bring disgrace to those who indulge in them, prove that moderation is essential for every human being, whether male or female, for it is only through moderation that we can avoid excess.

You might argue that courage is needed only by men. But that is not true. The best sort of woman must be manly and cleanse herself of cowardice, so that she will not be overcome by suffering or by fear.

If she cannot, how can she be chaste, if someone can compel her to endure disgrace by threatening her or torturing her? Women must be courageous, if (by Zeus) they are not to be inferior to hens and other female birds, who fight beasts much larger than themselves in order to defend their nestlings. How can it be that women do not need courage? That they are capable of taking up weapons, we know from the race of the Amazons who fought many nations in battle. If other women are deficient in this regard, the cause is lack of practice rather than lack of natural inclination . . .

Well then, suppose someone says, 'Do you think that men ought to learn spinning like women and that women ought to practise gymnastics like men?' No, that is not what I suggest. I say that because in the case of the human race, the males are naturally stronger, and the women weaker, appropriate work ought to be assigned to each, and the heavier tasks be given to the stronger, and the lighter to the weaker. For this reason, spinning is more appropriate work for women than for men, and household management.

Gymnastics are more appropriate for men than for women, and outdoor work likewise. None the less, some men might appropriately undertake some of the lighter work and work thought more appropriate to women, when the conditions of their body or necessity or time demand it. For all human work is a common responsibility for men and women, and nothing is necessarily prescribed for one sex or the other. Some tasks are more appropriate for one nature, others for the other. For that reason some jobs are called men's work, and others women's. As for matters that pertain to virtue, you would be justified in saying that these are equally the property of both, if we say that both possess no virtues different from the other.

It is reasonable, then, for me to think that women ought to be educated similarly to men in respect of virtue, and they must be taught starting when they are children, that this is good, and that bad, and that they are the same for both, and that this is beneficial and that harmful, and that one must do this, and not that. From these lessons reasoning is developed in both girls and boys, and there is no distinction between them. Then they must be told to avoid all base action. When these qualities have been developed both men and women will inevitably be sensible, and the well-educated person, whether male or female, must be able to endure hardship, accustomed not to fear death, and accustomed not to be humbled by any disaster, for this is how one can become manly. . . . If a man knows something about a particular skill, and a woman doesn't, or if the reverse is true, this shows that there is no difference in their education. Only about all the important things do not let one know and the other not, but let them both know the same. If someone asks me, which doctrine requires such an education, I would answer him that without philosophy no man and no woman either can be well educated. I do not mean to say that women need to have clarity with or facility in argument, because they will use philosophy as women use it. But I do not recommend these skills particularly in men. My point is that women ought to be good and noble in their characters, and that philosophy is nothing other than the training for that nobility.

## Marriage

(13a) He said that a husband and wife come together in order to lead their lives in common and to produce children, and that they should consider all their property to be common, and nothing private, not even their bodies. For the birth of a human being that such a union produces is a significant event, but it is not sufficient for the husband, because it could have come about without marriage, from some other conjunction, as in the case of animals. In marriage there must be complete companionship and concern for each other on the part of both husband and wife, in health and in sickness and at all times, because they entered upon the marriage for this reason as well as to produce offspring. When such caring for one another is perfect, and the married couple provide it for one another, and each strives to outdo the other, then this is marriage as it ought to be and deserving of emulation, since it is a noble union. But when one partner looks to his own interests alone and neglects the other's, or (by Zeus) the other is so minded that he lives in the same house, but keeps his mind on what is outside it, and does not wish to pull together with his partner or to cooperate, then inevitably the union is destroyed, and although they live together their common interests fare badly, and either they finally get divorced from one another or they continue on in an existence that is worse than loneliness.

# Tacitus

## ca. 55–117 C.E.

The historian Publius (or perhaps Gaius) Cornelius Tacitus was born about 55 C.E., during the reign of Nero, and lived until at least 117 C.E. Like Livy, the Roman historian with whom he is often compared, Tacitus wrote annalistic histories that chronicle events year by year; unlike Livy, Tacitus enjoyed senatorial rank and therefore was involved in "the making of history," as he understood history. Tacitus probably came from northern Italy or southern Gaul, but his familial status gave him connections to the Roman aristocracy, and he married the daughter of a Roman general and provincial governor, Agricola, whose biography he wrote. Tacitus held political office under the reign of Domitian, the cruel paranoid emperor who ruled from 81–96 C.E., and probably developed from personal experience the visceral suspicion of absolute power that colors so much of his work.

Tacitus wrote two annalistic histories. The earlier, his *Histories*, narrates the events of 69–70 C.E. and breaks off in the fifth book; Tacitus apparently intended to continue to the death of Domitian in 96 C.E. His final work, which is also fragmentary, is also his masterpiece. The *Annals* pick up where Livy intended to leave off, at the death of Augustus, and narrated down to the death of Nero in 68 C.E. Of the sixteen (or eighteen) books of the *Annals*, books 1–4 have survived, fragments of five and six, and books 11–16, though the end of book 16 is lost. We therefore have accounts of most of the reigns of Tiberius, Claudius, and Nero (Caligula, unfortunately, fell in the lost books). Tacitus is famous for his sophisticated rhetorical style—he was a famous orator and wrote a dialogue *On Orators*—and for his piercing psychological portraits. Scholars now view Tacitus' portraits as characterizations, masks that Tacitus applied to the characters of his drama rather than balanced, realistic representations, but they are gripping to read. The emperor Tiberius is especially well-drawn as the grim, reluctant ruler who slides deeper and deeper into suspicion and cruelty and lust as he withdraws from public contact. Tacitus is also a master at drawing a scene. Nero's murder of his mother Agrippina (14.1–12) or the death of Seneca (15.60–65) are brilliantly executed set-pieces in his longer narrative.

Tacitus claims that he needs to write about the emperors after Augustus because what was written during their reigns was falsified by fear, and what was written shortly after was marred by hatred. Thus he makes his famous claim to write *sine ira et studio*, "without anger or partisanship" (*Ann.* I.1). But throughout, Tacitus communicates his pessimism about the Imperial house, and the corruption and cruelty that inevitably erupt from their pursuit and exercise of power. In the opening chapters of the *Annals* below, Tacitus does not offer his direct opinion on Augustus and his rule. Rather, he reports the general opinions expressed at Augustus' death, both positive and negative. The critical assessment, however, is placed second and is given in more detail, and introduces the themes which will dominate much of Tacitus' narrative: dissimulation and pretense, surface appearances and hidden realities. Tacitus exploits the theme of degeneracy in his earlier ethnography *Germania*, in which he quietly juxtaposes the virtues of the primitive Germans with the vices into which the Romans, in Tacitus' opinion, have lapsed.

BSH

# from *Annals*

## Chapter I
## From Augustus to Tiberius

When Rome was first a city, its rulers were kings. Then Lucius Junius Brutus created the consulate and free Republican institutions in general. Dictatorships were assumed in emergencies. A Council of Ten did not last more than two years; and then there was a short-lived arrangement by which senior army officers—the commanders of contingents provided by the tribes—possessed consular authority. Subsequently Cinna and Sulla set up autocracies, but they too were brief. Soon Pompey and Crassus acquired predominant positions, but rapidly lost them to Caesar. Next, the military strength which Lepidus and Antony had built up was absorbed by Augustus.[1] He found the whole state exhausted by internal dissensions, and established over it a personal regime known as the Principate.

Famous writers have recorded Rome's early glories and disasters. The Augustan Age, too, had its distinguished historians. But then the rising tide of flattery exercised a deterrent effect. The reigns of Tiberius, Gaius, Claudius, and Nero were described during their lifetimes in fictitious terms, for fear of the consequences; whereas the accounts written after their deaths were influenced by still raging animosities. So I have decided to say a little about Augustus, with special attention to his last period, and then go on to the reign of Tiberius and what followed. I shall write without indignation or partisanship: in my case the customary incentives to these are lacking.

The violent deaths of Brutus and Cassius left no Republican forces in the field. Defeat came to Sextus Pompeius in Sicily, Lepidus was dropped, Antony killed. So even the Caesarian party had no leader left except the 'Caesar' himself, Octavian. He gave up the title of Triumvir, emphasizing instead his position as consul; and the powers of a tribune, he proclaimed, were good enough for him—powers for the protection of ordinary people.

He seduced the army with bonuses, and his cheap food policy was successful bait for civilians. Indeed, he attracted everybody's goodwill by the enjoyable gift of peace. Then he gradually pushed ahead and absorbed the functions of the senate, the officials, and even the law. Opposition did not exist. War or judicial murder had disposed of all men of spirit. Upper-class survivors found that slavish obedience was the way to succeed, both politically and financially. They had profited from the revolution, and so now they liked the security of the existing arrangement better than the dangerous uncertainties of the old régime. Besides, the new order was popular in the provinces. There, government by Senate and People was looked upon sceptically as a matter of sparring dignitaries and extortionate officials. The legal system had provided no remedy against these, since it was wholly incapacitated by violence, favouritism, and—most of all—bribery.

To safeguard his domination Augustus made his sister's son Marcellus a priest and a curule aedile—in spite of his extreme youth—and singled out Marcus Agrippa, a commoner but a first-rate soldier who had helped to win his victories, by the award of two consecutive consulships; after the death of Marcellus, Agrippa was chosen by Augustus as his son-in-law. Next the emperor had his stepsons Tiberius and Nero Drusus hailed publicly as victorious generals. When he did this, however, there was no lack of heirs of his own blood: there were Agrippa's sons Gaius Caesar and Lucius Caesar. Augustus had adopted them into the imperial family. He had also, despite pretended reluctance, been passionately eager that, even as minors, they should be entitled Princes of Youth and have consulships reserved for them. After Agrippa had died, first Lucius Caesar and then Gaius Caesar met with premature natural deaths—unless their stepmother Livia had a secret hand in them. Lucius died on his way to the armies in Spain, Gaius while returning from Armenia incapacitated by a wound.

Nero Drusus was long dead. Tiberius was the only surviving stepson; and everything pointed in his direction. He was adopted as the emperor's son and as partner in his powers (with civil and military authority and the powers of a tribune) and displayed to all the armies. No longer was this due to his mother's secret machinations, as previously. This time she requested it openly. Livia had the aged Augustus firmly under control—so much so that he exiled his only surviving grandson to the island of Planasia. That was the young, physically tough, indeed brutish, Agrippa Postumus. Though devoid of every good quality, he had been involved in no scandal. Nevertheless, it was not he but Germanicus, the son of Nero Drusus, whom the emperor placed in command of the eight divisions on the Rhine—and, although Tiberius had a grown son of his own, he ordered him to adopt Germanicus. For Augustus wanted to have another iron in the fire.

At this time there was no longer any fighting—except a war against the Germans; and that was designed less to extend the empire's frontiers, or achieve any lucrative purpose, than to avenge the disgrace of the army lost with Publius Quinctilius Varus. In the capital the situation was calm. The titles of officials remained the same. Actium had been won before the younger men were born. Even most of the older generation had come into a world of civil wars. Practically no one had ever seen truly Republican government. The country had been transformed, and there was nothing left of the fine old Roman character. Political equality was a thing of the past; all eyes watched for imperial commands.

Nobody had any immediate worries as long as Augustus retained his physical powers, and kept himself going, and his House, and the peace of the empire. But when old age incapacitated him, his approaching end brought hopes of change. A few people started idly talking of the blessings of freedom. Some, more numerous, feared civil war; others wanted it. The great majority, however, exchanged critical gossip about candidates for the succession. First, Agrippa Postumus—a savage without either the years or the training needed for imperial responsibilities. Tiberius, on the other hand, had the seniority and the military reputation. But he also possessed the ancient, ingrained arrogance of the Claudian family; and signs of a cruel disposition kept breaking out, repress them as he might. Besides, it was argued, he had been brought up from earliest youth in an imperial household, had accumulated early consulships and Triumphs, and even during the years at Rhodes—which looked like banishment but were called retirement—his thoughts had been solely occupied with resentment, deception, and secret sensuality. And then there was that feminine bully, his mother. 'So we have got to be slaves to a woman', people were saying, 'and to the two half-grown boys Germanicus and Drusus. First they will be a burden to the State—then they will tear it in two!'

Amid this sort of conversation the health of Augustus deteriorated. Some suspected his wife of foul play. For rumour had it that a few months earlier, with the knowledge of his immediate circle but accompanied only by Paullus Fabius Maximus, he had gone to Planasia to visit Agrippa Postumus; and that there had been such a tearful display of affection on both sides that the young man seemed very likely to be received back into the home of his grandfather. Maximus, it was further said, had told his wife, Marcia, of this, and she had warned Livia—but the emperor had discovered the leakage, and when Maximus died shortly afterwards (perhaps by his own hand) his widow had been heard at the funeral moaning and blaming herself for her husband's death. Whatever the true facts about this, Tiberius was recalled from his post in Illyricum (immediately after his arrival there) by an urgent letter from his mother. When he arrived at Nola, it is unknown whether he found Augustus alive or dead. For the house and neighbouring streets were carefully sealed by Livia's guards. At intervals, hopeful reports were published—until the steps demanded by the situation had been taken. Then two pieces of news became known simultaneously: Augustus was dead, and Tiberius was in control.

The new reign's first crime was the assassination of Agrippa Postumus. He was killed by a staff-officer—who found it a hard task, though he was a persevering murderer and the victim taken by surprise unarmed. Tiberius said nothing about the matter in the senate. He pretended that the orders came from Augustus, who was alleged to have instructed the colonel in charge to kill Agrippa Postumus as soon as Augustus himself was dead. It is true that Augustus' scathing criticisms of the young man's behaviour were undoubtedly what had prompted the senate to decree his banishment. But the emperor had never been callous enough to kill any of his relations, and that he should murder his own grandchild to remove the worries of a stepson seemed incredible. It would be nearer the truth to suppose that Tiberius because he was afraid, and Livia through stepmotherly malevolence, loathed and distrusted the young Agrippa Postumus and got rid of him at the first opportunity. But when the staff-officer reported in military fashion that he had carried out his orders, Tiberius answered that he had given no orders and that what had been done would have to be accounted for in the senate.

This came to the notice of Tiberius' confidant, Gaius Sallustius Crispus. It was he who had sent instructions to the colonel, and he was afraid that the responsibility might be shifted to himself—in which case either telling the truth or lying would be equally risky. So he warned Livia that palace secrets, and the advice of friends, and services performed by the army, were best undivulged; and Tiberius must not weaken the throne by referring everything to the senate. The whole point of autocracy, Crispus observed, is that the accounts will not come right unless the ruler is their only auditor.

Meanwhile at Rome consuls, senate, knights, precipitately became servile. The more distinguished men were, the greater their urgency and insincerity. They must show neither satisfaction at the death of one emperor, nor gloom at the accession of another: so their features were carefully arranged in a blend of tears and smiles, mourning and flattery. The first to swear allegiance to Tiberius Caesar were the consuls Sextus Pompeius (II) and Sextus Appuleius; then in their presence the commander of the Guard, Lucius Seius Strabo, and the controller of the corn-supply, Gaius Turranius; next the senate, army, and public. For Tiberius made a habit of always allowing the consuls the initiative, as though the Republic still existed and he himself were uncertain whether to take charge or not. Even the edict with which he summoned the senate to its House was merely issued by virtue of the tribune's power which he had received under Augustus. His edict was brief, and very unpretentious. In it he proposed to arrange his father's last honours, and stay by the side of his body. This, he said, was the only State business which he was assuming.

Nevertheless, when Augustus died Tiberius had given the watchword to the Guard as its commander. He already had the trappings of a court, too, such as personal bodyguards and men-at-arms. When he went to the Forum, or into the senate, he had soldiers to escort him. He sent letters to the armies as though he were already emperor. He only showed signs of hesitation when he addressed the senate. This was chiefly because of Germanicus, who was extremely popular and disposed of a large Roman force and hordes of auxiliary troops. Tiberius was afraid Germanicus might prefer the throne to the prospect of it. Besides, in deference to public opinion, Tiberius wanted to seem the person chosen and called by the State—instead of one who had wormed his way in by an old man's adoption, and intrigues of the old man's wife. Afterwards it was understood that Tiberius had pretended to be hesitant for another reason too, in order to detect what leading men were thinking. Every word, every look he twisted into some criminal significance—and stored them up in his memory.

At the senate's first meeting he allowed no business to be discussed except the funeral of Augustus. But first the emperor's will was brought in by the priestesses of Vesta. Tiberius and Livia were his heirs, and Livia was adopted into the Julian family with the name of 'Augusta'. Grandchildren and great-grandchildren had been named as heirs in the second degree. In the third degree came the most prominent men in the State; Augustus had detested a good many of them, but their inclusion bragged to posterity that he had been their friend. His legacies were in keeping with the standards of ordinary citizens, except that he left 43,500,000 sesterces[2] to the nation and people of Rome, a thousand to every Guardsman, five hundred each to the troops of the capital, three hundred to every citizen soldier, whether he belonged to a regular brigade or to an auxiliary battalion.

A discussion of the funeral followed. The proposals regarded as most noteworthy were those of Gaius Asinius Gallus and Lucius Arruntius. What Gallus wanted was that the procession should pass through a triumphal arch. Arruntius proposed that the body should be preceded by placards showing the titles of every law Augustus had passed and the names of every people he had conquered. Marcus Valerius Messalla Messallinus (I) also suggested that the oath of allegiance to Tiberius should be repeated every year. When Tiberius asked him to confirm that he, Tiberius, had not prompted this proposal, Messalla answered that it was his own idea—and that in matters of public importance he intended to use his own judgement and no one else's, even at the risk of causing offence. This show of independence was the only sort of flattery left.

Members clamoured that the body of Augustus should be carried to the pyre on the shoulders of senators. Tiberius, with condescending leniency, excused them. He also published an edict requesting the populace not to repeat the disturbances—due to over-enthusiasm—at the funeral of Julius Caesar, by pressing for Augustus to be cremated in the Forum instead of the Field of Mars, his appointed place of rest. On the day of the funeral the troops were out, apparently for protective purposes. This caused much jeering from people who had witnessed, or heard from their parents, about that day (when the nation's enslavement was still rudimentary) of the ill-starred attempt to recover Republican freedom by murdering the dictator Caesar—a fearful crime? or a conspicuously glorious achievement? Now, they said, this aged autocrat Augustus seems to need a military guard to ensure his undisturbed burial, in spite of his lengthy domination and the foresight with which his heirs, too, have been allocated resources for the suppression of the old order.

Then there was much discussion of Augustus himself. Most people were struck by meaningless points such as the coincidence between the dates of his first public office and his death, and the fact that he died in the same house and room at Nola as his father, Gaius Octavius. There was also talk about his numerous consulships—which equalled the combined totals of Marcus Valerius Corvus and Gaius Marius—of his tribune's power continuous for thirty-seven years, of the twenty-one times he was hailed as victor, and of his other honours, traditional or novel, single or repeated. Intelligent people praised or criticized him in varying terms. One opinion was as follows. Filial duty and a national emergency, in which there was no place for law-abiding conduct, had driven him to civil war—and this can be neither initiated nor maintained by decent methods. He had made many concessions to Antony and to Lepidus for the sake of vengeance on his father's murderers. When Lepidus grew old and lazy, and Antony's self-indulgence got the better of him, the only possible cure for the distracted country had been government by one man. However, Augustus had put the State in order not by making himself king or dictator but by creating the Principate. The empire's frontiers were on the ocean, or distant rivers. Armies, provinces, fleets, the whole system was interrelated. Roman citizens were protected by the law. Provincials were decently treated. Rome itself had been lavishly beautified. Force had been sparingly used—merely to preserve peace for the majority.

The opposite view went like this. Filial duty and national crisis had been merely pretexts. In actual fact, the motive of Octavian, the future Augustus, was lust for power. Inspired by that, he had mobilized ex-army settlers by gifts of money, raised an army—while he was only a half-grown boy without any official status—won over a consul's brigades by bribery, pretended to support Sextus Pompeius (I), and by senatorial decree usurped the status and rank of a praetor. Soon both consuls, Gaius Vibius Pansa and Aulus Hirtius, had met their deaths—by enemy action; or perhaps in the one case by the deliberate poisoning of his wound, and in the other at the hand of his own troops, instigated by Octavian. In any case it was he who took over both their armies. Then he had forced the reluctant senate to make him consul. But the forces given him to deal with Antony he used against the State. His judicial murders and land distributions were distasteful even to those who carried them out. True, Cassius and Brutus died because he had inherited a feud against them; nevertheless, personal enmities ought to be sacrificed to the public interest. Next he had cheated Sextus Pompeius by a spurious peace treaty, Lepidus by spurious friendship. Then Antony, enticed by the treaties of Tarentum and Brundusium and his marriage with Octavian's sister, had paid the penalty of that delusive relationship with his life. After that, there had certainly been peace, but it was a bloodstained peace. For there followed the disasters of Marcus Lollius (I) and Publius Quinctilius Varus; and there were the assassinations, for example, of Aulus Terentius Varro Murena, Marcus Egnatius Rufus and Iullus Antonius.

And gossip did not spare his personal affairs—how he had abducted the wife of Tiberius Claudius Nero, and asked the priests the farcical question whether it was in order for her to marry while pregnant. Then there was the debauchery of his friend Publius Vedius Pollio. But Livia was a real catastrophe, to the nation, as a mother and to the house of the Caesars as a stepmother.

Besides, critics continued, Augustus seemed to have superseded the worship of the gods when he wanted to have himself venerated in temples, with god-like images, by priests and ministers. His appointment of Tiberius as his successor was due neither to personal affection nor to regard for the national interests. Thoroughly aware of Tiberius' cruelty and arrogance, he intended to heighten his own glory by the contrast with one so inferior. For a few years earlier, when Augustus had been asking the senate to re-award tribune's powers to Tiberius, the emperor had actually let drop in a complimentary oration certain remarks about Tiberius' deportment, style of dressing, and habits. Ostensibly these were excuses; in fact they were criticisms.

After an appropriate funeral, Augustus was declared a god and decreed a temple. But the target of every prayer was Tiberius. Addressing the senate, he offered a variety of comments on the greatness of the empire and his own unpretentiousness. Only the divine Augustus, he suggested, had possessed a personality equal to such responsibilities—he himself, when invited by Augustus to share his labours, had found by experience what hard hazardous work it was to rule the empire. Besides, he said, a State which could rely on so many distinguished personages ought not to concentrate the supreme power in the hands of one man—the task of government would be more easily carried out by the combined efforts of a greater number.

But grand sentiments of this kind sounded unconvincing. Besides, what Tiberius said, even when he did not aim at concealment, was—by habit or nature—always hesitant, always cryptic. And now that he was determined to show no sign of his real feelings, his words became more and more equivocal and obscure. But the chief fear of the senators was that they should be seen to understand him only too well. So they poured forth a flood of tearful lamentations and prayers, gesticulating to heaven and to the statue of Augustus, and making reverent gestures before Tiberius himself.

At this juncture he gave instructions for a document to be produced and read. It was a list of the national resources. It gave the numbers of regular and auxiliary troops serving in the army; the strength of the navy; statistics concerning the provinces and dependent kingdoms; direct and indirect taxation; recurrent expenditure and gifts. Augustus had written all this out in his own hand. Furthermore, he had added a clause advising that the empire should not be extended beyond its present frontiers. Either he feared dangers ahead, or he was jealous.

The senate now wallowed in the most abject appeals. Tiberius remarked incidentally that, although he did not feel himself capable of the whole burden of government, he was nevertheless prepared to take on any branch of it that might be entrusted to him. 'Then I must ask, Caesar,' called out Gaius Asinius Gallus, 'which branch you desire to have handed over to you.' This unexpected question threw Tiberius off his stride. For some moments he said nothing. Then, recovering his balance, he replied that, since he would prefer to be excused from the responsibility altogether, he felt much too diffident to choose or reject this or that part of it. Gallus, however, who had guessed from Tiberius' looks that he had taken offence, protested that the purpose of his question had not been to parcel out functions which were inseparable; it had been to obtain from the lips of Tiberius himself the admission that the State was a single organic whole needing the control of a single mind. Gallus went on to praise Augustus and remind Tiberius of his own victories, and his long and splendid achievements as a civilian. All the same he failed to appease the indignation he had caused. Tiberius had hated him for years, feeling that Gallus' marriage to his own former wife, Marcus Agrippa's daughter Vipsania, was a sign that Gallus had the arrogance of his father Gaius Asinius Pollio (I)— and was over-ambitious.

Next Lucius Arruntius spoke in rather the same vein as Gallus. He too gave offence. Tiberius, in his case, had no longstanding hostility. But he was suspicious of Arruntius, whose wealth, activity, and talents were celebrated. Augustus, in one of his last conversations, had gone over the names of men who would be fit and willing to become emperor, or unfit and unwilling, or fit but unwilling. He had described Marcus Aemilius Lepidus (IV) as suitable but disdainful, Gaius Asinius Gallus as eager but unsuitable, and Lucius Arruntius as both fit and capable of making the venture, if the chance arose. (There is agreement about the first two names; but in some versions Arruntius is replaced by

Cnaeus Calpurnius Piso.) All those mentioned, apart from Lepidus, were soon struck down on one charge or another, at the instigation of Tiberius. Others who chafed his suspicious temperament were Quintus Haterius and Mamercus Aemilius Scaurus. What Haterius did was to ask: 'How long, Caesar, will you allow the State to have no head?' The fault of Scaurus was to say that, since Tiberius had not vetoed the consuls' motion by his tribune's power, there was hope that the senate's prayers would not be unrewarded. Tiberius lost no time in abusing Haterius. But the intervention of Scaurus, against whom his anger was more implacable, he passed over in silence.

Finally, exhausted by the general outcry and individual entreaties, he gradually gave way—not to the extent of admitting that he had accepted the throne, but at least to the point of ceasing to be urged and refuse. There is a well-known story about Haterius. He went into the palace to apologize, and, as Tiberius walked by, grovelled at his feet. Thereupon Tiberius crashed to the ground, either by accident or because he was brought down by the grip of Haterius—who was then all but killed by the guards. However, the emperor's feelings were not softened by the dangerous predicament of the senator, until Haterius appealed to the Augusta—as Livia was now called—and, at her urgent entreaty, was saved.

She, too, was flattered a great deal by the senate. It was variously proposed that she should be called 'parent' and 'mother' of her country; and a large body of opinion held that the words 'son of Julia' ought to form part of the emperor's name. He, however, repeatedly asserted that only reasonable honours must be paid to women—and that, in regard to compliments paid to himself, he would observe a comparable moderation. In reality, however, he was jealous and nervous, and regarded this elevation of a woman as derogatory to his own person. He would not even allow her to be allotted an official attendant, and forbade an Altar of Adoption and other honours of the kind. For Germanicus, however, he requested a special command. A mission was sent to confer it and at the same time to console Germanicus' sorrow at the death of Augustus. The same request was not made for Drusus because he was consul elect and in Rome.

The elections were now transferred from the Assembly to the senate. With regard to the number of praetors Tiberius adhered to the precedent established by Augustus and nominated twelve candidates. The senate asked him to increase the number, but he declared on oath that he would never do so.

Up to this time, although the most important elections were settled by the emperor, some had been left to the inclinations of the national Assembly drawn up by 'tribes'. The public, except in trivial talk, made no objection to their deprival of this right. The senate acquiesced gladly, since it relieved them from the necessity of undignified canvassing and outlay. Tiberius guaranteed that he himself would not recommend more than four candidates, who would have to be appointed without competition or rejection.

At the same time the tribunes petitioned to offer, at their own expense, an annual display which would take its name from the late emperor and be added to the calendar as the Games of Augustus. But it was decided to pay for them from public funds, and to allow the tribunes to wear triumphal robes in the Circus Maximus (they were not, however, to be permitted the use of chariots). It was not long before the organization of this show was transferred to the praetor who is concerned with lawsuits between citizens and non-citizens.

## Notes

[1] In this first paragraph, Tacitus refers to the following events: 753 B.C.E., the traditional start of the monarchy; 510 B.C.E., the expulsion of Tarquinius Superbus and the start of the Roman Republic; 451–449 B.C.E., Councils of Ten governed and wrote laws; 444–367 B.C.E. (at intervals) tribal commanders granted consular powers; 87–84 B.C.E., successive consulships of Lucius Cornelius Cinna; 82–79 B.C.E., successive dictatorships of Lucius Cornelius Sulla; 60–53 B.C.E., informal "First Triumvirate of Pompey, Crassus, and Caesar; 49–44 B.C.E., successive dictatorships of Julius Caesar; 43 B.C.E., official "Second Triumvirate" of Lepidus, Mark Antony, and Octavian (Augustus); 36 B.C.E., Lepidus dropped; 30 B.C.E., suicide of Mark Antony after loss at Battle of Actium.

[2] The Latin *sestertium* was one-fourth of a *denarius*. Comparative values are generally unhelpful, but during this time it seems that one *denarius* was the standard pay for a day's labor. See Gospel of Matthew 20:1–16.

# from *Germania*

## 7

They choose their kings for their noble birth, their commanders for their valour. The power even of the kings is not absolute or arbitrary. The commanders rely on example rather than on the authority of their rank—on the admiration they win by showing conspicuous energy and courage and by pressing forward in front of their own troops. Capital punishment, imprisonment, even flogging, are allowed to none but the priests, and are not inflicted merely as punishments or on the commanders' orders, but as it were in obedience to the god whom the Germans believe to be present on the field of battle. They actually carry with them into the fight certain figures and emblems taken from their sacred groves. A specially powerful incitement to valour is that the squadrons and divisions are not made up at random by the mustering of chance-comers, but are each composed of men of one family or clan. Close by them, too, are their nearest and dearest, so that they can hear the shrieks of their womenfolk and the wailing of their children. These are the witnesses whom each man reverences most highly, whose praise he most desires. It is to their mothers and wives that they go to have their wounds treated, and the women are not afraid to count and compare the gashes. They also carry supplies of food to the combatants and encourage them.

## 14

On the field of battle it is a disgrace to a chief to be surpassed in courage by his followers, and to the followers not to equal the courage of their chief. And to leave a battle alive after their chief has fallen means lifelong infamy and shame. To defend and protect him, and to let him get the credit for their own acts of heroism, are the most solemn obligations of their allegiance. The chiefs fight for victory, the followers for their chief. Many noble youths, if the land of their birth is stagnating in a long period of peace and inactivity, deliberately seek out other tribes which have some war in hand. For the Germans have no taste for peace; renown is more easily won among perils, and a large body of retainers cannot be kept together except by means of violence and war. They are always making demands on the generosity of their chief, asking for a coveted war-horse or a spear stained with the blood of a defeated enemy. Their meals, for which plentiful if homely fare is provided, count in lieu of pay. The wherewithal for this openhandedness comes from war and plunder. A German is not so easily prevailed upon to plough the land and wait patiently for har-vest as to challenge a foe and earn wounds for his reward. He thinks it tame and spiritless to accumulate slowly by the sweat of his brow what can be got quickly by the loss of a little blood.

## 19

By such means is the virtue of their women protected, and they live uncorrupted by the temptations of public shows or the excitements of ban-quets. Clandestine love-letters are unknown to men and women alike. Adultery is extremely rare, considering the size of the population. A guilty wife is summarily punished by her husband. He cuts off her hair, strips her naked, and in the presence of kinsmen turns her out of his house and flogs her all through the village. They have in fact no mercy on a wife who prostitutes her chastity. Neither beauty, youth, nor wealth can find her another husband. No one in Germany finds vice amusing, or calls it 'up-to-date' to seduce and be seduced. Even better is the practice of those states in which only virgins may marry, so that a woman who has once been a bride has finished with all such hopes and aspirations. She takes one husband, just as she has one body and one life. Her thoughts must not stray beyond him or her desires survive him. And even that husband she must love not for himself, but as an embodiment of the married state. To restrict the number of children, or to kill any of those born after the heir, is considered wicked. Good morality is more effective in Germany than good laws are elsewhere.

# Suetonius

Little is known about the dates of Gaius Suetonius Tranquillus' birth or death. He gained the friendship of Pliny the Younger, who helped him gain important administrative positions under the emperors Trajan and Hadrian, which he held until he, along with his patron Clarus, lost favor in 122 C.E. After this, nothing more is known about him. Of his works, his biographies of *The Twelve Caesars* survive intact.

Biography became a form of historical writing during the Hellenistic period, when Alexander the Great dominated political events so much that the story of his life and the events surrounding it was "history." During the Roman Republic, individuals holding annual magistracies could not determine the events of "history" to the same extent that the Hellenistic rulers could, and the impulse to biography was muted. The Romans favored a chronological, annalistic approach to history in which events shaped the humans as much as the humans shaped the events. This form of historiography is represented by Livy and Tacitus, who was a contemporary of Suetonius. In the emperors, however, the overlap of biography and history loomed large, and Tacitus as well seems to structure the books of his *Annals* around the reigns of emperors.

Suetonius abandons a chronological approach to his subject and proceeds through categories of personality and character and achievements. In the *Life of Nero*, excerpted below, Suetonius follows a general chronological pattern as he moves from Nero's ancestors to his birth to his early achievements that portended greatness to his accession to power. But Suetonius then divides his account between Nero's "good" acts and his "bad" acts and presents episodes or anecdotes for each, encouraging us to read Nero morally. In his presentation, Suetonius finds relevance in Nero's physical appearance, his studies, his aversions, and his sexual deviances (though few of these make their way into our excerpt). Suetonius used many sources in his research, including those hostile to his subjects, and he records invaluable details about Roman life. His biographical approach probably derives in part from the Roman practice of eulogy (*laudatio*), of which Augustus' *Achievements* and the *Laudatio Turiae* are related examples.

BSH

# from *Life of Nero (Vita Neronis)*

6. Nero was born at Antium on 15 December, A.D. 37, nine months after Tiberius' death. The sun was rising and his earliest rays touched the newly-born boy almost before he could be laid on the ground. Nero's horoscope at once occasioned many ominous predictions; and a significant comment was made by his father[1] in reply to the congratulations of his friends: namely, that any child born to himself and Agrippina was bound to have a detestable nature and become a public danger. Another promise of ill-luck occurred on the day of his purification: when Agrippina asked her brother Gaius to give the boy whatever name he pleased, he glanced at his uncle Claudius (later Emperor, and Nero's adoptive father) and said with a grin: 'I name him Claudius.' Since Claudius was then the butt of the Court, Agrippina was not amused, and ignored the suggestion. . . .

8. He had reached the age of seventeen when Claudius' death occurred, and presented himself to the Palace Guard that day in the late afternoon—ugly omens throughout the day having ruled out an earlier appearance. After being acclaimed Emperor on the Palace steps, he was taken in a litter to the Guards' Camp, where he briefly addressed the troops. He was then taken to the Senate House, where he remained until nightfall, refusing only one of the many high honours voted him, namely the title 'Father of the Country', and this because of his youth. . . .

11. He gave an immense variety of entertainments—coming-of-age parties, chariot races in the Circus, stage plays, a gladiatorial show—persuading even old men of consular rank, and old ladies, too, to attend the coming-of-age parties. He reserved seats for the knights at the Circus, as he had done in the Theatre; and actually raced four-camel chariots! At the Great Festival, as he called the series of plays devoted to the eternity of the Empire, parts were taken by men and women of both Orders; and one well-known knight rode an elephant down a sloping tight-rope. When he staged 'The Fire', a Roman play by Afranius, the actors were allowed to keep the valuable furnishings they rescued from the burning house. Throughout the Festival all kinds of gifts were scattered to the people—1,000 assorted birds daily, and quantities of food parcels; besides vouchers for grain, clothes, gold, silver, precious stones, pearls, paintings, slaves, transport animals, and even trained wild beasts—and finally for ships, blocks of city apartments, and farms.

12. Nero watched from the top of the proscenium.[2] The gladiatorial show took place in a wooden theatre, near the Campus Martius, which had

been built in less than a year; but no one was allowed to be killed during these combats, not even criminals. He did, however, make 400 senators and 600 knights, some of them rich and respectable, do battle in the arena; and some had to fight wild beasts and perform various duties about the ring. He staged a naval engagement on an artificial lake of salt water which had sea-monsters swimming in it; also Pyrrhic performances[3] by certain young Greeks, to whom he presented certificates of Roman citizenship when their show ended. At one stage of the *Minotaur* ballet an actor, disguised as a bull, actually mounted another who played Pasiphaë and occupied the hindquarters of a hollow wooden heifer—or that, at least, was the audience's impression. In the *Daedalus and Icarus* ballet, the actor who played Icarus, while attempting his first flight, fell beside Nero's couch and spattered him with blood.

Nero rarely presided at shows of this sort, but would recline in the closed imperial box and watch through a small window; later, however, he opened the box. He inaugurated the Neronia, a festival of competitions in music, gymnastics, and horsemanship, modelled on the Greek ones and held every five years; and simultaneously opened his Baths and gymnasium, and provided free oil for knights and senators. Ex-consuls, drawn by lot, presided over the Neronia, and occupied the praetors' seats. Then Nero descended to the orchestra where the senators sat, to accept the wreath for Latin oratory and verse, which had been reserved for him by the unanimous vote of all the distinguished competitors. The judges also awarded him the wreath for a lyre solo, but he bowed reverently to them, and said: 'Pray lay it on the ground before Augustus' statue!' At an athletic competition held in the Enclosure, oxen were sacrificed on a lavish scale; that was when he shaved his chin for the first time, put the hair in a gold box studded with valuable pearls and dedicated it to Capitoline Jupiter. He had invited the Vestal Virgins to watch the athletics, explaining that the priestesses of Ceres at Olympia were accorded the same privilege. . . .

16. Nero introduced his own new style of architecture in the city: building out porches from the fronts of apartments and private houses to serve as fire-fighting platforms, and subsidizing the work himself. He also considered a scheme for extending the city wall as far as Ostia,[4] and cutting a canal which would allow ships to sail straight up to Rome.

During his reign a great many public abuses were suppressed by the imposition of heavy penalties, and among the equally numerous novel enactments were sumptuary laws limiting private expenditure; the substitution of a simple grain distribution for public banquets; and a decree restricting the food sold in wine-shops to green vegetables and dried beans—whereas before all kinds of snacks had been displayed. Punishments were also inflicted on the Christians, a sect professing a new and mischievous religious belief; and Nero ended the licence which the charioteers had so long enjoyed that they claimed it as a right: to wander down the streets, swindling and robbing the populace. He likewise expelled from the city all pantomime actors and their hangers-on. . . .

I have separated this catalogue of Nero's less atrocious acts—some deserving no criticism, some even praiseworthy—from the others; but I must begin to list his follies and crimes. . . .

21. Appearances at Rome as well meant so much to Nero that he held the Neronia again before the required five years elapsed. When the crowd clamoured to hear his heavenly voice, he answered that he would perform in the Palace gardens later if anyone wanted to hear him; but when the Guards on duty seconded the appeal, he delightedly agreed to oblige them. He wasted no time in getting his name entered on the list of competing lyre-players, and dropped his ticket into the urn with the others. The Guards prefects carried his lyre as he went up to play in his turn and a group of colonels and close friends accompanied him. After taking his place and finishing his preliminary oration, he made Cluvius Rufus, the ex-Consul, announce the title of the song. It was *Niobe*; and he sang on until two hours before dusk. Then he postponed the rest of the contest to the following year, which would give him an opportunity to sing oftener. But since a year was a long time to wait, he continued to make frequent appearances. He toyed with the idea of playing opposite professional actors in public shows staged by magistrates; because one of the preators had offered him 10,000 gold pieces if he would consent. And he did actually sing in tragedies, taking the parts of heroes and gods, sometimes even of heroines and goddesses, wearing masks either modelled on his own face, or on the face of whatever woman he happened to be in love with at the time. Among his performances were *Canace in Childbirth, Orestes the Matricide, Oedipus Blinded*, and *Distraught Hercules*. There is a story that a young recruit on guard recognized him in the rags and fetters demanded by the part of Hercules, and dashed forward to his assistance. . . .

27. Gradually Nero's vices gained the upper hand: he no longer tried to laugh them off, or hide, or deny them, but openly broke into more serious crime. His feasts now lasted from noon till midnight, with an occasional break for diving into a warm bath, or if it were summer, into snow-cooled water. Sometimes he would drain the artificial lake in the Campus Martius, or the other in the Circus, and hold public dinner parties there, including prostitutes and dancing-girls from all over the city among his guests. Whenever he floated down the Tiber to Ostia, or cruised past the Gulf of Baiae, he had a row of temporary brothels erected along the shore, where married women, pretending to be inn-keepers, solicited him to come ashore. He also forced his friends

to provide him with dinners; one of them spent 40,000 gold pieces on a turban party, and another even more on a rose banquet. . . .

31. His wastefulness showed most of all in the architectural projects. He built a palace, stretching from the Palatine to the Esquiline, which he called 'The Passageway'; and when it burned down soon afterwards, rebuilt it under the new name of 'The Golden House'. The following details will give some notion of its size and magnificence. The entrance-hall was large enough to contain a huge statue of himself, 120 feet high; and the pillared arcade ran for a whole mile. An enormous pool, like a sea, was surrounded by buildings made to resemble cities, and by a landscape garden consisting of ploughed fields, vineyards, pastures, and woodlands—where every variety of domestic and wild animal roamed about. Parts of the house were overlaid with gold and studded with precious stones and mother-of-pearl. All the dining-rooms had ceilings of fretted ivory, the panels of which could slide back and let a rain of flowers, or of perfume from hidden sprinklers, shower upon his guests. The main dining-room was circular, and its roof revolved, day and night, in time with the sky. Sea water, or sulphur water, was always on tap in the baths. When the palace had been decorated throughout in this lavish style, Nero dedicated it, and condescended to remark: 'Good, now I can at last begin to live like a human being!' . . .

34. The over-watchful, over-critical eye that Agrippina kept on whatever Nero said or did proved more than he could stand. He first tried to embarrass her by frequent threats to abdicate and go into retirement in Rhodes. Then, having deprived her of all honours and power, and even of her Roman and German bodyguard, he refused to have her living with him and expelled her from his Palace; after which he did everything possible to annoy her, sending people to pester her with law-suits while she stayed in Rome, and when she took refuge on her riverside estate, making them constantly drive or sail past the windows, disturbing her with jeers and cat-calls. In the end her threats and violent behaviour terrified him into deciding that she must die. He tried to poison her three times, but she had always taken the antidote in advance; so he rigged up a machine in the ceiling of her bedroom which would dislodge the panels and drop them on her while she slept. However, one of the people involved in the plot gave the secret away. Then he had a collapsible boat designed which would either sink or have its cabin fall in on top of her. Under pretence of a reconciliation, he sent the most friendly note inviting her to celebrate the Feast of Minerva with him at Baiae, and on her arrival made one of his captains stage an ostensibly accidental collision with the galley in which she had sailed. Then he protracted the feast until a late hour, and when at last she said: 'I really must get back to Bauli,' offered her his collapsible boat instead of

the damaged galley. Nero was in a very happy mood as he led Agrippina down to the quay, and even kissed her breasts before she stepped aboard. He sat up all night, on tenterhooks of anxiety, waiting for the outcome of his scheme. On discovering that everything had gone wrong and she had escaped by swimming, when Lucius Agerinus, her freedman, entered joyfully to report that she was safe and sound, Nero, in desperation, ordered one of his men to drop a dagger surreptitiously beside Agerinus, whom he arrested at once on a charge of having been hired to murder the Emperor. After this he arranged for Agrippina to be killed, and made it seem as if she had sent Agerinus to assassinate him but committed suicide on hearing that the plot had miscarried. Other more gruesome details are supplied by reliable authorities: it appears that Nero rushed off to examine Agrippina's corpse, handling her limbs and, between drinks to satisfy his thirst, discussing their good and bad points. Though encouraged by the congratulations which poured in from the Army, the Senate, and the people, he was never either then or thereafter able to free his conscience from the guilt of this crime. He often admitted that he was hounded by his mother's ghost and that the Furies were pursuing him with whips and burning torches; and set Persian magicians at work to conjure up the ghost and entreat its forgiveness. During his tour of Greece he came to Athens, where the Eleusinian Mysteries were being held, but dared not participate when a herald ordered all impious and criminal persons present to withdraw before the ceremonies began.

Having disposed of his mother, Nero proceeded to murder his aunt. He found her confined to bed with severe constipation. The old lady stroked his downy beard affectionately—he was already full-grown—murmuring: 'Whenever you celebrate your coming-of-age and present me with this, I shall die happy.' Nero turned to his courtiers and said laughingly: 'In that case I must shave at once'. Then he ordered the doctors to give her a laxative of fatal strength, seized her property before she was quite dead, and tore up the will so that nothing should escape him.

35. Besides Octavia, he took two more wives—first Poppaea Sabina, a quaestor's daughter, at that time married to a knight, and Statilia Messalina, great-great-grand-daughter of Taurus who had twice been Consul and won a triumph. To marry Statilia he was obliged to murder her husband Atticus Vestinus, a consul. Life with Octavia had soon bored him, and when his friends criticized his treatment of her, he retorted: 'Just being an emperor's wife ought surely to be enough to make her happy?' He tried unsuccessfully to strangle her on several occasions, but finally pronounced that she was barren, and divorced her. This act made him so unpopular and caused so great a scandal that he banished Octavia and later had her executed on a charge of adul-

tery. Her innocence was maintained by the witnesses called by him to testify against her even under torture; so he bribed his old tutor Anicetus to confess (falsely) that he had tricked her into infidelity. Though he doted on Poppaea, whom he married twelve days after this divorce, he kicked her to death while she was pregnant and ill, because she complained that he came home late from the races. Poppaea had borne him a daughter, Claudia Augusta, who died in infancy.

There was no family relationship which Nero did not criminally abuse. When Claudius' daughter Antonia refused to take Poppaea's place, he had her executed on a charge of attempted rebellion; and destroyed every other member of his family, including relatives by marriage, in the same way. He committed an indecent assault on young Aulus Plautius and then put him to death, remarking: 'Now Mother may come and kiss my successor'; he explained that Agrippiria had been in love with Aulus and induced him to make a bid for the throne. There was also his step-son, Rufrius Crispinus, Poppaea's child by her former husband. Nero had the boy's own slaves drown him on a fishing expedition simply because he was said to have played at being a general and an emperor. He banished Tuscus, the son of his foster-mother and now prefect of Egypt, for daring to use the baths which he had built in preparation for the imperial visit to Alexandria. When his tutor Seneca repeatedly asked leave to retire, and offered to surrender all his estates, Nero swore most solemnly that Seneca had no cause to suspect him, since he would rather die than harm him; but he drove Seneca to commit suicide nevertheless. He promised Burrus, the Guards' Commander, a cough mixture, but sent poison instead; also poisoning the food and drink of the rich old freedmen who had originally arranged for him to be adopted as Claudius' heir, and had subsequently been his counsellors. . . .

38. Nero showed no greater mercy to the common folk, or to the very walls of Rome. Once, in the course of a general conversation, someone quoted the line:

When I am dead, may fire consume the earth,

but Nero said that the first part of the line should read: 'While I yet live,' and soon converted this fancy into fact. Pretending to be disgusted by the drab old buildings and narrow, winding streets of Rome, he brazenly set fire to the city; and though a group of ex-consuls caught his attendants, armed with tow and blazing torches, trespassing on their property, they dared not interfere. He also coveted the sites of several granaries, solidly built in stone, near the Golden House; having knocked down their walls with siege-engines, he set the interiors ablaze. This terror lasted for six days and seven nights, causing many people to take shelter in monuments and tombs. Nero's men destroyed not only a vast number of apartment blocks, but mansions which had belonged to famous generals and were still decorated with their triumphal trophies; temples, too, vowed and dedicated by the kings, and others during the Punic and Gallic wars—in fact, every ancient monument of historical interest that had hitherto survived. Nero watched the conflagration from the Tower of Maecenas, enraptured by what he called 'the beauty of the flames'; then put on his tragedian's costume and sang *The Sack of Ilium* from beginning to end. He offered to remove corpses and rubble free of charge, but allowed nobody to search among the ruins even of his own mansion; he wanted to collect as much loot and spoils as possible himself. Then he opened a Fire Relief Fund and insisted on contributions, which bled the provincials white and practically beggared all private citizens. . . .

40. At last, after nearly fourteen years of Nero's misrule, the earth rid herself of him. The first move was made by the Gauls under Julius Vindex, the governor of one of their provinces.

Nero's astrologers had told him that he would one day be removed from the throne, and were given the famous reply:

A simple craft will keep a man from want.

This referred doubtless to his lyre-playing which, although it might be only a pastime for an emperor, would have to support him if he were reduced to earning a livelihood. Some astrologers forecast that, if forced to leave Rome, he would find another throne in the East; one or two even particularized that of Jerusalem. Others assured him that he would recoup all his losses, a prediction on which he based high hopes; for when he seemed to have lost the provinces of Britain and Armenia, but managed to regain them both, he assumed that the disasters foretold had already taken place. Then the Oracle at Delphi warned him to beware the seventy-third year, and assuming that this referred to his own seventy-third year, not Galba's, he looked forward cheerfully to a ripe old age and an unbroken run of good luck; so much so that when he lost some very valuable objects in a shipwreck, he hastened to tell his friends that the fish would fetch them back to him. . . .

49. Finally, when his companions unanimously insisted on his trying to escape from the degrading fate threatening him, he ordered them to dig a grave at once, of the right size, and then collect any pieces of marble that they could find and fetch wood and water for the disposal of the corpse. As they bustled about obediently he muttered through his tears: 'Dead! And so great an artist!'

While he hesitated, a runner brought him a letter from Phaon. Nero tore it from the man's hands and read that, having been declared a public enemy by the Senate, he would be punished 'in ancient style' when arrested. He asked what 'ancient style' meant, and learned that the executioners stripped their victim naked, thrust his head into a wooden fork, and then flogged him to death with rods. In terror he snatched up the two daggers which he had brought along and tried their points; but threw them down again, protesting that the fatal hour had not yet come. Then he begged Sporus to weep and mourn for him, but also begged one of the other three to set him an example by committing suicide first. He kept moaning about his cowardice, and muttering: 'How ugly and vulgar my life has become!' And then in Greek: 'This certainly is no credit to Nero, no credit at all,' and: 'Come, pull yourself together!' By this time the troop of cavalry who had orders to take him alive were coming up the road. Nero gasped:

> 'Hark to the sound I hear! It is hooves of galloping horses.'

Then, with the help of his secretary, Epaphroditus, he stabbed himself in the throat and was already half dead when a centurion entered, pretending to have rushed to his rescue, and staunched the wound with his cloak. Nero muttered: 'Too late! But, ah, what fidelity!' He died, with eyes glazed and bulging from their sockets, a sight which horrified everybody present. He had made his companions promise, whatever happened, not to let his head be cut off, but to arrange in some way that he should be buried all in one piece. Galba's freedman Icelus, who had been imprisoned when the first news came of the revolt and was now at liberty again, granted this indulgence.

50. They laid Nero on his pyre, dressed in the gold-embroidered white robes which he had worn on 1 January. The funeral cost 2,000 gold pieces. Ecloge and Alexandria, his old nurses, helped Acte, his mistress, to carry the remains to the Pincian Hill, which can be seen from the Campus Martius. His coffin, of white porphyry, stands there in the family tomb of the Domitii, enclosed by a balustrade of stone from Thasos, and with an altar of Luna marble standing over it.

## Notes

[1] Nero's father was Gnaeus Domitius Ahenobarbus, consul in 32 C.E., who apparently died in 40 C.E.

[2] A proscenium theatre is one in which the audience occupies the front and sides of the stage. Nero is probably seated front and center on an upper tier.

[3] Originally a kind of war dance, here a matter of entertainment.

[4] Rome's port on the Mediterranean at the mouth of the Tiber, about 12 miles from Rome.

# Appendices

# Reading a Primary Text
# from Antiquity

Students often have difficulty approaching literature from the ancient world because of the challenge of distance, measured in both time and space. Geographical regions are unfamiliar (Where is the Deccan Plateau?) and names are difficult to pronounce (Amenemope can be quite a tongue-twister!). But the literature of the ancient world, each text, is an artifact or product of the activity of communication. As such (and if for no other reason), literature is a human product that can still communicate ideas to an audience, even a contemporary one. Keep in mind that what a text communicates to us may not be what its producer(s) intended to communicate, much less what was communicated to its original readers. Because you are studying ancient texts in order to better understand the cultures that produced them, your examination should begin with issues of original authorship, original audience, and original context. To assist you in that examination, we have compiled the following list of questions intended to get you started thinking critically and seriously about the literature of the ancient world. Look over the questions. Pick those that seem applicable to a particular reading. These questions are a great way to begin the initial examination of any text.

(1) How was this text composed? Was it authored—that is, was it the creation of a specific, identifiable individual? Do we or can we know who this individual is? Or was the text composed by combining previous texts into a larger "quilt"? (This is a process called redaction.)

(2) What kind of a text is it? Is it, for example, a law code, a hymn, a lamentation, a poem, or a narrative?

(3) If it is a narrative, who narrates it? Is the narrator someone "within" the narrative? Is it in the "third" person? Is there only one narrator? Is it a biography or autobiography?

(4) In what tense is it narrated? Is it told as though it is happening (present) or as though it has happened (past)? What biases and perspectives are self-evident in the text? What does this tell us about the author, the social group, or the larger community within which it functioned?

(5) Who was the intended audience? Who would have had access to the text? In what segment(s) of society would this text have been meaningful?

(6) Is there historical information that hints at the period in which a text was composed?

(7) What features of a text hint at the means by which it was composed? Do patterns of repetition (especially of epithets, other phrases, or of specific lines and other structures) suggest that the text was orally transmitted at some point? Would features of the text make it easier to memorize and recite?

(8) How does the text come down to us—i.e., how has it been transmitted? How many times, and into how many different languages, has a text been translated before it gets to us? Do we have reason to believe these translations are reliable? Are there competing different versions or editions of the text, or of various passages of the text? Why?

(9) What biases and perspectives are evident in the text? What does this tell us about the author, the social group, or the larger community within which it functioned?

(10) What is the text about? If it is a story concerned with a character and his or her actions, what are the prominent attributes of that character? You may want to consider gender, social position, or special qualities of the character.

(11) What time frame does the action encompass?

(12) Do the attributes of the text indicate what was valued about it by its readers or its audience?

(13) What does the text say about institutional and social structures of the culture that produced it?

(14) What worldview(s) is present in the text?

(15) Can we begin to understand the epistemology of the culture that produced the text?

(16) What are the points of comparison between the institutions, structures and worldview of the text with those of contemporary culture? What are the points of contrast?

(17) What can we learn from the text about the religious, economic, political and social conditions of the culture that created it?

(18) How does a particular text enhance your knowledge of the time period and subject that you are studying?

KG and KP

# Essay on Translation

Every text that is found in this reader, as well as every text you will read from the ancient world, has been translated into English. On the face of it, translation appears to be a relatively simple exercise, a matter of finding the English word that best renders the Sumerian cuneiform, Egyptian hieroglyphic, Chinese pictograph, Greek verb, Latin noun. For a very few texts, translation may be relatively easy. Some texts, after all, were written for mass consumption or for an audience that included both educated and uneducated. The laws of Hammurabi and the *Achievements* (*Res Gestae*) of Augustus were public documents, carved on stone for the obedience and admiration of all. The texts of the New Testament were written in the "common" (*koinê*) Greek, not without intentional structure or reference to other texts, but with an emphasis on clarity and simplicity. But the majority of the texts in this reader, and the vast majority of the texts in the ancient world, do not fall into such categories; they were written for a small, literate, upper-class audience that probably shared the values expressed within the works and understood the art that went into their creation. This is perhaps a good working definition for "literature," and the translation of literature from its original language is never a simple, straightforward matter. In this essay, I will present a few of the problems that face a translator, and I will conclude with the example of a Horation ode to demonstrate the potential elasticity of meaning—and to encourage you to learn other languages whenever possible.

First, consider this simple question: what is the real goal of the translator? Is it faithfulness to the original text, or what we might call "readability," a clear and enjoyable rendition? It may seem that these two are indivisible and should always be combined in any translator's mind as two sides of the same coin, but there are many factors that pit these two objectives against each other, and force the translator to attempt a middle ground between them, that may feel like Odysseus passing between Scylla and Charybdis.

For one, there is the matter of an author's style. An author may write tersely or floridly, openly or allusively; he may aim for a learned or a casual voice, in an authoritative or conversational mode, with a modern or archaic tone; she may prefer sentences that are short, effusive, intricate, or epigrammatic; he may favor verbs that are active, passive, or impersonal. The translator must make decisions not only about bringing words into English, but

542

bringing style as well. And styles, notoriously, change: what was popular then may not be popular now. For example, the Romans were schooled in rhetoric, and some authors, such as Cicero, favored long, elaborate, balanced sentences, which would tire most modern readers. The historian Tacitus, on the other hand, is regarded as one of the more difficult Latin authors because of his syntactical innovations and the general compression of his style. A literal rendering of Tacitus would require nearly as much work to decipher as the Latin text does, and would convey little of the dark, claustrophobic brilliance of his narrative. Modern translators will almost certainly choose to break Cicero's longer sentences into several sentences, and will flesh out Tacitus' implicit meaning with more words than he actually wrote. It is safe to say that translators strive to capture the tone, speed, atmosphere, and color of the original, elements that contribute to an author's style, but they strive to do so in language and expression that will not alienate the modern reader.

There is also the simple matter of vocabulary. Given the relative paucity of works that survive from the ancient world and the complete absence of native speakers, we are dependent on context and cross-reference to clarify obscure words. Some languages were completely lost: until the discovery of the Rosetta stone by Napoleon's soldiers in 1799, for example, there was no key to the decipherment of Egyptian hieroglyphics. Comparative material is rare for some languages. Even in Greek and Latin, the knowledge of which has never been lost, there are thousands of words that occur only once in extant literature (which scholars call *hapax legomena*, or "things once said"), leaving only context and root meanings, or etymology, as clues to their meanings. In such a case, the translator must decide whether to choose something that makes sense, or indicate his confusion in the text, or bury the possibilities in the relative obscurity of a footnote.

Of course, words can create the opposite problem as well. Meaning is notoriously elastic, and many words carry multiple connotations in their original language for which English offers no single equivalent. Puns or jokes are obvious examples, which may not "translate" even between English speakers. Another Latin example may help. In the first 25 lines of Vergil's *Aeneid*, the Latin verb *volvere* appears twice, once to describe Aeneas "undergoing" misfortune (line 9) and once to describe the Fates "spinning" destiny (line 22). Later in the first book, the same verb describes the winds stirring up the waves in a storm (line 86), and Jupiter unraveling the secrets of Aeneas' destiny for Venus (line 262). The verb basically means "to roll" and gives us our English derivatives "involve," "revolve," "evolve," "convolute," and their cognates, to name a few. But the translator can hardly choose one English word to fit all occurrences without compromising the sense of the individual passages. What the student loses, then, is not so much the meaning of the passage as it is a layer of imagery, which is created by the verbal echo in these passages, that connects Aeneas' sufferings with the flux of the sea and the progress of fate.

Fragmentary or elliptical texts present special problems. The *Epic of Gilgamesh*, the poems of Sappho, and the works of Aristotle all exist in forms that require a great deal of supplementation, and each translator must decide how much notation to give in order to indicate where the gaps in the text are, and what is conjecture. Some translators of *Giligamesh*, for example, privilege the narrative, and present the text as a seamless whole. Others, including Maureen Gallery Kovacs, make generous use of the ellipse to show where the text is broken and missing. The poems of Sappho survive only as quotations in the works of other writers or on scraps of papyrus, so we are not sure that we have a single complete poem by her. And Aristotle's works seem to survive as notes rather than as fully written treatises, and translators are often required to fill in his implicit meanings. Each of these require a translator to judge not only what is there but what isn't there, and to choose among filling in the gaps, offering conjectures about what is missing, or leaving them void.

As I hope it is clear, translators must make many decisions regarding the dichotomy between faithfulness and "readability." I talk above about decisions in response to specific textual challenges, but perhaps there is an even more basic way of asking the question: should a translator strive to locate the author in his or her original culture, or to make the author seem like a contemporary of ours? Should a translation consciously reveal that it represents the product of an ancient language and an ancient culture, or should it seem contemporary to its audience? If a historically accurate translation would require numerous footnotes to clarify the individuals or places mentioned within, a translator might opt to generalize or modernize: a reference to Scythia in an ancient text could be translated as "the far edge of civilization" or as "Afghanistan," for example, though neither communicates exactly where Scythia was nor how the Greeks or Romans regarded it. The more a translation appears as a "contemporary" product, the more quickly it will probably age, as well, given the short lifespans of idiom and style. For translators, of course, this means that translation is a never ending task—no translation will ever be so perfect that it will obviate the need for another.

Poetry is perhaps the greatest challenge for any translator; indeed, it has been said that poetry is that which is lost in translation. Poetry perhaps incorporates most of the problems mentioned above while adding a few more. Poetry is sometimes more indirect, often more allusive. Poetic devices in which one word "stands for" another in some way, such as metaphor, metonymy, synecdoche, and catachresis, present the translator with the question: should I use the allusive word or the word or idea alluded to? How much should I make what is implicit in the poem explicit in my translation?

Nor are the elements of poetry identical in all languages. For many speakers of English, poetry is at least partly defined by stress and rhyme. It may surprise many readers to learn that rhyme is virtually never used in some ancient languages, including Hebrew, Greek, and Latin, and that for many languages, pitch and meter determine poetic expression, making it more like song. Remember that the collection of early Chinese poetry is the *Shih-jing*, literally rendered as "song-word scripture." Differences in languages lead to different poetic forms and features. Most words in Greek and Latin are polysyllabic and contain more unstressed or short syllables than Chinese or, for that matter, English words contain. Chinese monosyllables led to poetic forms of 3 word lines, or 5 word lines, or 7 word lines, which used rhyme and alliteration, rather than to the elaborate metrical schemes of Greek or Latin lyric. Hebrew poetry privileges symmetry over metrical structure.

These general statements will probably make more sense with a specific example. I will use the fifth ode of Horace's first book of *Odes* to show some of the difficulties of translation that face a translator. The Latin appears below.

> Quis multa gracilis te puer in rosa
> perfusus liquidis urget odoribus
>   grato, Pyrrha, sub antro?
>     cui flavam religas comam,
>
> simplex munditiis? heu quotiens fidem          5
> mutatosque deos flebit et aspera
>   nigris aequora ventis
>     emirabitur insolens,
>
> qui nunc te fruitur credulus aurea,
> qui semper vacuam, semper amabilem       10
>   sperat, nescius aurae
>     fallacis! miseri, quibus
>
> intemptata nites! me tabula sacer
> votiva paries indicat uvida
>   suspendisse potenti                  15
>     vestimenta maris deo.

The poem is a short 16 lines, in four stanzas, each four lines long. The meter, i.e., the pattern of "long" (or stressed) and "short" (or unstressed) syllables, is a variation of the Asclepiadean, one favored by Horace. The core of all Asclepiadean meters is a "foot" called the choriamb, – ˘ ˘ –, (think of the baseball announcer's call, "Swing and a miss"). In *Ode* I.5, the choriamb is doubled in the first two lines of each stanza, with a caesura, or break, between them. Two syllables precede the first choriamb, and two syllables follow second choriamb. You can read the lines out loud and feel the beat and the caesura: *Quis multa gracilis | te puer in rosa/ perfusus liquidis | urget odoribus.* The third and fourth lines contain only one choriamb, and employ slightly different rhythms from each other. Each stanza observes a precise application of this elaborate meter.

Latin, like Greek, is an inflected language, which means that words change forms to indicate their function in the sentence. English bears vestigial inflection in nouns, pronouns, and verbs. For example, *boy* is singular, *boys* is plural; the pronoun *she* indicates the subject, *her* indicates the object; *we see* but *she sees*. But English communicates meaning primarily through word order: *The boy hit the ball* does not mean the same thing as *The ball hit the boy*, even though the words are the same. In Latin, in which nouns have many more forms, and in which nouns and adjectives agree with each other, word order is unnecessary for the determination of meaning. Greek and Latin poets, in a sense, can put the words anywhere. Horace chooses his placements here very carefully. In the first line, *gracilis* modifies *puer*, and *multa* modifies *rosa*. A slender boy, and lots of roses. *Te* is "you"; the poem is spoken as an address to Pyrrha, the lovely heart-breaker. Now notice the placements in line 1: *gracilis puer* surrounds *te*, and both are surrounded by *multa in rosa*. Nearly every noun in the poem is given only one adjective, and most adjectives precede their nouns, causing the reader to have patience: *liquidis . . . odoribus, grato . . . antro, flavam . . . comam* (clear…perfumes, pleasing…cave, yellow…hair). And what is the boy doing? Horace uses the verb *urget*. The English derivative "urges" is acceptible, but vague; "squeezes" seems a bit corny; "presses" sounds somewhat menacing. But the Latin verb contains all of these possibilities, and Horace has chosen the word for its ambiguity.

In the third stanza, Horace ends the first line with two words, *credulus aurea. Credulus* modifies the boy, who is "ready to believe," and *aurea* modifies Pyrrha, still *te* in that line. *Aurea* means "golden," and is consistent with the characterization of Pyrrha in the rest of the poem: her hair is blonde (*flavam comam,* 4), and she gleams (*nites,* 13). Even the name Pyrrha is Greek for "fiery" or "yellowish red." But Horace ends the third line of that stanza with the word *aurae*, which means "breeze" or "wind." The boy is *nescius aurae fallacis*, "ignorant of the deceptive breeze." By ending these two lines with a verbal echo, Horace draws a connection between the "gold" of Pyrrha and the changeable wind that portends a storm. No translator can really capture that.

With the exception of the first two words, *intemptata nites*, the last stanza is a sentence unto itself. The first word of that sentence is *Me* and its position is emphatic. The speaker now enters the poem in a first person voice (not necessarily to be taken as *Horace's* voice) and tells that he knows whereof he speaks. The final sentence is marked by compression and extreme separation of words: *me* is the subject of *suspendisse*, and *uvida* modifies *vestimenta* (wet . . . clothes). Slyly, almost grudgingly, the speaker admits that he too suffered shipwreck in the storms of love, suggesting though not stating that Pyrrha was the storm that wrecked him, and that he has survived to tell the tale. He dedicated his dripping clothes to the powerful god of the sea (*potenti . . . maris deo*).

If a translator cannot reproduce the meter, the verbal echoes, the interwoven word order, why should you read any translation of a Latin poem? What can you get out of it? Of course, you should be able to see something of the imagery, and grasp something of the metaphors and analogies. No matter what translation you read, you should be able to see the comparison between Pyrrha and the sea: now calm, shining, inviting, now threatening, devastating, ruinous. Most translations should catch the ambiguity between the metaphorical and the literal; the poem walks a fine line between describing a faithless girl as *like* the sea and describing actual storms and a shipwreck survivor. David West's translation below accompanies his edition of the Latin texts with commentary, and attempts only to render the Latin as literally as possible. West does not attempt to cast his translation in any meter, nor with any extraneous poetic devices.

Poets can offer their translations in meter, and some do. Milton produced a famous version that is about as close to the Latin as English can get (Milton, of course, wrote Latin poetry fluently and felt Latin meters in his bones). Nevertheless, he opts for iambics in his translation. This results in some awkwardness for modern English speakers: "slender" must be one syllable, and "thou untry'd" must be two. But he also reproduces some of Horace's language and word order, which can lead to confusion. What exactly are "liquid odours"? Is is clear that "he" is the subject of the verb "admire" in line 8? And when Milton says, "Who now enjoyes thee credulous, all Gold," he strains the English meaning of "credulous" and seems to apply it to "thee," though we know it refers to the subject, the boy. As masterful as Milton is, his version still requires some translation from his English into ours.

In a wonderful version, John Frederick Nims actually reproduces Horace's Asclepiadean meter, with its internal choriambs and pauses. To read Nims' translation is to feel, as much as a Latinless reader can, the pace and rhythm of the original. Of course, by privileging the meter, Nims has to give on other details. For Horace's *perfusus liquidis odoribus*, Nims gives us the choriamb "lotioned and soaped", which captures the sense but not the words of Horace; he updates Horace and loses something of the ridiculousness of Horace's suitor, dripping with pomade, which balances the final image of the speaker's dripping clothes. Nims creates a few details that are not in Horace: the grot is "cool," the rose is "rambling." Nims also adds immediacy by giving the boy direct speech, and by making the speaker a recent victim ("I? Just made it to shore, hung up my storm-drenched clothes"). This immediacy, however, is not in Horace, though it doesn't disserve him, either.

Poets can also take Horace more as a starting point and introduce their own poetic techniques into their translations—though at some point, the word "adaptation" might be more accurate than "translation." Heather McHugh takes the metaphor of the sea and storm and works variations on it. She is fond of the pun and the *double entendre*. In a delightful twist, she says the boy will curse the "breakers—God of his word, you of your faith." Though this pun is not in Horace, he did offer *aurea* and *aurae*, so McHugh can claim to be working in the same spirit. But she makes the seas largely internal—"his seas are barely stirred"—and the poem loses some of its grandeur. But this is a calculated effect on her part, and the alliteration and puns contribute to it. In the final version below, William Harris, a classicist, adheres least to Horace in meter, language, and detail, yet his poem is still arguably true to Horace's original.

Read the following translations—preferably aloud—and compare the rhythms, sounds, images, and tones. Each offers something valuable, though none, obviously, is exactly Horace.

## Horace, *Ode* I, 5 translated by John Milton (pub. 1673)

What slender Youth bedew'd with liquid odours
Courts thee on Roses in some pleasant Cave,
Pyrrha for whom bindst thou
In wreaths thy golden Hair,

Plain in thy neatness; O how oft shall he
On Faith and changèd Gods complain: and Seas
Rough with black winds and storms
Unwonted shall admire:

Who now enjoyes thee credulous, all Gold,
Who always vacant always amiable
Hopes thee; of flattering gales
Unmindfull. Hapless they

To whom thou untry'd seem'st fair. Me in my vow'd
Picture the sacred wall declares t' have hung
My dank and dropping weeds
To the stern God of Sea.

## Horace, *Ode* I, 5 translated by David West (pub. 1995)

What slim youngster, soaked in perfumes
is hugging you now, Pyrrha, on a bed of roses
      deep in your lovely cave? For whom
          are you tying up your blonde hair?

You're so elegant and so simple. Many's the time
he'll weep at your faithlessness and the changing gods
      and be amazed at seas
          roughened by black winds,

but now all innocence he enjoys your golden beauty
and imagines you always available, always lovable,
      not knowing that breezes are treacherous—
          I pity poor devils with no experience of you

and dazzled by your radiance. As for me,
the votive tablet on the temple wall announces
      that I have dedicated my dripping wet clothes
          to the god who rules the sea.

## Horace, *Ode* I, 5 translated by John Frederick Nims (died 1999)

Who's that slip of a boy, lotioned and soaped, who'll urge
Love on you in the cool grot by the rambling rose?
      Who've you tied back your golden
          Curls for, Pyrrha, in just your own

Simple elegant way? Oh what a shock in store
For him! "Count on the gods? Never again!" he'll groan,
      Dazed, ungainly, engulfed in
          Pitch-black hurricane-swirling seas.

Now he glories in you, thinking you purest gold;
Trusts you, "Always my own! Always my own true love!"

Trusts you, never suspecting
How torrential your summer air.

Those your glitter allures, put to no proof—beware!
I? Just made it to shore, hung up my storm-drenched clothes,
Votive gifts for the shrine of
Neptune, lord of the turning tide.

### Horace, *Ode* I, 5 translated by Heather McHugh (born 1948)

What slip of a boy, all slick with what perfumes,
is pressing on you now, o Pyrrha, in
your lapping crannies, in your rosy rooms?

Who's caught up in your net today, your coil
of elegant coiffure? He'll call himself
a sucker soon enough, and often, and rail

at the breakers—God of his word, you of your faith.
The darkest sort of thought will fill his form
when breezes bristle, mirrors roughen—just you wait!

So far, his seas are barely stirred. You are forever
fair to his fairweather mind, and golden
to his gullibility: no storms are forecast there,

and no distress. What blind and wretched men—
you've barely touched them, yet they find you gripping!
Whereas I have tendered my last and best

regards to the Gods of the wave, as temple tablets
will attest. I've thrown off the habit, and hung up
my wet suit there. (You see? It's dripping.)

### Horace, *Ode* I, 5 translated by William Harris

I can see you now, Pyrrha, with some girishaped boy in a whirl
Flounced on a bed of rosebuds while you allow him now
For a moment the luxury of pressing his suit.
Rumpled hair you catch with a neat whisk into a braid
Sweet as a picture in your starched frock. Oh he will weep

For changing seas and promises, wild billows laced
By black clouds, astonished and surprised,
Thinking he has you now all to himself,
Entire, attentive, quick to his every word,
As it will be forever.
All those poor fools
Who love the laughter not knowing all her mind.
A votive board of velvet shows the silver thanks
For cure of hand, or foot or head, and to the side
A figure of my small ship that foundered out at sea.

BSH